# THE LETTERS
# TO THE
# THESSALONIANS

VOLUME 32B

THE ANCHOR BIBLE is a fresh approach to the world's greatest classic. Its object is to make the Bible accessible to the modern reader; its method is to arrive at the meaning of biblical literature through exact translation and extended exposition, and to reconstruct the ancient setting of the biblical story, as well as the circumstances of its transcription and the characteristics of its transcribers.

THE ANCHOR BIBLE is a project of international and interfaith scope: Protestant, Catholic, and Jewish scholars from many countries contribute individual volumes. The project is not sponsored by any ecclesiastical organization and is not intended to reflect any particular theological doctrine. Prepared under our joint supervision, THE ANCHOR BIBLE is an effort to make available all the significant historical and linguistic knowledge which bears on the interpretation of the biblical record.

THE ANCHOR BIBLE is aimed at the general reader with no special formal training in biblical studies; yet it is written with the most exacting standards of scholarship, reflecting the highest technical accomplishment.

This project marks the beginning of a new era of cooperation among scholars in biblical research, thus forming a common body of knowledge to be shared by all.

*William Foxwell Albright*
*David Noel Freedman*
GENERAL EDITORS

THE ANCHOR BIBLE

# THE LETTERS TO THE THESSALONIANS

◆

A New Translation
with Introduction and Commentary

## ABRAHAM J. MALHERBE

YALE

THE ANCHOR YALE BIBLE

*Yale University Press*
New Haven & London

THE ANCHOR BIBLE
PUBLISHED BY DOUBLEDAY
a division of Random House, Inc.


THE ANCHOR BIBLE, DOUBLEDAY, and the portrayal of an anchor
with a dolphin are registered trademarks of Doubleday, a division of
Random House, Inc.

A hardcover edition of this book was published
in 2000 by Doubleday

Original Jacket Illustration by Margaret Chodos-Irvine


The Library of Congress has catalogued the hardcover edition as follows:


Library of Congress Cataloging-in-Publication Data
Bible. N.T. Thessalonians. English. Malherbe. 2000.
    The letters to the Thessalonians : a new translation with introduction and
commentary / by Abraham J. Malherbe.
      p.  cm. — (The Anchor Bible ; v. 32B)
Includes bibliographical references and indexes.

    1. Bible.  N.T.  Thessalonians—Commentaries.  I. Malherbe, Abraham J.
II. Title.  III. Bible.  English.  Anchor Bible.  1964 ; v. 32B.
BS192.2.A1    1964.G3 vol. 32B
[BS2725.3]
220.77 s—dc21
[227'.81077]                            00-021363
                                        CIP

First trade paperback edition published    2004

ISBN: 978-0-300-13948-6

PRINTED IN THE UNITED STATES OF AMERICA

For

My Children

*By Birth*

Selina Brooks

Cornelia Kleman

Abraham Johannes (Jan) Malherbe

and

*By Law*

Mark Brooks

Glenn Kleman

# CONTENTS

◆

# PREFACE

◆

In a letter to his publisher, Quintilian explains why he had delayed the publication of his book on rhetoric, on which he had worked for two years: "These two years have been devoted not so much to actual writing as to the research demanded by a task to which practically no limits can be set and to the reading of innumerable authors" (LCL 1.3). He justifies his delay by appealing to the advice of Horace, that a writer withhold a completed work for nine years (*The Art of Poetry* 386–389). Like all writers of commentaries, I am familiar with the difficulties Quintilian mentions, and I share Horace's desire to allow time for one's writing to mature before sending the manuscript to the publisher.

This volume was to have appeared long before now, but circumstances have conspired against me. That I have not been rushed to produce a book with even more imperfections than this one has been due to the understanding of Mark Fretz and Andrew Corbin, editors at Doubleday, and David Noel Freedman, editor of The Anchor Bible. Noel Freedman has been unfailing in his support and in the care with which he read everything I ventured to send him; I am truly grateful to him.

Paul's two letters to the Thessalonians, the earliest extant Christian writings, have fascinated me because they open windows onto newly founded Christian communities as no other documents do. They reveal the challenges recent converts faced and how Paul, aware of their problems, acted pastorally in writing to them. The pastoral dimension of Paul's writings, which was appreciated by the ancient commentators, in particular John Chrysostom and Theodoret, deserves more attention from modern scholars than it has received. I hope that this commentary will contribute to a greater awareness that Paul was as much concerned with the moral, emotional, and spiritual nurture of his converts as he was with their theological development.

This volume does not contain a glossary. The extensive subject index makes one unnecessary. This index will point the reader to those places where terminology, whose meaning is not immediately clear, is treated at some length. I prepared the subject index; my wife, Phyllis, the others. As always, I am thankful for her collaboration.

# MAP OF THE AEGEAN

◆

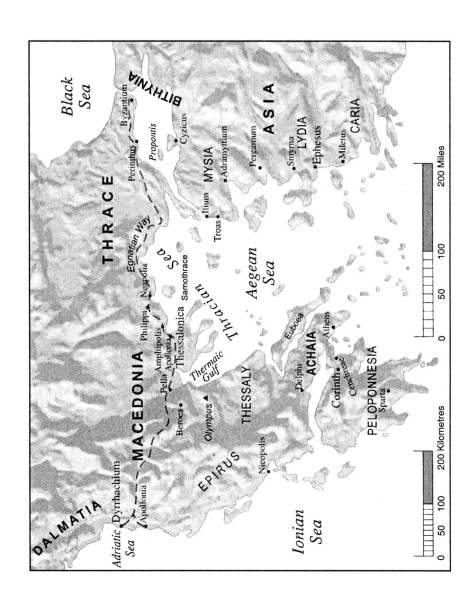

# PRINCIPAL ABBREVIATIONS

◆

| | | |
|---|---|---|
| AB | Anchor Bible | *Literature.* 2d ed. |
| ABD | *Anchor Bible Dictionary.* | Chicago, 1979. |
| | Edited by D. N. | Barn *Epistle of Barnabas* |
| | Freedman. 6 vols. New | BASOR *Bulletin of the American* |
| | York, 1992. | *Schools of Oriental* |
| ABRL | Anchor Bible Reference | *Research* |
| | Library | BBET *Beiträge zur biblischen* |
| AGJU | Arbeiten zur Geschichte | *Exegese und Theologie* |
| | des antiken Judentums | BC *The Beginnings of* |
| | und des | *Christianity.* Edited by |
| | Urchristentums | F. J. Foakes Jackson |
| AJP | *American Journal of* | and Kirsopp Lake. |
| | *Philology* | 5 vols. London, |
| AnBib | Analecta Biblica | 1920–1933. |
| ANRW | *Aufstieg und Niedergang* | BDF Blass, F., A. Debrunner, |
| | *der römischen Welt:* | and R. W. Funk, *A* |
| | *Geschichte und Kultur* | *Greek Grammar of the* |
| | *Roms im Spiegel der* | *New Testament and* |
| | *neueren Forschung.* | *Other Early Christian* |
| | Edited by H. Temporini | *Literature.* Chicago, |
| | and W. Haase. Berlin, | 1961. |
| | 1972– | BETL Bibliotheca ephemeridum |
| APFenn | Acta philosophica fennica | theologicarum |
| ARW | *Archiv für* | lovaniensium |
| | *Religionswissenschaft* | BEvT *Beiträge zur* |
| ASNU | Acta seminarii | *evangelischen* |
| | neotestamentici | *Theologie* |
| | upsaliensis | BFCT *Beiträge zur Förderung* |
| ATANT | Abhandlungen zur | *christlicher Theologie* |
| | Theologie des Alten | BGU *Aegyptische Urkunden aus* |
| | und Neuen Testaments | *den Königlichen* |
| AThR | *Anglican Theological* | *Staatlichen Museen zu* |
| | *Review* | *Berlin, Griechische* |
| BAGD | Bauer, W., W. F. Arndt, F. | *Urkunden.* 15 vols. |
| | W. Gingrich, and F. W. | Berlin, 1895–1983. |
| | Danker, *A Greek-* | BHT *Beiträge zur historischen* |
| | *English Lexicon of the* | *Theologie* |
| | *New Testament and* | Bib *Biblica* |
| | *Other Early Christian* | BibLeb *Bibel und Leben* |

| | | | |
|---|---|---|---|
| BJRL | Bulletin of the John Rylands University Library of Manchester | GNS | Good News Studies |
| | | GNTG | Grammar of New Testament Greek. |
| BN | Biblische Notizen | | Moulton, James H., |
| BNTC | Black's New Testament Commentaries | | Wilbert F. Howard, and Nigel Turner. 4 vols. |
| BR | Biblical Research | | Edinburgh; vol. I [3d |
| BWANT | Beiträge zur Wissenschaft vom Alten und Neuen Testament | | ed.], 1908; vol. II, 1919–1929; vol. III, 1963; vol. IV, 1976. |
| BZ | Biblische Zeitschrift | GRBS | Greek, Roman, and Byzantine Studies |
| BZNW | Beihefte zur Zeitschrift für die neutestamentliche Wissenschaft | GTA | Göttinger theologischer Arbeiten |
| CBQ | Catholic Biblical Quarterly | Hermas | Shepherd of Hermas |
| CIG | Corpus inscriptionum graecarum. Edited by A. Boeckh. 4 vols. Berlin, 1828–1877. | | (Mandates, Similtudes, Visions) |
| | | Hesperia | Hesperia: Journal of the American School of Classical Studies at |
| CJ | The Classical Journal | | Athens |
| 1 Clem | 1 Clement | | |
| 2 Clem | 2 Clement | HNT | Handbuch zum Neuen Testament |
| CNT | Commentaire du Nouveau Testament | HNTC | Harper's New Testament Commentaries |
| Colloq | Colloquium | | |
| ConBNT | Coniectanea biblica: New Testament Series | HR | History of Religions |
| | | HTKNT | Herders theologischer Kommentar zum Neuen Testament |
| CP | Classical Philology | | |
| CPJ | Corpus papyrorum judaicarum. Edited by V. Tcherikover and A. Fuks. 3 vols. Cambridge, Mass, 1957–1964. | HTR | Harvard Theological Review |
| | | HTS | Harvard Theological Studies |
| | | ICC | International Critical Commentary |
| Did | Didache | | |
| Diogn | Epistle of Diognetus | IG | Inscriptiones graecae. 14 vols. Berlin, 1873– |
| ÉBib | Études bibliques | | |
| EKKNT | Evangelisch-katholischer Kommentar zum Neuen Testament | Ign | Ignatius (Letter to the Ephesians, Letter to the Magnesians, Letter to the Philadelphians, Letter to Polycarp, Letter to the Romans, Letter to the Smyrneans, Letter to the Trallians) |
| ErJB | Eranos-Jahrbuch | | |
| ETL | Ephemerides theologicae lovanienses | | |
| EvT | Evangelische Theologie | | |
| ExpTim | Expository Times | | |
| FF | Foundations and Facets | | |
| FRLANT | Forschungen zur Religion und Literatur des Alten und Neuen Testaments | Int | Interpretation |
| | | JAC | Jahrbuch für Antike und Christentum |

| | | | |
|---|---|---|---|
| JBL | Journal of Biblical Literature | NEB | New English Bible |
| JEH | Journal of Ecclesiastical History | NICNT | New International Commentary on the New Testament |
| JETS | Journal of the Evangelical Theological Society | NIGTC | New International Greek Testament Commentary |
| JHS | Journal of Hellenic Studies | | |
| JRH | Journal of Religious History | NIV | New International Version |
| JRS | Journal of Roman Studies | | |
| JSNT | Journal for the Study of the New Testament | NovT | Novum Testamentum |
| | | NovTSup | Supplements to Novum Testamentum |
| JSNTSup | Journal for the Study of the New Testament: Supplement Series | NRSV | New Revised Standard Version |
| JTS | Journal of Theological Studies | NT | New Testament |
| | | NTAbh | Neutestamentliche Abhandlungen |
| KEK | Kritisch-exegetischer Kommentar über das Neue Testament (Meyer-Kommentar) | NTD | Das Neue Testament Deutsch |
| | | NTF | Neutestamentliche Forschungen |
| KJV | King James Version | | |
| KNT | Kommentar zum Neuen Testament | NTOA | Novum Testamentum et Orbis Antiquus |
| LCL | Loeb Classical Library | NTS | New Testament Studies |
| LEC | Library of Early Christianity | NTT | Nederlandsch Theologisch Tijdschrift |
| LD | Lectio divina | NTTS | New Testament Tools and Studies |
| LSJ | Liddell, H. G., R. Scott, H. S. Jones. A Greek-English Lexicon. 9th ed. with revised supplement. Oxford, 1996. | Numen | Numen: International Review for the History of Religions |
| | | OCD | Oxford Classical Dictionary. Edited by S. Hornblower and A. Spawforth. 3d ed. Oxford, 1996. |
| LXX | Septuagint | | |
| Mart Pol | Martyrdom of Polycarp | | |
| MH | Museum helveticum | | |
| MM | Moulton, J. H., and G. Milligan. The Vocabulary of the Greek Testament. London, 1930. Repr., Peabody, Mass., 1997. | OGIS | Orientis graeci inscriptiones selectae. Edited by W. Dittenberger. 2 vols. Leipzig, 1903–1905. |
| | | OT | Old Testament |
| MNTC | The Moffatt New Testament Commentary | PAmherst | The Amherst Papyri. 2 vols. Edited by B. P. Grenfell and A. S. Hunt. London, 1900–1901. |
| MTS | Marburger theologische Studien | | |
| MTZ | Münchener theologische Zeitschrift | PEleph | Elephantine Papyri. (BGU Sonderheft). |
| NCB | New Century Bible | | |

PEnt *Enteuxis: Requêtes et plaintes addressées au Roi d'Égypte au IIIe siècle avant J.-C.* Edited by O. Gueraud. Cairo, 1931.

PFreib *Mitteilungen aus der Freiburger Papyrussammlung.* 4 vols. Edited by W. Aly, M. Gelzer, and J. Partsch. Heidelberg, 1914–1986.

PG Patrologia graeca [ = Patrologiae cursus completus: Series graeca]. Edited by J.-P. Migne. 162 vols. Paris, 1857–1886.

PGiess *Griechische Papyri in Museum des oberhessischen Geschichtsvereins zu Giessen.* 3 vols. Edited by O. Eger, E. Kornemann, and P.-M. Meyer. Leipzig-Berlin, 1910–1912.

PHamb *Griechische Papyrusurkunden der Hamburger Staats- und Universitätsbibliothek.* 4 vols. Leipzig-Berlin, 1911–1988. Vol. 1, in three parts, edited by P.-M. Meyer (1911–1924).

PLond Bell *Greek Papyri in the British Museum.* 7 vols. (1893–1974). Vol. 6 (Numbers 1912–1929), edited by H. I. Bell. London, 1924.

PMerton *A Descriptive Catalogue of the Greek Papyri in the Collection of Wilfred Merton.* 3 vols. Edited by H. I. Bell, C. H. Roberts et al. London-Dublin, 1948–.

PMich *Michigan Papyri.* 19 vols. Various editors and publishers, 1931–1999.

POxy *Oxyrhynchus Papyri.* 65 vols. Edited by B. P Grenfell and A. S. Hunt. London, 1898–1998.

PParis *Notices et textes des papyrus du Musée de Louvre et de la Bibliothèque Impériale.* Edited by A. J. Letronne, W. Brunet de Presle, and E. Egger. Paris, 1865.

PPetr *The Flinders Petrie Papyri.* 3 vols. Edited by J. Mahaffy and J. G. Smyly. Dublin, 1891–1905.

PRyl *Catalogue of Papyri in the John Rylands Library.* 4 vols. Edited by A. S. Hunt et al. Manchester, 1911–1952.

Ps.- Pseudo-

PSakaon *The Archive of Aurelius Sakaon: Papers of an Egyptian Farmer in the Last Century of Theodelphia.* Edited by G. M. Parassoglou. Bonn, 1978.

PSI *Papiri greci e latini.* Pubblicazioni della Società Italiana per la ricerca dei papiri greci e latini in Egitto. 15 vols. Numerous editors. Florence, 1912–1979.

PVat A *I Papiri Vaticani di Aphrodito.* Edited by R. Pintaudi. Rome, 1980.

| | | | |
|---|---|---|---|
| PW | *Real-Encyclopädie der classischen Altertumswissenschaft.* 49 vols. Edited by A. F. Pauly, G. Wissowa, and W. Kroll. Stuttgart, 1893–1978. | SBLTT | Society of Biblical Literature Texts and Translations |
| PZeno Cairo | *Zenon Papyri. Catalogue général des antiquités égyptiennes du Musée du Caire.* 5 vols. Edited by C. C. Edgar. Cario, 1925–1940. | SBS | Stuttgarter Bibelstudien |
| | | SBT | Studies in Biblical Theology |
| | | SCHNT | Studia ad corpus hellenisticum Novi Testamenti |
| | | SD | Studies and Documents |
| | | SEÅ | *Svensk exegetisk årsbok* |
| | | SecCent | *Second Century* |
| RAC | *Reallexikon für Antike und Christentum.* Edited by T. Klauser et al. Stuttgart, 1950– | Semeia | *Semeia: An Experimental Journal for Biblical Criticism* |
| RB | *Revue biblique* | SHAW | Sitzungsberichte der Heidelberger Akademie der Wissenschaften, Philos.-Hist. Klasse |
| RÉG | *Revue des études grecques* | | |
| RelSRev | *Religious Studies Review* | | |
| ResQ | *Restoration Quarterly* | SHCT | Studies in the History of Christian Theology |
| RevPhil | *Revue de philologie* | | |
| RhM | *Rheinisches Museum* | SIG | *Sylloge inscriptionum graecarum.* Edited by W. Dittenberger. 4 vols. 3d ed. Hildesheim: G. Olms, 1986. Repr. of 1915–1924 original. |
| RHR | *Revue de l'histoire des religions* | | |
| RivB | *Rivista biblica italiana* | | |
| RNT | Regensburger Neues Testament | | |
| RSV | Revised Standard Version | SNT | Studien zum Neuen Testament |
| RTR | *Reformed Theological Review* | SNTSMS | Society for New Testament Studies Monograph Series |
| SANT | Studien zum Alten und Neuen Testament | | |
| SB | *Sammelbuch griechischer Urkunden aus Ägypten.* 21 vols. Vols 1 and 2 edited by F. Preisigke, 1915–1922. | SNTSU | Studien zum Neuen Testament und Seiner Umwelt |
| | | SP | Sacra pagina |
| | | ST | *Studia theologica* |
| SBFLA | *Studii biblici Franciscani liber annus* | Str-B | Strack, H. L., and P. Billerbeck. *Kommentar zum Neuen Testament aus Talmud und Midrasch.* 6 vols. Munich, 1922–1961. |
| SBLDS | Society of Biblical Literature Dissertation Series | | |
| SBLMS | Society of Biblical Literature Monograph Series | SUNT | Studien zur Umwelt des Neuen Testaments |
| SBLSBS | Society of Biblical Literature Sources for Biblical Study | SVF | *Stoicorum veterum fragmenta.* Edited by H. von Arnim. 4 vols. |

|          |                                                                 |       |                                                                      |
|----------|-----------------------------------------------------------------|-------|----------------------------------------------------------------------|
|          | Repr. Stuttgart: Teubner, 1964.                                 | UPZ   | *Urkunden der Ptolemäerzeit.* Edited by U. Wilcken. 2 vols. Berlin, 1922, 1937. |
| TANZ     | Texte und Arbeiten zum neutestamentlichen Zeitalter             | VD    | *Verbum domini*                                                      |
| TAPA     | *Transactions of the American Philological Association*         | WBC   | Word Biblical Commentary                                             |
| TBl      | *Theologische Blätter*                                          | WMANT | Wissenschaftliche Monographien zum Alten und Neuen Testament         |
| TDNT     | *Theological Dictionary of the New Testament.* Edited by G. Kittel and G. Friedrich. Translated by G. W. Bromiley. 10 vols. Grand Rapids, 1964–1976. | WUNT  | Wissenschaftliche Untersuchungen zum Neuen Testament                 |
| ThViat   | *Theologia Viatorum*                                            | YCS   | Yale Classical Studies                                               |
| TLZ      | *Theologische Literaturzeitung*                                 | ZNW   | *Zeitschrift für die neutestamentliche Wissenschaft und die Kunde der älteren Kirche* |
| TQ       | *Theologische Quartalschrift*                                   | ZPE   | *Zeitschrift für Papyrologie und Epigraphik*                         |
| TU       | Texte und Untersuchungen                                        | ZST   | *Zeitschrift für systematische Theologie*                            |
| TynBul   | *Tyndale Bulletin*                                              | ZTK   | *Zeitschrift für Theologie und Kirche*                               |
| TZ       | *Theologische Zeitschrift*                                      |       |                                                                      |

# The Letters
# to the
# Thessalonians:
# A Translation

◆

# 1 THESSALONIANS

◆

1 ¹Paul, Silvanus, and Timothy to the church of the Thessalonians in God the Father and the Lord Jesus Christ: grace to you and peace. ²We give thanks to God always for you all when without ceasing we mention you in our prayers, ³calling to mind before God our Father the work of your faith, the labor of your love, and the endurance of your hope in our Lord Jesus Christ, ⁴for we know, brethren, that you, whom God loved, he has chosen, ⁵for our gospel came to you not in word only, but also with power and the Holy Spirit and with a full conviction, fully in conformity with the kind of persons you know we proved to be among you for your sake; ⁶so you on your part became imitators of us and the Lord by receiving the word in deep distress and with joy inspired by the Holy Spirit, ⁷with the result that you became an example to all the believers in Macedonia and Achaia. ⁸For from you the word of the Lord has sounded forth not only in Macedonia and Achaia, but your faith in God has gone forth everywhere, so that we have no need to say anything; ⁹indeed, they themselves are reporting about us, namely, what kind of entrance we gained to you, and how you turned to God from idols to serve the living and true God, ¹⁰and to wait for his son from heaven, whom he raised from the dead, Jesus who delivers us from the wrath to come.

2 ¹For you yourselves know, brethren, that our entrance among you was not powerless; ²on the contrary, although we had earlier suffered and been insulted in Philippi, as you know, we were emboldened in our God to speak to you the gospel of God in the midst of a great struggle. ³For our exhortation is not motivated by error or impurity, nor is it made with guile, ⁴but as we have been approved by God to be entrusted with the gospel, so we speak, not as though we are seeking to please human beings, but God, who tests our hearts, ⁵for we never used flattering words, as you know, nor did we use any pretext for covetousness, as God is our witness; ⁶nor did we seek glory from human beings, either from you or others. ⁷Although we might have made harsh demands on you as apostles of Christ, yet we were gentle in your midst; as a nurse who cares for her own children, ⁸so we, having tender affection for you gladly determined to share with you not only the gospel of God but our very selves, because we had come to love you. ⁹For you remember, brethren, our labor and toil; working night and day in order not to burden any of you we preached the gospel of God to you. ¹⁰You yourselves are witnesses, and so is God, how holy, just, and blameless our behavior was to you believers; ¹¹you know that, as a father treats his own children individually, ¹²so we exhorted and comforted and charged you to conduct yourselves in a manner worthy of God, who calls you into his kingdom and glory.

[13]And for this reason we ourselves also give thanks to God without ceasing, because when you received the word of God that you heard from us you received it, not as a word that originated with humans, but as what it truly is, God's word, which is also at work in you who believe. [14]For you yourselves became imitators, brethren, of the churches of God which are in Judea in Christ Jesus, because you in your turn suffered the same things at the hands of your own countrymen as they for their part suffered at the hands of the Jews [15]who killed both the Lord Jesus and the prophets, and drove us out, and do not please God and oppose all people [16]by preventing us from speaking to the Gentiles that they may be saved so as to fill up constantly the measure of their sins. But wrath has come upon them until the end.

[17]But we, brethren, having been orphaned by being separated from you for a short time, in person but not in heart, most earnestly endeavored to see you face to face with great longing. [18]It is for this reason that we resolved to come to you, I, Paul, did so on more than one occasion, and Satan hindered us. [19]For what is our hope or joy or crown in which we shall exult—is it in fact not you?—before our Lord Jesus at his coming? [20]Yes! You are our glory and joy!

3 [1]Therefore, because we could hold out no longer, we gladly determined to be left in Athens alone, [2]and we sent Timothy, our brother and God's coworker in the gospel of Christ, to establish you and encourage you about your faith, [3]that no one should be agitated by these afflictions. For you yourselves know that we are appointed to this. [4]Indeed, when we were with you, we kept on telling you in advance, "We are bound to suffer tribulation," as it has indeed happened, and you know. [5]For this reason, when I for my part could hold out no longer, I sent to learn about your faith, lest the Tempter had tempted you, and our labor had been in vain.

[6]But Timothy has just returned to us from you and brought us the good news of your faith and love and that you have a good remembrance of us always, longing to see us as we do you— [7]for this reason we were comforted, brethren, because of you in all our anguish and distress through your faith [8]because now we live if you stand fast in the Lord. [9]What thanksgiving can we render God for you for all the joy with which we rejoice on your account in the presence of our God, [10]begging night and day with the utmost earnestness to see you face to face and complete what is lacking in your faith.

[11]Now may our God and Father himself and our Lord Jesus direct our way to you. [12]But as for you, may the Lord cause you to increase and abound in love for one another and for all, as we abound in love for you, [13]so as to establish your hearts blameless in holiness in the presence of our God and Father at the coming of our Lord Jesus with all his holy ones.

4 [1]Well then, brethren, we beseech and exhort you in the Lord Jesus that, as you received from us instruction about how you should conduct yourselves and so please God, as you are indeed conducting yourselves, you do so more and more. [2]For you know what precepts we gave you through the Lord Jesus.

3This is God's will, your sanctification, that is, that you abstain from immorality, 4that each one of you learn how to acquire his own wife in holiness and honor, 5not in lustful passion as the pagans do who do not know God, 6that he not trespass against or behave covetously in this matter against his brother, because the Lord is an avenger in all these things; indeed, we told you so before and kept on charging you. 7For God did not call us for impurity but in sanctification. 8Consequently, the person who rejects this rejects not man but God, who indeed gives his Holy Spirit to you.

9Concerning love for the brethren you have no need for us to write to you, for you yourselves are taught by God to love one another; 10indeed, you are doing it to all the brethren in the whole of Macedonia. But we exhort you, brethren, to do so more and more, 11and to make it your ambition to live a quiet life and to mind your own affairs and to work with your hands, just as we instructed you, 12so that you may conduct yourselves becomingly in the eyes of the outsiders and may depend on no one.

13We do not want you to be in ignorance, brethren, about those who are asleep, in order that you may not grieve as the rest do who have no hope. 14For if we believe that Jesus died and rose, so also God will gather through Jesus those who have fallen asleep to be with him. 15For this we tell you as a message from the Lord, that we who are alive, who are left until the coming of the Lord, shall by no means have precedence over those who have fallen asleep, 16because the Lord himself will descend from heaven, with a command, with the voice of an archangel and with the trumpet of God, and the dead in Christ will rise first; 17then we who are alive, who are left, will be snatched up together with them in the clouds to meet the Lord in the air; and so we shall always be with the Lord. 18So, exhort one another with these words.

5   1About the times and the seasons, brethren, you have no need to be written to; 2for you yourselves know accurately that the Day of the Lord so comes as a thief in the night. 3When they say, "Peace and security," it is then that sudden ruin comes upon them as birth pangs do upon a pregnant woman, and they shall in no way escape. 4But you, brethren, are not in darkness, for the Day to surprise you like a thief in the night, 5for you are all sons of light and sons of day. We do not belong to night or darkness. 6So then, let us not sleep as the rest do, but let us stay awake and be sober. 7For those who sleep do so at night and those who get drunk are drunk at night. 8But as for us, since we belong to the day, let us be sober, putting on the breastplate of faith and love and as a helmet the hope of salvation, 9because God did not destine us for wrath but to obtain salvation through our Lord Jesus Christ, 10who died for us in order that, whether we are awake or asleep, we might live with him.

11Therefore, exhort one another and build one another up, one on one, as indeed you are doing.

12We beseech you, brethren, to give recognition to those who labor among you and care for you in the Lord and admonish you, 13and to esteem them very highly in love because of their work. Be at peace among yourselves. 14And we exhort you, brethren, admonish the disorderly, comfort the discouraged, help the weak, be patient with all. [15]See to it that no one renders evil for evil to anyone, but at all times pursue what is good for one another and for all.

[16]Rejoice at all times,
[17]pray without ceasing,
[18]in everything give thanks, for this is God's will in Christ Jesus for you.
[19]Do not quench the Spirit,
[20]do not despise prophecies,
[21]but test every thing,
    hold fast to what is good,
[22]keep away from every form of evil.

[23]Now may the God of peace himself sanctify you completely, and may your whole spirit and soul and body be preserved blamelessly at the coming of our Lord Jesus Christ. [24]He who calls you is faithful and he will do it.
[25]Brethren, pray also for us.
[26]Greet all the brethren with a holy kiss.
[27]I adjure you by the Lord that this letter be read to all the brethren.
[28]The grace of our Lord Jesus Christ be with you.

# 2 THESSALONIANS

◆

1 ¹Paul, Silvanus, and Timothy to the church of the Thessalonians in God our Father and the Lord Jesus Christ: ²grace to you and peace from God [our] Father and the Lord Jesus Christ.

³We ought to give thanks to God always for you, brethren, as is proper, because your faith grows abundantly and the love of each individual one of all of you for one another is increasing, ⁴so that we ourselves do boast about you in the churches of God about your endurance and faith in all your persecutions and the tribulations that you are bearing.

⁵This is a clear proof of the righteous judgment of God, that you be made worthy of the kingdom of God, for which you are indeed suffering,

⁶since indeed it is just in God's sight to repay
those who afflict you with affliction,
⁷and you who are being afflicted with relief with us
at the revelation of the Lord Jesus from heaven with the angels of his power,
⁸with flaming fire, repaying with vengeance
those who do not know God
and those who do not obey the gospel of our Lord Jesus.
⁹They will pay the penalty of eternal ruin
from the face of the Lord
and from the glory of his might,
¹⁰when he comes
to be glorified in his saints
and to be marveled at in all who have believed
(for our testimony to you was believed)
on that day.
¹¹To this end we also pray for you always, that our God
may make you worthy of his call
and may fulfill every resolve to do good and work of faith in power,
¹²so that the name of our Lord Jesus may be glorified in you, and you
in him, according to the grace of our God and the Lord Jesus Christ.

2 ¹Now we beseech you, brethren, with reference to the coming of the Lord Jesus Christ and our gathering to him, ²not to be quickly shaken in mind nor to be emotionally wrought up, either by a spirit or by a spoken word or by a letter purporting to be from us, to the effect that the Day of the Lord has come.

³Let no one deceive you in any way. For [the Day of the Lord will not come] unless the apostasy comes first and the Man of Lawlessness is revealed, the Son of Perdition, ⁴who opposes and exalts himself over every so-called god or object

of worship so that he takes his seat in the temple of God, proclaiming himself to be God. [5]Do you not remember that while I was still with you I used to tell you these things?

[6]And you know now what it is that is exercising a restraining force, so that he may be revealed at his [proper] time. [7]For the mystery of lawlessness is already at work; only until he who is now restraining will be out of the way.

[8]And then the Lawless One will be revealed, whom the Lord Jesus will slay with the breath of his mouth and destroy by the appearance of his coming. [9]His coming will take place by the working of Satan, attended by all power and signs and wonders of falsehood, [10]and by all deceit of wickedness for those on the way to perdition, because they did not receive the love of the truth so as to be saved.

[11]And for this reason God sends them a power working to delude them, so that they should believe the lie, [12]that all should be judged who had not believed the truth but delighted in wickedness.

[13]But we ought to give thanks to God always for you, brethren beloved by the Lord, because God chose you as firstfruits for salvation through sanctification by the Spirit and belief in the truth. [14]To this he called you through our gospel, that you might obtain the glory of our Lord Jesus Christ.

[15]So then, brethren, stand fast and hold onto the traditions which you were taught, whether by our oral teaching or our letter.

[16]Now may our Lord Jesus Christ himself and God our Father who has loved us and given us eternal encouragement and good hope by grace [17]encourage and establish your hearts in every good work and word.

3    [1]For the rest, brethren, pray for us, that the word of the Lord may speed on and be glorified, as it does with you, [2]and that we may be delivered from the perverse and wicked men, for not everyone has faith.

[3]But the Lord is faithful, who will establish you and guard you from the Evil One. [4]We have confidence in the Lord about you, that what we command, you indeed are doing and will continue to do.

[5]May the Lord direct your hearts to the love of God and to the steadfastness of Christ.

[6]Now, we command you, brethren, in the name of the Lord Jesus Christ, withdraw from every brother who conducts himself in a disorderly manner and not in accordance with the tradition that you received from us. [7]For you yourselves know how you ought to imitate us, for we were not disorderly among you, [8]nor did we accept bread from anyone without paying, but in labor and toil, night and day, we kept at our work in order not to burden any of you. [9]It was not that we had no right [to be supported by you], but to present ourselves as an example for you to imitate. [10]Indeed, when we were with you, we used to give you this instruction, "If someone does not wish to work, let him not eat." [11]For we hear that there are some who are conducting themselves among you in a disorderly manner, doing no work at all, but being busybodies. [12]Such persons we command and exhort in the Lord Jesus Christ that, by working quietly, they are to eat their own bread.

13But as for you, brethren, do not become weary of doing good. 14But if anyone disobeys what we have communicated through this letter, that person you must mark so as not to associate with him, in order that he might be put to shame; 15nevertheless, do not regard him as an enemy, but admonish him as a brother.

16May the Lord of peace himself give you peace continually in every way. The Lord be with you all.

17The greeting with my own hand—of Paul, which is a sign in every letter, this is the way I write.

18The grace of our Lord Jesus Christ be with you all.

# GENERAL INTRODUCTION

♦

# INTRODUCTION

◆

When Paul arrived in Thessalonica in A.D. 49, he was experienced in preaching the gospel. He began to carry out his commission to be an apostle to the Gentiles immediately after his call (Gal 1:17; cf. Rom 15:15–16). Information about his work preceding the founding of the churches in Philippi and Thessalonica is relatively meager, compared with his later activity, and the texts that have to do with the early period are much disputed (Becker 1993: 1–124; Riesner, 204–96; Murphy-O'Connor 1996: 71–101; Hengel and Schwemer; contrast, Luedemann). Nevertheless, what seems clear is that Paul had been active in preaching in Damascus and Arabia (Gal 1:17; 2 Cor 11:32), Syria and Cilicia (Gal 1:21; cf. Acts 15:41; Tarsus: Acts 9:30; 11:25), Antioch (Gal 2:1–10; cf. Acts 11:25), and Cyprus and southern Asia Minor (Acts 13–14).

Thus, although 1 Thessalonians is the earliest extant letter of Paul's, it does not reflect the beginning of his missionary work but rather the work of a seasoned preacher. There is no indication that his strategy or his methods were new, or that 1 Thessalonians should be understood as his first effort at letter writing and that his style of writing letters would develop in his later letters; he had probably written other Christian letters in the decade and a half before 1 Thessalonians. The temptation should also be resisted to regard 1 Thessalonians as reflecting a rudimentary theology that would develop as Paul encountered the new circumstances that he would deal with in 1 and 2 Corinthians, Galatians, and Romans. The Paul we meet in 1 Thessalonians is already a mature thinker who brings to bear his theological convictions and pastoral experience on the problems and challenges of a newly founded church.

In the nineteenth century, the authenticity of 1 Thessalonians was questioned by some scholars, but the universal opinion today is that Paul wrote the letter, although its integrity has been questioned (see page 79). It is natural to examine the earliest Christian writing for clues to traditions that may open windows on the church before Paul, and to do so is important for our knowledge of the history of Christian theology. It may also allow us to appreciate Paul's letter better if we look at his teaching in comparison with that, for example, of the pre-Synoptic traditions (see NOTES and COMMENT on 1 Thess 4:12–18). But it will contribute little to our understanding of Paul's Thessalonian letters to read them against the background of an Antiochean theology that Paul is thought to have assimilated during his years of association with the church in Antioch (e.g., by Becker 1993: 83–140; against: Hengel and Schwemer, 11–15, 268–310; Söding 1997: 31–56). We shall understand 1 Thessalonians better, and appreciate it more, if we examine it as a witness to the way a Christian commmunity came into existence in a Greek metropolis and was nurtured by its founder.

# THESSALONICA

❧

Thessalonica was founded in 316 or 315 B.C. by Cassander, king of Macedon, who named the city after his wife, the half sister of Alexander the Great. It is situated on the Thermean Gulf and has one of the best harbors in the Aegean. It lay at the crossroads of major highways running in all four directions. The Egnatian Way was the major route connecting Rome with the East, and major trade routes running north and south made the city further accessible. This location early made Thessalonica a city of commercial importance, not only to Macedonia, but to regions beyond, as it is to this day. Towards the beginning of the first century A.D., the geographer Strabo called it the metropolis of Macedonia (*Geography* 7 Fragment 21), and the Thessalonian epigrammatist Antipater boasted that his city was the mother of all of Macedonia (*Greek Anthology* 9.428 LCL).

Thessalonica was the largest city in Macedonia, with an estimated population within the city walls of 65–80,000 people, and around 100,000 when those immediately outside the wall were included (Riesner, 301). By the first century, the city teemed with manual laborers, tradespeople, orators, and persons of other professions (Elliger, 89). Beyond the testimony of Acts 17:1–7, the earliest firm evidence of Jews in the city comes from the second century A.D. (a survey of the evidence in Levinskaya, 154–57), but given the diffusion of Jews throughout the eastern Mediterranean in the first century, there is no prima facie evidence against the witness of Acts. If the Thessalonian Jews followed the practice of their compatriots elsewhere, they would probably have engaged in trade and manual labor to make a living (see on Acts 17:5, pages 64–65). Like other foreigners in the city, they would not have taken an active part in the political life of the city and would have banded together to pursue their own interests (Elliger, 91–92).

As a reward for picking the winning side during the Roman civil wars, Thessalonica received the status of a "free city," which granted it a great deal of self-government. It enjoyed the advantages of the *Pax Romana*, and a considerable number of inscriptions show that the Thessalonians had a very positive attitude towards the emperors (see COMMENT on 1 Thess 5:3). The politarchs, who are mentioned in Acts 17:6–9, were the highest city officials. Holding annual magistracies, which could be held more than once, they varied in number, but there seem to have been five or six at once during the first century. Their major responsibility was to keep peace, and in pursuit of this aim they collaborated with the council (*dēmos*), whose meetings they convened (Horsley). It is not clear whether *dēmos* in Acts 17:5 refers to the city council or to the crowd that was stirred up by the Jews (see Elliger, 94–95; Taylor, 2460).

In addition to Judaism, other religions were represented in Thessalonica (see Edson; Elliger, 96–99). Heracles, the Dioscuri, Apollo, and Aphrodite are represented by the archaeological remains, as are Egyptian gods and cults. These cults were interconnected; the remains of a Serapeum, for example, contains inscriptions honoring Isis, Serapis, and Osiris, and elements of the cult of Dionysus may have been absorbed into the Egyptian cults. The imperial cult and its priests appear to have played a significant role in the city (Hendrix), but during the second and third centuries A.D. the main civic cult was that of the Cabiri, divinities associated with certain mystery sanctuaries. Attempts have been made to illuminate 1 Thessalonians by searching for clues in these cults, but the available evidence justifies no certainty about their practices or beliefs in Thessalonica in the first century (see COMMENT on 1 Thess 4:3–8; for methodological cautions, see Koester 1994).

# BIBLIOGRAPHY

◆

# 1. COMMENTARIES ON 1 AND 2 THESSALONIANS

◆

Alford, Henry
   1877   The Epistles to the Galatians, Ephesians, Colossians, Thessalonians, — to Timotheus, Titus, and Philemon. Vol. 3 of The Greek Testament. Boston: Lee and Shepard.
Auberlen, C., and C. J. Riggenbach
   1870   The Two Epistles of Paul to the Thessalonians. Translated by John Lillie. New York: Charles Scribner.
Best, Ernest
   1972   A Commentary on the First and Second Epistles to the Thessalonians. BNTC. London: Black.
Bornemann, W.
   1894   Die Thessalonicherbriefe. 6th ed. KEK. Göttingen: Vandenhoeck & Ruprecht.
Bruce, F. F.
   1982   1 & 2 Thessalonians. WBC. Waco, Tex.: Word.
Calvin, John
   1961   The Epistles of Paul the Apostle to the Romans and to the Thessalonians. Translated by Ross MacKenzie. Grand Rapids: Eerdmans.
Denney, J.
   1893   The Epistles to the Thessalonians. Expositor's Bible. London: Hodder & Stoughton.
Dibelius, Martin
   1937   An die Thessalonicher I.II. An die Philipper. 3d ed. HNT 11. Tübingen: Mohr (Siebeck).
Dobschütz, Ernst von
   1909   Die Thessalonicherbriefe. 7th ed. KEK. Göttingen: Vandenhoeck & Ruprecht.
Eadie, John
   1877   A Commentary on the Greek Text of the Epistles of Paul to the Thessalonians. London: Macmillan.
Ellicott, C. J.
   1864   A Critical and Exegetical Commentary on St. Paul's Epistles to the Thessalonians. Boston: Gould & Lincoln.
Findlay, C. G.
   1891   The Epistles to the Thessalonians. Cambridge: Cambridge University Press.
Frame, James E.
   1912   The Epistles of St. Paul to the Thessalonians. ICC. Edinburgh: T&T Clark.

Grotius, Hugo
1829    *Annotationes in Novum Testamentum.* Vol. 7. Groningen: Zuideman.
Holtz, Traugott
1986    *Der erste Brief an die Thessalonicher.* EKKNT 13. Zürich: Benziger.
Krodel, Gerhard
1978    *Ephesians, Colossians, 2 Thessalonians, The Pastoral Epistles.* Proclamation Commentaries. Philadelphia: Fortress.
Légasse, Simon
1999    *Les épîtres de Paul aux Thessaloniciens.* LD 7. Paris: du Cerf.
Laub, Franz
1985    *1. und 2. Thessalonicherbrief.* Würzburg: Echter.
Lenski, R. C. H.
1937    *The Interpretation of St. Paul's Epistles to the Colossians, to the Thessalonians, to Timothy, to Titus and to Philemon.* Minneapolis: Augsburg.
Lightfoot, J. B.
1980    *Notes on Epistles of St. Paul.* 1895. Repr. Grand Rapids: Baker.
Lünemann, Gottlieb
1885    *Critical and Exegetical Hand-Book to the Epistles to the Thessalonians.* Translated by Paton J. Gloag. New York: Funk & Wagnalls.
Marshall, I. Howard
1983    *1 & 2 Thessalonians.* NCB. Grand Rapids: Eerdmans.
Marxsen, Willi
1979    *Der erste Brief an die Thessalonicher.* Zürcher Bibelkommentare. Zürich: Theologischer Verlag.
1982    *Der zweite Thessalonicherbrief.* Zürcher Bibelkommentare. Zürich: Theologischer Verlag.
Masson, Charles
1957    *Les deux épîtres de Saint Paul aux Thessaloniciens.* CNT. Neuchâtel: Delachaux & Niestlé.
Menken, M. J. J.
1994a   *2 Thessalonians.* New Testament Readings. London: Routledge.
Milligan, George
1908    *St. Paul's Epistles to the Thessalonians.* London: Macmillan.
Moore, A. L.
1969    *1 & 2 Thessalonians.* NCB. London: Nelson.
Morris, Leon
1991    *The First and Second Epistles to the Thessalonians.* Rev. ed. NICNT. Grand Rapids: Eerdmans.
Neil, William
1950    *The Epistles of Paul to the Thessalonians.* MNTC. London: Hodder & Stoughton.
Ohlshausen, Hermann
1851    *Biblical Commentary on St. Paul's Epistles to the Galatians, Ephesians, Colossians, and Thessalonians.* Edinburgh: T&T Clark.
Plummer, Alfred A.
1918    *A Commentary on St. Paul's First Epistle to the Thessalonians.* London: Robert Scott.
Richard, Earl J.
1995    *First and Second Thessalonians.* SP 11. Collegeville, Minn.: Liturgical Press.

Rigaux, Beda, O. F. M.
  1956   *Saint Paul. Les épîtres aux Thessaloniciens.* ÉBib. Paris: Gabalda.
Roosen, A.
  1971   *De Brieven van Paulus aan de Tessalonicenzen.* Roermond, The Netherlands: Romen.
Schlatter, Adolf
  1950   *Die Briefe an die Thessalonicher, Philipper, Timotheus und Titus.* Stuttgart: Calwer.
Schlier, Heinrich
  1972   *Der Apostel und seine Gemeinde: Auslegung des ersten Briefes an die Thessalonicher.* Freiburg, Germany: Herder.
Staab, Karl
  1965   *The Thessalonicherbriefe. Die Gefangenschaftsbriefe.* RNT 7. Regensburg: Pustet.
Theodore of Mopsuestia
  1880   *Theodori Episcopi Mopsuesteni in Epistolas B. Pauli Commentarii.* 2 vols. Edited by H. B. Swete. Cambridge: Cambridge University Press.
Trilling, Wolfgang
  1980   *Der zweite Brief an die Thessalonicher.* EKKNT 14. Zürich: Einsiedeln.
Wanamaker, Charles A.
  1990   *Commentary on 1 & 2 Thessalonians.* NIGTC. Grand Rapids: Eerdmans.
Wohlenberg, G.
  1909   *Der erste und zweite Thessalonicherbrief.* 2d ed. KNT. Leipzig: Deichert.

# 2. BOOKS AND ARTICLES

◆

Aalen, Sverre
  1951   *Die Begriffe "Licht" und "Finsternis" im Alten Testament, im Spaetjudentum und in Rabbinismus.* Oslo: Dybwad.
Achtemeier, Paul
  1990   "*Omne verbum sonat:* The New Testament and the Oral Environment of Late Western Antiquity." *JBL* 109:3–27.
Adinolfi, Marco
  1976   "La santità del matrimonio in 1 Tess. 4,1–8." *RivB* 24:165–84.
Adkins, A. W. H.
  1976   "*Polypragmosyne* and 'Minding One's Own Business': A Study in Greek Social and Political Values." *CP* 71:301–27.
Aejmelaeus, Lars
  1985   *Wachen vor dem Ende: Die traditionsgeschichtlichen Wurzeln von 1 Thess 5:1–11 und Luk 21:34–36.* Helsinki: Kirjapaino Raamattutalo.

Allmen, D. von
  1981   *La famille de Dieu: La symbolique familiale dans le paulinisme.* Göttingen: Vandenhoeck & Ruprecht; Freiburg, Switzerland: Editions Universitaires.
Ameling, W.
  1985   *"PHAGOMEN KAI PIOMEN."* ZPE 60:35–43.
Arzt, Peter
  1994   "The 'Epistolary Introductory Thanksgiving' in the Papyri and in Paul." NovT 36:29–46.
Attridge, Harry W.
  1976   *First Century Cynicism in the Epistles of Heraclitus.* HTS 29. Missoula, Mont.: Scholars Press.
Aubin, Paul
  1963   *Le problème de la "conversion": Étude sur une terme commune a l'hellénisme et au christianisme des trois premiers siècles.* Paris: Beauchesne.
Aune, David E.
  1983   *Prophecy in Early Christianity and the Ancient Mediterranean World.* Grand Rapids: Eerdmans.
Aus, Roger D.
  1971   "Comfort in Judgment: The Use of the Day of the Lord and Theophany Traditions in 2 Thessalonians 1." Ph.D. diss., Yale University.
  1973   "The Liturgical Background of the Necessity and Propriety of Giving Thanks According to 2 Thess 1:3." *JBL* 92:432–38.
  1976   "The Relevance of Isaiah 66:7 to Revelation 12 and 2 Thessalonians 1." ZNW 67:252–68.
  1977   "God's Plan and God's Power: Isaiah 66 and the Restraining Factors of 2 Thess 2:6–7." *JBL* 96:537–53.
Baarda, T.
  1984   " 'Maar de toorn is over hen gekomen . . .' (1 Thess. 2:16c)." Pages 15–74 in *Paulus en de andere Joden.* Edited by T. Baarda, Jans Jansen, S. J. Noorda, J. S. Vos. Delft: Meinema.
Baasland, Ernst
  1988   "Die peri-Formel und die Argumentation(ssituation) des Paulus." *ST* 42:69–87.
Bailey, J. A.
  1979   "Who Wrote II Thessalonians?" NTS 25:131–45.
Bailey, R. E.
  1964   "Is 'Sleep' the Proper Biblical Term for the Intermediate State?" ZNW 55:161–67.
Balch, David L., Everett Ferguson, Wayne A. Meeks, eds.
  1990   *Greeks, Romans, and Christians* (Abraham J. Malherbe FS). Minneapolis: Fortress.
Baltensweiler, H.
  1967   *Die Ehe im Neuen Testament.* ATANT 52. Stuttgart: Zwingli.
Bammel, E.
  1959   "Judenverfolgung und Naherwartung: Zur Eschatologie der Ersten Thessalonicherbriefes." ZTK 56:294–315.
  1981   "Preparation for the Perils of the Last Days: 1 Thessalonians 3:3." Pages 91–100 in *Suffering and Martyrdom in the New Testament* (G. M. Styler FS). Edited by W. Horbury and B. O'Neil. Cambridge: Cambridge University Press.

Barclay, John M. G.
  1993    "Conflict in Thessalonica." *CBQ* 55:512–30.
Barnouin M.
  1977    "Les problèmes de traduction concernant II Thess ii.6–7."
          *NTS* 23:482–98.
Barr, James
  1962    *Biblical Words for Time*. SBT 33. London: SCM.
Bassler, Jouette M.
  1984    "The Enigmatic Sign: 2 Thessalonians 1:5." *CBQ* 46:496–510.
Baumert, Norbert
  1987    "*Omeiromenoi* in 1 Thess 2,8." *Bib* 68:552–63.
Baumgarten, J.
  1975    *Paulus und die Apokalyptik*. WMANT 44. Neukirchen-Vluyn: Neukirchen-
          er Verlag.
Beauvery, R.
  1955    "*Pleonektein* in I Thess. 4.6a." *VD* 33:78–85.
Becker, J.
  1976    *Auferstehung der Toten im Urchristentum*. SBS 82. Stuttgart: KBW Verlag.
  1993    *Paul: Apostle to the Gentiles*. Louisville, Ky.: Westminster John Knox.
Beker, J. C.
  1980    *Paul the Apostle: The Triumph of God in Life and Thought*. Philadelphia:
          Fortress.
Berger, Klaus
  1974    "Apostelbrief und apostolische Rede: Zum Formular frühchristliche
          Briefe." *ZNW* 65:190–231.
Berry, K. L.
  1995    "Friendship Language in Philippians 4:10–20." Pages 106–24 in Fitzgerald
          1996.
Best, Ernest
  1988    *Paul and His Converts*. Edinburgh: T&T Clark.
Betz, Hans Dieter
  1967    *Nachfolge und Nachahmung Jesus Christi im Neuen Testament*. BHT 37.
          Tübingen: J. C. B. Mohr (Paul Siebeck).
  1978    *Plutarch's Ethical Writings and Early Christian Literature*. SCHNT 4. Lei-
          den: E. J. Brill.
  1979    *Galatians: A Commentary on Paul's Letter to the Churches in Galatia*.
          Hermeneia. Philadelphia: Fortress.
  1994    *Paulinische Studien: Gesammelte Aufsätze III*. Tübingen: J. C. B. Mohr
          (Paul Siebeck).
Billerbeck, Margarethe
  1978    *Epiktet: Von Kynismus*. Philosophia Antiqua 35. Leiden: E. J. Brill.
  1979    *Der Kyniker Demetrius: Ein Beitrag zur Geschichte der frühkaiserzeitlichen
          Popularphilosophie*. Philosophia Antiqua 36. Leiden: E. J. Brill.
Bjerkelund, C. J.
  1967    *Parakalô: Form, Funktion und Sinn der parakalô-Sätze in den paulinischen
          Briefen*. Oslo: Universitetsforlaget.
Black, D. A.
  1984    *Paul, the Apostle of Weakness: Astheneia and Its Cognates in the Pauline Lit-
          erature*. New York-Bern: Peter Lang.

Black, Matthew
    1967    *An Aramaic Approach to the Gospels and Acts.* 3d ed. Oxford: Clarendon.
Boer, Willis P. de
    1962    *The Imitation of Paul: An Exegetical Study.* Kampen: Kok.
Boer, W. den
    1979    "Les historiens des religions et leur dogmes." Pages 1–44 in *Les études clas-
            siques aux xix^e et xx^e ss.* Edited by W. den Boer. Entretiens sur l'antiquité,
            class XXVI. Fondation Hardt. Geneva: Vandoeuvres.
Boers, Hendrikus
    1976    "The Form Critical Study of Paul's Letters. 1 Thessalonians as a Case
            Study." *NTS* 22:140–59.
Boismard, M.-E.
    1961    *Quatre hymnes baptismales dans la première épître de Pierre.* LD 30. Paris:
            Cerf.
Bolkestein, H.
    1939    *Wohltätigkeit und Armenpflege im vorchristliche Altertum: Ein Beitrag zum
            Problem "Moral und Gesellschaft."* Groningen: Bouma.
Bornkamm, Günther
    1969a   *Paul.* Translated by D. M. G. Stalker. New York: Harper & Row.
    1969b   *Early Christian Experience.* New York: Harper & Row.
Bousset, Wilhelm, and Hugo Gressmann
    1966    *Die Religion des Judentums im späthellenistischen Zeitalter.* HNT 21. 1903.
            4th ed. Repr., Tübingen: J. C. B. Mohr (Paul Siebeck).
Bradley, David G.
    1953    "The *Topos* as a Form in the Pauline Paraenesis." *JBL* 72:238–46.
Bradley, Keith
    1986    "Wet-Nursing at Rome: A Study in Social Relations." Pages 201–29 in *The
            Family in Ancient Rome: New Perspectives.* Edited by Beryl Rawson. Ithaca,
            N.Y.: Cornell University Press.
    1991    *Discovering the Roman Family: Studies in Roman Social History.* New York-
            Oxford: Oxford University Press.
Braun, Herbert
    1952–   "Zur nachapostolischen Herkunft des zweiten Thessalonicherbriefes."
    53      *ZNW* 44:152–56.
Braunert, Horst
    1962    "Ein rhetorischer Gebrauch von *ou monon . . . alla kai.*" *RhM* 105:226–36.
Broer, I.
    1983    "'Antisemitismus' und Judenpolemik im Neuen Testament. Ein Beitrag
            zum besseren Verständnis von 1 Thess 2,14–16." *BN* 20:59–91.
    1990    "'Der ganze Zorn is schone über sie gekommen': Bemerkungen zur Inter-
            polationsthese und zur Interpretation von 1 Thess 2,14–16." Pages 137–59
            in Collins 1990.
Bruce, Frederick F.
    1957    *Commentary on the Epistles to the Ephesians and the Colossians.* NICNT.
Brueggemann, Walter
    1968    *Tradition for Crisis: A Study in Hosea.* Louisville, Ky.: John Knox.
Brunt, John C.
    1985    "More on the *Topos* as a New Testament Form." *JBL* 104:495–500.

Buck, Charles, and Greer Taylor
1969    *Saint Paul: A Study in the Development of His Thought*. New York: Scribners.
Bultmann, Rudolf
1951    *Theology of the New Testament*. Vol 1. Translated by K. Grobel. New York: Scribner's.
Bussmann, Claus
1975    *Themen der paulinischen Missionspredigt auf dem Hintergrund der spätjüdisch-hellenistischen Missionsliteratur*. 2d rev. ed. Europäische Hochschulschriften 23.3. Bern-Frankfurt: Peter Lang.
Byrskog, Samuel
1996    "Co-Senders, Co-Authors and Paul's Use of the First Person Plural." ZNW 87:230–50.
Cadbury, Henry J.
1955    *The Book of Acts in History*. New York: Harper.
Cambier, J.-M.
1976    "Le jugement de touts les hommes par Dieu seul, selon la verité, dans Rom 2:1–3:20." ZNW 67:187–213.
Campenhausen, H. von
1957    "Die Begründung kirchlicher Entscheidungen beim Apostel Paulus." SHAW 2. Abhandlung.
1969    *Ecclesiastical Authority and Spiritual Power in the Church of the First Three Centuries*. Stanford: Stanford University Press.
Cancik, Hildegard
1967    *Untersuchungen zu Senecas Epistulae morales*. Spudasmata 18. Hildesheim: George Olms.
Carrington, P.
1940    *The Primitive Christian Catechism*. Cambridge: Cambridge University Press.
Cavallin, H. C. C.
1974    *Life after Death: Paul's Argument for the Resurrection of the the Dead. Part 1*. ConBNT 7:1. Lund: Gleerup.
Chadwick, Henry
1950    "I Thess. 3³: σαίνεσθαι." JTS 1:156–58.
Champion, L. G.
1934    *Benedictions and Doxologies in the Epistles of Paul*. Oxford: Kemp Hall.
Chapa, Juan
1990    "Consolatory Patterns? 1 Thess 4,13.18; 5,11." Pages 220–28 in Collins 1990.
1994    "Is First Thessalonians a Letter of Consolation?" NTS 40:150–60.
Clark, A. C.
1933    *The Acts of the Christian Apostles*. Oxford: Clarendon.
Clerici, Luigi
1966    *Einsammlung der Zerstreuten: Liturgiegeschichtliche Untersuchung zur Vor- und Nachgeschichte der Fürbitte für die Kirche im Didache 9,4 und 10,5*. Münster: Aschendorff.
Collins, Raymond F.
1984    *Studies on the First Letter to the Thessalonians*. BETL 66. Leuven: Leuven University Press.

1990    *The Thessalonian Correspondence.* BETL 87. Leuven: Leuven University Press.
1993    *The Birth of the New Testament: The Origin and Development of the First Christian Generation.* New York: Crossroad.

Coppens, J.
1975    "Miscellanées bibliques. LXXX. Une diatribe antijuive dans I Thess, II,13-16." *ETL* 51:90–95.

Cramer, J. A.
1963    *Catenae Graecorum Patrum in Novum Testamentum.* 1841. Repr., Hildesheim: Georg Olms.

Crawford, Charles
1973    "The 'Tiny' Problem of 1 Thessalonians 2,7: The Case of the Curious Vocative." *Bib* 54:69–72.

Crönert, W.
1906    *Kolotes und Menedemos.* Studien zur Palaeographie und Papyruskunde 6. Munich: A. L. G. Müller.

Cullmann, Oscar
1950    *Christ and Time: The Primitive Christian Conception of Time and History.* Philadelphia: Westminster.
1956    "The Tradition." Pages 59–105 in Cullmann, *The Early Church.* Philadelphia: Westminster.
1958    *Immortality of the Soul or Resurrection of the Body?* London: Epworth.
1966    "Der eschatologische Character des Missionsauftrags und des apostolischen Selbsbewusstseins bei Paulus. Untersuchung zum Begriff des *katechon* in 2 Thess. 2,6–7." Pages 305–36 in *Vorträge und Aufsätze 1925–1962,* 1936. Translated by Karlfried Fröhlich. Tübingen: J. C. B. Mohr (Paul Siebeck).

Dahl, Nils Alstrup
1941    *Das Volk Gottes: Eine Untersuchung zum Kirchenbewusstsein des Urchristentums.* Repr., Olso: A. W. Brøgger.
1967    "Paul and the Church at Corinth according to 1 Corinthians 1–4." Pages 313–35 in Farmer et al.
1975    "Form-Critical Observations on Early Christian Preaching." Pages 30–56 in Dahl, *Jesus in the Memory of the Early Church.* Minneapolis: Augsburg.

Dalfen, Joachim
1967    *Formgeschichtliche Untersuchungen zu den Selbstbetrachtungen Marc Aurels.* Inaug. diss. Munich.

Daube, David
1964    *The Sudden in the Scriptures.* Leiden: E. J. Brill.

Dautzenberg, G.
1969    "Theologie und Seelsorge aus Paulinischer Tradition: Einführung in 2 Thess, Kol, Eph." Pages 96–119 in *Gestalt und Anspruch des Neuen Testaments.* Edited by J. Schreiner. Würzburg: Echter Verlag.
1975    *Urchristliche Prophetie. Ihre Erforschung, ihre Voraussetzungen im Judentum und ihre Struktur im ersten Korinthebrief.* BWANT 6.4. Stuttgart-Berlin: Kohlhammer.

Davies, W. D.
1977    "Paul and the People of Israel." *NTS* 24:4–39.
1980    *Paul and Rabbinic Judaism: Some Rabbinic Elements in Pauline Theology.* 4th ed. Philadelphia: Fortress.

Deidun, J. J.
1981    *New Covenant Morality in Paul.* AnBib 89.
Deissmann, Adolf
1957    *Paul: A Study in Social and Religious History.* Translated by William E. Wilson. New York: Harper & Row.
1965    *Light from the Ancient East: The New Testament Illustrated by Recently Discovered Texts of the Graeco-Roman World.* Translated (1927) from the 4th German ed. (1923) by Harper & Row. Repr., Grand Rapids: Baker.
Delling, Gerhard
1963    "Partizipiale Gottesprädikationen in den Briefen des Neuen Testaments." *ST* 17:1–59.
1969    "Zum steigernden Gebrauch von Komposita mit ὑπέρ bei Paulus." *NovT* 11:127–53.
1970    *Studien zum Neuen Testament und zum hellenistischen Judentum: Gesammelte Aufsätze 1950–1969.* Göttingen: Vandenhoeck & Ruprecht.
1975    "Die Bezeichnung 'Gott des Friedens' und ähnliche Wendungen in den Paulusbriefen." Pages 76–84 in *Jesus und Paulus* (W. G. Kümmel FS). Edited by E. E. Ellis and E. Grässer. Göttingen: Vandenhoeck & Ruprecht.
Deming, Will
1995    *Paul on Marriage and Celibacy: The Hellenistic Background of 1 Corinthians 7.* SNTSMS 83. Cambridge: Cambridge University Press.
Denis, Albert-Marie
1957    "L'Apôtre Paul, 'prophète messianique' des Gentils: Étude thématique de 1 Thess., II,1–6." *ETL* 33:245–318.
Dewailly, L.-M.
1963    *La jeune église de Thessalonique: Les deux prémières épîtres de Saint Paul.* LD 37. Paris: Cerf.
De Witt, N. W.
1954a   *Epicurus and His Philosophy.* Minneapolis: University of Minnesota Press.
1954b   *St. Paul and Epicurus.* Minneapolis: University of Minnesota Press.
Dibelius, Martin
1935    *From Tradition to Gospel.* New York: Scribner's.
1972    *A Commentary on the Pastoral Epistles.* Translated by Philip Butolph and Adela Yarbro. Hermeneia. Philadelphia: Fortress.
Dick, Karl
1899    *Die schriftstellerische Plural bei Paulus.* Halle: Ehrhardt Karras.
Dihle, Albrecht
1962    *Die goldene Regel: Eine Einführung in die Geschichte der antiken und frühchristlichen Vulgärethik.* Göttingen: Vandenhoeck & Ruprecht.
Dill, Samuel
1925    *Roman Society from Nero to Marcus Aurelius.* London: MacMillan.
Dobbeler, Axel von
1987    *Glauben als Teilhabe.* WUNT 2:22.
Dobschütz, Ernst von
1904    *Christian Life in the Primitive Church.* Translated by George Brenner. London: Williams & Norgate.
Dodd, Charles H.
1963    *New Testament Studies.* Manchester: Manchester University Press.

# BIBLIOGRAPHY

1968    "The 'Primitive Catechism' and the Sayings of Jesus." Pages 11–29 in *More New Testament Studies*. Grand Rapids: Eerdmans.

Dodds, E. R.
1965    *Pagan and Christian in an Age of Anxiety: Some Aspects of Religious Experience from Marcus Aurelius to Constantine*. Cambridge: Cambridge University Press.

Donfried, Karl P.
1984    "Paul and Judaism: 1 Thessalonians 2:13–16 as a Test Case." *Int* 38:242–53.
1985    "The Cults of Thessalonica and the Thessalonian Correspondence." *NTS* 31:336–56.
1993    *The Theology of the Shorter Pauline Letters*. With I. Howard Marshall. Cambridge: Cambridge University Press.

Düring, Ingemar
1951    *Chion of Heraclea: A Novel in Letters*. Göteborg: Wettergren & Kerbers.

Dunn, James D. G.
1988    *Romans 1–8*. WBC 38A. Waco, Tex.: Word.

Dupont, Jacques
1952    *SYN CHRISTO: L'union avec le Christ suivant Saint Paul*. Bruges: Abbaye de Saint André.

Dupont-Sommer, A.
1961    *The Essene Writings from Qumran*. New York: Meridian.

Eckart, K.-G.
1961    "Der zweite echte Brief des Apostels Paulus an die Thessalonicher." *ZTK* 58:30–44.

Edson, C.
1948    "Cults of Thessalonica." *HTR* 41:105–204.

Ehrenberg, V.
1947    "Polypragmosyne: A Study in Greek Politics." *JHS* 67:46–67.

Elliger, Winfried
1978    *Paulus in Griechenland: Philippi, Thessaloniki, Athen, Korinth*. SBS 92/93. Stuttgart: Katholisches Bibelwerk.

Ellingworth, P., and E. A. Nida
1975    *A Translator's Handbook on Paul's Letters to the Thessalonians*. Helps for Translators 16. Stuttgart: United Bible Society.

Elliott, Neil
1994    *Liberating Paul: The Justice of God and the Politics of the Apostle*. Maryknoll, N.Y.: Orbis.

Ellis, E. Earle
1978    *Prophecy and Hermeneutic in Early Christianity*. WUNT 18. Tübingen: J. C. B. Mohr (Paul Siebeck).

Epp, Eldon J.
1966    *The Theological Tendency of Codex Bezae Cantabrigiensis*. SNTSMS 3.
1991    "New Testament Papyrus Manuscripts and Letter Carrying in Greco-Roman Times." Pages 35–56 in *The Future of Early Christianity* (Helmut Koester FS). Edited by Birger A. Pearson. Minneapolis: Fortress.

Evans, C. A.
1993    "Ascending and Descending with a Shout: Psalms 47.6 and 1 Thessalonians 4.16." Pages 238–53 in *Paul and the Scriptures of Israel*. Edited by C. A. Evans and J. A. Sanders. JSNTSSup 83. Sheffield: Academic.

Evans, Robert M.
1967   "Eschatology and Ethics: A Study of Thessalonica and Paul's Letters to the Thessalonians." Diss., University of Basel.

Exler, Francis Xavier J.
1923   *The Form of the Ancient Greek Letter: A Study in Greek Epistolography.* Washington, D. C.: Catholic University of America.

Farmer, William R., C. F. D. Moule, and R. R. Niebuhr, eds.
1967   *Christian History and Interpretation* (John Knox FS). Cambridge: Cambridge University Press.

Faw, Chalmer E.
1952   "On the Writing of First Thessalonians." *JBL* 71:217–25.

Fee, Gordon P.
1995   *Paul's Letter to the Philippians.* NICNT. Grand Rapids: Eerdmans.

Festugière, A.-J.
1961   "Lieux communs littéraires et thèmes de folk-lore dans l'Hagiographie primitive." *Wiener Studien* 74:139–42.

Field, Frederick
1899   *Notes on the Translation of the New Testament.* Cambridge: Cambridge University Press.

Fiore, Benjamin
1986   *The Function of Personal Example in the Socratic and Pastoral Epistles.* AnBib 105.

Fiorenza, Elisabeth S.
1983   *In Memory of Her: A Feminist Theological Reconstruction of Christian Origins.* New York: Crossroad.

Fitzgerald, John T.
1988   *Cracks in an Earthen Vessel: An Examination of the Catalogues of Hardships in the Corinthian Correspondence.* SBLDS 99. Atlanta: Scholars Press.
1996   *Friendship, Flattery and Freedom of Speech.* NovTSup. Leiden: E. J. Brill.
1997   *Greco-Roman Perspectives on Friendship.* SBLSBS. Atlanta: Scholars Press.

Fontaine, Jacques
1982   "Un cliché de la spiritualité antique tardive: *stet immobilis.*" Pages 528–52 in *Romanitas-Christianitas: Untersuchungen zur Geschichte und Literatur der römischen Kaiserzeit* (Johannes Straub FS). Edited by Gerhard Wirth. Berlin-New York: W. de Gruyter.

Forbes, Christopher
1995   *Prophecy and Inspired Speech in Early Christianity and Its Hellenistic Environment.* WUNT 2:75. Tübingen: J. C. B. Mohr (Paul Siebeck).

Fowl, Stephen
1990   "A Metaphor in Distress: A Reading of NEPIOI in 1 Thessalonians 2.7." *NTS* 36:469–73.

Fredrickson, David E.
1990   "Paul's Bold Speech in the Argument of 2 Cor 2:14–7:16." Ph.D. diss., Yale University.

Friedrich, Gerhard
1956   "Lohmeyers These über das paulinische Briefpräskript kritisch beleuchtet." *TLZ* 81:343–46.
1965   "Ein Tauflied hellenistischer Judenchristen: 1 Thess 1,9f." *TZ* 21:502–16.

1973 "1 Thessalonicher 5,1–11, der apologetischer Einschub eines Späteren." *ZTK* 70:288–315.

Fuchs, Ernst
1960 "Hermeneutik?" *ThViat* 7:44–60.

Funk, Robert W.
1966 *Language, Hermeneutics, and Word of God.* New York: Harper & Row.
1967 "Apostolic *Parousia*: Form and Significance." Pages 249–68 in Farmer et al.

Furnish, Victor P.
1971 "Fellow Workers in God's Service." *JBL* 80:364–70.
1984 *II Corinthians.* AB 32A. New York, NY: Doubleday.
1989 "Der 'Wille Gottes' in paulinischer Sicht." Pages 208–21 in Koch et al.

Gamble, Harry Y.
1977 *The Textual History of the Letter to the Romans.* SD, 42. Grand Rapids: Eerdmans.
1995 *Books and Readers in the Early Church: A History of Early Texts.* New Haven: Yale University Press.

Ganss, W.
1952 "Das Bild des Weisen bei Seneca." Diss., University of Freiburg.

Garlington, Don B.
1994 *Faith, Obedience, and Perseverance: Aspects of Paul's Letter to the Romans.* WUNT 79.

Gaventa, B. R.
1990 "Apostles as Babes and Nurses in 1 Thessalonians 2:7." Pages 193–207 in *Faith and History* (Paul W. Meyer FS). Edited by J. T. Carroll et. al. Atlanta: Scholars Press.

Geffcken, Johannes
1907 *Zwei griechische Apologeten.* Leipzig: B. G. Teubner.

Gerhard, G. A.
1909 *Phoinix von Kolophon.* Leipzig-Berlin: B. G. Teubner.

Gerhardsson, B.
1961 *Memory and Manuscript: Oral Tradition and Written Transmission in Rabbinic Judaism and Early Christianity.* ASNU 22. Uppsala, Sweden: C. W. K. Gleerup.

Geurts, N.
1928 *Het Huwelijk bij de Griekse en Romeinse Moralisten.* Diss., University of Utrecht. Amsterdam: H. V. Paris.

Geytenbeek, A. C. van
1963 *Musonius Rufus and Greek Diatribe.* Assen: van Gorcum.

Giblin, Charles H.
1967 *The Threat to Faith: An Exegetical and Theological Re-Examination of 2 Thessalonians 2.* AnBib 31. Rome: Pontifical Biblical Institute.

Giesen, H.
1985 "Naherwartung des Paulus im 1 Thess 4,13–18. Pages 123–50 in SNTSU. Linz: A. Fuchs.

Gillespie, Thomas W.
1994 *The First Theologians: A Study in Early Christian Prophecy.* Grand Rapids: Eerdmans.

Gilliard, F.
1989    "The Problem of the Antisemitic Comma between 1 Thessalonians 2.14 and 15." *NTS* 89:481–502.
Gillman, John
1985    "Signals of Transformation in 1 Thessalonians 4:13–18." *CBQ* 47:263–81.
Giusta, M.
1964,   *I dossografi de etica.* 2 vols.: vol. 1 (1964); vol. 2 (1967). Turin: Giapichelli.
1967
Glad, Clarence E.
1995    *Paul and Philodemus: Adaptability in Epicurean and Early Christian Psychagogy.* NovTSup 81. Leiden: E. J. Brill.
Goguel, M.
1925    *Introduction au Nouveau Testament.* 4 vols. Paris: Leroux.
Goppelt, L.
1970    *Apostolic and Post-Apostolic Times.* New York: Harper & Row.
Graafen, J.
1930    *Der Echtheit des 2 Thessalonicherbriefes.* NTAbh 14.5. Münster: Aschendorff.
Grabner-Haider, A.
1985    *Paraklese und Eschatologie bei Paulus: Mensch und Welt im Anspruch der Zukunft Gottes.* NTAbh N.F.4. Münster: Aschendorff.
Greeven, H.
1958    "Die missionierende Gemeinde nach den paulinischen Briefen." Pages 59–71 in *Sammlung und Sendung: Vom Auftrag der Kirche in der Welt.* Edited by J. Heubach & H. Ulrich. Berlin: Christlicher Zeitschriftenverlag.
Gregg, Robert C.
1975    *Consolation Philosophy: Greek and Christian Paideia in Basil and the Two Gregories.* Patristic Monograph Series, no. 3. Philadelphia: The Philadelphia Patristic Foundation.
Gregson, R.
1966    "A Solution to the Problem of the Thessalonian Epistles." *TQ* 38:76–80.
Grotius, Hugo
1641–   *Annotationes in Novum Testamentum.* 2 vols.: vol. 1, Amsterdam: J. T.
46      Blaev; vol. 2, Paris: Sumptibus Authoris.
Gundry, R. H.
1987    "The Hellenization of Dominical Tradition and the Christianization of Jewish Tradition in the Eschatology of 1–2 Thessalonians." *NTS* 33:161–78.
Guntermann, F.
1932    *Die Eschatologie des Hl. Paulus.* NTAbh 13.4/5. Münster: Aschendorff.
Gutierrez, Pedro
1968    *La paternité spirituelle selon saint Paul.* ÉBib. Paris: Gabalda.
Haacker, Klaus
1972    "Die Gallio-Episode und die paulinische Chronologie." *BZ* n.s. 16:252–5.
1988    "Elemente des heidnische Antijudaismus im Neuen Testament." *EvT* 48:404–18.
Hadorn, Wilhelm
1919    *Die Abfassung der Thessalonicherbriefe in der Zeit der dritten Missionsreise der Paulus.* BFCT 24:3–4. Gütersloh: Bertelsmann.

1919–  "Die Abfassung der Thessalonicherbriefe auf der dritten Missionsreise und
20     der Kanon des Marcion." ZNW 19:67–72.
1922   "Die Gefährten und Mitarbeiter des Paulus." Pages 65–82 in *Aus Schrift
       und Geschichte* (Adolf Schlatter FS). Edited by K. B. Bornhäuser. Stuttgart:
       Calwer.
Hadot, Ilsetraut
1969   *Seneca und die griechisch-römische Tradition der Seelenleitung.* Quellen
       und Studien zur Geschichte der Philosophie 13. Berlin: W. de Gruyter.
Haenchen, Ernst
1971   *The Acts of the Apostles.* Translated by Bernard Noble and Gerald Shin.
       Philadelphia: Westminster.
Hahn, Johannes
1989   *Der Philosoph und die Gesellschaft: Selbstverständnis, öffentliches
       Auftreten und populäre Erwartungen in der hohen Kaiserzeit.* Heidelberg-
       er althistorische Beiträge und epigraphische Studien 7. Stuttgart: Franz
       Steiner.
Hainz, Josef
1972   *Ekklesia: Strukturen paulinischer Gemeinde-Theologie und Gemeinde-Ord-
       nung.* Regensburg: Pustet.
Halamka, Ronald F.
1975   "I and II Thessalonians on Pastoral Care for Recent Converts." Ph.D. diss.,
       Concordia Seminary.
Hands, A. R.
1968   *Charities and Social Aid in Greece and Rome.* Aspects of Greek and Roman
       Life. Ithaca, N.Y.: Cornell University Press.
Hare, D. R. A.
1967   *The Theme of Jewish Persecution of Christians in the Gospel according to St.
       Matthew.* SNTSMS 6. Cambridge: Cambridge University Press.
Harnack, Adolf von
1910   "Der Problem des zweiten Thessalonicherbriefes." *Sitzungesberichte der
       königlichen preussischen Akademie der Wissenschaften.* Philosophisch-His-
       torischen Klasse, 1910, 560–78.
1928   "*Kopos (Kopian, Hoi Kopiontes*) im frühchristlichen Sprachgebrauch."
       ZNW 27:1–10.
Harnisch, Wofgang
1973   *Eschatologische Existenz: Ein exegetischer Beitrag zum Sachanliegen von
       1. Thessalonicher 4,13–5,11.* FRLANT 110. Göttingen: Vandenhoeck &
       Ruprecht.
Harrer, G. A.
1940   "Saul Who Also is Called Paul." HTR 33:19–34.
Harris, J. Rendel
1898   "A Study in Letter-Writing." *The Expositer.* 5th series. 8:161–80.
Hartman, Lars
1966   *Prophecy Interpreted: The Formation of Some Jewish Apocalyptic Texts and of
       the Eschatological Discourse Mark 13 Par.* ConBNT 1. Lund: C. W. K.
       Gleerup.
Helm, Rudolf
1906   *Lucian und Menipp.* Leipzig: Teubner. Repr., Hildesheim: Georg Olms,
       1967.

Hemer, Colin J.
1980    "Observations on Pauline Chronology." Pages 3–18 in *Pauline Studies* (F. F. Bruce FS). Edited by Donald A. Hagner and Murray J. Harris. Grand Rapids: Eerdmans.

Hendrix, H. L.
1984    "Thessalonicans Honor Romans." Th.D. diss., Harvard University.
1991    "Archaeology and Eschatology at Thessalonica." Pages 107–18 in *The Future of Early Christianity* (Helmut Koester FS). Edited by Birger Pearson. Minneapolis: Fortress.

Hengel, Martin
1991    *The Pre-Christian Paul*. Philadelphia: Trinity Press International.

Hengel, Martin, and Anna Maria Schwemer
1997    *Paul between Damascus and Antioch: The Unknown Years*. Louisville, Ky.: Westminster John Knox.

Henneken, Bartholomäus
1969    *Verkündigung und Prophetie im Ersten Thessalonicherbrief. Ein Beitrag zur Theologie des Wortes Gottes*. SBS 29. Stuttgart: Katholisches Bibelwerk.

Herzer, Jens
1998    *Petrus oder Paulus? Studied über das Verhältnis des Ersten Petrusbriefes zur paulinischen Tradition*. WUNT 103. Tübingen: Mohr Siebeck.

Hilgenfeld, A.
1899    *Acta Apostolorum Graece et Latine*. Berlin: G. Reimer.

Hill, David
1977    "Christian Prophets as Teachers of Instructors in the Church." Pages 108–30 in Panagopoulos.

Hock, Ronald F.
1980    *The Social Context of Paul's Ministry: Tentmaking and Apostleship*. Philadelphia: Fortress.

Hoffmann, Paul
1966    *Die Toten in Christus: Eine religionsgeschichtliche und exegetische Untersuchung zur paulinischen Eschatologie*. NTAbh N. F. 2. Münster: Aschendorff.

Holladay, Carl R.
1990    "1 Corinthians 13: Paul as Apostolic Paradigm." Pages 80–98 in Balch et al.

Holleman, Joost
1996    *Resurrection and Parousia: A Traditio-Historical Study of Paul's Eschatology in 1 Corinthians 15*. NovTSup 84. Leiden: E. J. Brill.

Holmberg, Bengt
1978    *Paul and Power: The Structure of Authority in the Primitive Church as Reflected in the Pauline Epistles*. Philadelphia: Fortress.

Holmstrand, Jonas
1997    *Markers and Meaning in Paul: An Analysis of 1 Thessalonians, Philippians and Galatians*. ConBNT 28. Stockholm: Almqvist & Wiksell.

Holtz, Traugott
1977    "'Euer Glaube an Gott': Zu Form und Inhalt von 1 Thess 1,9f." Pages 459–88 in *Die Kirche des Anfangs* (H. Schürmann FS). Edited by R. Schackenburg. Leipzig: St. Benno Verlag.
1982    "Der Apostel des Christus. Die paulinische 'Apologie' 1 Thess 2,1–12." Pages 101–16 in *Als Boten des gekreuzigten Herrn* (W. Krusche FS). Edited by H. Falcke, M. Onnasch, and H. Schultze. Berlin: Evangelische Verlagsanstalt.

1983    "Traditionen im 1 Thessalonicherbrief." Pages 55–79 in *Die Mitte des Neuen Testaments* (E. Schweizer FS). Edited by Ulrich Luz and Hans Weder. Göttingen: Vandenhoeck & Ruprecht.

Hommel, Hildebrecht
1956    *Schöpfer und Erhalter: Studien zum Problem Christentum und Antike.* Berlin: Lettner.

Hooker, Morna D., and Stephen G. Wilson, eds.
1982    *Paul and Paulinism* (C. K. Barrett FS). London: SPCK.

Horbury, William
1982    "1 Thessalonians ii.3 as Rebutting the Charge of False Prophecy." *JTS* 33:492–508.

Horn, F. W.
1992    *Das Angeld des Geistes: Studien zur paulinischen Pneumatologie.* FRLANT 154. Göttingen: Vandenhoeck & Ruprecht.

Horsley, G. H. R.
1994    "The Politarchs." Pages 419–31 in *The Book of Acts in Its Graeco-Roman Setting.* Edited by D. W. J. Gill and C. Gempf. The Book of Acts in Its First Century Setting, 2. Grand Rapids: Eerdmans.

Horst, P. W. van der
1978    *The Sentences of Pseudo-Phocylides.* Leiden: E. J. Brill.

Hughes, F. W.
1989    *Early Christian Rhetoric and 2 Thessalonians.* JSNTSup 30. Sheffield: JSOT Press.
1990    "The Rhetoric of 1 Thessalonians." Pages 94–116 in Collins 1990.

Hultgren, Arland J.
1985    *Paul's Gospel and Mission: The Outlook from His Letter to the Romans.* Philadelphia: Fortress.

Hunt, Allen R.
1996    *The Inspired Body: Paul, the Corinthians, and Divine Inspiration.* Macon, Ga.: Mercer University Press.

Hurd, John C.
1965    *The Origin of 1 Corinthians.* London: SPCK.

Huser, Fritz
1924    *Leib und Seele in der Sprache Senecas. Ein Beitrag zur sprachlichen Formulierung der moralischen Adhortatio.* Halle: Max Niemeyer.

Hyldahl, Nils
1980    "Auferstehung Christi-Auferstehung der Toten (1 Thess 4:13–18)." Pages 119–35 in *Die paulinische Literatur und Theologie.* Edited by S. Pedersen. Göttingen: Vandenhoeck & Ruprecht.

Jenks, Gregory C.
1991    *The Origins and Early Development of the Antichrist Myth.* BZNW 59. Berlin-New York: W. de Gruyter.

Jeremias, Joachim
1959    "Paarweise Sendung in Neuen Testament." Pages 136–43 in *Studies in Memory of Thomas Walter Manson 1893–1958.* Manchester: Manchester University Press.
1964    *Unknown Sayings of Jesus.* 2d ed. London: SPCK.

Jewett, Robert
1969    "The Form and Function of the Hellenistic Benediction." *AThR* 51:18–34.

1971a "The Agitators and the Galatian Congregation." *NTS* 17:198–212.
1971b *Paul's Anthropological Terms: A Study of the Use in Conflict Settings.* AGJU 10. Leiden: E. J. Brill.
1972 "Enthusiastic Radicalism and the Thessalonian Correspondence." Pages 182–232 in *SBL 1972 Proceedings.* 2 vols. SBL Annual Meeting.
1979 *A Chronology of Paul's Life.* Philadelphia: Fortress.
1986 *The Thessalonian Correspondence: Pauline Rhetoric and Millenarian Piety.* FF. Philadelphia: Fortress.
1993 "Tenement Churches and Communal Meals in the Early Church: Implications of a Form-Critical Analysis of 2 Thessalonians 3:10." *BR* 38:23–43.

Johanson, Bruce C.
1987 *To All the Brethren: A Text-Linguistic and Rhetorical Approach to 1 Thessalonians.* ConBNT Series 16. Stockholm: Almqvist and Wiksell International.

Johnson, Luke T.
1986 "The New Testament's Anti-Jewish Slander and the Conventions of Ancient Polemic." *JBL* 108:419–41.

Jones, C. P.
1986 *Culture and Society in Lucian.* Cambridge, Mass: Harvard University Press.

Judge, Edwin A.
1960a *The Social Pattern of Christian Groups in the First Century.* London: Tyndale.
1960b "The Early Christians as a Scholastic Community." *JRH* 1:4–15, 125–37.
1971 "The Decrees of Caesar at Thessalonica." *RTR* 30:1–7.
1983 "Cultural Conformity and Innovation in Paul: Some Clues from Contemporary Documents." *TynBul* 35:3–24.

Jülicher, Adolf
1931 *Einleitung in das Neue Testament.* 7th ed. Tübingen: J. C. B. Mohr (Paul Siebeck).

Jungkuntz, R.
1966 "Fathers, Heretics and Epicureans." *JEH* 17:3–10.

Kaesemann, Ernst
1969 "Pauline Version of the 'Amor Fati.'" Pages 217–35 in Kaesemann, *New Testament Questions of Today.* Philadelphia: Fortress.

Kaibel, G.
1878 *Epigrammata Graeca ex lapidis conlecta.* Berlin: G. Reimer.

Kamlah, E.
1963 "Wie beurteilt Paulus sein Leiden? Ein Beitrag zur Untersuchung seiner Denkstruktur." *ZNW* 54:217–32.
1964 *Die Form der katalogischen Paränese im Neuen Testament.* WUNT 7. Tübingen: J. C. B. Mohr (Paul Siebeck).

Karlsson, Gustav
1956 "Formelhaftes in Paulusbriefen?" *ErJB* 54:136–42.

Kaye, B. N.
1975 "Eschatology and Ethics in 1 and 2 Thessalonians." *NovT* 17:47–57.

Kemmler, Werner
1975 *Faith and Human Reason: A Study of Paul's Method of Preaching as Illustrated by 1–2 Thessalonians and Acts 17, 2–4.* NovTSup 40. Leiden: E. J. Brill.

Klauck, H.-J.
1982    *Herrenmahl und hellenistischer Kult: Eine religionsgeschichtliche Unter-suchung zum ersten Korintherbrief.* NTAbh N.F. 15. Münster: Aschendorff.
Klijn, A. F. J.
1982    "1 Thessalonians 4.13–18 and Its Background in Apocalyptic Literature." Pages 67–73 in Hooker and Wilson.
Klinghardt, Matthias
1996    *Gemeinschaftsmahl und Mahlgemeinschaft: Soziologie und Liturgie früchristlicher Mahlfeiern.* TANZ 13. Tübingen-Basel: Francke.
Kloppenborg, John
1993    "Philadelphia, theodidaktos and the Dioscuri: Rhetorical Engagement in 1 Thessalonians." *NTS* 39:265–289.
Klumbies, Paul-Gerhard
1992    *Die Rede von Gott bei Paulus in ihrem zeitgeschichtlichen Kontext.* FRLANT 155. Göttingen: Vandenhoeck & Ruprecht.
Knox, John
1950    *Chapters in a Life of Paul.* New York: Abingdon.
Koch, D.-A., ed.
1989    *Jesu Rede von Gott und ihre Nachgeschichte im frühen Christentum* (Willi Marxsen FS). Gütersloh: Gerd Mohn.
Koester, Helmut
1971    *Trajectories through Early Christianity,* with James M. Robinson. Philadelphia: Fortress.
1979    "1 Thessalonians—Experiment in Christian Writing." Pages 33–44 in *Continuity and Discontinuity in Church History. Essays Presented to George Huntston Williams.* SHCT 19. Leiden: E. J. Brill.
1980    "Apostel und Gemeinde in den Briefen an die Thessalonicher." Pages 287–98 in *Kirche* (Günther Bornkamm FS). Edited by Dieter Lührmann and Georg Strecker. Tübingen: J. C. B. Mohr (Paul Siebeck).
1982    *Introduction to the New Testament Volume II: History and Literature of Early Christianity.* Philadelphia: Fortress.
1985    "The Text of 1 Thessalonians." Pages 219–27 in *The Living Text* (Ernest W. Saunders FS). Edited by Dennis E. Groh and Robert Jewett. Lanham, Md.: University Press of America.
1990    "From Paul's Eschatology to the Apocalyptic Schemata of 2 Thessalonians." Pages 441–58 in Collins 1990.
1994    "Archäologie und Paulus in Thessalonike." Pages 393–404 in *Religious Propaganda and Missionary Competition in the New Testament World* (Dieter Georgi FS). Edited by L. Bormann et al. NovTSup 74. Leiden: E. J. Brill.
Kötting, B.
1978    "Genossenschaft." *RAC* 10:83–155.
Koskenniemi, Heikki
1956    *Studien zur Idee und Phraseologie des griechischen Briefes bis 400 n. Chr.* Annales Academiae scientarum fennicae. Series B, vol. 102:2. Helsinki: Suomalainen Tiedeakatemia.
Kraabel, A. T.
1981    "The Disappearance of the God-fearers." *Numen* 28:113–26. Repr. as pages 119–27 in Overman and MacLennan.

Kramer, Werner
1966    *Christ, Lord, Son of God.* SBT 50. Naperville, Ill.: Allenson.
Kraus, Wolfgang
1996    *Das Volk Gottes. Zur Grundlegung der Ekklesiologie bei Paulus.* WUNT 85.
        Tübingen: J. C. B. Mohr (Paul Siebeck).
Kreitzer, L. Joseph
1987    *Jesus and God in Paul's Eschatology.* JSNTSup 19. Sheffield: JSOT Press.
Krentz, Edgar M.
1992    "First and Second Epistles to the Thessalonians." *ABD* 6:515–23.
Kuck, David W.
1992    *Judgment and Community Conflict: Paul's Use of Apocalyptic Judgment
        Language in 1 Corinthians 3:5–4:5.* NovTSup 66. Leiden: E. J. Brill.
Kümmel, Werner Georg
1957    *Promise and Fulfilment: The Eschatological Message of Jesus.* SBT 23. Lon-
        don: SCM Press.
1975    *Introduction to the New Testament.* Rev. ed. Translated by H. C. Kee.
        Nashville, Tenn.: Abingdon.
Lachmann, K. L.
1842    *Novum Testamentum Graece et Latine.* Berlin: Reimer.
Lake, Kirsopp
1911    *The Earlier Epistles of St. Paul: Their Motive and Origin.* London: Riving-
        tons.
Lambrecht, Jan
1990    "Thanksgivings in 1 Thessalonians 1–3." Pages 183–205 in Collins 1990.
Lane Fox, Robin
1987    *Pagans and Christians.* New York: A. Knopf.
Langevin, Paul-Emile, SJ
1967    *Jésus seigneur et l'eschatologie: Exégèse de textes prépauliniens.* Studia.
        Travaux de recherche 21. Bruges: Desclée de Brouwer.
Lattimore, R.
1962    *Themes in Greek and Latin Epitaphs.* Urbana, Ill.: University of Illinois
        Press.
Laub, Franz
1973    *Eschatologische Verkündigung und Lebensgestaltung nach Paulus: Eine Un-
        tersuchung zum Wirken des Apostels beim Aufbau der Gemeinde in Thessa-
        lonike.* Regensburg: Pustet.
1976    "Paulus als Gemeindegründer (1 Thess)." Pages 17–38 in *Kirche im Werden:
        Studien zum Thema Amt und Gemeinde in Neuen Testament.* Edited by
        Josef Hainz. Munich: Paderborn.
1990    "Paulinische Autorität in nachapostolische Zeit (2 Thess)." Pages 403–17 in
        Collins 1990.
Lautenschlager, M.
1990    "Eite gregoromen eite katheudomen: Zum Verhältnis von Heiligung und
        Heil in 1 Thess 5,10." *ZNW* 81:39–59.
Levinskaya, Irina
1996    *The Book of Acts in Its Diaspora Setting.* The Book of Acts in Its First Cen-
        tury Setting 5. Grand Rapids: Eerdmans.
Liebeschuetz, J. H. W. G.
1979    *Continuity and Change in Roman Religion.* Oxford: Clarendon.

Lietzmann, Hans
1919    *An die Römer*. HNT 1. Tübingen: J. C. B. Mohr (Paul Siebeck).
Lieu, Judith M.
1985    "'Grace to You and Peace': The Apostolic Greeting." *BJRL* 68:161–78.
Lightfoot, Joseph B.
1893    "The Churches in Macedonia." Pages 237–50 in Lightfoot, *Biblical Essays*. London: Macmillan.
Lindemann, Andreas
1977    "Zum Abfassungszweck des Zweiten Thessalonicherbriefes." *ZNW* 68:35–47.
Lövestam, E.
1958    "Über die neutestamentliche Aufforderung zur Nüchterheit." *ST* 12:80–102.
1963    *Spiritual Wakefulness in the New Testament*. Lund: Ohlsson.
Lohmeyer, Ernst
1927    "Probleme paulinischer Theologie: I: Briefliche Grussüberschriften." *ZNW* 26:158–73.
Lohse, Eduard
1968    *Die Briefe an die Kolosser und an Philemon*. 14th ed. KEK. Göttingen: Vandenhoeck & Ruprecht.
Lucchesi, E.
1977    "Précédents non bibliques à l'expression néo-testamentaire: 'les temps et les moments.'" *JTS* 28:537–40.
Luedemann, Gerd
1984    *Paul: Apostle to the Gentiles. Studies in Chronology*. Translated by F. Stanley Jones. Philadelphia: Fortress.
Lührmann, Dieter
1990    "The Beginnings of the Church at Thessalonica." Pages 237–49 in Balch et al.
Lütgert, W.
1909    *Die Volkommenen in Philipperbrief und die Enthusiasten in Thessalonich*. BFCT 6. Gütersloh: Bertelsmann.
Lutz, Cora E.
1947    *Musonius Rufus: "The Roman Socrates."* YCS 10. New Haven: Yale University Press.
Luz, U.
1968    *Das Geschichtsverständnis des Paulus*. BEvT 49. Munich: Evangenlischer Verlag.
Lyons, George
1985    *Pauline Autobiography: Toward a New Understanding*. SBLDS 73. Atlanta: Scholars Press.
MacMullen, Ramsey
1966    *Enemies of the Roman Order: Treason, Unrest and Alienation in the Empire*. Cambridge, Mass.: Harvard University Press.
1974    *Roman Social Relations 50 B.C. to A.D. 284*. New Haven: Yale University Press.
1981    *Paganism in the Roman Empire*. New Haven: Yale University Press.
Malbon, Elizabeth C.
1983    "'No Need to Have Anyone Write'? A Structural Exegesis of 1 Thessalonians." *Semeia* 26:57–83.

Malherbe, Abraham J.
1968    "The Beasts at Ephesus." *JBL* 87:71–80 (=1989: 79–89).
1969    "Athenagoras on Christian Ethics." *JEH* 20:1–5.
1970a   "'Gentle as a Nurse': The Cynic Background to 1 Thess. 2." *NovT* 12:203–17 (=1989: 35–48).
1970b   "The Apologetic Theology of the *Preaching of Peter.*" *ResQ* 13:205–23.
1978    "Pseudo-Heraclitus, Epistle 4: The Divinization of the Wise Man." *JAC* 21:42–64.
1983a   "Exhortation in First Thessalonians." *NovT* 25:238–56 (=1989: 49–66).
1983b   *Social Aspects of Early Christianity.* 2d ed., enlarged. Philadelphia: Fortress.
1986a   "'Not In a Corner': Early Christian Apologetic in Acts 26:26." *SecCent* 5:193–210 (=1989: 147–63).
1986b   *Moral Exhortation: A Greco-Roman Sourcebook.* LEC 4. Philadelphia: Westminster.
1987    *Paul and the Thessalonians: The Philosophical Tradition of Pastoral Care.* Philadelphia: Fortress.
1988a   *Ancient Epistolary Theorists.* SBLSBS 12. Atlanta: Scholars Press.
1988b   "Herakles." *RAC* 15:559–83.
1989    *Paul and the Popular Philosophers.* Minneapolis: Fortress.
1990a   "Did the Thessalonians Write to Paul?" Pages 246–57 in *The Conversation Continues: Studies in Paul and John* (J. L. Martyn FS). Edited by R. Fortna and B. Gaventa. Nashville, Tenn.: Abingdon.
1990b   "'Pastoral Care' in the Thessalonian Church." *NTS* 36:375–91.
1991    "'Seneca' on Paul as Letter Writer." Pages 414–21 in *The Future of Early Christianity* (Helmut Koester FS). Edited by Birger A. Pearson. Minneapolis: Fortress.
1992    "Hellenistic Moralists and the New Testament." Pages 267–333 in ANRW II 26:3.
1995a   "God's Family in Thessalonica." Pages 117–28 in *The First Christians and Their Social World* (Wayne A. Meeks FS). Edited by L. Michael White and O. Larry Yarbrough. Minneapolis: Augsburg Fortress.
1995b   "Determinism and Free Will in Paul: The Argument of 1 Corinthians 8 and 9." Pages 231–55 in *Paul in His Hellenistic Context.* Edited by Troels Engberg-Pedersen. Minneapolis: Fortress.
1995c   "Paul's Self-Sufficiency (Philippians 4:11)." Pages 813–26 in *Texts and Contexts: Biblical Texts in Their Textual and Situational Contexts* (Lars Hartman FS). Edited by Tord Fornberg and David Hellholm. Oslo: Scandinavian University Press. Repr. as pages 125–39 in Fitzgerald 1996.
1996    "The Christianization of a *Topos* (Luke 12:13–34)." *NovT* 36:123–35.
1998    "Conversion to Paul's Gospel." Pages 231–44 in *The Early Church in Its Context* (Everett Ferguson FS). Edited by Abraham J. Malherbe et al. NovTSup 90. Leiden: Brill.
1999    "Anti-Epicurean Rhetoric in 1 Thessalonians." Pages 136–42 in *Text und Geschichte* (Dieter Lührmann FS). Edited by Stefan Maser and Egbert Schlarb. MTS 50. Marburg: Elwert Verlag.
Manson, Thomas W.
1962    "The Letters to the Thessalonians." Pages 259–78 in *Studies in the Gospels and Epistles.* Edited by Matthew Black. Manchester: Manchester University Press.

Marshall, I. Howard
1982 "Pauline Theology in the Thessalonian Correspondence." Pages 173–83 in Hooker and Wilson.

Marshall, Peter
1987 Enmity in Corinth: Social Conventions in Paul's Relations with the Corinthians. WUNT 2:23. Tübingen: J. C. B. Mohr (Paul Siebeck).

Martin, R. P.
1964 Worship in the Early Church. Westwood, N.J.: Revell.
1986 2 Corinthians. WBC 40. Waco, Tex.: Word Books.

Martin, Victor
1959 "Un recueil de diatribes cyniques. Pap. Genev. inv. 271." MH 16:77–139.

Marxsen, Willi
1968 Introduction to the New Testament: An Approach to Its Problems. Translated by G. Buswell. Philadelphia: Fortress.
1969 "Auslegung von 1 Thess 4.13–18." ZTK 66:22–37.

Maurach, G.
1970 Der Bau von Senecas Epistulae Morales. Bibliothek der klassischen Altertumswissenschaft, N.F., 2. Reihe, Band 30. Heidelberg: C. Winter.

Mayser, Edwin
1906– Grammatik der griechischen Papyri aus der Ptolemäerzeit. Berlin-Leipzig: W.
1938 de Gruyter.

McGehee, Michael
1989 "A Rejoinder to Two Recent Studies Dealing with 1 Thess 4:4." CBQ 51:82–89.

McNicol, Allan J.
1996 Jesus' Directions for the Future. New Gospel Studies 9. Macon, Ga.: Mercer University Press.

Mearns, C. L.
1981 "Early Eschatological Development in Paul: The evidence of I and II Thess." NTS 27:137–57.

Meeks, Wayne A.
1967 The Prophet-King: Moses and Johannine Christology. NovTSup 14. Leiden: E. J. Brill.
1983a The First Urban Christians: The Social World of the Apostle Paul. New Haven: Yale University Press.
1983b "Social Functions of Apocalyptic Language in Pauline Christianity." Pages 687–705 in Apocalypticism in the Mediterranean World and the Near East. Edited by David Hellholm. Tübingen: J. C. B. Mohr (Paul Siebeck).
1986 The Moral World of the First Christians. LEC 6. Philadelphia: Westminster.
1990 "The Circle of Reference in Pauline Morality." Pages 305–17 in Balch et al.
1993 The Origins of Christian Morality: The First Two Centuries. New Haven: Yale University Press.

Menken, M. J. J.
1990 "The Structure of 2 Thessalonians." Pages 373–82 in Collins 1990.
1993 "Paradise Regained or Still Lost? Eschatology and Disorderly Behaviour in 2 Thessalonians." NTS 38:271–89.
1994 "Getransformeerde traditie: christologie in 2 Tessalonicenzen." Inaugural address, Catholic University of Utrecht.

Merklein, H.
1992 "Der Theologe als Prophet: zur Funktion prophetischen Redens im theologischen Diskurs." *NTS* 38:402–29.
Merritt, Wayne
1993 *In Word and Deed: Moral Integrity in Paul.* Emory Studies in Early Christianity 1. New York: Peter Lang.
Metzger, Bruce M.
1994 *A Textual Commentary on the Greek New Testament.* 2d ed., (1st ed., 1971). London-New York: United Bible Societies.
Michaelis, Wilhelm
1925 *Die Gefangenschaft des Paulus in Ephesus und das Itinerar des Timotheus.* NTF 3. Gütersloh: Bertelsmann.
1945 "Der zweite Thessalonicherbrief kein Philipperbrief." *TZ* 1:282–86.
1961 *Einleitung in das Neue Testament.* 3d ed. Bern: Haller.
Michel, Otto
1936 "Zur Lehre vom Todesschlaf." *ZNW* 35:285–90.
1967 "Fragen zu 1 Thessalonicher 2,14–16: Antijüdische Polemik bei Paulus." Pages 50–59 in *Antijudaismus im Neuen Testament? Exegetische und systematische Beiträge.* Edited by W. Eckert et al. Abhandlungen zum christlich-jüdischen Dialog 1. Munich: Kaiser Verlag.
Mitchell, A. C.
1992 "The Social Function of Friendship in Acts 2:44–47 and 4:32–37." *JBL* 111:255–72.
Mitchell, Margaret M.
1989 "Concerning PERI DE in 1 Corinthians." *NovT* 31:229–56.
1992 "New Testament Envoys in the Context of Greco-Roman Diplomatic and Epistolary Conventions: The Example of Timothy and Titus." *JBL* 111:641–62.
Moffatt, James
1925 *An Introduction to the Literature of the New Testament.* New York: Charles Scribner's Sons.
Moore, George Foot
1927– *Judaism in the First Century of the Christian Era: The Age of the Tannaim.*
1930 3 vols. Cambridge, Mass.: Harvard University Press.
Morris, Leon
1956 "Kai hapax kai dis." *NovT* 1:205–208.
Moule, C. F. D.
1953 *An Idiom-Book of New Testament Greek.* Cambridge: Cambridge University Press.
Müller, Markus
1997 *Vom Schluss zum Ganzen: Zur Bedeutung des paulinischen Briefkorpusabschlusses.* FRLANT 172. Göttingen: Vandenhoeck & Ruprecht.
Müller, Peter
1988 *Anfänge der Paulusschule. Dargestellt am zweiten Thessalonicherbrief und am Kolosserbrief.* ATANT 74. Zürich: Theologischer Verlag.
Mullins, T. Y.
1962 "Petition as a Literary Form." *NovT* 5:46–54.
1964 "Disclosure: A Literary Form in the New Testament." *NovT* 7:44–50.

Munck, Johannes
    1959    *Paul and the Salvation of Mankind.* London: SCM.
    1962    "I Thess 1.9–10 and the Missionary Preaching of Paul." *NTS* 9:104–110.
    1967    *Christ and Israel: An Interpretation of Romans 9–11.* Philadelphia: Fortress.
Murphy-O'Connor, Jerome
    1974    *L'existence chrétienne selon Saint Paul.* LD 80. Paris: Cerf.
    1983    *St. Paul's Corinth: Texts and Archaeology.* GNS 6. Wilmington, Del.: Glazier.
    1996    *Paul: A Critical Life.* Oxford: Clarendon.
Nauck, W.
    1958    "Das *oun* paräneticum." ZNW 49:134–45.
Nicholson, John
    1994    "The Delivery and Confidentiality of Cicero's Letters." *CJ* 90:33–63.
Nickle, Keith
    1966    *The Collection: A Study in Paul's Strategy.* SBT 48. London: SCM.
Nock, A. D.
    1933    *Conversion: The Old and New in Religion from Alexander the Great to Augustine of Hippo.* Oxford: Clarendon.
    1954    "Bekehrung." RAC 2:105–18.
    1972    "Conversion and Adolescence." Pages 469–80 in *Essays on Religion and the Ancient World.* Edited by Zeph Stewart. Cambridge, Mass.: Harvard University Press.
Norden, Eduard
    1958    *Die antike Kunstprosa vom VI: Jahrhundert v. Chr. bis in die Zeit der Renaissance.* 2 vols. 3d ed. 1915. Repr., Darmstadt: Wissenschaftliche Buchgesellschaft.
O'Brien, Peter
    1977    *Introductory Thanksgivings in the Letters of Paul.* NovTSup 49.
    1982    *Colossians, Philemon.* WBC. Waco, Tex.: Word.
Ogg, George
    1968    *The Chronology of the Life of Paul.* London: Epworth.
Okeke, G. E.
    1980    "I Thess. ii.13–16: The Fate of the Unbelieving Jews." *NTS* 27:127–36.
Olbricht, Thomas H.
    1990    "An Aristotelian Rhetorical Analysis of 1 Thessalonians." Pages 216–36 in Balch et al.
Oliver, J. H.
    1971    "The Epistle of Claudius Which Mentions the Proconsul Junius Gallio." *Hesperia* 40:239–40.
Ollrog, Wolf-Henning
    1978    *Paulus und seine Mitarbeiter: Untersuchungen zu Theorie und Praxis der paulinischen Mission.* WMANT 50. Neukirchen: Erziehungsverein.
Osten-Sacken, P. von
    1971    "Gottes Treue bis zur Parusie." ZNW 68:176–99.
Otzen, P.
    1958    " 'Gute Hoffnung' bei Paulus." ZNW 49:283–85.
Overman, J. A.
    1992    "The God-fearers: Some Neglected Features." Pages 145–52 in Overman and MacLennan.

Overman, J. A., and R. S. MacLennan
1992   *Diaspora Judaism: Essays in Honor of, and in Dialogue with A. Thomas Kraabel.* South Florida Studies in the History of Judaism, 41. Atlanta: Scholars Press.
Palmer, D. W.
1981   "Thanksgiving, Self-defence, and Exhortation in 1 Thessalonians 1–3." *Colloq* 14:23–31.
Panagopoulos, J., ed.
1977   *Prophetic Vocation in the New Testament and Today.* NovTSup 45. Leiden: E. J. Brill.
Patte, Daniel
1983   "Method for a Structural Exegesis of Didactic Discourse: Analysis of 1 Thessalonians." *Semeia* 26:85–129.
Pax, Elpidius
1971   "Beobachtungen zur Konvertitensprache im erste Thessalonicherbrief." *SBFLA* 21:220–61.
1972   "Konvertitenprobleme im ersten Thessalonicherbrief." *BibLeb* 13:24–37.
Pearson, B. A.
1971   "1 Thessalonians 2:13–16: A Deutero-Pauline Interpolation." *HTR* 64:79–94.
Pease, A. S., ed.
1955   *M. Tulli Ciceronis De Natura Deorum.* 2 vols. Cambridge, Mass.: Harvard University Press.
Penna, Romano
1996   *Paul the Apostle.* 2 vols. Collegeville, Minn.: Liturgical Press.
Peterson, E.
1930   "Die Einholung des Kyrios." *ZST* 7:682–702.
Pfister, W.
1963   *Das Leben im Geist nach Paulus: Der Geist als Anfang und Vollendundg des christlichen Lebens.* Studia Friburgensia 34. Freiburg, Switzerland: Swiss University Press.
Pfitzner, Victor C.
1962   *Paul and the Agon Motif.* NovTSup 16. Leiden: E. J. Brill.
Plassart, André
1967   "L'inscription de Delphes mentionnant le proconsul Gallion." *RÉG* 80:372–78.
1970   "Lettre de l'empereur Claude au gouverneur d. Achaïe (en 52)." Pages 26–33 in *Les inscriptions du temple du IVe siècle.* Vol 3, pt. 4 of École française d. Athènes, *Fouilles de Delphes.* Paris: Boccard.
Plevnik, J.
1979   "1 Thess 5,1–11: Its Authenticity, Intention and Message." *Bib* 60:71–90.
1984   "The Taking Up of the Faithful and the Resurrection of the Dead in 1 Thessalonians 4:13–18." *CBQ* 46:274–83.
1997   *Paul and the Parousia: An Exegetical and Theological Interpretation.* Peabody, Mass.: Hendrickson.
Pobee, John S.
1985   *Persecution and Martyrdom in the Theology of Paul.* JSNTSup 6. Sheffield: University of Sheffield Press.

Praechter, Karl
  1973    *Kleine Schriften*. Hildesheim-New York: Georg Olms.
Preisigke, F.
  1915    *Sammelbuch griechischer Urkunden aus Ägypten*. Vol. 1. Strassburg: K. J.
          Trubner.
Preisker, Herbert
  1949    *Das Ethos des Urchistentums*. Gütersloh: Bertelsmann.
Prior, Michael
  1989    *Paul the Letter-Writer and the Second Letter to Timothy*. JSNTSup 23.
          Sheffield: JSOT Press.
Rabbow, Paul
  1954    *Seelenführung: Methodik der Exerzitien in der Antike*. Munich: Kösel-Verlag.
Radl, Walter
  1981    *Ankunft des Herrn: Zur Bedeutung und Funktion der Parusieaussagen des
          Paulus*. BBET 15. Frankfurt-Bern: Peter Lang.
Ramsay, W. M.
  1895    *St. Paul the Traveler and Roman Citizen*. London: Hodder and Stoughton.
Reed, Jeffrey T.
  1996    "Are Paul's Thanksgivings 'Epistolary'?" *JSNT* 61:87–99.
Reinmuth, E.
  1985    *Geist und Gesetz: Studien zu Voraussetzungen und Inhalt der paulinischen
          Paränese*. Theologische Arbeiten 44. Berlin: Evangelisch Verlagsanstalt.
Rensburg, J. J. van
  1986    "An Argument for Reading *nepioi* in 1 Thessalonians 2:7." Pages 253–59 in
          *A South African Perspective on the New Testament*. Edited by J. H. Petzer
          and P. Hartin. Leiden: E. J. Brill.
Richards, E. Randolph
  1991    *The Secretary in the Letters of Paul*. WUNT 2:42. Tübingen: J. C. B. Mohr
          (Paul Siebeck).
Riedweg, Christoph
  1994    *Ps.-Justin (Markell von Ankyron?) Ad Graecos De Vera Religione (bisher "Co-
          hortatio ad Graecos")*. 2 vols. Schweizerische Beiträge zur Altertumswis-
          senschaft 25. Basel: Friedrich Reinhardt.
Riesner, Rainer
  1994    *Die Frühzeit des Apostels Paulus: Studien zur Chronologie, Missionsstrategie
          und Theologie*. WUNT 71. Tübingen: J. C. B. Mohr (Paul Siebeck).
Rigaux, Beda
  1968    *Letters of St. Paul: Modern Studies*. Chicago: Franciscan Herald.
  1974–   "Tradition et rédaction dans 1 Th. v. 1–10." *NTS* 21:318–40.
  75
Rist, J. M.
  1969    *Stoic Philosophy*. Cambridge: Cambridge University Press.
Robertson, A. T.
  1934    *A Grammar of the Greek New Testament in the Light of Historical Research*.
          4th ed. Nashville: Broadman.
Roetzel, Calvin
  1986    "*Theodidaktoi* and Handwork in Philo and 1 Thessalonians." Pages 324–31
          in *L'Apôtre Paul: Personalité, Style et Conception du Ministère*. Edited by A.
          Vanhoye. BETL 73. Leuven: Leuven University Press.

Roller, Otto
1933    *Das Formular der paulinischen Briefe: Ein Beitrag zur Lehre vom antiken Briefe.* Stuttgart: Kohlhammer.
Romaniuk, K.
1993    "Les Thessaloniciens étaient-ils des paresseux?" *ETL* 69:142–45.
Roosen, Antoon
1977    "Das Zeugnis des Glaubens in 1 Thessalonicher 1,6–10." *Studia Moralia* 15:359–83.
Russell, D. A., and N. G. Wilson, eds.
1981    *Menander Rhetor.* Oxford: Clarendon.
Russell, D. S.
1964    *The Method and Message of Jewish Apocalyptic.* Philadelphia: Westminster.
Russell, R.
1988    "The Idle in 2 Thess 3.6–12: An Eschatological or a Social Problem?" *NTS* 34:105–119.
Sanders, Jack T.
1962    "The Transition from Opening Epistolary Thanksgiving to Body in the Letters of the Pauline Corpus." *JBL* 81:348–62.
Sandnes, Karl Olav
1991    *Paul—One of the Prophets?: A Contribution to the Apostle's Self-Understanding.* WUNT 2:43. Tübingen: J. C. B. Mohr (Paul Siebeck).
Schade, Hans-Heinrich
1981    *Apokalyptische Christologie bei Paulus.* GTA 18. Göttingen: Vandenhoeck & Ruprecht.
Schäfer, K.
1989    *Gemeinde als "Bruderschaft": Ein Beitrag zum Kirchenverständnis des Paulus.* Frankfurt: Peter Lang.
Schelkle, K. H.
1954    "Bruder." *RAC* 2:631–40.
Schenke, Hans Martin, and Karl Martin Fischer, eds.
1978    *Einleitung in die Schriften des Neuen Testaments: 1. Die Briefe des Paulus und Schriften des Paulinismus.* Gütersloh: Gerd Mohn.
Schille, Gottfried
1967    *Die urchristliche Kollegialmission.* ATANT 48.
Schippers, R.
1966    "The Pre-Synoptic Tradition in 1 Thessalonians II:13–16." *NovT* 8:223–34.
Schlier, Heinrich
1963    *Der Brief an die Epheser.* 4th ed. Düsseldorff: Patmos Verlag.
Schlueter, Carol J.
1994    *Filling Up the Measure: Polemical Hyperbole in 1 Thessalonians 2.14–16.* JSNTSup 98. Sheffield: JSOT Press.
Schmid, W.
1962    "Epikur." *RAC* 5:681–819.
Schmidt, J. E. C.
1801    "Vermutungen über die beiden Briefe an die Thessalonicher." Pages 380–86 in *Bibliothek für Kritik und Exegese des Neuen Testaments und älteste Christengeschichte* 2.3. Hadamar: Gelehrtenbuchhandlung.
Schmithals, Walter
1969    *The Office of the Apostle in the Early Church.* Nashville, Tenn.: Abingdon.

1972    *Paul and the Gnostics.* Nashville, Tenn.: Abingdon.

Schnider, Franz, and Weiner Stenger

1987    *Studien zum neutestamentlichen Briefformular.* NTTS 11.

Schoon-Janssen, J.

1991    *Umstrittene "Apologien" in den Paulusbriefen: Studien zur rhetorischen Situation des 1 Thessalonicherbriefes, des Galaterbriefes und des Philipperbriefes.* GTA 45. Göttingen: Vandenhoeck & Ruprecht.

Schrage, Wolfgang

1961    *Die konkrete Einzelgebote in der paulinischen Paränese. Ein Beitrag zur neutestamentlichen Ethik.* Gütersloh: Gerd Mohn.

1989    "Heiligung als Prozess bei Paulus." Pages 222–34 in Koch et al.

Schubert, Paul

1939    *Form and Function of the Pauline Thanksgivings.* BZNW 20. Berlin: Töpelmann.

Schulz, Anselm

1962    *Nachfolgen und Nachahmen: Studien über das Verhältnis der neutestamentlichen Jüngerschaft zur urchristlichen Vorbildethik.* Munich: Kösel Verlag.

Schwank, B.

1971    "Der sogenannte Brief an Gallio und die Datierung des 1 Thess." *BZ* n. s. 15:265–66.

Schweizer, E.

1945    "Der zweite Thessalonicherbrief ein Philipperbrief?" *TZ* 1:90–105.

Scott, James M.

1993    "Paul's Use of Deuteronomic Tradition." *JBL* 112:645–65.

Sellin, Gerhard

1983    " 'Die Auferstehung ist schon geschehen.' Zur Spiritualisierung apokalyptischer Terminologie im Neuen Testament." *NovT* 25:220–37.

Selwyn, Edward G.

1958    *The First Epistle of St. Peter.* London: Macmillan.

Sevenster, J. N.

1961    *Paul and Seneca.* NovTSup 4. Leiden: E. J. Brill.

Siber, Peter

1971    *Mit Christus Leben: Eine Studie zur paulinischen Aurferstehungshoffnung.* ATANT 61. Zurich: Theologischer Verlag.

Smith, Abraham

1995    *Comfort One Another: Reconstructing the Rhetoric and Audience of 1 Thessalonians.* Louisville, Ky.: Westminster John Knox.

Smith, David

1919    *The Life and Letters of St. Paul.* London: Hodder & Stoughton.

Smyth, H. W.

1959    *Greek Grammar.* Cambridge, Mass.: Harvard University Press.

Soden, Hermann von

1911    *Die Schriften des Neuen Testaments.* Vol. 1. Göttingen: Vandenhoeck & Ruprecht.

Söding, Thomas

1990    "Widerspruch und Leidensnachfolge. Neutestamentliche Gemeinden im Konflikt mit der paganen Gesellschaft." *MTZ* 41:137–55.

1992    *Das Trias Glaube, Hoffnung, Liebe bei Paulus: Eine exegetische Studie.* SBS 150. Stuttgart: Verlag Katholische Bibelwerk.

1997    *Das Wort vom Kreuz: Studien zur paulinischen Theologie.* WUNT 93. Tübingen: J. C. B. Mohr (Paul Siebeck).

Spicq, Ceslaus
1956    "Les Thessaloniciens 'inquiets' etaient-ils des paresseux?" *ST* 10:1–13.
1958    *Agapè dans le Nouveau Testament: Analyse des textes.* Vol. 3. ÉBib. Paris: Gabalda.
1969    *Les épîtres pastorales.* ÉBib. Paris: Gabalda.
1991    *Lexique théologie du nouveau testament.* Friburg: Cerf.

Stählin, G.
1973    "Um mitzusterben. Bemerkungen zur 2. Kor. 7.3." Pages 503–21 in *Neues Testament und christliche Existenz* (Herbert Braun FS). Edited by H. D. Betz and L. Schottroff. Tübingen: J. C. B. Mohr (Paul Siebeck).

Stalder, Kurt
1962    *Das Werk des Geistes in der Heiligung bei Paulus.* Zürich: EVZ Verlag.

Stanley, David
1959    "'Become Imitators of Me': The Pauline Conception of Apostolic Tradition." *Bib* 40:859–77.
1984    "Imitation in Paul's Letters: Its Significance for His Relationship to Jesus and to His Own Christian Foundations." Pages 127–41 in *From Jesus to Paul* (F. W. Beare FS). Edited by Peter Richardson and John C. Hurd. Waterloo, Ontario: Wilfrid Laurier University Press.

Steck, O. H.
1967    *Israel und das gewaltsame Geschick der Propheten. Untersuchungen zur Überlieferung des deuteronomistischen Geschichtsbildes im Alten Testament, Spätjudentum und Urchristentum.* WMANT 23. Neukirchen-Vluyn: Neukirchener Verlag.

Steen, Henry A.
1938    "Les clichés épistolaires dans les lettres sur papyrus grecques." *Classica et Mediaevalia* 1:119–76.

Stephenson, A. M. G.
1968    "On the Meaning of *enestēken hē hēmera tou theou* in 2 Thessalonians 2.2." Pages 442–51 in *Studia Evangelica* 4. TU 102.

Stone, M. E.
1990    *Fourth Ezra.* Hermeneia. Philadelphia: Fortress.

Stowers, Stanley K.
1981    "A 'Debate' over Freedom: 1 Corinthians 6:12–20." Pages 59–71 in *Christian Teaching: Studies in Honor of LeMoine G. Lewis.* Edited by E. Ferguson. Abilene, Tex.: Abilene Christian University Press.
1984    "Social Status, Public Speaking and Private Teaching: The Circumstances of Paul's Preaching Activity." *NovT* 26:59–82.
1986    *Letter Writing in Greco-Roman Antiquity.* LEC 5. Philadelphia: Westminster.
1990    "Paul on the Use and Abuse of Reason." Pages 253–86 in Balch et al.

Strobel, A.
1961    *Untersuchungen zum eschatologischen Verzögerungsproblem auf Grund der spätjüdisch-urchristlichen Geschichte von Habakuk 2,2 ff.* NovTSup 2. Leiden: E. J. Brill.

Stuhlmacher, Peter
  1968    *Das paulinische Evangelium: I Vorgeschichte.* FRLANT 95. Göttingen: Van-
          denhoeck & Ruprecht.
Suggs, M. Jack
  1960    "Concerning the Date of Paul's Macedonian Ministry." *NovT* 4:60–68.
Suhl, Alfred
  1975    *Paulus und seine Briefe: Ein Beitrag zur paulinischen Chronologie.* SNT 11.
          Gütersloh: Gütersloher Verlagshaus.
Sumney, J. L.
  1990    "'The Bearing of a Pauline Rhetorical Pattern on the Integrity of 2 Thessa-
          lonians." *ZNW* 81:192–204.
Swigchem, Douwe van
  1955    *Het Missionair Karakter van de Christelijke Gemeente volgens de Brieven van
          Paulus en Petrus.* Kampen: Kok.
Sykutris, Johannes
  1933    *Die Briefe des Sokrates und die Sokratiker.* Studien zur Geschichte und Kul-
          tur des Altertums 18:2. Paderborn: Ferdinand Schöningh.
Taatz, Irene
  1991    *Frühjüdische Briefe: Die paulinischen Briefe im Rahmen der offiziellen re-
          ligiösen Briefe des Frühjudentums.* NTOA 16.
Tarn, W. W.
  1961    *Hellenistic Civilization.* 3d ed. Revised by G. T. Griffith. New York:
          Meridian.
Taylor, Justin
  1996    "The Roman Empire in the Acts of the Apostles." Pages 2436–2500 in
          *ANRW* 2:26:3.
Theissen, Gerd
  1982    *The Social Setting of Pauline Christianity: Essays on Corinth.* Philadelphia:
          Fortress.
Thesleff, Holger
  1965    *The Pythagorean Texts of the Hellenistic Period.* Åbo: Åbo Academy.
Thraede, Klaus
  1963    "Untersuchungen zum Ursprung und zur Geschichte der christlichen Poe-
          sie II." *JAC* 5:125–58.
  1968–   "Ursprünge und Formen des 'Heiligen Kusses' im frühen Christentum."
  69      *JAC* 11/12:124–80.
  1970    *Grundzüge griechisch-römischer Brieftopik.* Zetemata 48. Munich: Beck.
Thyen, Hartwig
  1955    *Der Stil der Jüdisch-Hellenistischen Homilie.* FRLANT 65. Göttingen: Van-
          denhoeck & Ruprecht.
Tischendorf, Constantin von
  1872    *Novum Testamentum Graece.* Editio octava critica maior. Vol. 2. Leipzig:
          Giesecke & Devrient.
Treggiari, Susan
  1991    *Roman Marriage: Iusti Coniuges from the Time of Cicero to the Time of Ulpi-
          an.* Oxford: Clarendon.
Trilling, Wolfgang
  1972    *Untersuchungen zum zweiten Thessalonicherbrief.* Leipzig: St. Benno.

1981 "Literarische Paulusimitation im 2. Thessalonicherbrief." Pages 146–56 in *Paulus in den neutestamentlichen Spätschriften: Zur Paulusrezeption im Neuen Testament.* Edited by K. Kertelge. Freiburg-Basel-Vienna: Herder.

1987 "Die beiden Briefe des Apostels Paulus an die Thessalonicher: Eine Forschungsbericht." *ANRW* 2:25:4, 3365–3403.

Trillitzsch, Winfried

1962 *Senecas Beweisführung.* Deutsche Akademie der Wissenschaften zu Berlin: Schriften der Sektion für Altertumswissenschaft 37. Berlin: Akademie Verlag.

Tuckett, C. M.

1990 "Synoptic Traditions in 1 Thessalonians?" Pages 160–82 in Collins 1990.

Ulonska, H.

1987 "Christen und Heiden: Die paulinische Paränese in 1 Thess 4, 3–8." *TZ* 43:210–18.

Unnik, W. C. van

1968 "Den Geist löschet nicht aus (1 Thessalonicher V 19)." *NovT* 10:255–69.

1980 *Sparsa Collecta.* Vol. 2. NovTSup 30. Leiden: E. J. Brill.

Vielhauer, Philipp

1975 *Geschichte der urchristlichen Literatur.* Berlin-New York: W. de Gruyter.

Vilatte, Silvie

1991 "La nourrice grecque: un question d'histoire sociale et religieuse." *L'antiquité classique* 60:5–28.

Vögtle, Anton

1936 *Die Tugend- und Lasterkataloge im Neuen Testament.* NTAbh 16:4–5.

Vogel, W.

1934 "Eidenai to heautou skeuos ktasthai: Zur Deutung von 1 Thess 4,3 im Zusammenhang der paulinischen Eheauffassung." *TBl:* 13:83–85.

Volz, Paul

1934 *Die Eschatologie der jüdischen Gemeinde im neutestamentlichen Zeitalter.* Tübingen: J. C. B. Mohr (Paul Siebeck).

Vouga, François

1992 "Der Brief als Form der apostolischen Autorität." Pages 7–58 in *Studien und Texte zur Formgeschichte.* Edited by Klaus Berger, François Vouga, Michael Wolter, and Dieter Zeller. TANZ 7. Tübingen-Basel: Francke Verlag.

Walter, Nikolaus

1979 "Christusglaube und heidnische Religiösität in paulinischer Gemeinden." *NTS* 25:422–42.

Ware, James

1992 "The Thessalonians as a Missionary Congregation: 1 Thessalonians 1,5–8." *ZNW* 83:126–31.

1996 " 'Holding Forth the Word of Life': Paul and the Mission of the Church in the Letter to the Philippians in the Context of Second Temple Judaism." Ph.D. diss., Yale University.

Wehrli, F.

1969 *Die Schule des Aristoteles.* Vol. 5. 2d ed. Basel: Schwabe.

Weima, J. A. D.

1994 *Neglected Endings: The Significance of the Pauline Letter Closings.* JSNTSup 101. Sheffield: JSOT Press.

1996 "How You Must Walk to Please God." Pages 96–119 in *Holiness and Discipleship in the New Testament*. Edited by Richard N. Longenecker. Grand Rapids: Eerdmans.

Weima, J. A. D., and S. E. Porter
1998 *An Annotated Bibliography of 1 & 2 Thessalonians*. NTTS 26. Leiden: E. J. Brill.

Weiss, Johannes
1910 *Der erste Korintherbrief*. KEK.
1959 *Earliest Christianity: A History of the Period A.D. 30–150*. 2 vols. Translated by Frederick C. Grant. Previously published, 1937, *The History of Primitive Christianity*. Repr. New York: Harper & Row.

Weiss, W.
1993 "Glaube-Liebe-Hoffnung: Zu der Trias bei Paulus." ZNW 84:196–217.

Weizsäcker, Carl von
1907 *The Apostolic Age of the Christian Church*. Vol. 1. Translated by James Millar. London: Williams and Norgate.

Wengst, Klaus
1987 *Pax Romana and the Peace of Christ*. Philadelphia: Fortress.

West, J. C.
1914 "The Order of 1 and 2 Thessalonians." *JTS* 15:66–74.

Wette, W. M. L. de
1841 *Kurzgefasstes exegetischer Handbuch zum Neuen Testament*. Leipzig: Weidmann.

Wettstein, J. J.
1751– *Novum Testamentum Graecum*. 2 vols. 1751–52. Repr., Graz: Akademische
1752 Verlag.

White, John L.
1971 "Introductory Formulae in the Body of the Pauline Letters." *JBL* 90:91–97.
1972 *The Form and Function of the Body of the Greek Letter*. SBLDS 2. Missoula, Mont.: Scholars Press.
1984 "New Testament Epistolary Literature in the Framework of Ancient Epistolography." Pages 1730–56 in ANRW II 25:2.
1986 *Light from Ancient Letters*. Philadelphia: Fortress.
1993 "Apostolic Mission and Apostolic Message: Congruence in Paul's Epistolary Rhetoric, Structure and Imagery." Pages 145–61 in *Origins and Method: Towards a New Understanding of Judaism and Christianity* (John C. Hurd FS). Edited by Bradley H. McLean. JSNTSup 86. Sheffield: Sheffield Academic Press.

Whitton, J.
1982 "A Neglected Meaning for *Skeuos* in 1 Thessalonians 4.4." *NTS* 28:142–43.

Wichmann, Wolfgang
1930 *Die Leidenstheologie: Eine Form der Leidensdeutung im Spätjudentum*. Stuttgart: W. Kohlhammer.

Wiefel, Wolfgang
1975 "Die missionarische Eigenart des Paulus und das Problem des frühchristlichen Synkretismus." *Kairós* 17:218–31.

Wilcke, H. A.
1967 *Das Problem eines messianischen Zwischenreiches bei Paulus*. ATANT 51. Zürich: Zwingli Verlag.

Wilckens, Ulrich
    1963    *Die Missionsreden der Apostelgeschichte: Form- und traditionsgeschichtliche Untersuchungen.* WMANT 5. Neukirchen-Vluyn: Neukirchener Verlag.
Wiles, Gordon P.
    1974    *Paul's Intercessory Prayers: The Significance of the Intercessory Prayer Passages in the Letters of St. Paul.* SNTSMS 24. Cambridge: Cambridge University Press.
Wilhelm, F.
    1924    "Plutarchos *Peri Hesychias.*" *RhM* 73:466–82.
Wilson, J. M.
    1924    *The Acts of the Apostles: Translated from the Codex Bezae.* London: SPCK.
Windisch, Hans
    1924    *Der zweite Korintherbrief.* KEK.
Winter, Bruce W.
    1993    "The Entries and Ethics of Orators and Paul (1 Thessalonians 2:1–12)." *TynBul* 44:54–74.
    1994    *Seek the Welfare of the City: Christians as Benefactors and Citizens.* First Century Christians in the Graeco-Roman World. Grand Rapids: Eerdmans.
Witkowski, S.
    1911    *Epistulae privatae Graecae quae in papyris aetatis Lagidarum servantur.* Leipzig: B. G. Teubner.
Wolbert, Werner
    1981    "Vorbild und paränetische Autorität: Zum Problem der Nachahmung des Paulus." *MTZ* 32:249:70.
Wrede, William
    1903    *Die Echtheit des zweiten Thessalonicherbriefes.* TU 9:2. Leipzig: J. C. Henrich.
Wuellner, Wilhelm
    1990    "The Argumentative Structure of 1 Thessalonians as Paradoxical Encomium." Pages 117–36 in Collins 1990.
Yarbrough, O. Larry
    1984    *Not Like the Gentiles: Marriage Rules in the Letters of Paul.* SBLDS 80. Atlanta: Scholars Press.
Zahn, Theodor
    1953    *Introduction to the New Testament.* Vol. 1. Grand Rapids: Kregel.
Zeller, Dieter
    1979    "Christus, Skandal und Hoffnung. Die Juden in den Briefen von Paulus." Pages 279–302 in *Gottesverächter und Menschenfeinde? Juden zwischen Jesus und früchristlicher Kirche.* Edited by Horst Goldstein. Düsseldorf: Patmos Verlag.
    1996    "Selbstbezogenheit und Selbstdarstellung in den Paulusbriefen." *TQ* 176:40–52.
Zeller, Eduard
    1923    *Die Philosophie der Griechen in ihrer geschichtlichen Entwicklung.* 6 vols. 5th ed. Leipzig: Wellmann.
Zimmer, Friedrich
    1887    "1 Thess. 2.3–8 erklärt." Pages 248–73 in *Theologische Studien* (B. Weiss FS). Göttingen: Vandenhoeck & Ruprecht.

Zmijewski, Josef
    1986    *Paulus—Knecht und Apostel Christi: Amt und Amtsträger in paulinischer
            Schicht*. Stuttgart: Katholisches Bibelwerk.

# PAUL'S FIRST LETTER TO THE THESSALONIANS

◆

# 1 THESSALONIANS: INTRODUCTION

◆

## I. THE FOUNDING OF THE CHURCH

There is information in Phil 4:16 and Acts 17:1–16; 18:1–5 in addition to 1 Thessalonians itself about the founding of the church in Thessalonica and the events that led to the writing of the letter. It is proper to begin an investigation of the church's origin by examining what Paul himself has to say on the matter. Although information derived from Paul's letters permits us to sketch only a brief outline of his activities, 1 Thessalonians must serve as a control when we assess the account of Acts.

Two methodological premises, both rejected in this commentary, affect the reconstruction of the Pauline mission in Thessalonica. First, if one insists on using only those parts of Acts that can be corroborated by Paul's letters, a radically different chronology and, associated with it, reconstruction of his career and thought may emerge. The degree of skepticism with which Acts is treated in some reconstructions based on this minimalistic premise is extreme. Acknowledgment of the tendentiousness and other shortcomings of Acts as a historical source does not preclude a discriminating use of its evidence to supplement Paul's letters. All accounts of Paul's career are in fact indebted to Acts, and we do well to "beware of a too extravagant contempt for what Acts offers us" (Weiss 1959: 1:148). The matter of chronology will be taken up in the discussion of the date of 1 Thessalonians. Second, a different picture of Paul's relationship with the Thessalonians will also emerge if the letters addressed to them in their present form are viewed as compilations of fragments of letters written during a period of extended contact. The reconstruction that follows assumes the integrity of the letters (see page 79).

### A. THE EVIDENCE OF 1 THESSALONIANS

According to 1 Thessalonians, Paul had preached under unfavorable circumstances in Philippi before coming to Thessalonica (2:2). In Thessalonica, he had been successful in his mission, establishing a church that would soon become known throughout all Greece (1:2–10) and to which he ministered before leaving his converts (2:1–12).

In 1 Thessalonians Paul frequently reminds his readers of what he had told them, of what they knew, and of warnings he had given them (see pages 84–86).

These repeated reminders provide us with a glimpse of his initial instruction, given during his establishment of the church (Holmberg, 70–74). That this instruction was so structured in content and so uniformly used in the early Christian mission that it can be called a catechism (Selwyn, 365–466; Dodd 1968: 11–29) is to be doubted. Nevertheless, one can expect that the matters he refers to in the letter were indeed the ones that he typically stressed.

Paul's missionary preaching (1:9–10) and initial instruction (e.g., 5:1–2) certainly had a theological component (cf. Laub 1976: 20–26; Marxsen 1979: 17–22), but if the topics that he chooses to remind his readers of in the letter are any indication, he had emphasized Christian conduct more than doctrine (cf. 4:1–2). Paul is at great pains to remind the Thessalonians of the example he had set for them and the close relationship that he had fostered with them (1:5–6; 2:1–10). Furthermore, he had stressed the need for mutual love (4:9–10; cf. 3:12), thus developing a sense of community. The Christian community, however, was not to fall prey to the temptation of isolationism but was to love all people (3:12) and be especially careful to secure the approval of the larger society by being socially responsible and productive (4:9–12). Nevertheless, the founding of the church had been attended by tribulation (1:6; cf. 2:14), and Paul had warned his converts that it was the Christian lot to suffer tribulation (3:3–4). The picture that emerges from 1 Thessalonians is therefore one of sustained effort to form a community with its own ethos, yet with a positive view of its place in the larger society.

Nothing in this account of Paul's founding of the church represents the concerns his gospel frequently raised for Jews. The characteristic Pauline antitheses of law and gospel, faith and works, flesh and spirit, for example, are absent. Paul does not quote from the OT in the letter, and there are only a few places in the letter where he may allude to the OT (2:4, 16; 4:5, 6, 8; 5:8, 22), which suggests that he has in mind readers not nurtured on the Jewish Scriptures. Furthermore, on the assumption that Paul adopted a style of writing appropriate to the circumstances and background of his readers, the Hellenistic hortatory character of the letter confirms their Greek, and not Jewish, background (see pages 81–86).

The clearest evidence that Paul thinks of his readers as Gentiles is 1:9, where he says that they had turned from idols to serve a living and true God. This formulation of the preaching, which begins with God as the creator rather than with the OT promises that have been fulfilled in Christ, is derived from Hellenistic Jewish propaganda directed to Gentiles (see NOTES and COMMENT). Paul's comparison in 2:14 of the treatment that the Thessalonians had received from their own countrymen with the Judean churches' treatment by the Jews quite possibly points in the same direction.

This does not mean that there need have been no Jews in the Thessalonian church, as is sometimes claimed (e.g., by Marxsen 1968: 33; modified somewhat in 1979: 17–21). It is possible that, although there were Jews in the church, Paul in this letter has only Greeks in mind (Harnack 1910; for a fuller discussion see pages 352–53). Nevertheless, the letter clearly has a Gentile rather than a Jewish cast. What it does not tell us is where Paul first encountered these Greeks, where the church met, or how long Paul had stayed in Thessalonica.

## B. THE EVIDENCE OF ACTS

The Book of Acts partly confirms the information we gain from 1 Thessalonians and adds to it. The judgment that "all the individual events of Paul's activity in this city are legendary" (Koester 1982: 108) is too harsh. The most important features of the account furnish a credible picture (Bornkamm 1969: 62; Donfried 1984, 1985). But we must be cautious in using Acts, for it has its own interests, reflected in the events it chooses to describe as well as in the stereotypical features of those descriptions. This tendentiousness causes difficulties for any attempt at historical reconstruction, as does the fact that the information Acts provides at times appears at odds with Paul's letters.

Acts records that Paul, Silas, and Timothy had traveled from Philippi to Thessalonica by way of Amphipolis and Apollonia (17:1), all cities on the Egnatian Way. If Paul did not stop to preach along the way, the hundred miles or so between Philippi and Thessalonica could have been covered on foot in as few as three days, but more likely in six. Acts thus places the origin of the Thessalonian church very early in the so-called second missionary journey. If Paul had not preached in Amphipolis and Apollonia, as has been suggested (Lake, 62–63), it would then be the second church in Greece that he established.

That Paul usually was accompanied by coworkers is attested by Acts as well as by his letters (Judge 1960b; Ellis; Ollrog; Meeks 1983a: 133–34). Paul includes Silvanus and Timothy in the address of 1 Thessalonians (1:1), and later he refers to a mission to the Thessalonians on which he had sent Timothy after his own departure from Thessalonica (3:1, 6). The degree to which Paul retains the first person plural in the letter is not in keeping with his normal practice (see pages 86–90). If the plural is taken to include Silvanus and Timothy, as some scholars think, his use of it in his account of the church's origin (1:2–2:12) strongly suggests that Silvanus and Timothy were associated with him when he founded the church.

This accords with information provided by Acts, where Silvanus is named Silas (see NOTES and COMMENT on 1:1). According to Acts, Silas, who had been a leader in the church in Jerusalem (15:22) and a prophet (15:32), had set out with Paul on the mission from Antioch (15:40). Together they constituted the leadership of the mission in Philippi and Thessalonica. Timothy is said to have joined them at Lystra (16:1–3), but Luke consistently mentions only Paul and Silas (16:19, 25, 29; 17:4, 10) until after their departure from Thessalonica (17:14–15). This does not mean that Timothy joined Paul's company as a personal assistant to the senior missionaries (cf. Acts 13:5) and only later participated in the actual preaching (von Dobschütz 1909: 8; Hadorn 1922: 70). Paul's comments on Timothy in 1 Thessalonians and 2 Cor 1:19 show that Timothy fully participated in evangelization in Corinth a few months later. Luke's failure to mention Timothy in his account of the Macedonian mission may be due to his understanding that Paul and Silas were the leaders and to the traditional view that leaders operated in pairs (Jeremias 1959), but the precise roles of the three are not clearly identified.

In placing the founding of the church in Thessalonica after Paul's activity in Philippi, Acts agrees with 1 Thess 2:1, but what Acts adds about the founding of the church is more problematic. Whereas 1 Thessalonians reflects a Gentile church, Acts places Paul in the synagogue, "in accordance with his custom" (17:2). Luke repeatedly describes this custom (13:5, 14; 14:1; 17:10, etc.), which is important to him because of his understanding that Paul had first to preach to Jews before turning to Gentiles (13:46, 47; cf. 18:6; 28:23–29). The sequence, however important it may be to Luke, does not accord well with Paul's own statements. Paul describes his mission as being directed to the Gentiles (Gal 1:16; Rom 1:5, 13–15; 15:15–21), and from Gal 2:1–10 it might appear that he had agreed to confine himself to Gentiles while Peter would undertake the mission to the Jews. But these statements should not be taken absolutely; Paul also indicates that he attempted to win Jews by adapting himself to them (1 Cor 9:19)—a practice that his opponents in Galatia interpreted to his disadvantage (Gal 5:11; 1:10)—and that he submitted himself to the discipline of the synagogue (2 Cor 11:24) (Holmberg, 30; Meeks 1983a: 26). Thus, while Luke's interests obviously influence his description of the Jewish setting of the mission, there is reason to believe that Paul would have preached in the synagogue in Thessalonica (Haenchen, 506; Marxsen 1979: 17–20). In that setting, the manner of his preaching ("from the Scriptures", 17:2) and its content (the death and resurrection of the Christ, 17:3) are not surprising, even if expressed in typically Lucan terms.

Although Acts places Paul in the synagogue, it does not convey the impression that the response to his preaching resulted in a church consisting largely of Jews: "And some of them were persuaded, and joined Paul and Silas; as did a great many of the devout Greeks and not a few of the leading women" (17:4). The three groups mentioned as responding to his preaching are listed in an ascending order, which emphasizes the predominance of Gentiles among them. "Some" of the Jews were persuaded by Paul, the indefinite pronoun in the series indicating that they constituted the least significant of the three groups. On the other hand, a great many of the devout Greeks believed, as did not a few of the leading women. The latter presumably were not Jews either, and the understatement of the litotes ("not a few") emphasizes the large number of women of this class.

An important textual variant in Acts 17:4, which was preferred more in the nineteenth century (Lachmann; Ramsay 1895: 226–27, 235–36; Hilgenfeld) than in the twentieth (Wohlenberg, 3; Rigaux 1956: 21), elaborates on the Gentile response. The Western text reads: "And some of them were persuaded, and consorted with Paul and Silas, in the teaching: and many of the devout, and of Greeks a great multitude, and women, of the first rank, not a few" (J. M. Wilson, 81). The "and" between "devout" and "Greeks" makes for a response of three instead of two Gentile groups, thus further intensifying the contrast between the modest Jewish and enthusiastic Gentile responses to Paul's preaching. The above reading reflects the anti-Judaic tendency of the Western text (Epp 1966: 64–119), and for this as well as other reasons (Lake, 64; *BC* 3:162; Rigaux 1956: 21; Fiorenza, 21) the case for such a reading is weakened (but see the discussion in *BC* 4:204; Rigaux 1956: 21). Nevertheless, the variant merely reinforces the point, made elsewhere in Acts, that the majority of converts were Gentiles.

The enthusiastic Gentile response is characteristic of Luke's description of Paul's mission (Acts 13:48, 49; 18:6, 9, 10). These Gentiles, however, are usually identified as the Godfearers who worshiped in the synagogue (e.g., Haenchen, 509; Bruce 1982: xxii), and they could therefore not have been the persons Paul describes as having turned from idols to worship God (1 Thess 1:9; but see Hultgren, 138–41). Furthermore, Luke assumes that Gentile Godfearers were familiar with the OT (Acts 13:16–22, 26), and their numbers in the church therefore do not explain the comparatively few traces of the OT in 1 Thessalonians. The historical existence of the Godfearers as a group has been challenged (by Kraabel) but has been successfully defended (e.g., by Overman; Levinskaya, 51–82, 117–26). We are still left to locate Paul's preaching to Gentiles outside the synagogue and to determine whether Luke's account allows time for it.

The only chronological information that Acts provides about Paul's stay in Thessalonica is that "on three Sabbaths" (*epi sabbata tria*) he preached in the synagogue. The phrase has been understood as referring to his entire stay in the city (Lake, 64–66; Michaelis 1961: 219; Luedemann, 177), which would severely limit the opportunities Paul had to preach to Gentiles outside the synagogue. However, the three Sabbaths are clearly related to his activity in the synagogue (Haenchen, 507; Donfried 1985: 356). If the phrase means "three weeks," as has been claimed (Zahn, 212), it would imply that Paul preached in the synagogue during the week as well as on the Sabbath, thus increasing his evangelizing, but still only in the synagogue. This interpretation has little merit (Rigaux 1956: 23) and does not accommodate the evangelization of the Gentile readers Paul has in mind in 1 Thessalonians. On the basis of 1 Thess 2:1–12 it is possible to infer that, while on three Sabbaths Paul preached in the synagogue, during the week he preached elsewhere to Gentiles who had no connection with the synagogue (e.g., Frame, 4–5). This supposition makes room for the conversion of the readers of the letter, but it does not agree with Luke's stereotyped picture of Paul's transition from synagogue to Gentile mission.

Luke normally does not describe Paul's preaching to Jews and Gentiles as having taken place concurrently. Rather, he visualizes a sequence of events: Paul preaches in the synagogue and is rejected, whereupon he turns to the Gentiles, and his successful preaching to them in the city leads to his persecution (Acts 13:46–50; 18:5–17; with modification, 16:12–40; 19:8–41). Luke focuses on the initial preaching and the final persecution but is silent about Paul's activities between these events (Haenchen, 510). It should be noted that according to Acts 13:42–52, which is representative of the other instances in Acts in which Paul turns to the Gentiles (Haenchen, 417), the favorable response of the Gentiles comes after Paul has left the synagogue and includes Gentiles who were not Godfearers.

Paul's connection with Jason and the Christians who were associated with him further suggests that Luke wants his readers to envisage a scene similar to that in Corinth, where Paul is said to have moved his operations from the synagogue to the house of the Godfearer Titius Justus, where he enjoyed considerable success among the populace at large (18:4–11). Thus, while the stereotypical nature of Luke's narrative does create problems for any attempt at historical reconstruction, when justice is done to it, Acts' account of Paul's mission in Thessalonica appears to compress the recurring Lucan pattern that describes Paul preaching first in the synagogue and then in a setting where he converts Gentiles, thereby provoking Jewish opposition. Reconstructed thus, the pattern in Acts, if not the condensed version used to describe the Thessalonian mission, permits one to assume a period in which Paul preached to Gentiles after leaving the synagogue.

The chronological information in Acts regarding Paul's activity in Thessalonica is confined to the notice about his preaching in the synagogue, and nothing explicit is said about how long he stayed in the city after he left the synagogue. The account assumes, however, that Paul had been in the city long enough and had been sufficiently active in public for the charges brought against him to be possible and intelligible, and for his opponents to generate support and bring Paul and other Christians before the city authorities. The church was known to be associated with the house of Jason, who, perhaps because he was regarded by the authorities as the church's patron, was required, together with the church, to post bail for Paul (Malherbe 1983b: 97–98; Meeks 1983a: 62–63). Thus, when the tendentiousness of Acts is taken into consideration, there emerges the picture of Paul at work in Thessalonica for a period of at least some weeks beyond his initial activity in the synagogue.

Paul himself does not mention preaching in the synagogue nor the events that led to his persecution and departure from Thessalonica. He does, however, confirm the impression gained from Acts that he had been in Thessalonica considerably more than three weeks (1 Thess 2:9; Phil 4:16). Paul refers to his having worked in Thessalonica night and day to support himself while he preached in order not to burden his converts (2:9). The reference to this practice of his helps to lay the foundation for the exhortation in 4:9–12 that his readers likewise engage in manual labor in order to be financially independent. He therefore understood his practice to be paradigmatic, a matter on which 2 Thess 3:7–9 is explicit. However, his own manual labor could not effectively have served this function if it had been of such short duration. In addition, in Phil 4:16 he says that the Philippians had sent him financial aid on more than one occasion while he was in Thessalonica (Morris 1956; Suhl, 103–7). Given the distance between the two cities, the sending of these gifts would probably have taken weeks, if not months. This would allow time for bearers of the aid to travel from Philippi to Thessalonica, deliver the aid, return to Philippi, and then repeat the process (Haenchen, 511). And in Corinth, Paul worked at his trade before receiving help from Macedonia (Acts 18:1–5; 2 Cor 11:7–11). This sequence may very well have been important to Paul, for in addition to allowing him to advance his own practice as a model for his converts, it also expressed the willingness with which he carried out his commission as an apostle (1 Cor 9:15–18; Malherbe 1995a). The practice therefore functioned in his statements about and defenses of his apostolic self-understanding (2 Cor 11:10–13; Kaesemann; Hock). If we are justified in assuming the same sequence for Thessalonica, his sojourn there would have been extended into at least two or three months (von Dobschütz 1909: 17, suggests six weeks).

According to Acts 17:5–10, Paul's stay in Thessalonica came to an end when, out of jealousy over the missionaries' success in converting Gentiles (cf. 13:48–50), the Jews took some good-for-nothings from the marketplace, incited a riot, set the city in an uproar, and advanced on Jason's house with the intention of hauling his visitors out to the crowd. Paul and his companions, however, are not found. Luke creates the impression that they were in hiding (Lake, 70–71), for after their preaching and the response to it, they do not appear in public in Thessalonica. This is extraordinary, in view of Luke's tendency to stress the public nature of Christianity in general (Haenchen, 691–92; Malherbe 1989: 147–63) and of Paul's ministry in particular (Malherbe, 1986b). In the absence of the missionaries and on the grounds that he had extended hospitality to them, Jason and some Christians associated with him are dragged before the city authorities, who were responsible for dealing with offenses against "the decrees of Caesar" (Judge 1971). The charges of civil disturbance and treason are sufficiently grave for the authorities to demand bail from Jason and the other Christians. Presumably, Jason would have denied the charges (BC 4:206), but Acts concentrates on the danger in which the preachers find themselves by specifying that immediately, under cover of night, they are escorted from Thessalonica to Beroea (Haenchen, 506). This description of the secrecy with which the mission in Thessalonica ends is the more striking when it is compared with Paul's adamant refusal to leave Philippi in secret (16:35–40) and suggests that Luke intended to impress his readers with the extraordinary nature of Paul's mission in Thessalonica and its unusual termination.

Paul does not explicitly comment in 1 Thessalonians on his departure from Thessalonica, and opinions differ widely on whether certain statements can nevertheless be understood to allude to it. Marxsen (1979: 15, 20) claims that there is nothing in 1 Thessalonians even to indicate that Paul was forced to leave the city, and Suhl (95) takes Paul's repeated efforts to return (2:17–18) to imply that he had left voluntarily. Most writers, however, think that the passive in 2:17 ("we were made orphans") signifies that Paul's absence was imposed on him and bring 2:14 into the discussion, but with different results. Koester (1982: 109), regarding 2:14 as spurious, sees no evidence in the letter of a Jewish persecution at all. Haenchen accepts the genuineness of 2:14–15 and stresses that the Thessalonians were persecuted by their own race and not Jews, claiming that 2:15 reflects Paul's own experience, but is not connected with the events in Thessalonica: "2:14, 17 and 3:2f. lead us rather to suppose that Paul was driven out of Thessalonica by a Gentile anti-Christian movement, which erupted later against the community also and perhaps cost the Christians of Thessalonica a good deal more than the price of bail, even though the cases of death mentioned in 1 Thess

4:13 had evidently nothing to do with this persecution" (Haenchen, 513–14). Nevertheless, the majority of commentators relate Paul's references to the Thessalonians' tribulations or afflictions (1:6; 3:3–4), as well as his own experience at the hands of the Jews (2:15), to the events described in Acts (Zahn, 204; Milligan, 30; Frame, 112; Rigaux 1956: 447; Best 1972: 116). Some also consider it likely that "those who are asleep" (4:13) refers to Christians who had suffered martyrdom in the early days of the church (Lake, 88; Donfried 1985: 349–51; Pobee, 113–14).

In light of Paul's strongly expressed desire to renew his association with his converts and his assertion that his separation from them was involuntary (see NOTES and COMMENT on 2:17–18), it is striking that he does not explicitly mention the reason(s) for his departure and continued absence. His statements on this matter are as enigmatic as Luke's statements on Paul's departure from Thessalonica are extraordinary. On the assumptions that 2:15 is genuine, however, and that it refers to his ejection from Thessalonica and not to his early experience as a preacher (von Dobschütz 1904: 212–13), it appears that Paul does blame the Jews for his ejection from Thessalonica (see NOTES and COMMENT). Whether or not this agrees with Acts is not important for the interpretation of the letter, but it should be noted that, according to Acts, Paul apparently goes into hiding and ceases his preaching when the Jews organize against him. This would seem to agree well with what he says in 2:15–16.

## II. THE CHARACTER OF THE CHURCH

Attention has already been drawn to Paul's teaching as he founded the church (see page 56) and to the church's ethnic composition (see pages 56–57). The difficulties under which Paul left the church did not make it turn inward or become isolated; on the contrary, during the few months between the church's inception and the writing of 1 Thessalonians, the Thessalonians' conduct under hardship and their evangelizing in Macedonia and Achaia had made them exemplary (1:7–8), and Paul could compliment them on the bonds they had formed with other churches in Macedonia (4:10). It is important to appreciate the fact that this was no static church, but that it continued to expand and develop after Paul had left them. The church that Paul wrote to was no longer in all respects the one he had left behind (see COMMENT on 1 Thess 5:26–27). Nevertheless, it will be useful to sketch a profile of the church he established, reserving for later a fuller treatment of the circumstances and conditions he addressed in his letter (see pages 72–75, 77–78).

### A. THE EVIDENCE OF ACTS

The picture that Acts provides is not reflected in 1 Thessalonians. The statement that a large number of Greeks converted (Acts 17:4) and the supposition that 1 Thessalonians was written to separate groups (5:12, 14; see COMMENT on

5:26–27) have contributed to the view that the church was large (Rigaux 1956: 26). Luke does have a tendency to mention large numbers of converts (Acts 2:41; 4:4; 5:14), including in the Diaspora (13:48–9; 14:1; 18:8), but he does not explicitly describe the Thessalonian converts as large in number. The number of Greeks in 17:4 is large only relative to the other two groups ("some Jews," "not a few prominent women"); it does not specify the actual size of the congregation. Nor is it possible to derive a large membership from such passages as 1 Thess 5:12–14 (see NOTES and COMMENT). That the community is placed in Jason's house (17:5–6) would on the contrary seem to indicate that the church was small enough to be accommodated in a house, thus numbering at most a few dozen (cf. Suhl, 115).

As to the social level of the converts, Luke here reflects his tendency to mention the prosperous and the socially prominent, especially women (Malherbe 1986a). Although Acts 17:4 could be understood grammatically to refer to wives of prominent Greek men (Wohlenberg, 3; Lake, 71), the references to other prominent Macedonian women in 16:14–15 and 17:12 suggest that Luke has in mind Thessalonian women in their own right (Judge 1983: 22). The social prominence that women of favored status enjoyed in Macedonia is well known (Tarn, 98–100), and the mention of these women converts would suggest to Luke's informed readers that Christianity found especially favorable reception among the socially elevated.

The same picture emerges of Jason, the only Thessalonian at this stage of the church's history whose name we know. He is not the Jason mentioned in Rom 16:21 (Schille, 49; Ollrog, 30), who was a Jew. Jews sometimes adopted the Greek name as an alternative for Joshua (*BC* 4:205), but that Acts introduces him abruptly after Paul's break with the synagogue and makes him the object of the Jews' attack probably means that Luke thinks of him as a Gentile. Two factors suggest that he was a man of at least moderate wealth and influence (Meeks 1983a: 62–63). He owned a house large enough to accommodate Paul and his company as well, apparently, as the church, which points to his being a person of some financial substance, as were Phoebe of Cenchrea (Rom 16:2; cf. Judge 1983: 21) and Gaius of Corinth (Rom 16:23), who would render the same service of hospitality to the church (Theissen, 83–91). Furthermore, the success with which he and his Christian associates deflected the charge of treason may imply that they had some standing in the community or had friends in high places (Ramsay, 229).

It is sometimes suggested, on analogy to Aquila and Priscilla (Acts 18:2–3), that Jason was a tentmaker himself or that he had supplied Paul with shelter and work (*BC* 4:205; Haenchen, 512). That is not impossible (Hock, 31), but Luke says nothing about Jason's profession and, curiously, although he knows of Paul's working to support himself (Acts 18:3; 20:34), does not mention it in Thessalonica, where the practice was so important to Paul (1 Thess 2:9; 4:9–12; 2 Thess 3:3–13). Haenchen (511) is correct in his view that Luke's silence does not mean that he did not know of Paul's manual labor in Thessalonica. But Haenchen's explanation that Luke generally reserves such material for edifying contexts like

Acts 20:18–35, in which Paul is presented as the ideal missionary, does not account for Acts 18:3. There Luke's account of Paul's sojourn with Aquila and Priscilla ("and because he was of the same trade he stayed with them, and they worked, for by trade they were tentmakers") is as "prosaic" as mention of it in Thessalonica would have been. Luke does not simply fail to mention Paul's work; he describes Paul's converts (and Jason) as persons who are anything but manual laborers and, what is insufficiently appreciated, contrasts these Christians with the mob fired up by the Jews.

The term *agoraioi*, which describes the Jewish allies in Acts 17:5, deserves close scrutiny (Donfried 1984: 248). It is generally thought to have lost its etymological sense, as a designation for persons associated with the marketplace (e.g., Rigaux 1956: 29). Rather, on the basis of Plutarch, *Aemilius Paullus* 38.3, the word is usually taken to refer in a derivative way to agitators (Lake, 69; Bruce 1957: 326; Haenchen, 507). There it is said that Appius saw Scipio rush into the marketplace (*agora*) attended by men of low birth who had been slaves but who were now frequenters of the marketplace (*agoraioi*). These former slaves were able to gather a mob and force all issues by canvassing for them and shouting. The passage from Plutarch is remarkably similar to Acts 17:5 in describing the way people from the marketplace might be used to stir up a mob.

Furthermore, other associations are made with the term *agoraios* in this passage from Plutarch that help to clarify the Acts account of Paul's mission in Thessalonica. The connection with the marketplace that Plutarch makes is usually retained in other writings where the term is used, as is the description of the *agoraioi* as people of low birth. The term thus connotes a sharp class consciousness, as in Dio Chrysostom, *Oration* 1.33, where vulgar artisans and frequenters of the marketplace are contrasted with the freeborn and noble. This pertains equally to the Latin equivalent, *forensis*, in such passages as Horace, *The Art of Poetry* 244–50. Reflected in these passages is the low esteem in which manual labor and small trade, frequently associated with the *agoraioi*, were held (cf. Plato, *Protagoras* 347C; Dio Chrysostom, *Orations* 22.1; 27.5; 32.9; 36.25; 66.25; Lucian, *Philosophies for Sale* 27).

Seen against the background of such use of the term, the contrast between Paul's converts and the Jews' allies stands in sharp relief. The largest number of converts were prominent women, while the Jews enlisted good-for-nothings from the marketplace, small tradespeople, and manual laborers—types who were known for their propensity for civil disorder. The conflict between the Christian preachers and the Jews is not described as due to religious or theological differences, but social factors: the Jews are jealous of Paul's success among persons of high standing, and with the aid of low-class folk from the marketplace, they start a process that ultimately leads to Paul's being run out of town. If the Jews themselves were traders (D. Smith, 138), the social distinction would be sharper, but Luke provides no information about them. Luke's reasons for describing the events in this way are not clear. The conflict, as described, does fit his tendency to make much of converts of high social standing, but his suppression of information on Paul's employment, especially since he mentions it in chap. 18, suggests that special circumstances, probably in Thessalonica itself, were responsible for the nature of his account. What those circumstances were we do not know; for our present interest it is enough to recognize that Luke's description of the church is tendentious, and to be alert to the danger of interpreting Paul's statements in light of Acts.

## B. THE EVIDENCE OF 1 THESSALONIANS

In contrast to Acts, Paul describes the Macedonians as abjectly poor (2 Cor 8:2), a difference that cannot be explained by the surmise that the prominent women of Acts 17:4 had left the church by the time Paul wrote 1 Thessalonians (Deissmann 1957: 242–44). Paul reveals that he had engaged in manual labor when he founded the church (1 Thess 2:9) in order not to burden his converts and to provide them with an example to follow (2 Thess 3:6–13). The social setting he presupposes is that of a workshop, probably in someone's (Jason's?) house (Hock, 31). That he gives directions on manual labor in 1 Thess 4:10–12 shows that he thinks of the Thessalonians as still representing the artisan class. His statement on the Macedonians' profound poverty, however, should be seen for what it was, a rhetorical overstatement to shame the Corinthians into participating in the contribution for Jerusalem. The statement cannot mean that they were indigent, for they did make a financial contribution (2 Cor 8:4). Nevertheless, in view of the high cost of living in a commercial center like Thessalonica, it is likely that they, like Paul, would have had to work night and day to make a living (von Dobschütz 1904: 82; R. M. Evans, 90–91; Hock, 35), and Paul's concern not to burden them would have been especially appropriate.

The Thessalonians' social standing is also reflected in Paul's view of their relationship to the larger society. According to Acts, the church consisted of persons who, although they were opposed by the mob, made effective use of the judicial system to protect themselves. If they did not have friends at court or use competent attorneys to protect their interests, they themselves knew their way through the intricate legal proceedings (cf. Theissen, 97, on Corinth). The Thessalonians we meet in 1 Thessalonians, on the other hand, do not appear as persons sufficiently well-placed in society to take their case to court as a matter of course. In 1 Thessalonians, when Paul refers to their mistreatment by their countrymen, he does not appeal to civil authorities, but looks to divine retribution (2:14–16). His advice to the Thessalonians is that they should relate to non-Christians by loving them (3:12) and doing good to them (5:15), and more particularly, to secure their approval by not being meddlesome or a burden to society but by continuing in their manual labor (4:10–12).

The church in Corinth was characterized by considerable diversity and social stratification that impaired its life and worship (Theissen, 69–174). Evidence for a similar situation in Thessalonica has been sought in the Thessalonian correspondence. It has been argued that the church must have counted among its members some, but not many, persons from the "upper classes" who helped support the less fortunate, otherwise "there would not have been such a furor over the idlers" (R. M. Evans, 91–92). Perceived thus, the situation becomes more complicated when the matter of social standing is related to the ministering congregation as described in 1 Thess 5:12–15 and when the issue of authority or power is injected (R. M. Evans, 95–97). On this reading, in a church predominantly of one class, there was a negative reaction, reflected in the admonition of peace (1 Thess 5:13; cf. 2 Thess 3:15–16), to some members of the congregation who had assumed a leadership role.

The reaction is thought to have been due to resentment of this ministering group which had arisen out of the artisan class itself (Rigaux 1956: 581). They would have had functional, if not institutionalized authority, derived from the services they rendered the church (von Dobschütz 1909: 215–16; Holmberg, 101–102). The situation would have been further aggravated if the leaders continued in their normal employment and were therefore held up as examples to the idle (Wohlenberg, 115; Frame, 191–93; Rigaux 1956: 579). The friction thus caused would quickly have spread to the rest of the church (R. M. Evans, 96). There is, however, no firm evidence for this kind of disunity or tension in Thessalonica. The passages adduced (1 Thess 5:12–15; 2 Thess 3:15–16) do not support this reconstruction and are more naturally understood otherwise (see NOTES and COMMENT on these passages). Nor is there evidence of an institutional organization; Paul is concerned with how the church functions, not how it is formally structured. As there might have been some Jews in the church, so might there have been a few who were relatively well off, but 1 Thessalonians offers no evidence of either.

The people Paul has in mind are Gentiles whom he expects to support themselves by working with their hands. Yet we do well to heed the caution (Rigaux 1956: 27) not to think of the Thessalonians as a group of helpless people. It will be demonstrated in the commentary that Paul assumes that his readers will pick up nuances that were familiar to people who had listened with understanding to popular philosophers. His ethical injunctions, on the other hand, reflect the background of the workshop in which he had conducted his mission when he was with them (2:1–12). That he follows up his exhortation to brotherly love with directions on manual labor (4:9–12) further suggests that he thinks of the church as being in a social setting where such labor was still the norm. Read in one way, Paul's letters, including 1 Thessalonians, give the impression of scholastic communities meeting to discuss ethical and theological subjects (Judge 1960b). Although such an interpretation may be one-sided, the philosopher who gathers listeners around himself as he works at his craft was indeed a well-known ideal in antiquity, and 1 Thessalonians suggests that Paul operated in a similar manner in Thessalonica (Hock; Malherbe 1987).

A number of individuals mentioned in the New Testament are associated with Thessalonica and might conceivably contribute to our knowledge of the church. Aristarchus, whose name was common (BAGD, 106), is referred to in Acts as a Macedonian (19:29) or Thessalonian (20:4; 27:2). Later writers remembered him as a Jew who shared Paul's imprisonment (Col 4:10–11) after accompanying him on the journey to Jerusalem with the collection (Acts 19:29; 20:4) and after the trip to Rome (Acts 27:2; Ollrog, 45). The theory that he might have been converted during Paul's first visit to Thessalonica (O'Brien 1982: 249) is speculative and unconvincing, for his association with Paul dates from a much later period, particularly when Paul was active in Asia Minor (Schille, 52–53). If Aristarchus had been Paul's servant (Ramsay, 316; Bruce 1957: 305), it might explain why Acts is silent about him until he emerges as the Thessalonians' delegate to Jerusalem. Paul himself calls him his fellow worker (*synergos*) at the time the letter to Philemon was written (Phlm 24), which probably means that at that time he was a participant in the actual evangelizing of the Gentiles and not a servant (Ellis, 440–41; Ollrog, 63–72). Aristarchus thus first appears on the scene at least six years after the period with which we are concerned and therefore contributes nothing to our understanding of 1 Thessalonians.

The same is also true of other individuals who may be related to Thessalonica. According to Acts 20:4 a certain Secundus together with Aristarchus formed the team of Thessalonians accompanying Paul to Jerusalem. Based on an inscription in Thessalonica that refers to a Gaius Julius Secundus, some conjecture that the Secundus of Acts 20:4 is the same person as the Macedonian Gaius mentioned in Acts 19:29, who is similarly associated with Aristarchus (Zahn, 213), but this theory has no merit. References to Gaius are complicated by the popularity of the name (cf. Rom 16:23; 1 Cor 1:14; 3 John 1) and by textual variants. In Acts 19:29 the better manuscripts read "Gaius and Aristarchus, Macedonians," but according to Acts 20:4 Gaius was from Derbe. To resolve the problem, commentators have suggested that at 19:29 a variant be accepted which reads, "Gaius and Aristarchus, a Macedonian," which removes Gaius from Macedonia. Alternatively, Acts 20:4 can be emended to read, "and of the Thessalonians, Aristarchus and Secundus and Gaius, and the man from Derbe, Timothy" (Lake, 67), which makes Gaius a Thessalonian. Still another solution is to accept the Western text of 20:4 which, instead of Derbe, refers to Doberus, an obscure place in Macedonia (Clark, xlix-l; Cadbury, 40). It is thus only by emending the text that Gaius can be made a Thessalonian. As it is, he adds nothing to our knowledge of the church in Thessalonica. Nor does Demas, who was a Gentile (Phlm 24; Col 4:16) and is accused in 2 Tim 4:10 of abandoning Paul and going to Thessalonica. Whether he originally was from Thessalonica (Zahn, 213) is not known.

# III. FROM THESSALONICA TO CORINTH

## A. THE EVIDENCE OF 1 THESSALONIANS

According to 1 Thessalonians, after leaving Thessalonica Paul found his way to Athens. Repeatedly frustrated in his attempts to return to Thessalonica (1 Thess 2:17–18), he sent Timothy from Athens to the Thessalonians (3:1–2, 5). It is apparently on Timothy's return from Thessalonica that Paul wrote the letter. At the time of writing, Silas also was with him (1:1). It is not immediately clear from

1 Thessalonians itself where the letter was written. The reference to Athens in 3:1 was responsible for a widespread tradition in the early church that it was the place of origin, but there are good reasons to reject this interpretation (see pages 71–72). Paul's references to Macedonia and Achaia (1:7, 8; 4:10) throw more light on the matter when seen against the background of the way he customarily referred to these provinces. Recent objections that Paul's references are not to Roman provinces proper but to the general areas represented by them (e.g., Suhl, 94–95) do not affect the usefulness of the references for our immediate purpose.

Macedonia and Achaia were areas in which Paul had been active and continued to have influence. Philippi is mentioned in 2:2; it and Thessalonica were Paul's major Macedonian churches, and Paul's reference to Macedonia normally includes them both (e.g., Rom 15:26; 2 Cor 11:9; Phil 4:4–16). The order in which the two provinces are mentioned in 1:7–8 suggests that Paul had been active in Achaia after Macedonia, and we are left to discover what Paul could have meant by Achaia. The two major cities in Achaia from Paul's itinerary which concern us are Athens and Corinth. Athens is mentioned in the NT only in 1 Thess 3:1 and Acts 17:15, 16. There is, however, no evidence that there was a church under continuing Pauline influence in Athens or that Paul ever had this city in mind when referring to Achaia. The fact that Athens was a free city and technically not a part of Achaia has no bearing on the issue.

More to the point is that Paul later often associates Achaia with Corinth (e.g., 1 Cor 16:15; cf. Acts 18:12, 27), and he repeatedly refers to the church in Corinth as Achaia (e.g., 2 Cor 9:2; 11:10; Rom 15:26). But we should not think of this reference so narrowly as to include only the city of Corinth. Paul frequently relates the Corinthians to other Christians in the area (cf. 1 Cor 1:2, "together with all those . . . in every place"), and he also addresses Christians in the "regions of Achaia" (2 Cor 11:10) and "all of Achaia" (2 Cor 1:1). This indicates that, while Corinth may indeed have been the central and major location in Achaia for him, his reference to Achaia included churches elsewhere in the province.

This inclusive use of the designation "Achaia" represents Paul's later usage, years after the founding of the church in Thessalonica, and it need not necessarily mean that at the time he wrote 1 Thessalonians a number of churches had already been established in Achaia in addition to Corinth. Even allowing for rhetorical exaggeration, however (Vielhauer, 84; Suhl, 109), Paul's statements that the Thessalonians had become "an example to all the believers in Macedonia and Achaia" (1:7), that the word had sounded forth from them in Macedonia and Achaia, and that their faith had gone forth everywhere in Greece (1:8) indicate that Pauline churches quickly took their message beyond the cities in which they were established (see NOTES and COMMENT on 5:26–27). The months that had elapsed between his departure from Thessalonica and his writing of 1 Thessalonians were ample for the development he describes (see pages 72–73). This rapid expansion may have contributed to Paul's custom of speaking of provinces rather than cities (cf. Dibelius 1937: 5–6; Rigaux 1956: 385; Wiefel, 219–20), and his references to Macedonia and Achaia in 1 Thessalonians may have the same connotation as in his later letters. Pauline usage therefore suggests that he wrote the letter after he had been in Athens and had been active in Corinth and its environs.

## B. THE EVIDENCE OF ACTS

Once more, Acts agrees with information provided by Paul, adds to it, and appears at odds with part of it. According to Acts 17:10–18:5, under cover of darkness the Thessalonians sent Paul and Silas to Beroea, a major city about fifty miles southwest of Thessalonica, off the major highways (J. Taylor, 2462–63). Paul's reason for choosing Beroea is not stated. It may be wrong to assume that he hid in Beroea so that he could remain close to Thessalonica (Weiss 1959: 1:286–87), but such an assumption does fit the element of secrecy present in Luke's portrayal of Paul in Thessalonica. A striking parallel to Acts is found in Cicero, *Against Piso* 89, telling of another fugitive from Thessalonica who came to Beroea, a town out of the way, in disguise and at night.

The only other reference to Beroea in the NT is in Acts 20:4, which has been regarded by some as the basis for the account of Paul's activity there. On this theory, Paul kept to the Egnatian Way and took his mission to Illyricum (Rom 15:19), intending to go to Rome until he heard of Claudius's decree against the Jews (Acts 18:2) and was forced south to Athens and Corinth (Suhl, 92–96). It is tempting to find a place for a mission to Illyricum at this point in Paul's career. That mission could have taken place on another occasion, however, even if Rom 15:19 refers to Paul's own preaching and not to that of his churches or delegates (Bruce 1982: xxvi–xxvii). Yet, although there is insufficient reason to accuse Luke of inventing the Beroean sojourn, his hand is quite evident in the account. The converts this time include many Jews, who are contrasted with the Jews of Thessalonica, but again, as in Thessalonica, the converts also include a large number of prominent Greek women and men (17:11–12). Upon learning of the success of Paul's preaching, Jews from Thessalonica come to Beroea and incite the crowds against Paul, which leads to his departure for Athens, accompanied by some Beroeans, while Silas and Timothy remain in Beroea. The Beroeans are sent back with instructions to the two to join Paul in Athens as soon as possible (17:14–15). The Macedonian mission thus ends when Paul is once again forced out of a Greek city by Jews.

For the first time, while in Athens, Paul is alone (17:16–21). The response to his speech in the Areopagus is mixed (17:22–34), and he leaves for Corinth, where he joins Aquila and Priscilla and begins preaching in the synagogue every Sabbath (18:1–4). It is only when Silas and Timothy arrive from Macedonia that Paul begins to devote himself entirely to preaching to Jews (18:5). This account agrees with 1 Thessalonians in identifying a period of preaching in Athens and Achaia (Corinth) after the Macedonian mission, a return of Timothy from Macedonia (Thessalonica), and an association of Paul, Silas, and Timothy at a time when the letter could have been written. The account both adds details of the sojourn in Athens that are irrelevant here and describes events that are important for our understanding of 1 Thessalonians. These latter events will be discussed below, along with the date of the letter. Acts differs from 1 Thess 3:1–10 in that it does not state that Timothy and Silas had made it to Athens, but rather gives the impression that they only caught up with Paul in Corinth.

The comings and goings of Paul's companions are important for the dating of the letter, and various attempts have been made to harmonize Acts and 1 Thessalonians in regard to this issue. Ramsay (332–33), basing his view on the premise that it is Luke's style "to mention an intention and leave the reader to gather that it was carried into effect," maintained that Silas and Timothy must be understood to have joined Paul in Athens. Certainly Luke's statement in Acts 17:15 betrays his knowledge of a meeting of Paul, Silas, and Timothy in Athens. Another possibility, however, is that Luke simply made a mistake by confusing the arrival of Silas and Timothy from Beroea with the return of Timothy from Thessalonica (Lake, 73–75). Taking Acts at face value and combining it with Paul's letters makes possible a variety of other reconstructions. The most popular is that Silas and Timothy did join Paul in Athens and that from there Timothy was sent to Thessalonica and Silas to elsewhere in Macedonia, probably to Philippi (which would agree with 2 Cor 11:9 and Phil 4:14; Lake, 74; Milligan, xxx) or perhaps to Beroea (Rigaux 1956: 31; Vielhauer, 89).

Since Timothy's movements are easier to trace than those of Silas, most speculation has been centered on the latter. By stressing the plural in 3:1–2 (BC 4:224), it might be argued that Silas remained in Athens with Paul when Timothy was dispatched to Thessalonica. Not too much should be made of the plural "alone" and "we sent," however, since the plural *monoi* ("alone") could be understood as singular, especially since Paul uses the singular ("I sent") in 3:5 (von Dobschütz 1909: 14; Rigaux 1956: 31; Michaelis 1961: 221–22; see further pages 86–90). A refinement of this possibility leaves Silas in Athens after Paul departs for Corinth until Timothy returns from Macedonia and together they go to Paul in Corinth (Weiss 1959: 1:288). That would contradict Acts 18:5, however, which has both coming from Macedonia. Another possibility is that Silas remained in Athens until Paul left for Corinth, and then was sent on a Macedonian mission (Zahn, 214). Or Silas could have remained in Beroea to strengthen the church and not have gone to Athens (Dibelius 1937: 16; Masson, 7; Schenke and Fischer, 73).

It has also been suggested, despite 3:1–2, that Timothy, too, was never in Athens (von Dobschütz 1909: 15–16). The language ("to be left behind at Athens alone"), it is argued, does not require Timothy's presence in Athens; it was via the Beroeans who accompanied him to Thessalonica that Paul sent word to Timothy to leave Beroea and go to Thessalonica. This theory has the advantage of making 1 Thessalonians the first direct communication between Paul and the Thessalonians, which it may have been, for if Timothy had gone to Thessalonica from Athens, he would have had an opportunity to carry a letter from Paul to them. It is preferable, however, to accept the obvious meaning of 3:1–2, that Paul had sent Timothy to Thessalonica from Athens. Furthermore, the circumstances leading to the writing of the letter do not require that Paul's first communication with the Thessalonians be a letter (see pages 72–77).

In the final analysis, it is futile and unprofitable to speculate on the movements of Silas (Lake, 75). From the letter it would appear that after leaving the Thessalonians, Paul's attention remained focused on them rather than his coworkers (2:17–3:5), and we have no evidence that Silas returned to Thessalonica. What is certain is that he came from Macedonia with Timothy to Corinth. It is probable that he came from Philippi, for that would agree with the Pauline passages that are related to Paul's contact with Macedonia or Philippi while he was at Corinth, from which 1 Thessalonians was written (2 Cor 11:9; Phil 4:15–16; 1 Thess 1:1), and with Acts 18:5. But attempts to harmonize Acts with Paul's letters on this issue are incapable of proof (Kümmel 1975: 257), and they obscure what is important to both Acts and 1 Thessalonians.

It is striking that, according to Acts, the Macedonian mission, which was undertaken in response to a vision summoning Paul to Macedonia (16:9–10), met with so little obvious success. Paul's efforts are constantly frustrated, and he is forced out of one city after another. Thessalonica is of particular concern to Acts. Luke records no continuing contact between Paul and Philippi, Beroea is described as little more than a stopover, and after Macedonia, Athens is a disappointment (Rigaux 1956: 32). It is only when the travelers from Macedonia join Paul in Corinth that his mission there properly gets underway.

Acts depicts the loneliness of Paul in Athens (Haenchen, 534, 539) and, what is unusual for its accounts of Paul's founding of churches, records Paul's intention to maintain contact with his Macedonian converts through his intermediaries Silas and Timothy. The impression gained from Acts is one of Paul's frustration and anxiety about the beginning of his mission in Greece. In these respects Paul agrees with Acts and focuses on Thessalonica. Paul stresses his frustration at being unable to return to Thessalonica (2:17–18), and he maintains contact with the Thessalonians by sending Timothy to them (3:2, 5). Despite their different perspectives, Acts and Paul agree on these factors, which constitute the setting for the writing of 1 Thessalonians.

# IV. OCCASION AND PURPOSE OF THE LETTER

## A. OCCASION AND DATE

Paul conveys the impression in 1 Thess 1–3 that he is continuing his efforts to remain in contact with the Thessalonians (Weizsäcker, 287). The reconstruction of his and his associates' movements after leaving Thessalonica shows that he had used Timothy as his intermediary and that he wrote the letter from Corinth soon after Timothy and Silas arrived from Thessalonica (3:6–10; Acts 18:5). The reference to Athens in 3:1 led early interpreters to suppose that Timothy had returned to Athens and that Paul wrote the letter from there. That this interpretation was widespread is attested by its presence in the Marcionite Prologues, the subscriptions to many manuscripts (cf. Tischendorf, 776–78), and the introductions to some manuscripts (cf. von Soden, 344). Writing from Athens is a plausible interpretation, but cannot be accepted, because Paul's comment "we were willing to be left behind in Athens alone" would be peculiar if he were still there when he wrote (but see 1 Cor 15:32; cf. 16:8). There is, moreover, no evidence that Timothy did return to Paul in Athens after his mission to Thessalonica, and the evidence of Acts 18:5, combined with 1 Thess 1:1, is conclusive that Paul wrote the letter from Corinth, where Timothy and Silas were with him.

The tenor of the letter confirms this reconstruction. The letter reflects a young church (Koester 1982: 112–14) and is so positive in its intent to strengthen new converts that it is difficult to imagine what would have led Paul to write such a letter years later (Rigaux 1956: 46–47). The intensity of Paul's statements about his desire to return to the Thessalonians (2:17–3:6), with no mention of any intervening events between his departure and Timothy's mission to them (see NOTES and COMMENT on 2:14), leaves the impression that he had no definite information about them when he sent Timothy from Athens but that his anxiety about his new converts made him want to maintain contact with them (Best 1972: 8–11). All this makes no sense if a long period had intervened (von Dobschütz 1909: 17).

A calculation that the letter was written about four months after Paul's departure from Thessalonica would seem reasonable. A shorter period (Frame, 9) would not allow sufficient time for the travels of Paul and his associates or for his activities in Beroea, Athens, and Corinth. The following rough calculation suggests that about four months had elapsed since Paul's departure from Thessalonica, including the time needed to travel plus stays in the cities visited:

- Travel from Thessalonica to Beroea (Acts 17:10–13), 1 week.
- Travel from Beroea to Athens (Acts 17:14–15), 3 weeks.
- Return of Paul's companions to Beroea from Athens (Acts 17:15), 3 weeks.
- Timothy's journey to Athens and return to Thessalonica (1 Thess 3:1–3), 6 weeks.
- Timothy's journey from Thessalonica to Corinth (1 Thess 3:6–8; Acts 18:5), 4 weeks.

A longer period than what this timetable suggests—for example, one of six months (Jülicher, 58)—crowds Paul's stay in Corinth, about which we have more accurate chronological information.

In addition to these indications of relative chronology having to do with Thessalonica, the references in Acts to Gallio (18:12–17) and to Claudius's banishment of the Jews from Rome (18:2) make possible a fairly certain date for the writing of 1 Thessalonians. Older efforts at dating, which placed Paul's Macedonian mission in 52 (e.g., Lightfoot 1893: 245; von Dobschütz 1909: 17) and the writing of 1 Thessalonians in 53 (e.g., Wohlenberg, 9; Zahn, 207), did not have the advantage of an inscription (SIG 2:801) that locates Gallio's term of office in Corinth with considerable certainty and that therefore allows a more precise dating of Paul's activity. Recent investigation has led to the now widely accepted view that the inscription, which supplements other information on Gallio's tenure, shows him to have been proconsul in Corinth from late spring or early summer of 51 to the same time the following year (Plassart 1967; 1970; Ogg, 104–11; Oliver; Jewett 1979: 38–40; Hemer, 6–8; Murphy-O'Connor 1983: 141–50).

Paul remained in Corinth for eighteen months, during which time he was brought before Gallio (Acts 18:11–18). An opinion that has become traditional holds that it was at the end of Paul's stay and shortly after Gallio assumed office that the encounter between the two took place (Schwank; Jewett 1979: 38–40; Koester 1982: 102, 112; Furnish 1984: 22). This would mean that Paul had arrived in Corinth no later than the spring of 50 and that 1 Thessalonians was probably written at the very latest towards the end of that same year, but dates ranging from late 49 (Schwank) to late 51 (Koester) have also been suggested. These reconstructions have been challenged, however (Haacker 1972), and an alternative has recently been offered: Paul arrived in Corinth in the autumn of 50, encountered opposition by the time Gallio assumed office around the middle of 51, and as a result of Gallio's favorable decision remained in Corinth for almost another year, leaving just before another proconsul would take office and perhaps put his work at risk (Hemer, 6–8).

Despite their differences, these views agree that Paul was in Corinth by the autumn of 50. This accords with Claudius's edict, which resulted in Aquila and Priscilla's presence in Corinth by the time Paul arrived. The dating of the edict is problematic (see Rigaux 1956: 45; Jewett 1979: 36–38), but if Orosius, *History* 7.6.15, can be credited (Ogg, 99–103; Suhl, 325–27; Hemer, 6), it took place in 49, which would provide time for Aquila and Priscilla to have found their way to Corinth. That they had just recently come from Rome when Paul met them (Acts 18:2) would place Paul's arrival in Corinth early in 50. In sum, on this calculation, Paul would have arrived in Thessalonica in the summer of 49, left the city two or three months later, sent Timothy from Athens in late autumn or early winter, arrived in Corinth early in 50, and written 1 Thessalonians shortly thereafter, thus about six to eight months after he had founded the church in Thessalonica and about four months after he had left it. That Paul does not send greetings from the Corinthian church in 1 Thess 5:26, as he normally does in his letters written from other churches, may mean that the congregation in Corinth had not yet been well established.

Attempts have been made to date the letter both earlier and later. A chronology that rejects anything in Acts not corroborated by Paul's letters may place Paul in Macedonia as early as 40 (Suggs). Adopting this principle and giving greater precision to John Knox's historical reconstruction (Knox, 83–85), Gerd Luedemann proposes 41 as the date of Claudius's expulsion of the Jews and considers Paul's Macedonian mission to have occurred in the late 30s and 1 Thessalonians to have been written in the early 40s (164–71, 201). Luedemann acknowledges that Paul did appear before Gallio in 51 or 52 but contends that the appearance occurred during a later visit to Corinth (163–64, 195). He supports this historical reconstruction with an exegesis of 1 Thess 4:13–18 and 1 Cor 15:51–52, separating the texts by a period of eight to eleven years (201–44). The reconstruction thus attained does not convince, for it is overly skeptical of the evidence in Acts, runs into difficulties in the interpretation of details (Jewett 1979: 81–85), and of greatest importance, does not do justice to the impression Paul creates in 1 Thessalonians that the letter was written very soon after his mission in Thessalonica.

Yet another view is that the letter was written much later, probably from Ephesus or Athens, during Paul's third missionary journey. In support of such a late dating, argued for especially by Lütgert, Hadorn (1919; 1919–1920), Michaelis (1925; 1961: 221–25), and Schmithals (186), it is claimed that:

- 1:7–9 (cf. 4:10) has in mind a considerable period during which the Pauline mission was extended throughout Greece and probably Asia Minor ("everywhere")
- 2:14 presupposes some length of time during which persecutions arose
- 2:18 requires more time for Paul to have attempted a return to Thessalonica than the traditional dating permits
- 5:12 reflects a degree of organization that could not have evolved in a few months
- 4:13–18 shows that Paul had been away from Thessalonica long enough for some members of the congregation to have died
- and his absence was extended enough for opponents to have secured a footing in Thessalonica and for such problems as those addressed in 4:3, 11–12 to have arisen (see Best 1972: 10–11; Kümmel 1975: 257–58 for summaries of the arguments).

These arguments are not persuasive either and will receive attention in the NOTES and COMMENTS on the relevant passages (see also von Dobschütz 1909: 16–17; Rigaux 1956: 45–50; Best 1972: 10–11; Kümmel 1975: 258–59). The major objections to them are that:

- they do not do justice to the impression that Paul so deliberately creates, that his concern for the Thessalonians has been unbroken despite the obstacles that impeded his return
- they discount the evidence of Acts, which provides a natural historical context for the letter and makes understandable its tenor
- some of these reconstructions resort to an implausible partitioning of the letter to support their hypotheses.

# B. A LETTER FROM THESSALONICA?

First Thessalonians is the earliest extant Pauline letter (Kümmel 1975: 257; Marxsen 1979: 15) and thus the earliest preserved Christian writing (Vielhauer, 82). It may in fact be the first letter Paul wrote to a church; that cannot be proved (von Dobschütz 1909: 18–19), but it is likely that Paul had written letters before he wrote 1 Thessalonians. The events leading up to the writing of the letter may cast some light on the letter itself, and such prehistory must be explored for evidence of communication between Paul and the Thessalonians. A letter was thought of in antiquity as one half of a dialogue (e.g., Demetrius, *On Style* 223; Cicero, *To His Friends* 12.30.1), and in 1 Thessalonians Paul is continuing a conversation with the Thessalonians that had begun with his arrival in their city months earlier (Marxsen 1979: 9–11).

Paul gives no indication that he had sent Timothy from Athens in response to anything that he had heard from or about the Thessalonians. It was his anxiety about their faith that compelled him to maintain contact with them (2:17–3:5). His comments on Timothy's mission stress as its purpose the strengthening of their faith (3:2, 5) and provide no information on what else Paul might have communicated to them. Rendel Harris (173), however, surmised that Timothy carried a letter from Paul to them, traces of which he thought are discernible in 1 Thessalonians. This letter would have stressed Paul's desire to see them (2:17; 3:2, 6) and his concern whether his work with them had been in vain (3:5). That such concerns were conveyed by Timothy is highly likely; that a letter was required to do so is an assumption perhaps natural to scholars who are dependent on those of Paul's letters that have survived for their knowledge of his relations with his churches. Harris's suggestion of such a letter has not met with favor (see NOTES on 2:17–3:5; Malherbe 1990a: 248–49).

Harris also advanced the theory that the Thessalonians responded to Paul in a letter that was brought to him in Corinth by Timothy, to which 1 Thessalonians is the reply (167–73). Evidence of this letter is thought to be found in elements of epistolary form and the content of 1 Thessalonians. As to epistolary form, Harris considers "you always have a good remembrance of us" (3:6) and "we also [as you do in your letter] thank God constantly for this" (2:13) to be references to the thanksgiving period of the letter (cf. 1:2). As to the content of 1 Thessalonians, Harris thought the repeated statements that the readers knew what Paul was saying (e.g., 1:5; 2:1–2; 3:3; 4:2) and that they remembered (2:9) make possible a reconstruction of their letter to Paul.

Chalmer Faw regarded Harris's suggestion as ingenious, but judged his evidence elusive (cf. Moffatt, 126; Plummer, xviii). Faw thought that other elements of the form and content of 1 Thessalonians provided stronger evidence of a prior letter from the Thessalonians:

(1) Faw held that the introduction of a series of comments with *peri de* ("but concerning"; 4:9, 13; 5:1) or *de* ("but"; 5:12) compares with 1 Cor 7:1, 25; 8:1; 12:1; 16:1, 12, which are Paul's responses to written inquiries from the Corinthians (cf. 7:1). It is only in 1 Corinthians and 1 Thessalonians that Paul uses *peri*

*de*, but elsewhere in the NT it also very specifically has to do with replies (Mark 12:26; 13:32; John 16:11; Acts 21:25).

(2) Faw also argued that the transitions at 4:9, 13, and 5:12 would be very abrupt if they were not responses. More important, Paul is reluctant to discuss brotherly love and the times and seasons (4:9; 5:1) and only does so because his readers had asked him for advice on these subjects, but even then he goes on to tell them to continue in what they were already doing (4:1–2, 10). The content of the Thessalonians' letter, which was written by their leaders (5:12), can be determined, according to Faw, primarily from chaps. 4 and 5: it dealt with brotherly love (4:9–12), Christians who had died (4:13–18), and the time of the end (5:1–11). The letter was supplemented by Timothy's oral report, echoes of which are found in chaps. 1–3, particularly in comments revolving around thanksgiving and personal defense, although it is not always possible to distinguish Paul's two sources of information.

An investigation of epistolary conventions, especially in 2:17–3:10, which reflects the historical situation in which the letter was written, reveals significantly more epistolary elements than have previously been identified and helps to determine Paul's purpose in writing 1 Thessalonians (Malherbe 1990a; see NOTES on 2:17–3:10).

The epistolary elements in 2:17–3:5 expressing Paul's emotional need for communication (cf. Koskenniemi, 73–75) are associated with his sending Timothy to Thessalonica. They are precisely the kinds of statements that would have been natural in a letter written in Paul's circumstances. Paul's use of them to sketch the background against which he writes 1 Thessalonians is actually of much greater significance than their possibly pointing to a prior letter to the Thessalonians. By using the conventional epistolary phrases, Paul expresses his emotions towards his readers and does so in a manner that would convey his constant desire to remain in communication with them.

Paul's report of Timothy's return from Thessalonica contains further epistolary conventions (see NOTES and COMMENT on 3:6–10): the constant remembering of the absent friend and yearning to see him (3:6), joy and thanksgiving upon receiving a letter (3:8–9), and supplying the needs of a correspondent (3:10). These conventions make it probable that Paul had received a letter from the Thessalonians, brought by Timothy and supplemented by an oral report about conditions in Thessalonica. That Paul does not mention a letter does not mean that he did not receive one; he mentions no letter either in 1 Cor 16:17 or Phil 2:25–30, which comment on the bearers of letters without mentioning the letters.

Whether or not Paul had received a letter from the Thessalonians, these standard epistolary elements in the section dealing with the setting in which 1 Thessalonians was written heighten Paul's stress on the communication between himself and his converts. They support the conclusion, important for the interpretation of 1 Thessalonians, that chaps. 4 and 5 were written with a full awareness of the Thessalonians' circumstances and that they address points at issue in the church there. It would be an error to view the advice in these chapters as generally applicable paraenesis (see pages 82–83, 85) not related to conditions in Thessalonica. It is nevertheless significant that Paul does not mention such a letter (von Dobschütz 1909; Rigaux 1956: 55–56), but in 3:6 draws attention to Timothy's report. The purpose and result of Timothy's mission must therefore be examined more closely in order to determine the purpose of 1 Thessalonians, which was written in response to Timothy's report.

## C. TIMOTHY'S MISSION AND THE PURPOSE OF 1 THESSALONIANS

In 2:17–3:10 Paul describes Timothy's mission in a manner that highlights his own relationship with the Thessalonians. Timothy was sent at Paul's initiative, out of Paul's deep anxiety over them. With eloquence and pathos Paul expresses his desire to maintain contact. What he says about Timothy does not shift the focus from himself, for here Paul does not commend Timothy, as he does elsewhere in his letters when mentioning Timothy's intermediary function (e.g., 1 Cor 4:17; Phil 2:19–24). Paul had not heard from or about the Thessalonians since his abrupt separation from them, but he suspected that the separation had exacerbated the problems new converts normally experienced (Lake, 75–77; Donfried 1985: 350–51). He therefore sent Timothy for two apparent reasons.

Paul's first declared intention was that Timothy should strengthen the Thessalonians in their faith, lest they be dangerously agitated by "these afflictions" (see NOTES and COMMENT on 3:2–3, 5). One tradition of interpretation views these as the Thessalonians' tribulations, which may have been aggravated by the suffering they had experienced at the hands of their countrymen (2:14). Paul does not, however, make that connection. If Paul has the Thessalonians' affliction in mind, it is more likely that he is referring to the distress of the anguished heart (cf. 3:7; 2 Cor 2:4) experienced by converts to a new way of life, including Christians (Malherbe 1987: 46–48). Their initial reception of the gospel had been attended by such distress as well as by joy (1:6), and Paul had explained to them that affliction was to be their lot (3:3–4). Thus Paul the pastor, anxious about the possible effect his converts' psychological state had on their faith, sent Timothy to minister to their needs. He shared their distress and affliction, but Timothy's return with the news that they had not wavered in their faith comforted him (3:6–8; cf. 2 Cor 7:5–7). Paul is therefore confident of the soundness of their faith, and 1 Thessalonians reflects that confidence.

It is more likely that Paul is referring to his own afflictions (see COMMENT on 3:3). The context supports such an understanding of 3:3, which also comports better with the description of Timothy's report in 3:6, which reveals the major purpose of Timothy's mission. He brought back good news about the Thessalonians' faith and love, and reported further that they continued to hold Paul in good remembrance. This report allayed Paul's anxiety. The object of their love is not immediately apparent (see NOTES and COMMENT), but it is highly likely that Paul is referring in the first instance to their love for him (Marxsen 1979: 55), manifested in their good remembrance of him (Best 1972: 140). Paul's palpable relief upon receiving this report (3:6–8) draws attention to his relationship with them, which in reality was his major concern and his reason for sending Timothy to them. Timothy's report had greater significance than that the Thessalonians remembered Paul kindly (RSV), always thought kindly of him (NEB), or had pleasant memories of him (NIV). Paul's statement on their constant remembrance of him should be seen in the context of the paraenetic style he uses (see pages 83, 84, 85; COMMENT on 3:6–10).

Paul had been a model whom the Thessalonians had imitated so successfully that they had become examples to others (1:5–7). But now his enforced separation caused him to worry that they might no longer hold him in remembrance as their model. What was at stake was more than the absence of a moral paradigm, for Paul thought that his life could not be distinguished from his gospel (Rigaux 1956: 61–62; Laub 1976: 26–31; Koester 1982: 113). If the Thessalonians forgot him so soon, their faith would be in jeopardy. Strictly speaking, therefore, Paul's concerns for their faith and for their attitude towards him were inseparable. So Paul has learned, happily, that he is still their model, and as such he aids their continuing development by writing the letter, in which he completes what is yet lacking in their faith (3:10).

First Thessalonians is essentially a pastoral letter (von Dobschütz 1909: 20; Marxsen 1979: 24–25, 28). Throughout the letter Paul demonstrates an awareness of the conditions of recent converts (Pax 1971; 1972; Halamka; Malherbe 1987) with whom he has a cordial relationship and whose "faith required completion rather than correction" (Moffatt, 69; cf. Best 1972: 15).

# V. FORM AND FUNCTION OF THE LETTER

Although other outlines of 1 Thessalonians are possible (see Jewett 1986: 216–22 for a conspectus), the following outline of the letter is straightforward:

I.   Address, 1:1
II.  Autobiography, 1:2–3:13
   A.  Thanksgiving, 1:2–3:10
      1.  The Conversion of the Thessalonians, 1:2–10
      2.  Paul's Ministry in Thessalonica, 2:1–12
      3.  The Word under Persecution, 2:13–16
      4.  Reestablishing Contact, 2:17–3:10
   B.  Concluding Prayer, 3:11–13
III. Exhortation, 4:1–5:22
   A.  Introduction, 4:1–2
   B.  On Marriage, 4:3–8
   C.  On Brotherly Love and Self-Sufficiency, 4:9–12
   D.  Eschatological Exhortation, 4:13–5:11
      1.  On Those Who Have Fallen Asleep, 4:13–18

    2.  On the Day of the Lord, 5:1–11
  E.  On Intracommunal Relations, 5:12–22
    1.  On "Pastoral Care" among Members of the Church, 5:12–15
    2.  On the Evaluation of Prophecy, 5:16–22
IV.  Conclusion, 5:23–28

This outline assumes the literary integrity of the letter, an assumption that has been challenged by arguments that 1 Thessalonians is interpolated and/or that it is compiled of fragments of a number of Paul's letters (see the discussion in Collins 1984: 96–135). The most common hypothesis is that 2:13–16 or a part of it is an interpolation; widely rejected is the theory that 5:1–11 also comes from a later hand.

Compilation theories are complex. Based on a minute formal analysis that assumes that Paul was bound to a particular form of letter writing, one of these theories partitions the letter into numerous fragments that are interwoven with inauthentic material to form the present letter (Eckart). Another approach has been to divide 1 and 2 Thessalonians into four separate letters, made up of fragments from 1 and 2 Thessalonians. These four letters are thought to reflect a development of the Thessalonian situation (Schmithals 1972: 123–218). It has also been argued recently that 1 Thessalonians is made up of two separate letters into which 2:14–16 was interpolated after these two letters were combined, thus forming our present 1 Thessalonians (Richard, 11–19). The compilation theories have not been well received, and it is only 2:13–16 that calls for serious exegetical consideration as a possible interpolation.

Interpreters have sought to discover the purpose of 1 Thessalonians from its formal aspects, stressing either the autobiography in chaps. 1–3 or the paraenesis in chaps. 4–5 as providing the clue to Paul's purpose.

Some scholars have explained the extended autobiography as Paul's concerted effort to defend himself. The argument appeals especially to the antitheses in 2:1–9 as evidence of accusations that Paul denies. On this reading, the paraenesis in chaps. 4–5 was appended as a generally applicable exhortation and, with the possible exception of 4:13–5:11, not particularly related to the situation in Thessalonica. The letter is therefore regarded as apologetic.

Despite the absence of any reference in 1 Thessalonians to antagonism in Thessalonica among the Thessalonians or to Paul at the time the letter was written, interpreters who take the letter as essentially apologetic have detected opponents whom Paul supposedly had in view when he wrote (see Rigaux 1956: 58–61; Best 1972: 15–22; Marshall 1983: 16–20 for summaries of such hypotheses). These supposed opponents have been described as pagans (Zahn, 217–18), Jews (e.g., Milligan, xxxi; Frame, 9–10), or according to the church fathers, false apostles (cf. von Dobschütz 1909: 106–7). A further refinement is that they were spiritual enthusiasts (Lütgert; Hadorn 1919; Jewett 1972) or Gnostics (Schmithals 1972; Harnisch). The view that Paul faced competitors in Thessalonica depends more on reconstructions of the situations he eventually confronted in Galatia and Corinth than on the evidence of 1 Thessalonians itself.

Such hypotheses sometimes resort to partitioning the letter to gain support, and they import issues not implicit in the letter itself. Ultimately, they shatter on the cordiality and warmth of the letter, which do not fit polemic or apologetic, but rather are appropriate to the friendly, paraenetic style Paul adopted and then adapted to write the first Christian pastoral letter.

In contrast, it has been argued, on formal grounds, that the point of the whole letter is found in 4:1–2 and 4:10b–12 and that 4:1–5:11 constitutes the body of the letter (Bjerkelund, 134). The intent of the letter would thus be paraenetic, a judgment that is strengthened if one accepts the claim that all thanksgiving periods in Paul's letters—in this case, the extended autobiographical thanksgiving in 1:2–3:13 (see 1:2; 2:12; 3:9)—have either explicitly or implicitly a paraenetic function (Schubert, 16–20, 88–89). This view has much to commend it but needs to be modified by a broader view of paraenesis. The form of the letter is influenced by Paul's adoption of paraenetic style, and it will be seen that paraenetic features are present throughout the letter and that they perform a pastoral function.

Paul begins (1:3–7) and ends (3:6–10) the long autobiographical section of the letter with statements of thanksgiving that draw attention to his relationship with his readers. It is a relationship in which Paul, although separated from them, still exemplifies for the Thessalonians the gospel as it is lived out. This section has no other purpose than to strengthen the bond between himself and the Thessalonians, and so to prepare for the advice he will give in chaps. 4 and 5 (Jülicher, 59; Rigaux 1956: 61–62; von Campenhausen 1957: 8–9; Schlier 1972: 11). It delineates the personal example he wants them to continue remembering, and no part of this section is to be separated arbitrarily from the rest of the letter. This applies especially to 2:1–12, which is neither Paul's unburdening of his heart (thus Bornemann, 24–25; von Dobschütz 1909: 106–7) nor an apology, whether given in response to charges actually leveled against him or to charges that he merely anticipated (a possibility rejected by Marxsen 1979: 23–25). The antitheses in 2:1–12 do not reflect such charges, but are characteristic of descriptions of the ideal philosopher, to which Paul's paraenetic style is indebted (Malherbe 1970a). Paul, however, puts that style to a pastoral use (Malherbe 1987: 72–78).

The paraenetic style is used throughout the letter, and 2:1–12 must be integrated into the rest of the letter. Such self-descriptions were frequently offered by philosophers early in their addresses in order to establish themselves as trustworthy before they turned to advise their listeners or readers on practical matters. Paul's self-description functions in a similar manner, but in contrast to the philosophers, Paul stresses, not his own accomplishments or speech, but God's initiative and word (Malherbe 1983a: 246–49). Further distinguishing 1 Thessalonians from the philosophers' speeches and writings is the eschatological tone that suffuses the letter as a whole (cf. Koester 1979) and dominates the final prayer (3:10–13), which forms the transition between the autobiographical and properly paraenetic sections.

Paul begins the latter, paraenetic section by again referring to his work for the gospel and his overall Christian conduct to God and Christ (4:1–2). The subjects

he takes up had already been hinted at in the autobiographical section, particularly in 2:1–12, for instance, impurity (2:3; cf. 4:7), pleasing God (2:4; cf. 4:1),
covetousness or overreaching (2:5; cf. 4:6), manual labor (2:9; cf. 4:11), and
adapting exhortation to individual needs (2:11–12; cf. 5:11, 14). The example
that he had outlined and that gave shape as well as substance to his relationship
with the Thessalonians thus also serves to undergird his practical advice.

The several items Paul takes up may be designated as *topoi*, moral commonplaces, sometimes thought to be "self-contained, unitary teachings which have
but a loose, and often even an arbitrary, connection with their context" (Bradley
1953: 243). It is true that such moral *topoi* could be rather traditional in their
content and only loosely related to the situations to which they were addressed,
but this tendency should not be exaggerated. Contrary to Bradley's supposition,
moral philosophers were conscious of the need to adapt such teaching to particular circumstances (e.g., Seneca, *Epistle* 64.6–10; see page 82; COMMENT on
4:1–2). Therefore it is quite inadmissible to assume, on supposed analogy with
the philosophers' practice, that Paul's instruction had little or nothing to do with
the situation in Thessalonica.

Paul had very carefully prepared for the paraenetic section, which constitutes
his attempt "to complete what was lacking" in their faith (3:10), and there is no
reason to doubt that he addresses matters actually at issue in Thessalonica. He
had Timothy's report and probably a letter from the Thessalonians to inform him
of conditions in the church. The subjects he discusses, namely, marriage
(4:13–5:10) and relationships within the community (5:11–22), are precisely
those that would be of concern to a largely Gentile church. An attempt has been
made to isolate three groups whom Paul mentions in 5:14, namely, the disorderly, the fainthearted, and the weak (Frame, 11–12) and to identify instructions
directed to them (4:11; 4:13–5:11; 4:3–8 respectively), but such a schematization
is overly precise and does not contribute to the interpretation of the letter.

# VI. STYLE AND LANGUAGE

## A. PASTORAL PARAENESIS

It is generally agreed that chaps. 4 and 5 of 1 Thessalonians are paraenetic, but
the paraenetic style is actually reflected in the form and function of the letter and
is present throughout. To appreciate the importance of this style for 1 Thessalonians, it is necessary to understand paraenesis more broadly than in the purely
formal way Martin Dibelius did, whose opinion on the matter has influenced
scholars' understanding of paraenesis and its confinement in 1 Thessalonians to
chaps. 4 and 5.

Dibelius focused on the origins and form of paraenesis and applied his find-
ings to the hortatory sections of Paul's letters (e.g., Rom 12, 13; Gal 5:13–6:10;
Col 3, 4; 1 Thess 4, 5), which in style are different from the rest of the letters in
which they appear (Dibelius 1935: 238–39):

In particular (the hortatory sections) lack an immediate relation with the circumstances of the letter. The rules and directions are not formulated for special churches and concrete cases, but for the general requirements of early Christendom. Their significance is not factual but actual—not the momentary need but the universal principle.

. . .

Exhortation, therefore, had a broader basis than the Pauline mission. It was the common property of Christendom, i.e. it was the general duty of the primitive missionaries to give such directions to their churches, or at least to the churches composed of Christians of heathen origin to whom it was the most necessary.

. . .

Thus we see that the hortatory sections of the Pauline epistles have nothing to do with the theoretic foundation of the ethics of the Apostle, and very little with other ideas peculiar to him.

The NOTES and COMMENTS on chaps. 4 and 5 will show the last statement to be in error; the following survey of some features of ancient paraenesis will show that, while Dibelius correctly identified certain paraenetic characteristics, he worked with too narrow a view of the style, was not aware of differing ancient opinions about some paraenetic features, and absolutized what he thought paraenetic (for what follows, see Malherbe 1986b: 124–29; esp. 1992: 278–93; see COMMENT on 4:1).

Speakers who engaged in paraenetic discourse acknowledged that what they were saying was traditional and unoriginal, and so already known by the people listening to them (Isocrates, *To Nicocles* 40–41; Dio Chrysostom, *Orations* 3.25–26; 13.14–15; 17.1–2). Related to this feature is that paraenetic precepts are generally applicable. "Of course, there are slight distinctions, due to the time, or the place, or the person; but even in these cases, precepts are given which have a general application" (Seneca, *Epistle* 94.35). This is the characteristic that is fundamental to Dibelius's understanding of paraenesis. But even Seneca realized that selection, adaptation, and application remained tasks for the teacher (*Epistles* 64.7–10; 84; see Hadot, 179–90).

Some philosophers objected that since people already know what they are advised to do, precepts are superfluous, to which Seneca replied that knowing something does not mean that one will act upon it. Besides, "advice is not teaching; it merely engages the attention and arouses us, and concentrates the memory, and keeps it from losing grip" (Seneca, *Epistle* 94.11). He then provides three examples of moral teaching that his reader knows (*scis*) but does not practice. We therefore need to have our memories jogged (Isocrates, *Nicocles* 12; Seneca, *Epistle* 94.21, 25–26; Dio Chrysostom, *Oration* 17.2). By reminding someone of what he already knows (*oidate, scis*) one in effect is urging him to act on the knowledge he has. A related locution is to claim that the speaker has no need to speak on a particular subject, thus saying either explicitly or implicitly that one's auditors already know it (Isocrates, *Nicocles* 12).

A number of the characteristics of paraenesis are illustrated in Ps.-Isocrates, *To Demonicus* 9–11 (cited on p. 155): the use of personal examples (cf. Seneca, *Epistles* 25.6; 52.8; 94.40–41; see Fiore; Malherbe 1986b: 135–38); the call to imitate someone as your model (see Rabbow, 121, 156, 260–66), who is described in a series of antitheses; the reminder of the qualities of virtuous people (Ps.-Isocrates, *To Demonicus* 44; Plutarch, *Progress in Virtue* 85AB; Marcus Aurelius, *Meditations* 11.26); the advice given by father to son, whether the relationship is real or fictive (Ps.-Isocrates, *To Demonicus* 44; Ps.-Plutarch, *On the Education of Children* 4C, 8F, 9EF; Marcus Aurelius, *Meditations* 11.18.9).

Paraenesis found a place in letter writing, and by the first century A.D. the paraenetic letter had become a particular type among others recognized by handbooks that gave instruction in the styles in which various letters should be written (e.g., Ps.-Libanius, *Epistolary Styles* 52). Some of the letters of Cicero, Seneca and Pliny are paraenetic in nature and exhibit the characteristics that have been identified above.

Seneca frequently refers to models one should choose to guide oneself in one's conduct, and he used antitheses in describing the model, as he does in *Epistle* 52.8:

> Let us choose . . . from among the living, not men who pour forth their words with the greatest glibness, turning out commonplaces . . . but men who teach us by their lives, men who teach us what we ought to do and then prove it by their practice, who show us what we should avoid, and then are never caught doing that which they have ordered us to avoid.

A letter was only a substitute for the presence of an authoritative teacher like Seneca,

> for the living voice and the intimacy of a common life will help you more than the written word. You must go to the scene of the action, first, because men put more faith in their eyes than in their ears, and second, because the way is long if one follows precepts, but short and helpful if one follows examples. (Seneca, *Epistle* 6.5–6)

By referring to oneself as an example or model, one did more than delineate by one's own behavior particular qualities of character and demonstrate that they could be achieved.

> I mention this, not only to enforce my advice by example, but also that this letter may be a sort of pledge binding me to persevere in the same abstinence in the future. (Pliny, *Epistles* 7.1.7; cf. 2.6.6)

Letters also used the paraenetic theme of remembering. Seneca illustrates, after writing on the value of personal examples:

Happy is the man who can make others better, not merely when he is in their company, but even when he is in their thoughts! And happy also is he who can so revere a man as to calm and regulate himself by calling him to mind! One who can so revere another will soon be himself worthy of reverence. (Seneca, *Epistle* 11.9)

The paraenetic letters also claim that what is urged in them is not new and that no extended discussion is necessary (Seneca, *Epistles* 13.15; cf. 8.10; 99.32). There is therefore no need to write on the subject (Cicero, *To His Friends* 1.4.3; 2.4.2; Seneca, *Epistle* 24.6, 9, 11, 15; Pliny, *Epistle* 8.24.1). Statements like this did not rule out the giving of advice, but was a means by which the writer complimented his reader, thus actually laying the basis for giving advice. Related to this is the frequent statement that the reader was already doing what was being urged and that all that was required was that he continue to do so (Seneca, *Epistles* 1.1; 5.1; 25.4, 16; Cicero, *To His Brother Quintus* 1.1.8; Ign *Pol* 1:2).

It was observed above that the form of 1 Thessalonians serves a paraenetic function, the autobiographical section delineating the qualities of Paul, who presents himself as a model to be emulated. A number of the paraenetic features we have identified appear in this section. The first of a number of uses of *oidate* ("you know") occurs in 1:5, and then in quick succession in chap. 2 (vv 1, 2, 5, 11), and functions as a reminder of Paul's ministry (cf. *mnēmoneuete* in 2:9). Paul reminds them not merely to make them feel well disposed towards him; it is as imitators of him (1:6) that they are called to remember. The repeated *oidate* reminds them of the qualities that make Paul trustworthy and worthy of imitation.

The centerpiece of this self-presentation is 2:1–12, in which he describes himself in the antithetic style used by philosopher-preachers to describe themselves (see Dio Chrysostom, *Oration* 32.11, cited on p. 154). As we have seen, antithesis was also used in the description of historical examples. This self-presentation forms the basis for the practical advice Paul will give in chaps. 4 and 5.

The paraenetic character of the letter continues in 2:13–16. The repeated thanksgiving continues the paraenetic element that is present in all thanksgivings, and the theme of imitation occurs once more, but this time of an example other than Paul, namely, the churches in Judea. The theme of the section is the gospel, received by the Thessalonians, who then suffered for it, and preached by Paul, who suffered for doing so. The section describes the Thessalonians' and Paul's experiences after his departure from them and demonstrates that they continued to share affliction as a result of the gospel.

In 2:17–3:10 Paul provides information about the setting in which he wrote the letter. The first part of the section (2:17–3:5) is written in highly affective language, and the pathos reveals the deep affection Paul has for his converts. It is such friendship that forms the basis for paraenesis. Other paraenetic elements again appear: the familiar *oidate* as he reminds his readers of his initial instruction (3:3–4), and his joy he heard from the returning Timothy that they still remembered him favorably, that is, that they continued to hold him as their model (3:6). It is then on the basis of this relationship that he writes to supply what was deficient in their faith (3:10).

The content of chaps. 4 and 5 is paraenetic, even 4:13–17, which was written to console his readers, for consolation was viewed by the ancients as belonging to paraenesis. The two chapters teem with paraenetic markers: reminders of what the Thessalonians knew (4:1, 2, 6, 11; 5:2), that they have no need to be written to (4:9; 5:1), and that they are already doing what Paul wants them to do (4:1, 10; 5:11) but are to do so more and more (4:1–2, 10b).

As to style, then, 1 Thessalonians is clearly a paraenetic letter; indeed, it is one of the best examples of such a letter. The reason for the heavy use of the style may lie in the fact that Paul writes this letter to his recent converts to Christianity sooner after their conversion than he writes to any other of his converts. They still needed rather basic instruction in Christian behavior, and the letter is largely concerned with behavior rather than doctrine, thus the appropriateness of the paraenetic style. However, there is more to it than that.

What is noteworthy is the degree to which Paul elaborates on the relationship between himself and his readers. He uses the literary devices of paraenesis to describe that relationship, and the description has a paraenetic function. But the autobiographical section is also quite different from normal paraenesis in a number of ways. Although he uses the conventions of the moral philosophers, he is no philosopher but a preacher of the gospel. And the content of the message he had preached was not moral teaching aimed at personal betterment, but the word of God that aimed at generating faith. Most important, is that Paul could not separate himself from faith in the gospel, and that determined his relationship with his converts and made him different from his contemporaries.

The letter aims at nurturing the readers in this faith, and its paraenetic features perform what we would call pastoral care (Malherbe 1987: 68–78). The characteristics of recent converts are well ministered to by the paraenetic features of the letter (see pages 82–84):

1. Paul is presented as a trustworthy model who will continue doing what he had done when he was with them and in the intervening time before he wrote. As he had exhorted them (2:3, 12; 3:2) and sent Timothy to exhort, so he continues to do in the letter (4:1, 10, 18; 5:11). He had presented them with examples of conduct (2:9; 3:7), which he now calls on them to follow (4:11; 4:18).

2. The letter is adapted to the emotional condition of converts who are anxious and distressed. This is evident in his language, which is redolent with positive feeling designed to strengthen: thanksgiving (1:2; 2:13; 3:9), faith, hope, and love (1:2), power, Holy Spirit, full conviction (1:5), gentleness, self-giving, affection (2:7–8; cf. 1:4), endurance (3:1, 5), good news (3:6), yearning to see each other (2:17; 3:16), comfort (2:11–12; 3:7), joy (1:6; 2:19–20; 3:9). It is noteworthy that this language is almost totally confined to the autobiographical section of the letter, which describes the relationship from the perspective of Paul.

3. Disenfranchized by the larger society, the language of kinship is used to make them feel secure in a new fellowship (see NOTE and COMMENT on 1:4, on "brother," which is used fourteen times in the letter). To describe his re-

lationship with his readers Paul uses the images of nurse (2:7) and father (2:11), which he derived from the moral philosophers, and orphan (2:17), which he uses pastorally.

4. To converts who are uncertain about their knowledge of life in the faith, he repeatedly assures them that they do know.

5. To people who are uncertain about what to do, he assures them that they are already doing it and encourages them only to do so more and more. It is features such as these that make 1 Thessalonians a pastoral letter.

The identification of 1 Thessalonians as pastoral and paraenetic is not new. Patristic commentators, especially John Chrysostom and Theodoret, frequently comment on Paul's pastoral sensitivities and in the process use the language of paraenesis and psychagogy (on the latter, see COMMENT on 5:12–15). Thus, in the introductory summary to his *Commentary on 1 Thessalonians*, Theodoret says that Paul engages in paraenesis (PG 82:628–29) and throughout the commentary virtually identifies paraenesis with psychagogy (e.g., PG 82:636, 645, 648, 652).

## B. "WE" AND "I"

First and 2 Thessalonians are remarkable among Paul's letters for their almost exclusive use of verbs in the first person plural. In the first letter, Paul uses the plural verb forty-five times and, in addition, uses plural participles twenty times and the pronoun *hēmeis* ("we") forty-three times. The singular verb occurs only twice (3:5; 5:27), and the singular pronoun *egō* ("I") only once (2:18). In 2 Thessalonians, the first person plural verb appears seventeen times, a plural participle appears once, and the plural pronoun is used twenty-two times. The singular verb appears only twice (2:5; 3:17). Our discussion here is confined to 1 Thessalonians.

Paul mentions two cosenders, Silvanus and Timothy, in 1:1, and it is therefore natural to assume that they are included in the plurals throughout the letter and that Paul had special reasons for referring to himself in the few places where he uses the first person singular verb or the singular pronoun. The matter is complicated, however, by the fact that, with the exception of Romans, he mentions cosenders in all his other letters but then immediately begins to use singular verbs (e.g., 1 Cor 1:1, 4, 10; Phil 1:1, 3; Phlm 1, 4), although he uses the plural verb later (see Gal 1:1–2, 6; 3:23–25; 5:25–26; cf. 1 Cor 1:4, 10, 23; 2:6–16; the first plural dominates in 2 Cor 1–9, but alternates easily with the singular; see 3:23–3:3; Byrskog).

Despite Paul's inconsistency in using plural verbs, scholars have related these grammatical phenomena to the cosenders, thus extending his missionary practice of working with others to his style of letter writing. Different reasons have been suggested for Paul's mentioning cosenders: to make the letters less private in nature, to give more weight to what he has to say in the letters, to confirm the gospel by two or three witnesses, to honor the cosenders he mentions; or he mentions them because they are well known to his readers and might function as intermediaries between Paul and them, or more simply, they carried the letters in which they are mentioned to the trustees (summarized by Ollrog, 184). Most often, it has been argued that the plurals in 1 Thessalonians support the conclusion that Silvanus and Timothy were coauthors of the letter (Prior, 40; Murphy-O'Connor 1996: 19; Byrskog, 236–38). Joint authorship could have taken place in a number of ways. Someone else could have prepared a draft of the letter, which Paul then reworked, thus giving it his personal stamp. Or Paul could have done the actual composing of the letter in consultation with Silvanus and Timothy, breaking into the singular only in those places where he wanted to stress something that had a particular reference to himself. The most popular opinion is that Silvanus wrote the letter and that Paul interjected only twice (2:18; 3:5) and signed the letter (5:27).

Edward G. Selwyn (363–466) found evidence elsewhere in the NT to support the contention that Silvanus was Paul's secretary. Silvanus would have enjoyed such latitude in writing the letter for Paul, in the process leaving his own mark so clearly in the letter that it was natural to include him as coauthor through the use of the first person plural. Assuming that the Silvanus of the Thessalonian letters was the Silas of Acts 15:23 and 1 Pet 5:12, Selwyn interpreted the phrase *graphein dia* ("to write by"), which occurs in those two passages, as meaning that the church in Jerusalem and Peter used him as an executive secretary to compose the letters they wrote. The phrase does not, however, refer to a secretary's function, but more likely to that of a letter carrier (Richards, 73). Selwyn also argued that the terms used in Acts 15:32 to describe Silas's activity (*parakalein, epistērizein* ["to exhort," "to strengthen or confirm"]) occur so frequently in 1 and 2 Thessalonians and 1 Peter because he wrote all three letters. However, the statistical base on which Selwyn argues is too narrow; furthermore, the terms are natural to letters that are hortatory in nature.

Another objection to Silas as coauthor involves the interpretation of 1 Thess 3:1–2. Timothy could not be included in the first plural *epempsamen* ("we sent"), for he was the one who was sent, but Silas could be included. If the plural is taken as a real plural, it would mean that Silas was with Paul when Timothy was sent from Athens (so Zahn, 210). Although this is not impossible, there is no firm evidence that Silas had made it to Athens with Timothy (see pages 70–71). If he had made it to Athens, he would be included in the *monoi* ("alone") who remained after Timothy's departure.

On the face of the matter, it is unlikely that Silas should be included in the *monoi*, for to do so would lessen the pathos that Paul is so careful to create in 2:17–3:5. Furthermore, the singular *epempsa* ("I") in 3:5 and *egō men Paulos* ("I, Paul") in 2:18 show that he is stressing his personal anxiety in this context and that the singular *epempsa* and the plural *epempsamen*, which form an *inclusio*, are interchangeable. It should also be noted that the singular constructions are used here, where the epistolary situation is described, and in 5:27 (cf. 2 Thess 3:17), also an epistolary feature, where there is no doubt that Paul himself is writing.

Rather than a "real" plural, we may have to do with a majestic plural (Smyth, 1006) or, conversely, a plural of modesty (Smyth, 1008), an option favored by some patristic writers (see Rigaux 1956: 79). The most satisfactory understanding of the plural is that it is a literary or authorial plural (BDF §280), a usage found elsewhere in the NT (e.g., Heb 2:5; 5:11; 6:9, 11) and in Paul. In Paul's letters, the authorial plural may alternate with the singular, as it does in 1 Thessalonians (e.g., 2 Cor 1:1–14, 18 [after the singular in vv 15–17], 24 [after the singular in v 23]; 7:5–7 [the singular is in v 7]; singular and plural in 7:12–8:8).

Objections have been raised to the authorial plural on the basis of its use in ancient literature. The literary or authorial plural increased in usage in later Greek literature, but not in letters (Dick). Recent investigations have emphasized the latter but have focused too narrowly on letters that mention cosenders, of which there are relatively few anyway, and disproportionately on papyrus letters in Greek, whose content differs considerably from Paul's letters (Richards, 47; Murphy-O'Connor 1995: 16–18; Byrskog, 234–36). The situation is different when one takes into consideration the use of plural verbs in letters that do not mention cosenders, but which more closely approximate the character of Paul's letters, particularly 1 Thessalonians, which is paraenetic.

Seneca, Paul's contemporary, wrote such letters. That he wrote in Latin presents no impediment to introducing his letters into this discussion, for Latin letter writing was indebted to Greek epistolary theory and practice; it is only by historical accident that the letters preserved from the first century B.C. to the second century A.D. are primarily in Latin. The discussion of paraenesis above demonstrated how often the Latin letters of Seneca, Paul's contemporary, cast light on some major features of 1 Thessalonians, and their usefulness in illuminating Paul's letter will become more evident throughout this commentary. For now they will help clarify Paul's use of the plural in 1 Thessalonians. Seneca's letters differ from Paul's in that his relationship with Lucilius, his correspondent, ruled out the inclusion of a cosender, but otherwise their style is instructive for our present purpose.

Seneca uses a simple authorial plural, alternating it with the singular much in the way that Paul does (e.g., *Epistle* 78.7, after the singular in 1–6). He also uses the plural when referring to a general practice (*Epistles* 22.2; cf. 9.2) or to a condition shared with other people (*Epistles* 60; 74.11; 92.34). As is characteristic of paraenesis, he uses the hortatory subjunctive plural (*Epistles* 18.8; 24.15, followed by the singular). The effect of using the plural is that he places himself on the same level as his reader and creates a warmer tone (Huser, 82, 100).

Paul also uses the plural in specifying what he shares with his readers (God: 1:3; 3:11, 13; the Lord Jesus Christ: 1:3; 3:11, 13; 5:23, 28; the gospel: 1:5; what they believe: 4:14; what they experience: 3:3–4), as well as in the thanksgivings, which have an epistolary function (1:2, 3; 2:13; 3:9), and in epistolary clichés, which establish or nurture a friendly relationship with his readers (4:13; 5:1). For the most part, the first person plural is balanced by the pronoun *hymeis* ("you"), which in all its forms occurs at least 83 times in the letter. This fact is almost al-

ways overlooked in discussions of the plural in 1 Thessalonians. By repeatedly referring to his readers, particularly in the first three chapters, Paul reminds them
of his relationship with them (1:5–6 [with the focus on them in vv 7–9]; 2:1,
7–12, 17; 3:5–12; 4:1). For the rest, the plural is used in paraenesis (4:1, 2, 6, 10,
11, 13; 5:12, 14), on occasion in the form of a hortatory subjunctive (5:6, 8–10).
Related to the paraenetic use is the plural in claiming prophetic insight (4:15)
and its application (4:17).

By casting the net wider than is usually done, it thus appears that the plural is
explained as characteristic of paraenesis. The first person plural lends a warm
tone to the letter, which would be read aloud (5:27) and thus approximate a sermon. In Jewish and Christian preaching, the first person plural functioned in exactly this way (Thyen, 90–94). The inclusion of the cosenders at the beginning
of the letter does not any more determine the grammatical number throughout
this letter than it does in Paul's other letters. Their mention at the beginning of
this letter has a different significance.

Paul, Silas, and Timothy together had evangelized Thessalonica, and they
were again together in Corinth, where Paul wrote 1 Thessalonians. It is therefore
natural for Paul to mention Silas and Timothy, since they had just arrived from
Macedonia (Acts 18:5; 2 Cor 11:9). One might expect Paul rather to have mentioned them in the conclusion of the letter, where he mentions coworkers in his
other letters (see, e.g., 1 Cor 16:15–18, mentioning individuals with a special interest in Corinth). He instead mentions them in 1:1 because in chaps. 1–3 he reminds his readers of his association with them from the very beginning of the
church's existence, when Silas and Timothy were with him. This reminder
serves as the basis for the paraenesis in chaps. 4 and 5. Paul is careful in chaps.
1–3 to underline the continuity of his concern for them, and the mention of his
two coworkers brings to mind the initial joint effort that resulted in his readers'
conversion.

Mentioning Silas and Timothy with himself is the equivalent of the *oidate*
("you know") that he repeatedly uses to remind the Thessalonians of his ministry to them (1:5; 2:1, 5, 11; 3:3, 4). When he concludes the history of his contact
with them, he mentions Timothy's role in confirming his relationship with them
(3:3, 6), and from then on he no longer mentions his coworkers, for their literary purpose has been served. Given the circumstances in which the letter was
written, if anyone were to be included in the first person plural, it would be Timothy, for there is no further mention of Silas, and it is Timothy's return from
Thessalonica that was the occasion for the letter. But as we have seen, Timothy
cannot be included by virtue of 3:2, 5.

This does not mean that Paul's coworkers played an insignificant role in his
mission. In 1 Corinthians, for example, Paul discusses at length his relationship
with Apollos in preaching the gospel (3:6–4:5) and advances both of them as examples of note (4:6; cf. Phil 3:17). But he is also emphatic that he has a unique
relationship with the Corinthians that makes it possible for him to admonish
them in a unique way (4:14–21; see COMMENT on 3:6). The same attitude is
reflected in 1 Thessalonians.

## C. EPISTOLOGRAPHY

First Thessalonians shows that Paul was an accomplished letter writer, thoroughly familiar with the epistolary clichés of the time but free and creative in the way he used those conventions. The following clichés appear in 2:17–3:10, which reveals the epistolary situation—that is, it describes the events that led to the writing of the letter—and exhibits the characteristics of the so-called friendly letter:

1. The stress on being present in spirit although absent in body (the entire section, enclosed by formulaic statements in 2:17 and 3:10)
2. The yearning to see the readers (2:17; 3:6, 10)
3. The reference to an emissary through whom contact is established or maintained (3:1–5)
4. An expression of joy upon receiving a letter from one's readers or hearing about them (3:9)
5. Prayer to see one's readers (3:10)
6. A desire to see one's readers' needs fulfilled (3:10).

Elsewhere he uses the clichés of there being no need to write (4:9) and not wishing his readers to be ignorant (4:13).

The letter contains the constituent parts of Greco-Roman letters, but Paul modifies the conventions to conform his letter to the setting in which the letter would be read and the function he wished it to perform. Thus, in the prescript (1:1), the form of the ordinary letter is modified by the addition of "grace and peace." This makes it different from both the Greco-Roman and Jewish letters, but appropriate to the setting in which it would be read, the church gathered for worship.

The freedom with which Paul used epistolary conventions is particularly evident in his use of the thanksgiving period and the conclusion of the letter. The thanksgiving period is frequently found in pagan letters and became a fixed part in Paul's letters, sharing many formal features with the pagan thanksgivings. Its form in 1 Thessalonians is unique, however, in that it is extraordinarily long and that expressions of thanksgiving appear three times in this extended period (1:2; 2:13; 3:9), the first two being very similar in form. The thanksgiving performs its usual epistolary functions of introducing the major themes of the letter, setting its tone and reaffirming the bond between the writer and the recipients of the letter. In 1 Thessalonians, its particular function is paraenetic in that, by reminding the Thessalonians of what bound them together, he lays the foundation for the second part of the letter.

Paul's thanksgiving period is also different from the pagan ones in that it contains no health wish or supplication for the readers' well-being. Rather, the content of the thanksgiving is a prayer or prayer report (1:2–3; 2:13; 3:10; cf. 3:11–12), which, with 1:1, gives a liturgical cast to the letter. Paul's intention, that the letter be read to the church, is reflected stylistically in the alliterative *p* in 1:2 (see also 5:16–22).¨ Elements in the conclusion to the letter similarly exhibit Paul's creative adaptation of epistolary conventions. The Greco-Roman health wish appears, modified, in a prayer in 5:23, and the conventional greeting is adapted to the Christian communal context by the addition of "with a holy kiss" (5:26). Paul's modification of these conventions anticipates the reading of the letter in the Thessalonian assemblies (see 5:27) and are put to a pastoral purpose. So the prayer in 5:23–24 summarizes the main themes of the letter, thus reviewing the content of the letter. The prayer is given extra prominence by being separated from the greeting (5:26), with which it was usually combined in contemporary letter writing.

## D. OTHER FEATURES

Paul wrote 1 Thessalonians in a lively style. He did so, among other ways, by playing with prepositions (1:5), using asyndeta (2:11; 5:14–22), and by varying the word order, for example, by placing imperatives at the beginning of a series of sentences (5:14–15) and then at the end (5:16–22). Particularly striking is the emphatic style with which he wrote and the different ways in which he achieved emphasis.

Characteristic of the letter is its heavy use of personal and relative pronouns, beginning with 1:2 (see page 86) and extending throughout the letter, but occurring predominantly in the first half. The personal pronouns have the effect of making the letter more personal (e.g., 3:11), and with them Paul stresses his relationship with his readers, piling the pronouns on top of each other (e.g., ten in 1:2–5; eight in 3:6; seventeen in 3:6–10), as well as the relationships among members of the church (e.g., 5:12–13). In addition, they appear in positions of emphasis in sentences or clauses, for example, one pronoun stands before a string of nouns it modifies (1:3; cf. 2:19), and personal and relative pronouns otherwise appear at the beginning (1:6; 2:1, 10, 13; 2:17; 3:12; 4:16; 5:2, 4). Conversely, they appear at the end, the other position of emphasis, sometimes combined with each other (3:6; cf. 1:5–6).

Paul further creates emphasis through repetition: of an article (1:8, 10), of *ou* (["not"], 2:3–7; 2:17 [used with a participle instead of the more usual *mē*], of a phrase or word (e.g., 2:1, 2; 3:2, 5 ), and of *pās* (["every," "all"], 1:7, 8; 3:9; 4:10; 5:21–22). He also uses emphatic formulations (5:24, 27), elaborates a claim (2:6), makes comparisons (2:8; 5:2), mentions himself by name (2:18), uses rhetorical questions (2:19; 3:9), and stresses what he says through the emphatic use of *kai* (["and," "indeed"], 2:19; 4:14), *gar* (["Yes"], 2:20), *kai gar* (["indeed"], 4:10), and *loipon oun* (["Well, then"], 4:1).

Antithesis, heavily used in various ways in paraenesis (see COMMENT on 2:1–12), is the most characteristic manner in which Paul expresses emphasis, and he does so in different ways. The subject matter may express antithesis (2:1–2; cf. 5:5), as might contrasting sentences in a series (5:21–22). Normally,

however, the form of the antithesis is *ou* (or *mē* ["not"] or *oute* ["neither," "nor"])
... *alla* (["but"], 2:1–2, 3–4, 5–7, 13; 5:6, 9, 15), *ou monon* ... *alla* (["not only
... but"], 1:8), or *ou monon* ... *alla kai* (["not only... but also"], 1:5; 2:8), although a concessive participle may function as the negative part of the antithesis, followed by *alla* (["but"], 2:7). With one exception (4:4–5), the stress is on
the second member of the antithesis.

Paul writes with great intensity as he strengthens the bond between himself
and his readers. He does this with the images of a solicitous nurse (2:7–8), of a
kindly father (2:11), and of a bereft orphan (2:17), and by reminding them of his
preparedness to forgo his rights as an apostle (2:6) and his manual labor night
and day in order not to burden them (2:8–9). The section that describes the circumstances that led to his writing the letter (2:17–3:10) is full of pathos as he
heaps up affective language.

Finally, Paul's style in the letter is striking for the number of times that he uses
an *inclusio*, showing that the passion with which he writes did not contribute to
a lack of structure in his argument or exhortation. The entire letter is enclosed
by references to grace and peace (1:1; 5:23, 28), and the first part of the letter by
thanksgivings (1:2; 3:9). Smaller sections are similarly bracketed: 2:3, 12, on the
appeal (*parakalein*) he made in his ministry; 2:13, 16, the word under persecution; 2:17 and 3:10, his desire to see the Thessalonians; 3:2, 5, the purpose of
Timothy's mission to Thessalonica; 4:3, 7–8, holiness in sexual relations; 4:13;
5:8, the Christian hope, and within that section, 4:13, 18, grief and comfort. See
further, "Language and Style" in the Index of Major Subjects.

# VII. SUMMARY: PAUL'S FIRST LETTER TO THE THESSALONIANS

Paul's earliest extant letter was written from Corinth in A.D. 50 four or five
months after he had left the small church he had founded during a ministry of
three or four months. Frustrated in his attempts to return to Thessalonica, Paul
had sent Timothy from Athens, where Paul had gone from Macedonia, to establish his converts in their faith and ascertain that they still looked to him for guidance. Timothy, now accompanied by Silas, catches up with Paul, who in the
meantime had found his way to Corinth, and Timothy delivers a favorable report. To strengthen the young church, Paul writes this pastoral letter in which he
takes up issues that concern his recent converts.

# 1 THESSALONIANS:
# TRANSLATION,
# NOTES, AND
# COMMENTS

◆

# COMMUNICATING BY LETTER

◆

Attention is frequently drawn to Paul's modification of the epistolary frame, which was taught to children as early as the primary stage of their education. Paul was also thoroughly aware of other epistolary conventions as well as the theory that informed the practice of writing letters, which was taught in the upper levels of the educational curriculum (Malherbe 1988a). He modified those conventions to suit his own purposes and in the process created something new (Koester 1979). First Thessalonians should be read in light of what writers and recipients of letters understood to be involved in the writing of a letter.

A letter, it was said, should be "written in the same manner as a dialogue, a letter being regarded . . . as one of two sides of a dialogue" (Demetrius, *On Style* 223), since it is a substitute for an actual dialogue (Cicero, *To His Friends* 12.30.1). In such a "dialogue," the letter writer was to aim at speaking in exactly the same way he would have spoken had he been present, a desire Seneca expresses to his friend Lucilius: "I prefer that my letters should be just what my conversation would be if you and I were sitting in one another's company or taking walks together" (*Epistle* 75.1; cf. Ps.-Libanius, *Epistolary Styles* 2). A letter was therefore viewed as a sort of speech in written form (Cicero, *To Atticus* 8.14.1; 9.10.1), and it was expected that someone should so write that his letters would reveal his real self (Seneca, *Epistle* 40.1; see Thraede 1970: 7–8, 159–60). Consistency of character was thus a major issue when one wrote a letter, and letters played, where possible, on the past friendly association of writer and reader, and represented themselves as a continuation of that association (Ps.-Demetrius, *Epistolary Types* 1).

Paul seldom remained with a newly founded church for any length of time, and his anxiety for his churches was a heavy burden (2 Cor 11:28), frequently reflected in his laments about being separated from them (e.g., 1 Cor 5:3; Phil 2:12; cf. Col 2:5). In addition to coworkers who shuttled between himself and the churches (see 1 Cor 4:17; Phil 2:25–30), he made use of letters to maintain contact, although he would have preferred to visit them in person (e.g., 1 Cor 16:5–7; 2 Cor 1:15–16; Phil. 2:23). When there was tension between Paul and members of the churches to which he wrote, special attention was focused on the letters as adequate or true surrogates for his presence. This was so in his relationship with the Corinthians, some of whom detected sharp differences between Paul's demeanor in person and his demanding, harsh letters (2 Cor 10:10), which in their minds raised questions about his straightforwardness and integrity (2 Cor 1:15–2:4; 10:1–2; see Malherbe 1991: 413–17).

First Thessalonians is markedly different. It provides no explicit evidence that Paul was at odds with his readers, nor does the style of the letter suggest that there was any tension between Paul and them or that some people in Thessalonica were questioning his authority (thus Schmithals 1972: 135). The epistolary clichés of separation and yearning to see one's readers in order to render them some benefit are present in the section of the letter that describes the circumstances under which the letter was written (2:17–3:10), but there is no indication that Paul writes in this way to counter opposition of one sort or another. On the contrary, this section is striking for the pathos that suffuses it (see COMMENT) and is written out of Paul's joy that his yearning to reestablish communication with them had been satisfied by Timothy's successful mission to them and return to Paul. The section comes at the end of the first part of the letter in which Paul reprises his contacts with the Thessalonians from their conversion to the time of writing and in which he prods them to remember how close he and they were to each other. In this respect, the letter approximates in style a type of letter known as the "friendly letter." Even people in authority sometimes adopted this style in writing to their inferiors, not because they were in fact friends, but because they thought that nobody would refuse them anything when they wrote in a friendly manner but would rather submit to their wishes (Ps.-Demetrius, Epistolary Types 1).

Paul and his readers lived in a society in which the spoken word predominated (Achtemeier, 3–17), and his letters should be read in that light. Paul dictated his letters (cf. Rom 16:22; see Richards), and he expected them to be read aloud when the congregation met (cf. 1 Thess 5:27). This might suggest that Paul's letters could appropriately be examined according to the canons of ancient rhetorical handbooks (Betz 1984: 126–62), and 1 Thessalonians has been so viewed (Jewett 1986: 71–78; Johanson; Hughes 1990; Wuellner). Ancient epistolary theory, however, was never an integral part of the rhetorical systems (Malherbe 1988a: 1–11), and while Paul did use rhetorical elements in his letters, they are generally not those of the handbooks, nor did he construct his letters in the way an orator like Cicero did his speeches (Schnider and Stenger, 26–27).

It will emerge in this commentary that Paul made extensive use of the conventions of discourse used by philosophers who aimed at the moral and intellectual reformation of their listeners. Such philosophers, engaged in moral instruction, were acutely aware that their speech differed from that of the orators of the day (see Lucian, The Double Indictment 28), and when they did not reject out of hand such styles as epideictic, which orators used at festivals and funerals, they insisted that their own style be deemed appropriate (see Epictetus, Discourse 3.23.23–38). Paul's rhetoric shares elements with this popular philosophical speech, but also differs from it. If his speech is to be classified rhetorically, it is a "church rhetoric" (Olbricht). The liturgical elements contribute to the special nature of this rhetoric, as does the way Paul modifies other conventions and traditions he derives from his environment. What is of particular importance in attempting to understand how Paul thought the letter would function is to visualize the letter, in which Paul fills up what is lacking in their faith (3:10), being read to the Thessalonians gathered in someone's (Jason's?) home.

# I. ADDRESS, 1:1

◆

## TRANSLATION

1   ¹Paul, Silvanus, and Timothy to the church of the Thessalonians in God the
Father and the Lord Jesus Christ: grace to you and peace.

## NOTES

Paul uses Greek epistolary conventions, but modifies them. Basic to the standard
epistolary prescript, which also served as an address, were three parts, each of
which could be expanded (Exler, 24–60; Roller, 57–62; White 1984: 1733–34):
the name of the author, the addressees, and a salutation ("greetings"; *chairein*;
cf. Acts 23:26). This form of the address appears in Christian letters in the NT
only in Acts 15:29 and Jas 1:1. Paul already modifies the basic form in this, the
briefest address in all his letters, and would do so more extensively in his later letters.

   1:1. *Paul*. Originally known as Saul (Heb. *šā'ûl*), on his first organized mission
tour into Gentile territory he began to be called by the Latin name Paullus (Acts
13:9; cf. 13:7, the Roman governor was coincidentally named Sergius Paullus).
This was one of the three names that he would have had as a Roman citizen
(Harrer). First Thessalonians 1:1 and 2 Thess 1:1 are unique among Paul's epistolary addresses in not describing him as a servant of Christ (Phil 1:1), prisoner
of Christ (Phlm 1), or, most commonly, apostle (Rom 1:1; 1 Cor 1:1; 2 Cor 1:2;
Gal 1:1). There was evidently no need to assert his apostleship; on the contrary,
in 2:7 he mentions it only to make the point that he was ready to forgo his apostolic rights.

   *Silvanus*. With the exception of Romans, in all of his letters Paul names one
(1 Cor 1:1; 2 Cor 1:1; Phil 1:1; Phlm 1; cf. Col 1:1) or several (1 Thess 1:1;
2 Thess 1:1) persons as cosenders (cf. Gal 1:2 refers to unnamed persons; see
pages 86–90). For the sake of smoother English, the *kai* before Silvanus is not
translated. Silvanus and Timothy are also mentioned as cosenders of a letter in
2 Thess 1:1. Silvanus is the Latinized form of "Silas," which in turn was the Ar-
amaic form (*ša'îlâ*) of the Hebrew name "Saul" (Ollrog, 17–20). He is to be
identified with the Silas of Acts, who with Judas Barsabbas was sent by the
church in Jerusalem to Antioch (Acts 15:22, 32). According to Acts he was a
leader in the Jerusalem church and a prophet, and after returning to Jerusalem
(15:33), was selected by Paul to accompany him on the mission tour through
Asia Minor to Macedonia (15:40–16:40). Although Timothy is said to have
joined the company in southern Galatia (Acts 16:1–3), it is Silas who shared the
leadership with Paul in Philippi (Acts 16:19, 25, 29) and Thessalonica (Acts

17:4). Silas's movements after Beroea (Acts 17:14–15) are unknown until he and Timothy rejoined Paul in Corinth (Acts 18:5; see pages 67–71).

Silvanus is mentioned by Paul only in 1 Thess 1:1 and 2 Thess 1:1, which were written from Corinth, and for the last time in 2 Cor 1:19, which refers to his and Timothy's participation with Paul in the evangelization of Corinth. That Acts stresses his prominence and Paul always mentions him before Timothy testify to the high estimation in which he was held by both Luke and Paul. He has also been identified with the Silvanus mentioned in 1 Pet 5:12, who is there described in connection with the writing of that letter (Selwyn, 9–17). This identification is possible but not certain; Silvanus was a common name. Acts 15:23 has been taken to mean that Silas participated in the actual writing of the letter from Jerusalem to Antioch, but it cannot be demonstrated that he had an unusual part in writing either that letter or the letters to Thessalonica (see page 87). Paul's reference to "apostles" in 1 Thess 2:7 does not include Silvanus as an apostle of equal standing with himself (von Dobschütz 1909: 57–58).

*Timothy.* According to Acts 16:1–3, Timothy's mother was a Jew and his father a Greek, and he was already a Christian when Paul took him along on his mission. According to 2 Timothy, he had been brought up from infancy on the Scriptures (3:15) and shared the faith of his grandmother Lois and his mother, Eunice (1:5). This information cannot easily be reconciled with Paul's reference to Timothy as his "beloved and faithful child in the Lord" (1 Cor 4:17), which in the context (cf. v 15) implies that Paul had converted him. Of a different order is the commendation of Timothy in Phil 2:22, that he served with Paul in the gospel, metaphorically, "as a son with a father." Equally surprising, against the background of the notices in 2 Timothy is the statement in Acts 16:3 that Paul circumcised Timothy before including him in his party. What is certain is that Timothy joined Paul on this missionary tour and remained his closest associate, evidently without returning to his home church in Lystra, where Paul had first met him. With the exception of Silvanus and Sosthenes (1 Cor 1:1), Timothy is the only coworker of Paul who is mentioned as cosender of Paul's letters (with Silvanus in 1 Thess 1:1; 2 Thess 1:1; alone in 2 Cor 1:1; Phil 1:1; Phlm 1; cf. Col 1:1). Paul does not further describe or identify himself or Silvanus in the letter, nor does he add anything to Timothy's name. Timothy's recent mission and return would have made it superfluous (but see 1 Thess 3:2).

*to the church of the Thessalonians.* Paul usually addresses his letters by referring to the churches as situated in particular places, e.g., "to the church of God which is at Corinth" (1 Cor 1:2; cf. 2 Cor 1:1; Gal 1:2), "to Philemon . . . and the church in your house" (Phlm 1–2). Only here and in 2 Thess 1:1 does he describe the church in terms of the people of a certain locality who composed it (cf. Col 4:16), but his usual style of reference is present in 1 Thess 2:14, the only other place in the letter where he uses the word "church." The word translated "church" (*ekklēsia*) is used in the LXX for the community or people of God (Deut 23:2–3; 1 Chr 28:8; Neh 13:1), but in the world of Paul's Gentile converts, it described a civic assembly (cf. Acts 19:32, 39). Given Paul's Jewish heritage and the fact that he speaks of the "church(es) of God" in this letter (2:14) and elsewhere (e.g., 1 Cor 1:2; 10:32; 11:16; Gal 1:13), it is natural to suppose that Paul had this biblical background in mind when he addressed the Thessalonians and that he thought of them as the new people of God (Deidun, 10–11). It is not so clear, however, that Paul could have expected his recent Gentile converts to understand the term in this theological sense. We are therefore left to determine from the letter itself what Paul sought to convey.

*in God the Father and the Lord Jesus Christ.* The definite article before "Father" and "Lord," necessary in English, is not in the Greek, because *theos* and *kyrios* are almost proper names (BDF §254); furthermore, *theos* is preceded by a preposition (*en*), which frequently obviates the use of an article, and is followed by *patri*, which makes a further specification about *theos*. The *en* also governs *kyrios*. With this phrase Paul specifies that the *ekklēsia* of the Thessalonians is of a distinct character, which he defines in Christian and not OT terms (Dahl 1941: 210–11). The exact phrase is found only here and in 2 Thess 1:1, where, however, "our" is added to "Father." The *ekklēsia* has a special relationship with God and Christ. "In God" (*en theō*) is unusual for Paul and may be analogous to "in Christ" (see 4:16; cf. 2:14; 5:18) and "in the Spirit" (1:5; cf. Rom 8:9; Holtz 1986: 39), but "in God" is not normal Pauline usage. Paul does speak of boasting "in God" in Rom 2:17; 5:11, but that is not the same as being or existing in God. Acts 17:28 does have Paul speaking in Stoic terms of being in God, but those are Luke's words, not Paul's, and they describe the relationship of all humanity, not only the church, to God. In Eph 3:9, *en tō theō tō ta panta ktisanti* ("by God who created all things"; cf. Col 3:5), *en* is instrumental, and it makes sense to understand it similarly here, i.e., "the assembly of the Thessalonians brought into being by God the Father and the Lord Jesus Christ" (cf. 2:2 for another instrumental use of *en* with God; von Dobschütz 1909: 59; Best 1972: 62).

*God the Father.* God is described as Father in the salutations of all the letters bearing Paul's name. With the exception of 1 Thessalonians, all the letters specify that grace and peace come "from God our Father and the Lord Jesus Christ" (Rom 1:7; 1 Cor 1:3; 2 Cor 1:2; Eph 1:2; Phil 1:2; Col 1:2; Phlm 3), "from God the Father and the Lord Jesus Christ" (Gal 1:13; 2 Thess 2:2), "from God the Father and Christ Jesus our Lord" (1 Tim 1:2; 2 Tim 1:2), and "from God the Father and Christ Jesus our Savior" (Titus 1:4). First Thessalonians is thus unique in the Pauline corpus in not specifying God and Christ as the sources of grace and peace (but see Gal 1:1, 4); rather, the formula qualifies the nature of the church. Furthermore, the pronoun "our" is not used in 1:1. Where it does appear in 2 Thess 1:1, the relational aspect is clearly in view; its absence here draws attention, not to "our" relationship with God, but to the formulation "God the Father."

What Paul would have expected his readers to understand from this epithet appears from the creedal formulation in 1 Cor 8:6, that also has Gentile readers in view: "Yet for us there is one God, the Father, from whom are all things and from whom we exist, and one Lord, Jesus Christ, through whom are all things and through whom we exist," thus, God as Creator (cf. *Mart Pol* 19:2, *patēr pantokratōr* ["Father Almighty"]; Bultmann, 69–70). The description of the Creator as father is already found in Plato (*Timaeus* 28C; 37C), and via Stoicism

(Hommel) becomes Philo's favorite term for the Creator (e.g., *On the Cherubim* 44; *On the Creation of the World* 45, 46; *On the Migration of Abraham* 28, 193; *On the Special Laws* 1.41; 2.225). Understood thus, Paul addresses a church that owes its existence to the Creator of the universe.

*and the Lord Jesus Christ.* The church is further defined as being "in" Christ, which is also to be understood instrumentally: God the Creator brought the church into existence through the agency of the Lord Jesus Christ. That took place through the preaching of Christ. The Creator revealed the Lord Jesus Christ, his very own image, to Paul, who in consequence preached Jesus Christ as Lord (2 Cor 4:4–6; cf. Col 1:15; cf. Wis 7:22–28). Paul associates Jesus' lordship, which is confessed by the person who accepts his preaching, with Jesus' resurrection (Rom 10:9, 17), which also has a cosmic dimension (Phil 2:9–11; cf. Acts 2:36).

*grace to you and peace.* This salutation differs from those in Paul's other letters, which specify God as the source of grace (*charis*) and peace (*eirēnē*). It also differs markedly from the contemporary conventions of letter writing in ways that would have been immediately obvious to pagan readers. Pagan salutations were expressed in verbs, most frequently in the infinitive (e.g., *chairein*, "hail"; *eu prattein*, "do well"; *hygiainein*, "do well"; *eupsychein*, "be comforted"; Exler, 23–26), while Paul uses nouns quite unrelated in meaning to the pagan salutations. Early Christians recognized those differences and attributed them to the Jewish origins of Paul's greetings (e.g., Tertullian, *Against Marcion* 5.5; Lieu). Elements of the Pauline salutation do appear in Jewish letters, e.g., *chairein . . . eirēnē agathē*, "greetings and true peace" (2 Macc 1:1); "mercy and peace" (2 *Bar* 78:2); *charis kai eleos*, "grace and mercy" (Wis 3:9; 4:15), but the precise combination of "grace" and "peace" does not. It is not impossible but quite unlikely that to the Jewish "peace" (*shālôm*) Paul added *charis* by way of alluding to the Greek *chairein* (Weiss 1910: 4–5; Koskenniemi, 162; Taatz).

The argument has further been made that "grace and peace" was primarily liturgical and only secondarily epistolary in Jewish usage, and that Paul appropriated the blessing because he anticipated that his letters would be read to congregations gathered for worship (Lohmeyer; contra: Friedrich 1956). The precise Pauline formulation does not occur in Jewish liturgical texts, however, and it is likely that Paul combined "grace" with the Jewish "peace" to create a new form of epistolary address appropriate to his purpose and the setting in which he thought the letter would be read (see Kramer, 152–53, on Paul as the one who made the combination, but thinks that elements of the address come from the language of worship). The setting he had in mind was the congregation at worship, and more important than the possible derivation of the salutation is that one function it would perform was liturgical (Collins 1984: 139–40). This appears from the use again of "peace" and "grace" in benedictions at the end of the letter (5:23, 28) (Berger; see Schnider and Stenger). See further on 5:3, 24. For peace and grace as related to God and Christ, see COMMENT on 2 Thess 1:2.

## COMMENT

That Paul does not in the salutation call himself an apostle as he usually does in his letters is in keeping with the "friendly" nature of the letter. The setting in which the letter would be read is envisioned as cordial. The epistolary function of chaps. 1–3 is to lay the foundation on which the particular advice in chaps. 4 and 5 will be based, and that foundation is the relationship of which he reminds his readers. They knew what kind of person he had proved to be and had become his imitators (1:5–6); he had forgone his apostolic right to be harshly demanding, but on the contrary had been gentle like a nurse, giving of himself for their sakes (2:6–8); he had treated them like a father does his children (2:11) and, by being separated from them, experienced the anguish of an orphan (2:17). These images represent no consistent familial structure but are part of the pathos of the letter, rather than an appeal to authority, that contributes to the moral suasion with which Paul addresses his recent converts. That Paul does not identify himself as an apostle, which could, but need not necessarily have connoted his authoritative standing, is entirely in keeping with the nature of this letter.

It has been thought, however, that Paul's authority was inherent in the very nature of his letters, which differed from other ancient letters in that they were much longer (Roller, 38), had modified opening and closing formulae, and were unique as to their substance. It has also been suggested that Paul's letters have clear similarities to official Jewish letters (e.g., 2 Macc 1:1–9; 1:10–2:18), including the authority with which those letters were written (Taatz). Along the same line, it has been argued that characteristics of Paul's letters were derived from authoritative synagogal letters whose function was to transmit religious and theological instruction (Vouga). More particularly, authority has also been thought to be inherent in Paul's letters because they mediated revelation (Berger).

Whatever Paul's indebtedness to such possible precursors may have been, his letters are *sui generis* as to their form and content. Furthermore, no other known letters had ever been written by anyone like Paul. He had founded a community at the behest of God (2:2) and done so by means of proclaiming the divine message (2:4) in the preaching of which God was active (2:13). As its founder the community owed allegiance to him as he continued to nurture it. The letters were an integral part of the relationship between Paul and his churches, and it is impossible to separate them, as to their form and function, from that relationship. The arguments made for the other letters as authoritative do not apply to 1 Thessalonians because this letter differs from them precisely at those points where authority is thought to be located, e.g., in specifying God the Father as the source of the grace and peace that the apostle bestows. This letter is also unique in the high degree of concentration of those paraenetic features that stress the traditional, well-known quality of what is said rather than being revelatory (see pages 81–86).

To introduce the question of apostolic authority in the address is complicated by the inclusion of Silvanus and Timothy. Schmithals has recognized this and claimed, unconvincingly, that since Silvanus was an apostle (Schmithals

1969: 65–67), had Paul called himself an apostle, he would have extended the title to Silvanus and excluded Timothy, which would have been unacceptable to Paul (Schmithals 1972: 135–36). Why Silvanus is mentioned before Timothy, a much better known and ostensibly more consistently active participant in Paul's mission, has exercised the imagination of commentators from at least as early as John Chrysostom, who suggested that Timothy, with becoming youthful modesty, had asked Paul to mention him last (*Homilies on 1 Thessalonians* 1 [PG 62:393]). A more plausible reason is that Silvanus, a respected leader in the Jerusalem church (Acts 15:22), constituted with Paul a "yoke," or pair, of teachers required by Jewish custom (Jeremias). As Barnabas and Paul had the young John Mark to assist them on the first missionary journey (Acts 13:2, 6), so Paul and Silvanus took Timothy along on the second journey (Acts 16:1–3). Timothy's emergence as Paul's envoy to the Thessalonians (3:1–10) did not diminish Silvanus in Paul's eyes to the point that he would mention him after the youngster.

To focus on such matters, however, is to miss the point. Paul could have said more about his companions, for example, that they were active with him at the time, busy evangelizing Corinth, from where he was writing (2 Cor 1:19), or that they had brought financial aid from Macedonia (including Thessalonica?), which made it possible for him to devote himself completely to preaching (2 Cor 11:7–11; cf. Acts 18:5). He could also have referred to the person who would carry this letter to them or would accompany the letter, as he does elsewhere (Rom 16:1; 1 Cor 4:17; 16:10; 2 Cor 8:16–17; cf. Eph 6:21; Col 4:7). The focus in the letter, however, is on Paul's relationship with the Thessalonians. Timothy is only mentioned insofar as he plays a role in that relationship, just before and at the time of Paul's writing (3:1–10). One may asssume that Silvanus played no such role. The mention of Timothy in the greeting would evoke warm memories of Timothy's recent visit, what it accomplished, and the letter he likely brought from the Thessalonians to Paul.

Even such considerations obscure the fact that, whereas the senders receive no description in the greeting, the recipients are grammatically qualified, in a way that relates them to God and Christ. In this way the assembly (*ekklēsia*) of the Thessalonians to whom Paul writes is distinguished from other assemblies that existed in Thessalonica (John Chrysostom, *Homilies on 1 Thessalonians* 1 [PG 62:393]). *Ekklēsia*, which would not normally have had any sacral association in the minds of recent converts from paganism, is therefore qualified (Bruce 1982: 7; Holtz 1986: 38). Although socially humble and with little public influence, the Thessalonians Paul writes to are an assembly called into being by the Creator and Jesus Christ, which lends dignity to their existence (Marxsen 1979: 32). That this is only one of two times that Paul uses *ekklēsia* in 1 Thessalonians is no indication that he fails to develop an ecclesiology in the letter. The description of God the Father as progenitor of the church introduces the notion of the church as God's family, which is developed throughout the letter by means of a strong concentration of kinship language (Malherbe 1995a). On God's children, gathered to hear his words, Paul bestows the benediction, "grace to you and peace."

It is not clear for what group of people precisely the letter was intended. It is natural to think that the "church of the Thessalonians" constituted one group and "all the brethren" to whom the letter was also to be read (see COMMENT 5:26–27) another. The former may have been the group that had met in Jason's house (Acts 17:5–17); in any case, the constant reminders in the letter of the close relationship between Paul and his readers make it certain that in this letter Paul has in mind primarily the Gentile believers he had converted from paganism. In the few months since then, the Thessalonians themselves had been active in evangelization (vv 7–8), and "all the brethren" may refer to converts they had made, particularly in the environs of Thessalonica. If 2 Thessalonians was also written to the same church, but as its primary audience had a group of other brethren in mind, Paul would have founded that group as well (see pages 350–56). Paul therefore wants the letter to be circulated, as he also did some of his other letters (see 1 Cor 1:2; 2 Cor 1:1; cf. Col 4:16).

The letter to the Thessalonians, however, differs from those to the Corinthians in not mentioning in the address churches in Macedonia as he does ones in Achaia in writing to the Corinthians. A reason for the difference may be that the evangelization of Achaia took place during the eighteen months that Paul sojourned in Corinth (Acts 18:1–17) and presumably took place under his direction, whereas the word sounded forth to the Macedonians after Paul had left (1 Thess 1:8). Whether Paul had in mind that the actual letter he sent or a copy of it would be circulated we do not know, although the latter is more likely (see NOTE and COMMENT on 5:26–27 and pages 353–56). In any event, it appears that Paul felt it natural to instruct Christians whom he himself had not converted (see Rom 1:8–15; 15:18–24; cf. Col 1:3–8; 2:1–5). The primary audience of 1 Thessalonians, however, were those whom he had converted and from whom he was being forcibly separated.

# II. AUTOBIOGRAPHY, 1:2–3:13

## A. THANKSGIVING, 1:2–3:10

◆

As Paul modified the standard Greek epistolary address, so did he the elements following the address. Typically, a wish for the recipient's health followed the address or was combined with it. Then sometimes the author gave thanks to the gods for delivering himself from harm, which was in turn sometimes followed by a supplication to the gods on behalf of the recipients (White 1984: 1733–35; 1986: 200–202), and then came the body of the letter. In time, these elements assumed quite stereotyped forms, but not in a wooden way. Writers in fact exercised considerable freedom in expressing themselves without completely dispensing with convention.

Paul never petitions God for the physical health of his readers nor does he offer a supplication for their general well-being. Characteristic of his letters is his development of a thanksgiving period in which he thanks God, not for his own deliverance, but for the spiritual condition of his readers. Studies of Paul's thanksgivings have assumed that a fairly standard epistolary thanksgiving was in widespread use in the Hellenistic world and have taken great pains to identify its formal elements in the belief that Paul was indebted to this presumed practice (Schubert, who until recently was followed by most writers). It has become clear, however, that the thanksgiving period was not as firmly established an element in other letters as it is in Paul (Arzt; but see Reed) and that, while Paul does use rather fixed expressions in his thanksgiving periods, he is no slave to a schematic pattern (Lambrecht).

Much emphasis has also been laid on the epistolary functions of thanksgivings, the major ones being to introduce the basic themes of the letter, to set the letter's tone, and to establish or confirm a personal relationship between writer and reader. But it has recently been shown that the thanksgivings also have liturgical, pastoral, and hortatory functions, which represent their quintessential Pauline character (O'Brien 1977; Wiles).

First Thessalonians differs from all other letters, including Paul's own letters, in the degree to which thanksgiving dominates the beginning of the letter (see page 80). In 1:2–5 and 2:13 Paul expresses his thanks in carefully crafted formulations and in 3:9 concludes his narrative account of his relationship with his readers with yet another thanksgiving. This forms an *inclusio* that reveals how Paul understood matters between himself and the Thessalonians: they were a cause for joy and thanksgiving. The first three chapters are, then, an autobiographical thanksgiving (Lyons, 177–221). What triggered this sustained outburst was Timothy's report that the Thessalonians continued to love and remember Paul and yearned to see him (3:6–8). Paul gives thanks to God for what had transpired between them and in the process strengthens the bond between them. His expressions of thanks should therefore be seen in light of the immediate circumstance in which he wrote rather than be reduced to permutations of conventional formulas.

The first three chapters of the letter are autobiographical in a special way. They remind the Thessalonians of how they had come to conversion in response to Paul's preaching (1:2–10), of Paul's ministry with them (2:1–12), of their conduct, and of their persecution in consequence of their receiving the gospel from Paul (2:13–16), and of Paul's constant efforts to maintain contact with them (2:17–3:10). The prayer that concludes this section of the letter (3:11–13) once more highlights the extraordinary nature of Paul's relationship with his readers. The entire relationship, from its very beginning (1:3–5) to the day when they will together stand before God (3:13), is the result of God's action. That is Paul's ground for thanksgiving, which he utters so passionately and insistently that no epistolary convention can adequately contain it. So he breaks the formula open, extends it, and bends it to his will.

Paul writes in a self-referential way for a particular reason. His self-description is philophronetic, aiming at securing the goodwill of his readers in the manner of ancient letters of friendship (Boers). But it does more than that. This letter is written in paraenetic style, of which philophronesis was itself a part, which Paul uses for a pastoral purpose (see pages 81–86). It is in the nature of paraenesis that the practical advice that is given be justified by the character of the person who gives the advice. Whether always stated explicitly or not, advice on particular matters assumes a paradigm that it emulates. That is so in 1 Thessalonians, and chaps. 1–3 serve a paraenetic function (see COMMENT on 2:1–12). Paul reminds the Thessalonians of his behavior in a way that forms the basis for the practical directions that he will give in chaps. 4 and 5. But in describing himself, he is extremely careful to present himself as God's spokesman. It is the memory of the Thessalonians' response to God's message in the person of Paul that evokes his exuberant thanksgiving.

# 1. THE CONVERSION OF THE THESSALONIANS, 1:2–10

## TRANSLATION

1 ²We give thanks to God always for you all when without ceasing we mention you in our prayers, ³calling to mind before God our Father the work of your faith, the labor of your love, and the endurance of your hope in our Lord Jesus Christ, ⁴for we know, brethren, that you, whom God loved, he has chosen, ⁵for our gospel came to you not in word only, but also with power and the Holy Spirit and with a full conviction, fully in conformity with the kind of persons you know we proved to be among you for your sake; ⁶so you on your part became imitators of us and the Lord by receiving the word in deep distress and with joy inspired by the Holy Spirit, ⁷with the result that you became an example to all the believers in Macedonia and Achaia. ⁸For from you the word of the Lord has sounded forth not only in Macedonia and Achaia, but your faith in God has gone forth everywhere, so that we have no need to say anything; ⁹indeed, they themselves are reporting about us, namely, what kind of entrance we gained to you, and how you turned to God from idols to serve the living and true God, ¹⁰and to wait for his son from heaven, whom he raised from the dead, Jesus who delivers us from the wrath to come.

## NOTES

1:2. *We give thanks to God always for you all.* The first thanksgiving period extends from v 2 to v 10 and is one sentence in Greek. Paul gives thanks for the way in which the Thessalonians conduct themselves in consequence of having accepted his message (vv 2–5), compliments them for their preaching of the gospel (vv 6–8), and summarizes what they had responded to in their conversion (vv 9–10). The principal verb of this long, complicated sentence is *eucharis-*

*toumen* ("We give thanks"). On it depend three participles (*mneian poioumenoi, mnēmoneuontes,* and *eidotes*), which give further specification to the thanksgiving without being strictly parallel (Rigaux 1956: 369–70) and make vv 2–5 a subunit of vv 2–10. It is unusual for Paul to retain the plural, as he does here, after including others in the prescript (see 1 Cor 1:1, 4; Phil 1:1, 3). This is to be understood as an epistolary plural, which he also uses in 3:2 (*epempsamen,* interchangeable with *epempsa* in 3:5; for more extensive discussion of the issue, see pages 86–89).

For the second time in the letter Paul mentions God; he will do so eighteen more times by 2:15, wanting to impress on his readers that what had transpired was due to God's initiative. Here a thanksgiving to God introduces a recitation of God's place and role in their experience. Paul reports that he gives thanks to God always (*pantote*), a standard expression in his thanksgiving periods (1 Cor 1:4; Phil 1:4; 2 Thess 1:3; Phlm 4; cf. Col 1:3). It is thus formulaic, but it also marks the beginning of Paul's sustained effort in chaps. 1–3 to convey to his readers the importance of consistency and continuity, exhibited by *pantote* (2:16; 3:6; 4:17; 5:15–16), *adialeiptōs* (1:3; 2:13; 5:17), and *en panti* (5:18). Paul subtly paints a picture of himself as a model who is constantly rejoicing, praying, and giving thanks (Lyons, 205).

The phrase "for you all" could be construed either with what precedes or what follows (Frame, 75), but its association with *eucharistein* in Rom 1:4 (cf. 1 Cor 1:4) argues for the former. Paul here begins an extensive use of personal pronouns, an expression of his interest in fostering the personal relationship between himself and the Thessalonians. The preposition *hyper* might have been expected instead of *peri* here, but distinctions between the two prepositions were disappearing (BDF §§229.1, 231). The word *peri* often appears in prayers (5:25; cf. John 16:26; 17:9, 20; 3 John 2), including thanksgiving periods (Rom 1:8; 1 Cor 1:4; 2 Thess 1:3).

That Paul offers thanks for all need not imply that there were divisions in the church that he sought to heal by expressing his care for *all* of them. He uses "all" elsewhere in thanksgiving periods (Rom 1:8; Phil 1:3–4); moreover, if *peri pantōn hymōn* in thanksgivings revealed disunity, one would have expected it in the thanksgiving in 1 Cor 1:4 (cf. v 11), where it does not appear. It seems simply to be part of the liturgical style of this section of the letter, which is further enhanced by alliteration (*pantote peri pantōn . . . poioumenoi . . . proseuchōn . . . adialeiptōs*). Greek and Latin writers were fond of alliteration (*Rhetorica ad Herennium* 4.12.18, cautions against it), frequently playing on words beginning with labials, particularly *p* (e.g., Sophocles, *Ajax* 866, *ponos ponō ponon phere*; Herodotus 7.11, *poieein ē pathein prokeitai agōn*; Nepos 23.11.7, *pedestribus copiis pari prudentia pepulit adversarios*), including forms of *pās* (Democritus, *Fragment* 258 [Diels-Kranz], *para dikēn panta peri pantos*; Plato, *Menexenus* 247A, *dia pantos pasan pantos prothymias peirasthe echein*; 249C, *pāsan pantōn para panta ton chronon epimeleian poioumenē*; Lysias, *Funeral Oration* (2) 36, *pantachothen perieistekei plēthos polemiōn*). Paul shares this proclivity, using it at the beginning of his letters (1 Cor 1:4; 2 Cor 1:3–7; Phil 1:3–5; cf. Heb 1:1; Jas

1:2), thus aiming at a rhetorically impressive beginning in the oral reading of these letters (see also 5:16–22).

*when without ceasing we mention you in our prayers.* The first of the three dependent participles (*mneian poioumenoi*) is temporal: Paul is thankful whenever he mentions them, and he does that in his prayers. The participle does not have an object here (the Western and majority texts supply *hymōn*), but from the context (*panta hymōn*) and other thanksgiving periods (Rom 1:9; Phil 1:3; Phlm 4) it is clear that the readers are in view. The phrase *mneian poioumenoi* could also mean "remember" (BAGD, s.v. *mneia*), but it is part of an epistolary formula which reports that the writer constantly prays to the gods on behalf of his readers (Koskenniemi, 145–48; White 1986: 159–60, 200–202). Most commentators and printed editions of the Greek text take *adialeiptōs* to qualify what follows (*mnēmoneuontes*). In favor of taking it with "mention you in our prayers," however, are the presence of *adialeiptōs* and similar expressions (*ou dialeipō, dia pantos*) in the formula in papyrus letters (Koskenniemi, 145–48); Rom 1:9, where it does appear in this way; and the symmetry between *eucharistoumen . . . pantote* and *mnēmoneuontes . . . adialeiptōs.*

The non-Christian prayers most frequently had to do with the health of the correspondents, and reporting them functioned philophronetically, i.e., they assured the readers of the writer's friendly disposition towards them. Paul also uses the formula philophronetically, but modifies it dramatically. He does not mention physical health; rather, he develops the formula into a prayer report that focuses on his readers and introduces major themes that will be taken up in the body of the letter.

1:3. *calling to mind before God our Father.* The second dependent participle (*mnēmoneuontes*) is causal, providing the immediate grounds for Paul's thanksgiving, and states its content. The phrase *emprosthen tou theou* ("before God") in the Greek comes after "hope in our Lord Jesus Christ" and can be taken to refer to the eschatological nature of that hope (see Rom 8:24–26). In support of such an understanding is the use of *emprosthen tou theou* in an eschatological sense in 3:13 (cf. also 2:19, *emprosthen tou Kyriou hēmōn Iēsou*; see W. Weiss, 199–200, who stresses the forensic context). However, the use of the phrase in the third thanksgiving (3:9) for a petition to God made in the present suggests the option adopted here. It does make for a long clause but not a clumsy one, for understood thus the clause beginning with *mnēmoneuontes* and ending with *emprosthen tou theou* encapsulates the substance of what is remembered, not as a casual recollection, but as an activity before God. The position of the phrase at the end of the clause emphasizes this, in keeping with Paul's interest here to describe the Christian life in the three dimensions mentioned as in the presence of God. "God the Father" here is relational and describes God as he is addressed in prayer (Rom 8:15–16; Gal 4:6–7; cf. Matt 6:8–15). Stoics described God as a cosmic father (e.g., Diogenes Laertius, *The Lives of Eminent Philosophers* 7.147) and human beings as God's offspring (Seneca, *On Benefits* 3.28.1–2; *Epistle* 95.52; Epictetus, *Discourse* 1.13.3–5), but there were no Stoic communities of God's children called by their Father.

*the work of your faith, the labor of your love, and the endurance of your hope in our Lord Jesus Christ.* The entire verse after mnēmoneuontes consists of a series of genitives with ambiguous meanings (GNTG 3.218). The first genitive, hymōn, is possessive and qualifies ergou, kopou, and hypomonēs, which are genitives dependent on mnēmoneuontes. Pisteōs, agapēs, and elpidos are subjective, and tou Kyriou Iēsou Christou is objective, describing the object of hope. The one hymōn ("your") in Greek, linked to the three Christian qualities, is in an emphatic position (see also 2:19–20): it is something about the readers', not his own, circumstances that Paul calls to mind as cause for his thanksgiving.

Paul's recent converts are active in a threefold way, engaging in ergon and kopos and having hypomonē, all three members of this triad standing in the emphatic position relative to another triad, pistis, agapē, and elpis (see Marxsen 1979: 35). The stress in the prayer is, then, not in the first place on faith, love, and hope, but on the actions that issue from them (Wiles, 178). These three pairs of concepts range widely in meaning in pagan and biblical Greek as well as the NT itself. They are also central to Paul's thought, which makes it tempting, as the exegetical tradition shows, to generalize on the meaning of the language in 1:3 (see the interpretations of Wiles, 172–80; O'Brien 1977: 146–50). However, prudence dictates that the focus be on the context in which they are used. The context here (1:2–10) deals with the preaching and reception of the word, and the three terms stressing the effort of the Thessalonians describe the strenuousness with which they preached.

Ergon and kopos appear to be merely rhetorically distinct (see 5:12–13; 1 Cor 15:58), but hypomonē, while it also describes effort, nevertheless appears to be of a different order. In fact, however, all three terms have to do with the preaching of the word. Paul uses ergon with a wide range of meanings (BAGD, s.v. ergon), including (in the plural) the sense in which works of the Law are contrasted with faith (Gal 2:16; 3:2–5), a matter completely absent from 1 Thessalonians. This context suggests that ergon refers to preaching, as it does in Paul (1 Cor 3:13–15; Phil 1:22) and elsewhere (Acts 13:2; 14:26; 15:38; Söding 1992: 71–72, who widens the focus to capture other endeavors on behalf of the gospel and the church). Similarly, kopos and its verbal cognate, taken by Paul from the workshop, where it had the connotation of toilsome labor (cf. 1 Cor 4:12; 2 Cor 11:23; 1 Thess 2:9; 1 Tim 4:10; see Harnack 1928), describes his own missionary work (1 Cor 14:10; Gal 4:11; Phil 2:16; 1 Thess 3:5) and that of others (1 Cor 3:8; 16:16; 2 Cor 10:15).

The three terms thus describe the preaching of the gospel in an ascending order of intensity, culminating in hypomonē. Endurance (hypomonē) is frequently associated with eschatological trials (Mark 13:13; 2 Cor 1:6; 2 Tim 2:12), viewed from the perspective of hope (Rom 5:4; 8:24–25; 15:4; 1 Cor 13:7). Of these three terms, hypomonē especially has been taken here to describe the "endurance of our human condition as an expression of solid faith, hope and the love which has been given . . . by the Holy Spirit" (Garlington, 68, quoting Cambier, 191–92, with reference to Rom 2:7; 5:1–5). But hypomonē also describes the endurance in the midst of hardships with which Paul carried out his own ministry (2 Cor 6:4; 12:12; cf. Luke 21:19). Neither the word nor its cognates appear elsewhere in 1 Thessalonians, but the synonym *makrothymeō* is used in 5:14 in advice on how to act pastorally.

As important as the activity of the Thessalonians are its efficient causes: faith, love, and hope (contrast Rev 2:2). It is fruitless to speculate on Paul's possible source for this triad (see Söding 1992: 38–64, for a summary of possibilities); it does not appear anywhere before this occurrence, and it is reasonable to think that Paul was original enough to have formed it (see also W. Weiss, 204). The order varies in the places where the triad of qualities appears in the NT, the one of greatest importance in each context coming at the end, the position of emphasis: *pistis, agapē, elpis* in 1 Thess 1:3; 5:8; Col 1:4–5; *pistis, elpis, agapē* in Rom 5:1–5; 1 Cor 13:13; Heb 10:22–24; 1 Pet 1:21–22. The genitives *pisteōs, agapēs,* and *elpidos* are subjective: the Thessalonians' faith works, their love labors, and their hope endures (von Dobschütz 1909: 211–13).

Paul's preaching of the gospel sprang from his faith (2 Cor 4:13); so did that of the Thessalonians (cf. 1:8). From a different perspective, God's word was actively at work (*energeitai*) in the Thessalonian believers (2:13). Paul applauded preaching that was motivated by love (Phil 1:16), claimed to have demonstrated this to the Thessalonians when ministering to them (2:8), and advised them to love those who labored in the word (5:12–13).

In its more specialized meaning here, *hypomonē* is more than dogged determination in the face of hardships; it is given a different perspective by hope, the object of which is *tou Kyriou Iēsou Christou* ("the Lord Jesus Christ"), which stands in the position of greatest emphasis (von Dobschütz 1909: 211–13). Paul will elaborate on the content of hope later in the letter (4:13–5:8). Paul's thought about hope and ministry of the word is more fully expressed in his description of his own ministry in 2 Corinthians. The ministry of the Spirit is one that endures in glory (3:11), and that hope motivates Paul to speak with boldness (*parrēsia,* 3:12; cf. 7:4; Fredrickson; cf. 1 Thess 2:2). Despite the hardships that attended his ministry (4:7–12; 6:4–10, with *hypomonē* heading the list; Fitzgerald 1988: 166–201), hope sustains him (4:13–5:10, although he does not use *elpis*).

1:4. *for we know, brethren, that you, whom God loved, he has chosen.* The third participle (*eidotes*), grammatically dependent on *eucharistoumen,* is causal, providing the ultimate ground for Paul's thanksgiving (Eadie, 39; Frame, 77). More immediately, *eidotes* refers back to *mnēmoneuontes,* providing a reason for the Thessalonians' behavior that he mentions in his prayer, namely, that they have been called by God (Alford, 250; Wohlenberg, 24; von Dobschütz 1909: 24; Marshall 1983: 52). Having been called, they preached.

Paul addresses his readers as *adelphoi,* as he will thirteen more times in this short letter; in addition, he will use *adelphos* four times as a description of Christians. This frequency of usage shows that we have to do with more than the epistolary convention in so-called family letters of addressing as *adelphoi* persons not related by blood (on these letters, see Koskenniemi, 104–14; Stowers 1986: 71–76). The use of *adelphos* in 1 Thessalonians is much higher in number relative to Paul's other letters (e.g., ten times in Romans; twenty times in 1 Corinthians; three times in 2 Corinthians, all three of which are considerably longer than 1 Thessalonians) and is an important part of the fictive kinship that Paul develops in this letter and elsewhere (Schäfer).

Kinship language was used by other groups, for example, by mystery cults and philosophical schools, to whom a sense of community was important, but Paul's notion was derived from Judaism (Schelkle, 632–39; Kötting, 144–45; Meeks 1983a: 87). More specifically, what informed Paul's use here was the experience of the proselyte, estranged from previous relationships and seeking kinship of a different kind in the Jewish community (*Jos Asen* 12:11; 13:1; Philo, *On the Special Laws* 1.52; *On the Virtues* 103–4, 179; see Malherbe 1987: 43–46). This appears from Paul's modification of *adelphoi* as *ēgapēmenoi hypo tou theou* ("loved by God"). Proselytes were said to have been loved and called by God (*Gen Rab* 70.5; *Num Rab* 8.2; *Midr Tanh* 6; *Jos Asen* 8:9; Moore, 1.348–49; Pax 1971: 234–35). Paul applies this notion to Gentile converts to Christianity in Rom 9:24–25, changing Hosea 2:25 LXX, *eleēsō ten ouk eleēmenēn* ("I shall have mercy on her who has not received mercy") to *kalesō . . . tēn ouk ēgapēmenen ēgapēmenēn* ("I shall call her who was not beloved 'my beloved' ") (cf. *Ep Diogn* 4:4; Malherbe 1995a: 118). Paul normally uses *agapētos* ("beloved"; cf. 2:8); only here and in 2 Thess 2:13 (cf. Col 3:12) does he use the participle and does so to focus on God's election (see also 2:12; 4:7; 5:24; cf. Col 3:12; Jude 1) as an act of love (Rom 1:6–7; 11:28–29), the perfect tense expressing the enduring quality of that love.

*1:5. for our gospel came to you.* Paul now turns to his own preaching and its effects among the Thessalonians (vv 5–8). "For" (*hoti*) is epexegetical, describing how their election had taken place (so already Theodore of Mopsuestia [2.4]; and Lightfoot, Milligan, Rigaux, Best), rather than causal, providing a reason for making the assertion about his knowledge of their election (Ellicott, Alford, Frame, Wanamaker). Both are grammatically possible, but the former is the more likely because it correctly relates election to preaching, the subject that has occupied Paul in vv 2–4 and that he now further comments on in v 5 (see also 2 Thess 2:13–14). Furthermore, as Lightfoot points out, the phrase *eidenai ti hoti* in the NT is never causal but always epexegetical (e.g., in Rom 13:11; 1 Cor 16:15; 2 Cor 12:3–4; 1 Thess 2:1; cf. Acts 16:3). The causal reading agrees with a theological understanding that God's election (*eklogē, eklegesthai*) is supra- or prehistorical (appealing to Rom 9:11; 11:5, 7, 28; 1 Cor 1:27–28), which is to be distinguished from God's *klēsis* ("call"; e.g., von Dobschütz 1909: 69–70). The context here, however, provides no support for such a dogma.

Elsewhere in the letter Paul speaks of the gospel of God (2:2, 4, 9; cf. 8) or of Christ (3:2), but here of his own gospel (*to euangelion hēmōn*). *Euangelion* is a noun of action, and the construction *to euangelion hēmōn* is equivalent to *to euangelion to euangelisthen hyp' emou* ("the gospel that was preached by me"; Gal 1:11; cf. 2 Cor 4:3; 11:7). Paul draws attention to his part (*hēmōn*) in the proclamation of the gospel, thus accenting the personal aspect of preaching the gospel rather than its content, but then qualifies the nature of the event with an antithesis, *ouk . . . monon . . . alla kai* ("not only . . . but also"). Some manuscripts

(A C² K P) read *pros* for *eis* in the clause *ouk egenēthē eis hymās* ("did not come to you," read by א B C), but there is no real difference in meaning. Of greater significance is the repetitive use of forms of *ginesthai* in 1:5b, 6, 7; 2:1, 5, 7, 8, 10, 14, which suggests that *to euangelion hēmōn . . . egenēthē eis hymas* ("our gospel . . . came to you") is a topic sentence for the section 1:5b–2:14, in which Paul speaks of the Thessalonians' and his preaching (see Schubert, 19–20). The phrase *ginesthai eis* can simply mean "to arrive at" or "reach" (cf. Acts 21:17; 25:15; Gal 3:14), but this concentrated use of *ginesthai* where *erchesthai* or *einai* would have done equally well suggests a deliberate choice of the word to convey a sense of an eventful occurrence. This is borne out by the first of numerous antitheses in the letter.

*not in word only, but also with power and the Holy Spirit and with a full conviction.* Antithesis is a rhetorical device characteristic of Paul's style (Norden, 2.507–10; Weiss 1959: 2.411–16). Paul here begins using rhetorical and philosophical traditions, in the process modifying them to suit his immediate purpose. His modification of paraenetic conventions to make theological statements is particularly striking.

The connection between words and deeds had become commonplace in Paul's day (Festugière). The Sophists had been criticized for thinking that mere words would suffice in advising people (Plato, *Sophist* 234C; Xenophon, *On Hunting* 13.1, 6), and this criticism also came to be leveled at insincere philosophers (Lucian, *The Runaways* 15, 19). The commonplace became an important theme in popular moral philosophy, particularly among Stoics and Cynics (Helm, 40–42), who emphasized that a philosopher's words and deeds should conform, thus demonstrating his sincerity (Epictetus, *Discourse* 1.19.55–57; Seneca, *Epistle* 34.4; Lucian, *Demonax* 3; Julian, *Oration* 7.212D; cf. *1 Clem* 38:2; Ign *Eph* 15:1; Ign *Magn* 4:1). Anyone who expected his hearers to behave consistenly with what he said should himself do so (Seneca, *Epistle* 1.4). It was further claimed that it was much more useful to demonstrate briefly in action what was taught than to engage in extended verbal instruction (Dio Chrysostom, *Orations* 16.17, 21; 70.6; Seneca, *Epistles* 52.8–9; 75.45; Maximus of Tyre, *Oration* 36.5; Ps.-Crates, *Epistle* 21; Ps.-Diogenes, *Epistle* 15; Julian, *Orations* 6.189A; 7.124BC).

Consistency between speech and conduct is also required in the NT (Col 3:17; 1 John 3:18), and prophetic figures are described as mighty in word and deed (Luke 24:19; Acts 7:27). Paul rejected his Corinthian opponents' charge of vacillation by insisting that he was consistent in word and deed (2 Cor 10:10–11), and he describes his apostolic ministry as winning obedience of Gentiles in word and deed (Rom 15:18). In view of the widespread use of the commonplace and Paul's own use of it (Merritt), 1 Thess 1:5 is striking.

First, Paul uses an antithesis (as he also does in 2:13), unlike the other two places where he uses the commonplace (see further on v 8). This particular form of antithesis (*ouk . . . monon, alla kai* ["not . . . only, but also"]) expresses a difference between the two members of the expression, with the stress on the second, positive manner. The second member is not in contrast to the first, but embraces it, and the stress implies that the writer will shortly clarify the second member (Braunert), as Paul does elsewhere when he uses this form of antithesis (2 Cor 8:10–11, 21–22; 9:12–13; Phil 1:29–30; 2:27). Paul here uses the antithesis for stress rather than contrast (Kemmler, 156–59). He does not consider speech unimportant; on the contrary, his frequent use of *to euangelion tou theou* or *Christou* in chaps. 1 and 2, in 2:13 of his own preaching and in 1:8 of the Thessalonians', shows the importance that he attaches to preaching. But what is important for him here is how that preaching took place and what its effects were, and that he details in the second member of the antithesis.

The second noteworthy thing is that the second part of the antithesis does not refer to his *ergon* (contrast v 3) although in Rom 15:18 and 2 Cor 10:11 it does. When a philosopher spoke of his *ergon* in similar contexts, he drew attention to his own accomplishments or behavior as warrants for his demands. Paul here has no need to defend his conduct, as he does in 2 Corinthians, nor is it necessary to rehearse his credentials, as he does in Romans. Of importance, rather, is the manner in which the gospel came to them. *Alla kai* therefore does not contrast his speech with power (as in 1 Cor 4:19–20) and the Holy Spirit, but describes an extra dimension to his preaching: it took place *en dynamei kai en pneumati hagiō* ("in power and in the Holy Spirit"). The *en* can describe attendant circumstances or be instrumental (Moule, 79). In favor of the latter are 1 Cor 2:4, *en apodeixei pneumatos kai dynameōs* ("by the demonstration of the Spirit and power"), and Rom 15:19, *en dynamei pneumatos* ("by the power of the Spirit"), similar as to their meaning. The association of power and the Spirit is found elsewhere in the NT (e.g., Rom 15:13; cf. 1:4; esp. in Luke 1:17; 4:14; 24:49; Acts 1:8; 10:38). Paul conceived of the Holy Spirit as active in his preaching (1 Cor 2:4; 2 Cor 3:3; Gal 3:1–5) and responsible for the faith brought about by his preaching (1 Cor 2:4–5; 12:3). The power found expression in mighty works (Rom 15:18–19; cf. Heb 2:4), which he considered signs of his apostleship (2 Cor 12:12), but there is no indication that he thought of such objective demonstrations here.

On the contrary, *plērophoria pollē* ("with full conviction") refers to something subjective. The preposition *en*, added by some manuscripts (א A C P), is not to be read, for it would have continued the instrumental sense in its two previous occurrences, which would be inappropriate with *plērophoria*. This is an essentially Christian word and its meaning here is difficult to discern. The cognate verb can mean "to fill, fulfill" (2 Tim 4:5) or "to convince fully" (Rom 4:21; 14:5; Ign *Magn* 8:2), and the noun can have the sense either of "fullness" or "full assurance" (Col 2:2) or "conviction" (Heb 6:11; BAGD, 670). The word likely refers to Paul's conviction, although it is possible that the Thessalonians' assurance may be in view (Bruce 1982: 14). It more probably describes the manner in which he preached, taken up again in *eparrēsiasametha* in 2:2 (Findlay, 23–24; cf. Eadie, 42–43; Lightfoot 1980: 13–14; Koester 1980: 288; Zmijewski, 164–65), rather than "fullness" in the sense of the objective result of the Holy Spirit and power (Rigaux 1956: 377–79; Spicq 1991: 1253). The addition of *pollē* intensifies his claim to the conviction with which he had preached (analogous to *pasē parrēsia* in Phil 1:20; Acts 28:31, and *pollē parrēsia* in 2 Cor 3:16; 7:4; 1 Tim 3:13). Paul's assured conviction in speaking did not rest on rhetorical finesse or his own moral accomplishment, but on divine power (cf. 1 Cor 2:3–5; Rom 1:16). This distinguished him, on the one hand, from the rhetors and, on the other, from the self-confident popular philosophers, whose traditions he uses (Malherbe 1989: 15, 57; see COMMENT on 2:2).

*fully in conformity with the kind of persons you know we proved to be among you for your sake.* Paul's stress on the nature of his preaching is now bolstered by an appeal to what the Thessalonians know about him. His recollection of how the gospel came to them is in full conformity (*kathōs*) with what they themselves know about his behavior and demeanor with them at that time (cf. *kathōs* after *ou monon, alla kai* in Rom 4:16; *hōs* in Rom 9:24–25). This is the first of thirteen times that *kathōs* is used in the letter (1:5; 2:2, 4, 5, 13, 14; 3:4; 4:1 [twice], 6, 11, 13; 5:11), sometimes in conjunction with *oidate*. In addition, *kathaper* is used four times (2:11; 3:6, 12; 4:5). In all these occurrences, with one exception (4:5) the comparative conjunction is used in a positive way, mostly to underline conformity with what the Thessalonians knew or with God's will. It is language that assumes continuity and a history shared with the readers. This is the first of a number of occurrences of *oidate* in the letter (see also 2:1, 2, 5, 11; 3:3, 4; 4:2; 5:2), a characteristic of paraenetic style (see pages 82–86), and refers to something already known and accepted. For an appeal to what is known in connection with this form of antithesis, see Rom 5:3 and 1 Thess 2:8.

The personal relationship between Paul and his readers was formed when he conducted himself in a manner (*hoioi egenēthēmen*) that could not be separated from the manner in which he preached. Paul specifies two things about his preaching/behavior: it took place *en hymin* and *di' hymās*, both of which receive further attention in 2:1–12. *En* is to be retained with B D F G; without it, the sense would be "what kind of persons we became towards you." Paul likes to play on prepositions, sometimes for the sake of variety (e.g., in Rom 3:20; 2 Cor 1:11; 7:12; 8:7; Phil 3:9), sometimes in succinct formulas (e.g., Rom 11:36; 1 Cor 8:6). "Among you" (*en hymin*) reminds his readers of his association with them and hints at his public presence, like that of the popular philosophers who insisted that the genuine philosopher, in his attempts to improve his hearers, speak with *parrēsia* ("frankness") in public, *en tō mesō* (Diogenes Laertius *The Lives of Eminent Philosophers* 6.69; Epictetus, *Discourse* 3.22.55), for once people have seen what sort of person he is (*hopoios*), they are likely not to be vexed with him (Dio Chrysostom, *Oration* 33.5).

Paul differs from the philosophers in that he does not remind his readers of his ministry to the public at large, but to themselves, as in 2:7, *en mesō hymōn*. But like the philosophers, who out of goodwill sought to benefit their hearers (Dio Chrysostom, *Orations* 32.7, 8, 11, 20, 25; 38.9; 77/78.38; Malherbe 1987: 59), he had acted for his converts' sake (*di' hymās*). The earlier use of pronouns in the verse, *hēmōn . . . eis hymās*, is now intensified as he heaps up pronouns in vv 5 and 6, *en hymin, di' hymās, kai hēmeis . . . hēmōn*, to draw attention to and specify the nature of the relationship that he had established with them. He did not merely deliver a message, even one that had come with power and the Holy Spirit, and was preached with great conviction, but had proved to be a person of a certain quality (*hoioi egenēthēmen*) among them for their sake (cf. 2:8–12; 1 Cor 9:19–23; 2 Cor 4:5; 12:15; Phil 2:17). He elaborates on the thought in 2:10–12.

1:6. *so you on your part became imitators of us.* Paul now turns to the other side of their election, the way in which they received the gospel. Logically, v 6 is still dependent on *eidotes*, but the grammatical connection is beginning to loosen, hence recent editions (NA27) and translations (NIV, NRSV) print a new sentence beginning with *kai*. But *hoti* is still in control and v 6 should not be separated from v 5. The *kai* introduces the result of what precedes (BAGD, s.v. *kai* 2.f), specifying that, as Paul's relationship to the Thessalonians was effected by his preaching of the gospel to them, their relationship to him came about by their acceptance of the gospel.

The transition from the preaching of the gospel to its reception in terms of personal relationships is accentuated by the emphatic position of *hymeis*, which places the focus on his readers and their conduct. He had spoken of his manner of conduct (*egenēthēmen*); now he speaks of theirs (*egenēthēte*), their having become his *mimētai*. The notion of imitation implicit in the demand that one's words and deeds agree and thus provide an example to be followed now becomes explicit. As in all the other places where he speaks of imitation, with the exception of 2:14, Paul refers to imitation of himself (1:6; 1 Cor 4:16; 11:1; Phil 3:17; 2 Thess 3:7, 9; cf. Eph 5:1, of God). Paul's interest thus lies in the past, in what had transpired when they first believed. Precisely what he means by his readers' imitation must be determined from the context.

*and the Lord by receiving the word.* As it is not immediately obvious what Paul means by the Thessalonians' imitation of himself, so is it not clear in what way they imitated the Lord. The addition of *kai tou Kyriou* ("and the Lord") has been thought to be a self-correction, Paul catching himself after he had elevated himself as an example (Dibelius 1937: 5), more generally, as an addition due to Paul's modesty (von Dobschütz 1909: 72), merely as an afterthought (Stanley 1959: 866), or as an intensifying of what the community had been afforded (W. Michaelis in *TDNT* 4.670). Most commonly, it is thought that Paul has in view a sequence: he imitated Christ and the Thessalonians imitated him, he playing an intermediary role between Christ and them (Kamlah 1963: 224–25; Marxsen 1979: 38–39; Holtz 1986: 48–49). Such a view assumes that Paul and his readers had some knowledge of the life of Jesus (Frame, 82).

Rigaux (1956: 380–81) argues that the background is the ministry of Jesus, in which Jesus called people to follow himself (Matt 19:21) and take up their cross (Matt 10:38; 16:24; Mark 8:34), which is what Paul had done (2 Cor 4:10; cf. 1 Pet 2:21). Rigaux finds further support for his contention in the fact that *dechesthai ton logon* ("to receive the word") appears only here and in 2:14 in Paul and not in the LXX (for the synonymous *dechesthai to euangelion* see 2 Cor 11:4), but that it is used by Jesus, mostly in the parable of the Sower (Mark 4:20; Luke 8:13; *lambanein* Matt 13:20; Mark 10:16), with *meta charās* (Matt 13:20; Mark

4:16; Luke 8:13). The phrase then describes in Acts the reception of the gospel (8:14; 11:1; 17:11, *meta pasēs prothymias*). However, forms of *dechesthai* were quite commonly used (cf. Kemmler, 99, for drama and tragedy), among others, by moral philosophers to describe the reception of speech (e.g., Dio Chrysostom, *Oration* 33.15, 23, 44; Plutarch, *On Listening to Lectures* 39C,E; *On How to Tell a Flatterer from a Friend* 47E; *On Tranquility of Mind* 477F; *On Being a Busybody* 518F; *Table Talk* 1.613F; 3.650F), sometimes of a discourse resulting in a listener's conversion (Lucian, *Nigrinus* 4). Furthermore, when Paul speaks of the earthly Jesus, he does not have in mind a preacher or teacher but a self-denying Lord who had the benefits of others at heart (Rom 15:3; 2 Cor 8:9; 10:1; Phil 2:5–8; see Betz 1967: 143–45; Roosen 1979: 363).

How *dexamenoi* is understood affects the meaning of *mimētai*. If it is taken to describe action antecedent to *egenēthēte*, it could have a causal sense, the Thessalonians becoming imitators of Paul (2:2) and the Lord (2:15) in the suffering they endured because of receiving the word (Zmijewski, 166–67; Laub 1976: 29–30). It is preferable, however, to take *dexamenoi* as describing action contemporaneous with becoming imitators (thus Ellicott, 10; von Dobschütz 1909: 73). Then *dexamenoi* could be epexegetical, describing a correspondence between the modality of preaching and its accompanying circumstances (Roosen 1977: 363).

*in deep distress.* The word *thlipsis* carries a wide range of meanings, from external oppression to internal distress. It is common in the LXX, and it is possible "to differentiate, as in secular Gk., between external and internal afflictions, and in the case of the latter, between distress and anxiety" (H. Schlier in *TDNT* 3.141). It acquires a theological significance in the LXX, denoting the oppression and affliction of the people of God. In the NT, it describes a condition of believers (Rom 5:3; 12:12; Phil 4:14) and in particular refers to the eschatological tribulations (Matt 24:9, 21, 29; Rev 1:9).

*and with joy inspired by the Holy Spirit.* Their distress was accompanied by joy. The theme of joy in suffering is common in Judaism (e.g., 2 Macc 7:30; 4 Macc 10:20). Paul connects *chara* with *thlipsis* elsewhere (2 Cor 6:10; 7:4–5; 8:2), and it is not uncommon that the Holy Spirit is identified as responsible for joy (Luke 10:21; Acts 13:52; Rom 14:17; 15:13; Gal 5:22). But here joy has a special connection to the gospel (Laub 1973: 80–83): in the parable of the Sower the word was received *meta charās* (Matt 13:40; Mark 14:16; Luke 8:13), and the Philippian jailor is said to have rejoiced (*ēgalliasato*) upon believing in God (Acts 16:34).

1:7. *with the result that you became an example.* The manner in which they had become imitators in receiving the word resulted (*hōste*) in their becoming (*genesthai*) an example (*typos*) themselves. The pronoun *hymas*, grammatically unnecessary, is used for emphasis. Verses 7–8 now provide more information about the Thessalonians' activity spoken of in v 3. Paul had only implied in v 6 that he and the Lord had been *typoi*, but now is explicit about the Thessalonians being an example. Manuscript evidence for *typous* is strong (א A C D² F G), but *typos* (read by B D* 6 33) is to be preferred because a change to the plural, to agree with *hymas*, is more likely than the reverse. The singular views the church collectively rather than individuals as exemplary. It is a substantial compliment Paul pays his readers, for according to the conventional thinking on imitation their becoming an example in turn testifies to the dedication with which they had imitated Paul and the Lord (Seneca, *Epistle* 11.9).

*to all the believers in Macedonia and Achaia*. The present participle is substantival and became a common way to describe Christians (cf. 2:10, 13; Rom 4:11; 1 Cor 14:22). The present tense allows no restrictions to those who had already believed, a view held by John Chrysostom (*Homilies on 1 Thessalonians* 1 [PG 62:396]). He was followed by Oecomenius (*Commentary on 1 Thessalonians* 1 [PG 119:64]) and Theophylact (*Commentary on 1 Thessalonians* 1 [PG 124:1285]), who changed the present to the aorist. The clarification in v 8 makes it likely that Paul has in mind those who became believers as a result of the Thessalonians' exemplary preaching of the gospel. Paul is in a complimentary mood congenial to hyperbole. "All" (*pāsin*) cannot be taken literally if their imitation and exemplary behavior had to do with their reception and preaching of the word, for Paul had preached in Macedonia and Achaia before them. "Everywhere" (*en panti*) in v 8 is similarly complimentary. Paul had complimented them in his prayer report in vv 2–3; he now expands the compliment in geographical terms. Paul uses *en* twice, with Macedonia and Achaia, to make clear that he is referring to two separate provinces; when they are grouped together and contrasted with another place (v 8), one article suffices (GNTG 4.182). On Paul's use of these geographical references, see pages 68–69.

1:8. *For from you the word of the Lord has sounded forth not only in Macedonia and Achaia*. "From you" (*aph' hymōn*) is in the emphatic position, once more highlighting the readers' role in the spread of the word, and *gar* ("for") is explicative, introducing a clarification of the way in which they had become a *typos*. Verse 8 is an anacoluthon, and some commentators have suggested that a colon be placed after *Kyrios* (see Bornemann, 62–63), thus making two sentences: "For from you the word of the Lord has sounded forth" and "Your faith in God has gone forth, not only in Macedonia and Achaia, but everywhere." Their subjects (*ho logos tou Kyriou* and *hē pistis hymōn*) and predicates (*exēchētai* and *exelēluthen*) are synonymous. Then only v 8a would explain v 7. The second sentence would begin with the antithetic *ou monon . . . alla*, an unusual position in Paul (only in Rom 5:3, 11; 8:23; 9:10; 2 Cor 7:7). Henneken (59–61) has persuasively argued, however, that Pauline usage does not support the introduction of a colon here.

The prepositions *apo* and *ek* were at times used indiscriminately, as in Luke 8:35, *aph' hou ta daimonia exēlthen* ("from whom the demons had gone"). Although *ek* predominated, Paul used *apo* because he did not want to convey the idea that they were the source of the word of the Lord (cf. 1 Cor 14:36). That does not mean, however, that they did not preach the word, an opinion supported by the contention that then *hyph' hymōn* would be required (Eadie, 47; Milligan, 12). In NT Greek, "*hypo* with the agent with the passive or verbs with a passive meaning is . . . often replaced by *apo*" (BDF §210.2).

In v 3 he had already spoken of their preaching and used traditional terms to describe it. Here he refers to the gospel as the word of the Lord, the only place, in addition to 2 Thess 3:1, that he does so. For Paul the word is God's, with a vitality that comes from God and not man (1:5; 2:13; cf. 2 Thess 3:1). This is in marked contrast to Paul's description of his gospel and the circumstances attending his preaching (v 5). Paul does not draw this contrast in order to distinguish between his apostolic preaching and that of his converts (thus Ware), but because he wishes to say something further about the Thessalonians' faith that had caused them to preach (v 3) and made them an example to other believers (v 7).

Paul's description of the gospel as *ho logos tou Kyriou* ("the word of the Lord") is reminiscent of the OT (e.g., Jer 1:4, 11; Ezek 3:16; 6:1; 7:1), except that the Lord is now Jesus instead of God, and *tou Kyriou* is objective, the Lord as content of the message. The word resounded (*exēchētai*), whether as a trumpet (John Chrysostom, *Homilies on 1 Thessalonians* 2 [PG 62:399]; cf. Rom 10:18) or as thunder (Sir 40:13), Paul playing on the sense of hearing (cf. 2:13, *logos akoēs*). Paul sketches a picture of active preaching by the Thessalonians (Henneken, 62–63; different, Roosen 1977: 371 n. 26) in Macedonia and Achaia and beyond. Yet Paul was not simply concerned with the geographical extent of their preaching, but rather with the events that took place within those areas, hence he uses *en*, as in *en panti topō* ("everywhere"), rather than *eis* or *pros* (see 1:5 and variant). For the antithesis *ou monon . . . alla (kai)*, see NOTE and COMMENT on v 5.

*but your faith in God has gone forth everywhere.* As in v 5, the second part of the antithesis embraces and intensifies the first. Their preaching of the word of the Lord is now spoken of as their faith in God, as in v 3, although what Paul has in mind must be what was reported (v 9). According to Paul, faith comes from hearing the message of Christ's death and resurrection preached (Rom 10:5–17). The Thessalonians had received that message; now their faith impels them to preach it (cf. v 3). The repetition of the second article in *hē pistis hē pros theon* is grammatically unnecessary (BDF §269.2; GNTG 4.187, 221); it is repeated here for the sake of emphasis, specifying God as the object of their faith (*pros theon*; cf. *pros ton Kyrion Iēsoun*, Phlm 5). This is the only place where this formulation appears in the NT; it comes from Hellenistic Judaism (Holtz 1986: 53 n. 144 refers to 4 Macc 15:24; 16:22; Philo, *On the Life of Abraham* 268, 271, 273). Its content is summarized in vv 9–10.

The report about their faith, one assumes, was made by Christians, which could give further specification to *en panti topō* ("everywhere"). Places of worship were described as *topoi* (Helmut Koester in *TDNT* 8.198–99, 204–205), a usage also found in the NT (e.g., John 11:48; cf. Josephus, *Jewish Antiquities* 14.235). Paul uses it in this sense in the universalizing prescript of 1 Corinthians (1:2) in connection with Christians who call upon the name of the Lord Jesus Christ *en panti topō* ("in every place"; cf. 1 Tim 2:8), and it is quite possible that he has such a setting in mind here. Nevertheless, since "in every place" is in antithesis to Macedonia and Achaia, it may possibly have the extended geographical reference commentators give it (strongly argued by John Chrysostom, *Homilies on 1 Thessalonians* 2 [PG 62:399], who compares it with the spread of the

fame of Alexander of Macedon). In any case, the Thessalonians' evangelism
leads Paul to the kind of hyperbole frequently found in Hellenistic literature,
often in the introductions to works (e.g., Plutarch, *Romulus* 1; *Pyrrhus* 19; *Aristides* 1; Dio Chrysostom, *Oration* 51.3; Mark 1:5; Acts 19:10, 17; Rom 1:8; 10:18;
2 Cor 2:14; 3:2; Phil 4:5; Gal 1:5, 23).

*so that we have no need to say anything.* The phrase comes from the paraenetic
tradition (4:9; 5:1; see page 83), and once more Paul uses a paraenetic element
to compliment his readers. He does not say precisely what he has no need to say,
nor to whom he might say it, but the context shows he has their faith and a general report about it in mind. The word *lalein* may, however, in a more specialized way be used of the preaching of the gospel, as it does in 2:2, 4, 16; Rom
15:18; 2 Cor 2:17, and thus be analogous to *euangelizesthai* in 3:6. Both of these
words, which are normally used of preaching the gospel, are in this letter used
in connection with a report of the Thessalonians' faith, which in this context is
parallel to the gospel (Schlier 1972: 23–24; Roosen 1977: 375). The report of the
Thessalonians' faith and evangelism thus itself has an evangelical quality.

1:9. *indeed, they themselves are reporting about us.* "Indeed" (*gar*) introduces an
explanation of why it is not necessary to speak of the Thessalonians' faith. Paul
had heard about them from Timothy (see COMMENT on v 8), but he speaks
more generally. The construction is *ad sensum, autoi* referring to those in Macedonia and Achaia and everyplace. The knowledge of what these people were saying may partly have come to him from Timothy. The only other place where Paul
uses *apangello* is in 1 Cor 14:25, of an exclamation of faith, so the terms used to
describe reports about the Thessalonians and Paul are all evangelical in quality.

*namely, what kind of entrance we gained to you.* Paul considers his relationship
with the Thessalonians from two perspectives, his conduct and their response.
He here signals his intention to speak of the kind (*hopoia*) of *eisodos* he experienced, but reserves discussion of it for 2:1–12, where it is fleshed out. To be
noted here is that *eisodos* could carry the two meanings the RSV gives it, in v 9
("welcome," thus passive) and in 2:1 ("visit," thus active). The word is used in
the active sense in Acts 13:24; Heb 10:19; 2 Pet 1:11. That it also has the active
meaning in 2:1, which provides an explication of vv 9–10, and the prominent position of *peri hēmōn* argue for the active meaning (von Dobschütz 1909: 76).

*and how you turned to God.* The Thessalonians' response is described as a conversion, and it is given concreteness by reminding them of the content of what
they had accepted. During the first century, *pōs* was confused with *hōs* and took
over the function of *hoti* (GNTG 4.137), so that *pōs* here could be taken as introducing the fact of their conversion (Frame, 87; Best 1972: 81–82; cf. Acts
11:13). Coming so soon after *hopoia*, however, it is naturally read as modal in
sense, describing the manner of their conversion.

In recent years it has been argued that 1:9b–10 represents a scheme of preaching (also thought to be seen in Heb 5:11–6:2; Wilckens, 81–91) that Paul had inherited and here applies to the Thessalonians. Alternatively, the verses have been
thought to be a carefully structured piece of early Christian confessional tradition, perhaps a baptismal hymn of Gentile Christian origin (Friedrich 1965).

The existence of such a formula as well as Paul's dependence on it have received severe criticism by most recent commentators (see esp. Munck 1962; Holtz 1977: 459–88; 1986: 53–62; Wanamaker, 84–89). That Paul uses language derived from the so-called Hellenistic Jewish mission has been demonstrated (Bussmann), but there have been only unconvincing attempts to outline a scheme that Jews used and early Christians, including Paul, reproduced. Paul does not here give an outline of a missionary sermon he had preached in Thessalonica; more precisely, he summarizes what his converts had accepted and in the process partly uses traditional Jewish formulations also used by other Christians (Stuhlmacher, 258–62). These investigations have given insufficient attention to the Gentile recipients of the message, particularly to their response to the Christian message (Nock 1933: 212–55; Weiss 1959: 233–37) and to the fact that the phenomenon of conversion itself was well known in the pagan world (Nock 1933; 1954; 1972).

What Paul had described as his readers' *pistis . . . pros ton theon* (v 8), he now describes as their turning (*epestrepsate pros ton theon*, "you turned to God"). This is not typical Pauline language; he uses *epistrephein* elsewhere only in 2 Cor 3:16 and Gal 4:9, where he plays on the language of conversion (Langevin, 59–62). The occurrences in Acts (e.g., 3:19; 9:35; 11:21; 15:19; 26:18, 20) show that we have to do with a technical term describing conversion. Particularly relevant is Paul's preaching to the pagans in Lystra (Acts 14:15, *hymas apo toutōn tōn mataiōn epistrephein epi theon zōnta* ["you are to turn from these vain things to the living God"]), which has close affinities with our text.

The nature of the language of conversion is clearest in *Jos Asen* 11:10–11, where the convert reflects on the nature of the Jewish God: "But I have heard many saying that the God of the Hebrews is a true God and a living God [*theos alēthinos . . . kai theos zōn*] . . . . Therefore I will take courage too and turn to him [*epistrepsō pros auton*] and take refuge in him . . . ." See Tob 14:6 concerning pagans who turn to (*epistrepsousin*) and fear God truly (*alēthinos*) and abandon their idols. This usage was prepared for in the LXX, where *epistrephein*, although used mostly of Israel's (re)turning to God (e.g., Hos 5:4; 6:1; Joel 2:13), is also used of Gentiles' turning to God (e.g., Ps 21:28; Isa 19:22; Jer 18:8, 11). In the Testaments of the Twelve Patriarchs, the word describes Jews turning to God (e.g., *T. Iss* 6:3; *T. Dan* 5:9, 11; *T. Naph* 4:3) but also God turning Gentiles as well as Jews to himself (*T. Zeb* 9:7, 8). The term was also used by pagans of conversion to philosophy (Nock 1972: 470, 473; Aubin, 49–68). Philosophers might speak of turning to the divine in the pursuit of wisdom or truth (Epictetus, *Discourse* 2.20.22; cf. Ps.-Diogenes, *Epistle* 34.1; Lucian, *The Double Indictment* 17), but turning to God and away from all human values and opinions is the same as turning to oneself (*eph' hauton*), a coming to one's senses (Epictetus, *Discourses* 3.16.15; 22.39; 23.16, 137; 4.4.7; Marcus Aurelius, *Meditation* 9.42), and differs radically from the biblical idea of turning to God.

*from idols to serve.* The term *eidolon* in Greek usage described beings that were not in themselves evil. Other words were used to describe cultic images, and the appropriateness of venerating them was extensively debated, some philosophers taking a negative position on the matter (Plutarch, *On Tranquility of Mind* 477D; Ps.-Plutarch, *On Superstition* 167D; Oenomaus, according to Eusebius, *The Preparation of the Gospel* 5.36), others a positive one (Dio Chrysostom, *Oration* 12; Maximus of Tyre, *Oration* 2). See Geffcken, xx–xxix; Nock 1933: 221–27; Attridge, 13–23.

It was the LXX that made the term synonymous with false gods and used it to describe images of pagan deities (1 Chr 10:9; Ps 115:4; Isa 10:11). The Jewish polemic against religious images (Isa 44:9–20; Ep Jer) saw in idolatrous worship the cause of immorality (Wis 14:12). Paul shares this negative view of idols (1 Cor 8:4; 10:19; 12:2; Gal 4:9). Conversion from idols to God was for him much more than accepting a theological postulate about monotheism. The worshiper of idols has no knowledge of God or has rejected that knowledge and fallen into bondage to the idols, with dire moral consequences (Rom 1:18–32; Gal 4:8–9). The danger of lapsing into such servitude continued to be real to Paul's converts (1 Cor 10:7, 14; Gal 4:8–9) in spite of the commitment they made at their conversion to serve God rather than idols.

The infinitive *douleuein* complements *epestrepsate*, thus expressing the goal of conversion. To serve God requires total and exclusive allegiance (Matt 6:24; Luke 16:13), as a slave owes to his master (Rom 6:15–23). Service requires obedience (Rom 6:16–17), which is what Paul sought from the Gentiles in his mission (Rom 15:18; cf. 16:18–19; 2 Cor 10:5–6) and what they committed themselves to when they accepted Paul's message in their confession of faith (Rom 10:16–17). As slavery to false gods and their idols resulted in an immoral life, so serving God required a righteous and sanctified life (Rom 6:16–23), made possible by the knowledge of God (1 Thess 4:3–5; cf. 1 Pet 1:14–16), which was offered in preaching (2 Cor 4:4–6).

*the living and true God.* The nature of God, to whom the Thessalonians had turned and served is now doubly qualified. Paul's indebtedness to Hellenistic Jewish propaganda is evident in the epithet *theos zōn*. It was used in polemic, to distinguish God from idols (Dan 5:23 LXX; Bel 5, cf. 25 Theodotion; Jub 21:3–4; Jos Asen 11:9–10), and in a related use described God as the Creator (Sir 18:1; Bel 5; 1 En 5:1; 3 Macc 6:28). See Bousset and Gressmann, 358–60; Delling 1963: 9–26 for the use of the participle. In Jewish propaganda, then, it is to the living God that the Gentile converts turn (Esth 8:12q LXX; Jos Asen 11:10–11) in order to serve him (Dan 6:27–28 LXX, *esomai auto . . . douleuōn* ["I shall serve him"]).

So, too, in early Christian preaching to Gentiles, God is presented as the Creator (Acts 17:22–31) and described as the living God (Acts 14:15). This is thus the second time in the letter that God is described as the Creator (see NOTE and COMMENT on v 1). In a number of places in his letters Paul applies this missionary formulation to particular circumstances (Rom 9:24–26; 2 Cor 3:3; 6:16), as do other writers (1 Tim 3:15; 4:10, in connection with confessional formulas; Heb 9:14, *latreuōn theō zōnti*; Rev 10:22, modifying the epithet with a quotation of Exod 20:11). For Paul, the notion of God as the Creator has moral overtones (Rom 1:18–32; cf. Acts 17:28–31), as it did in Judaism (e.g., *Sib Or*

3.760–64, *pheugete latreias anomous, tō zōnti latreue* ["Flee unlawful worship; serve the Living One"]). The second description of God, as true (*alēthinos*), is equally well attested in Hellenistic Judaism. Both epithets appear in Jer 10:10, "But the Lord is the true God, he is the living God and the everlasting King," in contrast to idols, but the text does not appear in the LXX. The two do appear in Hellenistic Jewish propaganda that describes conversion (*Jos Asen* 10:10–11). By itself, the epithet of the true God describes him as the Creator (Josephus, *Jewish Antiquities* 11.55; *Sib Or* 5.499; Fragment 1.10), the only truly existent God (Philo, *On the Preliminary Studies* 159; *Ep Arist* 140), who is therefore to be distinguished from idols and false gods (Wis 12:27; Philo, *On the Special Laws* 1.332; *Sib Or* 5.493; Fragments 1.20; 3.46). This is the only place in Paul's letters where God is described in this manner (but see Rom 3:4), but the epithet is found in the Johannine literature (e.g., John 7:28; 17:3; Rev 3:4; esp. 1 John 5:20–21).

1:10. *and to wait for his son from heaven.* Paul had derived the first part of this description of the response to his preaching dealing with God from Hellenistic Judaism; as he now speaks of Jesus, he uses formulations for which he was probably indebted to early Christian christological reflection. Complete certainty about how he preached eludes us, but according to 2 Cor 4:1–6 he introduced God as Creator through the preaching of Christ (cf. 1 Cor 2:2). In 1 Cor 8:6, which also reflects preaching to Gentiles, Paul speaks of Jesus Christ as God's agent in creation, but here he speaks of Jesus as God's son from an eschatological perspective. In v 9, the infinitive *douleuein* ("to serve") introduced the theological part of the preaching, now *anamenein* ("to await") introduces the christological part. This is the only time *anamenein* occurs in the NT. Paul normally uses *apekdechesthai* ("to await eagerly") for eschatological waiting (Rom 8:19, 23, 25; 1 Cor 1:7; Phil 3:20). The tradition from which he derived the words appears to have been influenced by the LXX, where it is used of waiting with faith and full assurance for God's righteous judgment, mercy, and salvation (Jer 13:16; Isa 59:11; Jud 8:17; Sir 2:6–8). Paul thus signals the eschatological interest that will occupy him throughout the letter (2:19; 3:13; 4:13–18; 5:1–11; see esp. Munck 1962; Langevin, 67–73), which may account for the order in which he mentions the items from his preaching, the eschatologically charged claims about Jesus coming in the emphatic position at the end.

The designation of Jesus as God's son and that he would come from heaven suggests to some scholars that we here have to do with a pre-Pauline formulation (Kramer, 123–26). But this theory remains speculative and is not particularly helpful. The designation appears elsewhere in Paul's letters in this way only in 1 Cor 15:28. That the son will come out of the heavens (*ek tōn ouranōn*; cf. 1 Cor 15:47; John 3:31; 6:33) does not differ from his coming from heaven (*ap' ouranou*; 4:16); it reflects Paul's understanding that Christ had ascended into heaven (Rom 10:6). The plural shows Semitic influence (cf. 2 Cor 12:2; see further Luedemann, 254 n. 105).

*whom he raised from the dead.* Paul does not mention Jesus' resurrection in order to say something about how it showed him to be God's son (Rom 1:4), but because Christ's resurrection was preparatory to his return and the resurrection of Christians at his coming (see 4:14, 16 and the argument in 1 Cor 15:20–57; cf. Rom 8:11; 2 Cor 4:14). Christ's resurrection is an act of the living God, the Creator (cf. Rom 4:17, 24; 8:11): Paul always uses *egeirein*, with the exception of 4:14, 16, where he uses *anistanai*. Elsewhere, the generic article is used with *tōn nekrōn*, as it is here, only in Eph 5:14; Col 1:18; to use it or not is purely a matter of taste (GNTG 4.180).

*Jesus who delivers us from the wrath to come.* Paul identifies the resurrected son as Jesus (cf. Rom 6:11) and again uses the personal name when connecting his resurrection and return, when God will gather through Jesus and with him those who have fallen asleep (4:14; cf. 4:17). Paul had identified with the death of Jesus in his preaching (2 Cor 4:5, 11; see COMMENT on v 6). The Thessalonians had evidently been told that God had not destined them for wrath, but for salvation through Jesus, who had died for them (5:9–10). The subject of divine wrath appears for a third time in the letter (2:16; cf. 4:6) in a manner assuming that the readers were familiar with the subject and reflects the Jewish character of Paul's thinking. Greek dramatists and almost all philosophers criticized the anger of the gods of the myths as unworthy (Euripides, *The Bacchanals* 1348; Cicero, *De officiis* 3.102), but such criticism only witnessed to the widespread idea that the gods' anger required expiation. In contrast, the OT and later Jewish literature with few exceptions accepted the notion as integral to the nature of God (G. Stählin in *TDNT* 5.392–418), and it is to them that Paul is indebted.

Especially in such Jewish writings as the Sibylline Oracles, Gentiles are warned of God's firmly determined eschatological anger (3.545–72) because of, among other vices, their idolatry (5.75–89; 12.110–12). They are to seek their Deliverer (*rhystēr*) from wrath (3.561), repent, and seek God's forgiveness (4.159–70). God's wrath occupied an important place in Paul's teaching (Rom 1:18; 2:5, 8; 3:5; 5:9; 9:22) and preaching (1 Thess 1:10). The repetition of the article (*tēs orgēs tēs erchomenēs*) gives more weight to the participle, drawing attention to its essential feature, that wrath is certainly coming (Milligan, 15; Rigaux 1956: 396). This confidence is further heightened by the futuristic use of the present form of the participle (Lightfoot 1980: 18; BDF §323). From this certain wrath Jesus is the deliverer (*ho rhyomenos*), the present participle indicating a permanent function with a future application (cf. *hō kalōn* in 2:12; 5:24; Gal 5:8; Rigaux 1956: 395). *Rhyesthai*, less often used than its synonym *sōzesthai*, is used frequently in the LXX of God as the Deliverer (e.g., Dan 3:88; 8:4, 7, 11 LXX), the Creator who redeems his people Israel (Isa 49:7; 54:5). In the NT, the word is used eschatologically (cf. Matt 6:13) and is here attributed to God's son, who died for sinners and will save them from God's wrath (Rom 5:8–10; cf. Phil 3:20).

# COMMENT

*vv 2–5.* Paul's concentrated use of labials at the beginning of his first thanksgiving shows that he is writing with a view of how the letter would sound when read aloud. The letter would therefore function as a speech, and the liturgical features in these first verses contribute to the character of the speech as a sermon. Paul's epistolary thanksgivings may indeed reflect his practice of beginning his sermons with such a prayer (Rigaux 1968: 122). The worshipful tone already established in the salutation is now continued. This report of the thanksgiving Paul constantly gives is the first of five prayers or prayer reports in the letter (1:2–3; 2:13; 3:10; 3:11–13; 5:23), which appear in important places in the structure of the letter and make the letter different from ordinary friendly letters.

In this letter of exhortation Paul speaks from a perspective dominated by God, who is not described in the abstract but in his relationship with the Thessalonians, and Paul, as the initiator of that relationship and the recipient of thanksgivings and petitions. New converts like the Thessalonians needed to have such a perspective, offered them at their conversion, strengthened. It was not immediately obvious to them, as it was to Jews and Christians, that God should be the starting point for them in all things (*Ep Arist* 189, 200, 235). Indeed, some Corinthians still had questions about monotheism more than four years after the church there had been established (1 Cor 8:4–7), and Paul similarly places a heavy emphasis on God in 1 Corinthians.

Thanksgivings performed the formal function of introducing subjects to be taken up in the body of the letter (Schubert, 24), and this one does so, combining with it a hortatory function, which is extremely important to Paul in this letter (Wiles, 180; O'Brien 1977: 164–66). Paul's statement that he remembers them (v 3) is formulaic, but it will be echoed by their remembering him (2:9; 3:6), which serves a paraenetic purpose. The triad of Christian qualities, which for Paul is almost formulaic, functions in a similar manner. Paul speaks elsewhere in the letter of work (5:13), labor (2:9; 3:5; 5:12), and patience (5:14), so it is clear that he was aware of the thanksgiving's epistolary and hortatory functions. This becomes more evident when it is observed that the three efficient causes of the Thessalonians' activity—namely, their faith, love, and hope—are of concern to Paul throughout the letter. The triad appears again in 5:8, in connection with a series of hortatory subjunctives (beginning with 5:6), which there make explicit Paul's exhortation that is implicit here. The three terms also appear individually or in company with one or another of the three.

It is striking that most of the references to faith appear in the first three chapters, the autobiographical section of the letter. Paul studiously relates the Thessalonians' faith to his ministry before he proceeds to describe the practical implications of their faith in the second half of the letter. Christians are described as believers (1:7; 2:10, 13; applied to the Thessalonians in 4:14), yet Paul was concerned about their faith when he sent Timothy to them (3:2, 5–7), and even though he could comment on how widely their faith was known (1:8), at the time of writing he still knew that there was something lacking in it (3:10). Similarly, they had been divinely taught to love (4:9) and did indeed do so (3:6), but Paul nevertheless thought it necessary to pray that their love increase (3:10) and exhort them to exercise it (5:8, 13). And while he could confidently exclaim that the Thessalonians themselves were his hope (2:19), some details about their eschatological hope would still be given (4:13–5:11) in order to provide a basis for comfort and encouragement in the face of bereavement (4:18; 5:11) and in connection with his exhortation to the moral life (5:6–8).

Paul's procedure thus is to begin by mentioning in his first thanksgiving what his readers have achieved and then on that basis to urge them to greater heights (cf. 4:1, 9–10; 5:11), which is a procedure characteristic of paraenesis (see pages 84, 86), a style Paul adapts to his pastoral interests. An appreciation of this pastoral interest allows us to see the traditional *pantote* ("always") and *adialeiptōs* ("without ceasing") of the thanksgiving in a new light: Paul *never* forgets his readers, who may have felt abandoned (see NOTE and COMMENT on v 6; and cf. 2:17–3:10). That the thanksgiving so clearly performs formal and hortatory functions does not mean that it is not genuine in expressing thanks to God. The entire first chapter deals with the preaching of the gospel to and by the Thessalonians, and Paul's narrative of those events consistently has God at its center.

It is only in this chapter that Paul speaks of one of his churches as preaching the gospel (Ware; see further on the problem, Swigchem; Greeven). We do learn that some individuals who were associated with him were active in the spread of the gospel (e.g., Rom 16:6, 12–13; 2 Cor 1:19; 8:18; Phil 1:14–17; 4:3), and it has been argued that Paul's churches participated in his preaching through delegates they commissioned to serve as his coworkers (Ollrog, 129–32), but that is not certain. It is certain that his churches participated in his own work through their financial support (e.g., Rom 15:24; 1 Cor 16:6; 2 Cor 11:8–9; esp. Phil 1:4–8; 4:14–17). Paul also reminded the Corinthians of an evangelical dimension present in their worship (1 Cor 11:26; 14:20–25), and he came close to an outright mandate to preach at the end of his directions on abstaining from eating meat consecrated to idols (1 Cor 8:1–11:1). In that argument he illustrates his freedom to forgo his right to financial support by referring to his demeanor, which aimed at saving people (1 Cor 9:19–23; see Malherbe 1995b: 251–54), and concluding with a call that his readers imitate him as he does Christ (1 Cor 11:1). That, however, falls short of a clear-cut command to preach, and there is no indication either that the Thessalonians preached because Paul had commanded them to do so.

It emerges from vv 6–8 that the impulse to preach came from their relationship with Paul, but in vv 3–4 he provides another dimension: they preach, he knows (*eidotes*), because God had called them. Some patristic (Theodore of Mopsuestia 2:4 Swete) and some modern commentators refer this knowledge to the Thessalonians, so that it would be their consciousness of their election that led them to preach. The grammar, however, more naturally suggests that it is Paul who saw the connection. Ever alert to the pastoral side of Paul's letter, John Chrysostom correctly thought that Paul was praising his readers by referring to their election (*Homilies on 1 Thessalonians* 1 [PG 62:395]).

Paul takes great care at the beginning of the letter to stress his readers' relationship with God; he is equally careful to remind them of his own relationship with them and how it came about. He achieves this in a number of ways. He uses personal pronouns ten times in these four verses, four appearing in v 5, which describes his preaching and his relationship with them that resulted from this preaching. He further addresses them as brethren, thus introducing the language of kinship that he will constantly use in the letter. This relationship with the Thessalonians was not a matter of Paul's devising but of God's creation. Paul can call them brethren because God had loved them and called them through Paul's preaching, in which divine power was present. The community God called into existence (1:1) is one in which, as brothers, their social status is relativized (Phlmn 16; cf. Aristides, *Apology* 15.6–7). Because of their new relationship with God, they assumed moral responsibilities within the community that distinguished them from the larger society (4:5–6; 1 Cor 5:11–13; 6:2–6). The implications of these relationships within the church did not escape the notice of Christianity's critics (e.g., Lucian, *The Passing of Peregrinus* 13; Minucius Felix, *Octavius* 9.2; 31.8), whom the Apologists had to answer (e.g., Tertullian, *Apology* 39).

It is natural that Paul begins his letter by stressing his personal relationship with his readers, for that is in the nature of paraenesis, particularly in letters that sought to be substitutes for their writers' presence. In such letters the self-presentation of a writer served to establish firmly his relationship with his readers, a prerequisite for the advice that would follow (for this feature in Seneca's letters, see Hadot, 174–76; cf. Malherbe 1989: 32–34). It is a fundamental error to think that the characterization of the church in chap. 1 "moves this church out of the realm of personal relationship with the apostle into a universal horizon of participation in an eschatological event . . . . This also implies that the addressees are released from their dependence upon the writer," and therefore to think that in this respect (as in others) the thanksgiving radically departs from its conventional purpose of binding writers and readers more closely (Koester 1979: 36). Timothy had reported to Paul that the Thessalonians still looked to him as their paradigm (see NOTE and COMMENT on 3:6–8), and Paul here begins a delineation of that paradigm which extends through chap. 3, and provides the basis for the practical advice that he will give in chaps. 4 and 5. What makes the extended thanksgiving in this chapter different is that it stresses how the relationship between Paul and his readers came about, namely through God's initiative in their election and the exercise of his power in Paul's preaching.

God's power extended beyond Paul's speech. The grammatical subject in v 5, which describes Paul's preaching, is the gospel. It is Paul's gospel that is preached, but Paul's formulation draws attention to the way the gospel came, to its effect on Paul and the Thessalonians. Paul describes the gospel, not in terms of its content (cf. 1 Cor 2:2; 15:1–5), but totally in terms of its power and effect. This explains why Paul does not speak of his deeds, in antithesis to his words, which would have drawn attention to his own achievement, but of divine power. It is the gospel, coming in power and the Holy Spirit, which inspired deep confidence in Paul to preach. But Paul was more than merely an instrument; he could not in fact be separated from the gospel (Laub 1976: 26–31). What Paul says about the coming of the gospel in v 5a corresponds with his readers' knowledge (*kathōs oidate*) of his demeanor and conduct while he was with them. Paul embodied the gospel, acting totally for their sake (v 5a; cf. 2:8). It is this perception by the Thessalonians, Paul claims, that brought about their conversion and imitation.

vv 6–8. Paul had offered himself as a moral example to be followed when he founded the church in Thessalonica (2 Thess 3:7, 9), and in paraenetic style he reminds them of it in 2:9. The call to imitation by someone whose words and deeds conformed was a common paraenetic convention (see Seneca, *Epistles* 6.5–6; 11.8–10; Malherbe 1986b: 164–65; Hadot, 164–65; Fiore), and the question therefore arises as to whether 1:6 is also to be understood as referring to Paul as a moral paradigm (Malherbe 1987: 52–54). An argument of this commentary is that chaps. 1–3 serve a paraenetic function, and 1:6 may therefore itself be understood paraenetically. The paraenetic function of chaps. 1–3 does not, however, require that the imitation of which Paul speaks here, which took place when he preached in Thessalonica, was at that time moral in nature. A number of factors demonstrate how Paul's view of imitation differed from that of his contemporaries.

To begin with, it is noteworthy that this is the only place in his letters where Paul does not call on his readers to imitate himself (cf. 2:14) but reminds them that they had already become his imitators. This is striking in light of the fact that most of the moral philosophers whose hortatory conventions Paul uses were hesitant to call others to follow their own example, or even to offer recent virtuous individuals as worthy of imitation (see Malherbe 1989: 57–58). Especially for the Stoics, in theory the ideal virtuous person who could demand imitation was so distant a possibility that they questioned whether the ideal could in fact be realized, yet in practice they were ambiguous. Seneca, for example, held that the ideal good man appeared, like the phoenix, every five hundred years (*Epistle* 42.1), but he did not hesitate to adduce many examples, including his own (*Epistles* 42.1; 8.1), when providing instruction, and his frequent references to his own conduct must have been understood as exemplary by his reader (see Ganss). Cynics, however, were unambiguous in their claim to represent the ideal, which they had attained through their labors (Malherbe 1978: 58–59), and to call on people to follow their example. Paul's statement that his readers had imitated him seems to approximate the Cynics' confidence, but in reality he is quite different from them.

Precisely what Paul means by his readers' imitation is tied to his further statement that they had also imitated the Lord and that this had taken place in connection with their receiving the word. Paul thus once more changes a common moral hortatory convention to make a theological point about the reception of the gospel. In summary statements Paul claims to have held before his hearers the crucified Christ (1 Cor 1:23; 2:2; Gal 3:1), who died for the sins of others (1 Cor 15:3). First Thessalonians provides some indication of how Christ was presented in Paul's preaching to the Thessalonians. Of immediate relevance is that he died for their sake (5:10) and would deliver them from eschatological wrath (1:10). Paul comments further in vv 9–10 on what they had responded to, and that summary provides the context for these comments on Christ's vicarious death and eschatological deliverance.

Jesus' concern for others is a counterpart to Paul's own concern for the Thessalonians (*di' hymās*), and this must be part of what they had imitated. Furthermore, in what Paul himself suffered and endured (1 Cor 4:9–13; 2 Cor 4:8–11; 6:3–10; 11:22–12:10) he identified with the death of Christ (2 Cor 4:10; cf. 4 Macc 9:23; Ign *Rom* 6:3 for imitating someone's suffering). Suffering for others is intrinsic to Paul's understanding of the gospel, and to imitate him and the Lord means that one is prepared to sacrifice everything for others (1 Cor 10:23; 11:1; see Koester 1980: 289). Imitating Paul and the Lord therefore has nothing to do with the acceptance of authority or with a beginning of discipleship (thus W. Michaelis in *TDNT* 4.670), nor need the acceptance of the word have been a conscious commitment to imitate Paul and the Lord (Eadie, 45). What was proffered the Thessalonians was the gospel of the self-giving Lord preached by Paul, in whose life the gospel became transparent (Laub 1973: 84). Acceptance of that gospel had the effect of making the converts imitators of Paul and the Lord; it need not have extended to a conscious commitment to imitation (Schulz, 287; Holtz 1986: 49).

Paul's understanding of the Thessalonians' imitation finds further elaboration in his reminder that they had received the word *en thlipsei*. Given the relative frequency with which *thlipsis* and *thlibein* occur in the Thessalonian letters (1 Thess 1:6; 3:3–4, 7; 2 Thess 1:4, 6–7), noted for their eschatological interest and their concern with persecution (e.g., 1 Thess 2:14–16; 2 Thess 1:4–10; sometimes combined with Acts 17:5–9), it is to be expected that *thlipsis* in 1:6 would have been taken to have an eschatological significance (e.g., Koester 1980: 288–89; Collins 1984: 191–93, 291–93).

Most commentators think that *thlipsis* here refers to persecution and refer to Acts 17:5–9 (cf. 1 Thess 2:2) to identify the persecutors (Best 1972: 79; see the more extended discussion in Malherbe 1987: 46–48). The *thlipsis* may then be understood in light of the Jewish idea of the eschatological sufferings of the righteous (H. Schlier in *TDNT* 3.144–48; Collins 1984: 191–93, 291–93). But that cannot be true here, for Paul relates his readers' *thlipsis* to their reception of the gospel, not to persecution they encountered later, at the hands of their presumably Gentile countrymen (2:14). This persecution could not be the same as that described in Acts 17:5–9, which Luke lays at the door of the Thessalonian Jews, after Paul had made his converts, and the same applies to the persecution he describes in 2:15. It is closer to the truth that *thlipsis* encompasses both the reception of the gospel and all the problems that ensued (de Boer, 115–16).

The translation "deep distress" for *thlipsis* reflects an understanding that differs from the majority interpretation. Paul had preached in Thessalonica *en pollō agōni*, "in the midst of a great struggle" (2:2), which may refer to a combination of external dangers and anxiety (John Chrysostom, *Homilies on 1 Thessalonians* 2 [PG 62:401]; Neil, 35; Malherbe 1987: 47–48). While still in the city, he had forewarned his converts that it was the Christian's lot to endure tribulation (3:4) and later had sent Timothy to exhort them not to be unsettled emotionally by "these afflictions" (3:3), which is a reference to his own afflictions or anxieties. That he could preach with great conviction did not rule out personal distress. It is important that *thlibomenoi* stands at the head of the list of hardships in 2 Cor 4:8–10, which describes the ministry that identifies Paul with the death of Christ. The distress described by *thlipsis* can there be either external or internal for Paul (cf. 2 Cor 7:5); the other terms in this list, however, suggest that he primarily has in mind internal distress (Fitzgerald 1988: 172–74). The Thessalonians' reception of Paul's message about Christ meant that they identified with the tribulation of Paul and accepted the significance of Christ's suffering.

Another dimension of the Thessalonians' reception of the word was the distress of new converts, including those to philosophy and religion, as they experienced social, intellectual, and religious dislocation with attendant confusion, bewilderment, dejection, and even despair (see Malherbe 1987: 36–46; von Dobschütz, 73–74). The distress is captured in the prayer of Aseneth, a convert to Judaism: "I have no other hope but in Thee, Lord, for Thou art the father of orphans, the protector of the persecuted, and helper of the distressed (*thlibomenōn*) .... Look upon my orphan state, Lord, for I have fled to Thee" (*Jos Asen* 12:11; 13:11; see further Pax 1971: 240–41 on the *thlipsis* of the proselyte; Epictetus, *Enchiridion* 24, and H. Schlier in *TDNT* 3.139–40 for *thlipsis* in Epictetus's thought). The anxieties of converts may explain the *thlipsis* of Thessalonians, but such anxieties tend to characterize life after conversion, as the consequences of conversion (see 3:3–4). Paul, however, refers to *thlipsis* in conversion itself, and the response to his preaching must be examined for what in it could have caused the profound distress of which he speaks (Malherbe 1998: 231–44).

What is compressed in v 6 is expanded in Rom 1:18–2:16, which also utilizes elements from Hellenistic Jewish propaganda (Bornkamm 1969b: 47–70; Malherbe 1970b: 210–14). Paul's subject in Romans is the gospel, God's power to save (1:16), and to unfold that theme, Paul begins with a description of the human condition that makes God's salvation necessary. The moral dimension implicit in the items of the summary in 1 Thess 1:9–10 (God as Creator, idolatry, service to God, and divine judgment) becomes explicit and pronounced in Romans. Paul's intention in this opening section of Romans is to describe the human condition without Christ. Human beings are without excuse (Rom 1:20; 2:1; cf. 2:15) and subject to God's judgment (Rom 1:18; 2:2–6, 8, 16). This applies to Gentiles as well as Jews, for neither have pleased God but instead rejected his will for them in their lives (Rom 1:28–31; 2:21–22). Gentiles are culpable because they rejected the knowledge of God the Creator available to them in the creation and consequently lapsed into idolatry, the cause of sexual immorality (Rom 1:19–32; cf. Wis 14:12). They are storing up for themselves wrath on the day when God will judge them according to their works (Rom 2:5–8). Then they will experience inner turmoil (Rom 2:15–16), tribulation (*thlipsis*), and distress (*stenochōria*) because they had done evil Rom (Rom 2:8–9). This is eschatological judgment, but for Paul God's wrath is already revealed (Rom 1:18; see NOTE and COMMENT on 1 Thess 5:3–7; cf. Matt 3:7, 10; Luke 3:7, 9) and there is a continuation between the present and the future (Dunn 1.102). All this, Paul says, is according to his gospel (Rom 2:16).

The point of Paul's preaching, however, was not only to indict and cause anxiety and distress but to offer salvation to those who were indicted. Paul's gospel was a gospel of salvation (Rom 1:16) and demanded a decision that could not be delayed (2 Cor 6:1–2). The person who heard Paul's message was confronted by the prospects of destruction or salvation (2 Cor 2:14–17), which would cause profound anxiety. But acceptance of the gospel of Christ's vicarious death and his resurrection enabled believers to rejoice in the further *thlipsis* that would follow, knowing that they would be saved by Christ from God's wrath (Rom 4:24–25; 5:3, 9). Paul had preached such a gospel also to the Thessalonians. It offered them knowledge of God the Creator (1:9) that made possible a moral life (4:4). They had heard of the judgment that was coming (1:10; 4:6) but which already impinged on their lives and required them to live morally (5:3–5; cf. 2:16). They had also heard of Christ's death for them and that it was part of God's design to save them (5:9) and deliver them from God's wrath (1:10).

The Thessalonians' *thlipsis* is related to their imitation of the self-giving Paul and the Lord in receiving the word, which we have seen entailed identification with their self-giving. The picture that Paul presents in 2:2 of his ministry with the Thessalonians is not one in which he was free from anxiety, but one in which he was engaged in a profound struggle. We need not think, however, that Paul experienced unrelieved distress in his ministry. In his own life, as in that of his converts, tribulation was relieved by joy (e.g., 2 Cor 7:4; 8:2; cf. Rom 12:12). He exemplified in his ministry this combination of tribulation and joy. Identifying with the death of Christ, he too suffered and endured (1 Cor 4:9–13; 2 Cor 4:8–11; 6:3–10), in the process experiencing anxiety and joy (2 Cor 6:10; 7:4; cf. Rom 12:12), rejoicing at the prospect of salvation (Phil 1:18–19). By accepting Paul's gospel, the Thessalonians were similarly filled with deep distress and joy (1:6). Their anxiety would continue (3:3–4), but so should their joy (5:16), Paul providing an example (3:7–9).

We only have hints of the manner in which people responded when they accepted Paul's preaching (Malherbe 1987: 32–33), but it seems clear that the activity of the Spirit in prophets, at least, could result in a dramatic response of the total person (1 Cor 14:24–25). Conversion caused mixed emotions, for the message that brought about conversion cut to the very heart, laying open everything amiss in a person's life while holding out the promise of brighter prospects (see Lucian, *Nigrinus* 3–7, 35–37); for Paul, such a response to his preaching was the work of the Spirit, who was active in his preaching, engendering full conviction in himself, and was active in the Thessalonians, engendering joy in the midst of their distress. The message itself contained elements that would cause such a mixed response, which were quite different from the philosopher's call to a life of reason and virtue from the moral morass of irrationality.

Some converts to philosophy initially experienced deep disappointment because of their lack of knowledge and progress in their new life (e.g., Plutarch, *On Progress in Virtue* 77D). Paul's converts in Corinth seem not to have harbored any such self-doubt, but matters appear to have been otherwise with the Thessalonians. Paul's repeated references to what they already knew (see NOTE and

COMMENT on v 5) and were already doing (e.g., 4:1, 10; 5:11) would have the effect of building their confidence (see Malherbe 1987: 75–76). The hyperbolic reference to their exemplary character and evangelization in vv 7–8 is of the same order. Their preaching is implicit testimony to their own growth in faith, a report of which has gone forth everywhere.

In vv 6–8 Paul returns to the theme of his thanksgiving in vv 2–5, their labor in the gospel, but the perspective is now different. In v 4, he had claimed that they preached because of their election by God through his gospel; now he focuses on the relationship effected by their reception of the gospel. Paul and his gospel could not be separated, and to accept the gospel was in fact to accept it as represented by Paul and the Lord, the Lord as the content of what Paul preached, who had given his life for others, Paul as the one who gave himself to others in his preaching of that gospel. Imitation of Paul and the Lord caused them also to become an example to others, exemplifying the gospel and its inherent demand to be proclaimed.

The believers to whom they became examples could not have been those in Macedonia whom Paul had converted or, in addition, those who had become Christians after he had left Thessalonica, such as the Beroeans (Acts 17:10–12). Paul has been quite emphatic that the Thessalonians' imitation of himself took place through their acceptance of the gospel that he preached and exhibited in his life. That the Thessalonians as a result of their imitation themselves became an example to others therefore means that Paul has in mind those who came to faith as a result of his converts proclaiming the word in the way that Paul had done. The explanation in v 8 supports such an understanding.

The substantial compliment Paul pays them by saying that they in turn had become an example is once more pastoral. He differs from the convention of praising people in this manner, however, by not describing the Thessalonians as having become a paradigm through their developing moral excellence, but by accepting the word in deep distress and joy inspired by the Holy Spirit. Paul continues to adapt such conventions to a theologically informed pastoral care. Paul's pastoral concern is also evident in his geographical references. That there were Christians in Macedonia and Achaia, and in Judea (2:14), with whom the Thessalonians had much in common, meant that they were part of an extended network of believers. To be reminded of this would be of no little significance to a small band of Christians who may have felt abandoned by Paul and always faced the danger of being swallowed by the larger society (Riesner, 329–39).

Even allowing for Pauline hyperbole, the notice that the Thessalonian evangelism had extended beyond their city, to Macedonia and even Achaia, during the few months of the church's existence is remarkable. We have no information about how that took place, but we may infer from the mobility of society during the early Roman Empire that the Thessalonians, living on the Egnatian Way, had preached as they themselves traveled, or that persons they converted traveled and preached wherever they went (Malherbe 1983b: 62–65, 75–76, 95). Unfortunately, the individuals associated with Thessalonica in the NT appear much later and provide no information about the early months of the church's existence (see pages 66–67).

Paul does not say from whom he had heard about their faith and its expression in evangelism. He could not have received such a report before Timothy's mission, for he had been concerned about the stability of their faith in the face of tribulations and had sent Timothy precisely to strengthen their faith (3:2–5). Paul gives no indication even that he had heard about what may have been their condition and consequently sent Timothy; indeed, the impression he gives is that he sent Timothy out of his own need for assurance, because he knew that difficulties were bound to arise for them (2:17–3:5). The picture he sketches is an instantiation of the daily anxiety he had for his churches (2 Cor 11:28). Timothy reported upon his return that they were firm in their faith, that they still loved Paul and remembered him as their paradigm, news that relieved Paul of his anxiety about their faith (3:6–8). These are precisely the subjects Paul discusses in 1:3, 5–8. Paul here responds to Timothy's report by developing a theology of preaching and response that serves to strengthen his relationship with them. In the first instance, therefore, the news came to Paul from Timothy that, rather than wavering in their faith because of distress, they were preaching. That Paul generalizes the report once more magnifies their active faith. Paul does not, however, minimize their distress; he still thinks it necessary to find a place for it in the divine scheme of things (3:3–4), indeed in the very reception of the gospel (1:6).

What is remarkable about Paul's discussion of the Thessalonians' preaching of the gospel is how he connects it to their relationship with him. In his letter to another Macedonian church, he also speaks of people whose motivation to preach, whether noble or not, issued from their relationship with him (Phil 1:14–17), and Paul there also calls his readers to follow his example (Phil 1:29–30; cf. 3:17; 4:9). In 1 Thessalonians his evident purpose in doing so is to strengthen the relationship about which Timothy had assured him in order to lay a foundation for the advice he would give them in chaps. 4 and 5.

*vv 9–10.* Paul's explanation of why he need speak no more about their faith is not startling in light of his train of thought so far in the chapter, but it is nevertheless not what one might have expected. Paul might have said, we need not say anything about your faith, for people are talking about you (thus the correction of *pēri hymōn* for *peri hēmōn* by B and other witnesses); instead, he refers to what others are saying about him, thus once more connecting the Thessalonians' faith to himself and his entrance to them. People not only knew of the Thessalonians; they also knew that it was Paul's preaching that had brought them to faith in God. John Chrysostom, followed by other patristic commentators, saw in Paul's reference to his entrance an encomium to both himself and his readers, and thought that in reminding them of the content of his preaching he was engaging in comfort, encouragement, and exhortation (John Chrysostom, *Homilies on 1 Thessalonians* 2 [PG 62:400]; Theodore of Mopsuestia 2.8 Swete; Theophylact, *Exposition of 1 Thessalonians* 1 [PG 124:1285]).

In addition to its pastoral function, the account also has an epistolary function. Paul wrote to complete what was lacking in his readers' faith (3:10), and the response to his preaching summarized here is a summary of their faith in God (1:8). This summary catches a number of themes that are important in the letter, some of which have already been taken up earlier in chap. 1, others which will be taken up later. Attention has already been drawn to Paul's emphasis on God in the letter (see NOTE and COMMENT on vv 2, 4) as well as on faith, hope and love (see NOTE on v 3), and tribulation (see NOTE and COMMENT on v 6). Now Paul describes God in a way that prepares for much of what he will say about God later, for example, that God's judgment is assured (v 10; 2:16; 4:6; 5:9). That Christ saves from eschatological wrath (v 10) is repeated in 5:9, and the eschatological perspective dominates the letter throughout (e.g., 2:12, 16, 19–20; 3:13; 4:6; 4:13–5:10; 5:23).

The traditional Jewish elements in the summary should not lead to the assumption that what is in view was conversion to Jewish monotheism, on which followed a second, specifically Christian stage having to do with Jesus (correctly, Holtz 1977: 475–76; 1986: 61). From the start, the presentation of God is Christian, culminating in the saving work of Christ. Paul's usual way of referring to his preaching is to say that he had preached Christ crucified (1 Cor 1:23; 2:2; Gal 3:1; cf. 2 Cor 4:5). One may therefore be tempted to claim that here also it is Christ who predominates and to search for a description of God in vv 9–10 that distinguishes him from the God of the Jews as well as from the idols (Klumbies, 144–46).

For the sake of precision, however, it should be observed that Paul does not say that his summary in vv 9–10 is what he had preached, but that it is what they had converted to. The difference may appear to be slight, but formulating the issue thus allows Paul to focus on God and arrange the items chronologically in a way in which God predominates. Thus, the summary begins with a reminder that the readers had converted to God from idols, not the traditional order, from idols to God (Acts 14:15). "God" is then repeated and further characterized as living and true, Jesus is described in his relationship to God and as the object of God's action in his resurrection, and the last item in the summary speaks of God's wrath. God is the one who acts, from creation to eschatological judgment. The response to him that conversion calls for is service. Jesus, God's son, is here an eschatological figure who was raised from the dead and will deliver from God's judgment those who convert. Conversion requires that they await his coming from heaven.

The *thlipsis* caused by Paul's gospel continued, not only because of the unsettling elements in Paul's message (see COMMENT on v 6) or because of the social reorientation his converts had to go through as they redefined their relationships with society (Holmberg, 70–72). Conversion also required an intellectual metamorphosis: converts had to change their understanding about the divine and service to him, their understanding of human nature in relation to the divine, the cosmic scheme of things, and their moral accountability. All this, particularly the focus on morality, would have been thought by Paul's contemporaries to belong to the realm of philosophy rather than religion. But according to Paul, the mandate to undergo a metamorphosis of the mind had as its purpose "to prove what is the will of God, what is good and acceptable and perfect" (Rom 12:2), a statement that introduces the detailed ethical advice Paul gives in Rom 12–15.

That Christian morality should be grounded in religious belief and practice was not self-evident and required constant explanation and repetition. In pagan thought, cultic requirements of ritual purity aside, there was no essential connection between religion and morality, and religious conversion generally did not call for commitment to moral transformation (Nock 1933: 138, 155; Walter, 426–27; Meeks 1993: 18–36). A. D. Nock could find only four instances of such moral change associated with conversion to a cult, but change of a sort required by Christianity he found only in the time of Julian, when people were converted back to paganism from Christianity (Nock 1972: 475–76).

The moral dimension of the commitment Paul called for was already present in his mission preaching and continued in his earliest teaching to his new converts (Lührmann). It is significant that when Paul "fills up what (was) lacking" in the Thessalonians' faith (3:10) by giving detailed moral instruction, he introduces the section of the letter in which he does so by reminding them that he had taught them to please God (4:1), describes as God's will what he advises them to do (4:3), and concludes the section with a summary statement of God's design to save through the death of Christ (5:9–10). In this paraenetic section there are constant reminders of what his readers already know (4:1–2, 6, 9, 11; 5:1–2). The summary in 1:9–10 is itself a reminder and already serves a hortatory function as the readers are made to recall their conversion and its moral commitments (Meeks 1993: 33–36).

# 2. PAUL'S MINISTRY IN THESSALONICA, 2:1–12

In 2:1–12 Paul reminds the Thessalonians of his ministry with them, thus taking up the subject he introduced in 1:5b and returned to in 1:9–10. It is important, form critically, to decide how this autobiographical section of the letter relates to the thanksgiving. Is it part of the thanksgiving, or is it introduced by the thanksgiving, thus constituting the beginning of the body of the letter? If it is the latter, 2:1–12 would reveal Paul's primary intention in writing. Attention has therefore been drawn to the eschatological endings of Paul's thanksgiving periods which Schubert (4–9) thought marked the climax of those periods. There has, however, been disagreement on whether an eschatological climax is constitutive of a Pauline thanksgiving period, since Romans and Philemon lack one (O'Brien 1977: 261), or whether 1:10 should be viewed as such a climax. Another approach has been to examine formulas thought to mark the transition from thanksgiving to body to clarify where the thanksgiving ends and the body begins.

The view of this commentary is that chaps. 1–3 constitute a long thanksgiving in which Paul thanks God for what had transpired between himself and the Thessalonians. One of a thanksgiving's functions is to introduce themes that will be taken up later in the letter, and 2:1–12 does precisely that. It is frequently overlooked that in the "transitions" that have been discerned, the perspective changes from the addressees to the writer (Schnider and Stegner, 43–44), which is what happens here. Paul now writes in some detail about himself, not in defense, but to provide in his own person an example of the sort of life he will encourage his readers to live later in the letter. In the process of doing so, he affectively strengthens the bond between himself and his converts, thus laying the foundation on which he will base his exhortation. In this self-description he makes use of language he borrowed from the popular philosophers of his day and adapts it according to his own self-understanding and the needs of his readers. A more detailed treatment of this material and the function to which Paul puts it is reserved for the introduction to the COMMENT.

# TRANSLATION

2  ¹For you yourselves know, brethren, that our entrance among you was not powerless; ²on the contrary, although we had earlier suffered and been insulted in Philippi, as you know, we were emboldened in our God to speak to you the gospel of God in the midst of a great struggle. ³For our exhortation is not motivated by error or impurity, nor is it made with guile, ⁴but as we have been approved by God to be entrusted with the gospel, so we speak, not as though we are seeking to please human beings, but God, who tests our hearts, ⁵for we never used flattering words, as you know, nor did we use any pretext for covetousness, as God is our witness; ⁶nor did we seek glory from human beings, either from you or others. ⁷Although we might have made harsh demands on you as apostles of Christ, yet we were gentle in your midst; as a nurse who cares for her own children, ⁸so we, having tender affection for you, gladly determined to share with you not only the gospel of God but our very selves, because we had come to love you. ⁹For you remember, brethren, our labor and toil; working night and day in order not to burden any of you we preached the gospel of God to you. ¹⁰You yourselves are witnesses, and so is God, how holy, just, and blameless our behavior was to you believers; ¹¹you know that, as a father treats his own children individually, ¹²so we exhorted and comforted and charged you to conduct yourselves in a manner worthy of God, who calls you into his kingdom and glory.

# NOTES

2:1. *For you yourselves know, brethren.* The conjunction *gar* ("for") introduces either an explanation of what precedes, provides a reason for what precedes, or is resumptive, meaning almost "however" (Milligan, 16) or "indeed," which is its meaning here. It may join this sentence to the immediately preceding summary of what Paul's readers had responded to (1:9b–10), but since Paul now writes of his earlier preaching, it is more likely that a connection is made either with 1:5 or 1:9a. The repetition of *eisodos* suggests that 2:1 explains 1:9. The topic is the gospel (2:2, 4, 8, 9), however, which was introduced in 1:5, so over-ly fine distinctions need not be made. Paul draws a contrast between what was generally known about his mission in Thessalonica (1:9a) and what his readers themselves know (2:1). The contrast is strengthened by the emphatic position of *autoi* and the repeated use of *oidate* in this section (vv 1, 2, 5, 11), which reminds the Thessalonians (*mnēmoneuete* in v 9) of details about Paul's ministry among them.

*that our entrance among you.* The translation is smoother than the Greek, which emphatically makes *eisodos* the object of the Thessalonians' knowledge: "For you yourselves know, brethren, our entrance to you, that it did not take place in vain." Conceptually, *eisodos* is related to Paul's notion that God opens a door for him to preach the gospel in the midst of adversity (1 Cor 16:9; 2 Cor 2:12; cf. Col 4:3). Quite different is Epictetus's view of suicide as a door that God opens for the philosopher (*Discourses* 1.24.19; 3.8.6; 13.14).

Paul does, however, use terminology and images in 2:1–12 that are common in descriptions of philosophic missionaries, and that may be the case here. The word *eisodos* is used of the entrance to philosophy (Lucian, *Hermotimus* 73–74). Paul's *eisodos pros hymās* ("entrance among you"), however, more likely is a formulation equivalent to the philosophers' *eisienai pros* (Plutarch, *A Letter of Condolence to Apollonius* 111F; Epictetus, *Discourses* 1.30.1; 3.1.1), *eisienai eis* (Epictetus, *Discourse* 3.23.23; Dio Chrysostom, *Oration* 32.4, 20; cf. 7, 10 for *eisienai* used absolutely), and *ienai eis* (Dio Chrysostom, *Oration* 32.8). These formulations are the equivalent of coming *eis to meson* ("into the midst") or being *en tō mesō* ("in the midst," 2:7; see NOTE and COMMENT on 1:5). For the philosophers, such phrases described their public involvement, including their speech, which required courage, especially in view of the crowds' unpredictability. Crates, an early Cynic, was called the "Door Opener" because of his habit of entering every house (*eis pāsan eisienai oikian*) and admonishing its residents (Plutarch, *Table Talk* 2.632E; Diogenes Laertius, *The Lives of Eminent Philosophers* 6.86), and according to one textual tradition of Julian, *Oration* 6.200B, the Greeks inscribed the entrances to their houses, "Entrance [*eisodos*] for the Good Genius Crates." Paul differs from the philosophers in that it is God who gives him the boldness to speak (cf. v 2).

*was not powerless.* When used figuratively, *kenos* can mean either "powerless" or "fruitless," thus describing either character or result. Paul generally uses the word in the latter sense (1 Cor 15:10, 58; 2 Cor 6:1), but also uses it in the former sense of his preaching (1 Cor 15:14). In addition, he uses it in a specialized sense dependent on Isa 49:4, *kenōs ekopiasa* ("I labored in vain"; see 3:5; Gal 2:2; Phil 2:16; cf. Gal 4:14), but his use here is different (contra Denis).

The meaning of *kenōs* is best understood in light of the philosophical tradition to which Paul is indebted in this section. Philosophers distinguished themselves from professional orators, who spoke for display but did not engage in a contest (an *agōn*; *Rhetorica ad Alexandrum* 1440b13). Such speech the handbooks on rhetoric described as empty (*inanis* or *vacuus*), which reflected as much the characters of the speakers as their speeches (Quintilian 12.16–17), for they merely aimed at pleasing (Quintilian 12.73–74; cf. Dio Chrysostom, *Oration* 31.30). Flatterers, too, were accused of claiming their speech to be frank, contriving a counterfeit boldness (*parrēsia*) that was soft, weightless (*abarē*) and slack, empty (*kenon echousa*), etc. (Plutarch, *On How to Tell a Flatterer from a Friend* 59CD). In contrast, philosophers, in the most vivid terms, described their speech as contests (Plutarch, *On Progress in Virtue* 80B). This contrast between empty and powerless speech and emboldened frankness is also present in this Pauline text.

There are two further, related, reasons for taking *kenē* to mean "powerless" here. This section takes up 1:5, where Paul's preaching is described in a contrast between mere speech and power, which is similar to his thought here. More important, the second member of the antithesis in 2:1–2, the first of five complex antitheses in eight verses, has to do, not with the result but the character of his ministry.

*2:2. on the contrary, although we had earlier suffered and been insulted in Philippi, as you know.* The emphasis is on this second, positive member of the antithesis, introduced by *alla* ("on the contrary") and ending with *en pollō agōni* ("in the midst of a great struggle"). Within this long contrast there is another contrast, between Paul's own misfortune and conflict and his empowerment by God to preach the gospel. This entire statement is proof that his entrance had not been *kenos*. The passive aorist participles are concessive ("although"), thus heightening the boldness with which he preached in Thessalonica, in contrast to what he had experienced in Philippi. The Thessalonians knew of these experiences (see Acts 16:19–24, 35–40; cf. Phil 1:29–30), because either Paul and his companions or those who had brought him financial aid from Philippi (Phil 4:16) had told them about the hardships he had endured in Philippi.

It is futile to seek greater precision by distinguishing between *paschein* and *hybrizein*, for example, by arguing that the former describes physical suffering, the latter illegal treatment. The two words described different aspects of the same experience. The noun *hybris* is used in 2 Cor 12:10 at the end of the list of hardships, a rhetorical device Paul had inherited from the moral philosophers (Fitzgerald 1988). The word appears frequently in descriptions of the crowds' reaction to philosophers who, rather than flattering them, admonished them to improve themselves (Dio Chrysostom, *Orations* 9.9; 32.21; 72.10; Ps.-Diogenes, *Epistle* 20; Ps.-Heraclitus, *Epistles* 4.4; 8.3), and in such contexts appears in conjunction with *paschein* (e.g., Musonius Rufus, Fragment 10; Dio Chrysostom, *Oration* 34.34). While *paschein* describes suffering in general in such contexts, *hybrizein* tends to refer to the accompanying insults or abuse that might cause depression in most people.

*we were emboldened in our God to speak to you the gospel of God.* Both the tense and the meaning of *eparrēsiasametha* strengthen the contrast between Paul's actions in Philippi and those in Thessalonica. The ingressive aorist marks a decisive moment, he "began to be bold in speaking." The word *parrēsia* and its cognates describe a freedom of speech that had its roots in Athenian democracy but by Paul's day had come to have moral overtones. Originally, the free citizen had the right of free speech; then the philosopher, freed morally by his reason or his clear perception of what was correct, had the right, indeed the responsibility, in friendship to be frank in helping others by correcting them (H. Schlier in *TDNT* 5.871–86; Fredrickson; Glad, 104–25; and esp. Fitzgerald 1996).

Paul's reminder of his emboldened speech introduces the subject of the rest of the section, in which he lays out the motivation and manner of his work among his readers. Normally, *parrēsia* refers to frank speech, as it does in the NT (Acts 14:3; 18:26; 19:8; Phlm 8), but it also refers to confidence or boldness (Eph 3:12; Phil 1:20; 1 Tim 3:13). The two notions are combined in the word itself, especially when it is further strengthened, as in *pollē parrēsia* ("much boldness," 2 Cor 3:12; 7:4). It is also combined with *lalein*, as in *meta parrēsias . . . lalein* ("to speak with boldness," Acts 4:29, 31; cf. 9:27–28), and with *gnōrizein*, as in *en parrēsia gnōrisai to mystērion tou euangeliou* ("to make known with boldness the mystery of the gospel," Eph 6:19).

Paul's formulation here differs from such descriptions as well as those of the philosophers, who tended to use *tharsos* or *tharrein* with *parrēsiazein* to describe their courage or confidence to speak (Epictetus, *Discourse* 3.22.96; Dio Chrysostom, *Orations* 4.15; 6.57; 11.27; Plutarch, *On How to Tell a Flatterer from a Friend* 68D; esp. Musonius Rufus, Fragment 9, for the brave man's courage in speaking). Had Paul said simply *eparrēsiasametha en pollō agōni* ("I spoke boldly in the midst of a great struggle"), he would have sounded like the philosophers from whom he derived the term *parrēsiazesthai*. However, by adding what stands between *eparrēsiasametha* and *en pollō agōni* he radically changes the understanding of *parrēsia* by introducing two themes that run through the remainder of the section, both relating to God in his ministry.

The terms *eparrēsiasametha* and *lalein* enclose the words *en tō theō hēmōn* ("in our God"), which qualify Paul's emboldened speaking. The *en* is instrumental (see NOTE and COMMENT on 1:1), affirming that it is God who emboldens Paul to speak, but it is not clear whether *hēmōn* ("our") is intended to distinguish the Christians' God from pagan gods or whether, more likely, it describes their relationship with God, as Paul's use of "my God" does elsewhere (Rom 1:8; 2 Cor 2:21; Phil 1:3; 4:19).

Paul further differs from the philosophers in the content of what he is emboldened to speak about, *to euangelion tou theou* ("the gospel of God"). In 1:5, he had spoken of his gospel, but in this section, where he mentions God nine times, stressing God's role in his ministry, he refers to the gospel as God's (vv 2, 8, 9; cf. Rom 1:1; 15:16; 2 Cor 11:7) and to God, who had entrusted the gospel to him (v 4). So, here *tou theou* is not the object, but is a genitive of origin, the gospel that comes from God (Eadie, 57).

*in the midst of a great struggle.* The *agōn* that Paul refers to has been understood in three ways. On the basis of Acts 17:5–9 and interpreting 1 Thess 1:6 as referring to opposition, *agōn* has been similarly understood (Best 1972: 91–92; Wanamaker, 93). Thinking that the contest contrasts Paul's difficulties in Philippi with a happier experience in Thessalonica, Dibelius (1937: 7) thought that *agōn* refers to Paul's effort in preaching. A third view holds that the reference is to Paul's emotional struggle while preaching (Rigaux 1956: 405). These interpretations are not mutually exclusive when *agōn* is situated in the context of the philosophers' description of their endeavor.

As noted above, philosophers described their endeavor as a contest or struggle (see Pfitzner, 16–37), contrasting themselves to the emptiness or powerlessness of the sophists' speeches. Stoics, and especially Cynics, were fond of this athletic metaphor to describe the philosophic life (Epictetus, *Discourse* 3.22.51, 59; *Enchiridion* 51). Theirs, they held, was the real contest, requiring constant effort, unlike that of the degenerate athletes, who posture but do not enter the struggle (Dio Chrysostom, *Oration* 32.20). This contest was primarily internal, against various desires and passions, and personal, against such hardships as hunger, cold, thirst, anger, fear, and pleasure, although hardships imposed by others, such as exile or low esteem were also included (Dio Chrysostom, *Orations* 8.11–16, 20; 9.12; Ps.-Diogenes *Epistle* 31.4; Ps.-Heraclitus, *Epistle* 4.7). To a much lesser extent, the struggle was also against evil persons (Seneca, *On the Firmness of the Wise Man* 2.2; Lucian, *The Fisherman* 17).

Paul uses this athletic image in 1 Cor 9:24–27 (cf. Phil 3:14) to describe the effort he constantly put forth in his ministry. He also does so here, contrasting it to merely powerless speech. There is no need to exclude the possibility that he also has external opposition in mind, but what he mentions in vv 3–6 (error, uncleanness, guile, a desire to please, greed, desire for reputation) are precisely the sort of internal vices moral philosophers considered their antagonists in their struggle for virtue. Paul differs from them in two ways: his concern was not his own virtue but the preaching of the gospel, and God qualified him for his ministry.

2:3. *For our exhortation.* Paul offers, from here through v 12, an explanation of the motives and methods of his preaching. The *gar* ("for") connects this explanation to the entire clause *eparrēsiasametha en tō theō hēmōn lalēsai*, thus unfolding what it means to be emboldened by God to preach the gospel. This preaching is now described by the comprehensive term *paraklēsis* ("exhortation"), which allows Paul greater lattitude to explain why and how he preached. The verb admits of a wide range of meanings in common Greek usage, including "to call to," "to beseech," "to comfort," and "to exhort" (O. Schmitz in *TDNT* 5.774–76).

The word group and its Latin equivalents (*adhortatio, exhortatio, hortatio*) appear frequently in lists describing the various means of persuasion available to the philosophers who sought to influence people's behavior (Musonius Rufus, Fragment 49; Philo, *On the Life of Joseph* 73–74; Seneca, *Epistles* 94.21, 39; 95.34, 65). The term frequently describes consolation or is used in the lists in connection with other words describing consolation. Some commentators have thought that consolation is what Paul means here (Denis, 259–68; Kemmler, 168–73), an interpretation that would gain strength if the entire letter were to be understood as a letter of consolation (see Chapa 1994: 150, 159–60, for discussion and literature, and COMMENT on 4:13–18).

Most commentators correctly understand *paraklēsis* to mean "exhortation" or "appeal." As *lalein* in vv 2 and 4 makes evident, the reference here is to the address itself, and not the content of the speech. The present verb *estin* or *ginetai* ("is") must be supplied; Paul's description is of what he habitually does, not only what he had done in Thessalonica. The reference could be to an appeal that Paul made, or God made through Paul (see 2 Cor 5:20; 6:1), but that is not so different from "exhortation" unless the appeal is thought to be limited to the kind of preaching behind 1:9b–10. The majority of interpreters, however, take *paraklēsis* to refer to the gospel in a more general sense, somewhat akin to *peithein* ("to persuade," 2 Cor 5:11; Gal 1:10). The formulation *logos tēs paraklēseōs* ("word of exhortation") is used of a sermon that leads to conversion (Acts 13:15) as well as a long, theologically grounded moral discourse (Heb 13:22), and Paul appears to have both in mind here, as he moves from his readers' conversion (1:5, 9) to his ministry with them (2:3–12).

The variegated character that *paraklēsis* has for Paul appears from the fact that it seldom appears by itself, as it does in Rom 12:1 (Grabner-Haider, 7–8). Most frequently, it is interpreted or given precision by an accompanying word or words from the moral philosophers' vocabulary. The noun and verb are used nine times in this letter, which also contains nine other terms describing moral exhortation: 2:3, *paraklēsis*; 2:12, *parakalein, paramytheisthai* ("to comfort"), *martyresthai* ("to charge"); 3:2, *stērizein* ("to establish"), *parakalein*; 3:7, *parakalein*; 4:1, *parakalein*; 4:2, *parangelia* ("precept"); 4:6, *diamartyresthai* ("to charge"); 4:10, *parakalein*; 4:11, *parangellein* ("to give precepts"); 4:18, *parakalein*; 5:11, *parakalein oikodomein* ("to build up"); 5:12, *erotān* ("to beseech"), *proistanai* ("to care"), *nouthetein* ("to admonish"); 5:14, *parakalein, nouthetein, paramythein, antechestai* ("to help"), *makrothymein* ("to be patient").

The variety of terms associated with *parakalein* demonstrates the richness the word had for Paul. As for the immediate context, it is important that *paraklēsis* (v 3) and *parakalein* (v 12) form an *inclusio* to Paul's explanation of God's emboldening of his speech. It is Paul as exhorter, kerygmatic, and moral, who was so emboldened.

*is not motivated by error.* Again, *estin* or *ginetai* must be supplied. Paul's exhortation does not have its origin (*ek*, "from") in some lack of genuineness or misperception on his part. It is not necessary to see in this negative statement any eschatological significance (Denis, 268–75) or see Paul as distancing himself from heretics (Schmithals 1972: 143–45) or rebutting a charge of false prophecy (Horbury). Paul does use *planē* of eschatological error (2 Thess 2:11; cf. Matt 27:64), and it is used in connection with heresy (Eph 4:14; 2 Pet 2:18; 3:17), but there is evidence of neither in this context. In 2 Cor 6:8 *planos* ("impostor") is contrasted with "true" and "genuine," and that is likely the sense here (cf. the contrast between *alētheia* and *planē* in Rom 1:25, 27). Herbert Braun classifies passages in which the words *mē planāsthe* ("do not be deceived") occur (1 Cor 6:9; 15:33; Gal 6:7; Jas 1:16) as Stoic (H. Braun in *TDNT* 6.244–45), but the word *planē* and its cognates were in fact used by and of philosophers other than Stoics.

The term *apatē* ("deceit") and its cognates were more commonly used to describe false philosophers (e.g., Dio Chrysostom, *Oration* 32.9), who flattered people (Dio Chrysostom, *Oration* 48.10), but *planē* was also used (Crönert, 36; Euripides, *Rhadamanthus*, Fragment 660), and *planān* and *apatān* were used interchangeably (Dio Chrysostom, *Oration* 4.34–35, 37; Ps.-Cebes, *Table* 4–5; cf. Dio Chrysostom, *Oration* 4.114–15). The charlatans' behavior was scandalous, for it was the philosophers' task to teach people who had fallen into error about good and evil (Epictetus, *Discourses* 1.8.3–4; 3.22.23; 23.34; Marcus Aurelius, *Meditation* 9.42.6). Given Paul's indebtedness to the philosophers throughout this section, *planē* should probably be understood in light of that tradition, as a denial of ignoble motivation to preach. Paul differs from the philosophers, however, in that this is not an asseveration of his integrity, as in the philosophers, but a reference to God's entrusting the gospel to him (v 4a).

*or impurity.* The construction is exactly parallel to the previous clause: "nor is it motivated by impurity." The impurity Paul has in mind may be sexual, particularly because of its association with *planē*, which can have sexual overtones (Rom 1:27; 2 Pet 2:18; 3:17), and it is used in this sense in 4:7 (cf. 2 Cor 12:21; Gal 5:19; cf. Eph 4:19; 5:3). However, since Paul is here explaining the boldness with which he spoke, and the terminology he uses is derived from the philosophers, it is reasonable to seek clarification from them. According to Epictetus, the true Cynic will first purify his reason, his governing principle, before seeking to correct others (*Discourse* 3.22.19, 93; cf. Billerbeck 1978: 72–73), in contrast to the charlatan who dares to admonish without having purified himself of even the grossest immorality (Dio Chrysostom, *Oration* 77/78.36–38). That Paul is thinking along these lines is suggested by the antithesis in vv 4b–6, where, characteristically, it is God who tests the heart, discovering in it no desire to flatter or hunt for reputation. That God discovers purity of intention in Paul, however, does not exclude purity of morals as well.

*nor is it made with guile.* The *en* ("with") now describes the manner of his ministry. Guile (*dolos*) belongs to the language of polemic (see 2 Cor 12:16; cf. 4:2, in a list of hardships) and is not confined to any one tradition. It also appears in descriptions of the ideal philosopher (Dio Chrysostom, *Orations* 32.11 [*adolōs*]; cf. 12.48) or the ideal statesman who, like a father, will exercise leadership *adolōs kai katharōs* ("without guile and with purity"; Philo, *On the Life of Joseph* 68; cf. Julian, *Oration* 8.241CD, *katharās enteuxeōs, tēs adolou kai dikaias homilias* ["pure association, candid and just conversation"]; cf. Lucian, *Hermotimus* 59; Gerhard, 162–63).

**2:4.** *but as we have been approved by God to be entrusted with the gospel, so we speak.* As in the first antithesis, where the emphasis lay in the second, positive member, which specified God's action (vv 1–2), so also it does in this second antithesis (vv 3–4). The speech (*lalēsai*) of v 2 is now elaborated (*houtōs laloumen*, "so we speak," v 4b). Paul speaks in conformity with God's action. The adverb *kathōs*, in addition to introducing a comparison here ("as"), may have a causal sense: Because Paul had been approved by God, he preaches (cf. 1:4). Having earlier spoken of the boldness with which he had preached (*eparrēsiasametha ... lalēsai*), he now turns to qualities of character exemplified in his preaching. They are in contrast to the vices rejected in the negative in v 3, and the entire discussion in vv 3–12 is an unfolding of his *paraklēsis* and for the most part is described in a series of antitheses.

Paul has been qualified by God: "we have been approved [perf., *dedokimasmetha*] to be entrusted with the gospel" (GNTG 4.147). As to its meaning, *dokimazein* corresponds to *axioun* ("to deem worthy" or "to make worthy"; cf. 2 Thess 1:11; 1 Tim 1:12). Unlike the philosophers, who examined themselves for their fitness to undertake the philosophic task, for Paul it is God who tested him and approved him. This is in the tradition of the OT prophet, who is called by God, a tradition reflected in Paul's allusion in Gal 1:15 to Jer 1:5 (cf. Isa 49:1). He has in mind his call to be an apostle (see Gal 2:7, where the same expression, "to be entrusted with the gospel," is used; cf. 1 Cor 9:17). This notion was so basic to Paul's self-understanding that opponents who challenged the legitimacy of his apostleship would call for proof (*dokimē*) that Christ was speaking (*lalein*) in him (2 Cor 13:3; see the extensive use of the word group in vv 3–8).

*not as though we are seeking to please human beings, but God.* A new antithesis now explains v 4a, and is in turn explained by a complex antithesis in vv 5–7. The participial clause defines *laloumen* negatively. The participle (*areskontes*) retains the full sense of the present ("going about aiming to please") and is more emphatic because *ouch* ("not") is used instead of the more usual *mē* (GNTG 1.231–32; Milligan, 19). With *hōs* ("as though") the participle expresses intention.

Genuine philosophers insistently claimed that they did not seek to please people, particularly the crowds, in order to gain reputation or glory (*doxa*) from them (Dio Chrysostom, *Orations* 34.31–33; 66.26; Ps.-Plutarch, *On the Education of Children* 6B; Ps.-Crates, *Epistle* 35.2; Ps.-Diogenes, *Epistle* 11; see Glad, 112–14). To do so, they claimed, would be to behave like flatterers, the very antithesis to the frank speaker (Plutarch, *On How to Tell a Flatterer from a Friend* 51F, 53A). For the idea in the moral philosophical tradition, see Zeller 1996: 43–44.

Paul operates on a different level, informed by the characteristically OT goal of pleasing God (Gen 5:22; 6:2; Ps 25:3; 114:9; but see Epictetus, *Discourse* 1.30.1) rather than being a pleaser of persons (*anthrōpareskos*; Ps 52:6; cf. Ps.-Plutarch, *On the Education of Children* 4D; Eph 6:6; Col 3:22). Paul thinks of pleasing God primarily in moral terms (Rom 8:8; 1 Cor 7:32 [*kyriō*]; 1 Thess 4:1), but he also uses it, as he does here, of preaching the gospel. With the goal of doing everything for God's glory (*doxa*), not his own, he can nevertheless say that he attempts to please all people, seeking their advantage (*symphoron*), not his own (1 Cor 10:31–33; cf. 9:19–23). This attitude proved problematic (cf. Gal 1:10–11), even though he attempted to be clear that he was not encouraging self-gratification but seeking the good of others, as Christ had done (Rom 15:1–3; 1 Cor 11:1).

*who tests our hearts.* The phrase *hōs . . . areskontes* carries over; it is Paul's intention to please God. The description of God as the one "who tests our hearts" is an allusion to Jer 11:30 (cf. 12:3) and once more reveals Paul's prophetic self-understanding. By using the present participle *dokimazonti* ("who tests") Paul shows that he thinks of the testing that resulted in his being entrusted with the gospel as continuing. For Paul, "heart" describes the total inner person, the real self, in contrast to what a person may appear to be to others, and its dominant quality is to strive and to will (Bultmann 1951: 1.222). That he uses the plural and "our" is not evidence that he here includes Silas and Timothy (Henneken, 98–103; contra: Denis; on the editorial, epistolary, or authorial plural, see pages 86–89).

2:5. *for we never used flattering words, as you know.* The conjunction *gar* ("for") introduces a confirmation of what Paul has just said about the nature of his speech. The Greek reads, literally, "for not at any time were we [*egenēthēmen*] attended by a word [*en logō*] of flattery [*kolakeias*]." The *en* describes attendant circumstances, and *kolakeias* is a genitive of quality or definition (Moule, 78). "Word" takes up *lalein* (v 2), *paraklēsis* (v 3), and *laloumen* (v 4). As in v 3 three negatives formed the first member of an antithesis, so here three negative clauses (vv 4–6) form the first member of an antithesis whose second member concludes this long sentence in v 7. The general statement "not at any time" is confined to his behavior by "as you know": The Thessalonians themselves can vouch for him on the basis of what they had observed in Thessalonica (see NOTE on 1:5; cf. 2:1).

Flattery was opposed to frank speech (see Plutarch's discourse on friendship and *parrēsia*, *On How to Tell a Flatterer from a Friend*; Fitzgerald 1996) and the subject was just below the surface in v 3 and in Paul's denial that he had tried to please people. Flattery had been listed as a major vice for centuries (e.g., Dio Chrysostom, *Oration* 32.26, with *apatē*; Vögtle, 201; Glad, 23–36) and was used with comparative frequency by Philo and by Josephus (J. Schneider in *TDNT* 3.817–18). It is therefore striking that this is the only occurrence of *kolakeia* and its cognates in the NT, and that its synonym, *thōpeia*, does not occur at all. Paul's inclusion of the word here is most likely due to its appearance in descriptions of the ideal philosopher, to which he is indebted (Dio Chrysostom, *Oration* 32.11; Ps.-Heraclitus, *Epistle* 4.3).

*nor did we use any pretext for covetousness, as God is our witness.* The second negative clause is still dependent on *egenēthēmen*. The phrase *en prophasei pleonexias*, lit., "in a pretext of covetousness," is to be understood on analogy to *en logō kolakeias*, *en* describing attendant circumstance and the genitive *pleonexias* defining the pretext (Moule, 37–38; see Papyrus Geneva 271, col II, 26–28 [V. Martin, 85]; Lucian, *The Passing of Peregrinus* 13). The Thessalonians could vouch for Paul's speech; God testifies to Paul's motivation rather than to any outward act (cf. 2:10; Rom 1:9; 2 Cor 1:23; Phil 1:8, all early in his letters; cf. Lucian, *Phalaris* 1, beg.; contrast Diogenes Laertius, *The Lives of Eminent Philosophers* 8.22: philosophers should not call on God to witness). Greed was regarded as a major vice (G. Delling in *TDNT* 6.266–74; for fairly systematic discussions, see Horace, *Satire*, 1.1; Dio Chrysostom, *Oration* 17; cf. Malherbe 1996: 124–30), and Paul includes the word group in lists of vices (Rom 1:29; 1 Cor 5:10–11; 6:10; cf. Eph 4:19; 5:3, 5; Col 3:5). For a description that shares elements with this context, see 2 Pet 2:3, 14.

Paul was sensitive to the problem when raising money (2 Cor 9:5) but did not escape charges that he and Titus had taken financial advantage (*pleonektein*) of

the Corinthians (2 Cor 12:17–18). There is no evidence that he is here countering such accusations; this is his way of distancing himself from avaricious
preachers (see Apollonius of Tyana, *Epistle* 59, with flatterers; Lucian, *Nigrinus*
23–24; Diogenes Laertius, *The Lives of Eminent Philosophers* 6.51) in the same
manner that genuine philosophers did (Dio Chrysostom, *Oration* 32.11 ["not for
gain"]; cf. Gerhard, 58–62).

2:6. *nor did we seek glory from human beings, either from you or others.* The
present participle *zētountes*, still dependent on *egenēthēmen* to form a periphrasis, now describes Paul's intention not to seek glory (*doxa*) from any human
being. He had already implicitly denied seeking glory when he spoke of flattery
and pleasing people, now he is emphatically explicit, first in a general denial
("from human beings"), then in more specific denials ("from you," "from others"). This is now the third statement, introduced by a negative, with which Paul
confirms that he did not seek to please human beings but God. The stress here,
however, is on human beings. The change in the prepositions from *ex* (lit., "out
of") to *apo* ("from") does not appear to have any great significance (*GNTG*
4.259; but see NOTE on 1:8).

One might have expected Paul to say that he did not seek glory from humans
but did from God, as he said of his intention to please or not to please. Only in
a very few places, however, does Paul speak of his glory. In 2 Cor 6:8, he contrasts *doxa* with *atimia* ("dishonor"), and something like "honor" or "reputation"
is probably what it means in 1 Thess 2:6. Mostly, *doxa* has to do with Paul's ministry (2 Cor 3:7–11, "splendor," RSV; cf. 4:7), which he carries out for God's
glory (1 Cor 10:31; cf. 2 Cor 1:20; 4:17; cf. 8:19; 2 Thess 1:12). When he does
speak of his glory in 2:20, it has an eschatological reference (but see 2 Cor 3:18).
The same eschatological perspective is present in this self-description, which
finds its goal in v 12: Paul's aim is conduct worthy of God, who calls people into
his kingdom and glory. It would be incongruous for Paul to speak of his glory
without that eschatological element (cf. 2 Thess 1:5, 10).

There is no indication that Paul's reputation or lack of it was an issue in Thessalonica (see 3:6). Paul mentions it here because it was a standard part of the description of the ideal philosopher (Dio Chrysostom, *Orations* 32.11; cf. 66),
made necessary by the large number of sophists (Dio Chrysostom, *Oration* 12.5)
who craved reputation, notoriety, and honor (Dio Chrysostom, *Oration* 32.6, 10;
Lucian, *The Passing of Peregrinus* 13). Reputation is frequently associated with
wealth by the moral philosophers (Ps.-Crates, *Epistle* 8; Diogenes Laertius, *The
Lives of Eminent Philosophers* 6.93; Stobaeus, *Anthology* 4.82) and is part of the
stock description of charlatans. Paul's self-description in these verses denies that
he was guilty of craving self-gratification, money, or honor, the triad of vices already combined by Aristotle (*Nicomachean Ethics* 1.4 1095a23; cf. Plutarch, *On
Talkativeness* 502E; see Praechter, 69–70) but most frequently associated with
false philosophers (cf. the systematic treatment by Dio Chrysostom, *Orations*
4.84, 91–132; 66.1; see Gerhard, 97–90; Praechter, 60–61).

2:7. *Although we might have made harsh demands on you.* Paul further explicates his denial that he had sought *doxa* in another antithesis. This time the first

member is not a negative statement, as it has been in vv 1–6, but is introduced by a concessive participle, *dynamenoi*. The participle does not depend on *egenēthēmen* but is subordinate to *zētountes*, which it explains. The aorist tense of the participle refers specifically to his behavior in Thessalonica, not his experience in general, as a present participle would have done.

The *en* is adverbial, "to be harsh or burdensome" (Moule, 78). The meaning of *baros* is disputed. Paul's use of cognates of *baros* in v 9 and elsewhere (2 Thess 3:8; 2 Cor 11:9; 12:16) of financial support suggests that it means "burden" here and that, with the word, Paul alludes to *pleonexia* (Vulgate, *oneri esse*; Field, 199; many commentators). The participle, however, is connected to the immediately preceding clause. Furthermore, the meaning of the clause in which it appears is clarified by the second member of the antithesis, which speaks of gentleness. The word *baros* could also mean that Paul did not seek glory, although he could have acted *in gravitate*, with apostolic dignity, as a person with some weight. While *baros* does admit of such a meaning (Eadie, 64, cites Diodorus Siculus, *Library of History* 4.61; 16.8; Polybius, *Histories* 4.32.7; 30.15.1), in that sense it would not clearly be in contrast to gentleness. The meaning of *baros* must be different.

The subject matter of vv 1–12 is the nature of Paul's emboldened speech, and the meaning of the phrase *en barei dynamenoi* is discovered in ancient discussions of *parrēsia*. To the crowds who listened to philosophers the very word philosopher was harsh (*bary*), because of the demands that philosophers made of them (Maximus of Tyre, *Oration* 4.6). Philosophers knew that their *parrēsia* required them to modulate their speech (see NOTES on vv 11–12), at times being harsh (Dio Chrysostom, *Oration* 77/78.36; Diotogenes, 75,1–8 Thesleff; Glad, 71–98), and a certain type of Cynic with a pessimistic view of the human condition thought that the crowds could only be benefited by harsh scolding (Malherbe 1989: 16–20, 39–41).

Philosophers who made a profession of harshness did find people who admired them for it (Lucian, *Philosophies for Sale* 10). In fact, their opponents charged that their biting speech was designed to gain them *doxa* (Plutarch, *On Progress in Virtue* 81CE; see Dio Chrysostom, *Oration* 4.125–28, for a vivid description of the phenomenon without using *doxa*). That Paul in discussing his emboldened speech should deny having sought glory from people despite being able to make harsh demands is thus quite in keeping with the traditions he is using.

*as apostles of Christ.* This is the only time that Paul uses *apostolos* in this letter and is the earliest use of the term in all his letters. Some commentators, thinking that the plural "apostles" must include Silas and Timothy, who were not apostles in the special way the Twelve and Paul were (1 Cor 9:1; 15:3–10), have held that "apostle" here must have the more general meaning of envoy or missionary that it has elsewhere in Paul (Rom 16:7; 1 Cor 4:9; Phil 2:25). That is unlikely, however, for the issue here, related to Paul's manual labor (see NOTE and COMMENT on v 9), is so personal to Paul that Silas and Timothy could not be included. Paul still uses an epistolary plural (see pages 86–89) as he expresses his view of an apostolic prerogative he could have claimed.

Paul never refers to his apostleship in order to claim special privileges, al
though his apostleship does furnish him certain rights. Thus in 1 Cor 9:1–6, he
asserts his right to financial support only to forgo it (Malherbe 1995b). His procedure is the same here, although the subject of the illustration in that passage,
forgoing one's right to financial support, is not. Paul's defense of his apostleship
in 2 Cor 10–13 is instructive. While asserting his apostleship (11:5; 12:11–12)
and his apostolic right to adopt a harsh manner of speech (10:7–11; cf. 13:10),
he chose to be mild when present (10:1–2). He does threaten harsh treatment
(13:1–5, 10; cf. 1 Cor 4:21), but his opponents know that he is mild of mien and
criticize him for it (10:10). At his most diplomatic, in Phlm 10, he also forgoes
his right to *parrēsia*, choosing rather to exhort, as an old man and a prisoner! See
1 Pet 5:3; Mark 10:42 and parallels for domineering church leaders.

The Thessalonians also know of the way in which Paul had spoken when he
was with them, but again there is no evidence that they criticized him for it. Paul
mentions his right to demanding speech simply for rhetorical purposes. By introducing it only to reject it in the second member of the antithesis, he places
the weight on the second part, his gentleness.

*yet we were gentle.* What Paul says in vv 7b–8 is in antithesis to his denial that
he had sought glory. He closes this last antithesis in the series in a manner different from the previous ones. He uses *alla* ("but," here translated "yet" because
of the concessive *dynamenoi*) here as in all the preceding antitheses, but in
those he had described God's action in the second part, the position of emphasis (vv 2, 4). But here, Christ is mentioned in the first part and Paul's demeanor
in the second (cf. also v 8). From here on Paul lays the stress on the style of his
ministry.

The major text critical problem in the letter occurs here. The textual evidence
(P66 ℵ* B C* D* F G Ψ*) favors reading *egenēthēmen nēpioi* ("we were infants")
over *egenēthēmen ēpioi* ("we were gentle"; ℵ2 A C2 D2 Ψ2 The Majority Text).
Furthermore, *nēpioi* is the more difficult reading, and *ēpioi* (elsewhere in the NT
only in 2 Tim 2:24) in the manuscripts in which it occurs can be understood as
an attempt to make the text more easily intelligible (see Spicq 1958: 3.107–10).
The variant readings could be explained in terms of transcriptional error. It
could be described as a case of haplography, that is, the n in *nēpioi* was inadver-
tently omitted after the immediately preceding final n in *egenēthēmen*. Conversely, dittography could explain the *nēpioi* as the result of inadvertent repetition of the final n in *egenēthēmen*.

The problem is an old one, patristic commentators already having come down
on both sides, as their successors would in every generation since (see Crawford,
69–70). Despite the weight of textual evidence, however, the majority of interpreters and translations have read *ēpioi* (but see Crawford, van Rensburg, Fowl,
Gaventa), primarily on the grounds that *nēpioi* would be too incongruous, since
the change in metaphor from infants to nurses in the same verse would be in-
comprehensible, and the fact that Paul uses the image of infants unflatteringly
elsewhere (Rom 2:20; 1 Cor 3:1; 13:11; Gal 4:1, 3). Thus the extreme difficulty
of the reading in this case works against it (Metzger, 630). Another reason for pre-

ferring *ēpioi* is that it fits in the traditions about bold speech that Paul has been using (so also Koester 1985: 224–26). The philosopher's speech, at times harsh, should also be *ēpios*, it was held, reflecting a philanthropic attitude rather than an unreserved dourness, such as characterized some pessimistic Cynics (for the evidence, see Malherbe 1989: 42–43).

*in your midst.* For *en mesō hymōn*, see on *eisodos*, v 1. The expression "is as if one should say, we are as one with you, not taking the higher lot" (John Chrysostom, *Homilies on 1 Thessalonians* 2 [PG 62:403]; cf. Luke 22:27). It refers, in addition, to an event the Thessalonians had observed.

*as a nurse who cares for her own children.* Paul illustrates the gentleness he claims by means of a comparison (*hōs ean . . . houtōs* ["as . . . so"]) with a wet nurse's care of the children in her care. Such women were a well-known feature of Roman society (Bradley 1986; 1991; cf. Vilatte). One of their qualifications was kindness, and they were remembered for it (Malherbe 1989: 43). The word *trophos* occurs only here in the NT, but the language of nurture is applied to learning, as it was in the Greek world (1 Cor 3:2; Heb 5:12–14; 1 Pet 2:2). The image of a bird warming (*thalpein*) her eggs or caring for her young is found in the OT (Deut 32:6; Job 39:14), but it is universal (cf. Plutarch, *On the Cleverness of Animals* 962E). More important for us is the use of *thalpein* to describe the solicitous care for someone who is ill (Alciphron, *Epistle* 4.19.9) and, particularly, in context with *ektrephein* ("to nourish"; cf. Eph 5:29) of intellectual nurture (Plutarch, *On Listening to Lectures* 48C; cf. Sir 15:2–3).

It is the Greek and not Jewish (Gutierrez, 91–101) usage that informs Paul's application of the image of the nurse. The image of the gentle nurse who knows her charges and cares for them was used in contrast to harsh, indiscriminate *parrēsia*. What was important was that one be timely in delivering sharp reproof (Malherbe 1989: 136–45). Warning against untimely frankness and stinging reproof, Plutarch adduces the example of nurses: "When children fall down, the nurses do not rush up to berate them, but they take them up, wash them, and straighten their clothes and, after all this is done, then rebuke and punish them" (*On How to Tell a Flatterer from a Friend* 69BC; Malherbe 1989: 43–45; see further on vv 11–12).

The pathos with which Paul writes is enhanced by reference to the nurse's "own" children. The pronoun *heautēs* retains its reflexive force ("her own") despite the fact that reflexive pronouns by Paul's time functioned as personal pronouns (as in v 12; BDF §283). The reflexive pronoun in the genitive in the attributive position stresses a relationship or possession in contrast to others, as in v 8; 4:4; 2 Thess 3:12 (Zimmer, 267–68; contrast Gal 4:25). In 1 Cor 7:2, it is used interchangeably with *idios*. Paul thus intensifies the image by referring to a special degree of gentleness, that of a woman already known for gentleness in work for which she is paid, for her own children. See further on v 11.

2:8. *so we, having tender affection for you, gladly determined.* The apodosis of the comparison is introduced by *houtōs* ("so"), which goes with *eudokoumen* ("gladly determined"). The comparison with a nurse is thus made in the first place to describe the deliberate decision to deal with the Thessalonians in a certain manner. Used of divine determination (1 Cor 1:21; 10:5; Gal 1:15), *eudokoun* is also used by Paul to describe his own free decision in regard to different aspects of his ministry (Rom 15:26–27; 2 Cor 5:8; 12:10; 1 Thess 3:1). The imperfect tense of the verb expresses a continuous determination to give himself to his converts.

The translation, "having tender affection," attempts to render *omeiromenoi*, a present participle that modifies *eudokoumen*. This word occurs only in Job 3:21 and Ps 62:2 Symmachus in the OT, and its precise meaning is no clearer today than it was to ancient lexicographers, who sought to explain it by *epithymein* ("to desire" or "to yearn for"), an explanation that is supported to a degree by grave inscriptions from the fourth century A.D. (*CIG* 2.4000; Milligan; Baumert). But the meaning "to long for" or "to yearn for" cannot be sustained for our passage, for Paul describes his feeling when he was still with the Thessalonians. Attempts at etymological explanation have completely failed.

The comparison with a nurse suggests that the word may describe a nurse's cooing over her charges (Wohlenberg, 52–53). Paul may have used the word for its onomatopoeic effect. The image of the nursery is also used in Ps.-Socrates, *Epistle* 25.2:

> For there is nothing dearer to me than philosophy and the discourses that deal with philosophy. I was nurtured [lit., "nursed"] from my youth up, as one might say, in the Socratic lullabies in every appropriate and holy place, partly in the Academy, and partly in the Lyceum.

For a negative view of philosophers who croon myths as nurses do to children, see Julian, *Oration* 7.204A, 206D.

*to share with you not only the gospel of God but our very selves, because we had come to love you.* Once more an antithesis elaborates a statement. The form *ou monon . . . alla kai* ("not only . . . but") is used because the second member embraces the first, stresses it, and will itself shortly be clarified (see NOTE on 1:5). The infinitive *metadounai* takes two objects, the gospel and Paul's *psychē* ("soul"). Paul's preaching was more than oral communication; it was a giving of himself (see NOTE on 1:5), which is the emphatic point of comparison with the nurse. By sharing his *psychē*, Paul shared himself totally (cf. Acts 15:26). Bruce (1982: 32) comments: "The *psychē* is here the seat of affection and will (cf. *mia psychē*, Phil 1:27; *sympsychos*, Phil 2:2; *isopsychos*, Phil 2:19). The meaning is not simply 'we were willing to give [lay down] our lives for you' but 'we were willing to give ourselves to you, to put ourselves at your disposal, without any reservation.' "

The passages Bruce cites reflect the ancient topos on friendship (Malherbe 1995c: 815), to which the idea of sacrificing or offering oneself also belongs (G. Stählin in *TDNT* 9.152; cf. Seneca, *Epistle* 9.10–11; John 15:13). John Chrysostom commented on this passage by producing a long discussion of friendship (*Homilies on 1 Thessalonians* 2 [PG 62:403–6]). Paul's reason (*dioti*) for his willingness to share himself, that he had come to love them, fits well with this interpretation. His love for the Thessalonians and his consequent care found their counterpart in the solicitousness of a wet nurse. There is no need for the romanticism that draws out the metaphor of suckling as a transmission of vital power (so Lünemann, 472; Alford, 257).

2:9. *For you remember, brethren, our labor and toil.* "For" can be resumptive, picking up *alla* (v 7) and further illustrating *oute zētountes . . . doxan* ("nor seeking glory," v 6; Frame, 102) only loosely tie what follows to the preceding, thus meaning "in effect" (Rigaux 1956: 423) or "and" (Best 1972: 103); or be causal, introducing proof of his love for them. In view of how manual labor was viewed in Paul's society and the importance he attached to his own practice (see COMMENT), the last is to be preferred. He also makes a connection between love and manual labor in 4:9–12. Paul now moves from an image (of the nurse) to historical practice (his manual labor) to underscore his self-giving to his readers.

Having discussed his motivation and demeanor in preaching, he now affirms that the more specific manner in which he conducted his ministry was undertaken freely (*eudokoumen*) and not as an obligation. He describes his labor in affective terms that properly represent the way it was viewed, and further strengthens the bond necessary for the paraenesis of chaps. 4 and 5. The present indicative, *mnēmoneuontes*, in this case is stronger than the imperative: he remains in their memory. As he had remembered their *kopos* in 1:3, they remember his. Up to now, Paul had referred to his readers' knowledge (1:5; 2:1, 2, 5), now he is explicit about their recollection, a feature of paraenesis (see pages 82, 83, 84).

In 1:5, *kopos* was used in a figurative sense, labor in the gospel. The association of the word with the hard labor of the workshop (Harnack 1929) is accentuated by the addition of *mochthos*, used only by Paul in the NT and always in association with *kopos* (2 Cor 11:27; 2 Thess 3:8). The two words occur elsewhere in combination (T Job 24.2; BAGD, 528), *mochthos* describing the fatiguing, painful side of labor (Spicq 1991: 1050–51). Paul thus wishes to convey, not just that he had worked, but the strenuous and exhausting demands of labor on him, which he had undertaken willingly (*eudokoumen*) out of his love for them.

*working night and day in order not to burden any of you we preached the gospel of God to you.* The demanding nature of his work is further accentuated by his reminder that he had worked night and day (*nyktos kai hēmeras*), the genitive meaning that he had worked during the night and day, not throughout night and day, which would have required the accusative. The normal working hours were from sunrise to sunset, but there is evidence that laborers sometimes had to start working before sunrise in order to earn their bread. Some manual laborers could attain relative financial security by practicing their trades, but an itinerant tentmaker like Paul (Acts 18:3; cf. 1 Cor 4:12; 9:6; 2 Thess 3:10), although able to be self-sufficient (Phil 4:14), would still be poor (2 Cor 6:10) and suffer deprivation (1 Cor 4:11; 6:5; 11:27). On the subject, see Hock, 31–35.

Paul's purpose in working so hard was not to burden (*pros to mē epibarēsai*) any of his converts, by which he would also incidentally distinguish himself from many freeloading and avaricious preachers of the day (see NOTE on v 5). He uses *epibarein* (2 Thess 3:8), *katabarein* (2 Cor 12:16), and *abarēs* (2 Cor 11:9) elsewhere to make the same point, but here, as the context shows, he offers his unwillingness to burden them as proof of his love for them. Furthermore, the present participle *ergazomenoi* denotes action contemporaneous with the main verb *ekēryxamen*: Paul's hard labor accompanied his preaching of God's gospel to them (*eis hymās*). The use of *eis* with the recipients of a message (cf. Mark 14:9; Luke 24:47) is a Semitism and the equivalent of a pure dative (1 Cor 9:27; BDF §207, 1; Moule, 69). Once more, the self-portrait he sketches is one in which his preaching is inextricably connected with a giving of himself.

2:10. *You yourselves are witnesses, and so is God.* The absence of a connecting particle leaves the relationship of the description of Paul's pastoral care in vv 10–12 to what precedes unclear. Verses 10–12 could still be controlled by *alla* in v 7 (Frame, 103), or be closely related to v 9 (Dibelius 1937: 9; Wanamaker, 100), or (with v 13) be a conclusion to v 9 in which Paul offers the ultimate proof of his selflessness (von Dobschütz 1909: 98), or be a more general summary of what he had described in detail in vv 1–9 (Ellicott, 24; Lünemann, 474; Wohlenberg, 54), or be a move from a characterization of Paul's evangelism to his pastoral care (Marshall 1983: 72; Roosen 1971: 58).

These verses conclude Paul's self-description but, as vv 11–12 will show, are not a general summary of what precedes, but a quite detailed description of Paul's ministry in Thessalonica. Furthermore, while logical and chronological distinctions can be made between evangelism aiming at conversion and post-conversion nurture, it is not useful to make them here. During his relatively short stay in Thessalonica, Paul would still have been striving to convert some people at the time that he was caring for some already converted. He has both in mind as he reminds his readers, "those who believe" (cf. 1:7), how he had conducted himself during the entire period with them (Holtz 1986: 87).

The asyndeton has a rhetorical effect, lending strength to what follows. So does Paul's calling the Thessalonians and God as witnesses to his conduct. He concludes with an appeal to the Thessalonians' own knowledge as he had throughout his self-description (vv 1–2, 5, 9) and will again in v 10. That "you" stands in the position of emphasis ("yourselves" supplied in English to bring this out) indicates that his major interest is in reminding his readers of what they had observed. (Cf. Isocrates, *Nicocles* 46, "you yourselves are my witnesses.") God also is adduced as witness to elevate the relationship to a higher level. For the same order, see 1:6; 2:5, 15 (cf. Rom 1:9; 2 Cor 1:23; Phil 1:8 for God as witness).

*how holy, just, and blameless our behavior was to you believers.* The translation smooths what would read, literally, "how holily and justly and blamelessly we became among you believers." Adverbs with *einai* or *ginesthai* could function as adjectives (BDF §434) or, more likely, could be taken as secondary predicates defining the form and manner of *egenēthēmen* (GNTG 3.226; Ellicott, 24). The dative *hymin* ("to you") is more problematic. It likely is not a dative of advantage, indicating how Paul had acted for their sake. The view, already held by patristic commentators, that *hymin* is a dative of opinion or credit (GNTG 3.239; cf. Matt 18:17; 1 Cor 1:18), is probably correct (see Lünemann, 479). That Paul further

specifies *hymin* as "believers" does not mean that he did not care about the opinion of nonbelievers (cf. 4:12). Rather, he defines the circle to whom he had extended the pastoral care described in vv 11–12, those whom God calls into his
kingdom and glory, thus maintaining the focus on his relationship with them
(v 10).

The stringing together of adverbs at the beginning of the description shows the
importance Paul attaches to the behavior they describe. The first two are positive, the third negative. The former, taken together (*hosiōs kai dikaiōs*), appear
three other times in the NT (Luke 1:75; Eph 4:24; Titus 1:8) and not in the LXX.
This is a Greek construction which, since Plato (*Gorgias* 507B), described the
sensible man's action as regards people as just (*dikaios*), and as regards the gods,
holy (*hosios*) (Polybius, *Histories* 22.10.8; Dio Chrysostom, *Oration* 69.2; PParis
63 [*UPZ* p. 625, 14–18], but used without specific reference by Diogenes Laertius, *The Lives of Eminent Philosophers* 6.5).

The negative adverb (*amemptōs*) is used in the NT only here and in 5:23,
where the reference is eschatological (thus also the adjective, 3:13; cf. *anegklētos*
in 1 Cor 1:8; Col 1:22 [with *hagios* and *amōmos*]). In view of v 12b, the eschatological perspective may be present, but the *hymin* shows that he has in mind
the way he appeared while preaching the gospel (cf. Phil 2:15–16, with *amōmos*).
The viewpoint is similar to that of the Pastoral Epistles, where blamelessness is a
qualification of church functionaries (1 Tim 3:2 [*anepilēmptos*]; 1 Tim 3:10;
Titus 1:6, 7 [*anegklētos*]).

2:11. *you know that, as a father treats his own children individually.* The translation attempts to render a clause that contains three comparatives and no finite
verb, reading, literally, "even as you know [*kathaper oidate*] how [*hōs*] each one
of you as [*hōs*] a father his own children." Paul uses *kathaper* instead of *kathōs*
(1:5; 2:2, 4–5) for the sake of variety. Having already said that they were witnesses
to his conduct, he again refers to their knowledge as a way of introducing his reminder of his pastoral care. The first *hōs* introduces the main feature of his care,
the second a metaphor that strengthens his description. The terminology and
imagery he uses to describe his care are derived from the moral philosophers, but
not so the goal of that care.

Paul uses the image of the father in a wide-ranging manner to describe his relations with his converts (Gutierrez; von Allmen; Best 1988: 29–58). He became
their spiritual father through the gospel (1 Cor 4:15; Phlm 10; cf. 1 Tim 1:2) and
addressed them as his children (1 Cor 4:17). In addition to using it of his spiritual paternity, he also used such language metaphorically (*hōs patēr*, Phil 2:22;
*hōs tekna*, 2 Cor 6:13) as he does here (*hōs patēr*). The imagery was used in Judaism (e.g., Prov 3:1; 4:1; Sir 7:3; 39:13), but Paul's use of it here is more indebted to the Greek tradition of moral instruction, where the teacher spoke as father to his disciples, whom he called his children (Malherbe 1989: 54–55; 1992:
283; Plato, *Phaedo* 116A). The image was thought particularly apt because of the
favorable disposition of fathers to their children (Philo, *On the Life of Moses*
1.328; Musonius Rufus, Fragment 8 [p. 64, 14 Lutz]; Iamblichus, *The Life of
Pythagoras* 31.198). Such a father adapts his instruction to the nature and emo-

tional condition of his children (Ps.-Plutarch, *On the Education of Children* 13DEF). The notion of modulating his care is implicit in Paul's claim that he had treated them individually, lit. "each one of you" (*heis hekastos hymōn*; see *heis ton hena*, 5:11; cf. Acts 20:31). The nurse's ministrations were used in Paul's day of gentle adaptability (see NOTE on v 7), which he now applies to the father. Theophylact saw this similarity between the nurse and father (*Commentary on 1 Thessalonians* 2 [PG 124:1292]), and John Chrysostom was impressed by Paul's not neglecting anyone (*Homilies on 1 Thessalonians* 3 [PG 62:407]). Since such use stresses the relationship between a father and his children, the reflexive character of the pronoun ("his own") is to be retained (see NOTE on v 7).

The need for individual instruction was generally recognized in ancient psychagogy, the endeavor that aimed at moral and intellectual growth and combined spiritual exercises, psychotherapy and psychological counseling (Malherbe 1992: 301–4; Glad, 17–23; see further NOTES and COMMENT on 5:11, 12–15). Plato has Socrates say that he came "to each one of you individually like a father or an elder brother and [urged] you to care for virtue" (*Apology of Socrates* 31B). Even philosophers who spoke to large crowds realized the necessity of private instruction. Dio Chrysostom maintained that the good philosopher would lead people to virtue "partly by persuading (*peithōn*) and exhorting (*parakalōn*), partly by abusing (*loidoroumenos*) and reproaching (*oneidizōn*) . . . taking them aside privately one by one (*idia hekaston*) and also admonishing (*noutheton*) them in groups" (*Orations* 77/78.38; cf. 13.31; 32.6). Converts to philosophy in particular needed such measured attention (Rabbow, 267–75; Glad, 137–52).

*2:12. so we exhorted and comforted and charged you.* Paul now specifies the different types of care in which he had engaged, adapting them to his converts' individual needs. Such adaptation is fully in line with the moralists, who varied their speech according to their listeners' needs (Seneca, *Epistles* 94.39, 49; 95.34, 65; Clement of Alexandria, *Christ the Educator* 1.1,9; Hadot, 168–72; Glad, 58–69). Paul encourages his readers at much greater length in 5:11–22 to follow the same practice. This is the second bracket of the *inclusio*, beginning in v 3, that explains Paul's *paraklēsis*. Within this *inclusio* Paul has gradually moved from a description of his ministry in general to an emphasis on his conduct in Thessalonica, and here he summarizes the nature of his pastoral care. The three participles are grammatically still dependent on *egenēthemen* (v 10) and specify further how his conduct was holy, just, and blameless.

Of the three activities Paul describes, *parakalein* ("to exhort") is the most general and inclusive (see NOTE on v 3). The nature of his exhortation is specified more particularly in the two that follow, *paramytheisthai* ("to comfort") and *martyresthai* ("to charge") (Grabner-Haider, 11–13; Holtz 1986: 90). The three are not synonymous (so von Dobschütz 1909: 101) but represent nuances in the range of Paul's care. Paul always uses *paramytheisthai* or its cognates with some form of the word group *paraklēsis* (5:14; 1 Cor 14:3; Phil 2:1), and *parakalein* could by itself also describe consolation or comfort (cf. 4:18). He has in mind a particular kind of comfort, the condolence or consolation expressed in the literary type *paramythētikos logos* or *consolatio* (see further COMMENT on 4:18; 5:14; Malherbe 1990b: 387–88; Chapa 1994). Such consolations addressed people who were bereaved or suffered other distresses such as poverty, social criticism or scorn (Cicero, *Tusculan Disputations* 3.57–58). People were also prepared for misfortunes or distress they might encounter (Cicero, *Tusculan Disputations* 3.28–60, 77; 4.12, 14, 37, 60, 64; Seneca, *Epistles* 2.15; 91.4; Epictetus, *Discourse* 3.24.103–4). This premeditation of hardships was part of the moral philosopher's psychagogy (bibliog. in Malherbe 1990b: 387 n. 58). Consolation thus conceived partakes of the nature of exhortation more than it does of the sympathy characteristic of modern condolences. Paul reminds his readers in 3:3–4 that when he had still been with them, he cautioned them about tribulations and distress (*thlibesthai*) to come. For what these might have been, see COMMENT on 1:6 and 3:3–4.

Towards the other end of the spectrum of care was Paul's charging his converts to conduct themselves in a certain manner. The word *martyresthai* means to make an emphatic declaration (Gal 5:3; Eph 4:17) and differs from *diamartyresthai* only in that the latter is stronger than the former and is parallel to *keleuein* ("to command"), as in *CPJ* 153,82, 89 (cf. Acts 20:21). In 4:6 Paul provides an insight into the subject matter on which he had strictly charged his readers.

*to conduct yourselves in a manner worthy of God.* The purpose (*eis to* plus infinitive) of the activity described with the participles is radically different from the moralists, whose traditions Paul has been using and modifying. The moralists sought to lead people to virtue, a fulfillment of human potential, while Paul views human conduct in relation to God (see COMMENT on 1:10; more fully on 4:1–8). The translation "conduct" renders *peripatein*, lit., "to walk about," a notion is used in a moral and religious sense only in the LXX (Prov 28:6; Isa 59:9), and especially by Paul (4:1; 1 Cor 7:17; 2 Cor 4:2; Phil 3:17–18; H. Seesemann in *TDNT* 5.944–45). It is equivalent to the more Greek *anastrephein* (2 Cor 1:12; cf. Eph 2:3; 1 Tim 3:15; cf. *anastrophē* [Gal 1:13; cf. Eph 4:22; 1 Tim 4:12]) or *politeuesthai* (Phil 1:27; cf. Acts 23:1).

The adverb *axios* ("in a manner worthy") occurs in Pauline literature with *peripatein* (cf. Eph 4:1; Col 1:10), *politeuesthai* (Phil 1:27), and *prosdechesthai* (Rom 16:2), thus only in ethical contexts. It essentially means "suitably" and is given fuller expression by a noun in the genitive, with which it is used (resp. *klēseōs, kyriou, euangeliou, hagion* ["call, Lord, gospel, saints"]), which provides the motivation for the obligation expressed in the verb (von Dobschütz 1909: 101). The view that the moral life is to be congruent with God is characteristically Jewish and Christian, but Stoics could use similar religious language to express the goal of living in cosmic harmony (cf. Epictetus, *Enchiridion* 15, of conducting oneself [*anastrephesthai*] so as to be worthy [*axios*] of the banquet of the gods).

*who calls you into his kingdom and glory.* The language of God's call is from the OT (esp. Isa, e.g., 41:9; 42:6; 43:1; 45:3). The textual evidence for the present participle, *tou kalountos* (B D G 33 81), is stronger than that for the aorist, *tou kalēsantos* (ℵ A lat sy co), and should be read as such. The aorist assimilates to Paul's more usual practice (e.g., Rom 8:30; Gal 1:6, 15; 5:13), although he also uses the present elsewhere (Rom 9:12; Gal 5:8). In 1:4–5 Paul had spoken of the Thessalonians' election, which had taken place through the preaching of the gospel. He elaborates on it in 2 Thess 2:13–14: the call had taken place by the sanctification of the Spirit and belief in the truth, and its goal was to obtain the glory of Christ. The same moral element is present in 4:7, where the aorist is also used. In 2:12 and 5:24, the present participle is important. With other present-participial descriptions of God (*zōn*, 1:9; *didōn*, 4:8), it describes a God who is active, requiring a life of a particular quality in view of the eschaton (cf. 5:4–5; Collins 1984: 237–41).

Paul further describes the ultimate goal of his work in terms of God's kingdom and glory. The pronoun (*heautou*) is here without reflexive force (see NOTE on v 7). He mostly speaks of the kingdom as a future reality (1 Cor 15:24, 50), the inheritance of which requires pure lives (1 Cor 6:9–10; Gal 5:21). As the Day of the Lord, while still future, determines existence now (5:1–8), so does the kingdom (Rom 14:17; 1 Cor 4:20). "Glory" (*doxa*) may form a hendiadys with kingdom (cf. Mark 10:37, *doxa*; Matt 20:21, *basileia*). However, the importance that *doxa* has in Paul's eschatological thinking suggests that it be seen as a particular aspect of the transformation Christians experience now through their faith and hope (Rom 5:2) of resurrection (Rom 8:18–21; 1 Cor 15:40–43; Phil 3:20–21). See COMMENT on 2 Thess 1:9–12.

# COMMENT

## Introduction

Paul's self-description in 2:1–12 has been thought important for deciding what the relationship was between Paul and the Thessalonians and therefore what he sought to achieve by writing the letter. A major line of interpretation has been that this section is an apology in which Paul defends himself against charges brought against him, either by Gnostics (Schmithals, 136–55), or enthusiastic radicals—akin to opponents thought to have been active as well in Corinth (Lütgert; Jewett 1972; 1986: 149–57, 169–70)—or Jews (Frame, 9–12, 90), or by the larger, non-Christian society (Bruce 1982: 27–28; Marshall 1983: 61). So influential has this line of interpretation been that even writers who do not think that Paul was responding to actual charges continue to refer to Paul's "apology" or "defense" (Best 1972: 16–18; Palmer; Schoon-Jansen, 39–65).

Other interpretations of the section have also been offered. Denis has argued that Paul here presents himself as messianic prophet. Von Dobschütz (1909: 107) considered the section a digression in which Paul, depressed by his separation from his converts, justifies himself despite the fact that the actual situation did not require him to do so. Marxsen (1979: 44) thought the section prophylactic: Paul speaks of the past, when he had to distinguish himself from rival preachers, as a warning to his readers to be on guard against other preachers.

Holtz (1986: 94) has connected the section with v 13, relating the Jews to problems that Paul's readers encountered in the larger society, a consequence of the readers not having fully accepted Paul's word.

Dibelius (1972: 11–12) discovered no immediate need for Paul to have defended himself, but in view of the similarities between Paul's self-description and those of philosophical preachers who had to distinguish themselves from charlatans, he argued that Paul did the same. I extended this line of investigation by situating Paul more firmly in the context of the philosophers while identifying points where he differed from them (Malherbe 1987: 3–4; 1989: 35–48, 58–60; 1992: 294–98). The relevance of the materials I introduced into the discussion has to various degrees been widely accepted but with different interpretations, particularly with respect to the function to which Paul puts the material in 1 Thessalonians (Boers, 153, 158; Palmer; Collins 1984: 184–85; Lyons, 177–201; Wanamaker, 90–91; Richard, 104–109). But the philosophical interpretation has also been rejected, it being argued that Paul is distinguishing himself from sophists (Winter 1993).

The way in which Dio Chrysostom, a younger contemporary of Paul, describes himself (*Oration* 32.11–12), is instructive:

But to find a man who in plain terms [*katharos*] and without guile [*adolos*] speaks his mind with frankness [*parrēsiazomenon*], and *neither* for the sake of reputation [*doxēs*] nor for gain, *but*, out of good will and concern for his fellow-men stands ready, if need be, to submit to ridicule and to the disorder and uproar of the mob—to find such a man as that is *not* easy, *but* rather the good fortune of a very lucky city, so great is the dearth of noble, independent souls and such the abundance of toadies [*kolakōn*], mountebanks, and sophists. In my own case, for instance, I feel that I have chosen that role, *not* of my own volition, *but* by the will of some deity. For when divine providence is at work for men, the gods provide, *not* only good counsellors who need no urging, *but* also words that are appropriate and profitable to the listener.

This self-description is very similar to vv 1–8 in content as well as the antithetical style in which it is couched.

This discourse of Dio was delivered at the invitation of the people of Alexandria, and there is no indication that by using antitheses Dio was countering any charges that had been brought against him. He also begins other speeches he had been invited to deliver with self-descriptions designed to distinguish himself from other public speakers, in order to present himself as trustworthy (e.g., *Orations* 12.1–16; 33.1–8; 34.1–6; 35.1–2). In *Oration* 32 Dio presents the most systematic description of the ideal philosopher in all his orations, after a brief description of a variety of philosophers and orators (8–10). The antitheses thus function in a general way to distinguish him from the throng of preachers, but within the self-description itself they stress the qualities central to the ideal philosopher.

Antitheses became customary in descriptions of the ideal philosopher, and their use was thus not confined to self-descriptions. They were a means by which short characterizations could be made emphatically (Dio Chrysostom, *Oration* 77/78.37–38; Maximus of Tyre, *Oration* 25.1; Julian, *Oration* 6.200B–D), or an entire discourse could be structured antithetically (e.g., Epictetus, *Discourse* 3.22.9, 50). Important for our purpose is that the ideal, described in antithetic form, was offered as an example to be imitated (Lucian, *Demonax* 1–8; Maximus of Tyre, *Orations* 36.5; cf. 15.9).

Antitheses were also a characteristic means of emphasis in paraenesis, including the use of personal examples (see COMMENT on 1:6). The classic text that also illustrates a number of other paraenetic characteristics (the father's example, call to remember and imitate) is Ps.-Isocrates, *To Demonicus* 9–11:

Nay, if you will but recall [*anamnēstheis*] also your father's principles, you will have from your own house a noble illustration of what I am telling you. For he did *not* belittle virtue *nor* pass his life in indolence; *on the contrary*, he trained his body by toil, and by his spirit withstood dangers. *Nor* did he love wealth inordinately, *but*, although he enjoyed the good things at his hand as became a mortal, *yet* he cared for his possessions as if he had been immortal. *Neither* did he order his existence sordidly, *but* was a lover of beauty, munificent in his manner of life, and generous to his friends; and he prized more those who were devoted to him than those who were his kin by blood; for he considered that in the matter of companionship, nature is a much better guide than convention, character than kinship, and freedom of choice than compulsion. But all time would fail us if we should try to recount all his activities. On another occasion I shall set them forth in detail; for the present, however, I have produced a sample of the nature of Hipponicus, after whom you should pattern your life as an example, regarding his conduct as your law, and striving to imitate and emulate your father's virtue.

A writer might also describe his own life in detail, in antithetic form, in order to provide a basis for the practical advice he would give (Isocrates, *Nicocles* 12–47 for the personal example, 48–62 for the paraenesis proper).

The same features characterized letters in which writers sought to influence the behavior of their readers. A handbook on letter writing describes paraenesis antithetically as advising someone to do some things and abstain from others, and then provides a sample of the style of a paraenetic letter: "Always be an emulator, Dear Friend, of virtuous men. For it is better to be well spoken of when imitating good men than to be reproached by all men while following evil men" (Ps.-Libanius, *Epistolary Styles* 51; cf. 5). Writers of such letters sometimes explicitly referred to their own examples, which enforced their advice and also expressed a commitment to continue in the same manner of life (Pliny, *Epistle* 7.1). Sometimes, as in the case of Seneca, they did so implicitly (*Epistle* 32.1; see Trillitzsch, 69–70; Cancik, 58–61).

Paul writes in this tradition, and the antitheses, which have been a major means by which putative opponents have been identified (Schmithals 1972: 137; Mearns, 145; Jewett 1982: 208–15), are paraenetic and not apologetic. They extend well beyond vv 1–12, in places where they could not be apologetic (1:5, 8; 2:13, 17; 4:7, 8; 5:6, 9, 15). In this they are like other paraenetic elements that occur throughout the letter (see pages 81–86). The autobiography in chaps. 1–3 serves a paraenetic purpose, and we have observed how Paul introduces themes in chap. 1 that he will take up later (see Palmer). He does the same thing in vv 1–12, which has an exemplary function (Kamlah 1964: 198).

There is a direct correlation between what Paul says about himself here and what he later advises his readers to do, either explicitly or implicitly (impurity: 2:3/4:7; love: 2:8/3:12; 4:9; 5:13; labor: 2:9/4:11; blamelessness: 2:10/5:23; individual attention: 2:11/5:11; exhortation: 2:12/5:11; charging: 2:11/4:6; comfort: 2:12/4:18; 5:14; God's calling associated with the moral life: 2:12/5:23–24). The correlation extends beyond particular words to the persona of Paul and what is required of the Thessalonians. The Paul who is described here is a gentle, understanding leader who adapted himself to the circumstances and conditions of his converts when he was in Thessalonica. The letter continues in that mode, and the Paul who emerges from recollection and the letter itself is a model for the readers to follow (Malherbe 1987: 68–78).

This connection between Paul's self-presentation and his detailed advice shows that he had actual circumstances in Thessalonica in mind when he described himself in this way. He knew conditions there from Timothy's report (3:6) and perhaps from a letter the Thessalonians had written to him (see COMMENT on 3:6–10; Malherbe 1990a). Paul writes to "fill up" what he had learned to be lacking in their faith (3:10).

## Comment

Paul's use of Greco-Roman traditions about philosophers is intense in this section. This is evident from the similarity of these verses to Dio Chrysostom's description of the ideal philosopher as well as other features that have been identified in the NOTES. By using these traditions Paul by no means presents himself as a philosopher. We shall notice that at key places in this autobiographical section he differs significantly from the perspective behind these traditions. It was natural for Paul's converts to use traditional categories to express their understanding of his ministry, and he sometimes engaged them in similar terms as he corrected misperceptions conveyed by these traditions (Malherbe 1989: 91–119). Here, however, he gives no indication that he is correcting any misunderstanding about himself. He is simply using categories natural to himself and his audience in an effort to firm up the relationship between themselves (Malherbe 1995b: 243–44, 254–55).

The section falls into three subsections, all dealing with Paul's activity in Thessalonica. In vv 1–2 Paul reminds his readers in general terms of his entrance among them, in vv 3–9 he describes his exhortation as to his motivation and character, and in vv 10–12 he closes with a detailed summary of his pastoral method and the goal of his efforts.

*vv 1–2.* Paul resumes discussion of his *eisodos,* which he had treated in 1:9–10 in terms of the content of the message to which the Thessalonians had responded. With the phrase *kathōs oidate* Paul again reminds his readers of his ministry to them (cf. 1:5). The emphasis with which he reminds them, plus the stereotyped nature of the phrase and his frequent use of it throughout the letter (1:5; 2:1, 2, 5, 11; 3:3, 4; 4:2; 5:2), shows that it is not an epistolary "disclosure formula" (White 1971: 93–94), but is paraenetic.

The significance of the fact that Paul's self-description in this section serves a paraenetic function is not slight. From 1:5–6 it emerged that Paul could not make a distinction between the gospel and his own person as he proclaimed it. This section takes up his reference to his *eisodos*, but the focus is now totally on Paul and his preaching, with no interest at all in the content of the message, although he refers to the gospel repeatedly (vv 2, 4, 8, 9). Thus, Paul again does not think of his preaching as separate from his own life, but the latter is now viewed from the perspective of its providing an example for others to follow in their moral lives. The distinction that form critics have made between kerygma and ethics proves much too sharp so far as 1 Thessalonians is concerned (Lührmann).

In the first antithesis in this section, Paul is utterly brief in stating that his entrance was not powerless. The distinction customarily made between "powerless" and "fruitless" for *kenos*, describing either character or result, may be overly sharp, although the balance tips in favor of the former. Plutarch illustrates how *kenos* could refer to the entire endeavor in which public speakers might engage (*On Listening to Lectures* 41B–D). In philosophic discussion, Plutarch says, we should set aside the reputation (*doxa*) of the speaker and pay attention to the substance of what he says, "for as in war so also in lectures there is plenty of empty show [*ta kena*]." He then describes the whole demeanor of such a speaker: his gray hair, his figure, his serious brow, his bragging about himself, and the success with which he brings a clamoring and shouting crowd to its feet. Such speakers give an empty pleasure (*kenēn hedonēn*) and receive an even more empty renown (*kenoteran doxas*). This is what Paul did not do, and his interest lies in the second member of the antithesis.

In contrast, Paul refers to hardships he had experienced in Philippi. By doing so he would secure the goodwill of his readers (cf. Cicero, *On Invention* 1.16.22), particularly since they had already been informed of those experiences. Referring to difficulties one had overcome could be a form of self-praise, a topic ancient authors discussed in great detail (Fitzgerald 1988: 107–14; cf. Betz 1978: 356–93). It was held, among other things, that frank speech (*parrēsia*) that pleads for justice gives scope to self-praise and that self-praise is made endurable by not claiming honor for oneself but attributing it to God (Plutarch, *On Praising Oneself Inoffensively* 541D, 542E). Paul does refer to God, but in a manner quite different from the philosophers. Philosophers held that one should be impervious to the violence of the mob and be wholly unaffected as one suffers and is insulted (Dio Chrysostom, *Oration* 34.34). The philosopher should consider as injuries none of the things that people consider him to suffer as injuries and should not be disturbed by them but should forgive rather than retaliate (see Musonius Rufus, Fragment 10, which is entirely devoted to a discussion of *hybris*). Such hardships are credentials for the philosopher, proving him trustworthy, and justify the demands he makes of people. Paul differs radically in that he does not encounter hardships impassively; rather, it is precisely in the depth of undergoing them that he experiences the divine power that sustains him and brings the realization that the power is God's (2 Cor 12:9–10). Paul can claim to be sufficient in all circumstances, even using the Stoic word *autarkēs* to describe himself thus, but he revalues the word: he is not self-sufficent, but can make do with what is at hand because he is divinely empowered (Phil 4:11–13; Malherbe 1995c). The hardships therefore do not function as a self-commendation but display God's power in his ministry.

Paul specifies that he had been emboldened by God to preach the gospel, which is the subject of the section. Philosophers derived their right (*exousia*) to speak frankly from the moral freedom they had attained through their own efforts (Fredrickson, 70–82), but Paul derived his freedom to speak boldly from the Lord (2 Cor 3:13, 17). He is loath to speak about rights except to correct people who claimed rights that they justified with appeals couched in philosophical terminology (e.g., 1 Cor 6:12; 8:9; 9:1–12; 10:23; see Malherbe 1995b). Paul spoke no less confidently than the people whose terminology he uses, but the full conviction that characterized his preaching was accompanied by divine power and the Holy Spirit (see NOTE on 1:5).

*vv* 3–9. As he had in vv 1–2, Paul in vv 3–4 introduces something in the first member of an antithesis by way of sharpening the real point of interest, which is taken up in the second. Everything he says in v 3 could have been said by a genuine philosopher. Error, impurity and guile are regularly associated with charlatans, who lack integrity. Serious philosophers of every stripe, however, required a would-be philosopher to engage in serious introspection and self-evaluation before undertaking the correction of others.

The need for this self-assessment was expressed in different forms, such as the command of the Delphic oracle, "Know thyself," quoted by Plutarch at the beginning of his discussion of *parrēsia* (*On How to Tell a Flatterer from a Friend* 65F; cf. Julian, *Oration* 6.188AB). It could also be a demand to take inventory of one's capacities before making a deliberate decision to follow a new plan of life (Epictetus, *Discourse* 3.22.12, 19–20), or be described as a requirement to purge one's mind by the aid of reason and set it free (Dio Chrysostom, *Oration* 77/78.40). The language in which this activity is described may be religious, making use of the Delphic oracle, or popular piety, as the Stoics did when they wanted to ensure that a person's desire to undertake the role of philosopher was in keeping with his proper role in the cosmic scheme of things (e.g., Epictetus, *Discourse* 3.22.1–2, 23, 53–54; Malherbe 1995b: 243, 246–47). Basically, however, such language served to heighten the need for self-assessment.

Paul departs dramatically from such a view. His philosophical contemporaries, whose language he uses, would have contrasted the ignoble motivations and method of v 3 with such noble motivations as goodwill and friendship (Dio Chrysostom, *Oration* 12.12), claiming that they aimed only at the benefit of their hearers, in the process constantly having to affirm their own capacity to do so

(Dio Chrysostom, *Oration* 34.4–5). As their self-assessment had to do with human capacity, so their altruistic motives were concerned with human achievement. Paul, in contrast, uses the statement in v 3, which a good philosopher could also have made, as a foil to affirm that he had been approved by God to be entrusted with the gospel. Paul did not become an apostle after a period of introspection that led him to the conviction that he was fit for the task. His view is rather that matters had transpired according to God's design (Gal 1:15), that Christ had laid hold of him (Phil 3:12), and that he had no other choice than to preach (1 Cor 9:16–17). Furthermore, he felt that God had chosen him despite what he had been (Gal 1:23; cf. 1 Cor 15:9) and that his sufficiency came from God (2 Cor 3:5).

The notion of approval presupposes a prior testing (BAGD, 202). Paul thinks of the action as being entirely God's. Paul is entrusted with the gospel, which is God's (v 2), and acts in conformity with God's initiative as he speaks (*houtōs laloumen*). It can therefore not be otherwise than that his speech is designed to please God, not people. The first part of the antithesis ("not . . . to please human beings") is part of the traditional discussion of preachers, but the second part ("but God, who tests our hearts"), which is what Paul really wishes to affirm, comes from the language of the prophets (see NOTE on v 4). Paul here reinterprets the philosophers' description by using language of the prophet's call as he does in 1 Cor 9:16–17 (Malherbe 1995b: 244–51).

The three negative clauses that follow in vv 5–6 describe how Paul spoke in conformity with God's entrusting the gospel to him and his desiring to please God. The topics of these clauses (flattery, greed, and seeking glory), as, indeed, the major theme that they expand (to be pleasing), are all standard in discussions of the philosophers and other public speakers. What makes Paul's use different is that they are all brought to bear on how he had conducted himself in relation to God, who continues to test his heart. He once more adapts contemporary conventions to express his unique self-understanding to people who were familiar with these conventions.

Verse 7 marks a change in the way Paul uses antitheses. Up to now, they had been used to stress God's activity, which was mentioned in the second member (vv 2, 4). From now on, Christ (v 7) and God (v 8) are mentioned in the first part, and some aspect of Paul's ministry receives emphasis by being placed in the climactic second part. Paul carefully sketches a certain style of ministry in the remaining verses of this section that is particularly important for his later exhortation, whether that exhortation is implicit, as in his prayers, or is explicit in the directions he gives. The exhortation throughout correlates with this self-description.

Paul describes himself in emotive language that is designed to foster a warm personal relationship between himself and his readers. He begins with a reminder that he had been willing to forgo a right. That he chooses a harsh, demanding demeanor as the right he was willing not to insist on is important for two reasons: it sets the tone for the rest of the self-description, and he eliminates ecclesiastical status, that of apostle, from consideration. The image of the nurse provides a dramatic contrast and is the first signal that Paul will use images from the household to describe his relationship with the Thessalonians. He uses the language of kinship throughout the letter but does so without presenting a domestic hierarchy. He has addressed his readers as brothers (see NOTE on 1:4), now he acts like a nurse, later he will remind them that he had treated them like a father treats his children (v 11), and still later he will be a deprived orphan (2:17). What is important for Paul is not the structure that the image of the household might provide, but the relationships within the household. Elsewhere, he may use the imagery in a harsh way (e.g., 1 Cor 3:1–2; 4:15–21), but in this letter he consistently uses it to present himself as gentle, caring, and solicitous.

The image of the gentle nurse (v 7) is derived from a tradition that required demanding *parrēsia* to be modulated. In applying the image to himself (*houtōs*), Paul develops it in a different direction from that tradition to speak of his deliberate decision, out of love for them, to share himself with them (v 8). Rather than being acquisitive ("seek glory"), Paul shares (*metadounai*). At this point, he departs from the philosophers whose imagery he uses.

Philosophers would, like the understanding nurse, adapt their style of discourse to the need of the moment, but the better class of moralist was ever aware of the charge of wanting to please people, thereby showing a lack of integrity, relinquishing his proper role, and losing his freedom. Dio Chrysostom's manly and high-minded philosopher, committed to help people, would vary his speech, but precisely then exercise care to protect his individuality decently (*euschēmonōs*) and steadfastly, never leaving his proper station (*taxis*) (*Oration* 77/78.38; cf. Epictetus, *Discourse* 3.22.2–8). This concern for their integrity and doing what was proper to their call would make it impossible for them to speak of sharing their souls with their audiences.

Paul's claim that he had given himself to his converts demonstrates that he did "not understand gentleness as a device, but as a commitment" (Koester 1979: 42). Paul's giving of himself in his ministry was inextricably connected to his understanding of the gospel as the message of Jesus' giving of himself for others (see COMMENT on 1:5–6). He makes that connection here, as the statement about sharing God's gospel in the first part of the antithesis is amplified in the second, namely, that he had shared his soul with them because he had loved them. He then provides further clarification by reminding them of his working in Thessalonica.

How Paul could regard his work, which was that of a tentmaker (Acts 18:3), as an act of self-giving becomes clear when one considers how manual labor was viewed in first century Greco-Roman society and by Paul. A generalization is frequently made that runs as follows: Greeks and Romans looked down on manual labor, while Jews did not, but rather expected that every man should teach his son a trade and that a rabbi should learn a trade if he were not financially able to support himself otherwise. Paul is then thought to have represented the high Jewish assessment of work, although it is acknowledged that he did not completely comply with this view. Two other problems call this understanding into question. First, Jews did not uniformly hold manual labor in high esteem, as is evident from the scribal ideology represented by Sir 38:24–39:11. Second, the rabbinic traditions that do represent views like these are later than Paul (Hock, 23–24). The attitudes towards manual labor were more complex, and so were Paul's practice and his interpretation of it.

Polite society had contempt for manual laborers, considering such work servile and humiliating (Cicero, *De officiis* 1.50; see Hock, 35–37). We do not know where Paul learned his trade or what precisely his social background was (Hengel 1991: 15–17). What is clear, however, is that the Paul we know from his letters did belong to a social level and exhibited a literary culture considerably higher than the proletariat in which an earlier scholarly generation had placed him (Malherbe 1983b: 29–59). The attitude towards manual labor that he reveals in his letters reflects that of the well situated in his society. He lists working with his hands as one of the hardships he suffered (1 Cor 4:12); it is in his mind when he says that by refusing to accept financial reward, instead offering it free of charge, presumably by supporting himself, he became a slave to all (1 Cor 9:19), and the same attitude is present when he says that he had abased himself by preaching gratis (2 Cor 11:7).

Not everyone, however, looked down on people found in the workshops. Some philosophers included workshops among the places where they taught, and the Cynics continued the Socratic practice of doing so, and by the early Empire various Cynics, in their own way ideal figures, were represented as teaching in workshops, particularly as shoemakers. This is not to say that reference to these philosophers was intended to teach people to take up trades; Cynics were also known for begging.

What the practice did was to illustrate how these philosophers exemplified certain virtues, such as self-sufficiency, by working at physically demanding trades (Ps.-Socrates, *Epistles* 12, 13; Hock, 38–40). The philosopher demonstrates "by his own labor the lessons which philosophy inculcates—that one should endure hardships, and suffer the pains of labor with his own body, rather than depend on another for sustenance. What is there to prevent a student while he is working from listening to a teacher speaking about self-control or justice or endurance?" (Musonius Rufus, Fragment 11 [p. 83 Lutz]). The examples of such individuals made the point that attaining virtue did not require endless discussion but a practical life committed to high values.

What remained an ideal for some, Paul put into practice and offered himself as an example to be followed (2 Thess 3:7–12). It is important to note that already when he founded the church in Thessalonica his manual labor occupied an important part of his ministry. One reason for working was not to burden his converts. The paraenetic use of his practice is also present in 1 Thessalonians. In 2:9 he reminds them of his work, and in 4:10–12 commands his readers to work, again reminding them that he had earlier commanded them to do so.

Paul's refusal to take money from people while evangelizing them offended some Corinthians, who evidently thought that Paul's rejection of their offer showed that he did not love them (2 Cor 11:7–11). Paul differed from other preachers who demanded financial support, and his practice became a bone of contention, some people claiming that, while Paul did not directly make demands that burdened them, he did so through envoys he sent to them (2 Cor 12:15–18). The polemic is intricate, but for our present purpose it is worth noting that Paul insisted that his work was an expression of love (2 Cor 11:11), as it is in 1 Thess 2:9.

Of greatest significance for understanding 1 Thess 2:9 is Paul's discussion in 1 Cor 9 of his practice of forgoing financial support. Throughout the early part of the chapter (vv 1–15) he claims the right to support but does not exercise the right. He interprets his decision by discussing determinism and free will. He had no choice as to whether or not to preach; necessity was laid upon him (vv 16–17). But he was free to decide on the manner in which to preach, and he chose to preach free of charge. Paradoxically, he decided to exercise his freedom by becoming a slave to others in order to gain some (vv 18–19; cf. Gal 5:13). The freedom to serve is then exhibited in his practice of conforming to the circumstances of people in order to save them, doing everything for the sake of the gospel (vv 21–23; cf. 10:31–11:1; on the argument, see Malherbe 1995b). The argument drives to the heart of Paul's self-understanding as an apostle (v 1).

The argument in 1 Cor 9 is explicit and sustained because conditions in the Corinthian congregation required it to be so. The same self-understanding is also present in 1 Thess 2, but Paul more calmly and briefly introduces the subject of his working in his self-description. His interest is not first and foremost in a policy that ensured his converts financial relief. Had that been the case, he would have had to refer in some way to the financial contributions of support that he had received on more than one occasion from the Philippians while he was in Thessalonica (Phil 4:15–16). Nor had he been challenged in any way on financial matters, for then one would have expected a response made with the asperity of 2 Cor 11:7–11.

Paul's reference to his working is part of his systematic self-description that has a paraenetic purpose. It appears in the large antithesis to his relinquishing of his apostolic right to be harshly demanding. The entire second part of the antithesis (vv 7b–9) shows how different he was, and the same elements present in his other discussions of his work, particularly 1 Cor 9, surface here. Although God had tested and approved Paul to be entrusted with the gospel (cf. 1 Cor 9:17) and emboldened him to speak, Paul gladly made the decision as to how he would carry out that task. Like a gentle nurse he shared not only the gospel but his very self with his converts because he loved them. His manual labor was proof of his love as he worked and toiled, night and day, not to burden any of them. For further reflection on these verses and the consequence of Paul's teaching on love, see COMMENT on 4:9–12. The affective language in vv 7b–9, including "not to burden," contrasts with the harshness that he could have adopted. This is intrinsic to his preaching of the gospel, not merely adventitious to it, even with so noble a motive as to help others (cf. Acts 20:34). Dio Chrysostom could boast that he shared (*metadous*) with others the little he had (*Oration* 3.15); Paul, with God's gospel, had shared (*metadounai*) himself.

Paul's frequent references to his manual labor suggest that he spent considerable time in the workshop; otherwise it is unlikely to have caused the problem it did for the Corinthians or to have had the argumentative value Paul took for granted in his letters. Public speakers had various options as to where to speak, but Paul appears to have preached primarily in relatively private contexts such as households (Stowers 1984; Meeks 1983a: 75–77). Households could also be where teaching artisans like Paul plied their trade, and Paul appears to have done so in Thessalonica (see Acts 18:3 for Corinth; Hock for the practice in general and for Thessalonica, pages 60–61; Malherbe 1987: 7–20). Paul thinks of the Thessalonians as manual laborers (1 Thess 4:10–13; 2 Thess 3:7–12), and in v 9 he relates his labor to his preaching the gospel to his readers ("to you"). The picture that emerges is of a tentmaker preaching to his fellow workers while cutting and stitching.

*vv 10–12.* The classic text that describes Paul's adaptability (1 Cor 9:19–23) has its counterpart in these verses. The problems that preachers' adaptability caused themselves are absent from this letter. Indeed, Paul's adaptability is provided as a model for his readers to follow (5:11, 14); God is called upon as witness to his integrity in practicing it (v 10), and its goal is described in terms of God's standards and actions under an eschatological perspective (v 12).

Paul follows a similar method in giving a theological cast to 1 Cor 4:14–21, also at the end of an autobiographical section of the letter (chaps. 1–4) and before giving detailed advice (chaps. 5–15). There, too, he makes full use of the standard paraenetic themes: the advisor as father, addressing the readers as children, paraenetic language (*parakalō* ["I urge"]), calling them to imitation, and reminding them. Paul differs from standard paraenesis, however, in the way the entire text is given a theological cast: Paul's spiritual paternity is real, not merely metaphorical, having been effected in Christ, by means of the gospel. Christ is to determine Christian conduct; the Corinthians' conduct must meet the standards of the kingdom of God.

Paul does not spell out the same paraenetic elements in vv 10–12 that he does in 1 Corinthians, but they are nevertheless present. What the theological framework of vv 10 and 12 enclose is quite conventional (see NOTES). Unlike 1 Cor 4:15, 21, where he uses the father image to pose punishment or gentle treatment as options, here Paul thinks of a father in different terms, a figure, not of authority, but of understanding. Homer had described a gentle (*epios*; cf. v 7) father (*Odyssey* 2.47; *Iliad* 24.77), and such a father became a feature of the psychagogic tradition. He was one who did not speak with arrogance founded on official authority, but spoke out of solicitude (Philo, *On the Life of Moses* 1.328). For Paul, a father is someone who assumes the responsibility of providing for his children (2 Cor 12:14; cf. Seneca, *On Benefits* 5.5.2–3). Paul's use of such an affective image was most appropriate in writing to people whose recent conversion had resulted in strained family relationships (cf. Luke 12:51–53; Mark 10:29–30; and see Malherbe 1987: 48–52).

## 3. THE WORD UNDER PERSECUTION, 2:13–16

Paul continues his thanksgiving in a form similar to his first thanksgiving in 1:2–5 (Schubert, 17–27; O'Brien 1977: 153–54) and picks up the themes of that thanksgiving. The earlier thanksgiving led to a consideration of the Thessalonians' reception of the word in tribulation (1:6–10) and to an account of Paul's ministry, carried out in a great struggle (2:1–12). This thanksgiving, too, introduces a section (2:14–16, 17–3:10) in which suffering, tribulation, and the word dominate. Paul thanks God that the Thessalonians had received his preaching as God's word (v 13), in the process suffering at the hands of their countrymen (v 14) as Paul suffered at the hands of Jews (vv 15–16). The close parallels between 2:13–16 and 1:2–10 are not evidence that this pericope is an interpolation that interrupts the flow between 2:12 and 2:17 (argued by Eckart; Pearson); Paul does repeat himself here, but he also does so elsewhere, for example, in 1 Cor 8 and 10:1–11:1; 12 and 14 (Hurd, 27–30), so that this pericope is not as unusual as it might at first glance appear.

The thanksgiving performs its epistolary function by introducing the subject of persecution, which is continued in the theme of tribulation that runs through the section that follows (3:1–5, 7). The thanksgiving also functions didactically and paraenetically. In vv 1–12 Paul stressed that what he had preached was the gospel or word of God; he now thanks God that the Thessalonians had received it as such, rather than as words of his own devising. Verses 13 and 16 form an *inclusio*, showing that he is primarily concerned with the preaching and receiving of the gospel.

Paul's stress on suffering suggests that he was concerned lest his readers' misfortunes had led them to regard his preaching as a human word. That they had not done so is cause for thanksgiving (v 13). He then encourages them by stressing their solidarity in their suffering with the churches in Judea, Jesus, the prophets, and Paul himself (vv 14–15) and by assuring them of God's judgment of those who through their persecution would hinder the preaching of the word (v 16).

A hypothesis has been advanced that traditions are used in the pericope in a way that is un-Pauline and that we therefore have to do with an interpolation made by a later redactor (see esp. Pearson, who has offered the most cogent and coherent argument in favor of the hypothesis). The main problem is thought to be v 16c, and the extent of the supposed interpolation varies (suggested as vv 15–16, 14–16 or 13–16), depending on how the traditions used are viewed. In defense of the hypothesis, arguments have been advanced on formal, historical, but primarily theological grounds that Paul could not have written these verses (see the summaries of the arguments by Lyons, 203–7; Wanamaker, 29–33; Schlueter, 26–29). In addition, vv 13–16 have been thought to be a fragment of one of a number of letters Paul had written to the Thessalonians that were combined by a later redactor (Schmithals 1972: 123–218; Eckart).

These theories have been advanced over the last two hundred years and have frequently been rejected, not least of all, on methodological grounds (Broer

1983; 1990; Jewett 1986: 33–46; Collins 1984: 96–135). The position of this commentary is that the pericope was written by Paul and that it belongs in the position in which the textual tradition has transmitted it (see also Holmstrand, 42–46). The issues raised in discussion of the redactional and interpolation theories will be taken up as appropriate in the NOTES and COMMENT.

## TRANSLATION

2 [13]And for this reason we ourselves also give thanks to God without ceasing, because when you received the word of God that you heard from us you received it, not as a word that originated with humans, but as what it truly is, God's word, which is also at work in you who believe. [14]For you yourselves became imitators, brethren, of the churches of God which are in Judea in Christ Jesus, because you in your turn suffered the same things at the hands of your own countrymen as they for their part suffered at the hands of the Jews [15]who killed both the Lord Jesus and the prophets, and drove us out, and do not please God and oppose all people [16]by preventing us from speaking to the Gentiles that they may be saved so as to fill up constantly the measure of their sins. But wrath has come upon them until the end.

## NOTES

2:13. *And for this reason.* The *kai* ("and") connects v 13 to v 12, and continues the thought of that verse while adding something new. It frequently appears with *dia touto kai* ("for this reason also") elsewhere (e.g., Mark 6:14; John 5:16; Heb 9:15; Barn 8:7; Ign *Magn* 9:2), but in Paul only here and in 2 Thess 2:11, which may be why it was omitted by some manuscripts. The reason (*dia touto*) for his thanksgiving is that God continues to call them (v 12), to which he will add another reason, that they had received the word.

*we ourselves also give thanks to God without ceasing.* The second *kai* ("also") can go with "we ourselves," as the word order might seem to indicate. Understood thus, and particularly in light of the emphatic position of *hēmeis* ("we ourselves"), it could appear that Paul is stressing that he too, in addition to others, presumably the Thessalonians, was giving thanks. The hypothesis that Paul is responding to the thanksgiving in a letter the Thessalonians had written him (Harris; Malherbe 1990a) or is the work of an editor who has stitched this fragment of our Pauline letter to others (Schmithals 1972: 133–34) is unnecessary. Paul could simply be responding to the Thessalonians' joy and thanksgiving about which he had heard from Timothy (cf. 3:6–10 for the thanks Timothy's report causes).

The *kai* more likely, however, goes with "give thanks," for the phrase *dia touto kai* "is so fixed . . . that *kai* can even be separated from the verb which it emphasizes" (BDF §442.12; cf. 3:5; Col 1:9). The emphasis achieved by the removal of the *kai* from its logical order is brought out in Moule's translation, "that is in fact [*kai*] why we give thanks" (Moule, 161). Paul does not stress that it is *he* who gives thanks but that God's call is a reason for thanksgiving. For the literary form of this prayer report, particularly the significance of *adialeiptōs* ("without ceasing"), see NOTES and COMMENT on 1:2.

*because when you received the word of God that you heard from us.* The *hoti* ("because") does more than introduce the content of Paul's thanksgiving. It is causal, offering another, complementary reason for his thanksgiving: the Thessalonians had answered God's call by receiving the word. For God's election or call as taking place through preaching, see NOTES on 1:4–5; 2:12; and cf. 2 Thess 2:13–14. Paul picks up the topic of 1:5, the reception of the word, and elaborates it. Fundamental to Paul's understanding is that the word is heard and faith engendered by it (Rom 10:14–18). For this understanding of *akoē*, see Isa 53:1, which is cited in Rom 10:16 and John 12:38; cf. Gal 3:2, 5; Heb 4:2. This active sense, rather than a passive one, which understands *akoē* as the message or tradition that was received (Milligan, 28; Gerhardsson, 265; Schippers), agrees with the dynamic nature of God's word described in this verse.

In an extremely compact construction Paul draws attention to three aspects of the preaching: he preached, but it was God's word that he preached, and the Thessalonians received it as such. The awkwardness of the construction *par' hēmōn tou theou* ("from us of God"), which modifies "the word that you heard from us," draws attention to Paul's concern to bar any distinction between his and God's word.

The participle *paralabontes* ("you received"), the first of two different words describing the Thessalonians' response to his preaching, anticipates the second one (*edexasthe*) and describes action contemporaneous with it. The verbs *paralambanein* and *(para)didosthai* in combination elsewhere in Paul (1 Cor 11:23; 15:3; 1 Thess 4:1, 2) describe the transmission of tradition and correspond to the rabbinic *qibbēl* and *masar* (Davies 1980: 347–50). It is therefore possible that *paralabontes* here also refers to the reception of tradition, particularly if *logos akoēs* were understood similarly. *Paralambanein* does not, however, appear with *(para)didosthai*, but with *dechesthai*, which describes the reception of preaching, as it also does in 1:6 (see NOTES). Furthermore, in 1 Cor 15:1 and Gal 1:9 it refers to the reception of the gospel, as it also does in Matt 13:20; Mark 10:16.

*you received it, not as a word that originated with humans, but as what it truly is, God's word.* The second verb describing the Thessalonians' response (*dechesthai*) does not have precisely the same meaning as *paralambanein* (but see 2 Cor 11:4). In Plutarch, *On Listening to Lectures* 39C, it describes the person who "has the habit of listening with restraint and respect, takes in and masters a useful discourse [*ōphelimon logon edexato kai katesche*], and more readily sees through and detects a useless or false one." Frequently *dechesthai* simply describes reception of the gospel or word of God (Acts 8:14; 11:1) but more usually goes beyond recording the outward acceptance of the preaching, as *paralambanein* appears to do. Thus it describes a reception with all eagerness (Acts 17:11), with joy (Luke 8:13), in deep distress and with joy (1 Thess 1:6), and in Jas 1:21 it characterizes the acceptance of the practical consequences generated by the implanted word (cf. v 18, the word of faith), which is capable of saving souls. There is a similar expansion here of the object of the Thessalonians' reception. Once more an antithesis is used for the sake of emphasis, and "word of God" forms an *inclusio* to the assertion that Paul's preaching had no human origin but was truly of God.

*which is also at work in you who believe.* Grammatically, this relative clause, introduced by *hos kai*, could modify either "God" or "word," but the distinction need not be made too sharply. It is God who calls (v 12), and *hos kai* in 4:8 and 5:24 refers to God, but here Paul stresses the preached word as the means through which God acts. The word is the special theme in the verse, and Paul adds that in addition to ("also") being God's word, it is active. Had Paul wished to describe God as the subject of *energein*, it is likely that he would have used the active form of the verb, as he does elsewhere (1 Cor 12:6; Gal 2:8; 3:5; Phil 2:13), instead of the middle, as he does here. The notion of the word as vital appears in 1 Pet 1:26 (cf. Plato, *Phaedrus* 276A, for the spoken word as living and breathing), where conversion is also in mind. The closest parallel is Heb 4:12, which, however, has to do with judgment. Paul thinks of the gospel as God's power, but only for those who believe (Rom 1:16; 1 Cor 1:18). He could have ended the sentence with "you," but the addition of "who believe" underscores the importance of faith in this letter (see NOTES and COMMENT on 1:3, 7, 8).

2:14. *For you yourselves became imitators, brethren.* As Paul had drawn attention to himself with the emphatic *hēmeis* in connection with his thanksgiving (v 13), here the emphatic position of *hymeis* focuses on his readers: "For you it is, brethren, who became imitators." The explicative *gar* ("for") connects the Thessalonians' reception of the word with their suffering for it. That the word was active in them resulted in their suffering at the hands of their countrymen. Paul had instructed them that suffering would be inevitable (3:3–4), so the connection he makes here could not have been unexpected. As in 1:6, a connection is made between reception of the word and imitation, but here Paul thinks of the community rather than individuals. Furthermore, while in 1:6–8 he drew attention to the positive result of their acceptance of the word in relation to other believers, here he is concerned with a negative result, their mistreatment by non-Christians.

In a formal sense, this is the only place where Paul does not refer to imitation of himself or Jesus, but of someone else (Holtz 1986: 100–101), but he does refer to other churches' examples to undergird his exhortation (e.g., 1 Cor 16:1; 2 Cor 8:1–6; cf. Rom 15:26–27; Meeks 1990: 312), so the charge that this use of the imitation theme is not Pauline (Pearson, 87–88) is not apt. As in 1:6, Paul does not here exhort his readers to imitation, but recalls that they already had become imitators. He does not use the theme of imitation in the conventional paraenetic manner (see COMMENT on 1:6); rather, he compliments them, in this way revealing his pastoral concern for his recent converts. He expresses that concern once more by adapting a paraenetic theme.

*of the churches of God which are in Judea in Christ Jesus.* The formulation is similar to Gal 1:22, except that here the church is described as God's possession (cf. Rom 16:16, "of Christ"). See also 1 Cor 10:32; 11:16, 22; 2 Thess 1:4; and, with a geographical location, 1 Cor 1:2; 2 Cor 1:1. Turner (GNTG 3.212) argues that the genitive describes an ill-defined relationship that may be called "mystical" and is interchangeable with the formula "in Christ," as in this sentence. Perhaps more significant is that Paul so describes the church when he refers to his own persecution of it, evidently to underline the gravity of his wickedness in doing so (1 Cor 15:9; Gal 1:13; cf. the variant reading in Phil 3:6).

In this letter, *ekklēsia* occurs only in 1:1, of an assembly created by God, and here, where God's suffering Judean churches are imitated. This reference to God's church therefore does not reflect on Paul's error but honors the Thessalonians. Paul has particular churches in mind, those who at the time of writing existed in Judea. He thus continues his geographical references, adding Judea to Macedonia, Achaia and "everywhere" (1:7–8). "Judea" may refer to Palestine generally, as it does in Luke 1:5; Acts 10:37; 21:20; Strabo, *Geography* 16.479–80; Josephus, *Jewish Antiquities* 1.160; Tacitus, *Histories* 5.9. The plural, "churches," may be further evidence that he has more than Jerusalem in mind (Holtz 1986: 99–100).

If "in Christ Jesus" is taken to go most closely with "Judea," its addition may be seen as an effort to distinguish the Christian assemblies from their Jewish counterparts (so Frame, 109). It does more than that, however, if the description of the Judean churches is seen in light of 1:1, where the church of the Thessalonians is described in terms of its relationship to God, its creator, and Christ, God's agent in that creation (see NOTES on 1:1).

*because you in your turn suffered the same things at the hands of your own countrymen.* Paul specifies in what way they had become imitators of the Judeans, namely that they had suffered. But what those sufferings were is not stated, nor is it clear what Paul understood by *symphyletai* ("countrymen"). *Symphyletai*, occurring only here in the NT, could have either an ethnic sense, referring to the Gentile Thessalonians, from whom at least the majority of Paul's readers came (see NOTE on 1:9), or a local sense, referring to the inhabitants of Thessalonica, who could have included Jews (cf. *sympolitai*, "fellow citizens," in Eph 2:19). The latter meaning accommodates Acts 17:5–9 (Marshall 1983: 78–79; Donfried 1984: 247–48), although Paul could have had in mind sufferings they endured after his departure from Thessalonica, which he had foreseen when he was still with them (3:3–4). The comparison with sufferings under Jews suggests an ethnic sense. The point of the references to the relationship between Christian and non-Christian Jews in vv 14–16 is to draw an analogy between their conflicts and those between the Thessalonian Christians and their countrymen (Michel 1967: 51–52). John Chrysostom, ever prepared to find a pastoral intention and assuming the opposing countrymen to have been Jews, understood Paul to be offering a "great consolation": "It is no wonder that they did this to you, seeing that they did it to their own people" (*Homilies on 1 Thessalonians* 3 [PG 62:408]). The reference to Judean Christians would have had a pastoral effect whether or not the "countrymen" were Jews, for it would once more have reminded the readers that they were part of a fellowship that extended beyond their city or even Greece (see also 1:7–8).

*as they for their part suffered at the hands of the Jews.* The translation "they for their part" (Bruce 1982: 47) renders *kai autoi* (lit., "and you"), because in it is a reciprocal reference to *kai hymeis* ("you in your turn"; Eadie, 181). Again the nature of suffering is not clearly specified (see COMMENT), although v 15 may point to physical violence. What is important for Paul is not the details of the persecution but that it was in opposition to the acceptance of the word, in the case of the Thessalonians as well as the Judeans.

2:15. *who killed both the Lord Jesus and the prophets.* Paul now elaborates on the actions of the Jews, who are the grammatical antecedents to "who." He does not speak of all Jews, but of those who acted against their fellow Jews. The comma that is printed between vv 14 and 15 in Greek editions of the text and in modern translations is wrong, for it would set off a nonrestrictive clause that does not limit the action described to particular Jews, but would generalize it (see Gilliard for the grammatical and textual arguments). Paul uses a tradition about the killing of the prophets (see COMMENT) but adapts it by relating it to the execution of Jesus and opposition to his own ministry.

The definite article *ton* functions as a relative pronoun ("who") that introduces a number of dependent clauses that qualify the antecedent. He attributes actions to the Jews on five objects, all introduced by *kai* ("both," "and"). The translation takes the first *kai* ("both") to go with "the Lord" as the second *kai* goes with "the prophets." It could also go with the participle, "who both killed the Lord Jesus and the prophets," and be followed by another *kai* ("and") with a participle describing a further action, "and drove us out." It is preferable, however, to take *kai* with the nouns, for Paul describes the Jews' actions in terms of the persons who were the objects of those actions (the Lord Jesus, the prophets, Paul, God, all people).

Each person introduced by *kai* stands in an emphatic position. This is most striking in the first case, where "the Lord" is separated from "Jesus" by the participle to stress the heinousness of their actions. Paul normally refers to Christ as having been crucified rather than killed (1 Cor 1:23; 2:2; Gal 3:21), which points to Roman responsibility for Jesus' death, evidently under the influence of "the rulers of this age," that is, demonic powers (1 Cor 2:8–9). But Paul here shares the view of an old kerygmatic tradition (Acts 2:33, 36; 3:15; 4:10; 7:52; cf. Mark 12:1–9). His use of the more generic term and his identification of Jews as complicitous in Jesus' death (the only place in his letters where he does so) are due to the tradition of the killing of the prophets that he is using (2 Chr 36:15–16; Neh 9:27, 30; Jer 2:30; *Pesiq. Rab.* 26 [129a]; Hare, 137–41; see also 1 Kgs 19:10, cited in Rom 11:3; cf. Matt 23:27; Luke 13:34; Acts 7:52; and for the tradition, see Steck). These were OT prophets rather than Christian ones, as the addition of *idious* ("their own") in some manuscripts seeks to make clear.

*and drove us out.* Having spoken of the Thessalonians' reception of the word under persecution, Paul now turns to his preaching in the face of persecution, attaching himself to the tradition of the persecuted prophets (cf. Matt 5:11–12). He says three things about the Jews' actions, each introduced by *kai*, each identifying a different, yet related dimension of his circumstances. The verb *ekdiōkein*, appearing in its compound form only here in all of Paul's letters and in Luke 11:49, could mean "to persecute severely" (BAGD, 239, citing a variant reading in Luke 11:49) or refer to expulsion, which is the more likely meaning here, although the latter could be part of the former. Paul normally uses the simple form of the verb (e.g., Rom 12:14; 1 Cor 4:12; 15:9; Gal 1:13, 22; Phil 3:6). The aorist tense refers to a past event, which suggests Paul's expulsion from Thessalonica at the instigation of the Jews there (Acts 17:5–10, continued in Beroea, 13–14). This is supported by 2:17, which expresses Paul's yearning to overcome his involuntary separation from the Thessalonians and introduces his reminder of the steps he had taken to correct the situation (2:17–3:10).

*and do not please God.* Paul now turns to the present, charging that the Jews displease God, which is not part of any tradition, but a conviction Paul developed during his work as a missionary. The fourth *kai* in the series is epexegetic, introducing a further specification, that by expelling him the Jews displeased God. With this theological description of their expulsion, Paul again extends his notion of pleasing God beyond the more usual moral one to his preaching of the gospel, as he had also done in v 4. His testing by God guaranteed that he spoke to please God and not people.

*and oppose all people by preventing us from speaking to the Gentiles that they may be saved.* The fifth *kai* in the series introduces the last object of Jewish action. Not only do they displease God by their actions, they are hostile (*enantios*, occurring only here in Paul) to all people. This is not a condemnation of Jews in the style of their ancient critics who, like Tacitus, thought that "against all people they feel hate and enmity" (*Histories* 5.5; cf. *Annals* 15.44; Josephus, *Against Apion* 2.121; Philostratus, *Life of Apollonius* 5.33; Diodorus Siculus, *Library of History* 34.1). Such attitudes were caused by Jewish separatism, interpreted as due to their misanthropy, which is not what is in view here. Pagan criticism was social; Paul's is theological. Furthermore, Paul does not speak of hostility by all Jews, as is evident from the fact that he has just implicitly complimented the Judean churches. He is speaking specifically of those Jews who were preventing him from preaching to the Gentiles, the purpose of his call (see NOTES on v 4). There is no *kai* before the present participle (*kōluonton*, "preventing"), which is subordinate to what precedes and explains how their hostility was expressed.

*so as to fill up constantly the measure of their sins.* Contrast Matt 3:15. Paul viewed his mission to the Gentiles under an eschatological aspect (2:19; 2 Cor 6:1–2; cf. Mark 13:10), in particular, to save his listeners from divine wrath (1:10; 5:9; cf. Rom 5:9), and he interprets opposition to his preaching similarly (Bammel 1959: 307–8; Holtz 1986: 107). The translation "so as" renders *eis to* with the infinitive, which could express either purpose or result (BDF §402.2) but which in Paul almost always expresses purpose (GNTG 3.143), as it does elsewhere in 1 Thessalonians (2:12; 3:10; 4:9). It expresses purpose here, placing the Jewish action in the plan of God. It was God's purpose, not the Jews', that their actions should fill up the measure of their sins. For this use of the prepositional clause to describe God's purpose, see Rom 1:20, 24; 4:11, 16; 7:4; cf. Lünemann, 484. The clause could depend on all of vv 15–16a, encompassing all the opposition Paul has mentioned, or, more likely, only on v 16a, which is grammatically more natural and in keeping with Paul's focus on preaching in this pericope. *But wrath has come upon them until the end.* The contrastive particle *de* ("but") introduces an explicit statement of what has been implicit so far in v 16: The Jews hindered Paul from preaching to the Gentiles so that the Gentiles might be saved from God's wrath, in the process constantly filling up the measure of their sins, leading to their punishment. But, Paul now affirms, God's wrath is not deferred; it has already come upon them. The construction *phthanein epi* appears only here in Paul (also in Matt 12:28; Luke 11:20). The emphatic position of *ephthasen* ("has come") at the beginning of the clause shows that Paul wants to stress God's action in contrast to the Jews' actions. The aorist tense of *phthanein* has caused interpreters difficulties. It can be taken to refer to a past historical event (see COMMENT), or if brought into relation with the future wrath of 1:10, the tense could be thought of as a prophetic future (Frame, 114). It has also been considered equivalent to *ēngiken* ("has drawn near"), with an appeal to Matt 12:28 (Rigaux 1956: 452).

The meaning of the phrase *eis telos*, which qualifies the anticipatory realization of God's ultimate wrath has been much debated. This precise formulation, also used in the Gospels (Matt 10:22; 24:13; Mark 13:13; Luke 18:5; John 13:1), occurs only here in Paul's letters (he uses *heōs telous* in 1 Cor 1:8; 2 Cor 1:13, and *eis to telos* in 2 Cor 2:13). It could be modal, meaning "completely," "totally," "in the highest measure" (von Dobschütz 1909: 115; BDF §207.3; Moule, 70; Holtz 1986: 115). The parallelism to *pantote* ("constantly") in the preceding clause, however, requires a temporal sense, which in turn offers three possibilities: (1) "finally," "in the end" (Luke 18:5), (2) "forever" (Ps 76:8; 78:5; 102:9 LXX), (3) "to the end" (Matt 10:22; 24:13; Mark 13:13). The last has most to commend it, for a number of reasons.

The other occurrences of "wrath" in 1 Thessalonians (1:10; 5:9) are eschatological and agree with the present and future sense in Romans (1:18; 2:5, 8; 3:5; 4:15; 5:9; 9:22; 12:19; 13:4, 5), the only other letter in which Paul uses the term. Furthermore, the use of the phrase in the Synoptic traditions, dealing with persecution of preachers (Matt 12:22–23; Mark 13:12–13) and preaching until the end comes (Matt 24:3–14), suggests that Paul is using language commonly used of preaching in the face of opposition. He intensifies it with his declaration that God's eschatological wrath has already come on his Jewish opponents. His polemic is extremely sharp in view of the repeated assurances in the LXX that God would not punish Israel utterly (e.g., 2 Chr 12:12; Amos 9:8; Dan 3:34; cf. Wis 26:5; 18:20; *T. Levi* 5.6; *T. Dan* 6.5). What God had done to the Egyptians who pursued the Israelites (Wis 19:1), he now did to the Jews who persecuted Paul, and his punishment is moving towards the eschatological end.

# COMMENT

*v 13.* The presence of a second thanksgiving period, especially so late in the letter, is unusual in Paul's letters, and so is the fact that in form it is very similar to

1:2. Furthermore, the argument has been made that the so-called apostolic parousia of 2:17–3:13, also thought to be a Pauline epistolary convention, is introduced by vv 11–12 and not vv 13–16 (Funk 1967). Our pericope can then, partially on these grounds, be regarded as an interpolation (Pearson, 89–91) or a rhetorical digression (Wanamaker, 108–10). These peculiarities could be explained as due to the fact that this is Paul's earliest extant letter and that his epistolary style was not yet firmly fixed (see Baarda, 30–32). This is, however, only the earliest extant letter of Paul, not necessarily the earliest letter he had written—after a ministry of fifteen years or more before writing 1 Thessalonians! We cannot, therefore, assume that 1 Thessalonians represents a rudimentary epistolary form that would be refined in his other letters, written during the relatively short period of approximately nine years. The letter must be understood in its own terms.

It is significant that a third expression of thanks appears at the end of the autobiographical section in 3:9 and that it forms an *inclusio* with 1:3–5. Paul considers the relationship between himself and the Thessalonians, described in chaps. 1–3, as a cause for joy and thanks. That relationship came into being through Paul's preaching of the word and the Thessalonians' reception of it, which Paul has described in some detail up to this point in the letter, all the time stressing God's role in his preaching and his readers' election through the gospel. The fulsome way in which Paul gives thanks for their reception of the gospel underscores this, secures their goodwill by complimenting them, and has the further paraenetic effect of encouraging them to let the divine word continue to be active in them.

*v 14.* Reception of the gospel entailed distress, which concerned Paul from the start and caused him to set in motion the events that resulted in this letter (1:6; 3:1–5). It is this aspect of suffering associated with the gospel that Paul now emphasizes. Paul's Gentile converts had to be taught why reception of "good news" should involve suffering. To the Philippians, Paul presented their suffering as something granted by Christ, not to be passively endured but to be experienced as an *agon* ("contest" or "struggle," Phil 1:29–30; see 1 Thess 3:2; Walter, 423–25). In 2 Thess 1:3–4, also in a thanksgiving period, he insists that he has good cause to boast in the Thessalonians' conduct under persecution. Here he thanks God that when they received God's word they saw it for what it really was, and that he was the mediator of that word, which was still active in them. By introducing the subject of suffering in this way, Paul leaves no doubt that his and their experiences were not adventitious but flowed from their acceptance and profession of God's word (Marxsen 1979: 47).

Paul is concerned with the Thessalonians' suffering at the hands of their countrymen, probably having in mind their Gentile neighbors. He does not say what they suffered and certainly does not say that they endured a systematic persecution (contra: Pearson, 87) or, for that matter, any persecution at all (for a list of hypothetical sufferings, see Collins 1993: 112). Since neither Acts nor 1 Thessalonians gives any indication that they were persecuted, it is more likely that they suffered "public insults, social ostracism and other kinds of non-violent opposition" (Hare, 63; Barclay, 514–15: harassment, perhaps extending to physical abuse), just as the recipients of 1 Peter did (cf. 1:12, 15; 3:9, 15–16; see Söding 1990: 141–43). It is impossible to say with certainty whether the Thessalonians suffered because of anything they did or simply because of their being Christians (cf. 1 Pet 5:16; see de Boer, 98–108), and there is no indication that they consciously set out to imitate the Judeans. The notion of imitation is associated with preaching in 1:6–8 (see COMMENT), and it may be implied here that they encountered opposition because they preached. Such a reading may be supported by the reference to God's preached word as active in them and by Paul's reference to opposition to his own preaching (vv 15–16). In any event, these sufferings would complement the distress normally experienced by new converts (see COMMENT on 1:6) and, like that experience, require pastoral attention.

There has been much speculation as to why Paul mentions churches in Judea rather than any other place as ones the Thessalonians imitated (see de Boer, 103–106; Best 1972: 113). That the importance of the Judean churches, or even the primacy of the Jerusalem church, in early Christianity may have been a reason misses the point and is in any case more Lukan than Pauline. Another view of the Judean churches is one that sees them in need and may better explain why they came to mind.

Paul attached great importance to the contributions for Christians in Judea that he raised from his Gentile churches throughout his mission in the eastern Mediterranean (Gal 2:9–10; 1 Cor 16:1–4). His Gentile converts knew the circumstances of those churches (Rom 15:25–27), and the Macedonians themselves contributed generously to that need even though they themselves were poor and suffered affliction (2 Cor 8:1–5). In Paul's thinking, then, affliction and need characterized the Macedonians as well as the Judeans, and given the latter's chronological priority, it is natural that he describes them as the ones imitated. There may be yet another reason why he refers to the suffering of the Judean churches. He himself had persecuted them, his fellow Jews (Gal 1:13, 22–23), and it is not unnatural, although certainly ironic, that when he was himself persecuted by Jews, he thought of the churches he had persecuted.

Paul does not, however, say in v 14 that the Judean churches had been persecuted, but rather that they and the Thessalonians had suffered the same things. If Paul had in mind the Thessalonians' social ostracism, that would be what he had in mind with reference to the Judeans. Scholarly discussion, however, has speculated about Jewish persecution of Christians in Judea. Since Acts describes such persecutions before Paul wrote 1 Thessalonians (7:57–8:3; 12:1; cf. 9:29) and Paul mentions his own persecution of those churches (Gal 1:13, 22), it would seem clear that at least up to the time of the death of Herod Agrippa I in A.D. 44 Christians were from time to time persecuted in Judea (see Goppelt, 56–60; Jewett 1971a; Schlueter, 39–53). However, it has been claimed that after Herod there were no Jewish persecutions of Christians until a decade after Paul wrote and that this is further evidence of an interpolation that reflects later Christian experience (Pearson, 86–87).

Besides arguing from silence, this assertion assumes that Paul refers to persecutions in v 14, which he does not, and that they were taking place when he wrote, which is not what he says. The aorist (*epathete*, "you suffered") indicates that he had an earlier experience in mind, and we simply do not know what that was. It is important, however, to note how Paul viewed the non-Christian Judeans. When he took the contribution, which he was organizing during the period when he wrote to the Thessalonians, to Jerusalem, he anticipated danger from "the disobedient." The reaction that he expected may have been due to the special significance of the contribution as uniting Jewish and Gentile Christians (Nickle, 100–143). This made Paul quite uncertain whether even the Judean Christians would find it acceptable (Rom 15:30–32; cf. Acts 21:17–36, which does not mention the contribution, but see the hint in 24:17, 26). Nevertheless, that he did plan the contribution indicates that he hoped it would be accepted, and that must have made him constantly sensitive to the at-times strained relations between Christian and non-Christian Jews in Judea.

v 15. Paul turns to the violence of the Jews and goes beyond the Judean churches and their Jewish opponents. From here on it is his own experience of being persecuted that drives him to his outburst. Paul understood himself to be a prophet (see NOTE on 4:15), and it is therefore natural for him to identify with the fate of the prophets. He quickly moves from the killing of the Lord Jesus and the prophets to his own expulsion, expressed in verbs in the aorist tense ("killed," "drove out"), to the significance of their actions, expressed in the present ("do not please," "[are] hostile," "preventing"), leading to their final indictment because they thwarted the purpose of his mission and brought down God's judgment upon themselves. It is this focus that colors his use of "the Jews." In v 14, "the Jews" describe non-Christian Jews in opposition to their fellow Judeans, but by using the Jewish tradition of the killing of the prophets against Jews who opposed him, Paul increases the intensity, and the clauses that follow qualify "the Jews." The term therefore does not describe a race or a people with a particular history, but persons who are known from the particular actions Paul details. For Paul, the immediately defining action is their violent obstruction of his efforts to preach the gospel.

As the references in the NOTES show, the tradition of the killing of the prophets was widespread in Judaism, and Paul could have derived it directly from Jewish sources (thus Tuckett). However, the same key words, most of which are not Pauline in the precise way in which they appear in this pericope, are found in Matt 23:29–38: *apokteinein* ("to kill"), *prophētai* ("prophets"), *diōkein* ("to persecute"), *plēroun* ("to fill") (cf. Schippers, 232–34). Despite methodological reservations about allowing the collocation of un-Pauline terms to lead to the conclusion that Paul actually took it from a pre-Synoptic Christian tradition (Broer 1983: 71–72), there are factors to support this conclusion. Among them are the nonchronological order, in which the Lord Jesus is mentioned before the prophets (cf. Justin, *Dialogue* 16.4; contrast Acts 7:52), and the designation of Jesus as Lord (cf. Phil 2:5–11) which suggests the Gentile mission as the context in which the tradition was redacted (Steck, 274–75; Michel 1967: 54–55; Mark 12:1–9 reflects a similar context).

Paul uses the tradition in a pre-Synoptic form and applies it to himself. There is no cogent literary or theological reason why this tradition should require the pericope to have been written after Matthew, and to hypothesize that Matthew could have written thus only after the destruction of Jerusalem (Pearson, 92–94). Such a theory does move the theological offense from Paul to Matthew and an unknown redactor, but the pericope is quite intelligible in the context of the Gentile mission and, indeed, of Paul's own mission.

The picture that Paul sketches here of an itinerant missionary ejected from the city (cf. Matt 23:34, understanding *diōxete* as "will drive out") agrees with his description of his hardships, among which were persecutions at the hands of Jews, evidently in a number of different locations (2 Cor 11:24–27). This description of his treatment by Jews assumes that in his mission Paul at times placed himself in a situation where he fell under the jurisdiction of the synagogue. Despite skepticism about the accounts in Acts, according to which Paul preached in synagogues (e.g., 13:14–43; 17:1–4, 10–12; 18:1–4), it would appear from 1 Cor 9:20–22 and 2 Cor 11:24–27 that he indeed did so (Meeks 1983a: 26).

According to Acts, Paul did not last long in any synagogue; his success led to his withdrawal from the synagogues and ultimately his ejection from the cities through the machinations of Jews (Acts 13:44–51; 17:5–9, 13–14; cf. 18:12–18). Although Paul himself does not say why and under what circumstances he had left Thessalonica, the passive in 2:17, "we were made orphans," may signify that he did not leave voluntarily (see pages 61–62). It is only extreme skepticism about what Acts has to offer and the hypothesis that Paul did not write 2:13–16 that raise serious doubt that Paul here refers to his expulsion by Jews, probably engineered in the way Acts describes.

Other passages where the notion of pleasing or not pleasing God appears show how problematic it was in Paul's ministry. Paul contributed to the problem by the way in which he used it to describe his evangelistic method. To the Corinthians, he uses it as part of an argument about freedom to forgo one's right, in which he presents himself as an example. Although he had been called by God to preach and was under obligation to do so, nevertheless he preached voluntarily, demonstrating his freedom by the way in which he chose to carry out his mandate: he accommodated himself to people's circumstances for the sake of the gospel (1 Cor 9:16–22; see Malherbe 1995b), an approach that he describes as pleasing people in all respects (1 Cor 10:32–33).

Paul's opponents found in this adaptability a basis for their accusations. The Galatians charged that he was pleasing people and not God, to which Paul responded with a vehemence almost matched by vv 15–16 (Gal 1:6–10). To support his denial of the charge, he adduces his apostolic call as part of God's predetermined plan (Gal 1:11–17). His affirmation of his integrity in v 4 is not dissimilar: he pleases God and not people, for God had tested him, and in conformity with that testing he spoke (*lalein*).

In 1 Corinthians and 1 Thess 2:4 Paul was paradigmatic, and in Galatians apologetic. In both passages he speaks of pleasing God in contexts where he stresses the immutability of God's decision or God's testing him to preach the gospel. Here he is polemical, turning the charge on those who oppose his ministry: they are the ones who do not please God. He will go on in v 16 to claim that their actions, too, are part of a larger scheme of things.

*v 16.* Paul's identification of Jewish hostility with their hindering him from preaching to the Gentiles places his other statements in proper perspective. Paul does have a tendency to generalize (see 1:7–8; cf. Rom 12:17–18; 1 Cor 7:7; 15:19; 2 Cor 3:2; Phil 4:5). "All people," however, does not refer to humanity in general as the objects of Jewish hostility, but more precisely to the Gentiles whom Paul wanted to save by his preaching (cf. 1 Cor 15:1–2; 9:22), in view being the deliverance from God's eschatological wrath (1:10; cf. 5:9). In his self-description in vv 1–12 Paul had expounded on his motivation and method of "speaking" (vv 2, 4). His interest throughout this pericope is in the negative reaction to this word, either to those who receive it or those who preach it. He uses "all," not to generalize, but probably to mark the transition from his comments on Jewish hostility against Jewish Christians in Judea to Jewish hostility against the Gentiles whom he wished to save. The type of hostility he has in mind is alluded to in Matt 23:13 and Luke 11:52 and described in Acts 17:5–10, 13–14; 18:5–6. He writes as if he expects his readers to understand his reference, which is not surprising, in light of Acts 17:5–9 (see pages 61–62). Johannes Weiss suspected that Paul wrote these words shortly after he broke with the synagogue in Corinth (Weiss 1959: 1.195; Haacker 1988: 409–10). Paul, however, does not dwell on the details of the opposition but proceeds to locate it in a larger framework.

Paul constructs the divine scheme within which Jewish opposition fits with the aid of apocalyptic traditions. The idea of filling up the measure of one's sins, after which punishment is meted out, belongs to a Jewish tradition also reflected in a pre-Synoptic tradition that Paul uses here. Similar language occurs elsewhere (Gen 15:16; Dan 8:23; 2 Macc 6:14; Ps.-Philo, *Biblical Antiquities* 26.1–3), as does the notion that humans have a fixed limit to their actions, good and evil (2 *Bar* 56:2), established by God (4 Ezra 4:34–37; 7:74; 2 *Bar* 21:8; 48:2–5). In Matt 23:31–32, in a polemic against the scribes and Pharisees, the idea is combined with the tradition of the killing of the prophets (cf. Luke 11:47–52), which may suggest that Paul has in view everything he has attributed to the Jews since v 15. He would thus be returning to past actions, an interpretation strengthened if the aorist tense of *anaplērōsai* and *ephthasen* were understood to refer to the past, but the text is more problematic.

The aorist tense of the articular infinitive, "to fill up the measure," need not in itself indicate either action in progress or action completed, for it is indefinite, like a substantive (Frame, 113). To take it as a reference to past actions is rendered difficult by the presence of *pantote* in a position of stress at the end of the clause. This adverb cannot mean "in every way," as equivalent to *pantos* or *pantelōs* (suggested by von Dobschütz 1909: 114), for in every occurrence in Paul's letters it means "always" or "continually," as it does in this letter (1:2; 3:6; 4:17; 5:15, 16). The adverb describes the action of the infinitive as progressive, with the aorist viewing the action collectively, as one (Frame, 113). The present participle, "preventing," on which the clause depends, shows that the action continues, and the last clause of the sentence places the statement in an eschatological perspective, relating past and present action to the future. This present eschatological reality sharpens the polemical edge of Paul's indictment.

The eschatological dimension of v 16 enables us to grasp the meaning of the clause and the reason for Paul's sharpness. The eschatological perspective under which Paul conducted his mission included present as well as future dimensions. Paul preached about a future salvation (1:10; cf. Rom 5:9–10) that was already a present reality (1 Cor 1:18; 15:2). Similarly, the divine wrath from which his message promised salvation was future (1:10; 5:9; Rom 2:5; 5:9) but was already revealed and experienced (Rom 1:18; see COMMENT on 1:6). For the idea, see *1 En* 84:4, "and your wrath shall rest upon the flesh of the people until the great day of judgment." In 2 Thess 1:4–6 Paul makes a connection between present oppression and future retribution, but here he looks at the other side: people who actively oppose his preaching already experience God's wrath (cf. Rom 1:18; 1 Cor 1:18). This is in sharp contrast to those who are being called into the kingdom (v 12), which also has both present and future dimensions.

That God's anger came or would come upon Israel or individual Israelites is an idea frequently found in the OT (e.g., Num 12:9; 2 Chr 19:2; 25:15; 28:9; Zech 7:12). The idea is combined with *phthanein*, which means "to arrive" or "to come before" (G. Fitzer in *TDNT* 9.88–92) in *T. Levi* 6.11, "the wrath of the Lord has come upon them utterly" (*ephthasen de hē orgē kyriou ep' autous eis telos*), in a construction so similar to our verse that it appears to have been a common expression. There is no evidence of dependence one way or another, and while *T. Levi* 6.11 is not eschatological, 1 Thess 2:16 is. *Phthanein* appears seven times in the NT, once with the ordinary meaning of "to come to" (2 Cor 10:14), once in connection with God's scheme of redemption (Rom 9:31) and five times in eschatological contexts.

The eschatological use of the term is important. In Matt 12:28 and Luke 11:20 *ephthasen* describes the proleptic arrival of God's kingdom through Jesus' ministry in which divine power is manifested through his exorcisms (Kümmel). Paul retains this proleptic sense in Phil 3:16, where he distinguishes between proleptic attainment and final realization (see vv 12–14). The same distinction is also present in 1 Thess 4:15, where the issue is not merely one of precedence in temporal order but of eschatological attainment as well. In our passage the verb has the same eschatological connotation. The Jews, who hindered Paul from preaching to Gentiles so that the latter could now lay hold of a salvation still to be fully realized in the future, have now proleptically experienced God's wrath that will also be fully realized in the future (1:10; 5:9).

The starkness of Paul's language is like that of Jewish apocalyptic writings (see Baarda, 56–59, for what follows; cf. 1QS 4.12–13; 5.12–13), but whereas they called upon the faithful to hate their oppressors (e.g., 1QS 1.4, 10–11; Josephus,

*Jewish War* 2.139), Paul leaves vindication to God (cf. Rom 12:19–21). He does not exult in their punishment (e.g., *1 En* 62:11–12), nor does he ask God to destroy them (e.g., *1 En* 84:6; cf. Ps 69:25), nor does he curse them (e.g., 1QS 2.5–10). Like the apocalyptists, however, Paul did accept the reality and justice of God's wrath (Rom 12:19; cf. 1QS 10.16–18). It is tempting to ameliorate the harshness of such language by noting that it does not exclude the possibility of change, as Paul the former persecutor of Christians had himself changed (Baarda, 59; cf. 1QS 10.20–21), but that dulls the edge of Paul's language.

That edge is particularly sharp if the aorist *ephthasen* is taken to refer to a historical event (for lists of such events, see Baarda, 51–52; Wanamaker, 30–31). The destruction of the temple in A.D. 70 is often suggested, which could mean that the so-called interpolation comes from a time after the destruction, when it was viewed as punishment for the killing of Jesus (Pearson, 82–84), or, if the aorist were taken as prophetic, that the destruction was similarly viewed, but as an event that still had to take place (Eadie, 90–91; Findlay, 56–57; cf. Lightfoot 1980: 35–36). Among events that had already occurred at the time of writing, Claudius's banishment of the Jews from Rome in A.D. 49 has been advanced as Paul's most likely reference, for it would have been fresh in Paul's mind when he wrote, shortly after the arrival of Aquila and Priscilla from Rome (Acts 18:1–3), and because the banishment was thought by Jews to have had eschatological significance (Bammel 1959). Other events include the killing of thousands of Jews in A.D. 49 (Josephus, *Jewish Antiquities* 20.102, 112–17; *Jewish War* 2.225–27), the great famine around A.D. 47 (Acts 11:28; Josephus, *Jewish Antiquities* 20.51, 101), the suppression of the insurrection led by Theudas (Acts 5:36; Josephus, *Jewish Antiquities* 20.98), and the death of Herod Agrippa I in A.D. 44 (Acts 12:23).

Interpretations which see a reference to a historical event or combination of events run into trouble with the finality of Paul's statement, which, when taken purely historically, on the face of it does not agree with Rom 9:1–5 and 11:25–26, which express hope for Israel's future. Numerous attempts have been made to harmonize 1 Thessalonians and Romans (see Schade, 54–56; Schlueter, 54–62, for summaries). The solution has been found, for example, in Paul's early theology in 1 Thessalonians, which would come to fruition in Romans (Davies 1977), or in the difference in perspective on his mission in 1 Thessalonians, carried out while he was expecting an imminent parousia, and in Romans, where the parousia is delayed and his mission expands (Okeke). It has also been suggested that Paul had in mind only a minority of Jews (Coppens), or that *eis telos* is to be understood as meaning that God's wrath has come upon the Jews up to the end, when they will be given an opportunity to be saved (Munck 1967: 63–64), or that Paul's use of the Deuteronomic tradition implies hope for the ultimate salvation of Israel (Scott, 651–57), or that Paul "adds some new information in Rom 11:25ff., namely, that at the end God's mercy will be extended to Israel in a mysterious way and all Israel will be saved" (Donfried 1984: 252).

By recognizing that Paul is speaking about his immediate situation in which he was being prevented from preaching to the Gentiles, the need to harmonize the pericope with Romans' history of salvation is removed (Zeller 1979: 260). That recognition, however, should not blind our eyes to the fact that speaking of himself and his Jewish opponents is not done in isolation, but to make clear to the Thessalonians what happened to them when their countrymen turned against them (Marxsen 1979: 49–50; Penna, 296).

The intensity with which Paul writes is increased by the tradition of the killing of the prophets and the apocalyptic language that he uses in v 16. That does not absolve Paul (Luz, 290–91); on the contrary, Paul is highly polemical, but it is an intra-Jewish polemic in which he engages (Michel 1967; Broer 1983: 73–77). It is in the nature of polemic to verge on vituperation and hyperbole, and Paul does so elsewhere in his letters where he has Christians in mind (e.g., 2 Cor 10–13; Gal 1:6–8; Phil 3:2, 18–19). In this he was no different from pagan and Jewish authors who were familiar with this particular kind of rhetoric (Schlueter, 75–110; Johnson). The persecution that Paul was experiencing at the time he wrote and the sense that Satan was threatening his work (v 18; cf. 3:5) heated his polemical language, as they also did the pathos with which he goes on to describe his attitude towards his readers (vv 17–20).

# 4. REESTABLISHING CONTACT, 2:17–3:10

## INTRODUCTION

Paul now comes to the end of his extended autobiographical thanksgiving that began in 1:2. The intensity with which he has just spoken of his persecution continues, but changes from polemic to pathos as he describes the circumstances that led to his writing of the letter. Having reminded his readers of the history of the church's founding and their association with him, he now comments on their separation and his efforts to overcome it.

In addition to traveling to Thessalonica himself or sending an emissary, Paul could have communicated with the Thessalonians by means of a letter. Not being able to go himself, he sent Timothy, and he now writes, after Timothy's return, but says nothing about any correspondence that may have preceded 1 Thessalonians. Nor does he say anything about how he had learned about the Thessalonians' circumstances that finally caused him to send Timothy. The impression that he relentlessly creates is that it was his emotional need that finally drove him to initiate contact through Timothy. But he would have heard about them from others (see NOTES and COMMENT on 1:8–9; 2:13–14), and we have to reckon with the possibility that Paul and the Thessalonians had written to each other before he wrote 1 Thessalonians.

Paul seldom identifies the sources for what he knew about his churches when he wrote to them, and only once does he refer to a letter a church had written him (1 Cor 7:1). He does not consistently provide such information even in 1 and 2 Corinthians, in which he is more explicit than he is anywhere else about his absence, letter writing, and the sources for his knowledge about the Corinthians (Malherbe 1991: 415–17; Dahl 1967). His reticence to provide such information about the background to 1 Thessalonians, then, should not lead us to assume that there had been no prior contact between Paul and the Thessalonians by letter, and we should be alert to any clues pointing to a possible correspondence between them (see Malherbe 1990a). That notwithstanding, what is most important for our purpose is Paul's intention in writing 1 Thessalonians, and that will be discovered best by close examination of the impression he creates in the letter before us.

Paul begins his account of the circumstances that led to the writing of 1 Thessalonians by vividly describing his separation from his readers in language that reappears at the end of the section. It thus forms an *inclusio* that exhibits the main interest of 2:17–3:10. Paul expresses his desire to see them in person as well as the conviction that supernatural powers are involved (2:18; 3:10). Up to this point in the letter, Paul had emphasized God's role in forming the bond between himself and the Thessalonians through his preaching and their reception of the gospel. Now that they are separated, Satan has kept Paul from returning to them (2:18) and, Paul feared, might have tempted them (3:5). Paul's perspective, however, is broader; it is formed by the coming of the Lord Jesus, when the Thessalonians will be shown to be Paul's hope, joy, crown to boast in, and joy before the Lord (2:19–20) and will have hearts that are blameless and holy before God (3:13). In the meantime, Paul makes petitions before God that their separation may be overcome (3:9–10; cf. 1:3).

Paul moves through his account of their separation in chronological sequence. He is in anguish over being separated from them and had made repeated attempts to return to them (2:17–20). When that failed, he had sent Timothy to them because he was worried that his hardships might have destabilized them (3:1–5). Timothy had returned with a report that brought Paul great relief, joy and thanksgiving, and left him with the desire to see them and complete what was lacking in their faith (3:6–10).

Form critics have viewed the section beginning with 2:17 in different ways and therefore described its significance differently. For example, it has been described as both the opening (Richard, 134–35) and the closing (White 1972: 142–43) of the body of the letter, thus with varying views of the main purpose of the letter. Connected with the thanksgiving (1:2–10), the apostolic apology (2:1–12) and the apostolic parousia (2:17–3:11; Funk 1967), its purpose has been seen to secure goodwill (Boers, 155) or, with 2:1–12, has been regarded as a self-recommendation (Schneider and Stenger, 50–59). Such formal studies tend to be overly formalistic and precise (Lambrecht, 198–200; White 1993: 148–49), and neglect the communicative function of the section.

That function is clear when it is appreciated how much 1 Thessalonians has in common with a "friendly letter" and how closely in structure this section of 1 Thessalonians approximates the corresponding section of Philippians. Philippians is a letter of friendship (Fitzgerald 1996: 107–60), and to a considerable degree, the same elements appear in this section and in Phil 2:12–30: expression of a desire to see his readers (2:17 ‖ Phil 2:24); circumstances responsible for the delay (2:18 ‖ Phil 2:23); the sending of emissaries (3:1 ‖ Phil 2:19–25); the description of his converts as a crown of boasting (2:19 ‖ Phil 2:16); the Day of the Lord (2:19; 3:12 ‖ Phil 2:16); his readers as blameless (3:13 ‖ Phil 2:15); the danger of his having run in vain (3:5 ‖ Phil 2:16); there is a lack to be filled (3:10 ‖ Phil 2:30). In both letters, Paul strengthens his personal relationship with his readers before giving them detailed practical advice.

Paul uses the conventions of the so-called friendly letter in 2:17–3:10 with much the same aim as the sample of such a letter in Ps.-Demetrius, *Epistolary Types* 1:

Even though I have been separated from you for a long time, I suffer this in body only. For I can never forget you or the impeccable way we were raised together from childhood up. Knowing that I myself am genuinely concerned about your affairs, and that I have worked unstintingly for what is most advantageous to you, I have assumed that you, too, have the same opinion of me, and will refuse me in nothing.

Like Ps.-Demetrius, Paul wishes to secure goodwill: he has recalled in detail his past relations with the Thessalonians, and now he intensifies the emotion before he provides advice in chaps. 4 and 5. The friendship implicit in this style provides the basis for his paraenesis (Malherbe 1992: 291–92).

The language of the NT has been described as more emotionally charged than that of Jews or Greeks (see Malherbe 1983b: 38–40), and that certainly applies to this section. Paul's language in 2:17–3:13 is striking for its pathos (Johanson, 101–109; Olbricht, 230), even exaggerated as affective expressions are piled up (Weiss 1959: 2.402–3): brethren (2:17; 3:2, 7), orphaned by being separated (2:17), not in heart (2:17), most earnestly endeavored (2:17), to see you face to face (2:17; 3:10), with great longing (2:17), we resolved to come to you (2:18), I, Paul did so on more than one occasion (2:18), Satan hindered us (2:18), hope (2:19), joy (2:20; 3:9), before the Lord Jesus or God (2:19; 3:9, 13), coming (2:19; 3:13), glory (2:20), hold out no longer (3:1, 5), to be left behind alone (3:1), God's coworker (3:2), to strengthen (3:2, 13), to exhort (3:2, 7), faith (3:2, 5, 6, 7, 10), to be agitated (3:3), tribulations (3:3, 7), the Tempter tempted (3:5), labor in vain (3:5), bring good news (3:6), love (3:6, 12), have a good remembrance (3:6), longing to see (3:6), were comforted (3:7), distress (3:7), we live (3:8), stand in the Lord (3:8), thanksgiving to God (3:9), night and day (3:10), pray most earnestly (3:10), complete what is lacking (3:10), God our Father (3:11), the Lord Jesus (3:11; cf. 2:19), direct our way (3:11), to increase your love and make it abound to one another and to all people (3:12), hearts blameless in holiness (3:13), with all his holy ones (3:13). With such language Paul binds his converts to himself before beseeching and exhorting them to follow the precepts he had given them (4:1–2).

# a. PAUL'S ANGUISH OVER BEING SEPARATED, 2:17–20

## TRANSLATION

2  17 But we, brethren, having been orphaned by being separated from you for a short time, in person but not in heart, most earnestly endeavored to see you face to face with great longing. 18It is for this reason that we resolved to come to you, I, Paul, did so on more than one occasion, and Satan hindered us. 19For what is our hope or joy or crown in which we shall exult—is it in fact not you?—before our Lord Jesus at his coming? 20Yes! You are our glory and joy!

## NOTES

2:17. *But we, brethren.* The *hēmeis* ("we") is emphatic, Paul drawing attention to himself as the subject rather than the object of action (as in vv 15–16). The *de* ("But") could mark a contrast with the Thessalonians (v 14) or the Jews (vv 14–16), simply be a transition particle ("now," as in 3:6, 11), or be resumptive, continuing his description of his life with the Thessalonians (v 12) or adding his longing to his thanksgiving (v 13). The sharp change in style, marked by "But we," from polemic to pathos, suggests that he is picking up on v 13. He reverts to kinship language ("brethren"), which is important in this letter (see NOTE on 1:4).

*having been orphaned by being separated from you.* The passive *aporphanis-thentes* ("having been orphaned") may indicate that Paul had left Thessalonica against his will (see pages 61–62). Paul now uses language that serves both epistolary and pastoral purposes, although the two cannot properly be separated. The epistolary convention of stressing one's desolation and desire for contact is reflected in his description of himself as an orphan (see BGU 385, 4–6; PSI 1161, 11–19 for the loneliness of daughters in writing to their parents). The repetition of *apo* ("from") with *hymon* expresses strongly the idea of separation. That one was spiritually present although absent in body was one of the most common themes in ancient epistolographic theory and practice, e.g., in PLondBell 1926: 17–18, "Even though in body I have not come to your feet, yet in spirit I have come to your feet," and in Ps.-Demetrius, *Epistolary Types* 1, cited above (see Koskenniemi, 38–42; Thraede 1970: 39–46, 78–80, 95–97; cf. 1 Cor 5:3–4; Phil 1:27). See also Plato, *Phaedo* 116A: Socrates was like a father to his disciples; when bereft of him, they would spend the rest of their lives as orphans.

The absent writer could also use this convention paraenetically when he exhorts his readers to live as though he were present (Seneca, *Epistles* 32.1; cf. 11.9; 25.5–6; Phil 2:12). Behind this practice is the nonepistolary paraenetic use, e.g., in Xenophon, *On Hunting* 12.19–22; Isocrates, *Nicocles or the Cyprians* 51, after the delineation of the moral paradigm in 29–47 (see 37), and towards the beginning of the paraenesis proper in 48–64; Lucian, *Nigrinus* 6–7.

*for a short time, in person but not in heart.* Paul minimizes his separation in two ways. First, he hastens to stress its temporariness by combining two phrases, *pros kairon* ("for a season," cf. 1 Cor 7:5; Luke 8:13) and *pros hōran* ("for an hour," cf. 2 Cor 7:8; Gal 2:5; Phlm 15) into an intensive phrase, *pros kairon hōrās* (lit., "for a season of an hour"). Second, he limits his separation by claiming that it is only physical and emphatically not in heart. Although remote from *aporphanisthentes*, the negative particle *ou* ("not") is to be construed with it and is more emphatic than the more usual *mē* with the participle would have been (see NOTE on 2:4). For the phrase "in person but not in heart," see 2 Cor 5:12; cf. 1 Cor 5:3; Col 2:5.

*most earnestly endeavored to see you face to face with great longing.* Paul continues to pile up words describing intense feeling. The adverb *perissoterōs*, although comparative in form, probably has a superlative meaning ("most earnestly"), as it does in 2 Cor 1:12; 2:4; 7:15 (but see the discussion in Rigaux 1956: 459–60). The word *spoudazein* ("to endeavor") appears frequently in ancient letters in connection with the circumstances of their being written (e.g., POxy 939, 16, 18; PSakaon 36, 18; SB 1077, 8). The translation "endeavored to see" renders the aorist plus infinitive, *espoudasamen . . . idein*, a construction common in letters, where the aorist expresses the occasion for writing and the author's mood when he wrote. The meaning of the finite verb, however, is not stressed in the letters; its main function is rather to give a certain nuance to the verb in the infinitive (Koskenniemi, 194). If this applies to Paul, the accent here would be on Paul's wanting to see them in person, which is further emphasized by his adding, "with great longing." This is one of the few places in the NT where *epithymia* ("longing") is used in a good sense (cf. Luke 22:15; Phil 1:23). Here it is the equivalent of *pothos* (see NOTE on 3:6), frequently used in letters to describe the longing of absent friends (e.g., Libanius, *Epistles* 268.1; 525.1; see Thraede 1970: 166, and 95–97 for a discussion of 1 Thess 2:17).

*2:18. It is for this reason that we resolved to come to you.* Paul uses *dioti*, which stands for *dia touto hoti* ("it is for this reason that") and is stronger than the simple causal *hoti* ("because"), to connect firmly his desire to see them with his great longing for them. If a comma or semicolon rather than a period separated vv 17 and 18, *dioti* would introduce a subordinate clause, which would make the connection still stronger (Rigaux 1956: 460–61). The difference between *boulesthai* and *thelein*, both of which describe a wish, is not clear, but since *ethelēsamen* ("resolved") corresponds to *espoudasamen*, "we resolved" is preferable to "we wished." For the use of "to come to you" in describing the epistolary context, see Rom 1:10–13; 15:22–23; cf. PPetr 2.11.1, 3, "If you can, and nothing hinders you, come to . . . ."

*I, Paul, did so on more than one occasion.* Paul emphasizes that he had more than once undertaken to come to them. The emphasis is achieved by using the particle *men* (lit., "on the one hand") without a corresponding *de* ("on the other hand") and lapsing into the singular, particularly using his own name. For *men* in anacoluthon, as here, and where it emphasizes Paul's emotional state, see Rom 10:1 (BAGD, 503.2a). The solitary *men* retained its emphatic nature ("indeed") without always implying a contrast (Smythe §2897), so Paul is not contrasting himself to others, for example, Silas or Timothy.

The emphasis is further heightened by "I, Paul," which is also understood by some commentators as Paul distinguishing himself from his supposed coauthors, who on this theory would have been represented in the plural forms of the verb used up to this point in the letter (Best 1972: 126; Bruce 1982: 55). Those plurals, however, are editorial or epistolary plurals (see pages 86–89), from which Paul departs in 2:18–3:5 because of the intense emotions he expresses. More significant than his use of *egō*, however, is that Paul refers to himself by name in the body of the letter. In 1 Cor 3:4, 5, 22 he does so, but there he refers to what others have said. More important are 2 Cor 10:1 and Phlm 22 (cf. Eph 3:1), in both of which his name heightens the emotion, which appears to be the function of using his own name. The same is true in letters of friendship, in which there is a strong sense of physical separation, which is also the case in all three occurrences in Paul (cf. Gregory Nazianzen, *Epistles* 64.5; 93; Chariton, *Chaereas and Callirhoe* 8.4.5–6, in all of which, however, the name appears at the close of the letter; cf. 1 Cor 16:21; see Koskenniemi, 124). The emotion is heightened by the addition of *kai hapax kai dis*, "on more than one occasion" (cf. Phil 4:16; for the meaning of the phrase, see Morris 1956).

*and Satan hindered us.* Although Paul reverts to the plural ("us"), he is thinking of himself: Satan prevented him from going, but he could send Timothy (3:2). Paul had an acute sense that his freedom of movement was curtailed (e.g., Rom 1:10–13; 15:22–23; cf. 1 Cor 16:5–7; Acts 16:6–10). He gives no indication as to how he was hindered in Athens (for suggestions, see Frame, 121–22; Rigaux 1956: 462; G. Stählin in *TDNT* 3.855–57). More important to him is that Satan (cf. "the Tempter" in 3:5) was active in opposing his ministry. His separation from his converts has now been elevated to a supernatural level. It is striking that Paul's references to Satan under one name or another appear in letters either written to Corinth (1 Cor 5:5; 7:5; 10:10; 2 Cor 2:11; 4:4; 6:15; 11:3, 14; 12:7) or from Corinth (Rom 16:20; 1 Thess 2:18; 2 Thess 2:9).

2:19. *For what is our hope or joy or crown in which we shall exult—is it in fact not you?* Paul now provides the reason for his repeated resolve to return to them. With a rhetorical climax so passionate that it fractures his syntax, he rushes to an exclamation that brings him and his readers before the returning Christ. To the church fathers, Paul's description of his converts sounded like a mother speaking to her little children (Theophylact, *Exposition of 1 Thessalonians* 2 [PG 124:1296–97]; Oecomenius, *Commentary on 1 Thessalonians* 2 [PG 119:76–77]). Satan may thwart his movements at the present, but his readers are proof that his ultimate goal will be reached.

The three words are strung together by *ē*, accented grave (lit., "or"), which comes close to being a copulative conjunction in interrogative sentences (BDF §446). The rhetorical question and the compliment he pays his readers with it bring them into his own eschatological expectation. It is less important to decide whether the copula to be supplied should be "is" or "will be" than to recognize that the reference to the entire question is future.

The intensely personal way in which Paul writes shows that the plural ("our") is editorial. The Thessalonians are related to *Paul* in this special way. It is a remarkable statement, not that Paul has hope for them (cf. 2 Cor 1:7), but that they *are* his hope. To refer to people as one's hope was not unusual (e.g., *Greek Anthology* 7.453). Of special interest are instances in which individuals are described so in letters, particularly where the writer expresses his longing for his correspondent (Cicero, *To His Friends* 14.4.6; Basil, *Epistle* 146.1; Libanius, *Epistle* 1529.2; see Thraede 1970: 168). Paul holds the view that his own eschatological hope is bound up with his converts' spiritual condition as they jointly stand before the Lord (see on 1:3; 2:19; cf. 1 Cor 3:8). Joy, also, has an eschatological reference (Rom 12:12; 15:13; cf. 14:17; see Luke 1:14; 2:10; 1 Pet 1:8; 1QS 1:8). As it is here, "joy" is combined with "crown" in Phil 4:1, which, in view of the immediately preceding verses (3:20–21), is to be understood eschatologically.

The phrase "crown of boasting" comes from the OT (Prov 16:31; Ezek 16:12; 23:42), and "crown" is used figuratively in other ways in Jewish sources, e.g., the crown of glory (*T. Benj* 4:1; 1QS 4:7; 2 Bar 15:8; cf. 1 Pet 5:4). However, the image Paul uses is that of the crown bestowed on the victor in the Greek games (Pfitzner, 76–129). He applies the metaphor to his own life (Phil 3:12–14) and elaborates on it as applied to his ministry, where the crown that he will receive is an eschatological reward (1 Cor 9:24–27).

The *kauchesis* Paul has in mind here is the exultation or joy he will feel over the church he had established (John Chrysostom, *Homilies on 1 Thessalonians* 3 [PG 62:409]). Paul thinks that he and his converts will exult in each other in the Day of the Lord (2 Cor 1:14), but they will, in a special way, be the crown he will receive for having completed his race successfully. Therein lies the reason for exultation (Phil 2:14). For the use of *kauchāsthai* (lit., "to boast") to describe exultant joy, see Rom 5:2–3, and for this understanding here, see the variant *stephanos agalliaseōs* ("crown of joy") in A and *exultationis corona* in Tertullian, *On the Resurrection of the Flesh* 24. For the crown as a sign of joy, see W. Grundmann in *TDNT* 7.622, and for the figurative use in Judaism, 7.626, 627, 629–30.

Paul interrupts his question with another rhetorical question that gives the answer: "Is it not in fact you?" Most editors and commentators accent the *e* that introduces this interruption grave, which would make it the third copulative conjunction in the sentence. It is preferable, however, to accent it circumflex, which would make it an adverb introducing a question that does not permit an alternative (so Bruce 1982: 53). The *ou* ("not") indicates that the expected answer is "yes." The *kai* ("in fact") could mean "also" here, Paul implying that he included other Christians in this praise (Richard, 131: "Does that not include you?"), but his focus is so strongly on the Thessalonians and his language so emphatic that it is preferable to take the *kai* as providing further stress.

*before our Lord Jesus at his coming?* Paul concludes the interrupted sentence by making explicit when his readers will be shown to be his hope, joy, and crown to exult in. Whereas in 3:13 they appear together before God (cf. on 1:3), here their appearance is before the Lord Jesus, as though it is he who will judge the success of Paul's ministry. See 2 Cor 5:10, the judgment seat of Christ, and Rom 14:10, the judgment seat of God; cf. 1 Cor 4:4–5. For Christ sharing God's prerogatives, see further NOTES on 3:11, 12. This is the earliest occurrence of *parousia* ("coming") in the NT, but the formulaic use of it elsewhere in the letter (3:13; 5:23; cf. 4:15) shows that Paul did not introduce it into Christian usage. Outside these passages and 2 Thess 2:1, 8, the word is used in Paul's letters of Christ's coming only in 1 Cor 15:23. See COMMENT on 4:15.

2:20. *Yes! You are our glory and joy!* The causal conjunction *gar*, translated here as "Yes!" strengthens the second answer to the question by affirming what was asked (BDF §452.2). The *hymeis* ("you") is in the emphatic position: "You it is who are." For someone described as a person's glory, see Macrobius, *Commentary on the Dream of Scipio* 1.1.1, and esp. Seneca, *Epistle* 20.1: Lucilius will be Seneca's glory if Seneca succeeds in nourishing him philosophically. Paul did not seek glory from anyone, the Thessalonians included (2:6); instead they are his glory and will appear to be so at the coming of Christ (see further on 2 Thess 1:10).

# COMMENT

Paul frequently comments on his separation from his churches and his desire to remain in contact with them by means of emissaries or letters (Rom 1:8–13; 15:14–33; 1 Cor 16:1–12; 2 Cor 7:5–16; Phil 2:25–30; see Lyons, 209; Malherbe 1991: 445). When occasion demanded, he was sharp in such comments (e.g., 1 Cor 4:14–21; 2 Cor 1:1–2:13); at other times he wrote with great warmth (e.g., Phlm 21–22), as he does here. It is the nature of the relationship with his readers at the time that determines the tone of his comments, whether they are sharp or whether he builds on the friendly relationship that already exists and strengthens it in order to provide a firm basis for the detailed advice he then proceeds to give.

Paul's description of his anguish over being separated from his converts is expressed in a number of epistolary conventions: the use of family language (orphan), bodily absence but spiritual presence, a desire to see one's correspondents, one's resolve to go to them, and referring to oneself by name. These epistolographic features are part of the pathos with which Paul writes and expresses his need for communication, as they do in ancient letters. Coming, as they do, immediately before Paul's description of Timothy's mission, through which Paul reestablished contact with them, it has been suggested that they are evidence of a letter Paul had written the Thessalonians and Timothy had delivered to them (Harris). In that letter Paul would have expressed his desire to see them (2:17; 3:2, 6) and his concern whether his work among them had been in vain (3:5).

It is quite likely that such concerns were expressed when Timothy went to them, but the evidence is not strong enough to support the claim that they were made in a letter rather than raised by Timothy. These elements do not lead up to a letter but to Timothy's mission, which was to reestablish contact. The description of this mission, we shall see, is itself replete with similar epistolographic expressions. Furthermore, they appear in a letter written after contact had been reestablished. Their function can only be fully established after the entire sequence of events leading up to the writing of 1 Thessalonians has been examined. It is already clear, however, that by constantly stressing a desire to communicate, Paul sharpens the focus on 1 Thessalonians as the fulfilling of his desire to do so.

At this point, we can make two observations. First, the conventional nature of the language dismisses the notion that Paul is here making an apology for his absence (Frame, 116–17). Second, Paul does not provide any information his readers would not already have received from Timothy. What is more important than what he says is how he says it, and implicit in how he describes the situation is that it is now not only the church that needs him but that he needs the church (Marxsen 1979: 52).

The pathos with which Paul writes 2:17–3:10 is a continuation of the emotion of the preceding autobiographical description, particularly of 2:1–12, which has a paraenetic function. For example, he had suffered and been insulted, and had spoken while in a great struggle (2:2), he had made no demands as an apostle, but was gentle like a mothering nurse (2:7), had tender affection for them, loved them, gave himself for them and worked with his hands night and day in order not to burden them (2:8–9). As a father treats his own children individually, so he had adapted his ministry to their individual needs (2:11–12). Paul writes this pastoral letter in a style that is congruent with the demeanor in which, he says, he conducted himself during his ministry to them (contrast the charge in 2 Cor 10:10).

Paul's pastoral purpose is evident in his use of the metaphor of the orphan. While accomplishing the epistolary function of describing the anguish of separation, the metaphor is particularly significant as a pastoral device in dealing with recent converts. When he had described himself as providing pastoral care, he had used parental images (2:7, 11); now he moves from an image of siblings ("brothers"), used primarily in the vocative in the letter (exceptions: 3:2; 4:6, 10; 5:26–27), to one of a child in its most vulnerable state, that of orphan. The way in which he had used the two other images heightened the caring nature of his ministry. The image of an orphan describes Paul in the most poignant way possible as in need. One could have expected Paul to say that his separation had made him bereft of his Thessalonian children (Field, 200; cf. Plato, *Phaedo* 116A; but see Eadie, 93) or that the Thessalonians had been orphaned by his absence (John Chrysostom, *Homilies on 1 Thessalonians* 3 [PG 62:408]), but Paul wrenches the metaphor to extract the most emotion possible from it (see also Gal 4:20). Implicit in the metaphor as he uses it is that he is in need of their help.

It would be wrong, however, to think that Paul seeks sympathy; he rather expresses empathy with them, for it was new converts who were called orphans (*Jos Asen* 12:14; 13:1), and who were also described as loved by God (see NOTE on 1:4). Such converts required special consideration, and the concentration of kinship language in this letter is one way in which Paul strengthens the new relationships within the church (Malherbe 1987: 44, 48, 63–65, 77). The way he stands the metaphor on its head, that *he* is the orphan, shows the extent to which he goes to express his need to reestablish contact. More important, since in fact contact has been established, is that it reveals the relationship that Paul presents as the context for the writing of 1 Thessalonians. He does not write as an authoritative and demanding apostle, but as someone who knows what it means to be in the orphan state in which his readers find themselves.

The need implicit in Paul's description, however, is modified. For example, that he is spiritually present although absent in body has a paraenetic edge: they are to conduct themselves as though he were actually present (see NOTE on 2:17). It is also noteworthy in this regard how he juxtaposes his descriptions of himself and them. He is orphaned, has a great desire to see them, but is thwarted by Satan; they, on the other hand, are his hope, joy, crown of boasting and glory. This is an expression of confidence in them and can be interpreted as an effort to secure their goodwill, but it is no different from an exhortation. In lavishing such praise he expects them to live up to it (Weiss 1959: 2.403).

Paul expresses confidence in yet another way when he declares that the Thessalonians will be the crown in which he will boast before the Lord Jesus when he comes (2:19). The image is of Paul as victor in a race (see further NOTE on 3:5), with God awarding him the crown of victory. What is striking here is that it is his converts who are his crown. The salvation for which he strives is not only a personal one; the fruit of his ministry, a faithful community he had founded, will justify his exultation before the Lord, who will judge him victorious (W. Grundmann in *TDNT* 7.629–30).

Paul often refers to an eschatological reward he hopes to receive for his efforts in preaching the gospel (Lyons, 210–11). As he does here, he uses the image of the winner of a race receiving a prize in 1 Cor 9:24–27 (*brabeion* instead of *stephanos*; also in Phil 3:14). The expectation of an eschatological reward also appears without the metaphor of a crown (e.g., 2 Cor 1:14). What is most striking in the passages that describe Paul's expectation of an eschatological reward for his carrying out his apostolic ministry is the frequency with which Satan appears in the context (1 Cor 3:10–15; cf. 4:1–5; 9:24–27; cf. 10:9–13; 2 Cor 4:1–5; 11:13–15; 1 Thess 2:18–19).

# b. TIMOTHY'S MISSION TO THE THESSALONIANS, 3:1–5

## TRANSLATION

3 ¹Therefore, because we could hold out no longer, we gladly determined to be left in Athens alone, ²and we sent Timothy, our brother and God's coworker in the gospel of Christ, to establish you and encourage you about your faith, ³that no one should be agitated by these afflictions. For you yourselves know that we

are appointed to this. ⁴Indeed, when we were with you, we kept on telling you in advance, "We are bound to suffer tribulation," as it has indeed happened, and you know. ⁵For this reason, when I for my part could hold out no longer, I sent to learn about your faith, lest the Tempter had tempted you, and our labor had been in vain.

## NOTES

3:1. *Therefore, because we could hold out no longer.* The phrase *dio mēketi ste-gontes . . . epempsamen* ("Therefore, because we could hold out no longer . . . we sent") is virtually repeated in v 5, *dia touto kagō mēketi stegōn epempsa* ("For this reason, when I for my part could hold out no longer, I sent"), except for the plural in v 2 and the singular in v 5. Since the verbs *epempsamen* and *epempsa* refer to the same action by Paul, the plural must be epistolary (Moule, 119). The *inclusio* thus formed describes the occasion and purpose of Timothy's mission to the Thessalonians.

Paul was eager to see the Thessalonians (2:17) and for that reason (*dioti*) had resolved to go to them, but was hindered by Satan (2:18). He therefore (*dio*) sent Timothy. Read this way, *dio* sums up the main points of 2:17–20 (von Dobschütz 1009: 129; Frame, 125; Rigaux 1956: 466). The more immediate connection with 2:19–20, however, stresses that it was because of his high regard for them that he sent Timothy.

The translation, "because we could hold out no longer," understands the participle as causal, rather than temporal, in light of Paul's specification of the reasons for his actions. The use of *mēketi* with the participle (cf. Rom 15:23; Acts 13:24) is normal (BDF §430). The verb *stegein*, which appears in the NT only in vv 1 and 5 and in 1 Cor 9:12; 13:7, originally meant "to cover," "to protect," or "to keep out," but allowed an internal meaning, "to hold back," and then came to mean "to endure" (W. Kasch in *TDNT* 7.585; POxy 1775.10). The translation "hold out" is an attempt to render the latter as well as retain the original sense. It is synonymous with *pherein* (Rom 9:22; Heb 12:20; 13:13) and *hypopherein* (1 Cor 10:13; 2 Tim 3:11; see von Dobschütz 1909: 129–30). The causal reading of the participle strengthens the *ad sensum* translation that Paul "could not" hold out. Philo, *Against Flaccus* 63 (*mēketi stegein dynamenoi* ["unable any longer to endure"]), is frequently cited in support of such a reading. If the participle expresses an imperfect intention, however, it would be equivalent to *mellontes stegein*, "since we intended no longer to bear the situation" (Frame, 125). The utter desolation that Paul describes favors the translation adopted.

*we gladly determined to be left in Athens alone.* John Chrysostom noted that Paul said *eudokēsamen* ("gladly determined") instead of *eilometha* ("chose"; John Chrysostom, *Homilies on 1 Thessalonians* 3 [PG 62:410]). *Eudokein* describes a free choice, with the connotation of a preference over something else (von Dobschütz 1909: 130, refers to 2 Cor 5:8; Sir. 25:16). Theophylact adds *proekrina-men*, "we selected the option of" (*Exposition of 1 Thessalonians* 3 [PG

124:1297]). See further NOTE on 2:8. Paul wishes to communicate to his readers that he was not totally at the mercy of his circumstances. He did choose another option some time later, when he left Athens for Corinth (Acts 18:1).

The reference to Athens does not imply that Paul wrote the letter from Athens, as some ancient authors inferred (see pages 71–72). "Athens" does not appear with eudokēsamen, but is in an emphatic position, between kataleiphthēnai ("left") and monoi ("alone"). This has led some commentators to discover here Paul's great sacrifice to remain alone in the great city, and to flesh out his circumstances with the aid of Acts 17:16–34—as if Acts presents a picture of a Paul desolate in spirit! Not much is to be made of the reference to Athens. Paul's readers would have learned of his circumstances in Athens from Timothy, and Paul does not dwell on his circumstances other than to describe how concerned he was about the Thessalonians. That he was "left alone" echoes "having been orphaned by being separated from you" (2:17).

It is not immediately obvious who the subject of eudokēsamen is. It may be Paul and Silas (Frame, 126; Bruce 1982: 60), people in Athens other than Silas (Best 1972: 131), or Paul, if it is an epistolary plural (von Dobschütz 1909: 130; Dibelius 1937: 16; Roosen 1971: 73; see pages 86–89). In favor of an epistolary plural are the problematic reference of monoi ("alone") to more than one person, the extremely personal nature of Paul's language in 2:17–3:5, and the fact that epempsamen (v 2) must be an epistolary plural. Furthermore, while Silas did join Paul in Corinth (Acts 18:5; cf. 2 Cor 1:19) and was with him when he wrote 1 Thessalonians (see 1:1), his movements after Beroea (Acts 18:10–15) are uncertain, and there is no evidence that he, like Timothy, had joined Paul in Athens (see pages 70–71).

The only other place where Paul uses kataleipein is in a quotation of 1 Kgs 19:18 in Rom 11:3 (cf. Eph 5:31, quoting Gen 2:24). The phrase kataleipesthai monos occurs in the LXX (Gen 32:24; 42:38; Isa 3:26; 49:21; Jud 13:2; 1 Macc 13:4; cf. John 8:9). The verb is different from katamenein ("to remain behind"; cf. remanere in the Vulgate), and its passive form, plus the emphatic nature of the construction, conveys a feeling of solitariness approximating that of someone abandoned. The word is used by Aristotle to describe leaving a friend in the lurch (Rhetoric 2.4.26) or abandoning a child (Rhetoric 3.16.5). Paul uses the word, not to blame anyone for leaving him alone (contrast 2 Tim 4:10, 16), but purely for its emotional value.

3:2. and we sent Timothy, our brother and God's coworker in the gospel of Christ. Paul was separated from the Thessalonians against his will (2:17), but he increased his anguish by sending Timothy out of his own volition to his recent converts. Timothy would act as Paul's emissary to his churches on other occasions. Paul expresses his affection for and trust in Timothy when he commends him on those occasions (1 Cor 4:17; 16:10–11; Phil 2:19–22). Here, he is described more restrainedly as simply "our brother" and "God's coworker," a description even less full than the commendations of other persons who do not appear to have been as close to him as Timothy (e.g., 2 Cor 8:18, 22; Phil 2:25; cf. Col 4:7–8). Timothy had been with Paul when the church in Thessalonica was founded and had just returned from his mission there (v 6), so there was no need for Paul to commend him to his readers.

The description of Timothy as Paul's brother may be an example of the fictive kinship that Paul has been developing throughout the letter (see NOTE on 1:4). It has been suggested, however, that the term at times refers to a relatively limited group of workers who were engaged in missionary activities rather than to disciples in general (Ellis, 13–22). This is likely in some cases (e.g., 2 Cor 8:18; 9:3, 5; 12:18; Phil 1:14) and certain in others (2 Cor 8:23), especially when "brother" is used with other descriptions that designate one of Paul's evangelistic colleagues (e.g., Phil 2:25, "Epaphroditus, my brother and coworker and fellow soldier, and your messenger and minister to my need"), and may be the case in 1 Thess 3:2.

The boldness of the description of Timothy as also "God's coworker" (*kai synergon tou theou*) created difficulties that can already be observed in the textual tradition (Metzger, 563; Best 1972: 132–33). One variant, indeed, the best attested, removed the offensive synergism by writing *diakonon* ("minister") for *synergon* (ℵ A P Ψ 81 629* vg). The reading *kai synergon tou theou* (attested to by D* 33 it^(d, 86*) Ambrosiaster) is to be preferred because it is more difficult and best accounts for the other readings. Other attempts to mitigate the perceived problem were to delete the words *tou theou* ("of God"; B 1962) or make them qualify "the gospel of Christ" (arm).

While relatively limited in his characterization of Timothy, Paul's description of him as God's coworker is unusually laudatory. Paul had been at great pains to describe his own ministry in terms of his relationship to God (2:1–6) and to the Thessalonians (2:7–12). Timothy had reported to Paul that they still believed in God and loved Paul (3:6). In the fulsome manner in which Paul writes upon receiving Timothy's news, it is natural that he describes Timothy in relation to himself ("my brother") and God ("God's coworker"). The designation *synergos theou* is unusual, but it is not unique, and it belongs to a larger complex of terms that describe the preaching of the gospel as work and preachers as workers (see NOTE on 1:3). The term is not exclusively Pauline, but Paul did give it a special cast that described his mission as one undertaken in the company of others (Ollrog, 67).

Euodia and Syntyche were Paul's coworkers in the gospel (Phil 4:3); Timothy is God's coworker in the gospel. In 1 Thess 2:2, 8, 9 Paul had referred to the gospel as God's, meaning that it originated with God. Here it is the "gospel of Christ" (cf. Rom 15:19; 1 Cor 9:12; 2 Cor 2:12; 9:13, etc.), where *tou Christou* is objective and refers to Christ as the content that defines his work.

*to establish you and encourage you about your faith.* As Paul had been vivid in describing his need for contact, now he is vivid in describing the purpose of Timothy's mission in terms of their need. The two terms (*stērizein*, "to establish," and *parakalein*, "to encourage") used to describe the purpose (*eis to* plus infinitive) of Timothy's being sent to Thessalonica belonged to Paul's lexicon of exhortation (see NOTE on 2:3). They are often used in the NT in close proximity to each other (Rom 1:11–12; 1 Pet 5:10–11) or together, as they are here (also in Acts

14:22; 15:32; 2 Thess 2:17). Since *parakalein* is the more general word and receives specificity from words with which it is used, Paul's main aim was "to establish" the Thessalonians.

The original meaning of *stērizein* and its cognates was "to make firm," "to support," and it took on the transferred meaning of "to confirm" or "to strengthen." The moral and religious meaning came from Judaism (G. Harder in *TDNT* 7.655; Spicq 1991: 1428–32) and is represented particularly by Philo, who attributes stability in the face of confusion ultimately to God (e.g., *On Dreams* 1.158; 2:11; *On Flight and Finding* 49; *On the Special Laws* 2.202; *On Rewards and Punishments* 30; contrast Epictetus, *Gnomologium* 39 [Schenkl, 487]). This transferred meaning is found in 1 Thess 3:2 and in Luke 22:32 in a pastoral sense, and in eschatological contexts in 1 Thess 3:13; Jas 5:8; 1 Pet 5:9–11.

Paul had sent Timothy to stabilize them because he feared that they might have been shaken or agitated (v 3; cf. 2 Thess 2:2; and for standing firm, 1 Thess 3:8; 2 Thess 2:15). Paul's stated reason for sending Timothy was his uncertainty about his recent converts' faith. "Faith" (*pistis*) appears in vv 2 and 5 and with *epempsamen* and *epempsa*, forms an *inclusio*, thus marking the subject of vv 1–5. Paul wanted Timothy to encourage the Thessalonians about their faith (*hyper tēs pisteōs hēmōn*, the *hyper* substituting for *peri*; Moule, 65; GNTG 4.270). The singular *epempsa*, parallel to the plural, shows that the latter is an authorial and not real plural (see pages 86–89).

3:3. *that no one should be agitated by these afflictions.* Paul's concern that the Thessalonians be strengthened in their faith now focuses more narrowly: nobody (*mēdena*, "not one") should be disturbed (cf. 2:12; 5:11 for interest in individuals). The construction, *to mēdena sainesthai* ("that no one be agitated") is an example of the substantivized infinitive, which with *to mē* is the equivalent of a *hina mē* clause (BDF §399.3; see Rom 14:13, 21; 2 Cor 10:2; 1 Thess 4:6). This is an exception to the more usual use of a preposition before the articular infinitive to express purpose (Moule, 140; see 1 Thess 3:5).

The meaning of *sainesthai* ("to be agitated"), occurring only here in the Bible, has been understood differently. The basic meaning, of the wagging of a dog's tail, led to its use to describe greeting, fawning over or flattering someone, but it also came to describe agitation (F. Lang in *TDNT* 7.53–56). The derived meaning of seducing or beguiling has been adopted for 1 Thess 3:3 by some commentators, particularly those who think that Paul in this letter confronts opponents who were leading his converts astray (e.g., Frame, 127–28). The older translations, patristic commentaries, and most modern interpreters have understood the word to describe being moved, shaken, or unsettled. It is the equivalent of the Latin *quasso* and cognates, which describe being shaken emotionally (Lucretius, 3.600; cf. Cicero, *Tusculan Disputations* 4.29). Two texts strongly favor this understanding. Diogenes Laertius, *The Lives of Eminent Philosophers* 8.41, gives an account of an assembly "so shaken [*sainomenoi*] by a report of Pythagoras that they wept and wailed." In another fragmentary text, Origen states that, in dealing with controversial issues, "all the questions about the faith [*peri pisteōs*] which disturbed [*esēnen*] us have been examined" (Chadwick). In light of Paul's charge to Timothy to establish (*stērizein*) the Thessalonians (see NOTE on v 2), this is the logical meaning (see esp. Rigaux 1956: 470–71).

The nature of the tribulations (*thlipseis*) that upset the Thessalonians has been much disputed. Most commentators, on the basis of Acts 17:1–9 and 1 Thess 2:13–16, understand the reference to be to persecutions, seen as eschatological woes, but there is no evidence in the letter itself to support such an interpretation. Another interpretation, which shares a concern of this commentary with the emotional and psychological state of Paul's readers, thinks that "Paul refers to the alienation caused by the converts' adoption of a new value system which radically changed their social, cultic, and religious affiliation and loyalties" (Richard, 149). A refinement of the eschatological perspective is that Paul fears that the Thessalonians might be shaken by their anticipation of the ultimate apocalyptic reality (Bammel 1981). This interpretation has much to commend it in light of Paul's statement that they had accepted his preaching with tribulation and joy (see COMMENT on 1:6).

It is not certain, however, that it is the Thessalonians' tribulations that Paul has in mind, for it is not clear what the antecedent of *tautais* ("these") is. The reference could be to the experiences of the Thessalonians (Frame, 128), of Paul (John Chrysostom, *Homilies on 1 Thessalonians* 8 [PG 62:442]; von Dobschütz 1909: 134–35; Holtz 1986: 127), or both (Best 1972: 135). That it refers to Paul's experiences is suggested by the fact that, beginning with 2:17, Paul in a new section describes, with great pathos, his desolation at being separated from his readers. Timothy's mission was the result of Paul's yearning for them. Furthermore, 3:7 shows that Paul was relieved of *his* distress by Timothy's return and also shows that *thlipsis* in this chapter does not refer to external pressures but to internal distress. Thus, once more Paul compliments his readers: he had assumed that they knew that he was distressed because he was separated from them and were in danger of being unsettled by his distress (see v 5). Exactly how this concern of theirs was related to their faith is not yet clear.

*For you yourselves know that we are appointed to this.* Paul begins and ends his final statement (end of v 4) about his reason for sending Timothy to Thessalonica with *oidate* ("you know"). The *autoi gar oidate* ("you yourselves know") stands in an emphatic position and refers to their own knowledge of yet another feature of his ministry to them (cf. 2:1, 2, 5, 11). The reason (*gar*) nobody should be unsettled by Paul's distress is that he had instructed them in the matter during his work with them. The subject of *keimai* ("we are appointed"), which serves as the passive of *tithēmi* (cf. 5:9), is Paul (von Dobschütz 1909: 135; Holtz 1986: 128). But Paul's tribulation was shared by his converts when they imitated him in their reception of his preaching (see COMMENT on 1:6). His instruction on the matter flowed from that reality. Paul thought of his suffering as divinely determined (see COMMENT on 2:14 and 2 Thess 1:3–4), and his frequent references to it show how intrinsic it was to his self-understanding (e.g., 2 Cor 4:7–12; 6:3–10; 11:23–33). Thinking of his own life as paradigmatic in this respect, he at times referred to his suffering for hortatory purposes (e.g., 1 Cor 4:9–13; see Fitzgerald 1988: 117–48).

3:4. *Indeed, when we were with you, we kept on telling you in advance, "We are bound to suffer tribulation."* With the phrase *kai gar hote pros hymās ēmen proelegomen* ("Indeed, when we were with you we kept on telling you in advance") Paul introduces with great emphasis an actual statement he had made when he instructed them. The identical construction appears in 2 Thess 3:10, where it also introduces an earlier statement that provides a basis for his argument.

The emphasis is achieved in four ways. First, the clause *kai gar* ("indeed," "in fact") adds a new and important thought to what Paul has just said (Smythe §2814). Second, he specifies that he had made the statement when he was with them (*pros hymās*), something he also does in 2 Thessalonians (2:5; 3:1, 10) when he stresses something important to his argument. Third, he uses the word *prolegein*, which, in addition to its obvious predictive meaning (see end of v 4), also connotes a warning (see 2 Cor 13:2; Gal 5:21, in each of which the word is repeated, "warned you before and I warn you now"). Fourth, he uses the imperfect tense (*proelegomen*) to describe ongoing action; it was no casual item in his instruction.

Paul continues his emphasis by quoting his own words, cast in an emphatic form. The *hoti* could be recitative or introduce indirect discourse unchanged (Frame, 129; Rigaux 1956: 473); the similarity to 2 Thess 3:10, where he does quote something, suggests that it is recitative. By using *mellomen* with the infinitive rather than a simple future, Paul stresses the certainty of the tribulation that is destined to come (cf. Rom 4:24; 8:13, the only other places where Paul uses *mellein* with a present infinitive).

The elements of certainty and prediction are both present in the construction. Since the Thessalonians had seen tribulation in Paul's life and received the gospel in tribulation, suffering was not a mere prospect when Paul instructed them. What Paul had stressed then was the certainty of its occurring. A striking parallel is found in Acts 14:22, where Paul and Barnabas are said to be *epistērizontes tas psychas tōn mathētōn, parakalountes emmenein tē pistei kai hoti dia pollōn thlipseōn dei hēmās eiselthein eis tēn basileian tou theou* ("strengthening the souls of the disciples, exhorting them to continue in the faith, and saying that through many tribulations we must enter the kingdom of God"). Paul now stresses the predictive element for pastoral purposes, which it would also have had when he taught his converts that distress was sure to come (see COMMENT).

*as it has indeed happened, and you know.* The phrase *kathōs kai* ("as indeed") is used five other times in 1 Thessalonians (2:14; 4:1, 6, 13; 5:11; cf. 2 Thess 3:1) where the *kai* lends even stronger emphasis than that already present in *kathōs* without the *kai* (2:4, 13; 4:1, 11). The emphasis is extended further with the addition of *kai oidate* ("and you know"; cf. 2:1; 3:3; 4:2, 10; 5:2). The addition is still dependent on *kathōs*, and with it is a feature of paraenetic style (see pages 81–86) that Paul uses pastorally throughout the letter. The emphatic conclusion (vv 3b–4) of his account of Timothy's mission functions pastorally by stressing that there was continuity in Paul's experience from the very beginning: there is no need for surprise or consternation (cf. 1 Pet 5:12).

3:5. *For this reason, when I for my part could hold out no longer.* Paul now concludes his account of the origin of Timothy's mission that he began in v 1 with language almost identical to v 1. The reason he repeats his inability to endure the separation from his converts is to prepare for an elaboration of the reason for Timothy's mission, now given almost completely in terms of his own need.

The *dia touto* ("For this reason") points forward to what more will be said about why Timothy was sent. If the plural Paul had been using, with the exception of 2:18, had been real, which was the position of older commentaries, then the *kagō* ("I for my part") would be Paul's way of distinguishing himself from the others included in the plural, in particular, Silas (Rigaux 1956: 474). If the plurals are epistolary, as has been argued in this commentary, then the *kai* in *kagō* simply lends prominence to *egō*. The emphasis achieved in 2:18 by mentioning his own name is here achieved by *kagō* and the singular *epempsa*.

*I sent to learn about your faith.* Since the opening words of v 5 resumed vv 1–2, Paul does not have to mention that it was Timothy whom he had sent. On the singular *epempsa*, see v 2 and page 87. The purpose of the mission is stated differently from vv 2–3 in two ways. First, the reference to their faith is briefer and different, Paul being the intended beneficiary rather than the Thessalonians. Through Timothy he wishes to learn about their faith. What was said in vv 2–3 no doubt carries over, but it is significant that the focus is now on the Thessalonians in relation to Paul and his ministry. The second difference lies in the added dimension that is given to his ministry by the words that follow.

*lest the Tempter had tempted you.* With *mē pōs* ("lest") Paul expresses the apprehension with which he had sent Timothy (BDF §370.2). The aorist *epeirasen* ("had tempted") indicates that at the time he sent Timothy, Paul had feared that the Tempter (cf. Matt 4:3) had already tempted them, and the subjunctive *genētai* ("had been") implies his uncertainty about the outcome of the temptation. An insight into Paul's thinking is provided by 2 Cor 2:5–11, in which Paul, after emotionally referring to the tribulation and anguish with which he had written to the Corinthians on a prior occasion, cautions them not to abandon a member of the congregation who was still under the congregation's censure. By not restoring the person to the church's fellowship, he would lapse into excessive sorrow and be taken advantage of by Satan (see 1 Cor 7:5 for Satan tempting people because of their lack of self-control; cf. 10:8–10).

*and our labor had been in vain.* Paul is now explicit that his concern was whether his ministry had been successful, measured by the perseverance of his converts. For his use of *kopos* to describe evangelical activity, see NOTE on 1:3 and 5:12 (*kopiān*). The idea of not laboring in vain implies concerted effort to be completed successfully and in that respect is similar to the image of the crown that he hoped to receive for winning his race (see COMMENT on 2:19). His language is that of Isa 49:4, which he uses elsewhere to express his conviction that his apostleship was in the prophetic tradition. Paul uses the language of labor and the race together in Phil 2:16 and interchangeably in Gal 2:2 (*mē pōs eikē kekopiake*) and 4:11 (*mē pōs eis kenon trechō ē edramon*). These passages reveal Paul as working in the gospel for his eschatological reward without presum-

ing that he would receive it (cf. Phil 3:12–14). Also similar to 1 Thess 2:18 is
Satan's role, here tempting the Thessalonians, there interdicting Paul's movements (see further 2 Cor 11:12–14).

## COMMENT

The main purpose of 2:17–3:10 is to describe the circumstances leading to the
writing of 1 Thessalonians, and the main point of that description is 3:6–10,
Paul's response to Timothy's report that his mission had been successful. Paul's
account of the sending of Timothy to reestablish contact with the Thessalonians
should therefore be seen in light of that response. Paul's account of Timothy's
commissioning and return contains conventions that were used in connection
with the sending of emissaries and acknowledgment after completion of their
mission. Awareness of those conventions will cast light on Paul's words. Even
though the account of Paul's commission in 3:1–5 is repetitive, it is brief and
concentrated.

Paul begins his description of Timothy's mission as a consequence (*dio*) of the
deprivation he had experienced by virtue of his enforced separation from the
Thessalonians (2:17–20). Paul had stressed that while he was subject to circumstances beyond his control, he acted out of his own volition: although orphaned
(*aporphanisthentes*), he had earnestly endeavored (*perissoterōs espoudasamen*) to
see them; he had resolved (*ethelēsamen*) to come to them, but Satan had hindered (*enekopsen*) him. Now, once again, continuing in deeply affective language, Paul describes how, undaunted by his restrictive circumstances, he had
gladly determined (*eudokēsamen*) to remain in Athens while sending Timothy
back to Thessalonica.

The expression of one's own or one's emissary's eagerness (e.g., by using
*spoudaios* and its cognates) to see or establish contact with one's correspondent
was an epistolary convention (see NOTE on 2:17) also used by Paul. The formulaic character of such expressions should not obscure the fact that Paul could
use them diplomatically (e.g., 2 Cor 8:16–17, 22; Phil 2:28). In 1 Thess 2:17–3:5
Paul uses the convention pastorally. He did not send Timothy because he had
learned something about the Thessalonians; he did so out of his sense of deprivation, gladly determining to send Timothy and be left alone, abandoned, as it
were, in Athens. This is how his recent converts felt, alienated from society and
in tension with family and friends (see COMMENT on 1:6), and by describing
himself in this way, Paul communicates his empathy with his readers (cf. "orphaned" in 2:17). Paul's claim that he sent Timothy because he found his separation unbearable is found in vv 1–2 and 5, the two brackets to the *inclusio*, which
differ in what they describe as the purpose of Timothy's mission to Thessalonica.

According to vv 1–3a, Timothy was sent, in essence, to continue the pastoral
care Paul had engaged in when he was in Thessalonica. As Paul had exhorted
(*parakalein*; 2:3, 12), so Timothy was to do (v 2). Paul feared that his distress
might trouble them so much that their faith might be shaken. Elsewhere in the
letter, Paul describes faith as faith in God (1:8), which he explicates in a sum-

mary of what his converts had accepted (1:9–10; cf. 4:14). This message of Paul's was, to Paul's mind, inseparable from his own ministry (Rigaux 1956: 61–62; Laub 1976: 26–31; Koester 1982: 113), which he conducted with profound distress combined with joy (cf. 2 Cor 7:4; 8:2; Rom 12:12), both of which the Thessalonians had experienced when they became imitators of Paul in their acceptance of his message (1:6).

In Phil 4:14 Paul complimented the Philippians for having shared his tribulation, a sign of friendship (Cicero, *On Friendship* 22; Plutarch, *On Having Many Friends* 96A,CD; Lucian, *Toxaris* 7). Paul therefore did not consider participation in his distress a problem. The Thessalonians' circumstances, however, had deteriorated since he had left them, and in 2:13–16 he addressed that problem. Now he recalls their concern about the distress his separation and repeated unsuccessful attempts to return to them caused them, and of his fear that his failure to do so might have a deleterious effect on their faith. Patristic commentators thought that Paul was concerned because he knew that pupils are upset by their teachers' trials (e.g., Theophylact, *Exposition of 1 Thessalonians* 3 [PG 124:1297]).

Paul assumes that the Thessalonians had heard of his circumstances before he sent Timothy and that the report would have painted a dire picture of the conditions in which he found himself. That the report had the effect on the Thessalonians he describes and is not a rhetorical ploy is likely in view of the autobiographical description in 1:2–2:12, which recalls what the Thessalonians themselves as well as others knew of the relationship they had with Paul. That Paul was correct in his surmise appears most clearly from the Thessalonians' response to Timothy's mission. They assured Timothy that they still loved Paul and remembered him well and that their faith was intact (3:6). At the same time, probably in a letter they sent Paul via Timothy, but in any case through him (see Malherbe 1990a), they requested Paul's advice about certain practical matters, which he gives in chaps. 4 and 5, and which he describes as the filling up of what was lacking in their faith (3:10). What they particularly lacked was an understanding of how God is active in the Christian life, which explains the emphasis on God in the letter (see NOTES and COMMENT on 1:2, 4, 9).

The second, related motivation for Timothy's mission, already just visible below the surface in vv 1–3, comes into full view in the second bracket of the *inclusio*. Now Paul describes the reason for the mission in terms of his own interest: he wanted to learn about their faith out of fear that the Tempter had tempted the Thessalonians and that his ministry had been in vain (v 5). Again their faith is tied to Paul and his ministry. By using the image of strenuous labor for his ministry, which conveyed a notion of intense effort, like that of the race he was striving to win, Paul presents himself as vigorous on their behalf. It is noteworthy that he does not describe the Thessalonians as derelict in any way. As Satan had frustrated him in his work (2:18), so he fears the Tempter may have acted on his converts. Once more, Paul shares something with them.

This pastoral method of stressing what one shares with those one seeks to help is also present in Paul's calling upon his readers to remember his ministry among them. He does so to the point of quoting some of the actual words he had spoken to them. His pastoral method is further present in recalling that when he was with them he had warned them to anticipate distress that would come later, in addition to what they had experienced in their conversion (1:6). Anticipation of hardship or misfortune was a standard feature of ancient consolation. John Chrysostom already understood that Paul was following this particular method (Homilies on 1 Thessalonians 4 [PG 62:417]; he refers to John 14:29). This method of therapy assumed that hardships were destined to fall on human beings because fate so decreed and that when they did, people should not be surprised (see esp. Cicero, Tusculan Disputations 3.30; Seneca, Epistles 24.15; 91.4; see Malherbe 1987: 57–58; 1990b: 387–88). Paul, too, stresses very emphatically that hardships are inevitable, but for him they belong to God's purpose (cf. 5:9) and are not the dictates of impersonal fate. It was necessary for Paul to stress that hardships were part of God's scheme and did not happen by chance, for his Gentile converts, unlike Jewish converts, would be surprised (cf. 1 Pet 4:12) that conversion to the Creator (see NOTE on 1:9) would cause hardship.

Timothy's work with the Thessalonians marked his emergence as an important associate of Paul despite his youth (cf. 1 Tim 4:12; Titus 2:15; Acts 16:1–3). Unlike his commendations of Timothy when he sent him on missions (1 Cor 4:17; 16:10–11; Phil 2:19–23) or in his commendations of other envoys (2 Cor 8:16–19, 23a; Phil 2:25–30), Paul is quite brief in his description of Timothy here. There was no need to write at length about Timothy, for Timothy had just returned from a successful completion of his mission and, in fact, had had more contact with the Thessalonians than Paul had with them. Nevertheless, Paul describes Timothy in terms conventionally used in connection with the dispatching of emissaries. Although he chooses to use that language for its value in the present letter, it is not unreasonable to suppose that his words reflect what he had thought about Timothy and his mission at the time he sent him.

In sending an emissary it was important to state clearly the relationship between the sender and the person sent for at least two reasons. It was expected that the emissary would be received as the sender himself would be received (M. M. Mitchell 1992: 645–49; see Matt 10:41–42; Rom 16:1–2; Did 11:4), and the emissary had power and authority to speak on behalf of the sender (M. M. Mitchell 1992: 649–51; see Luke 10:16; John 12:49; 1 Cor 4:17). Paul is careful to specify the relationships that obtained when sending out emissaries. For example, Titus is called his koinōnos and synergos (2 Cor 8:23), and Epaphroditus his adelphos, synergos, and systratiōtēs and the Philippians' apostolos and leitourgos (Phil 2:25).

In 1 Thess 3:2, Timothy is simply called Paul's brother (cf. 2 Cor 8:18, 22; Phil 2:25), and rather than refer to him as his synergos in his commendation as he does to other emissaries (2 Cor 8:23; Phil 2:25), Paul calls him God's coworker. The familial language is in keeping with Paul's use of kinship language throughout the letter, even if it does designate Timothy as a missionary. More striking is his calling Timothy God's coworker, which evokes a sense of concerted effort, just as Paul's *kopos* does.

Missionary activity is frequently described simply as "the work" (Acts 14:26; 15:38), or as "the work of the Lord" or "of Christ" (1 Cor 16:10; Phil 2:30), or the work to which the Holy Spirit calls someone (Acts 13:2), or as an individual's work (1 Cor 3:13–15; 9:1; cf. Phil 1:22). Preachers are called *ergatai*, "workers" (Matt 9:37; 2 Tim 2:15; negatively: Luke 13:27; 2 Cor 11:13; Phil 3:2). Paul refers to his associates simply as his *synergoi* (Rom 16:21; 2 Cor 8:23; Phlm 1, 24), or specifies that they are his coworkers in Christ (Rom 16:3, 9) or the gospel (Phil 4:3; cf. 3 John 8, "in the truth"), or specifies the goal of their collaboration (2 Cor 1:24, the Corinthians' joy; cf. Col 4:11, "for the kingdom of God").

The closest parallel to 1 Thess 3:2 is 1 Cor 3:9, *theou gar esmen synergoi* ("for we are God's coworkers"). The claim that in the latter passage the meaning is that they are coworkers for God (Furnish 1971) may find support in the fact that Paul goes on to say that they are God's field (*geōrgion*) and building (*oikodomē*), that is, that they belong to God. But if that were so, one could have expected Paul to use *misthōtos* ("hired worker"), particularly in view of *misthos* ("wage" or "reward") in v 8, or *ergatēs* ("laborer"), which would have fit well here (cf. Demosthenes, *Oration* 35.32, *hoi peri tēn geōrgian ergatai*, "workmen engaged in farming"). The latter could also have found support elsewhere in the NT, where remuneration of workers (*ergatai*) in the gospel is in view (Matt 10:10; 1 Tim 5:18; cf. 1 Cor 9:13).

The context of 1 Cor 3:9 casts considerable light on Paul's understanding of *synergos tou theou*. Throughout 1 Cor 3: 5–13 Paul stresses the personal responsibility of evangelists but is careful to emphasize that it is God who is the major actor. That does not imply, however, that the phrase means that the evangelists worked with each other for God (correctly, Henneken, 23–24). They work with God, but at his behest, as Paul explains in 2 Cor 5:20–6:2 (Furnish 1984: 340). The notion that God is the effective force in Paul's mission without in any way diminishing Paul's own and his converts' efforts is present elsewhere in his letters (Gal 2:8; Phil 1:5–6; 2:13; see Ware) and is implicit in his description of his own ministry and the active word of God (1 Thess 2:1–13). It is in this sense that Timothy, too, is God's coworker.

When commending Timothy to the Philippians, Paul claimed a special relationship with Timothy, like that between a father and his son (Phil 2:19–23). Of particular relevance is his commendation of Timothy in 1 Corinthians. In sending Timothy, evidently to accompany or carry the letter, Paul cautions that Timothy would remind (*anamnēsei*) the Corinthians of his ways; Timothy would engage in paraenesis that pointed to Paul as their spiritual father, who is to be their paradigm (1 Cor 4:14–17; see pages 83–85). Timothy does the work of the Lord (*to ergon tou kyriou ergazetai*) as Paul does, and they are to receive him hospitably and send him back to Paul (1 Cor 16:10–11). Paul's description of Timothy's mission in 1 Thess 3 is quite similar to what is said of him in 1 Corinthians. Timothy continues Paul's pastoral work (3:2–3), and the account of his return focuses on the relationship between Paul and the Thessalonians (3:6).

## c. TIMOTHY'S RETURN AND REPORT, 3:6–10

### TRANSLATION

3   6But Timothy has just returned to us from you and brought us the good news of your faith and love and that you have a good remembrance of us always, longing to see us as we do you—7for this reason we were comforted, brethren, because of you in all our anguish and distress through your faith 8because now we live if you stand fast in the Lord. 9What thanksgiving can we render God for you for all the joy with which we rejoice on your account in the presence of our God, 10begging night and day with the utmost earnestness to see you face to face and complete what is lacking in your faith.

### NOTES

3:6. *But Timothy has just returned to us from you.* Paul contrasts (*de*, "But") vv 6–7 with what precedes, but it is not obvious whether the contrast is between Paul's *thlipseis* (v 3) and his comfort (v 7) or between his sending of Timothy (v 5) and Timothy's return (v 6). If it is the former, *arti* ("now," "just") would go with the main verb, *pareklēthēmen* ("we were comforted," v 7), and thus both reach far backwards and forwards in the text. That is possible (see Lünemann, 503), but Paul's interest in vv 1–5, as shown by the two brackets of the *inclusio*, was in sending Timothy to overcome the separation between himself and the Thessalonians. Timothy's return, however, is described with a genitive absolute, which is subsidiary to the main verb. The sense of the participle is temporal: now that Timothy has just returned, Paul hastens to respond. But it is also causal, providing a reason for Paul's comfort. First Thessalonians was thus written shortly after Timothy's arrival (see pages 72–74). Paul again piles up pronouns, eight in this verse, to stress his personal relationship with the Thessalonians (cf. 1:4–6) and reverses the chronological order ("to us from you") to highlight Timothy's arrival.

*and brought us the good news of your faith and love.* The second genitive absolute, *Timotheou . . . euangelisamenou* ("brought . . . the good news"), is likewise subsidiary to the main verb and provides an additional ground for Paul's comfort. The verb *euangelizesthai* ("to tell good news") is always used in the NT in the technical sense of preaching the gospel, and this exact phrase, *euangelizesthai tēn pistin*, but with a different meaning, is used in that sense in Gal 1:23. Most commentators, however, consider this the only nontechnical use in the NT. Paul must, however, have used it to convey more than another verb, such as *legein* ("to tell") or *anangellein* ("to announce"), would have done. It is especially important that Timothy's good news had to do with faith, love, and re-membrance of Paul. This is an expansion of what one might have expected, a re-port about their faith (v 2), to include comment on their love for Paul and a good remembrance of him. All three matters involved their relationship to him and the gospel they had received from him (see COMMENT).

*and that you have a good remembrance of us always.* Paul's account of Timo-thy's report expands to show what had been at the heart of his concern about the Thessalonians: how they conceived of their relationship to him. The construc-tion *echein mneian . . . agathēn pantote* ("to have a good remembrance always") is different from *mneian poieisthai . . . adialeiptōs* ("to mention . . . without ceas-ing") in 1:2 (despite 2 Tim 1:3) and has a different significance, one not captured by modern translations (e.g., RSV: "remember us kindly"; NEB: "always think kindly of us"; NIV: "always have pleasant memories of us"). The interpretation that sees in the phrase Paul's relief that the Thessalonians still held him in high regard despite a charge by opponents that he had deserted the Thessalonians (Frame, 132; Best 1972: 140) is not on target.

It should be recognized that Paul's language is conventional in two ways. First, in letters of friendship writers stressed that their absent friends were constantly (e.g., *adialeiptōs, aparaleiptōs*) remembered (see Ps.-Demetrius, *Epistolary Types* 1, quoted on page 181; Koskenniemi, 123–27; see NOTE on 1:3). Second, in paraenesis it was common to call to mind someone after whom to model onself, a practice Paul had already reflected in 2:9 (cf. 2 Thess 3:7; see pages 83–85). According to Timothy, the Thessalonians still remembered Paul in this way.

*longing to see us as we do you.* The participle *epipothountes* ("longing") de-scribes a manifestation of their good remembrance of Paul and provides yet an-other detail about Timothy's report. Paul used *epipothein* and its cognates to de-scribe intense emotion in his relationship with his churches (e.g., 2 Cor 5:2; 7:7, 11; 9:14; Phil 1:8; 4:1; cf. 2:26, of Epaphroditus). Of special interest is its use to describe an unfulfilled desire to see his readers, as here, for which he substitutes a letter (Rom 1:11; 15:23; cf. 2 Tim 1:4). Ancient letters teem with expressions of longing (*pothos, epithymia* [see NOTE on 2:17], etc.; for the motif, see Thraede 1970: 90, 165–68, with reference to 1 Thess 3:6, 10 on p. 97). This is one more epistolographic cliché in a series that Paul uses in this context. Paul goes beyond the simple use of a cliché, however, by attributing his knowledge to Timothy's report, thus making it a compliment to them, and adding that he, too, longs to see them. By placing the pronouns next to each other (*hēmeis hymās,* "we you") at the end, before breaking off the sentence, Paul heightens the emo-tion. Paul's account of Timothy's report demonstrates how successful he consid-ered Timothy's mission to have been.

*3:7. for this reason we were comforted, brethren, because of you.* With *dia touto* ("for this reason") Paul resumes the thought begun in the two genitive absolutes before his revealing excursus. Since this transitional phrase always begins a sen-tence in Paul's letters (e.g., 3:5; cf. Rom 1:26; 4:16; 5:12; 1 Cor 11:10; 2 Cor 13:10), the previous sentence is not completed. At the end of v 6 he had turned from the report about the Thessalonians to his own longing for them, now he abruptly turns to the effect of Timothy's report on him. He had sent Timothy to exhort (*parakalesai*) and strengthen them (v 2), and now Timothy's good news comforted (*pareklēthēmen*; cf. 4:18) him.

Calling them "brethren" lends some poignancy to what he says, namely, that he is comforted *eph' hymin* ("because of you"). With verbs of feeling the preposition *epi* often describes the ground or cause of the action described in the verb (BDF §235.2). In view of v 2, *hyper tēs pisteōs* ("about your faith"), one might have expected him to say that he was comforted "by your faith" or by a report concerning their faith. But by mentioning them first and grounding his comfort in them, Paul once more strengthens the personal bond with them.

*in all our anguish and distress through your faith.* The *epi* ("in") here is temporal (cf. 2 Cor 1:4, *epi pasē tē thlipsei*; 7:4; Phil 1:3), and "all" is intensive (2 Cor 1:4; 7:4; 1 Pet 5:7; cf. 1 Thess 3:9, *pasē tē chreia*). It is difficult to distinguish between *anangkē* and *thlipsis* as to meaning, and the construction *pasē tē anangkē kai thlipsei* connects them still farther. The noun *anangkē* has a sense of necessity (Matt 18:7; Luke 14:18; 1 Cor 7:37; 9:16) or compulsion (2 Cor 6:4; Phlm 14). It may refer to external actions (2 Cor 12:10) and then have an eschatological meaning (Luke 2:23; 1 Cor 7:26). The term is also used of emotional anguish, with *thlipsis* and *stenochōria*, another synonymous term for emotional difficulties, in 2 Cor 6:4. This is the meaning of the word in 3:7, for its association with *thlipsis* points to v 3, where *thlipsis* refers to Paul's feeling of desolation caused by his separation from the Thessalonians. Now that Timothy has come and reported good news about them, Paul intensifies his description of his distress, thereby heightening the comfort that Timothy's report brought to him. The Thessalonians themselves were the cause of Paul's comfort, and their faith was the means by which (*dia tēs hymōn pisteōs*) it was effected, the attributive position of the possessive pronoun lending greater emphasis (GNTG 3.190).

*3:8. because now we live if you stand fast in the Lord.* The *hoti* ("because") introduces further clarification of Paul's comfort. He had feared that the Thessalonians might have become emotionally unsettled in their faith because of his *thlipseis*, and he sent Timothy to exhort them (vv 2–3). Now (equals *arti*, v 6) the report of their faith gives him new life because they stand fast (*stēkete*) in the Lord. Paul's claim that he now lives is no allusion to eternal life (some church fathers; see Rigaux 1956: 480), and interpretations along the line of Lünemann (505), "we are in full strength and freshness of life, we do not feel the sorrows and tribulations which the outer world prepares for us," are overblown.

Two things appear to be behind Paul's language. It was commonplace to speak of the preparedness of friends to live and die together (e.g., Euripides, *Orestes* 317–18; *Ion* 852–53, 857–58; Horace, *Odes* 3.9.24; Athenaeus, *Deipnosophists* 6.249B; cf. 2 Kgs 15:21; see Stählin). Such language was used in letters to express hyperbolically the devastation of physical separation, for example, "I beg you to send for me; else I die because I do not see you daily" (PGiess 17). Related to this is the idea that a letter saved the recipient (PMich 8.482, 22–24).

This language of well-being belonged to the varied terminology that was used to describe the joy occasioned by receiving a letter (Koskenniemi, 75–77) or the arrival of a friend. The latter is the case here, and 2 Cor 7:3–7 is a significant parallel. There Paul uses the same terminology to describe the arrival of Titus after a period during which Paul had experienced intense distress:

> you are in our hearts to die together and to live together . . . I am filled with comfort [*paraklēsei*]. With all our affliction [*epi pasē thlipsei*] I am overjoyed [*hyperperisseuomai tē charā*] . . . we were afflicted at every turn [*en panti thlibomenoi*]. But God . . . comforted [*parekalesen*] us by the coming of Titus . . . but also by the comfort with which he was comforted by you [*pareklēthē eph' hymin*], as he told us of your longing [*epipothēsin*], your mourning, your zeal for me, so that I rejoiced still more [*mallon charēnai*].

In this text Paul uses conventions to good effect in attempting to reestablish a close tie to the Corinthians. The same elements appear in 1 Thess 3:6–8, but more concisely, for his relationship with his readers had not been strained, as those with the Corinthians had been.

Paul does, however, sound a note of caution: "if you stand fast in the Lord." Normally, *ean* is used with the subjunctive (BDF §372.1a); this use with the indicative may make the condition just hypothetical enough to add a hortatory element to it (Alford, 265; Lünemann, 505; W. Grundmann in *TDNT* 7.637). Paul's life depends on their standing fast (*stēkete*) in the Lord. Paul uses *stēkete* in the indicative (Phil 1:27, "stand fast in the spirit"), but mostly in the imperative: "stand" (Gal 5:1; 2 Thess 2:15); "stand in the faith" (1 Cor 16:13); and "stand in the Lord" (Phil 4:1; 1 Thess 3:8).

*Stēkein* is primarily a NT word (W. Grundmann in *TDNT* 7.736–38), but it conveys the meaning of the Latin *stare*, "to stand firm," in a military sense, which took on a moral or spiritual sense in late Stoicism (Fontaine). It is similar in meaning to *histēmi* in Eph 6:11, 13, 14 (Schlier 1963: 290, refers to Thucydides, *History of the Peloponnesian War* 5.104; Xenophon, *Anabasis* 1.10.1; 4.8.19; Polybius, *Histories* 4.61; Dionysius of Halicarnassus, *Roman Antiquities* 9.28.50). Paul was familiar with the Stoic use of martial imagery (see Malherbe 1989: 91–119), which in the sense that interests us is preserved mostly in Latin sources. Unlike the Stoics, who would stand fast in the security provided by their reason, for Paul security is defined by being in Christ.

3:9. *What thanksgiving can we render God for you.* Paul now concludes the thanksgiving that began in 1:2 and was renewed in 2:13. It was usual in letters to thank the gods, upon receipt of a letter, that communication had been effected (e.g., POxy 1481, 9–10; PVat A, 8). An exclamation, in the form of a rhetorical question, is introduced by *gar*, which is not rendered in the translation. With self-evident conclusions, especially with strong affirmations or an interrogative, it can mean "then" (BDF §452.1; BAGD, s.v. *gar*, 3). The rhetorical question indicates that Paul's thanksgiving is the result of everything that immediately precedes, in particular, Timothy's report that contact with the Thessalonians had been restored.

This thanksgiving differs in form from 1:2 and 2:13, and also in the fact that it does not specify that Paul constantly (*pantote, adialeiptōs*) gives thanks. The aorist, *dynametha* . . . *antapodounai*, expressing punctiliar action, describes Paul's thanksgiving as his immediate reaction to Timothy's news (O'Brien 1977: 156). The Thessalonians were the ground for his comfort (v 7), but it is God whom he thanks. The rhetorical question signifies that, while it is appropriate to render (*antapodounai*, "to recompense"; cf. Ps 116:12 [115:3 LXX]) thanks to God, it could not be done adequately. For intercessory prayers framed as questions to God, see 2 Sam 24:17; Isa 6:11; 2 *Bar* 81:1–2 (Wiles, 186).

*for all the joy with which we rejoice.* The cause (*epi* plus dative; cf. *eph' hymin*, v 2) of Paul's thanksgiving is the joy he experienced (cf. 1 Cor 1:4; Phil 1:3, 5). The language is emphatic, "all" lending intensity and "all the joy" presenting a contrast to "all our anguish and distress" (v 7). The Hebraism "joy with which we rejoice" (cf. Isa 66:10 LXX; John 3:29; GNTG 2.419; 4.69) further accentuates Paul's joy. Paul's thanksgiving has its counterpart in ancient letters that express joy because the writer had received a letter (e.g., PEleph 1, 2–3; PHamb 1.88, 3; see Koskenniemi, 75–77).

*on your account in the presence of our God.* Paul's focus on the Thessalonians intensifies. "You," which appears ten times in vv 6–10 (v 7: "because of you," "your faith"; v 8: "if you stand fast"; v 9: "for you"), now continues, "on your account." As it does in 1:3, the phrase *emprosthen tou theou* ("in the presence of God") refers to the present (contrast 2:19; 3:13).

3:10. *begging night and day with the utmost earnestness to see you face to face.* Grammatically, *deomenoi* ("begging") depends on *chairomen* ("we rejoice"), but the connection is loose and not causal, as though Paul's rejoicing led to his prayer (O'Brien 1977: 158). For *deisthai* in a similar context, see Rom 1:10. The word is stronger than *proseuchesthai* and embodies a sense of personal need ("I beseech"). It was used frequently in petitions addressed to kings (Milligan, 42).

The intensity in the word is further strengthened by *hyperekperissou* ("with the utmost earnestness"), one of a number of compounds with *hyper* that Paul is fond of constructing to express emphasis (e.g., in Rom 5:20; 8:26, 37; 2 Cor 9:14; 11:23; Phil 2:9; 2 Thess 1:3; see Delling 1969, esp. 143–49). The intensity is further strengthened by "night and day," which functions adverbially in the way *pantote* does in 1:2. The expression says nothing about early Christian prayer practice (see O'Brien 1977: 158 n. 85). It conveys the same sense present in the letter of the homesick soldier who wrote, "If you wish just a little to see me, I do so a lot [to see you] and I pray daily [*kath' hēmeran*] to the gods to grant me quickly a good opportunity to come [to you]" (PMich 3.203, 17–18; cf. BGU 1.246, 12–13; POxy 528, 6ff.; PGiess 17).

*and complete what is lacking in your faith.* Paul's petition has a twofold purpose: to see the Thessalonians and to complete what is lacking in their faith. This marks a turning point in the letter as Paul decisively turns to the future. He now adds a second purpose to the desire to see them (cf. 2:17). The grammatical construction *eis to idein* . . . *kai katartisai* suggests what he intended his desired visit to accomplish: Timothy was to stabilize them in their faith (v 3); Paul wants to augment it. In the first thanksgiving, he had given thanks for the work that issued from their faith (1:3); now he has a desire to correct a deficiency in their faith. The meaning of this sentence has been made difficult by the relative infrequency with which *katartizein* ("to complete") and *hysterēma* ("what is lacking") are used, and how they are related to the Thessalonians' faith.

Faith here must mean one's total response to God, which could be inadequate or deficient (e.g., Rom 14:1; 2 Cor 10:15; see Best 1972: 145). It has been debated whether Paul has in mind doctrinal or practical matters or both (von Dobschütz 1909: 147, who refers to 4:1ff. and 4:13ff.). The petitions for love and holiness in vv 12–13 and the fact that Paul takes up these topics in 4:2, 9; 5:13 suggest that they must be included (O'Brien 1977: 159). A fuller understanding must take into consideration that the Thessalonians' faith was tied to their relationship with Paul (see NOTES on vv 3 and 5). The term *hysterēma* used here in the plural, was used infrequently in ancient literature (U. Wilckens in *TDNT* 8.593), and is used in the NT only once (Luke 21:4) outside the Pauline literature, where it appears eight times (including Col 1:24). It occurs five times with various forms of *plēroun* ("to fill"), thus having the sense of a deficiency that could be corrected (1 Cor 16:17; 2 Cor 9:12; 11:9; Phil 2:30; Col 1:24). This appears to be formulaic and not to have a negative sense (Holtz 1986: 138).

Formulations like this appeared frequently in letters and performed the function of expressing one's intention to satisfy or supply the want (*apoplēroun to endeon*) caused by one's physical separation from one's readers (Basil, *Epistle* 297). Stated in a different way, a letter completes or substitutes for one's physical presence (*dia grammatōn plērō ta tēs parousias*; Gregory Nazianzen, *Epistle* 68.1). Related to this notion of filling up a correspondent's need is the very common convention of inviting one's readers to express their need (*chreia*; Koskenniemi, 68–69; Steen, 128–30). Such invitations took forms like "please do not hesitate to write me about anything you need (*peri hōn ean chreian echeis*)" (POxy 930; PSI 333). The verb *chrēzein* ("to need") was also used frequently, as was *hysterein*, which functioned as an equivalent in letters (e.g., PEnt 86, 3.11; PZeno Cairo 59025, 2.12; PMerton 83, 23–24).

Paul's concern with the Thessalonians' *hysterēmata* fulfills the same epistolary function to express his intention in writing the letter. He is more precise in describing his intention, however, by using *katartizein* rather than some form of *plēroun*. The surface meaning of *katartizein* is to mend something, such as a net (Mark 1:19), but of greater relevance to 1 Thessalonians is the derived pedagogic and psychagogic meaning the verb and its cognates had assumed (e.g., Plutarch, *Cato the Younger* 65.5; *Alexander* 7). It is used pedagogically in Luke 6:40 and pastorally in Gal 6:1 (cf. Heb 13:21, of God). The variety of psychagogic terms with which it appears in 2 Tim 3:16–17 (*ōphelimos, didaskalia, elegmos, epanorthōsis, paideia*) and 1 Pet 5:10 (*stērixei, sthenōsei, themeliōsei*) shows how the Thessalonians' deficiencies were to be completed—by Paul's pastoral letter.

# COMMENT

With vv 6–10 Paul comes to the final and main part of 2:17–3:10. Paul describes Timothy's report as the successful climax to repeated attempts on his part to satisfy his yearning to see the Thessalonians. The way in which he describes Timothy's report and his reaction to it explains the warm tone of 1 Thessalonians, which was written in response to Timothy's news from Thessalonica. By ending the autobiographical section of the letter, which begins in 1:2, in this way, Paul vividly describes the relationship with his readers that will provide the basis for his advice in chaps. 4 and 5. It is a relationship that has never been marked by tension or misunderstanding; on the contrary, it has been characterized by mutual yearning to bridge the distance separating them.

Paul progressively becomes clearer about the significance that Timothy's mission had for him. From v 2, it would appear that Timothy was sent to benefit the Thessalonians, but from v 5 it becomes clear that Paul wanted to learn about their faith lest his own ministry, to which their faith was inextricably connected, had been rendered ineffectual by the Tempter. Timothy's report (v 6) evoked a response from Paul so extravagant that it highlights what was at the heart of his concern.

Timothy reported on three matters, the Thessalonians' faith, love, and remembrance of Paul. It is unsatisfactory to point out that Timothy reports favorably on two elements (faith and love) of the triad of 1:2 but that Paul had to write further about hope in 4:13–5:10 (von Dobschütz 1909: 140; Rigaux 1956: 478). Nor is it adequate to identify God as the object of the Thessalonians' faith, each other or all people as the objects of their love, and Paul as the one they remembered (Bruce 1982: 66; Marshall 1983: 94–95; Wanamaker, 133–34), and to let the matter rest with that observation. All three elements in fact focus on Paul and represent three dimensions of the Thessalonians' relationship with him.

The importance that Timothy's report about the Thessalonians' faith had for Paul is evident from his comments in chap. 1, which was written in light of that report. In hyperbolic fashion, Paul claims that a report about their faith in God has gone forth everywhere so that no further comment is required, for everyone knows about the Thessalonians' response to his preaching (1:8–9). Paul had just given an account of their conversion that presents his life as inextricable from his message, and of the Thessalonians as having become imitators of him when they accepted his message (1:5–7). This faith moved them to preach the gospel (1:5, 7–8), thus assuring that Paul had not run in vain (3:5; cf. Phil 2:16; see Ware 1996). This theology of preaching, written in response to Timothy's report about their faith, further strengthens his relationship with them and is a commentary on 3:6.

The love about which Timothy reported could be their love for God (cf. Rom 8:28; 1 Cor 2:9; 8:3; 2 Thess 3:5). It could also be love for Christ (cf. Phlm 5, where love and faith are combined), for other Christians (cf. Gal 5:6, faith working through love), or for all people (1 Thess 3:12). In 1 Thessalonians, however, love is also closely connected to the work of ministry. According to 1:3, the Thessalonians' labor (*kopos*) in the gospel issued from their love (cf. Phil 1:16; 1 Thess

2:8), and in 5:12 Paul urges them to love those who labor (*kopiōntas*) among them and otherwise act pastorally because of their work. Paul had feared that his own labor (*kopos*) might have proved in vain because the Tempter had rattled the Thessalonians' faith. Now he is relieved by the report of their faith and their love for him. That love strengthens the relationship within which their faith finds stability (Marxsen 1979: 55).

That Paul's major concern had been how the Thessalonians viewed him becomes clearest from Timothy's report that they had a good remembrance of him always, which was a manifestation of their love for him (Best 1972: 140). The remembering of a mentor was a feature of the instruction by ancient moral preachers, and Paul's statement must be viewed in the context of that practice. The person whose words agreed with his life could be called upon as a moral paradigm (see COMMENT on 1:6; 2:8) who demonstrated in his own life what his teaching meant and that its goals could be achieved. Paul had used this method of instruction when he founded the church in Thessalonica (2 Thess 3:7–10), and he does so in 1 Thessalonians, when he provides an autobiographical account in chaps. 1–3 to support his explicit paraenesis in chaps. 4 and 5 (see COMMENT: Introduction on 2:1–12).

A disciple continued to be guided by the exemplary life of his teacher in his absence by remembering him (pages 83–84). This theme of remembrance appears in the moral literature (e.g., Ps.-Isocrates, *To Demonicus* 9; Cicero, *To His Friends* 2.1.2; Seneca, *Epistle* 11.9). A particularly instructive example is provided by Lucian, *Nigrinus* 6–7, which describes the attitude of a new convert to philosophy to his absent teacher:

Then, too, I take pleasure in calling his words to mind frequently, and have already made it a regular exercise: even if nobody happens to be at hand, I repeat them to myself two or three times a day just the same. I am in the same case with lovers. In the absence of the objects of their fancy they think over their actions and their words, and by dallying with these beguile their lovesickness into the belief that they have their sweethearts near; in fact, sometimes they even imagine they are chatting with them and are as pleased with what they formerly heard as if they were just being said, and by applying their minds to the memory of the past give themselves no time to be annoyed by the present. So I too, in the absence of my mistress Philosophy, get no little comfort out of gathering together the words that I then heard and turning them over to myself. In short, I fix my gaze on that man as if he were a lighthouse and I were adrift at sea in the dead of night, fancying him by me whenever I do anything and always hearing him repeat his former words. Sometimes, especially when I put pressure on my soul, his face appears to me and the sound of his voice abides in my ears. Truly, as the comedian says, "He left a sting implanted in his hearers."

This text captures the major elements present in the convention of calling the moral paradigm to remembrance: that recollection encompassed the teacher's actions and words, and that it comforted students in the absence of their masters while they yearned for their teachers.

Paul uses this tradition of exhortation to describe his relationship with the Thessalonians. They always have a good remembrance of him and yearn to see him, conditions that enable him now to complete with confidence what was lacking in their faith. The "good remembrance" of him that they have, according to Timothy's report, Paul fills out in chaps. 1–3, which serve as a commentary on *mneia agathē*. In good paraenetic fashion, Paul tells them nothing they do not already know, but reminds them by recounting the history they share with him and by prodding their memory with the often repeated "(as) you know" and reminding them of particular actions. The relationship between them began when they became imitators of him when they accepted his message (1:6), and by referring to their "good remembrance always," Paul asserts that the relationship has remained intact from the beginning.

Paul's reference to the hortatory scheme of example-imitation-remembrance has a further significance. By referring to his own behavior as an example to be followed, the responsible moral teacher made a commitment, as expressed by Pliny (*Epistle* 7.1.7): "I mention this, not only to enforce my advice by example, but also that this letter may be a sort of pledge binding me to persevere in the same abstinence in the future." Such a commitment is implicit in Paul's use of this hortatory tradition and underlies v 10. It has obvious pastoral implications for a small community of recent converts in need of reassurance.

Paul attributes this knowledge about the Thessalonians to Timothy. Evidently this is the specific information he had sent Timothy to get (v 5). In addition, he had received general reports about the Thessalonians' evangelism (1:8), and, purportedly, news it was known that they preached as a result of their conversion by Paul (1:6–7, 9). Nowhere is there any explicit indication that the Thessalonians had communicated with Paul, either by letter or through an oral message they sent with Timothy. It is most likely that Paul's churches did sent oral messages to Paul via his messengers, but Paul is surprisingly reticent about acknowledging such communications. Only in 1 Corinthians (7:1) does he refer to a letter he had received from one of his churches.

There are a number of traditional epistolary elements in 2:17–18 (being orphaned by being separated, bodily absence but spiritual presence, endeavoring to see one's correspondents face to face), and they have been considered evidence of a letter Paul had sent to the Thessalonians with Timothy (Harris). That evidence has generally been judged insufficient proof that such a letter had been written. There are many more epistolographic elements in 3:6–10, however, which, with other features in the letter, have been taken as evidence that the Thessalonians had written a letter to Paul, that Timothy had brought this letter to him, and that he responded by writing 1 Thessalonians.

The NOTES have drawn attention to the concentration of epistolographic clichés and conventions in these verses: v 6, remembrance and longing; v 8, dying daily, thanksgiving to the gods that communication has been effected, and joy upon receiving a letter; v 10, writing to meet a need. In addition to these features, it has been thought (especially by Faw) that the strongest evidence for a letter from the Thessalonians is found in Paul's introduction of a series of comments with *peri de* ("but concerning"; 4:9, 13; 5:1) or *de* ("but"; 5:12). This use of the phrases is compared with 1 Cor 7:1, 25; 8:1; 12:1; 16:1, 12, which are frequently thought to be Paul's responses to written inquiries from the Corinthians. Furthermore, it is argued that the transitions at 4:9, 13 and 5:12 would be very abrupt if they were not responses (Faw). The content of this letter, according to this theory, can be determined primarily from chaps. 4 and 5, which show that the letter dealt with brotherly love (4:8–12), Christians who had died (4:13–18), and the time of the end (5:1–11). On this reading, Paul's letter would be primarily didactic in nature. The Thessalonians' letter is also thought to have been supplemented by Timothy's oral report, echoes of which are found in chaps. 1–3, particularly in comments in connection with thanksgiving and personal defense, although it is not always possible to distinguish between Paul's two sources of information.

The hypothesis of a letter from the Thessalonians has been accepted by some interpreters (e.g., Frame, 9, 107; Masson, 1–8; Fuchs), regarded as possible by others (e.g., Milligan, xxx, 126; Lake, 86–87; Kummel 1975: 260), and as improbable by perhaps the majority (e.g., von Dobschütz 1909: 19; Rigaux 1956: 55–56; Vielhauer, 87). The objections most frequently raised are that Paul would have mentioned such a letter at 3:6 and that too much weight is attached to Paul's use of *peri de*: "one example of Paul's method does not create an essential pattern" (Best 1972: 15). Indeed, the significance that *peri de* is often assumed to have in 1 Corinthians is highly debatable (Mitchell 1989: 190–92). The use of the formula in ancient letters and treatises is much wider and not useful as an indication that Paul responds to a letter when he uses it (Baasland; Mitchell 1989). It may introduce a response to a letter, but frequently it simply introduces a new topic or introduces a response to an oral report (Malherbe 1990a: 250–51).

The overinterpretation of the *peri de* formula does not contradict the view that when it occurs in 1 Thessalonians Paul is answering a letter (incorrectly, D. G. Bradley; Boers). Ancient epistolographic practice shows that the formula could introduce a response to a written inquiry, not that it always did. The other epistolographic elements in vv 6–10 increase the probability that Paul derived his information from a letter written by the Thessalonians as well as Timothy's report about them. That Paul does not mention this letter is not surprising in view of his general practice. Paul seldom provides details about circumstances attending the writing of his letters. In fact, in 1 Thess 3:10, he does not even refer to the letter he is writing, nor does he tell us in his Corinthian letters, where he is more forthcoming about his epistolographic practice, who carried his letters to Corinth (Malherbe 1990a: 254–55).

Of great relevance are two instances in his letters where he mentions messengers between himself and two churches but does not mention letters, although in each case it is generally correctly assumed that the messengers carried a letter in which they are mentioned. In 1 Cor 16:17 Paul expresses joy over the arrival of Stephanas, Fortunatus, and Achaicus, for they had supplied the needs of the Corinthians by refreshing their and Paul's spirits. No letter is mentioned, but it is almost universally thought that Stephanas brought the letter in which the Corinthians asked Paul for advice (see Hurd, 49–50; Dahl 1967: 324–25). It is noteworthy that in addition to requesting advice the letter stressed mutual affection, but that the epistolographic clichés are applied to the intermediaries and their mission rather than the letter they brought to Paul.

The same thing is true of Phil 2:25–30, which is a commendation of Epaphroditus, who is usually thought to have been the bearer of Paul's letter to the Philippians (see Malherbe 1990a: 257 n. 42). Paul introduces the commendation with "I thought it necessary to send," which has been identified as an epistolary formula which was used to introduce an intermediary who was also the bearer of a letter (Koskenniemi, 81–87, 122; see PRyl 235, 12ff.; PLondon Bell 1925, 3ff. for the exact formula). Other epistolary conventions are Epaphroditus's yearning to see the Philippians and the prospect of joy when they are united. Once again, the mission of the bearer of a letter is described in epistolary terms without any mention of a letter he carried.

Given the preponderance of the epistolary conventions in vv 6–10, it is highly probable that Timothy brought a letter from the Thessalonians in which they expressed their yearning to see Paul and asked him for advice on a number of matters. We do not know why Paul does not mention such letters; it may be that he did not value letters as highly as the live communication by means of emissaries (M. M. Mitchell 1992). The society in which Paul lived placed a premium on oral communication, the "living and abiding voice" (Papias, according to Eusebius, *Ecclesiastical History* 3.39.4).

If Paul did receive a letter from the Thessalonians, it would be of the greatest importance for the interpretation of 1 Thessalonians, especially of chaps. 4 and 5. He would then be addressing actual circumstances in the church rather than delivering moral instruction that was, in the nature of paraenesis, as widely assumed, so general in character that it could not be taken to reflect any particular situation (incorrectly, D. G. Bradley). Such a view misunderstands the nature of ancient paraenesis (see pages 82–83); furthermore, it fails to do justice to Paul's depiction of the epistolary situation in 2:17–3:10, especially 3:1–5, where he claims to have initiated contact with the Thessalonians, partly in order to learn about their circumstances. Whether or not Timothy conveyed that information orally or whether it was supplemented by a letter from the Thessalonians, as is more probable, when Paul wrote to mend the deficiencies in their faith, he did so on the basis of a firm knowledge of conditions in Thessalonica.

It is important to appreciate the significance of the epistolary elements in 3:6–10, whether or not they reflect a letter from the Thessalonians. Paul uses these clichés in the first place to describe the relationship within which he gives advice. As we have seen, they strengthen that relationship in which the Thessalonians remembered Paul as their mentor, which was the prerequisite for paraenesis. In describing the purpose of the letter he is writing (v 10), Paul uses language (*katartizein*) that describes a psychagogic and paraenetic enterprise. In

1 Thessalonians, Paul puts these elements to use in a unique way to create the first Christian pastoral letter (see pages 88–89; Malherbe 1987: 68–78).

# B. CONCLUDING PRAYER, 3:11–13

◆

The autobiographical part of the letter having come to an end, Paul now concludes the first major part of the letter with yet another extended prayer. Paul petitions God to allow him to return to the Thessalonians and asks the Lord to prepare them for the coming of the Lord Jesus. As to its form, the prayer has been described as a benediction (Champion; Jewett 1969) or, more precisely, a prayer wish (Wiles, 52–63). The ultimate origin of certain elements in the prayer has been discovered in Jewish practice (Wiles, 23–29), but the more immediate origin of the prayer is likely to have been pre-Pauline Christian worship (Champion; Jewett 1969).

This is the only place where Paul adds a prayer of this kind after a thanksgiving; elsewhere such prayers appear, among other places, after paraenesis (e.g., Rom 15:5, 13; cf. Heb 13:20–21). In 1 Thessalonians it appears in the transition to (3:11–13) and after (5:23) the detailed paraenesis, thus enclosing paraenesis. The prayer is closely related to its context and functions as a transition between chaps. 1–3 and 4–5. Paul's separation from the Thessalonians and his desire to see them, which is the theme of 2:17–3:10, is repeated in the first petition (v 11), and his interest in the stabilizing of the Thessalonians (v 2) appears in the second (v 13). At the same time, the major topics of chaps. 4 and 5 are anticipated in the prayer. The holiness for which he prays (v 13) comes up again in 4:3–8, love of the brethren and their relationship to non-Christians is treated in 4:9–12 (see also 5:12–13), the coming of the Lord is treated at some length in 4:13–5:10 (see also 5:23). The prayer thus functions both pastorally and paraenetically.

## TRANSLATION

3  ¹¹Now may our God and Father himself and our Lord Jesus direct our way to you. ¹²But as for you, may the Lord cause you to increase and abound in love for one another and for all, as we abound in love for you, ¹³so as to establish your hearts blameless in holiness in the presence of our God and Father at the coming of our Lord Jesus with all his holy ones.

## NOTES

3:11. *Now may our God and Father himself.* The particle *de* does not here have its usual adversative force, as though the prayer that it introduces were contrasted with anything that precedes. It marks a transition (BDF §171.2; "now," "then") and introduces Paul's prayers in 1 Thessalonians (here and in 5:23 where the entire phrase also occurs) and 2 Thessalonians (2:16; 3:5, 16; cf. Rom 15:5, 13). It is striking that instead of addressing God directly in prayer ("Do you, O God, direct . . ."), Paul begins with the reflexive pronoun *autos* ("himself"). A comparable use of *autos* is found elsewhere (Rom 8:16, 26; 1 Cor 15:28; 2 Cor 8:19; 11:14), apart from Paul only in Rev 21:3. It may retain some of its emphatic force (*GNTG* 4.41, citing 4:16; 5:23; 2 Thess 2:16; 3:16). These words have a liturgical ring (Wiles, 30–31) and may come from a Hellenistic community (Jewett 1969: 22–23). For addressing God as Father in prayer, see Rom 8:15–17; Gal 4:6.

*and our Lord Jesus direct our way to you.* God the Father and the Lord Jesus were connected in the liturgical address of the letter (see NOTE on 1:1), but the use of the personal pronouns here makes the tone more personal (Holtz 1986: 142 n. 707). Here Paul goes further by connecting God and Jesus in his prayer and using a singular verb in his petition. It is unnecessary to claim that the prayer is directed to God and that the Lord Jesus is to be understood as the agent through whom God is expected to act in reply to the petition (Wiles, 55 n. 3; Holtz 1986: 142). The prayer shows no interest in the relationship between Jesus and God; furthermore, the singular verb relates the actions to both (Best 1972: 147; cf. 2 Thess 2:16–17), and in v 12 it is the Lord's actions for which Paul prays. See 2:19 for Christ exercising the divine prerogative of judging.

The verb is in the aorist optative (*kateuthynai*), which is frequently used in prayers in the NT (Rom 15:5, 13; 1 Thess 3:11–12; 5:23; 2 Thess 3:5, 16; 2 Tim 1:16, 18; 4:16; Heb 13:21). By the time of Paul, the optative in Greek was found mostly in prayers, formulas, and oaths (Wiles, 32). The construction ("direct our way") is to be understood in its literal sense (Luke 1:79; *1 Clement* 60:2; for the metaphorical sense, see 2 Thess 3:5).

3:12. *But as for you, may the Lord cause you to increase and abound in love.* The prayer continues as Paul now focuses on the Thessalonians, the *de* ("But") retaining its adversative force, as is evident from the emphatic position of *hymās,* "as for you" (Frame, 147), which is further enhanced by its appearance immediately after another *hymās* (*tēn hodon hēmōn pros hymās; hymās de;* see NOTE on 1:5). Paul had just prayed for divine action in regard to himself; now he asks that the Lord favor the Thessalonians. In view of vv 11 and 13, *kyrios* must refer to Jesus, although here *kyrios* is used without a further identifier (see also 1:6, 8; 3:8; 4:15–17; 5:2, 12, 27; but in 4:6 it is used of God; see 1 Cor 4:6). Paul also addresses Jesus in prayer in 2 Cor 12:8 and probably in 2 Thess 3:3, 5, 16 (cf. 2 Tim 1:16, 18; Acts 7:59–60).

The two verbs in *pleonasai kai perisseuai* ("to increase and abound") are synonymous and are used together for the sake of emphasis (so also in 2 Cor 4:15; Rom 5:20). Paul sometimes increases the emphasis even more with the composite verb *hyperekperisseuein* (Rom 5:20) or another emphatic construction, e.g., "And this is my prayer, that your love may abound yet more and more (*eti māllon kai māllon perisseuē*)" (Phil 1:9). John Chrysostom describes Paul as speaking of excessive love and the unbridled frenzy of love because he uses these verbs instead of *auxanein* (*Homilies on 1 Thessalonians* 4 [PG 62:419]). See also the emphatic construction, with *pleonazein*, in 2 Thess 1:3.

*for one another and for all, as we abound in love for you.* Love is one of the triad of endowments that appears in 1:3 and 5:8 as brackets to the major part of the letter. Up to this point in the letter, Paul has referred to the Thessalonians having been loved by God when they converted (1:4) and by himself when he preached to them (2:8), and he thanked God for their own love for those to whom they in turn preached (1:3). What had relieved Paul most about Timothy's report was that they loved Paul (3:6). Paul will go on to speak about their love for one another (4:9) and particularly for those who care for them spiritually (5:13). Most striking here, however, are Paul's holding up his own love as a standard for them and his inclusion of "all" as objects of their love (see also 5:15, for the same formulation, to pursue the good, *eis allēlous kai eis pantas*). Rather than all people generally, it is likely that Paul has in mind pagans who were present in the Christian assemblies (see NOTES on 5:12, 15). For Paul's ambiguous attitude in 1 Thessalonians towards non-Christians, see COMMENT on 4:9–12.

3:13. *so as to establish your hearts blameless in holiness.* Although there is no verb for praying, the prayer continues (Wiles, 61). The Lord's gift of increasing the Thessalonians' love has an eschatological goal (*eis to* plus the infinitive, cf. 2:12, 16; 3:2, 5, 10), the establishing of their hearts. Paul had sent Timothy to the Thessalonians to stabilize (*stērixai*) them (3:2); now he prays that by making their love abound, the Lord may establish (*stērixai*) their hearts, by which he means their entire, not only the inner, person (cf. 2 Thess 2:17; Jas 5:8). This language is derived from the LXX (e.g., Ps 111:8; Sir 6:37; 22:16). He has also expressed his interest in the stability of the Thessalonians in other ways (1:3, *hypomonē*; 3:8, *stēkete*).

Paul then specifies in a number of ways how their hearts will be established. The blamelessness he mentions is eschatological, as in 5:23 (see NOTE on 2:10), and has in view their relationship with God rather than people (Phil 3:6; cf. Luke 1:6). He specifies still further that they will be established blameless in holiness. This form of the word *hagiōsynē* appears elsewhere in the NT only in Rom 1:4 and 2 Cor 7:1, both of which may derive from non-Pauline tradition. Up to this point, holiness has only been associated with the Spirit (1:5, 6). Here Paul draws attention to the Thessalonians' holiness, as is also the case in 5:23, which similarly has an eschatological perspective. This reference to holiness anticipates the application of the idea to the moral life in 4:3–8.

*in the presence of our God and Father.* Paul now specifies that it is God who will judge whether their increase in love will have reached its intended goal. Once more he invokes the presence of God (1:3; 3:9), this time thinking eschatologically (cf. 2:19, "before our Lord Jesus at his coming"). Paul was aware of God's testing and judging of himself, qualifying him to preach the gospel (2:4).

"Our God and Father" is so formulaic (cf. v 11) and God is described as Father so frequently in liturgical language (e.g., Rom 1:7; 6:4; 8:15; 15:16; Gal 1:1; Phil 2:11) that unless something in the text draws attention to the epithet (e.g., 1:1; 1 Cor 8:6), no special significance is to be seen in it in any particular context. Paul's calling God "Father" here does not have the effect of providing the comfort that God, in judging the Thessalonians, will act like a loving father (so a long exegetical tradition represented by Rigaux 1956: 490; Richard 1995: 166).

*at the coming of our Lord Jesus with all his holy ones.* In his preaching to the Thessalonians, Paul had spoken of God's judgment and Jesus' return, describing Jesus as delivering them from divine wrath (1:10). He now associates Jesus with judgment when the Lord comes, but the expected outcome seems to be positive (see NOTE on 2:19). It is likely that Paul derived the term *parousia* from pre-Pauline churches (Schade, 27; Best 1972: 351–52). The term also appears in Matt 24 of the return of the Son of Man in judgment (Matt 24:37–42). See further on 4:15.

The *hagioi* ("holy ones") who will accompany the Lord Jesus could be Christian saints or angels. In favor of the former is that the term is frequently used to describe Christians, by Paul (e.g., Rom 8:27; 1 Cor 1:2; 6:1–2; Phil 4:22) and other writers (Acts 9:13, 32; Heb 6:10). In favor of understanding the reference to be to angels are the following (summarized by Bruce 1982: 73–74; Richard, 177–78):

1. The term is used in the OT (e.g., Dan 7:17, cf. 10), in Jewish literature (e.g., 1 En 1:9) and in the NT (Matt 13:41; 25:31; Mark 8:38; 13:27) of angels who will be in attendance at the final judgment. Paul reflects that use in 2 Thess 1:7.

2. It is generally thought that Paul is here dependent on Zech 14:5, "The Lord your God will come, and all the holy ones with him." In Matt 25:31, also reflecting this passage, "holy ones" is changed to "angels."

3. This understanding agrees with 1 Thess 4:16–17, according to which the dead in Christ will be raised when the Lord returns and only then join him in the air.

## COMMENT

Although Paul had been relieved of his anxiety about the Thessalonians by Timothy's report, he still wanted to see them in person, and he comes back to the theme in his prayer (v 11). In his Corinthian correspondence, Paul expressed a similar desire (1 Cor 16:5–7; 2 Cor 1:15–16), yet his strained relations with the Corinthians at the same time made him ambivalent about visiting them (1 Cor 4:18–21; 2 Cor 1:23). There is no ambivalence in 1 Thessalonians about his desire to visit them and no evidence anywhere else that would cast doubt on the genuineness of his first petition. It was only after a considerable lapse of time that Paul made it back to Thessalonica, for he had not yet returned when he wrote 2 Thessalonians.

The only information from Paul about a subsequent visit to Macedonia comes from 1 Cor 16:5 and 2 Cor 2:13 (cf. Acts 19:21; 20:1), which describe his efforts, towards the end of his work in the eastern Mediterranean, to gather the contribution for the saints in Judea (Rom 15:25–26). Thessalonica is not mentioned, but it is likely that Paul had visited the church on that tour and that it contributed to the collection (see Acts 20:4; cf. 1 Cor 16:3–4).

Paul's prayer is paraenetic in that he focuses in his second petition on two aspects of the Thessalonians' behavior, their love and its eschatological aim, holiness before God. He will go into detail on these in the following two chapters. This marks a change, for, whereas up to now he has been concerned with the relationship between himself and the Thessalonians, from now on his interest will be in their relationships with each other and the larger society and how those relationships are to lead to blamelessness in holiness before God.

Paul's love for them is the model for their love for others (v 12, *kathaper kai hēmeis eis hymās*, "as we for you"). He had already reminded them of how he had demonstrated that love (2:8), but the weight now lies elsewhere, *eis allēlous kai eis pantas* ("for one another and for all"). From now on, the reflexive pronoun *allēloi* ("one another") dominates (4:9, 18; 5:11, 15), as the personal pronouns *hēmeis* and *hymeis* ("we" and "you") have predominated so far in the letter. Every bit of advice that he will give has a communal dimension.

Paul's sense of the importance of the communal dimension of the faith has been expressed in a number of ways up to this point, e.g., the creation of the church by God (1:1), the long description of how Paul founded the church through his preaching and nourished it (1:2–3:10), and his studied use of kinship language. He demonstrated his love for them with his willingness to endure hardships while preaching to them, in the process providing an example for them to follow (2:8; Wiles, 59–61; cf. 1 Cor 13:4–7; Holladay, 94–97).

According to Paul, love summarizes all social obligations (Rom 13:8–10; Gal 5:12–15) and is to be the bonding element in the relations between members of the congregation to which he is writing. This is similar in some respects to the Epicureans of Paul's day (Malherbe 1987: 40–41, 102). For Paul, however, love was not something utilitarian, as friendship was for the Epicureans, something needed to attain a goal (Diogenes Laertius, *The Lives of Eminent Philosophers* 10.120; rejected by Cicero, *On Friendship* 27–28, 30; Seneca, *Epistle* 9.17; see Berry, 111–13). Paul prays for a dramatic increase in their love, to be engendered by God, with an eschatological goal (see also 1 Cor 13:8–13 for the eschatological dimension of love).

The blamelessness before God for which Paul prays is one in holiness, their condition before God when the Lord Jesus comes with all his holy ones. Here Paul represents apocalyptic tradition, which also connects the holy ones with the end (Dan 7:18, 22, 25, 27; 1QH 3:22; 4:25; 1QM 3:25). Despite Ps 29:5; 95:6; 96:12; 144:5, which speak of the divine presence, "in holiness" here does not mean "in the sphere of holiness," to which "in the presence of God" stands in apposition (Richard, 176–77).

Paul has in mind the Thessalonians' holiness, which God will complete at the coming of the Lord Jesus Christ (5:23). The Thessalonians had been sanctified by the Spirit when they were called by God through Paul's preaching of the gospel (2 Thess 2:13–14; cf. 1 Pet 1:2, 22). That sanctification took place at a particular moment in time (note the aorist tense in 1 Cor 6:11), but it constantly comes to realization in the Christian's moral life, with eternal life the end (cf. Rom 6:19–23). Paul will apply this understanding to a particular problem in 4:3–8.

# III. EXHORTATION, 4:1–5:22

◆

The autobiographical account of chaps. 1–3 is a long thanksgiving that introduces chaps. 4 and 5, which are Paul's main purpose in writing the letter (Bjerkelund, 134). The autobiography functions paraenetically in that it presents Paul as a paradigm for the Thessalonians, strengthens Paul's relationship with them to support his detailed advice and anticipates the advice he will give in chaps. 4 and 5. The prayer in 3:11–13 serves as a transition and introduces, after an introduction (4:1–2) to the last two chapters of the letter, the topics Paul will now take up, all of which are viewed from a communal perspective: the sanctified life in sexual matters (4:3–8), the church's relationship to outsiders (4:9–12), and the coming of the Lord (4:13–5:11). In addition, he will discuss at some length the Thessalonians' attitude to each other in their mutual ministry (5:12–22). Paul discusses these subjects because they were important to his readers. They may have written him for advice on these issues, but he would in any case have heard from Timothy what their needs were (see COMMENT on 3:6–10), and he now writes to complete what was lacking in their faith (3:10).

It is impossible to determine with certainty what Paul wrote in response to a letter from the Thessalonians, had he received such a letter, and what he wrote in view of Timothy's report about them. Paul did not always identify the sources for his knowledge about his churches when he wrote to them. Even in 1 Corinthians, where he identifies some of his sources (1:11; 7:1), he does not do so throughout the letter (see Dahl 1967). The similarity in structure of 1 Cor 1–7 to 1 Thess 1–4 may nevertheless be significant in this regard.

As 1 Thess 1–3 is paradigmatic, so is 1 Cor 1–4 (cf. 1 Cor 4:6, 14–16). In 1 Corinthians, Paul then gives directions on matters touching sexual behavior (chap. 5) and relations to the larger society (6:1–11) before turning to matters about which the Corinthians had written him (7:1). In chaps. 5 and 6 Paul avoids identifying his sources for conditions in the Corinthian church, but there is no doubt that he is addressing actual circumstances in the church and that he is not merely giving advice that may be generally applicable.

In 1 Thessalonians Paul also discusses sexual matters (4:3–8) and community relations (4:9–12) before dealing in greater detail with other issues. In 1 Corinthians, Paul is intent on cultivating behavior within the church that will define its relationship with its social environment before turning to matters that are almost completely intramural (cf. 5:11–13; 6:1–4). Although Paul's discussion in 1 Thessalonians is much briefer, he reflects the same interests in 1 Thess 4:6, 12.

That Paul wrote to the two churches in similar ways does not mean that he wrote *pro forma*, without addressing actual conditions in the churches. He had taught on both subjects when he had founded the church (4:6, 11), and his continuing interest in them shows the importance he attached to them. It may well be that Paul in 1 Thessalonians writes in light of Timothy's report on matters in which Paul was interested, and it is quite likely that in at least 4:9–12 and probably in 4:13–18, he responds to a letter from them.

# A. INTRODUCTION, 4:1–2

◆

Paul prefaces his detailed advice with a brief introductory comment written in paraenetic style, stresses that his directions agree with his former teaching, provides theological warrants for those directions, and states the goal of the behavior he inculcates.

Some commentators think that vv 1–2 introduce 4:3–12, but the majority opinion is that vv 1–2 introduce the entire last two chapters of the letter and provide the perspective from which Paul's precepts in them are to be viewed. The general, programmatic nature of these verses supports the latter view. Furthermore, vv 3–12 consists of two discrete sections: the *inclusio* formed by the references to sanctification and God in vv 3 and 7–8 make vv 3–8 a self-contained unit, and the phrase *peri de* ("now concerning") in v 9 marks a transition to a new subject.

## TRANSLATION

4 ¹Well then, brethren, we beseech and exhort you in the Lord Jesus that, as you received from us instruction about how you should conduct yourselves and so please God, as you are indeed conducting yourselves, you do so more and more. ²For you know what precepts we gave you through the Lord Jesus.

## NOTES

4:1. *Well then, brethren.* This is the only place in the NT where *loipon oun* is used. Some manuscripts omit *oun*, probably for that reason, and because of an uncertainty about the meaning of the phrase that is shared by modern commentators. At issue is whether *loipon* in its adverbial use is temporal ("finally") or inferential ("therefore"). In favor of the former it is frequently argued that *loipon oun* sometimes appears in a transition to the closing section of a document (BAGD, 480, cites *UPZ* 78.43; POxy 119.13; 2 Cor 13:11; Phil 4:8), which is also taken to be the sense in 1 Thess 4:1. Furthermore, *oun* is already inferential, so *loipon*, which could otherwise be inferential, it is argued, could not have the same meaning here.

Arguments in support of an inferential meaning proceed from *oun*, observing that it is used elsewhere to introduce paraenesis, as it does here (Rom 12:1; Gal 5:1; 6:10; cf. Eph 4:1; Col 3:5; see Nauck). Given the paraenetic nature of the letter and that *(to) loipon adelphoi* ("therefore brethren") elsewhere in Paul's letters also introduces paraenetic statements (Phil 3:1; 4:8; 2 Thess 3:1), the paraenetic interpretation is to be preferred, and the construction to be regarded as emphatic (Milligan, 46; Rigaux 1956: 496). The translation "well then, brethren" (see LSJ, s.v. *loipon*, 5) attempts to state more succinctly what is expressed in the freer but accurate paraphrase, "And now, brethren, to apply more directly what we have been saying" (Milligan, 45).

*we beseech and exhort you in the Lord Jesus.* Paul begins his exhortation by using a literary form of petition that had originated in formal petitions and was later adopted for informal requests (Mullins 1962). Such petitions consisted of a recital of the background the petitioner considered important for his petition, a verb or verbs of petition, an address, a courtesy phrase (e.g., "if you deem it worthy") and the desired action. The form, somewhat adapted, is present here. The background is pointed to by *loipon oun*, the verbs *erōtōmen* ("we beseech") and *parakaloumen* ("we exhort") express the petition, the addressees are called *adelphoi* and the desired action is expressed in the subordinate clause of purpose introduced by *hina*. With minor modifications, Paul uses the same formula elsewhere (Rom 12:1; 15:30; 1 Cor 1:10; 2 Thess 2:1–2). The major difference is that instead of a courtesy phrase, Paul modifies his exhortation theologically in a prepositional phrase ("in the Lord Jesus").

That we have to do with an epistolary form is certain, but to claim that it is therefore not paraenetic (Bjerkelund, 109, 189; followed by Holtz 1986: 151) is to make Paul captive to a narrow formalism that he successfully escaped. As he had bent other epistolary forms to serve his theological interests, so he modifies this form to serve his paraenetic aims. The verbs Paul uses, *erōtān* and *parakalein*, are more personal than other verbs used in official petitions, and *erōtān*, in particular, is more familiar, as though the petitioner and person petitioned were on the same social level (Mullins 1962: 48). Paul makes the appeal more personal still by addressing his readers as brethren.

The verbs Paul uses here are part of his lexicon of exhortation in which *parakalein* and its cognates predominate but are interpreted by other hortatory terms that accompany them (see COMMENT on 2:3). Paul uses *erōtān* elsewhere only three times, always in conjunction with terms conveying a sense of close relationship ("brethren" in 5:12 and 2 Thess 2:1; "true yokefellow" in Phil

4:3). The position of *erōtān* before *parakalein* makes clear that Paul is not making an authoritative demand (for the same order, see PFreib 39; POxy 744, 6).

Paul's appeal is made "in the Lord Jesus," which could qualify only *parakaloumen*. The latter is frequently regarded as a more authoritative mode of speech than *erōtōmen* and thus refers to the authority with which Paul spoke (e.g., by Rigaux 1956: 497; Deidun, 177). However, *parakaloumen* takes its meaning from *erōtōmen*, and where it is used elsewhere in this epistolary formula, the preposition *dia* and not *en* is used (Rom 12:1; 15:30; 1 Cor 1:10; cf. 1 Thess 4:2). It is therefore better to understand "in the Lord Jesus" as qualifying both the subject and objects of the verbs (von Dobschütz 1909: 156). Paul's exhortation takes place within a relationship defined by the Lord Jesus, so the communal perspective of the advice he will give is already part of the introduction.

*that, as you received from us instruction.* The content of Paul's exhortation is introduced by *hina* ("that"), which also occurs in the corresponding position in other uses of the epistolary formula (Rom 15:30; 1 Cor 1:10). It is omitted by a strong textual tradition (א A D² Ψ byz syrʰᵃʳᶜˡ), probably because it is left hanging until it is repeated (*hina perisseuēte māllon*, "that you may do so more and more") to complete the sentence. This grammatical awkwardness makes the reading harder and therefore supports retention of *hina*.

The first *hina* clause provides specificity to the exhortation, whose end is given in the second *hina* clause: the Thessalonians are to be more abundant in their conduct by living according to the tradition they had received from Paul. Once again the paraenetic *kathōs* ("as") appears to underline conformity with what the readers know (see NOTE on 1:5), in this case, the moral instruction they had received from Paul. In 2:13, the reference was to their reception of the gospel; here it is to a manner of life. There is no Greek word behind "instruction"; it is an interpretation of the articular indirect interrogative sentence that follows (see GNTG 3.182).

*about how you should conduct yourselves and so please God.* Paul gave instructions, not only that they should live to please God, but specified how (*pōs*) they were obligated (*dei*, "should") to do so. Obligation in ethical matters is expressed with *dei* in a variety of moral traditions (e.g., Lev 5:17; Xenophon, *Memorabilia* 1.2.42; *Ep Arist* 159, 227) and also elsewhere in Paul (e.g., Rom 12:3; 2 Thess 3:7). For Paul's use of *peripatein* ("conduct") for the manner of life about which he had instructed them, see the discussion of 2:12. There his goal was that they conduct themselves in a manner worthy of God; here it is that they please God (the two notions are combined in Col 1:10). The *kai* is consecutive ("and so"; BDF §442.2). Paul again uses *peripatein* in v 12, but its appearance in vv 1 and 12 does not constitute an *inclusio* (so Yarbrough, 67–68). The subject matter of vv 3–12 is too diverse in nature for an *inclusio*, and Paul's concern with conduct extends well beyond v 12.

The idea of pleasing God as the goal of human conduct is derived from the OT (e.g., Gen 5:22, 24; 6:9; 17:1; Lev 10:20; Num 25:27; Ps 55[56]:13; 68[69]:31; 114[116]:9). It was necessary for Paul to stress this connection between religion and morality (see COMMENT on 4:3–8), and he uses *areskein* ("to please") and its cognates elsewhere in a moral sense (Rom 8:8; 12:1–2; 1 Cor 7:32; 2 Cor 5:9; cf. Eph 6:6; Col 3:22). The language, however, may not have been completely foreign to his Gentile readers, for this language of piety was also used by moral philosophers who described the aim of the moral person as following or pleasing God (e.g., Ecphantos, ap. Stobaeus, *Anthology* 4.7.65=82.24 Thesleff). For the Stoic Epictetus this meant to live in harmony with the cosmic order (*Discourses* 1.12.8, cf. 7; 2.23.42, and see 1.30.1; 2.14.12–13; 18.19; 4.4.48; cf. Seneca, *Epistle* 74.20–21, extolling the love of reason). His teacher, Musonius Rufus (Fragment 16 end), held that by living rationally, which was to live philosophically, one did the will of God.

Paul combines Jewish and Greek ideas in Rom 12:1–2, where he uses the same epistolary formula that he uses here. Basic to his appeal is not some sense of universal reason, as is the case in Epictetus, but divine mercy, yet the appeal itself is cast in a combination of traditional biblical and Greek philosophical language: living sacrifice, pleasing God, rational service, conformity to this age versus metamorphosis by renewal of the mind, proving what is the will of God, namely, what is good, pleasing and perfect (see Lietzmann, 103). In Rom 12:1–2 Paul uses the language of philosophic conversion to philosophy to introduce precepts that constitute the paraenetic section of Romans (chaps. 12–14).

Stoics like Seneca spoke of a metamorphosis of the mind and of moral precepts which were necessary to one's moral development (Seneca, *Epistles* 94.48; cf. 6.1; see Maurach, 42 n. 58, 81 n. 21; Hadot, 59–60, 103–26). Paul also refers to precepts (v 2), and he uses paraenetic devices in the section of the letter that vv 1–2 introduce, but here he differs from Rom 12:1–2 in stating that it is adherence to the tradition they had received from him that will be pleasing to God. See Heb 13:20–21 for a completely nonphilosophical use of much of the same terminology.

*as you are indeed conducting yourselves, you do so more and more.* The first of the two clauses is neither parenthetic (Bruce 1982: 79) nor an interruption (Holtz 1986: 153), nor is it to be omitted, as is done by some manuscripts. It is part of the paraenetic style of the letter, which continues in the second clause and in v 2 (cf. also 4:10; 5:11; see Malherbe 1992: 286–87; pages 84, 86). This particular style was appropriate to exhortation that took place between friends and was warm and complimentary.

The attitude expressed in such situations is that it was really superfluous to give advice, for the reader or hearer was already engaged in the desired action (Cicero, *To His Friends* 6.10b.4; Seneca, *Epistle* 25.4; Ign *Pol* 1:2; Ign *Eph* 4:1; 8:1; Ign *Rom* 2:1; Ign *Trall* 2:2). What the exhorting person could do was simply encourage the reader that he continue in what he was already doing (Seneca, *Epistles* 1.1; 5.1; 13.15; 24.16; cf. Cicero, *To His Brother Quintus* 1.1.36). Paul does this in the second clause, introduced by a second (untranslated) *hina*, which introduces the content of his appeal. By using this style at the beginning of his detailed advice, Paul once more exhibits his cordial relationship with the Thessalonians. He does not command them as an authoritative apostle but beseeches and exhorts them to please God in their manner of living.

4:2. *For you know what precepts we gave you through the Lord Jesus.* Paul continues to use the conventions and language of paraenesis. It is frequently pointed out that *parangelia* ("precept") and its cognate *parangellein* most often describe authoritative demands (e.g., Acts 5:48; 16:23–24), as the verb does in 2 Thessalonians (3:4, 6, 10, 12; cf. 1 Cor 7:10; 11:17), and it is understood that *parangelia* has the same meaning here (O. Schmitz in *TDNT* 5.764; Wanamaker, 149; Richard, 181) and in v 11.

Some commentators acknowledge that the word does not have an imperatival quality here, but are unwilling to soften it too much since they think that Paul is speaking from a position of authority (e.g., Best 1972: 157; cf. Rigaux 1956: 499). Accordingly, it is then claimed that Paul uses the circumlocution *parangelias edōkamen* rather than "what we commanded" in order to accentuate concrete injunctions (Deidun, 180). Rather than discover any reference or allusion to apostolic authority in the letter, however, we have seen that Paul constantly uses the conventions of paraenesis on the basis of a relationship that he describes as gentle, loving, self-giving, and so on. The images of nurse and father suggest a different understanding of *parangelia* (Murphy-O'Connor 1974: 107–8).

In a context such as this it is more natural to understand *parangelia* as the equivalent to the Latin *praeceptum* or the Greek *parangelma*, a precept addressed to life in particular situations (cf. Milligan, 47, for the equivalence). *Parangelma* was the more common term for precept (see Ps.-Isocrates, *To Demonicus* 44; Plutarch, *Advice [Parangelmata] to Bride and Groom; Precepts [Parangelmata] of Statecraft*; cf. Zeno, "to heed the precepts [*parangelmasin*] on how to live" [*ap.* Stobaeus, *Anthology* 3.106; 3.245, 9–10 Wachsmuth]; Philo of Larissa, "precepts [*parangelmata*] on health" [*ap.* Stobaeus, *Anthology* 2.7.3; 2.41, 4 Wachsmuth]). *Parangelia*, however, was also used (e.g., Aristotle, *Nicomachean Ethics* 2.2 1104a7). The use of precepts was discussed extensively in connection with the nature of paraenesis (e.g., Seneca, *Epistles* 94.1, 14, 32; 95.1; see Giusta, 1.162–63). A particularly pressing question was raised as to why precepts were needed if they represented not new but traditional advice and the persons they were addressed to were already doing what the precepts urged them to do.

In answer to such questions it was said that precepts were useful, among other reasons, because they reminded people of what they knew they were to do (Seneca, *Epistles* 94.21; cf. 13.15). Friendship between people made them sensitive about telling each other how to live (Cicero, *To His Friends* 2.1.2; *To His Brother Quintus* 1.1.36), and moralists went to great lengths to stress that they were merely calling their readers to remember. Pliny accordingly introduces a letter in which he repeatedly reminds his readers as follows: "The love I bear you obliges me to give you, not indeed a precept (for you are far from needing a preceptor), but a reminder that you should resolutely act up to the knowledge you already have, or also improve on it" (*Epistle* 8.24.1).

Paul's introduction to his paraenesis belongs to this tradition. The reason (*gar*, "for") he need only encourage them to do more and more of what they were already doing was that they knew (*oidate*) the precepts he had given them (cf.

Seneca, *Epistle* 94.26; see also Isocrates, *To Nicocles* 40). The frequent repetition of (*kathōs*) *oidate* ("[as] you remember") in this letter (1:5; 2:1, 2, 5, 11; 3:3, 4; 4:2; 5:2) jogs the memory (cf. 2:9). Where Paul differs from the paraenetic tradition is that the advice he gives does not possess any validity because it is self-evidently good and therefore has become common coin, or because it is given by a friend. In v 1 Paul had addressed his readers as brethren and by using the formula "in the Lord Jesus" had indicated that his exhortation was given within and intended to be received by a community defined by Jesus. Now he states more strongly that his precepts were given "through [*dia*] the Lord Jesus," the *dia* describing Christ as the efficient cause of his appeal (see BAGD, s.v. *dia*, A.III.1.d; cf. Rom 12:1; 15:30; 1 Cor 1:10; 2 Cor 10:1). Paul's precepts are specifications of how his readers are to please God in their conduct.

# COMMENT

Since *loipon oun* does not merely introduce a final series of issues that Paul raises now that he has achieved his main purposes in the first three chapters, but is inferential, it remains to decide to what the last two chapters are linked. It has been suggested that Paul links them to the judgment (3:13), or, more particularly, to the Thessalonians' blamelessness at the time of judgment (3:13), or to 3:10–13, or to 3:6 (see von Dobschütz 1909: 155). The connection has also been thought to be more generally to the history of the church described in chaps. 1–3 (Frame, 141–42; Best 1972: 154; Holtz 1986: 151) or to the relationship between Paul and the Thessalonians (Lightfoot 1980: 51).

Paul has carefully described in 3:6–9 the circumstances that led to his writing of the letter and has clearly anticipated in 3:10–13 the topics he would treat in chaps. 4 and 5. It is therefore reasonable to see him as linking his detailed advice to those circumstances. He recounted them to provide both a reason and a basis for his advice: he will give further instructions because there were still deficiencies in their faith, and he will do so because he learned from Timothy that his readers still looked to him for guidance.

By making so close a connection with the Thessalonians' need, a view of paraenesis is assumed that differs from a widely held one (see pages 81–82). It has for some time been assumed, to a considerable extent on formal grounds, that the traditional character and general applicability of paraenesis meant that paraenesis had nothing to do with the actual situations to which it was addressed (D. G. Bradley; correctly, Brunt; Schrage 1961: 37–48). On the face of it, such a wooden formalism is improbable, but there are also other reasons why it should be rejected.

The ancient writers who wrote about paraenesis and provide us with examples of it had a different view. Seneca, one of the major sources for our knowledge of paraenesis, knew of a debate about the nature and use of precepts. Some people thought that despite small distinctions due to time, place or the person who used them, precepts were of a general application (*Epistle* 94.35). Seneca had great respect for traditional wisdom but resisted the mindless gathering and dissemination of precepts (see Hadot, 179–90). They should be digested and blended into a harmonious whole through reason (*Epistle* 84). The serious person should increase the lode of wisdom and, like a physician, give attention to when and how the precepts are to be applied (*Epistle* 64.8–10). According to Plutarch, if one keeps relevant *parangelmata* as god-given, one will be able to adapt them to all the circumstances of life (*A Letter of Condolence to Apollonius* 166DE).

Paul applies his precepts in chaps. 4 and 5, which, as to their content, have parallels in other NT moral instructions, particularly Rom 12–13 and 1 Peter, esp. 1:13–22. Some scholars have thought it possible to identify baptismal catechetical material in such passages (Carrington; Selwyn, 18–24, 362–466; Davies 1980: 109–46). Such a catechism would have been indebted to Jewish instruction to proselytes, used traditions of Jesus' teachings, and assumed its form in the instruction of Gentile converts (Dodd 1968). Paul was aware that he was using traditional material, as is evident from his use of technical terminology for the transmission of (e.g., 1 Cor 11:2, 23; 15:3; 1 Thess 2:13; 2 Thess 2:15; 3:6) and holding to tradition (1 Cor 11:2; 15:1–2; 2 Thess 2:15; see Cullmann 1956: 63–64).

Paul does refer to a body of teaching that his converts had received from him, probably soon before or after baptism. It evidently contained a summary and exposition of his missionary preaching (1 Cor 15:3–4), teaching about the Lord's Supper (1 Cor 11:23–24), and moral rules, after the fashion of Jewish *halakot* (1 Cor 4:17; cf. Rom 6:17; 1 Cor 11:2; Phil 4:9; 2 Thess 3:6; cf. Col 2:6). First Thessalonians has figured prominently in attempts to reconstruct this catechesis, for its frequent references to what the Thessalonians had learned from Paul at the time of their conversion provide more immediate access to such instructions than any other NT document does. In this connection, 4:1–12 is considered of the greatest importance, for it is claimed to have close affinities with OT holiness codes (e.g., Deut 7:6–7; 14:2; 26:18–19; Exod 19:6; Lev 20:26), one of whose purposes was to separate Israel from the nations (cf. 1 Thess 4:6; see Deidun).

It is impossible to determine with any degree of certainty what the content or the form of Paul's original instruction was. At best, the passages usually identified as having been catechetical constitute a minimum; Paul speaks on these subjects because they required attention at the time when he wrote. Presumably, many other topics (e.g., worship) required no discussion, for the early converts to whom he wrote had no problems about them when he wrote, and therefore called for no comment. Paul wrote on these topics, not by way of providing comment on a catechism, but because he knew that the Thessalonians needed his instruction and advice.

The paraenetic markers in chaps. 4 and 5 (4:9; 5:1–2; cf. 4:1, 13, 15) and the designation of his instructions as precepts should not lead to the view that, rather than speaking with apostolic authority, Paul is providing guidelines which are to function as aids in a process of moral growth (Murphy-O'Connor 1974: 107–8). What provides the perspective for his precepts is not whether he writes with apostolic authority, but that his precepts are given through the Lord Jesus and that they apply to a community defined by the Lord Jesus.

# B. ON MARRIAGE, 4:3–8

◆

The first exhortation on a particular topic is given as a call to holiness in sexual behavior. In form it is an *inclusio*: God and *hagiasmos* ("holiness") occur in vv 3, 4, and 7 (see also the opposites, *porneia* ["immorality"] in v 3 and *akatharsia* ["impurity"] in v 7), and the pericope concludes (*toigaroun*, "consequently") with a warning not to disregard God, who gives his Holy Spirit (v 8). The structure of vv 3–6, which constitute one long sentence, is governed by a number of infinitives that develop what Paul means by holiness in the situation he envisages (see esp. Adinolfi). "Holiness" is in apposition to "the will of God" and is explicated by the infinitival clause "that you abstain [*apechesthai*] from immorality." The matter at issue, the desirability and quality of marriage, comes to light in vv 4–6. The infinitive *eidenai* ("that . . . you learn") in v 4, to which *ktāsthai* ("to acquire") is complementary, is imperatival and is a further explication of the theme of holiness (Baltensweiler, 138). The articular infinitives (*to mē hyperbainein kai pleonektein*, "not to trespass and behave covetously") in v 6 give further specification to the two preceding ones (Giblin, 19).

## TRANSLATION

4 ³This is God's will, your sanctification, that is, that you abstain from immorality, ⁴that each one of you learn how to acquire his own wife in holiness and honor, ⁵not in lustful passion as the pagans do who do not know God, ⁶that he not trespass against or behave covetously in this matter against his brother, because the Lord is an avenger in all these things; indeed, we told you so before and kept on charging you. ⁷For God did not call us for impurity but in sanctification. ⁸Consequently, the person who rejects this rejects not man but God, who indeed gives his Holy Spirit to you.

## NOTES

4:3. *This is God's will, your sanctification.* The exhortation is introduced by *gar* ("for"), which is not translated, for here it is explanatory (BAGD, s.v. *gar*, 2) with a sense expressed in the paraphrase, "Well, to be explicit, God's will is this" (Frame, 146). The *gar* explains v 1 rather than v 2. The *touto* ("this") points forwards (cf. 4:15; 1 Cor 11:17; 2 Cor 2:1; 8:10; 13:9) to the infinitives in the long sentence that extends through v 6. It stands at the head of the sentence, but its position of emphasis need not imply that Paul intends a contrast with what pagans or Jews thought constituted the divine will (Bornemann, 165–66); it rather lays stress on sanctification as being at the heart of Christian morality. The same phrase appears in 5:18, where it points backwards.

Paul speaks of God's will in terms of his own apostleship (1 Cor 1:1; 2 Cor 1:1; cf. Col 1:1), of God's directing him in carrying out his mission (Rom 1:10; 15:32; perhaps 1 Cor 16:12), of Christian rejoicing, prayer and thanksgiving (1 Thess 5:17–18), and of Christian moral conduct, as he does here (Rom 12:2; cf. Col 1:9–10; 1 Pet 4:1–2). Behind the last is a Jewish use that saw God's will as fixed in Torah (e.g., Ps 39[40]:8; 2 Macc 1:3–4; cf. G. Schrenck in *TDNT* 3.54 for rabbinic references) and obedience to it as pleasing God (T Iss 4.1–3; 2 Bar 4:4). Paul was familiar with this usage (Rom 2:18; 1 Thess 4:1), but for him the will of God is not confined to the Law but is to be proved by a transformed mind to determine what is pleasing to God, perfect and good (Rom 12:1–2; cf. Phil 1:9–10; see Furnish 1989: 215–17).

In this bracket of the *inclusio*, *hagiasmos* ("sanctification"), which is in apposition to *thelēma tou theou*, is a noun describing action (cf. 2 Thess 2:13; Heb 12:14; 1 Pet 1:2), not a state or a condition, which is usually described by *hagiōsynē* (cf. 3:13; 2 Cor 7:1). The action required by the readers is further detailed in the infinitives that follow, which mark a progression in thought. Now Paul's exhortation in v 1, that his readers engage in conduct that is required to please God, is given specificity by these infinitives, which have the force of imperatives. Sanctification therefore requires human effort. In the second bracket (v 7), however, *hagiasmos* describes God's action. There are thus two aspects to sanctification, divine initiative and human endeavor (Stalder, 200–38).

Paul's prayer in 5:23, that God sanctify the Thessalonians completely, and his mention of God's will in 5:18 do not mean that 4:3a is to be understood as a heading to all of chaps. 4 and 5 (thus Furnish 1989: 214; Weima 1996). The tight form of the *inclusio* here shows that Paul is viewing this particular moral item through the lens of holiness.

*that is, that you abstain from immorality.* The infinitive *apechesthai* ("to abstain") is epexegetic, Paul clarifying what sanctification means in this context. Its occurrence in such passages as Acts 15:20, 29; 1 Pet 2:11, in addition to 1 Thess 4:3; 5:22, has led to the surmise that it was a technical term derived from catechesis aimed at distinguishing Christian from pagan morality (Selwyn, 372–73). Instruction of this sort did take place, but the hypothesis of a catechism cannot be proved.

The word *porneia* has been understood in a number of different ways (see Collins 1984: 310). It could refer to fornication, that is, illegitimate sexual behavior between unmarried persons (in support of this meaning, 2 Cor 12:21; Gal 5:19; Col 3:5 are frequently cited). It has also been thought to refer to incest (cf. 1 Cor 5:1) and sometimes particularly to marriage within the degrees of consanguinity prohibited by Lev 18:6–18 (Matt 5:32; 19:9; Acts 15:20, 29; 21:25 are cited in support; Baltensweiler, 141–42). These meanings are possible, even if the passages adduced to support them are not always apt.

It is far more probable that *porneia* here has a general sense of immorality, including fornication (Rigaux 1956: 502; Best 1972: 160). The word *porneias* is preceded in 1 Thess 4:3 by a definite article that has a generic quality (von Dobschütz 1909: 163), which is further brought out in some manuscripts which either replace the article with *pasēs* ("all"; ℵ² Ψ 104 365) or add *pasēs* to the article (F Gᶜ). It is not different from *akatharsia* ("impurity") in v 7 and with *en pathei epithymias* ("in lustful passion") shows that Paul has in view general pagan immorality. This is what Jews, including Paul, thought characteristically pagan (*Jub* 25:1; Rom 1:24, 26, with its references to *epithymia, akatharsia, pathē atimias,* parallel 1 Thess 4:4–5). Teaching against such behavior was part of basic Jewish instruction in moral behavior (e.g., *T Sim* 5.3; *T Reub* 4.6; cf. Str-B 4.356–83; F. Hauck and S. Schulz in *TDNT* 6.588–90).

*4:4. that each one of you learn how.* The infinitive *eidenai* is parallel to *apechesthai* and defines the positive side of sanctification (Ellicott, 52). By using *hekastos hymōn* ("each of you") instead of the general *hymās* ("you"), Paul individualizes his direction (cf. Col 4:6; see the addition of *hina*, on analogy to 2:11, by B² B³ Chrys and some Latin manuscripts). The meaning of *eidenai* partly depends on its relationship to *ktāsthai* ("to acquire"), the next infinitive in the series. If a comma were placed after *skeuos* ("wife"), thus separating *eidenai* and *ktāsthai,* and *eidenai* were taken to have the same meaning it has in 5:12 ("respect"), the meaning here would be "that each of you respect his own wife" (thus Frame, 146–48). The majority of the commentators, however, correctly regard *ktāsthai* as dependent on *eidenai* and understand *eidenai,* followed by a complementary infinitive, to mean "to learn how" (cf. Luke 12:56; Phil 4:12).

*to acquire his own wife.* This is one of the most disputed texts in the entire letter. The difficulties revolve around the meaning of *ktāsthai* and of *skeuos.* The verb is used of marriage, e.g., by Musonius Rufus (Fragment 12 [86, 7 Lutz]), of "a woman who has a lawful husband" (*kektēmenē andra nomimon*). However, its meaning, which in the present generally is "to acquire," "to get," is here determined by how *skeuos* ("vessel") is understood. *Skeuos* is used figuratively here, as it is elsewhere in Paul (Rom 9:21, 22, 23; 2 Cor 4:7; cf. 2 Tim 2:20, 21; Heb 9:21). Three meanings, with minor variations, have been proposed.

One interpretation understands *skeuos* to refer to the male sexual member. Largely on the basis of 1 Sam 21:5 (but see also *Greek Anthology* 16.243; Aelian, *Nature of Animals* 17.11), it is argued that *kelî,* the Hebrew equivalent of *skeuos,* is used in this way and that *skeuos ktāsthai* in 1 Thess 4:4 could have the sense of "to control one's sexual urge" or "to master oneself" (Whitton; against, Eadie, 127). This would fit the general prohibition against *porneia* in v 3, and Paul does speak of honor and dishonor when referring to the genitalia in 1 Cor 12:23–24. The principal difficulty with this view is that it fails to do justice to *heautou* ("his own"; see Vogel). Although reflexive pronouns could serve as personal pronouns (see 2:12; BDF §283), they need not always do so (see NOTE on 2:7). Furthermore, its attributive position here (cf. 1 Cor 7:2) stresses one person's possession in contrast to that of someone else, in this case, that of the brother against whom one should not trespass or act covetously (v 6).

One of the two most widely held interpretations understands *skeuos,* more broadly, to mean "body," especially in its sexual aspect (for patristic commentators who represent this view, see C. Maurer in *TDNT* 7.365 n. 48; cf. Rigaux 1956: 504–6; Marxsen 1979: 60–61; McGehee). There is Hebrew precedent for referring to humans as vessels, but in their totality rather than of their bodies as vessels (*TDNT* 7.360–61). The philosophical use of the term has also been thought to be relevant. The term *skeuos*, however, is not used of the body as a vessel containing or imprisoning the soul in Greek philosophical writings before the first century, but the notion does appear in such literature from the second century on. That the paucity of the philosophical sources, particularly in Greek, from the period may be responsible for this is suggested by the fact that *vas*, qualified by *animi* (Cicero, *Tusculan Disputations* 1.52; *animae* understood in Lucretius *On the Nature of Things* 3.440) does appear in Latin witnesses to Greek philosophy. Although this view of *skeuos* influenced certain Jewish writers, it is absent from Paul and other NT writers. The closest parallels to 1 Thess 4:4 are 2 Cor 4:7, where *skeuos* is qualified by *ostrakinos* ("earthen"), and 1 Pet 3:7, where it is qualified by *asthenesteron* ("weaker") and is in any case too obscure in its meaning to be helpful.

Two major difficulties work against this interpretation. First, the meaning of *ktāsthai* is normally ingressive ("to acquire," "to gain possession of"), which makes no sense if *skeuos* refers to one's body. On the basis of a few papyrus examples, it has been argued that the present infinitive *ktāsthai* here has the same meaning as the perfect infinitive *kektēsthai* ("to possess") and that the words in question could refer to someone "taking possession of his body" (Milligan, 49; cf. then the derived meaning reflected in the NIV: "to control his own body"). That is not the natural meaning of *ktāsthai*; furthermore, we shall see that the verb was used of marrying a wife. The second difficulty is that the reflexive *heautou* makes no sense when *skeuos* is understood as body (Schrage 1989: 229–30).

The other widely held interpretation is reflected in the translation "to take a wife for himself" (RSV; see *TDNT* 7.365 n. 49 for patristic commentators who represent this view; cf. Collins 1984: 311–12; Holtz 1986: 157–58). The exact phrase *skeuos ktāsthai* does not occur anywhere else in Greek literature, but there is evidence that Hebrew usage that had to do with marriage and sexual relations influenced Paul's choice of words, which are also similar to other Greek formulations (*TDNT* 7.360–62, 366).

The Hebrew *kelî* ("vessel"), as were other terms, was used by some rabbis as a euphemism for a woman engaged in sexual relations (Yarbrough, 72–73). Also relevant to the argument is the Hebrew *ba'al 'iššâ*, which in the OT is used ingressively, of getting married (Deut 22:13; 24:1; Ruth 4:5), and duratively, of engaging in sexual relations (Isa 54:1). The Hebrew *ba'al 'iššâ* corresponds to the Greek *ktāsthai gynaika*, "to take a wife" (Sir 36:24; Ruth 4:5; Xenophon, *Symposium* 2.10; cf. Musonius Rufus, cited above). It is in this linguistic context that Paul formed his phrase *skeuos ktāsthai*.

While there is thus sufficient evidence to support the supposition that *skeuos* refers to a wife, interpreters differ on whether *ktāsthai* is ingressive or durative. In support of the latter, the argument has been advanced that in the Jewish sphere, to which Paul belonged, there was a shift in the meaning of *ktāsthai* from the ingressive to the durative, parallel to a similar development in the meaning of *ba'al*. In this interpretation, the meaning of 1 Thess 4:4 would be "that every one of you know how to hold his own vessel in sanctification and honour (i.e., live with his wife in sanctification and honour)" (*TDNT* 7.366, followed, for example, by Best 1972: 162; Holtz 1986: 158).

Such an interpretation is not implausible, and the formulation *hekaston hymōn to heautou skeuos ktāsthai* ("that each one of you acquire his own wife") instead of the more normal *ktāsthai hekaston hymōn heautō skeuos* ("that each of you acquire a wife for himself") may support this understanding. However, the genitive *heautou* is stronger than the dative *heautō* and contrasts a marriage entered in holiness and honor to defrauding and being covetous of his brother in sexual matters. Furthermore, the evidence for the durative sense of *ktāsthai* is not strong enough to sustain this interpretation, and it is more probable that Paul is directing the Thessalonians to marry rather than fall prey to sexual immorality, as he also does in 1 Cor 7:2.

*in holiness and honor.* This is the positive member of an antithesis whose negative one (v 5) serves to place the stress on the positive one. The phrase is adverbial and modifies *ktāsthai*. Depending on how that verb is understood, this phrase would describe either conduct within marriage or, the interpretation represented here, the manner in which the marriage is to be entered. The single preposition *en* ("in") with two nouns unites them to form a complex in which *hagiasmos*, the active noun expressing the subject of the *inclusio* (vv 3–8), predominates.

Paul provides further details about his readers' sanctification by contrasting it with pagan lustful passion, which suggests that he has in mind sexual matters rather than a general attitude (contra: Holtz 1986: 159). More is implied in the term than not compromising one's relationship with God (Masson, 48) or the state of those consecrated to God, who are to let a religious feeling permeate their marriage (Frame, 150). Paul's understanding of sanctification is not simply a matter of attitude or feeling; rather, he thinks of a condition brought about by the Holy Spirit and of a process that continues (see COMMENT). The realism with which Paul views holiness versus sexual immorality is evident from 1 Cor 6:12–20, where he modifies popular moral philosophical traditions, as he does here. In marriage, sanctification is so palpable a quality in the Christian that it extends in some way even to an unbelieving partner in marriage (1 Cor 7:14). This is not the same as praying and thinking about God upon entering the wedding chamber (Tobit 8:1–10, referred to by von Dobschütz 1909: 166). It is from such a perspective of holiness that Paul's discussion of marriage should be viewed.

The significance of the single *en* is that *timē* ("honor") is to be seen from the perspective of holiness. It is therefore fundamentally incorrect to think that "holiness involves a relationship with God and honor suggests a relationship between human beings" (Collins 1984: 316–17). Commentators have not quite known what to do with Paul's reference to honor. For example, references to Rom 1:24 do not help to clarify how honor is related to marriage (Rigaux 1956: 507; Best 1972: 164–65). In contrast to the view that what is in mind here is behavior appropriate to the general norm (Holtz 1986: 158), it has also been thought that honor "is the respect which is to be shown to the wife, to which she has a claim as a creature of God" (J. Schneider in *TDNT* 8.174), and that Christians would have a more precise idea than pagans of what is honorable or dishonorable because of *agapē* ("love"; Masson, 48). References are dutifully made to Heb 13:4, where marriage itself is regarded as honorable, and to 1 Pet 3:7, where honor is to be bestowed on the wife. In addition to sharing with 1 Pet 3:7 the use of *skeuos* for wife, 1 Thess 4:4 shares with it a concern with honor for the Christian wife.

Moral philosophers, whose hortatory language Paul has been using in this chapter, also reflected on sexual conduct, honor and marriage. Musonius Rufus, Paul's contemporary, held that sexual relations outside marriage were dishonorable (Fragment 12 [86, 26–27 Lutz]). Plutarch, among others, thought that one could marry for dishonorable reasons and that, even within marriage, sensual pleasure is short, but not so honor, kindness and affection (*agapēsis; The Dialogue on Love* 754, 769A; cf. Musonius Rufus, Fragment 13A). Aristotle held that within marriage the man should receive the larger measure of honor (*Nicomachean Ethics* 8.14 1163b, 1–5), but Xenophon required husbands to honor their wives (*Hiero* 3.4; *Oeconomicus* 7.42; see also Ps.-Aristotle, *Concerning Household Management* 3.23–25 [143, 25 Rose]) and thought that husbands and wives should honor each other and that in addition the wife should honor her husband's parents (*Advice to Bride and Groom* 143B). Paul's advice that each Thessalonian man acquire his own wife "in honor" would therefore not have sounded strange to his contemporaries. What set him apart was his view that the honorable relationship was to be defined by what he understood as sanctification.

4:5. *not in lustful passion.* In a simple but long antithesis (this time not in the *ou . . . alla* form he has used earlier in the letter, e.g., 1:5, 6; 2:1–2, 3–4, 8), Paul contrasts pagan sexual morality to the Christian conduct he has just described. The negative member of the antithesis serves to strengthen the positive one. The contrast could be to the earlier warning against illegitimate sexual behavior (v 3) and not represent the view that pagans live in sexual lust with their wives, which is what v 5 may be taken to mean (Holtz 1986: 160). That reference, however, is too remote, and furthermore, the contrast is clearly defined by the preposition: *en hagiasmō kai timē* ("in holiness and honor"), *mē en pathei epithymias* ("not in lustful passion"). The similarity in language to Rom 1:24 (*epithymiai . . . atimazesthai*) and 1:26 (*pathē atimias*), where he describes pagan sexual life as other Jews did (cf. T Jos 7.8, *pathos epithymias ponērās*, "passion of evil lust"), has contributed to commentators' focus on Paul's condemnation of pagan sexual indulgence (cf. *pathos* next to *epithymia* in a list of vices in Col 3:5). In fact, however, Paul shares much with his moral philosophical counterparts.

Paul's language (*pathos epithymias*) was derived from the Stoics. They defined *pathos* ("emotion" or "passion") as an irrational and unnatural movement of the soul, as an impulse in excess (*pleonazousa; SVF* 3.39; cf. Cicero, *Tusculan Disputations* 3.7; 4.11; see also *SVF* 3.377, *pleonazousa . . . hyperteinousa*). It is a troubled movement of the soul, an intemperate longing, disobedient to reason, that may rightly be termed desire or lust (Cicero, *Tusculan Disputations* 3.23–24). The word receives further specificity in 1 Thess 4:4 when it is combined with *epithymia*, which Stoics regarded as one of the *pathē*, a craving opposed to reason (*SVF* 3.391; Diogenes Laertius, *The Lives of Eminent Philosophers* 7.113). One should discipline or train (*paidagōgein*) one's desires, for example, rather than indulge in extramarital sex (Musonius Rufus, Fragment 12 [86, 40 Lutz]) or hit on (*epitygchanein*) someone else's wife (Musonius Rufus, Fragment 7 [56, 27 Lutz]).

On the subjects of sex and marriage Paul shared more than language with his philosophical contemporaries. They also cautioned against sexual indulgence in relation to marriage. They contrasted the hedonistic life of a bachelor to the disciplined married life, a reason why some men did not want to marry (*SVF* 3.255,32–256,2). They frequently discussed the reasons why one should marry (see Yarbrough, 46–52, 80–81), and warned against marrying because of a woman's beauty and thus become a slave of pleasure (*SVF* 3.254, 7; 256, 3–4; Musonius Rufus, Fragment 13B; Hierocles, *On Duties* [*ap*. Stobaeus, *Anthology* 4.22.24; 4.506, 15 Hense]). Within marriage, sexual intercourse was to be engaged in only for procreation (e.g., Musonius Rufus, Fragment 12 [86, 4–8 Lutz]), and marriage should be characterized by companionship, love and devotion (e.g., Musonius Rufus, Fragment 13A).

Paul's familiarity with the philosophical traditions raises the question as to how his comment on pagan lustful passion is to be understood. That he is not merely indulging in traditional polemic, however far off the mark it may be, appears from what he goes on to say.

*as the pagans do who do not know God*. Paul qualifies what he says about the lustful passion with which his readers should not enter marriage: it is the behavior of pagans who do not know God. The comparative *kathaper kai* (cf. 3:6, 12; Rom 4:6; 2 Cor 1:14) draws a comparison with and contrast to the way each of the Thessalonians is to acquire his own wife and the way pagans bereft of a knowledge of God habitually do (see NOTE on 4:13 for *kathōs kai*). As the honor with which the former act is dominated by holiness, so the lustul passion of the latter is qualified as conduct ignorant of God. Paul thus goes beyond merely using philosophical terminology: he provides a theological interpretation of sexual behavior.

Instead of understanding lustful passion as opposition to reason, as the philosophers did, Paul asserts that its cause was ignorance of God. In this he was Jewish. The epithet that Gentiles do not know God comes from the OT (Job 18:21; Ps 78[79]:6; Jer 10:25), but Paul does not appear to have any particular OT passage in mind. Paul shares the Jewish view that the moral life is grounded in a knowledge of God and that idolatry is the source of immorality (Wis 14:12, 22–27; *Sib Or* 3.29–45; 1 Cor 10:7–8). Romans 1:18–32 shares such thinking and is frequently adduced to clarify 1 Thess 4:5. There Paul does make the connection between rejection of the knowledge of God and immorality, but his purpose in using this tradition in Romans is to indict Gentiles (cf. *anapologētoi*, "without excuse," in 1:21; 2:1, and the harsh tone throughout), whereas in 1 Thess 4:4 he uses it in exhortation to the sanctified life.

Paul does not refer to the Gentiles in this way primarily to draw a contrast between them and Christians as the people of God (thus Yarbrough, 78–81). The epithet appears in the larger context of a discussion about the sanctified life (vv 3–8) and is, more immediately, in grammatical contrast to *en hagiasmō* in v 4. His meaning is clarified by 1 Pet 1:14–16, where the same tradition is used in paraenesis: Lusts belonged to a period of ignorance; now that the readers have come to know a holy God, they are themselves to be holy. Paul's focus in writing to his recent converts is similar, not so much on pagan lustfulness as on God, who is the source of their holiness.

4:6. *that he not trespass against or behave covetously in this matter against his brother.* The last two infinitives (*to mē hyperbainein kai pleonektein*) are different from the preceding ones in that they have an article. The presence of the article and the meaning of the verbs in the infinitive have raised questions about how v 6 is related to vv 3–5. The articular clause may revert to *hagiasmos* (v 3) and represent a specific exemplification of sanctification (Ellicott, 54; Eadie, 131; Holtz 1986: 155–56), it may stand in apposition to all of vv 3–5, with the article having an emphatic resumptive force ("I say," "I mean," Findlay, 87), it may be taken more narrowly as in apposition to *eidenai* (v 4) and as representing a further explanation of *apechesthai* (v 3; Best 1972: 165–66), or it may have a final sense, "so as not to trespass against" (Lightfoot 1980: 56; Bruce 1982: 81).

Another line of interpretation has laid stress on the asyndeton at the beginning of v 6 and regarded the article as marking a rhetorical break and a change of subject (Dibelius 1937: 21–22; von Dobschütz 1909: 167). The article has then been taken to require that the entire clause, "that he not trespass against or behave covetously in this matter against his brother," be considered as parallel to *ho hagiasmos hymōn* ("your sanctification") and as a second exponent of the subject matter of the will of God (v 3). Also seeing in the article a break between the two infinitives it introduces and the preceding ones, yet another interpretation retains the connection with sanctification and regards the article as in apposition to *hagiasmos* and as providing a further explanation of it (Holtz 1986: 162–63).

There is insufficient ground for excising v 6 from Paul's treatment of sanctification in vv 3–8; indeed, the asyndetic construction itself suggests a close connection with what precedes (Frame, 152). Furthermore, the articular infinitive is often used in apposition (Smyth, 2035; Robertson, 1078; cf. Rom 4:13), and the infinitive with *to mē* is not unusual (incorrectly, Richard, 188) but is used in apposition by Paul elsewhere (Rom 14:13; 2 Cor 2:1), as it is used here, in apposition to vv 4–5.

The major reason for detecting a shift in subject in v 6 is not Paul's grammar but his use of *pleonektein*, which in turn is thought to give specific meanings to *hyperbainein* and *tō pragmati*. The basic meaning of *pleonektein*, which in addition to this verse occurs in the NT only in 2 Corinthians, is "to overreach," "to be greedy or covetous," and thus "to take advantage" (2 Cor 2:11; 7:2) or "to defraud" (perhaps 2 Cor 12:17, 18). For the same construction, *pleonektein ton adelphon*, see Dio Chrysostom, *Oration* 17.8. Paul used *pleonexia* of greed in 1 Thess 2:5, and a number of commentators think that the verb here is to be understood in the commercial sense of "to defraud" (see the summary of the arguments supporting this viewpoint in Collins 1984: 317–18). Covetousness and sexual immorality were regarded by Jews as the major pagan vices, and Paul combines *porneia* and *pleonexia* in Rom 1:29–31; 2:21–22; 13:13; 1 Cor 5:9–11; 6:9–10; 2 Cor 12:20–21; Gal 5:19–21, thus making use of a traditional formula (Reinmuth, 22–41). This supports the view that in 1 Thess 4:6 he also has avarice in mind.

On the basis of this understanding, *hyperbainein* ("to transgress"), which occurs only here in the NT, is also understood commercially. The word can be understood absolutely, "to sin" (BAGD, s.v. *hyperbainō*). John Chrysostom held a view in this direction by thinking of a transgression of boundaries established by God (*Homilies on 1 Thessalonians* 5 [PG 62:424]; cf. Dio Chrysostom, *Oration* 17.12, to transgress *to dikaion*, the principle of justice). It is more likely, however, that *hyperbainein* and *pleonektein* both have *ton adelphon autou* as object (Frame, 152; *TDNT* 5.745; Holtz 1986: 161). So also *prāgma*, which admits of a wide range in meaning ("thing," "event," "deed," "matter," "occurrence") determined by its context, is then here understood commercially (J. Schneider in *TDNT* 5.740; Schrage 1989: 230).

The commercial interpretation is to be rejected for a number of reasons. First, the unity of the context, which deals with sanctification in sexual behavior, militates against it (Collins 1984: 318–19). Covetousness should be read in continuity with and in light of the discussion of *porneia* and marriage, not as a new topic. Second, by reading v 6 as in apposition to vv 4–5, continuity rather than change becomes more evident. The commercial language already appears in v 4 in the command to acquire (*ktāsthai*) one's own wife; now Paul turns to consider a man's relationship with his brother in the matter of his brother's wife. Whereas Paul had advised his readers not (*mē*) to enter marriage in lustful passion (v 5), now he gives a command not (*mē*) to infringe on the rights of his brother. In mind here is the fellow Christian. The question of the narrowness of Paul's focus on intracommunal Christian relations, raised by some commentators, is not to the point. Paul was responding to concerns Timothy raised about attitudes within the Thessalonian church, and Paul has this particular situation in mind.

Third, the command not to transgress and behave covetously by engaging in adultery fits well with ancient discussions of adultery. The word *pleonektein* occurs in such discussions. Hierax, for example, speaks of the greedy who snatch away others' wives (*ap.* Stobaeus, *Anthology* 4.9.54 [3.367,16–19 Hense]; cf. Dio Chrysostom, *Oration* 17.14, for the snatching away of Helen and of Menelaus's possessions). A synonym (*lichneuein*) is also used by Epictetus (*Discourse* 2.4.8, 10) where he charges the adulterer with snatching away and greedily coveting what belongs to someone else. The noun *lichneia* is also associated with adultery in other such texts from the moralists (Epictetus, *Discourse* 4.8.13; Musonius Rufus, Fragment 4 [44, 17–18 Lutz]; Stobaeus, *Anthology* 2.31.123).

Such usage is consonant with the view of Musonius Rufus (Fragment 12 [86, 21–22 Lutz]; cf. Lysias 1.4), that the adulterer wrongs (*adikei*) the husband of the woman he corrupts (so also Clement of Alexandria, *Christ the Educator* 2.10; Origen, *Commentary on 1 Corinthians* 6:11 [*ap.* Cramer, 5.107, 17–18]; John Chrysostom, *Homilies on 1 Thessalonians* 5 [PG 62:424]). The view that it was only the husband who was thought to be wronged by adultery (F. Hauck in *TDNT* 4.732–33) is incorrect (see, e.g., Ps.-Aristotle, *Concerning Household Management* 1.4.1).

*because the Lord is an avenger in all these things.* Dio Chrysostom thought that the divine by its very nature punished the covetous (*Oration* 17.16), and the view that the gods watched over marriage was not unusual (e.g., Musonius Rufus, Fragment 14 [94, 25–31 Lutz]; Dio Chrysostom, *Oration* 7.135) nor was the view that they punished adultery (see Treggiari, 200). Paul's thinking, however, was informed by the OT, and we may here have an allusion to Ps 93(94):1. It is not clear whether he has in mind God or Christ, who is also thought of by him as judge (see NOTE on 2:19; Schade, 270 n. 154). The description of the judge as an avenger (*ekdikos*) makes it likely that he is referring to God, who was so described in the Jewish tradition (see Holtz 1986: 164 n. 105; in addition to Ps 93[94]:1, see *T Reub* 6.6; *T Levi* 18.1; *T Gad* 6.7; *Jos Asen* 23:13; and for the NT, Rom 12:19; Heb 10:30), but Christ is equally described by him as judge (see NOTE on 2:19; 3:13, and esp. 2 Thess 1:8). By referring to "all these things," Paul includes everything he has brought up since v 3.

*indeed, we told you so before and kept on charging you.* This is the ninth time that Paul uses *kathōs* in the letter. It is characteristic of paraenetic style and stresses that a speaker's present and past words or actions are in conformity with each other ("even as" see NOTE on 1:5). The construction here, *kathōs kai . . . kai*, is emphatic (see NOTE on 3:4), hence the translation "indeed." Paul's consistency in his instruction is summarized in the verbs; its subject was the vengeance of God.

Some commentators understand *proeipamen* ("we told you before") as Paul's prediction that the judgment would take place (for *prolegein* used of prediction, see 3:4), but the word probably has the connotation of a warning implicit in announcing a future event about whose certainty there should be no doubt (as in 2 Cor 13:2; Gal 5:21). The certainty of the divine wrath had been part of his original preaching (see NOTE on 1:10; cf. 2:16). The importance the subject had for Paul is further brought out by the durative imperfect ("kept on") and meaning ("charging") of *diemartyrametha*. The perfective force of *dia* in the verb makes it stronger than *martyresthai* ("to charge") in 2:12, lending an imperatival force to it (cf. Luke 16:28; Acts 8:25; 20:21; 1 Tim 5:21; 2 Tim 2:14; 4:1).

4:7. *For God did not call us for impurity but in sanctification.* The reason (*gar,* "For") why Paul had spoken so emphatically about God's vengeance is found in the nature of their call. The call of God of which Paul speaks took place through his preaching of the gospel (see NOTE on 2:12) and is viewed from a negative and positive side, once more formulated antithetically, with the stress in the second, positive member of the antithesis. The emphasis in this verse is on the ethical dimension of the call; in v 8 it is on God. The two prepositions do not have the same meaning here, as is sometimes claimed (e.g., Holtz 1986: 165).

The *epi* in *epi akatharsia* could express either purpose or result (BAGD, s.v. *epi*, II.1.b.e). Most commentators elect the former ("for impurity"), but it has also been argued that Paul has in mind the impurity that characterized his readers' pre-Christian existence (see Rom 6:19; cf. Eph 4:19; 5:3; von Dobschütz 1909: 171) and that Paul means that God called them because of or in view of their impurity (Masson, 49–50; Horn, 124). The heat of Paul's rhetoric, however, shows that he has in mind their present condition. His language has become more insistent and sharp in v 6, and the intensity will be increased still further in v 8. He is not merely reminding them of their call but is drawing their attention to its moral consequences. The sharpness of his rhetoric and his reference to God as an avenger must have been called for by circumstances in Thessalonica. By *akatharsia* he could mean something other than sexual immorality (see NOTE on 2:3), but the context (esp. vv 4–5) suggests that he has sexual behavior in mind (see Rom 1:24; 2 Cor 12:21; Gal 5:19; cf. Col 3:5). In either case, Paul has exemplified (2:3) what he now commands.

The *en* in *en hagiasmō* ("in sanctification") describes neither the purpose of God's calling (Best 1972: 168) nor its result (Lünemann, 519; Frame 155), but its modality (von Dobschütz 1909: 171). It is through God's call that they are sanctified (cf. 2 Thess 2:13–14), that they became *hagioi klētoi* ("saints by calling"; 1 Cor 1:2; 2 Cor 1:1; Bruce 1982: 86; Laub 1973: 59). As a counterpart to *akatharsia*, Paul thinks of moral holiness. Whereas in v 3 sanctification was viewed in terms of his readers' responsibility, now it is described as God's action (cf. 1 Cor 6:11).

4:8. *Consequently, the person who rejects this rejects not man but God.* Paul ends his discussion with a new sentence that draws an emphatic, warning conclusion from what he has said (the intensive *toigaroun*, "consequently," "for that very reason," appears elsewhere in the NT only in Heb 12:1, in exhortation). Paul has repeatedly related what he has said about sexual morality to God (vv 3, 6); now as explicitly and sharply as possible he does so again by asserting (again antithetically) that rejection of his words would be a rejection of God.

Paul had earlier stressed that God was the effective force behind his preaching (2:2, 4, 12) and was active in the message they had received (2:13). Now their moral life is most emphatically grounded in God's action. He has specified what God's will, not his own, is in the matter (v 3), and to neglect God's will (cf. Mark 7:9; Luke 7:30; John 12:48) is tantamount to rejecting God (cf. Exod 16:8; 1 Sam 8:7). The language is so common, particularly when reflecting Christian mission (Luke 10:16; cf. Matt 10:40), that there is no need to think that Paul was defending himself (see COMMENT: Introduction on 2:1–12).

*who indeed gives his Holy Spirit to you.* The second bracket to the *inclusio* begun in v 3 is expanded by describing God as giving his Holy Spirit to Paul's readers. This characterization of God is introduced by the intensive *ton kai* ("who indeed"; for the ascensive *kai*, see Matt 5:47; 1 Cor 2:10; 2 Cor 1:8) to stress that God is the source of "his" Holy Spirit. The thinking is that of such passages as Ezek 36:27; 37:14, and this is the closest that Paul comes to refer the giving of the Holy Spirit to an OT passage. Whether he is merely speaking "biblically" (von Dobschütz 1909: 173) or is consciously adapting Ezek 37:14 (Horn, 126–27) is difficult to determine.

Some manuscripts read the aorist participle, *donta* ("gave"), perhaps under the influence of Rom 5:5; 2 Cor 1:22; 5:5; Gal 4:6 (Schrage 1989: 226). Had Paul used the aorist, he would have thought of the giving of the Spirit in conversion, when they were called (cf. the aorist *ekalesen* in v 7; *elabete* in Gal 3:2; the Spirit with the aorists in 1 Cor 6:11). The present, under the influence of the OT texts, may be atemporal, describing God as the Giver of the Spirit (Pfister, 16), but more likely he has in mind God's continuing to make the Spirit available for their sanctification (cf. the present *kalōn* in 2:12; 5:24).

## COMMENT

It is not immediately obvious why Paul wrote on sexual morality and marriage or why he wrote in the way he did. One view is that sexual immorality was a common theme and that one need not suppose that conditions in Thessalonica called forth Paul's instruction (Dibelius 1937: 19–20). An opposite view is that circumstances in Thessalonica were responsible for Paul's writing on the subject and that he had learned of those circumstances either from a letter the Thessalonians had written him, asking for advice (Faw; Best 1972: 154, 162), or from Timothy (Bruce 1982: 87–88; Wanamaker, 158–59).

It is unlikely that vv 3–8 were a reply to a request for information. As an answer to such a request, Paul's discussion would be unreasonably brief if his converts asked for direction in sexual matters: Get married, thus avoiding sexual immorality, and do not covet someone else's wife. This discussion is dramatically brief and lacking detailed advice, compared with 1 Cor 7, where Paul does give advice in response to a request for it. Furthermore, Paul is emphatic that he is not telling them something new (4:1–2), but that his commands are merely a reminder of what he had told them at some length (the imperfect tense in v 6). It is therefore much more likely that Paul is writing in view of what he had learned from Timothy about what the Thessalonians needed.

A wide variety of suggestions has been advanced about what the situation in Thessalonica was. One is that Paul, the Jew, was acutely aware of the different, low state of pagan sexual morality and that he feared either that his recent converts might revert to their pre-Christian ways (Rigaux 1956: 502–3), especially under pressure from outsiders (Weima 1996: 104–6), or that they had already succumbed (Wanamaker, 158–59). The permissive attitude, frequently thought to have been generally held, is illustrated by Cicero, *In Defense of Marcus Caelius* 48:

However, if there is anyone who thinks that youth should be forbidden affairs even with courtesans, he is doubtless eminently austere . . . , but his view is contrary not only to the licence of this age but also to the customs and concessions of our ancestors. For when was this not a common practice? When was it blamed? When was it forbidden? When, in fact, was it that what is allowed was not allowed?

The attitudes and practices Cicero mentions were indeed widespread, but as the NOTES demonstrate, his rhetorical questions would lose their force a century later, when the moral philosophers, some of whom were Paul's contemporaries, held quite different views of sexual morality.

Attempts have also been made to relate the sexual practices Paul warns against to practices associated with certain cults in Thessalonica. The cults of Dionysus (Donfried 1985: 337–38), the Cabiri (esp. Jewett 1986: 127–32; already Rigaux 1956: 502; Donfried 1985: 338–40), and Samothrace (Donfried 1985: 340–41), whose interconnectedness is sometimes stressed, have come under consideration. The Thessalonians may have been tempted by such cultic practices, but we do not know as much about these cults as is sometimes supposed, and it is difficult to judge the claims made since no close exegesis of the Pauline text has yet been offered to support them. It is futile to speculate what the purported practices, pagan or Christian, in Thessalonica may have been (Koester 1994).

It has also been suggested that it was Paul's awareness of cultic practices in the setting in which he wrote 1 Thessalonians, rather than conditions in Thessalonica, that was responsible for his taking up the subject. On the theory that he wrote from Athens, the practices associated with Aphrodite have come under consideration (Ulonska). Without reference to a particular cult, it has also been thought that conditions in Corinth, where he most likely wrote the letter, influenced his perspective (von Dobschütz 1909: 168–69). Paul's letter, however, was written in response to what he heard about circumstances in Thessalonica from Timothy (see COMMENT on 3:6–10), and there is no evidence that his situation in Corinth determined what he wrote.

A view that has received very little support is that Paul responded to a problem that the Thessalonians had dealing with inheritance law (Baltensweiler 1967: 135–49). Of greater interest to commentators has been the possibility that Paul sought to address views contrary to his own that were causing problems in the congregation in Thessalonica. These problems were caused, according to these theories, by spiritual "enthusiasts" given to libertinism (Lütgert, 67–71) or, more precisely, by Gnostic libertinists (Schmithals 1972: 156–58). Another view identifies opponents to Paul in Thessalonica who mounted an intellectual challenge to the authenticity of the traditional ethics that he espoused, insinuating that Paul's ethics derived from humans rather than God (Jewett 1986: 105–6). The approach to the letter that discovers opponents who make the text more understandable does not do justice to the literary or rhetorical nature of the letter (see COMMENT on 2:1–12) and works with a view of early Christianity that places a premium on confrontation and polemic at the expense of the continuity that the church's history presupposes.

The most recent extensive study of vv 3–8 is that of Larry Yarbrough (66–87). Yarbrough argues that Paul did not write on sexual morality and marriage because the Thessalonians were living immorally and that Paul had to answer specific questions brought by Timothy. Nor did he write because these were standard topics discussed by moral philosophers. Rather, Paul writes on these topics

> because the traditional formulation of the precepts he knew distinguished believers from non-believers and citing them would remind the Thessalonians of who they were, which would in turn encourage them to continue in their efforts to lead a life pleasing to God. (87)

Very important to Yarbrough are Tob 4:12 and *T Levi* 9.9–10, which are not only similar to 1 Thess 4:3b–5 in form but also distinguish the (Jewish) community from the surrounding world (69–70, 86). "Paul employs traditional polemic concerning marriage . . . in the service of general paraenesis" (87).

Yarbrough strengthens his argument by taking vv 3–8 to belong to a larger discussion of Christian conduct (vv 1–12), which allows him to bring Paul's comments on brotherly love (v 9) and outsiders (v 12) into the discussion of marriage and sexual behavior. Familial relations within the community draw attention to the boundaries that exist and are important, for the exclusiveness they imply is a motivation to live in a certain way. Of great importance in this respect is the centrality of God in Paul's paraenesis. Paul refers to God or the Lord Jesus eight times in vv 1–12 as the sources of his precepts, and describes the Thessalonians as the people of God (1:1, 4, 9–10; 3:13; 5:5, 23–24). The life they are to live as God's people is to be holy, which distinguishes them from those who belong to the world.

Yarbrough's treatment of vv 3–8 marks a distinct advance over other interpretations. It makes an effort to understand the pericope in its literary context, recognizes its paraenetic character, explores the moral traditions, pagan as well as Jewish, with which it has affinities, and seeks to discover the function of the passage. Yarbrough does not quite succeed, however, in situating vv 3–8 firmly in its literary context. He does not relate the pericope to 3:6–13 and therefore slights the epistolary situation, nor does he examine Paul's use of the traditions with sufficient exegetical rigor, consequently missing the way in which Paul modifies them. Yarbrough is correct that sanctification is important to Paul's discussion, but does not recognize the force of the *inclusio*, which separates vv 3–8 from vv 9–12, nor its function, which is to indicate that the entire pericope is to be seen under the aspect of sanctification. Separation or distinctiveness is only one dimension of sanctification, and it is incorrect to see separation as the focus of the pericope.

The NOTES show that Paul's discussion betrays an awareness of the moral traditions concerning marriage even more than has been recognized. This is also true of Paul's discussion in 1 Cor 7 (see Deming). At the same time, Paul differs from these traditions in important ways. He does not go on at great length about the reason for marrying or the relationship between husband and wife as they do (see Geurts; van Geytenbeek, 62–71; Yarbrough, 7–63, 80–81). Paul is so brief that a superficial reading may leave the impression that he sees marriage primarily as a way to avoid sexual immorality (vv 3–4; cf. 1 Cor 7:2), a view shared by some rabbis (*B. Qidd.* 29b; see Yarbrough 22–23).

That Paul is concerned with more than promoting marriage as an anodyne against sexual immorality is clear from the way in which his discussion is shot through with religious and theological language that qualifies everything he says about his warrants for his instruction, and the motivation, manner and end of the behavior he inculcates. In the introduction to chaps. 4 and 5 he claims that his instruction took place in (v 1) or was given through the Lord Jesus (v 2) and had as its goal conduct that would please God (v 1). Then in the six verses in which he discusses marriage, he uses such language nine times: the will of God (v 3), sanctification (vv 3–4), knowledge of God (v 5), the Lord as avenger (v 6), God's calling (v 7), holiness (v 7), rejection of God (v 8), God as giver of the Holy Spirit (v 8).

The sheer preponderance of theological language already shows clearly how different the texture of his treatment is from that of the philosophical sources he modifies. God stands behind Paul's paraenesis (Horn, 125). More significant even than the pervasiveness of the language are its Jewish cast and the rubric within which Paul uses it. As he had reached for Jewish traditions when speaking about judgment (2:16), so he does when speaking about the moral life. Old Testament passages shimmer through in vv 6 and 8 more visibly than they do anywhere else in the letter. Sanctification, a notion he derives from the OT, is the rubric within which he describes the will of God and to which all the other language in vv 3–8 belongs (see Deidun, although his overemphasis distorts the text). The few other references to holiness and sanctification in 1 Thessalonians (3:12; 5:23) appear in eschatological contexts, and it is incorrect to see the theme as dominating the entire letter (Weima 1995: 99–103; cf. Dewailly, 77–78).

According to the OT, God is the Holy One who sanctifies (Isa 41:14; 43:3; Lev. 20:8; 21:8; 22:32; cf. 2 Macc 14:36; 1QS 10:12; on what follows, see esp. Schrage 1989). God chose Israel, a holy people (Deut 7:6; cf. *Jub* 2:12, 20; 1QSb 4:27), with a call that has an imperatival element to it (Lev 19:2; Deut 14:2). Paul thought of Christians as chosen by God through the gospel and as sanctified at a particular moment, at the time of their conversion (1 Thess 1:4–5; 2 Thess 2:13–14).

Paul's use of the the passive to describe sanctification at conversion (1 Cor 6:11) and the passive participle to describe Christians as sanctified (1 Cor 1:2; Phil 1:1) shows that he thinks of God as the main actor in that sanctification, which is punctiliar in nature. The same is also true when he speaks of sanctification by the Spirit (2 Thess 2:13; cf. Rom 15:16; 1 Cor 6:11; 1 Pet 1:2). But as in the OT, there is an imperatival element to the call to holiness (Rom 6:18–20; 12:1–2). All human conduct is to be holy (Rom 12:1–2; cf. 1 Pet 1:15), and concrete directions are given as to what that conduct should be (1 Thess 4:3–6). Sanctification is thus a process in which Christians exercise responsibility as well as a condition that is brought about by God.

The faithful response is not, however, exclusively human. For example, at one point Paul speaks of sanctification as the Christian's fruit (RSV: "return"; NRSV:

"advantage"), issuing from service to God (Rom 6:22); at another he speaks of the qualities of the Christian life as the fruit of the Spirit (Gal 5:22). In addition to the sanctification of individuals, Paul thinks of sanctification in corporate terms. In fact, the only place where *hagios* is used in the singular is Phil 4:21, but even there it has a plural sense (Fee, 457: *pās* functions distributively). The church is the temple of the Holy Spirit (1 Cor 3:16–17).

Sanctification does set Christians apart from the world (Rom 12:1–2), yet they do not escape from it, but lend a particular kind of presence to it, that of a new family whose moral standards are different (1 Cor 5:9–13; cf. 6:1–11). In 1 Thessalonians, the attitude towards non-Christians is relatively positive. Although nonbelievers have no hope (4:13) and have harassed the Thessalonians (2:14), they are to be loved (3:13) and not retaliated against (5:15). The love Christians have for their brethren does not create a conventicle living in disregard of society's opinion of them; on the contrary, brotherly love, which is divinely taught, is the basis for a community whose conduct seeks approval from the larger society, "the outsiders" (4:9–12).

It would be incongruous if Paul's main emphasis in vv 3–8, immediately preceding so positive an attitude towards non-Christians, were to separate Christians from them. As observed in the NOTE on 4:6, the stress is not on the negative part of the antithesis, the lustful passion of the pagans who do not know God, but on the positive part, the injunction to acquire a wife in holiness and honor (v 5). In the antithetical style typical of paraenesis, the negative part is a foil to draw attention to the positive action that is commanded. The contrast would have special meaning for converts who had only recently converted from paganism.

Light is thrown on vv 3–8 by a discussion of sexual immorality in 1 Cor 6:12–20, where Paul inveighs at some length against sexual immorality and also adduces a number of theological reasons to support his advice. In the dialogical style of the diatribe he engages an interlocutor on the issue of freedom in sexual behavior (Stowers 1981). The dialogue begins with the interlocutor introducing a viewpoint, evidently that of some Corinthians, in the form of a Stoic slogan on the wise man's freedom ("all things are lawful to me"), which Paul counters with another ("but not all things are expedient").

The Corinthians were familiar with such philosophical traditions (Malherbe 1995b: 335–36), but Paul ceases the philosophical discussion after the interlocutor's Cynic-sounding claim that food is for the belly and the belly for food (v 13; cf. Diogenes Laertius, *The Lives of Eminent Philosophers* 6.69). He then continues his opposition to the Corinthian position with a series of theological affirmations on the judgment, the Lord's ownership of the body (v 13), the resurrection (v 14), Christians' bodies as members of Christ's body (vv 15–16), Scripture (v 17), and the body as temple of the Holy Spirit and divine ownership of the body (v 18).

In the NOTES it has been shown that Paul works with the same kind of philosophical traditions that are found in 1 Corinthians. There is no evidence that the Thessalonians expressed their self-understanding in the same terms that the Corinthians did, but Paul's consistent use of these traditions supports the surmise that Paul expected his Thessalonian readers to understand them. His heavy use of theological affirmations to support his moral instruction is to be understood in the light of how Paul's contemporaries supported their moral claims.

It is clear that philosophy provided moral instruction with a theoretical framework as well as rationale (Ps.-Plutarch, *On the Education of Children* 7DE; Musonius Rufus, Fragments 8; 16), but it does not appear that there was an essential connection between religion and ethics. With very few exceptions, conversion to a cult did not require moral transformation (see COMMENT on 1:9–10). Whether there was a connection between religion and morality beyond initiation is a matter under dispute (see Malherbe 1989: 61 for bibliography). It may be that the separation between them, which may not have been universal, is a modern notion projected onto ancient religion by historians of religion (den Boer), but the least that the debate on the issue demonstrates is that there was no necessary connection.

Regardless of what pagans thought of how morality and religion were related, what is important in attempting to understand ancient Jewish and Christian moral texts is that Jews and Christians thought their morality to be superior because it was grounded in their religion. The comparison appears most clearly, but not exclusively, in their apologetic writings, which, though ostensibly addressed to outsiders, were in fact addressed to their own communions with the purpose of strengthening them vis-à-vis an unfriendly society. The *Epistle of Aristeas* is explicit. At a series of banquets, the seventy-two translators of the LXX are each asked essentially philosophical questions, in response to which each answer includes a reference to God (182–300). The king repeatedly compliments them, as he does most fully in 200–201:

> When all had expressed approval and signified it by applause, the king said to the philosophers, of whom not a few were present, "I think the virtue of these men is extraordinary and their understanding very great, for having questions of such a sort addressed to them they have given proper replies on the spur of the moment, all of them making God the starting-point of their reasoning." And the philosopher Menedemus of Eritrea said, "True, Your Majesty; for inasmuch as all things are governed by providence, and these men are right in holding that man is a creature of God, it follows that all power and beauty of discourse have their starting point from God."

The point of the Jewish apologist is clear: the morality of Jews is superior because every aspect of their lives is governed by their belief in God and obedience to his law. Philosophy is not rejected; on the contrary, the philosophers accept Jewish wisdom as essentially philosophical.

Christian apologists followed in this tradition. The one, true God instructs in religion and ethics (Theophilus, *To Autolycus* 3.9, 11), and instruction in morality begins with and requires belief in one God, the Creator (Diogn 7; cf. Herm *Mand* 1). Christian morality is not a matter of human devising but is uttered and taught by God (Athenagoras, *Embassy* 11, on the philosophical affinities of which see Malherbe 1969).

Lactantius reflects this attitude in his criticism of Roman religion: "For the worship of God being taken away, man lost the knowledge of good and evil" (*The Divine Institutes* 5.5). He intones the superiority of Christianity: "What is the religion of the gods? . . . I see nothing else in it than a rite pertaining to the fingers only. But our religion teaches justice . . . has its existence altogether in the soul of the worshipper . . . has the mind itself for sacrifice" (*The Divine Institutes* 5.20). The argument may be contentious, but the judgment is correct that "the fact that Christian religion linked worship and moral conduct so explicitly and emphatically must have worked in its favour with educated Romans. The nature of traditional paganism made it difficult to give ethics an explicitly and central part to it. Christianity indisputably did so" (Liebeschuetz, 265; see also 271–75).

The apologists interpreted and defended existing communities when they emphasized the essential connection between their morality and religion. Paul emphasized the connection pastorally as he nurtured the newly founded congregation in Thessalonica. It is likely that Timothy had told Paul that there was need to write on the matter. The situation looks similar to Paul's description of his ministry in 2:1–12. Timothy had reported to Paul that the Thessalonians still looked to Paul as their model, yet Paul goes on to present a picture of himself as their model. He reminds them repeatedly of things they already knew, so he does not provide new information about his behavior but rather stresses the religious and theological dimensions of the motivation, warrants, method and goal of his ministry. The importance of this description of the Thessalonians' model appears in 4:3–8, where the same elements appear, now of the Thessalonians' behavior. In 2:1–12 Paul describes himself in terms similar to the (self-)descriptions of his philosophic contemporaries; in vv 3–8 he similarly uses language used by the moral philosophers in discussing marriage, but modifies it by describing sexual behavior in terms of a sanctified life. In doing so, he explicates, in one aspect of life, the moral claims implicit in his readers' acceptance of the gospel (see COMMENT on 1:9–10).

# C. ON BROTHERLY LOVE AND SELF-SUFFICIENCY, 4:9–12

◆

From a discussion of sexual morality within the church Paul turns to a new subject in vv 9–12, which constitutes a single unit. What was expressed in a prayer in 3:12 is now treated as a moral obligation (Bornemann, 176). The discussion begins with love between members of the church, to which is attached advice on social conduct and manual labor that have as their aims self-

sufficiency and the favorable opinion of non-Christians. The connection between vv 9–10a and vv 10b–12 has been problematic for some commentators
who, impressed by the adversative nature of de ("But") in v 10b and what they
understand as new subject matter thereafter, think that the two sections could
not be connected (e.g., Dibelius 1937: 23). According to them, the close proximity between the two sections is due simply to the fact that they both deal with
furtherance of the Christian life (Lührmann, 524).

A number of factors, however, suggest that vv 9–12 are in fact a unit. In the first
place, Paul had already connected love for the community with manual labor
when he referred paradigmatically to his own conduct in 2:8–9, thereby laying the
foundation for this directive. Secondly, love within the church does not rule out
concern about non-Christians. In 3:12, love for each other is balanced by love for
"all," probably non-Christians in the Christian assemblies, and in chap. 5 the community, which is to tend to its own nurture and love those who extend care (5:13),
and is to pursue the good of each other and of all people (5:15). Thirdly, the grammatical structure is not as loose as is sometimes averred (e.g., by Lünemann, 523),
but is tight (see Ellicott, 59). Rather than marking a breach with what precedes,
the de, which is slightly adversative, redirects attention from a general statement
about love for the church to a particular, practical manifestation of that love.

Fourthly, parakaloumen de ("But we exhort") does not introduce a new subject but is followed by five infinitives, the first one of which is dependent on it
and still refers to the church's love for each other. The other infinitives are connected by kai ("and") three times, which succinctly but clearly specifies how love
for the brethren is to be demonstrated. Finally, love (or friendship) and self-sufficiency were frequently discussed together by the moral philosophers (see
NOTES), whose concerns and terminology Paul represents and adapts in this
section, in which he gives the earliest extant Christian direction in social ethics.

## TRANSLATION

4   9Concerning love for the brethren you have no need for us to write to you,
for you yourselves are taught by God to love one another; 10indeed, you are
doing it to all the brethren in the whole of Macedonia. But we exhort you,
brethren, to do so more and more, 11and to make it your ambition to live a quiet
life and to mind your own affairs and to work with your hands, just as we instructed you, 12so that you may conduct yourselves becomingly in the eyes of the
outsiders and may depend on no one.

## NOTES

4:9. Concerning love for the brethren. After having discussed sexual morality within the church, Paul turns to relations within the church and the church's relationship to the larger society (cf. 1 Cor 5; 6:1–11). The phrase peri de can introduce a response to an inquiry made by letter (see 1 Cor 7:1), but it does not
always do so (see COMMENT on 3:6–10). As was the general custom (see D. G.

Bradley; Baasland), Paul frequently uses the phrase to introduce a new subject (1 Cor 7:1, 25; 8:1, 4; 12:1; 16:1, 12; cf. 2 Cor 9:1). Paul would in any case have learned from Timothy that the Thessalonians needed instruction on the subject of love towards each other, but it is quite possible that he is here responding to a request that they made in a letter (Milligan, 126; Frame, 140, 157; Faw). Judging from vv 9–12, they would have asked, not merely whether to love each other, but about the wider implications of that love.

Paul uses a word (*philadelphia*) for love of the brethren that was used by non-Christians of love for blood relations (see Plutarch, *On Brotherly Love* 478A-492D, the only systematic study of the subject, on which see Betz 1978: 231–63). Brotherly love was known "as the near-proverbial virtue of the Dioscuri, the divine twins, Castor and Polydeuces" (Kloppenborg, 283). Perhaps *philadelphia* came into Christian usage through Hellenistic Judaism, where it and its cognates were also used of blood relations (e.g., 4 Macc 13:21, 23, 26; 14:1; 15:10; Philo, *On the Embassy to Gaius* 87, 92), but it also frequently described a relationship with Israel (e.g., 2 Macc 15:14 of Jeremiah; see Schäfer, 134–58). In the NT, the word group is used only in paraenesis, figuratively, of fictive kinship (Rom 12:9–10; 1 Thess 4:9; Heb 13:1; 1 Pet 1:22; 3:8; 2 Pet 1:7). It is used in some of these passages of a particular type of love (Rom 12:9–10; 1 Thess 4:9; 1 Pet 1:22; 2 Pet 1:7), which was also described with a characteristic Christian term (*agapē*).

Although *philadelphia* and its cognates in a figurative sense were not completely absent from pagan Greek (see Ps.-Socrates, *Epistle* 28.12), the analogous relationship was described as friendship (*philia*), a social virtue of the utmost importance to the ancients (see Fitzgerald 1997), especially to the Epicureans (see COMMENT). Paul does not use *philia* or *philos* ("friend"), but he does use extensively the clichés customarily used in discussing friendship and friends (Fitzgerald 1996). Part of the ancient treatment of friendship was a discussion of the problem of how friendship could require the mutual giving and receiving of benefits between friends while maintaining self-sufficiency (*autarkeia*) as a virtue (e.g., Cicero, *On Friendship* 30; Seneca, *Epistle* 9.3, 5). Paul used the categories of this discussion when acknowledging assistance he had received from the Philippians while maintaining that he was *autarkēs* (Phil 4:11; see Malherbe 1995c). In 1 Thess 4:9–12, he similarly deals with love for the brethren in a discussion framed by *philadelphia* (v 9) and lacking nothing (v 12).

*you have no need for us to write to you.* The Greek literally reads, "you have no need to write to you." Some manuscripts (א² D* F G Ψ) read *echomen* ("we have"), others (H 81 Aug) have a passive, *graphesthai* ("to be written," cf. 5:1). Both variant readings are attempts to make the sentence easier, hence the more difficult reading is preferred, and *hēmās* ("for us") is to be supplied to render the sense of the clause. In a reply to a request for information about love for the brethren this might seem a bit chiding: "You don't need any more information." However, the rhetorical character of Paul's language conveys a quite different sense. This is a case of *paralipsis*, in which one pretends to pass over something one in fact mentions (BDF §495.1; see also 5:1; 2 Cor 9:1; Phlm 19; cf. *UPZ*, 238, II, 4, *perisson hēgoumai diexodesteron hymin graphein*, "I consider it superfluous to write to you more fully"). Letters by definition fulflled definite needs (Ps.-Libanius, *Epistolary Styles* 2), so such statements had special functions. Here the epistolary cliché functions paraenetically and is of the same order as similar phrases in other letters (e.g., Cicero, *To His Friends* 1.4.3; cf. 2.4.2). It is another way in which Paul reminds his readers of what they already know (see NOTE on v 2). As the continuation of this verse and v 10 show, Paul is actually complimenting his readers on their knowledge of and love for each other (cf. Seneca, *Epistle* 47.21: that Lucilius needs no exhortation is a mark of good character).

*for you yourselves are taught by God to love one another.* Paul's emphatic reason ("for you yourselves") why he need not write is not antithetic, contrasting their knowledge with someone else's (cf. 2 Thess 1:4). Rather, it is of a piece with the other paraenetic statements about what they already know (cf. 2:1, "For you yourselves know"; also 3:3; 5:2; see pages 82, 86). Paul writes in this way in order to encourage them to love (John Chrysostom, *Homilies on 1 Thessalonians* 6 [PG 62:429]). So far, he has described his readers as loved by God (1:4) and by himself (2:8); he has complimented them on their love (1:3, the object unspecified); but he has also prayed that their love for one another might increase (3:12), and he will again exhort them to love (5:8, 13). Thus, while Paul acknowledges that they loved him (3:6) and even all the Macedonians (4:10b), he is concerned about reciprocal relations within the church (*allēlous*; cf. 3:12).

This is the first time that *theodidaktos* ("taught by God") appears in Greek literature. Paul's paraenetic reminder is strengthened by referring what they know to God's teaching (see Epictetus, *Discourse* 1.25.1–6: instruction is unnecessary, for they have received instructions directly from God). It has been suggested that Paul has in mind some kind of internal teaching the Thessalonians had (e.g., Jer 31:33–34), or teaching they received from prophets in their midst (cf. 5:20; cf. Ps.-Socrates, *Epistle* 1.10, of predicting, *didaskontos tou theou* ["while God was instructing me"]), or teaching from Jesus (John 13:34), or his own teaching under inspiration by God and the Spirit (see Theophilus, *To Autolycus* 2.9). Given Paul's earlier emphasis that he had spoken God's word to them (2:2, 4, 8, 9) and that the Thessalonians had received his teaching as God's word (2:13), the latter is the most probable meaning. In addition to Jer 31:33–34, a number of other OT passages could have informed Paul's language: Jer 38:33–34 (see Deidun, 33–35); Isa 54:13 (quoted in John 6:45; cf. *Pss Sol* 17:35); Ezek 37:14.

The word Paul uses, *theodidaktos*, appears to have been coined by him. He seems to have done so on analogy to other compound words with *didaktos*, which enjoyed wide currency in philosophical circles. Some philosophers, especially those of a Cynic bent, described themselves as *autodidaktoi* ("self-taught"; see Stobaeus, *Anthology* 4.32.11 [5.782,17–20 Hense]; Maximus of Tyre, *Oration* 10.5; for the idea, Juvenal, *Satires* 13.19–22) or *autourgoi tēs sophias* ("self-made philosophers"; see Xenophon, *Symposium* 1.5; Dio Chrysostom, *Oration* 1.9, cf. 63) in order to stress the wisdom they acquired from practice rather than study.

Many philosophers claimed to have been "untaught" (see Pease, 1.382) and as *adidaktoi*, possessing an innate knowledge (e.g., Dio Chrysostom, *Oration*

12.42; Julian, *Orations* 6.183B; 7.209C). It was especially Epicurus and his followers who, rejecting conventional education and depending on the untutored instinct, claimed to be *adidaktoi* (see Cicero, *De finibus* 1.71 [*parum eruditus*]; Sextus Empiricus, *Against the Mathematicians* 11.96) and were roundly criticized for it (e.g., by Plutarch, *Against Colotes* 1122E; collections of references in Pease, 1.381; E. Zeller, 3.1, 374 n. 2). Paul's rejection of Epicurean attitudes in vv 11–12 (cf. also on 5:3) strengthens the surmise that this formulation fits into his use of anti-Epicurean language.

It has recently been suggested that Paul's use of *theodidaktos* is analogous to Philo's use of *autodidaktos* to describe an individual who receives his wisdom directly from God rather than any human teacher (Roetzel). This is improbable, however, for *theodidaktoi* is by nature an emphatic coinage, with an implicit contrast between *philadelphia* as a divine teaching and a human teaching. This need not mean, however, that Paul is saying that his readers were not dependent on his instruction in the matter (so Koester 1979: 39). A suggestion that the term was coined in view of the popularity of the Dioscuri paradigms of friendship is unlikely. According to that view, Paul coined the new term to evoke them as examples to imitate (Kloppenborg, 287). Paul's stress in chap. 2 that he spoke for God, the theological warrants for his advice in 4:1–8, and the paraenetic function of the term, similar to "you have no need for us to write to you" (v 9) and "just as we have instructed you" (v 11), make such judgments incongruous.

*4:10. indeed, you are doing it to all the brethren in the whole of Macedonia.* With *kai gar* ("indeed") Paul emphasizes what he has just said by adding a new and important thought (see NOTE on 3:4), with which he strengthens the confidence with which he expressed himself in v 9. Once more the paraenetic compliment ("you are doing it") appears (cf. 4:1; 5:11). The Thessalonians' love reaches out, first to each other (v 9), then to *all* the brethren in the *whole* of Macedonia. The hyperbole (cf. 2 Cor 1:1, "the whole of Achaia") is designed as a compliment (see NOTES on 1:7–8), but a special relationship may have existed among the Macedonian churches (see Phil 4:16).

Paul does not say how the Thessalonians exhibited their love, but their hospitality to travelers was one likely expression of love. Another was their labor in preaching the gospel, an activity that issued from their love (see NOTE on 1:3). If Paul wrote 1 Thessalonians soon after Silas and Timothy arrived in Corinth with financial aid from Macedonia that enabled him to devote himself fully to preaching (2 Cor 11:7–9; cf. Acts 18:5), he would have had another demonstration of their love. But Paul does not mention the Thessalonians' financial support in his letters to them, and his reason for not doing so eludes us. Some manuscripts (א² B D¹ H Ψ byz) repeat *tous* after *adelphous*, thus emphasizing the attributive position of what follows. Other manuscripts (א* A D* F G 629 lat) omit *de*. The meaning is essentially the same.

*But we exhort you, brethren, to do so more and more.* With the slightly adversative *de* ("But") Paul introduces a sentence that continues to the end of v 12. The *de* does not introduce a new subject (Ellingworth and Nida, 88). The exhortation to increase what they were already doing picks up the words of v 1 and gives a practical focus to the general statement of the church's love for each other. *Parakaloumen* ("we exhort") introduces five infinitives, the first of which (*perisseuein* ["to abound"]) depends on and complements it. The sentence at the beginning looks backwards, urging that Paul's readers abound in love for the brethren, and then forwards, specifying in greater detail how that is to take place. Paul here completes what was lacking in their belief that they were to love each other (3:10).

4:11. *and to make it your ambition to live a quiet life and to mind your own affairs.* The *kai* ("and") is explicative ("namely," "that is"; Lenski, 321), introducing an explanation of how their love is to abound. The infinitive *philotimeisthai* ("to make it your ambition"), itself dependent on *parakaloumen*, in turn has three infinitives (*hēsychazein* ["to live a quiet life"], *prassein* ["to do"], *ergazesthai* ["to work"]) depending on it. On a superficial grammatical level these three infinitives are strung together, but there is a progression in thought (cf. also vv 3–6; Ellingworth and Nida, 88).

The word *philotimeisthai* and its cognates appear in the LXX only in the more Hellenistic books (e.g., 2 Macc 2:21; 3 Macc 4:15; 4 Macc 1:35; Wis 14:18; 18:3). We here have to do with a characteristically Greek idea whose significance in 1 Thess 4:11 can be disclosed by examining it in the context of Greek social philosophy and practice.

*Philotimeisthai* means "to love or seek after honor" and in that sense is equivalent to *philodoxeisthai*, "to seek fame or glory" (e.g., Aristotle, *Rhetoric* 1.5.9; Xenophon, *Memorabilia* 3.12.4; Pollux, *Onomasticon* 5.158). Used with the infinitive, as it is here, it describes the earnest striving or ambition for something (Xenophon, *Oeconomicus* 21.6; Plato, *Phaedrus* 232A). The intensity of the emotion or endeavor appears from the frequency with which the word group appears with *spoudazein* ("to be eager or earnest") and its cognates (Epictetus, *Discourse* 4.4 title; Philo, *On the Creation of the World* 81; *On Dreams* 2.55; *On the Embassy to Gaius* 60; Plutarch, *Themistocles* 5.4; *On Talkativeness* 504A; *On Stoic Self-Contradictions* 1036B). Although early writers used the word also in a bad sense, in the Greco-Roman period it was generally used positively (LSJ, 1941). When the ambition was beneficent, the word could be used as the equivalent of generosity (Plutarch, *Cicero* 3.1; *Phocion* 31.3); it could, among other things, describe hospitality (Philo, *On the Life of Abraham* 110) and also refer to the ambition of common folk (Philo, *On Husbandry* 63).

For the most part, however, *philotimeisthai* came to describe the endeavor of the ambitious man who, in the hope of reputation (*doxa*), chose the political life and became involved in public affairs (Philo, *On Rewards and Punishments* 11). Greco-Roman society was driven by an intense desire for recognition which drove especially the upper classes to compete in dispensing benefactions to cities, special causes and institutions (Bolkestein, 152–56; 258–59; Hands, 26–61). Some moral philosophers, however, questioned whether honor or reputation should be so highly regarded (SVF 1.559, 560), holding that it was a matter of indifference whether one had a good reputation or not (SVF 1.190; Teles, *On Self-Sufficiency* 11,9 Hense).

The Epicureans were even sharper in their rejection of the ambitious drive for honor and reputation. They organized themselves in communities whose stated principle was to withdraw from public life and not to engage in public affairs or politics (Philodemus, *On Frankness* 7; Vatican Fragment 58; Diogenes Laertius, *The Lives of Eminent Philosophers* 10.119). They claimed not to care for the praise of the mob (Epicurus Vatican Fragment 29), holding that there was no security in being famous and highly regarded (Epicurus, *Principle Doctrine* 7) and that joy could not be gained through wealth, honor, and the respect of the mob (Vatican Fragment 81). There is evidence, however, that some Epicureans did covet respect (Hahn, 159–60) and did experience tensions caused by their social philosophy (see Malherbe 1987: 43).

The Epicurean lack of *philotimia* was a scandal to moral philosophers like Plutarch, who placed a high value on what they regarded as a social virtue (see Plutarch, *That Epicurus Actually Makes a Pleasant Life Impossible* 1098E, 1099D, 1107C) and were themselves able to be benefactors to their own cities (see Hahn, 156–65). Epicurus withdrew from public life, Plutarch maintained, and had no passion for honor (*timē*), something that Plutarch found totally unacceptable (1098D). People who are socially ambitious (*philotimoi*) and care for reputation (*philodoxoi*) cannot lead an inactive or quiet life (*hēsychazein*), Plutarch held, but should enter politics and be involved in public affairs (*politeuomenoi kai prassontes ta koina*) (*On Tranquility of Mind* 465F–466A). This collocation of social and political terminology shows the context within which Paul's directions in 1 Thess 4:9–12 receive their meaning.

Paul extends his explanation of how his readers are to let their love abound: they are to make it their ambition "to live a quiet life and mind [their] own affairs" (*hēsychazein kai prassein ta idia*). With this oxymoron, which is diametrically opposed to Plutarch's view of things, Paul emphatically draws attention to the two infinitives that follow. The oxymoron has struck commentators (e.g., Milligan, 54; Best 1972: 174; Bruce 1982: 90), but its precise meaning has remained unclear to the point that it has been suggested that Paul here writes about the religious rather than the political realm (Bornemann, 181). It is true that in the other two places where Paul uses *philotimeisthai* (Rom 15:20; 2 Cor 5:9) he does so, but here he continues to instruct his readers in their social responsibilities.

The first infinitive, dependent on *philotimeisthai*, is *hēsychazein* ("to live a quiet life"), which had long described withdrawal from active participation in political and social affairs (=*apragmonein*: e.g., Chion, *Epistle* 3.5; *idiopragia, ta hautou prattein*: e.g., Plutarch, *On Stoic Self-Contradictions* 1043 A–D). In the late Roman Republic and early Empire, the temptation was particularly strong to look for calm, away from political involvement and social struggles (MacMullen 1966: 46–94; cf. Festugière, 53–67).

Sometimes a principled desire to retire from the demands of society to pursue a higher spiritual good is difficult to distinguish from a romanticization of the countryside, which had become a literary commonplace (see Horace, *Satires* 2.6; *Epistles* 1.10; 1.14; Pliny, *Epistles* 1.9; 4.1; Martial, *Epigram* 3.58; Plutarch, *Frag-*

ment 143; see the discussion in Dill, 174–75, itself not without romanticization). Serious philosophers of all sorts did, however, yearn for *hēsychia*, the quiet life (see Wilhelm for a collection of much of the material from popular morality). The Stoic Seneca, for example, thought of retirement as an opportunity to meditate and engage in more noble activities than those from which one resigned (*Epistle* 68.10; cf. 56; 73; for philosophers preparing their students for social service, see Hahn, 75–76). Cynics held differing views (Maximus of Tyre, *Oration* 15.4, but see 6; Dio Chrysostom, *Oration* 20.14, but see 26). The true Cynic found the notion of retirement congenial, and it was not un-Cynic to romanticize the traditions of the noble savage and the countryside, where simple values were the norm (Dio Chrysostom, *Orations* 7; 36; cf. 1.51). In Diogenes, Cynics had a hero who rejected the conventions of the city (see Rist, 59–60). Some thought of their garb as weapons with which to keep people away (Ps.-Lucian, *The Cynic* 19; but see Dio Chrysostom, *Oration* 35.4). Exile was bound to contribute to a jaundiced view of the entanglements and corruption of urban life (Dio Chrysostom, *Orations* 13.34–37; cf. 6.25; Epictetus, *Discourse* 1.10.2; see Wilhelm) and to provide an opportunity to teach one's followers by one's own example (e.g., Musonius Rufus, Fragment 11).

The widespread interest in the contemplative life pursued in the company of friends is illustrated by the nontechnical account of the protagonist in an epistolary novel from the first century A.D.:

I had thus such a natural bent for a quiet life [*hēsychia*] that even as a young man I despised everything that could lead to an active and disturbed life. When I was settled in Athens I did not take part in hunting, nor did I go on shipboard to the Hellespont with the Athenians against the Spartans, nor did I imbibe such knowledge as makes men hate tyrants and kings, but I associated with a man who is a lover of a quiet life [*hēsychia*] and I was instructed in a most godlike doctrine. The very first precept was: seek stillness [*hēsychia*]. For that is the light of philosophy, whereas politics and meddlesomeness [*polypragmosynē*] wrap it in gloom and make the way to philosophy hard to find for those who search. (Chion, *Epistle* 16.5, translation by Ingemar Düring, modified)

Chion then goes on to speak of learning about God and justice (*dikaiosynē*) (6, cf. 8), and living the quiet life with a friend (7).

The kind of quietism so popular in the first century had a venerable history that casts light on 1 Thess 4:11. Although Greek social and political discussion had early valued the person who lived quietly and minded his own affairs and did not meddle in other people's affairs (Ehrenberg; Adkins), it was Plato's formulation that continued to exert influence on later writers. According to Plato, " 'to do one's own business [*ta hautou prattein*] and not to be a busybody [*polypragmonein*] is justice [*dikaiosynē*],' is a saying that we have heard from many and have very often repeated ourselves" (*Republic* 4.441DE). The philosopher lives quietly and tends to his own affairs (*labōn hēsychian kai ta hautou prattein*) (Re-

*public* 6.496D; cf. *Gorgias* 526C). But it is not only the intellectuals who are in view. The state is well run when craftsmen work at their own trades, not touching the affairs of others, but each person doing his own work and tending to his own affairs (*ta de heautou hekaston ergazesthai te kai prattein*) (*Charmides* 161E–162B), when the cobbler cobbles and the carpenters practice carpentry (*Republic* 4.443CD). Such language later occurs in writers as different as Dio Cassius (*Roman History* 60.27) and Ps.-Socrates (*Epistles* 24–26; for the influence of Plato, see Sykutris, 78–79).

In practice, living quietly and tending to one's own affairs was not without its problems. Seneca knew that sluggishness would set in and ambition revive (*Epistle* 56.8–10), and his attitude towards society was finely calibrated. Holding that life in retirement should be superior to that of society, he knew that condemnation was implicit in withdrawal from society, and he warned against incurring society's displeasure (*Epistle* 14.8, 14). His desire was not to repel society (*Epistle* 5.2–3), but to make retirement obvious rather than conspicuous by parading it (*Epistle* 19.2). Plutarch had no patience with Stoics like Seneca. Attacking Chrysippus, who thought that retirement and attending to one's own affairs were matters of social decency (*asteia*), Plutarch accused Stoics of being inconsistent and unprincipled in the ways they supported themselves (*On Stoic Self-Contradictions* 1043A–1044B).

Seneca was aware of the danger of being identified with the Epicureans when encouraging retirement (*Epistle* 68.10; cf. Plutarch, *On Stoic Self-Contradicitons* 1033C). Plutarch's virulent attacks on the Epicureans show what Seneca feared and further demonstrate the common currency of the issues Paul addresses in his instruction to the Thessalonians. Plutarch charged that Epicurean quietism threatened the state (*Against Colotes* 1125C). He questioned their honesty (*Against Colotes* 1108C) and ascribed every imaginable ignoble motive to their desire "to live unknown," an ideal he held to be impossible (*Is "Live Unknown" a Wise Precept?*). The Epicureans denied any ambition, but Plutarch claimed that to be held in low esteem was painful, and nothing is held in lower esteem than to be without friends, inactive, atheistic, sensual and indifferent, which was the "esteem" in which Epicureans were held (*That Epicurus Actually Makes a Pleasant Life Impossible* 1100BC; *Is "Live Unknown" a Wise Precept?* 1128A–C, 1129A–D, 1130E).

*and to work with your hands, just as we instructed you.* The *kai* before *ergazesthai* is explicative, as the *kai* before *philotimeisthai* had been. Thus, as their ambition to live quietly and mind their own affairs explains how the Thessalonians are to abound in loving each other, so their manual labor explains the nature of their quietism and tending to their own affairs. Paul had supported his instruction that they work with the example of his own manual labor (2 Thess 3:7–12) and in this letter had referred to his example as a demonstration of his love for them (2:8–9; cf. 2 Cor 11:11). The community's love cannot be separated from its work (H. Preisker, 113–14; Schrage 1961: 262; Schäfer, 165).

The language and the discussion we have traced were found among the elite who reflected on the matter. The moral philosophers who provide so much insight into the moral reflection of the period were themselves from a financially more privileged level (Hahn, 69–72, 78–80, 156–60) and were self-conscious about the matter of social class. They admired the uncompromising Cynic challenge to adopt a life of virtue and could use Cynicism in characterizing the ideal philosopher (see Seneca's admiration for Demetrius [Billerbeck 1979]; Lucian, *Demonax*; Ps.-Lucian, *The Cynic*; Epictetus, *Discourse* 3.22, a special case [Billerbeck 1978]; Hahn, 79–80). But that did not prevent them from severely criticizing the Cynics (Hahn, 111–14), who in general represented the economic and social level of Paul's converts (see Hahn, 172–81).

Plato's references to the crafts show that they too were part of the discussion of social quietism (*Charmides* 161E–162B; *Republic* 4.443CD), and the issue became acute in the early Roman Empire. Concerned with people at the low end of the social scale, the satirist Lucian, who, ironically, had himself abandoned sculpture after being apprenticed (*The Dream*; see Jones, 6–10), criticized craftsmen who abandoned their trades upon converting to philosophy, especially in response to Cynic preaching (*The Runaways* 17; *The Double Indictment* 6; *Philosophies for Sale* 11). He denied that such people did any good in either private or public life and accused them of making no contribution to the world (*Icaromenippus* 30–31). The serious philosopher's insistence that he was following a higher calling than those who practiced their trades or professions would hardly have satisfied his critics (cf. Dio Chrysostom, *Orations* 80.1; cf. 31.2–3; Maximus of Tyre, *Oration* 15.9).

4:12. *so that you may conduct yourselves becomingly in the eyes of the outsiders.* The *hina* ("so that") could introduce the result of the preceding actions (so Masson, 52; Ellingworth and Nida, 90). It makes more sense, however, to understand it as introducing purpose, Paul changing from the infinitives to the *hina* clauses as he moves "from the object to the purpose of his exhortation" (Frame, 163, comparing 1 Cor 10:32–33).

The *hina* could pick up *parengeilamen*, in which case Paul's original purpose in instructing the Thessalonians to work would have been that they act becomingly to outsiders (von Dobschütz 1909: 181; Lenski, 322). The greater likelihood is that *hina* picks up *parakaloumen* in v 10b (Rigaux 1956: 522) and that v 12 is connected to vv 10b–11 both syntactically and in terms of content (Roosen 1971: 90; Ellingworth and Nida, 90). Love has been the subject all the way through, and in v 12 Paul states the purpose of demonstrating love in the way he has taught (contra: Lightfoot, 61).

Commentators discover a double purpose here, to behave becomingly and to be economically independent (e.g., Frame, 163; Best 1972: 177; Holtz 1986: 179), and some think that the first clause refers to *to philotimeisthai hēsychazein kai prassein ta idia* ("to make it your ambition to live a quiet life and to mind your own affairs") and the second to *ergazesthai tais chersin hymōn* ("to work with your hands") (e.g., Lünemann, 526; Ellicott, 60; Bornemann, 182). We have seen, however, that the four infinitives are intimately related to each other, and it would be artificial to separate them. The same is also true of the actions described by the subjunctives in this verse, with which Paul ends his exhortation.

In 2:12, Paul was concerned that his readers conduct themselves worthily of God (*peripatein . . . axiōs theou*), and in 4:1 he reminded them that he had instructed them how to conduct themselves and please God (*peripatein kai areskein theō*). Now he turns to how they should relate to society. Commentators frequently assert that *pros tous exō* means "with a view to the outsiders," as in Col 4:5, and not "in the view of the outsiders" (e.g., Bornemann, 182; Rigaux 1956: 520). The difference is not at all clear (e.g., Frame, 163, makes the same distinction in his grammatical notes, but in his commentary paraphrases, "with a view to the opinion of non-Christians"; cf. Best 1972: 170, "in the judgment of outsiders"). The traditions Paul has been using frequently had to do with criticism of social behavior, and that is what he wishes to prevent.

If it was difficult for the elite who sought a quiet life to escape criticism; it was impossible for manual laborers to do so. In the crowded commercial sections of the city where they worked and lived Paul's readers enjoyed little privacy (for urban conditions, see MacMullen 1974: 62–87; for Christians, see Lane Fox, 63). It is not unexpected, then, that Paul's exhortation that they conduct themselves becomingly in the eyes of outsiders (*euschēmonōs pros tous exō*) is flanked by admonitions of an economic order (manual labor, financial independence).

Paul continues to reflect the positive attitude towards non-Christians expressed in 3:12 (cf. 5:15; for non-Christians as "outsiders," see 1 Cor 5:12–13; Col 4:5; 1 Tim 3:7; cf. Mark 4:1). He did not advocate that his converts withdraw physically from society, but required a quality of life from the "brothers" that was different from that of society (1 Cor 5:9–13). Despite the different social levels they addressed, Paul is much like Seneca in this respect.

In describing the desired behavior as becoming (*euschēmonōs*), Paul uses the adverb of a word group that was widely used in company with such words as *prepein* ("to be fitting"; e.g., Dio Chrysostom, *Oration* 7.125–26) and *kosmiōs* ("orderly"; e.g., Plato, *The Statesman* 307E; Lucian, *The Dream* 13; *Hermotimus* 19; *The Carousal* 35) to describe the social virtues of seemliness, propriety and orderliness. The suggestion frequently made, that Paul is here advising behavior opposite to that of the disorderly (*ataktoi*) mentioned in 5:14 (cf. 2 Thess 3:6; Lünemann, 526; Eadie, 146), finds support in the places where *euschēmonōs* and its cognates appear with various forms of *taxis* ("order") (cf. 1 Cor 14:40; and see Dio Chrysostom, *Oration* 31.53; Ps.-Musonius, *Letter to Pancratides* 2, 4; Aelius Aristides, *Oration* 46.364D). Paul is, then, addressing an actual situation in which some members of the church were acting unbecomingly, and he inculcates behavior that would be acceptable to social norms. In Rom 13:12–14, such behavior is determined by the rapid approach of the Day of the Lord (cf. 1 Thess 5:1–9), but it is striking that in 1 Thess 4:9–12, rather than introduce eschatology, Paul restricts his language to contemporary social terminology.

Paul is quite explicit about what the seemly behavior should be: to continue in manual labor. This concern was widespread. The socially well-situated Epicurean Philodemus worried about what kind of employment was appropriate and, rejecting manual labor, decided that as a gentleman farmer one would find, in retirement with one's friends, the most seemly (*euschēmonestatēn*) form of revenue (*On Household Management* Col XXIII, 17 p. 64 Jensen). On a social level closer to that of Paul's readers, Lucian held that the artisan could strive to produce something that is seemly (*The Dream* 13).

Dio Chrysostom, in his idealization of country folk and the poor, who epitomized for him the simple life others sought in retirement (see Hock, 44–45), thought that the poor, hospitable people whom he described as living *euschēmonōs* (*Oration* 7.81–83), had opportunities of making a living that were neither unseemly (*aschēmonas*) nor injurious to men who were willing to work with their hands (7.125). People from the favored classes looked down on manual laborers (see Hock, 35–36) and, as in the case of Philodemus, did not think it seemly for themselves. But for the lower economic classes they thought it quite the proper thing to do (for more nuance on the subject, see further at COMMENT on 2:9).

*and may depend on no one.* The *kai* is explicative and introduces an explanation of precisely what is meant. Paul concludes this extended discussion of brotherly love with the final statement of purpose, that they have need of "no one" or of "nothing." Although there is not much difference in meaning between the two renderings, it is more likely that the former is correct. In 2:8–9, the paradigmatic foundation for this advice, Paul's interest was not in self-sufficiency for its own sake, but for its significance to his relationship with the Thessalonians: because he loved them, he did not burden them, but worked to support himself. Similarly here, in advice on brotherly love, he exhorts them to gain financial independence of each other. The topics of love (friendship) and self-sufficiency were joined in contemporary moral discussions (see NOTE on v 9). That independence, gained by their manual labor, would appear becoming to outsiders.

## COMMENT

Some commentators think that in 4:9–12 Paul discusses two topics, brotherly love (vv 9–10) and manual labor with its special consequences (vv 11–12). Taken thus, Paul's comments on love may then be regarded as catechetical in nature (von Dobschütz 1909: 178; Dodd, 13–14; see NOTES on vv 1–2) and not be related to a concrete situation in Thessalonica, while the directions on manual labor had in mind a situation in need of correction.

Most commentators think that the two topics are related, that Paul is correcting some Thessalonians who were abusing the love of the congregation by refusing to work, and instead looking to the church for their livelihood. Paul would have learned of this situation either directly from Timothy or from a letter from the Thessalonians brought by Timothy. A variant of such an interpretation is that the actual problem did not yet exist but that Paul anticipated that it would soon arise. Most attention has focused on the failure to work, the possible reasons for this idleness, and the behavior that accompanied it. Partly because the connection between love and idleness is not explicitly made by Paul, it has not been examined in detail, and quite diverse interpretations of the situation have been offered.

The traditional interpretation is that some Thessalonians thought that the coming of Christ was so imminent that they saw no reason to work and thereby prepare for the future (e.g., Rigaux 1956: 519–21; Best 1972: 175; Bruce 1982: 91; Jewett 1986: 172–75). Support for this interpretation is found in the example of groups in Christian history whose eschatological views affected their social behavior in such a manner, and in the strong eschatological interest of 1 and 2 Thessalonians. Several factors make this interpretation improbable. The connection between idleness and eschatology is not made anywhere in the Thessalonian letters; indeed, except for *theodidaktoi*, Paul's treatment of the problem is bereft of anything theological. This is striking, especially after the theologically pregnant discussion in the immediately preceding verses.

Furthermore, there is no evidence in 1 Thessalonians that the Thessalonians expected an imminent end. Had they done so, Paul would have exacerbated the problem in 5:1–10. There, precisely because they had deferred the Parousia, under the influence of the false prophets' teaching (5:3), he intones the unexpectedness and certainty of the Day of the Lord so strongly that its imminence came to be misunderstood by his readers (see 2 Thess 2:1–2).

Furthermore, the Epicurean overtones in his language in 4:11 and in 5:3, 6 would be strange in the extreme if his readers had fervent eschatological views. This language was used by and of philosophers whose behavior was not determined by any eschatology at all. Paul uses the language by design and gives their behavior an unfavorable, Epicurean coloring (Malherbe 1999).

Finally, the traditional eschatological interpretation fails to do justice to the social factors in the text, not least of which is that the discussion is framed by brotherly love and self-sufficiency. It also fails to recognize the social and political nature of the language in which the issue is discussed.

Another eschatological interpretation is more nuanced and detailed. According to this view, Paul's preaching of the coming of Christ had created in his converts, already when he was with them, an exaggerated "enthusiasm" that relativized the importance of the normal pursuits of this life, including working for one's bread. Instead, they depended on the material support of fellow Christians and, with an elitist self-understanding engendered by their eschatological outlook, preached this message to outsiders and meddled in their affairs, in the process criticizing and irritating them (Marxsen 1979: 62). On this understanding, the disorderly (*ataktoi*) of 5:14 are the problem, and 2 Thess 3:6–15 provides more details about their activities. A further refinement has also been added, that the disorderly, who may have made their demands in the Spirit (1 Thess 5:19–22), were one of three groups, the other two being the fainthearted and the weak (cf. 5:14), into which the church was divided (Frame, 157, 160–61).

This interpretation has in its favor that it looks to Paul's original work in Thessalonica as the possible source of the problem. It is unsatisfactory, however, for a number of reasons. While it is quite likely that Paul's eschatological message had an emotionally destabilizing effect on his converts (see NOTE and COMMENT on 1:6), there is no indication that it led to idleness. And while it is likely that the idlers were identical to the disorderly of 5:14, it is methodologically wrong to read the situation reflected in 2 Thess 3:6–15, which addresses a later development, into these verses (Lenski, 322).

A third eschatological interpretation shares some features with this one while taking an independent course. The reason some of the members of the Thessalonian church gave up working, it is claimed, was that they were too busy preaching the gospel to outsiders, who had socially harassed them because of their new faith. In retaliation, they attacked pagan morals and ideology, and emphasized the certainty of the impending judgment of their critics. It is to be expected that they would meet with the antagonism of those critics who saw in them features like those of the Cynics who abandoned their trades in order to meddle in other people's affairs (Barclay, 520–25).

This interpretation loosens the Thessalonians' idleness somewhat from eschatology, or at least sees the relationship differently, but it still discovers a connection not found in the text. And while it ostensibly refrains from taking 5:14 and 2 Thess 3:5–13 into account, it nevertheless lets them in the back door by bringing the meddlesome Cynics into the discussion and identifying the Thessalonian activity as preaching. The Cynic analogy is apt, as has been illustrated in the NOTES, but it is fundamentally wrong to view the passage as though the main focus were the relations between the church and a hostile society. On the contrary, the view of the outsiders, when they do come in for brief mention, is benign: they will find Christian conduct becoming when it is an appropriate expression of the Christian community's love for each other. There is also no indication in the letter that Paul has preaching to pagans in view; his interest in the first place is in conduct and the mutual relations within the church, which might win the favor of outsiders.

The connection between eschatology and idleness, despite the popularity of the interpretation that had argued for it, has long been denied (e.g., already by de Wette in 1841). The situation in Thessalonica has, for example, been thought to be the result of other influences, such as a form of Gnosticism whose characteristics are illuminated by the Pastoral Epistles (Lütgert, 75–76; Schmithals 1972: 158–60). More soberly, it has been pointed out that, given the pervasiveness of eschatology in the letter and the way it is used to support the rest of the exhortation, one would have expected it to receive attention here, particularly if it were in some way responsible for the problem Paul is correcting. In this judgment, the reason for the Thessalonians' idleness was probably a local one that Paul anticipated would cause problems later (Kaye).

The history of interpretation of 4:9–12 demonstrates that important features of the text are neglected when a notion external to the text itself, such as eschatology, is imported to provide coherence to Paul's statements. The attention shifts from the text itself, particularly from its syntax and the discipline that it should exercise on interpretation, to a construct made largely on the basis of an idea about the possible social effects of a particular eschatological outlook, an idea that is elaborated largely with the aid of 2 Thessalonians. The same criticism applies to the attempt to interpret vv 11–12 in light of patron-client relationships, for it conflates these verses with 2 Thess 3:6–13 (as done by Winter 1994: 41–60).

The text does not point forward, however, but backward, to the time when Paul as God's spokesman delivered to the Thessalonians the divine teaching of brotherly love (v 9) and instructed them to work with their hands (v 11). It is appropriate, then, to explore the significance of that earlier period for any light it may cast on 4:9–12.

Before turning to Paul's description of his ministry when he was with his readers, it is necessary to examine vv 9–12 for information about the epistolary situation that may contribute to our understanding of this text. Paul's statement that he need not write to the Thessalonians on brotherly love does not mean that he was not replying to a request from them for further instruction on the subject, a request communicated either by letter or by Timothy (Holtz 1986: 173). It is merely one of a number of statements of paraenetic force (others are: taught by God, they already love, they are to do so more and more, he had instructed them, he exhorts them; see pages 82–86). These statements, in addition to their hortatory function, compliment his readers and remind them that this advice is not new.

In 4:9–12, brotherly love and manual labor are connected, as they are in 2:8–9; Paul's reminder of his own exemplary conduct while he was with them. In 4:9–12 Paul clarifies the communal implication of his conduct during his founding of the church, presenting it as a continuation of his earlier instruction. Paul's interest is primarily in relations within the church. As his own behavior took on a special significance in the social context in which he lived, so would the Thessalonians', but in both instances his focus is on relationships in the church.

There were actual circumstances within the church to which Paul replies. This appears from the presence of the disorderly (5:14), a notion frequently associated with unbecoming conduct (see NOTE on 4:12). Paul had heard about their situation upon Timothy's return and in his reply completes one element lacking in their faith (3:6–10). That Paul does not accuse his readers of anything and that the tone of his paraenesis is complimentary and hortatory support the surmise that he is responding to an inquiry from them, probably made in a letter, about the nature of brotherly love. There is no reason not to accept at face value Paul's description of them as extraordinarily loving.

Paul's exhortation for them to do so more and more (cf. *hyperekperissōs* in 5:13) is paraenetic, and marks the transition from the explicit discussion of brotherly love to a clarification of how it is to be exercised. He thus moves to the practical problem, but his tone in vv 11–12, while less warm that it was in vv 9–10, indicates that the problem was not as severe as some have thought it to have been and certainly not severe enough to have caused divisions within the church. Paul is addressing the church as a whole, not first one group who extends loving care and then another who abuses it by not supporting themselves. There were some individuals who did not work, but Paul writes as though the church as a whole were uncertain about the limits of love for the brethren.

In early Christian paraenesis, *philadelphia* and *agapē* are expected to be expressed in a practical manner through the extension of hospitality (Rom

12:9–10, 13; Heb 13:1–2; 1 Pet 4:8–9; cf. 1:22). Given the importance of hospitality in the life of the house churches Paul and others established, the practice could easily become burdensome (see Malherbe 1983b: 66–69, 92–112), especially to a church as remarkable for its communal love as the Thessalonian church was. It would be natural, even for this church, after extending hospitality for some months after its founding, to inquire of Paul whether brotherly love obligated them to give material aid without regard to a person's ability to secure his own livelihood.

They would naturally have put the question to Paul in such a form as, "Who may depend on the church's love for financial support?" Paul, however, answers as though the question had been, "How do I express my love?" thus turning it around in a manner reminiscent of Luke 10:25–37. By answering the question in this way, Paul gives instruction that is applicable to all, not only to the idlers in the church. His instruction is positive and is given nonpejoratively, as is fitting in reponse to a question rather than to a complaint or accusation. The picture that emerges is of a church wrestling with a problem that has begun to emerge as a result of their generosity.

Paul considered love for others a Christian obligation. In Rom 13:8 he thus modifies a common ancient maxim, that one is not to owe anyone anything (see Pausanias, *Description of Greece* 1.23.10; Diogenes Laertius, *The Lives of Eminent Philosophers* 3.43; Dihle, 74 n. 2), by adding, "except to love one another." In 1 Thess 4:9–12 he interprets love as meaning not to burden another. In preparation for this advice, he had in 2:8–9 described his own behavior in similar terms, thus making a paraenetic use of his manual labor, as he would again in 2 Thess 3:7–10. The matter is more complicated, however, for his own practice was more problematic and 4:9–12 does not consist of a simple directive to work.

In 2:8–9 Paul reminds his readers of his conduct while with them in a context within which he uses the conventional description of the ideal philosopher to describe himself. By working to support himself, he had put into practice what was held by some to be the philosophical ideal. He differed from that ideal, however, by freely deciding to give himself to those he had come to love by working to support himself and thus not to burden them. This was all the more remarkable because he thought of manual labor as a hardship (1 Cor 4:12), slavish (1 Cor 9:19), and abasing (2 Cor 1:7), the attitude of those who did not have to work with their hands to earn a living.

Paul presented this giving of himself as an expression of love. In ancient culture it would have been regarded as an act of friendship, and John Chrysostom expatiated at great length on the passage by writing about Paul's friendship (*Homilies on 1 Thessalonians* 2 [PG:403–6]). At the heart of Paul's practice was his self-understanding, that his manual labor was undertaken as an act of free will (*eudokoumen*) which he demonstrated in his willing alignment of himself with God's purpose (see COMMENT on 2:9). Paul does not, however, stress that dimension of his practice in the Thessalonian letters but rather makes his references to it function paraenetically in one way or another.

It is clear why Paul makes a paradigmatic use of his practice in writing to the Thessalonians after the problem of idleness had arisen. There is, however, no evidence that any of the Thessalonians were idle during Paul's sojourn with them, nor is there any basis for the view that Paul worked to teach a higher Jewish work ethic to Greeks who scorned work (see COMMENT on 2:9). It would indeed have been remarkable had the major purpose of Paul's labor been paradigmatic. He was, after all, from a favored social level that allowed him to choose freely (*eudokoumen*) whether or not to work, an option not normally open to manual laborers, who worked out of necessity. Furthermore, he received financial assistance from the Philippians on more than one occasion during his relatively short stay in Thessalonica (Phil 4:14–16), so his own work could not have been as central to his self-support and, therefore, as exemplary at the time as it would later become in his letters. It is possible, however, that experience had taught him that his converts might abandon their employment as some converts to Cynicism did (see NOTES on 2:9 and 4:11; cf. Malherbe 1987; Hock, 42–47), and that his practice was also prophylactic.

His emphasis more likely, however, was on love as the basis for the church's life, and that was at the root of the problem that developed. John Chrysostom correctly saw that love was the main thing involved, and sought to explain its significance by writing at length about friendship. That was the natural thing for the ancients to do, but importing the conventions of friendship into Christian relationships proved to be problematic. Luke could use the clichés describing friendship ("one soul," "all things in common") to describe the ideal Jerusalem church (Acts 4:32; see A. C. Mitchell), but Paul's churches encountered difficulties when they understood their relationship with Paul in terms of the conventions of friendship.

Two principles basic to ancient discourse on friendship were in tension with each other. One was that friends shared benefits (Cicero, *On Friendship* 26), which resulted in endless discussion about what and when such gifts were to be given and how they were to be received (e.g., Cicero, *On Benefits* 2.1.2; 4.40.3, 5). Most of the moralists insisted that the need to give benefits resided in the giver rather than the receiver, or else the basis of friendship would be purely utilitarian, which was held to be the Epicurean view (Diogenes Laertius, *The Lives of Eminent Philosophers* 10.120; Cicero, *On Friendship* 27–28). In tension with the need to give and receive benefits was the virtue of self-sufficiency: How could self-sufficiency, accepted by all as a virtue, be maintained when one's relationship with a friend finds expression in giving and receiving benefits? The tension was alleviated basically by concentrating on the character and motive of the giver as determining the nature of the relationship (see Berry, 112–14, for the different views of self-sufficiency in relation to friendship).

These problems surfaced in Paul's churches. His converts in Corinth defined their relationship with him in terms of friendship and expected Paul to accept their financial support. Offered in the spirit of friendship, acceptance of their gift would entail certain obligations (see P. Marshall, 165–258). Paul refused, not because he did not love them, but because he understood himself to be different from other preachers (2 Cor 11:11–12). A less troublesome church, the one in

Philippi, appears to have sent him, as friends, financial aid to meet his needs (Malherbe 1990a: 254 and n. 44; Berry, 108–9). In response, Paul uses the clichés of friendship but relativizes his need (Phil 4:11; see Malherbe 1995c). It is noteworthy that Paul is uneasy with the idea of self-sufficiency in these discussions. In writing to both sets of correspondents, he speaks of self-sufficiency, but he describes it in a way that would have appeared odd to his contemporaries: self-sufficiency is possible because the Corinthians and he are enabled by divine power to be so (2 Cor 9:8; Phil 4:11–13).

We have no evidence that Paul used the conventions of friendship in his initial contact with the Philippians or Corinthians. It was they who defined their relationship with him in categories natural to themselves, and they did so over a period of months or years after Paul's departure from them. When Paul did respond, he did so carefully, using the friendship language in a nuanced way, as he does in Philippians, to strengthen the close bond with the church, but changing the meaning of the language. There is no evidence either that Paul used the conventional friendship language to describe his relationship with his converts while he was in Thessalonica. What Paul shared with the discussions of friendship was the bond his actions helped to create between himself and his converts (cf. Lucian, *Toxaris* 6, 37; see Rom 5:17), and it was his manual labor as a demonstration of that love that was important.

Love and self-sufficiency, the two elements in tension in reflections on friendship, frame the discussion in 1 Thess 4:9–12 and may suggest that the Thessalonians had applied the conventions of friendship to their own relationships. This passage differs from 1 and 2 Corinthians and Phil 4, however, in that it deals with relationships within the Thessalonian church rather than with the church's relationship with Paul and that it was written less than six months after Paul had left the newly founded church. Furthermore, Paul is responding to a request for direction about the church's internal relations rather than to a gift or an offer of a gift that requires justification of his attitude or at least an explanation of it.

Paul's reply to the Thessalonians' request reveals a concern about the broader social dimensions of communal love. It is important to note that for Paul, this social concern is in the first instance an intracommunal one. Some Thessalonians had become idle and may themselves have described this as expressive of their desire *hēsychazein kai prassein ta idia* ("to live a quiet life and mind your own affairs") and appealed to the love of the church to make this possible. Whether they or Paul introduced this language into the discussion, what is significant is how Paul now uses it to clarify how the church's love is to be expressed. The Thessalonians must, ironically, make it their ambition to be quiet and tend to their own affairs by working with their own hands (see 4:13; 5:3 for further use of Epicurean characterizations of the Thessalonians' conduct; Malherbe 1999). It is particularly ironic, for they had a reputation beyond their own city for doing good (1:7–8; cf. 4:10). Paul's use of the language is in total agreement with the philosophical and social discussions identified in the NOTES.

Society knew of and criticized manual laborers, who converted and abandoned their trades like some of those who converted to Cynicism and thereby upset the social order. It also knew of people like the Epicureans who withdrew from social involvement to pursue the ideal of a quietistic and private life. That Paul's converts, although being on the economic level of the Cynic converts and from the same context, were in his eyes in danger of lapsing into a kind of Epicureanism is suggested by a number of factors.

1. His major concern is with the church's love for each other, which is analogous to Epicurean friendship.

2. His ironic use of *philotimeisthai*, a striving the Epicureans rejected, would carry a special sting for people affecting an Epicurean attitude.

3. The way the Epicureans are in view in his discussion of the issues represented in vv 9–12.

Whether it was the Thessalonians or Paul who first used language especially amenable to Epicureans is not absolutely clear, but it could have been they who did so. It need not be thought incongruous that the manual laborers in Thessalonica could have done so. Workshops were often the setting for philosophical discussion (Hock, 37–40), and the Christian congregations engaged in activity that might be regarded as scholastic (Judge 1960b). Furthermore, Paul expected his language, whose philosophical background is incontrovertible, to be understood by his readers.

Paul, however, was clearly sensitive to the possible charge that someone who lived quietly and privately might appear Epicurean whether that person described himself as an Epicurean or not, and he uses the Epicurean language in a critical way, to distinguish Christians from Epicureans (cf. 4:13; 5:3, 6). Ancient Christians were later lumped together with Epicureans (e.g., Lucian, *Alexander the False Prophet* 25, 38), and Paul already may have been aware that social critics called Christians, and other persons of whom they disapproved, Epicureans (Jungkuntz). Paul's requirements that the Thessalonians engage in manual labor and be careful to act in a manner becoming to outsiders would distinguish Christians from Epicureans, who valued neither but considered communal life based on friendship the ideal.

Paul assumes that Christian behavior motivated by love would impress non-Christians favorably. It is puzzling that commentators think that Paul is unclear about why the Thessalonians' behavior should commend them to outsiders, and assume that Paul had a missionary purpose in mind (so van Unnik 1980; Laub 1973: 175; Holtz 1986: 180). An interest in preaching to outsiders is found in Col 4:2–6, but here Paul writes about conduct. Elsewhere in Paul as well as other writers, Christian conduct does have an evangelical thrust (1 Cor 10:32; cf. Matt 5:16; 1 Pet 2:12; 3:1–6; 2 Clem 13), but there is no indication that this is so here. Nor is there any hint of polemic or apologetic in his words (correctly, Deidun, 26–27). Paul is simply urging his readers to certain behavior in the concrete social context in which they live.

Paul's churches existed in crowded urban centers, and he was much concerned with the way in which they defined themselves in their social settings (Meeks 1983a: 84–107). Here it is socially responsible Christian conduct, at the heart of which is the Thessalonians' love for each other that would commend them to outsiders. It is not that their behavior is to be designed to please outsiders, for they are to please God (v 1; for the danger, see Tertullian, *Idolatry* 14); rather, Paul assumes that in this respect Christian morality finds an echo in pagan moral thought. His use of the philosophical language in v 11 already assumes that.

Paul shared the ambivalence of other early Christians about pagan morality. On the one hand, they were thankful to have escaped from pagan immorality (1 Cor 6:9–11; Eph 2:1–3; Titus 3:3; 1 Pet 1:18), to which they were now superior (1 Thess 4:5; 1 Cor 5:1). On the other hand, in their moral exhortation they presupposed that pagan society sufficiently shared their own standards to respond positively to their behavior. This is especially so in the later writings of the NT and thereafter but is already found in Paul (in addition to 1 Thess 4:12, see 1 Cor 10:32; cf. Col 4:5; 1 Tim 3:7; 6:1; Titus 2:5, 8, 10; 1 Pet 2:12, 15; 3:1, 16; *1 Clem* 1:1; 47:7; Ign *Trall* 8.2).

The love shown by Christians for each other when in need drew the attention of outsiders (Lucian, *On the Passing of Peregrinus* 13; Tertullian's report of pagan response in *Apology* 39; even the slander in Minucius Felix, *Octavius* 9), and it has been suggested that it was this virtue, which was also honored by pagan moralists, that was perhaps the strongest single cause for the spread of Christianity (Dodds, 136–38; cf. Lane Fox 323–25). Paul's exhortation, however, commends Christian social responsibility, grounded in love, and not dependence on others, as seemly behavior. John Chrysostom also knew of Christians who were called "Christ-mongers" by pagans who saw those Christians as taking advantage of others when they were able to help themselves (*Homilies on 1 Thessalonians* 6 [PG 62:430]). Christians could not escape observation from outsiders, even in Paul's day. Paul is closer to Chrysostom, but he is not as defensive.

# D. ESCHATOLOGICAL EXHORTATION, 4:13–5:11

◆

As Paul continues to complete what was lacking in the Thessalonians' faith (3:10), he turns to an extensive discussion of eschatology, which falls into two parts (4:13–18 and 5:1–11). In addition to their subject matter, these two sections share some similarities in form. Each begins with an epistolary cliché dealing with the recipients' knowledge about the subject introduced, uses the term *adelphoi* ("brethren") in the vocative, and uses *peri* ("about") to introduce a new subject (see 4:13; 5:1). They also end in a similar manner, with a confident statement about the believers' being with the Lord (4:17; 5:10) and with an encouragement to exhort each other (4:18; 5:11). The larger discussion is enclosed by *elpis* ("hope"; 4:13; 5:8), which, with the theme of the eschatological community (4:17–18; 5:10–11), provides the perspective from which the details between these two brackets are to be seen.

Paul conveys more doctrinal information here than he has heretofore done in chap. 4, and his purpose may therefore appear to be didactic rather than paraenetic. However, the information is provided for reasons that have to do with conduct. Paul's readers were evidently grieving because they were uncertain about what their relationship would be with those of their number who would have died by the time the Lord came (4:15). In addition, they were affected by a false security that some had preached (5:3). To urge the Thessalonians to appropriate behavior, Paul first corrects the doctrinal misunderstandings and, on the basis of correct knowledge, urges his readers to correct their behavior (see *hōste*, "so then," 4:18; *ara oun*, "therefore," 5:6; *dio*, "therefore," 5:11). Paul is addressing conditions in Thessalonica about which he had learned from a letter written by the Thessalonians (4:13–18) and from Timothy (5:1–10).

# 1. ON THOSE WHO HAVE FALLEN ASLEEP, 4:13–18

The structure of 4:13–18 is straightforward. The subject of the pericope (Christians who have died) and Paul's intention in writing (that his readers not grieve) are stated in v 13. Paul seeks to accomplish his goal in two ways. First, in v 14 he adduces his and his readers' belief in the death and resurrection of Jesus, from which he draws the inference that God through Jesus will gather all Christians who had died. He then strengthens this inference with an explanation that he calls a word of the Lord. He applies this message from the Lord to the immediate situation, a fear of some of his readers that those alive at the coming of the Lord will in some way have an advantage over those who will have died by then (vv 15–17). He concludes with an exhortation that they comfort each other (v 18), which thus forms an *inclusio* to the pericope that began with a concern for his readers' grief (v 13).

## TRANSLATION

4   13We do not want you to be in ignorance, brethren, about those who are asleep, in order that you may not grieve as the rest do who have no hope. 14For if we believe that Jesus died and rose, so also God will gather through Jesus those who have fallen asleep to be with him. 15For this we tell you as a message from the Lord, that we who are alive, who are left until the coming of the Lord, shall by no means have precedence over those who have fallen asleep, 16because the Lord himself will descend from heaven, with a command, with the voice of an

archangel and with the trumpet of God, and the dead in Christ will rise first;
17then we who are alive, who are left, will be snatched up together with them in
the clouds to meet the Lord in the air; and so we shall always be with the Lord.
18So, exhort one another with these words.

## NOTES

4:13. *We do not want you to be in ignorance, brethren.* The Greek has a postpositive *de*, which is not translated, as it was not in v 9. It is merely a transitional connective (see also 5:1, 12) and has no adversative force here. Paul uses the vocative *adelphoi* ("brethren") in transitions or when he introduces a new idea (e.g., 2:1, 17; 4:1; 5:12, 14; 2 Thess 3:1, 13), as he does here. Attempts have been made to relate vv 13–18 to vv 9–12 by suggesting that what Paul advises his readers in this pericope is an expression of the love he has just spoken of and that the eschatological fervor some interpreters think underlies vv 11–12 now becomes explicit. There is no ground in the text for such surmises: Paul does not mention love in this pericope, and eschatology does not play a role in vv 9–12. It is best to regard this as a new beginning (von Dobschütz 1909: 184).

The phrase *ou thelomen . . . hymās agnoein* ("We do not want you to be ignorant") and its positive form, *thelō* (or *boulomai) hymās eidenai* ("I wish you to know") were epistolary clichés that quite frequently but not always appeared towards the beginning of letters (see Milligan, 55; Koskenniemi, 77–79; Mullins 1964). These phrases, similar to *gnōrizō hymin* ("I make known to you"; 1 Cor 12:3 [cf. 1]; 15:1; Gal 1:11), are by nature emphatic disclosures and introduce a new section of a letter. They also introduce information (White 1986: 207), but Paul's varied use of the negative (Rom 1:13; 11:25; 1 Cor 10:1; 12:1; 2 Cor 1:8) and positive (1 Cor 11:3; cf. Col 2:11; see Phil 1:12 [*boulomai*]) forms makes it impossible to draw rigid conclusions about their significance.

It has been thought that with this phrase Paul introduces material that had previously been unknown to his readers (Luedemann, 214–15) or that he corrects "some misconception the community has about a topic he has already discussed with them" (Richard, 232–33). A more prudent view is that Paul uses the phrase to introduce material whose significance the readers did not sufficiently appreciate (Wilcke, 113) or that he wants to emphasize (Harnisch, 22, appealing to Rom 11:25; 1 Cor 10:1; 12:1) or, better, clarify (Giesen, 126) its existential relevance. Exegesis will have to determine which possibility is correct in any particular text.

The issue is important for 1 Thessalonians, because it affects one's understanding of Paul's mission instruction, the nature of the problem he is addressing, and therefore his intention in writing. If the phrase is understood to introduce completely new information, it is thought, Paul would not initially have instructed his converts about their resurrection. On this understanding, his main purpose here would be doctrinal teaching. Such a view is based on too rigid a view of epistolary forms, and cannot be sustained by exegesis of the pericope. It will appear that Paul focuses on a major detail, the eschatological gathering of the faithful, an item in the apocalyptic tradition with which his readers were familiar. On that basis he will seek to assuage their grief.

*about those who are asleep.* Because *peri* ("about") does not stand at the beginning of the sentence does not mean that Paul is not replying to a letter (so von Dobschütz 1909: 186); he begins with the epistolary formula for the sake of emphasis. Paul could be writing in response to a request from his readers about members of their number who had died, made either in a letter or sent via Timothy, or he could have heard from Timothy that they were grieving. However he heard, he addresses actual concerns in Thessalonica. The textual evidence is divided between the present, *koimōmenōn* ("are asleep"; ℵ A B 33 326) and the perfect, *kekoimōmenōn* ("have fallen asleep"; D F G K L Ψ), but the former is preferred because it is favored by the older manuscripts and because it is more likely to have been altered into the more usual perfect (cf. Matt 27:52; 1 Cor 15:20) than the reverse (Lightfoot 1980: 63; Metzger, 564–65).

The verb *koimāsthai*, which in the NT is always in the passive, is a euphemism for death and is used instead of the more usual terms describing death or dying (*apothnēskein*, e.g., Rom 7:2, 3; 8:13; in 1 Thess 4:14; 5:10, only of Jesus' death; *nekros*, e.g., 1 Thess 4:16; cf. 1 Cor 15:16, 32, 35; *teleutān*, e.g., Matt 2:19; Mark 7:10; Acts 2:39, not in Paul). Paul uses *koimāsthai* only in 1 Corinthians (7:39; 11:30; 15:6, 18, 20, 31) and in 1 Thessalonians (4:13, 14, 15), and only in 1 Cor 11:30 and 1 Thess 4:13 in the present tense.

Two questions arise about the significance of the present tense. Does it more readily lend itself to a future awakening than the perfect would have done (so Milligan, 55)? Does it include, in addition to Christians who had already died, those who were likely to die before the Parousia (so Dibelius 1937: 24; Masson, 53)? This is probably to read too much into the present tense, which is more probably timeless and equivalent to a substantive, "the sleepers" (so Frame, 166; Holtz 1986: 188). In mind, as the context shows, are Christians, not all the dead (so the contrast between "you" and "the rest" in v 3; "the dead in Christ," in v 16). The latter are left out of consideration altogether, for Paul is addressing a particular pastoral problem, the grief of his readers.

The description of death as sleep is natural and was widespread (see Hoffmann, 186–202; H. Balz in *TDNT* 8.548–49, on *hypnos*). It appears in Greek and Latin literature from Homer onwards (*Iliad* 11.241; e.g., Sophocles, *Elektra* 509; Aelian, *Miscellaneous Stories* 2.35; Cicero, *On Old Age* 81; Catullus 5.46) and on epitaphs (Lattimore, 82–83). It also appears in the LXX (e.g., Gen 47:30; 1 Kgs 2:10; Isa 43:17). Jewish use has been thought more relevant to the NT. Words describing death as sleep appear on Jewish epitaphs, sometimes expressing hope in life after death, whether a resurrection is in view or not (Cavallin, 166–68; see Delling 1970: 40, for the formula, "Sleep in peace"). In some writings, the terms have in view death before an awakening in a resurrection (e.g., Dan 12:2; 2 Macc 12:44–45; 1 En 92:3; 4 Ezra 7:32).

*in order that you may not grieve as the rest do who have no hope.* With *hina* ("in order that") Paul introduces his purpose for supplying the new information: he wants them to cease grieving. The present subjunctive with *mē* prohibits the continuation of something (*GNTG* 3.74–75), thus indicating that Paul was writing to people who were grieving about their dead. The succinctness of Paul's treatment of the problem suggests that he was replying to a specific matter of concern about which they had inquired (Lünemann, 528). What this concern was must be determined from the manner in which Paul writes to provide comfort.

Paul uses *lypein* to describe an inward sorrow, rather than another word that could describe a visible demonstration of grief (e.g., *thrēnein* [Luke 7:32]; *klaiein* [1 Cor 7:30]; *odyresthai* [2 Cor 7:7]; *penthein* [Rev 18:11]). Paul discusses the subject at great length in 2 Corinthians, particularly in chap. 7, where he shows some acquaintance with the philosophical views on grief without developing his discussion in a philosophical direction (R. Bultmann in *TDNT* 4.313–24, esp. 320–21). Here, by contrast, he shows no interest in the nature of grief nor any positive goal it might have (contrast 2 Cor 7:9–11, *kata theon lypē* ["a godly grief"]). The cause of the Thessalonians' grief is clear: their incomplete understanding of matters pertaining to Christians who had died, and Paul's attitude towards this grief is equally straightforward: it is prohibited.

Paul is not writing in the tradition of philosophical reflections on the nature of grief as an emotion, but is writing the earliest Christian condolence or consolation in a manner that echoes a consolation tradition that utilized philosophical elements. The consolation literature called for grief to cease (Kaibel, 345, 3–4; Lattimore, 218; cf. 253 n. 299), and the prohibition *mē lypēs* ("do not sorrow") appeared on epitaphs (SB, nos. 3514, 3515, 3516, 5715, 5751, etc.). Although the latter were addressed to the deceased, their consolatory intention for those who read them is obvious.

The significance of *kathōs kai* ("as") has proven to be problematic. From the Antiochians onwards, the phrase has been thought to introduce a contrast between Christian and pagan attitudes towards grief (see Hoffmann, 210–11). Thus, Paul does not command the Thessalonians not to grieve at all, but not to grieve with the same motive, manner, and measure as the pagans. This interpretation, in effect, reads the commonplaces of ancient consolations into Paul's brief statement. It does not do justice to the similarity between *kathōs kai* to *kathaper kai* in v 5, which introduces a negative comparison that functions antithetically. Paul is thus making an absolute prohibition, but what it means here must be determined by the context. Is he forbidding any grief at all in any circumstance surrounding the death of Christians, or is he forbidding any grief at all in reply to the specific question the Thessalonians had addressed to him? The latter appears to be the case.

Paul had described non-Christians using in-group language so far: "those who do not know God" (v 5), "the outsiders" (v 12). Now they are "the rest" (*hoi loipoi*), which may have a more theological connotation than "outsiders," as appears from use of the term elsewhere (cf. Eph 2:3). Luke replaces Mark's *hoi exoi* (Mark 4:11) with *hoi loipoi* to describe those who do not understand the parables (Luke 8:10; cf. 18:9). The term is also used in 1 Cor 7:12 of people to whom the Jesus tradition (v 11) does not apply, and it does so in 1 Thess 5:6, cf. 2. In

Rev 9:20 the fuller expression, *hoi loipoi anthrōpōn* ("the rest of men") is used of Gentiles.

It is reasonable to suppose that *hoi loipoi* in 4:13 does not merely refer to non-Christians as a social group but to those to whom the teaching of Jesus does not apply. There may be a contemptuous note in the expression (see M. Black, 176–77). Paul thus has in mind not only Gentiles (so von Dobschütz 1909: 188) but also Jews (so Holtz 1986: 189), as vv 14–17 also show. The "rest" are further characterized as "having no hope" (cf. Eph 2:12, "who have no hope and are without God"). Paul does not thereby refer to pagan or Jewish views of the hereafter; he is speaking of Christian hope, which has a very particular content, the relevant ramifications of which he will now set out in support of his urging his readers to comfort each other.

**4:14.** *For if we believe that Jesus died and rose.* Paul advances the reason (*gar*, "For") why his readers should not grieve. The *ei* ("if") with the indicative assumes as fact what it introduces (BDF §372.1; cf. Rom 5:15; Col 3:1) and has a causal sense ("since"). The plural verb includes the Thessalonians (see 1 Cor 15:11). They had accepted Paul's message of the resurrection of Jesus (1:10). Paul's readers knew the significance of Christ's death (5:10), but his interest here is in the resurrection. Paul never speaks of Jesus as having fallen asleep; the closest he comes is in 1 Cor 15:20, where Jesus is described as "the first fruit of those who have fallen asleep." Theodoret (*Interpretation of 1 Thessalonians* 4 [PG 82:648]) thought that Paul used *apethanen* ("died") to stress the reality of Jesus' death but used *koimōmenous* psychagogically to encourage the Thessalonians who were discouraged.

A number of features suggest that Paul is using traditional Christian language. Only here and in v 16 does he use *anisthasthai* ("rose") of resurrection (even in Rom 15:12 and 1 Cor 10:7, where it is not used of the resurrection, it appears in OT citations; cf. Eph 5:14), although he does use the noun *anastasis* (e.g., Rom 1:4; 1 Cor 15:12, 13, 21). While other writers use *anistasthai* of resurrection (e.g., Mark 9:9, 10; Luke 24:46; Acts 2:24, 32), Paul uses *egeirein* ("to raise"), normally in the passive, to describe Christ's resurrection by God (e.g., Rom 6:4, 9; 1 Cor 15:4, 12, 13; the active in 1 Cor 6:14), which is the content of the confession made in response to his preaching (Rom 10:9). Also striking is his relatively rare use of the name Jesus when speaking of Christ's resurrection (Rom 8:11; 2 Cor 4:14; 1 Thess 1:10; see Kramer, 199–202). These features have led some commentators to the view that Paul is using an earlier creedal formula, but support for this view is weak (e.g., contradicting it are Harnisch, 33; Luedemann, 215–16), and it is more likely an independent formulation (cf. Rom 14:9). More significant than the form of the faith statement is that its content, the resurrection of Christ, points forward. The same sequence was present in the preaching they had accepted (1:10).

*so also God will gather through Jesus those who have fallen asleep to be with him.* The sentence has appeared grammatically incorrect for, having begun with a conditional clause, it now continues with a comparative clause (*houtōs kai*, "so also"). One expects the second clause to be symmetrical with the first, "since we believe, so we believe that [or: it is necessary to believe that]," and this may therefore be an instance of ellipsis. That does not solve the problem, however, for the contents of the two clauses are different. One would expect that Paul's affirmation of Christ's resurrection would be followed by one of the resurrection of Christians (as in 1 Cor 6:14; 2 Cor 4:14 [*syn autō*]), but Paul moves to the gathering at the Parousia of those who had fallen asleep. It is best to understand *houtōs* as drawing an inference from the preceding, as it does elsewhere in Paul (e.g., Rom 1:15; 6:11; see LSJ, s.v. *houtōs*, II).

The grammatical awkwardness of the second clause heightens its effect, and the *kai* further strengthens what is stated in the apodosis. The subject changes from Christ to God, who will act through Christ as his agent. The *kai* does not, however, refer narrowly only to God but to everything that follows in the sentence (Rigaux 1956: 535, who refers to Gal 4:3; Rom 6:11; 1 Cor 2:11; 9:14; 14:12; 15:42, 45). God will gather those who have fallen asleep, the aorist participle *tous koimēthentas* (used in a middle sense; Milligan, 57), being parallel to the aorist verb describing Christ's death.

The translation renders the sense of the sentence, not its Greek word order, which is awkward: *ho theos tous koimēthentas dia tou Iēsou axei syn autō*, literally, "God those who had fallen asleep through Jesus will gather with him." It is not immediately obvious whether *dia tou Iēsou* ("through Jesus") goes with *tous koimēthentas* ("those who had fallen asleep") or with *axei* ("will gather"). If it goes with the former, what it signifies is unclear, suggestions including martyrdom, contact with Christ, and most commonly, that it is the equivalent of *en Christō* (v 16; cf. 1 Cor 15:18; Rev 14:13; see the range of possibilities discussed in Eadie, 152–53; Best 1972: 188–89). These interpretations are forced and do not render the normal sense of *dia* with a genitive of person.

It is more natural to read *dia tou Iēsou* with *axei* and to understand it as a genitive of instrument or agent. This is in keeping with Paul's use of *dia* with Christ. God, who raised Christ and will raise Christians (Rom 8:11; 1 Cor 6:14), effects their resurrection through Christ (1 Cor 15:21) and will render judgment through Christ (Rom 2:16). Paul concludes this eschatological section by affirming that God has appointed Christians to be saved through Jesus Christ (5:9). That verse is syntactically related to a reference to hope in the preceding verse (5:8) as 4:14 is, which thus signifies that hope consists in what God accomplishes through Jesus.

A literal translation of *axei syn autō* would be "will lead [or bring] with him," but the action described is the eschatological gathering, hence the translation "will gather . . . with him." The theme of God gathering his people finds expression in the OT (e.g., Isa 11:12; 43:5; Jer 38:10; Ezek 11:17; Zech 12:3; cf. 2 Macc 2:7, 18; see Clerici, 65–92). It is described in Matt 24:31 (*episynagein*) as done by angels at the behest of the Son of Man (see Hyldahl, 133). Matthew here apparently clarifies Mark 13:27, which has the Son of Man sending out the angels and gathering (*episynagein*) his elect, but Mark does not say that the angels are his agents in the gathering.

In 1 Thess 4:14, it is God who gathers, without specification here of how that will be accomplished. Paul does not use the form *episynagein* (but see *hēmōn episynagogēn ep' auton* ["our gathering together to meet him"], 2 Thess 2:1) but uses one that stresses the association with Christ, which is further intensified by placing it at the end of the sentence. The unusual construction emphasizes the comforting assertion that God had not abandoned those who had died (see Siber, 29–30). The meaning of *syn autō* is equivalent to *eis to einai autous syn autō* ("that they might be with him"), already understood thus by Theodore of Mopsuestia (*Commentary on 1 Thessalonians* 4 [2.27 Swete]). This is the detail about which Paul does not want his readers to be ignorant and is the fundamental statement he makes in providing comfort to the Thessalonians (Radl, 134–35), and it is explained in vv 15–17. Paul concludes with the promise that all Christians together (*hama syn autois*) will be snatched up to meet the Lord in the air, "and we shall always be with the Lord [*syn kyriō*]," (v 17; cf. 5:10, *hama syn autō*; cf. 2 Cor 4:14; Col 2:12; 3:14).

4:15. *For this we tell you as a message from the Lord.* The *gar* ("For") signals that Paul will now provide information on how the eschatological association with Jesus will come about. The particle is thus explicative and does not provide a second ground for his prohibition in v 13. The *touto* points forward to the explanation that begins with *hoti* ("that").

## A Message from the Lord

The Greek reads *logō kyriou* ("a word of the Lord"). Two major issues concern this "word of the Lord": What does it refer to, and what should be attributed to it from vv 15–17? Paul does not quote the word of the Lord, but applies it to the situation at hand, which makes it impossible to answer either question with certainty. Nevertheless, the issues are important for the history of christological and eschatological tradition and for understanding Paul's reasoning in this passage.

Three major possible meanings of "a word of the Lord" have been suggested. The first is that Paul has in mind an actual statement made by Jesus, as he has in 1 Cor 7:10; 9:14; 11:23, the only other places in his letters where he explicitly refers to a teaching of Jesus. In those places, it is claimed, he alludes to passages in the Synoptic tradition which are in varying degrees but not precisely similar to what he attributes to Jesus in 1 Corinthians. A number of passages have come under consideration as representing, in different ways, the type of sources to which Paul is indebted in 1 Thess 4:15–17 (Luz, 327–28, has collected Matt 10:39; 16:25, 28; 20:1ff.; 24:31, 34; 25:6; 26:64; Luke 13:30; also John 5:25; 6:39–40). Such passages, however, with the exception of Matt 24:30, provide very close similarities but no exact parallels, so the Gospel traditions are generally ruled out as Paul's source here (but see Marshall 1983: 125–27). It has also been thought that Matthew and Paul used common apocalyptic traditions (McNicol, 29–44) or that Paul shares words with John 11:25–26 (Gundry, 164–66).

A variation of this view is that Paul may have had access to an *agraphon*, a statement of Jesus not preserved in the Gospels (cf. Acts 20:35; so esp. Jeremias 1964: 80–83; Frame, 171; Morris 1991: 140–41). While possible, the hypothesis cannot be verified and ultimately contributes little to the exegesis of 1 Thess

4·15–17. Another variation, that Paul refers to the general eschatology of Jesus as it is known from the Gospels (Rigaux 1956: 538–39), is equally unhelpful, for it raises unanswerable questions about Paul's knowledge of such teaching. A second possibility is related to the first one. It holds that Paul uses a tradition closely related to Matt 24 and its parallels but supplements and interprets it in light of Jewish apocalyptic speculation based on Dan 7:13 and 12:2–3. On this understanding, in v 15 Paul makes a statement that he claims is based on a word of the Lord. In vv 16–17 he then provides support for his statement with words similar to the Synoptic eschatological tradition, passages from Daniel, and other Jewish apocalypses (Hartman, 187–90). The relevance of the apocalyptic language cannot be disputed, but completely different conclusions have been drawn from its presence in vv 16–17. For example, one view is that this is Paul's elaboration of Jesus' words also found in Matt 24:30–31 (Hyldahl, 130–31), while another is that the kernel of vv 16–17 derives from a Jewish apocalypse that Paul understood to be a saying of the risen Lord (Luedemann, 231).

A third possibility, one that enjoys wide acceptance, is that the reference is to a prophetic word. The reasoning goes as follows (see Luz, 327–28): In 1 Cor 7:10; cf. 7:6, 12, 25; 9:14, Paul refers to commands of the Lord that are related to but not identical with statements in the Synoptic tradition, and their source must be found elsewhere. The passages in 1 Corinthians speak, not of Jesus, but of the Lord, who for Paul is the exalted Lord, and they are therefore to be understood as prophetic declarations made by the authority of the Lord, and the same is true of 1 Thess 4:15–17. That Paul is here speaking in the prophetic tradition is further evident from his words *legomen en logō kyriou*, which in the OT represent claims to speak for God (the exact words appear in the LXX: 1 Kgs 21:35; cf. 13:1, 2, 5, 32; Hos 1:1; Ezek 34:1; 35:1; see Siber, 39–43; Henneken, 92–95; see also NOTE on 2:15).

If it is accepted that Paul refers to a prophetic word received from the exalted Lord, it still has to be decided whether he received it directly from the Lord or by way of a tradition that ultimately went back to a prophetic revelation. On the face of it, it is not unlikely that Paul could be referring to a word he had himself received from the Lord. He uses language to describe experiences of his own which provide a context for such an understanding: revelation (Gal 1:12; 2:2; 2 Cor 12:1, 17; 1 Cor 14:7; cf. Eph 3:3); vision (2 Cor 12:1); being snatched into the third heaven (2 Cor 12:2) or into Paradise (2 Cor 12:4); and ineffable words (2 Cor 12:4) (Wilcke, 130). The closest parallel to 1 Thess 4:15–17 is 1 Cor 15:51–52, which is very important in this respect, for there Paul claims to speak a mystery (cf. Eph 3:3).

That Paul does not use *logos* elsewhere to describe what he received during such experiences is not the problem some see it to be (Wilcke, 130–31; Hoffmann, 219), for Paul's use of the prophetic claim, *legomen en logō kyriou*, is clearer evidence than the other terms he uses. Recent scholarship has argued that in 1 Cor 2:6–16 Paul either describes himself as standing in the succession of OT prophets (Sandes) or as a Christian prophet (Gillespie; Hunt). A long line of interpreters have taken the view that he also does so in 1 Thess 4:15–17, from patristic commentators (e.g., John Chrysostom, *Homilies on 1 Thessalonians* 8 [PG 62:439]; Theodoret, *Interpretation of 1 Thessalonians* 4 [PG 82:648]) to the great commentators of the nineteenth century (e.g., Ellicott, 63; Lünemann, 73–98; Eadie, 154–55) to commentators from the beginning to the end of the twentieth century (e.g., von Dobschütz 1909: 194; Henneken, 73–98; Best 1972: 193; Merklein; Donfried 1993: 39–40). This view has the strongest evidence in its favor, hence the translation "message from the Lord."

Many scholars, however, prefer to think that Paul took material from a Jewish-Christian apocalypse and ascribed it to the exalted Lord. An analogy for this is found in Mark 13, "where a Jewish apocalypse clearly glimmers through as the kernel (13:7–8, 12, 14–22, 24–27) of the apocalyptic speech" (Luedemann, 231). The *logos kyriou* need not designate a single statement, but could be used of a complex of doctrine or of parts of such a complex (Hartman, 182). On this understanding, extensive redaction criticism must be undertaken to lay bare what Paul understood to be the word of the Lord (see esp. Luedemann, 213–37).

The three verses (15–17) have been subjected to intense examination for their witness to the history of eschatological and christological traditions (reflected in Holleman, 22–31). It is generally agreed that the *hoti* ("For") in v 16 marks a new stage in Paul's argument and that v 18 is an exhortation on the basis (*hōste* ["so"]) of what precedes. The "word of the Lord" is therefore to be found in v 15 or vv 16–17. Some scholars have thought that it is confined to v 15b (Lünemann, 128; von Dobschütz 1909: 193–94; Holtz 1986: 185; Merklein, 410–15) but that the verse is not a direct citation (Wilcke, 132–33). On such an understanding, vv 16–17 are Paul's explication of the word of the Lord.

An increasing number of scholars argue for the reverse, that vv 16–17 contain the Lord's word and that v 15b is Paul's summary and application of it. The matter is complicated by the fact that Paul's own language is found throughout vv 15–17, which makes it difficult to distinguish between allusion and application. Redaction criticism has peeled off the Pauline layer to reveal the following word of the Lord (so Luz, 329; Siber, 38; Harnisch, 42–43; Luedemann, 225; Collins 1984: 160–61):

> The Lord, with a cry of command,
>    with the voice of an archangel
>    and the trumpet of God
>    will descend from heaven.
> The dead in Christ will rise.
> Those who are left will be snatched together with them in the clouds
>    to meet the Lord in the air.

This would represent a late stage in the development of the pre-Pauline tradition. That tradition could be traced further back to a Son of Man tradition that had been taken over by the "Lord tradition" (Marxsen 1969: 30).

Reconstructions like this, leaving one breathless with their precision, are of greater significance for their contribution to our knowledge of the development of early Christology and eschatology than for the exegesis of 1 Thessalonians. The pervasiveness of the Pauline language throughout vv 15–17 may in fact make any tradition behind the text irrecoverable. The view that Paul spoke as a prophet, which is most likely correct, would relativize whatever may have been traditional in his words. One would expect him to have used traditional categories and expressions natural to the immediate situation. For a proper understanding of what he is about, the stress should be on how his comments function to assuage the grief of his readers, which is the true function of the pericope, and why he found it necessary or useful to identify what he said as a prophetic word.

*that we who are alive, who are left until the coming of the Lord.* The *hoti* ("that") introduces the content of the message from the Lord. This explanation of why the Thessalonians should not grieve is remarkable, for having just said what God will do, Paul now states what the living will not do at the coming of the Lord. The pronoun *hēmeis* ("we") is in contrast to *tous koimēthentas* (cf. vv 16b–17) and is modified by *hoi zōntes* ("who are alive") and *perileipomenoi* ("who are left"). The temporal limit is established by *eis tēn parousian tou kyriou* ("until the coming of the Lord"), but Paul's focus is not confined to the Parousia. The present participles describe those who are now living, who are left, some of whom are grieving for the dead. Their existence is eschatological, bracketed by Jesus' resurrection and his coming.

By using the first person pronoun, Paul includes himself with those who will still be living at the Parousia, as he does in 1 Cor 15:52. Elsewhere, however, he identifies himself with those who will be raised (1 Cor 6:14; 2 Cor 4:14; 5:1; cf. Phil 1:20). This has led to the view that Paul's eschatology evolved as he faced new circumstances (e.g., Dodd 1963: 108–11; see the survey of developmental theories in Gillman, 263–66). Patristic commentators already struggled with the problem that Paul would have been proved to be wrong in 1 Thess 4:15 if his words were taken literally. John Chrysostom held that Paul was not speaking of himself but of those who would be alive at the Parousia (*Homilies on 1 Thessalonians* 7 [PG 62:436]; cf. Theodoret, *Interpretation of 1 Thessalonians* 4 [PG 82:648]); Oecomenius explained that Paul was speaking of living souls (*Commentary on 1 Thessalonians* 4 [PG 119:92]); and Theophylact thought that Paul was not speaking of himself but that by adding "those who are alive, who are left" he signified by his own person all those who would live to the end (*Exposition of 1 Thessalonians* 4 [PG 124:1313]). See further, Theodore of Mopsuestia, *Commentary on 1 Thessalonians* 4 (Swete 2.29, esp. n. 3).

Some commentators are still reluctant to think that Paul thought he would be alive at the Parousia (e.g., Marshall 1983: 127), but the majority are of the opinion that he did think so (e.g., Holtz 1986: 197–98), while others relativize the issue by holding that Paul always had both possibilities open to him (Best 1972: 195–96). Ellicott (64) does not want to attribute too much significance to "living" and "survive": "At the time of writing these words he was one of the *zōntes* and *perileipomenoi*, and as such he distinguishes himself and them from the *koimōthentes*, and naturally identifies himself with the class to which he and they belonged." This is as good an attempt as can be made to support the view that Paul did not think he would survive to the end, but it does not do justice to *eis tēn parousian tou kyriou* ("until the coming of the Lord"). The dogmatic interest that drives this line of interpretation obscures the consolatory function of Paul's words (see COMMENT).

The "living" are clearly in contrast to "those who had fallen asleep." So too is "who are left," but the precise meaning of these words is not immediately obvious. The passive of *perileipō* (found in the NT only here and in v 17) expresses the result of a subtraction, that which remains (Spicq 1991: 1229). The ultimate origin of the term is sometimes thought to be the OT notion of the Remnant, although it is not certain that *perileipesthai* was used in this connection (see V. Herntrich in *TDNT* 4.196–209). Of more immediate relevance is thought to be the apocalyptic idea of those who will survive the Messianic Woes. Especially important are certain passages from 4 Ezra, e.g., "And it shall be that whoever remains after all I have foretold you shall himself be saved and shall see my salvation at the end of the world" (6:25; cf. 7:27–28; 9:8; 13:48). Passages like these inform the apocalyptic tradition some scholars think are behind the word of the Lord that Paul redacts.

Although precisely the same term is not used in the apocalyptic writings, the apocalyptic idea may be behind Paul's use of *perileipesthai*. Paul, however, uses the word, with *zōntes*, to describe people who have not yet died, not people who have survived the Messianic Woes. The same contrast with death is also found in 4 Macc 12:6; 13:18. Given Paul's practical purpose of providing comfort in the face of death, it is worth considering whether the term is not related to the consolation literature. Again, the exact word does not occur, but Plutarch, although he has a different view of postmortem existence from Paul's, uses a fragment from Pindar in an instructive manner.

In a consolatory mood, Pindar (Fragment 131) says of the soul that, when the body follows death's command, something living is yet left (*zōon d'eti leipetai*), an image of life, and this alone is a gift of the gods. Plutarch cites the fragment in a consolation (*A Letter of Condolence to Apollonius* 120D) to support his argument for the immortality of the soul. He quotes it again in *Romulus* 28.6–8 and comments on it: The soul returns to the gods when it is set free from the body. "We must not . . . violate nature by sending the bodies of good men with their souls to heaven, but implicitly believe that their virtues and their souls in accordance with nature and divine justice" will pass progressively through the stages of heroes and demigods to that of the gods. Paul and Plutarch agree that what is left by death eventually triumphs. They differ on almost everything else, except that the language they share is designed to comfort.

## The Coming of the Lord

The basic meaning of *parousia* ("coming") is presence, arrival or coming. It is used in this way by Paul in 1 Cor 16:17; 2 Cor 7:6, 7; 10:10; Phil 1:26; 2:12. In all other places where the word occurs in the NT, it is in the technical, eschatological sense of the coming of the Lord (Jas 5:7; 2 Pet 1:16; 3:4; 1 John 2:28), the Day of the Lord (2 Pet 3:12), or the Son of Man (Matt 24:27, 37, 39; cf. 3). It is used by Paul in an eschatological sense primarily in his Thessalonian letters, of the coming of the Lord (1 Thess 2:19; 3:13; 4:15; 5:23; 2 Thess 2:1; cf. 1 Cor 15:23) and of the Lawless One (2 Thess 2:9), with a temporal sense, "at the Parousia," "until the Parousia."

Paul is the earliest NT writer to use *parousia* in its technical meaning, but the expectation of Christ's eschatological coming did not originate with him (see Rigaux 1956: 196–208; A. Oepke in *TDNT* 5.858–71; Best 1972: 359–71). That this expectation was already part of the Aramaic-speaking church before Paul is evident from Paul's use of *maranatha* ("come Lord") in 1 Cor 16:22. The Synoptics show that the tradition of the coming of the Son of Man preceded Paul's use of *parousia* to describe it (e.g., Mark 14:62 and Matt 26:64; Mark 8:38, Matt 16:27, and Luke 9:26). Paul uses other terms to describe the same event, for example, the verbal form *erchesthai* ("to come"; 1 Cor 4:5; 11:26; 2 Thess 1:10), the *apokalypsis* ("revelation") of the Lord (1 Cor 1:7; 2 Thess 1:7; Rom 2:5; cf. 1 Pet 1:7, 13; 4:13) and Day of the Lord (1 Cor 5:5; 1 Thess 5:2; cf. "that day": 2 Thess 1:10; "the day": Rom 13:12).

These other terms describing the eschatological climax are derived from Jewish sources, but there is no unambiguous evidence that *parousia* was used in this technical sense in pre-Christian Judaism. It was derived from pagan Greek usage, of the ceremonial arrival of a king or ruler with honors or of the coming of a god to help people in need. It is not unreasonable to suppose that the word would have had such connotations for Paul's Greek readers (Gundry). It is remarkable that the word in its technical sense is largely confined to 1 Thessalonians. It is supplanted in the Pastoral Epistles by *epiphaneia* ("appearance"), an even more religiously charged Hellenistic word (1 Tim 6:14; 2 Tim 1:10; 4:1, 8; Titus 2:13; cf. 2 Thess 2:8, combined with *parousia*). The term "second coming" appears for the first time in the latter half of the second century, when it describes the glorious coming of Christ in contrast to his humble coming in the flesh (e.g., Justin, *Apology* 52.3; *Dialogue* 14.8).

shall by no means have precedence over those who have fallen asleep. With *ou mē* ("by no means") and the subjunctive *phthasōmen* ("will have no precedence") Paul in the most emphatic way negates something in regard to the future (BAGD, s.v. *mē*, D; BDF §365). The *parousia* is the reference point. The participles *zōntes* and *perileipomenoi* describe the condition of those who are alive in contrast to those who had fallen asleep in the period before the Parousia. The phrase *ou mē phthasōmen* likewise describes a contrast between the survivors and the sleepers, but it has in view what will not take place at the Parousia.

The negative phrase could oppose something hypothetical that is contrary to Paul's understanding, but it is so strong that it sounds like a denial of an opinion actually held by some people in Thessalonica. The latter is more likely in view of the parallel in 5:3, *ou mē ekphygōsin* ("they will by no means escape"), said about some people who propound erroneous eschatological teachings. What is denied with *ou mē phthasōmen* is what caused the Thessalonians' grief, which Paul now assuages (see COMMENT).

Paul has already used *phthanein* in an eschatological context in 2:16, where it described the proleptic realization of God's wrath (see COMMENT). This is the only place in the NT where the word is used without a prepositional clause as it is in 2:16, and the word is generally thought to have its original sense here, "to go before or precede someone" (e.g., Milligan, 59; Frame, 173; G. Fitzer in *TDNT* 9.90), and to be the equivalent of *prophthanein* (Matt 17:25). Paul's explicitness in laying out the chronological sequence in vv 16–17 shows that the temporal element is here present in *phthanein*, but some commentators incorrectly restrict the word to this meaning (e.g., Best 1972: 180), translating the phrase "will certainly not have any temporal advantage." There is also a qualitative element in the word, hence the polyvalent translation, "(not) to have precedence" (thus Bruce 1982: 99) over those who had fallen asleep. It is this misconception about the relationship between the living and the dead at the Parousia that caused the Thessalonians' grief (see COMMENT).

4:16. *because the Lord himself will descend from heaven.* With the explicative *hoti* ("because"), parallel to *gar* in v 15, Paul explains the assertion he has just made. His elaboration will make use of apocalyptic imagery, but whether he derived it directly from Judaism or from earlier Christian apocalyptic tradition is impossible to determine with certainty and fortunately is unimportant. What is important is that Paul represents the apocalyptic scenario as a message from the Lord that he offers in a way designed to address his readers' immediate needs.

Immediately following the denial of what the living faithful will experience, Paul emphatically turns to what the Lord will do. In v 14 it had been God who would act through Jesus as his agent; now the divine gathering is described in terms of Jesus' role. The long sentence, which elaborates the ground of comfort, begins with "Lord himself" and ends with "and so we shall always be with the Lord" (vv 16–17). With the emphatic *autos ho kyrios* ("the Lord himself") Paul may wish to stress, in contradistinction to some Jewish expectations in which the Messiah played no decisive role at the end (Best 1972: 196), that Jesus would be at the center of the action (see also Isa 63:9, "but the Lord himself saved them," cited by Bruce 1982: 100). A more likely reason for the emphasis is found in the text itself. The *parousia* is always connected in 1 Thessalonians with the *kyrios* (2:19; 3:13; 4:14; 5:23), and Paul wants to make clear to his readers what it is that the *Lord* will do at his coming in which they can take comfort. It is not the case that they find themselves in a scheme of things in which the Lord's coming simply marks a terminus. Rather, the Lord himself will act dramatically in ways that the apocalyptic language seeks to capture.

With other Christians, Paul thought of Jesus as in heaven (Rom 8:34; 10:6; cf. Acts 2:33; Eph 1:20; Col 3:1), from which he would come to save his own (Phil 3:20; cf. Acts 1:9–11). Paul prefers *ap' ouranou*, the singular without the article, as he has it here (cf. *ex ouranou*: 1 Cor 15:47; 2 Cor 5:2; Gal 1:8), but he uses the plural in 1 Thess 1:10 (cf. 2 Cor 5:11; Phil 3:20) with no difference in meaning. The parallels in the Synoptic Gospels have the Son of Man descending (Mark 13:24–27; Matt 24:29–31; Luke 21:25–28).

*with a command, with the voice of an archangel and with the trumpet of God.* The descent of the Lord is described as accompanied by three military sounds, each introduced by an *en* ("with") of attendant circumstance (cf. Luke 14:31; Eph 5:26 for this use of *en*). The last two sounds are qualified by genitives and are connected by *kai* ("and"), which suggests that they explain the first (thus von Dobschütz 1909: 195; Frame, 174). It is not clear who issues the command (*keleusma*). In view of v 14 it may be God (cf. Philo, *On Rewards and Punishments* 117, on God, who with a single *keleusma* can gather together [*synagein*] all the exiles from the uttermost parts of the earth). On the other hand, the emphatic *autos ho kyrios* makes it natural to think of the Lord as the subject, and v 16b suggests that the command is directed to the dead (cf. John 5:28; 11:43). In Matt 24:31, the Son of Man sends out the angels with the sound of a loud trumpet to gather his elect.

Archangels are not mentioned in the OT. Michael, called the archangel in Jude 9, the only other place in the Bible where the term occurs, is called "one of the rulers" in Dan 10:13 and "the great *archōn*" in Dan 12:1. Late Judaism knew the names of seven archangels (*1 En* 20:1–7 Greek names Suru'el [Uriel], Raphael, Raguel, Michael, Saraqa'el, Gabriel, Remiel), but the NT shows no interest in their names nor, indeed, in them as a group. In Rev 5:1 and 7:2 (cf. chap. 19) an angel speaks for God with a loud voice.

Paul is more reticent than the Son of Man tradition about the role of angels at the Parousia (cf. 3:13), but if "the voice [*phōnē*] of an archangel" explains command, angels may also function as the means through whom the Lord communicates. In 2 Thess 1:7 they are the agents through whom the descending Lord will exercise his power, but here their martial nature is confined to their voicing the Lord's command.

The dramatic nature of the Lord's command is enhanced by its connection with "the trumpet of God." The OT already speaks of the sounding of "the great trumpet" (Isa 27:13; cf. Joel 2:1, 15), which God himself may be said to sound (Zech 9:14). The trumpet is associated with theophanies (Exod 19:13, 16, 19; 20:18) and found a place in the expectation of the Day of the Lord (Zeph 1:16–18), when it will announce punishment (1QM 2.16–3.12; 7.13, 15; 4 Ezra 6:23; cf. *Life of Adam and Eve* 22, for the archangel Michael sounding the trumpet; see Baumgarten, 96 n. 196). The seven angels with seven trumpets announce the seven calamities in Rev 8–9, and a voice (*phōnē*) as of a trumpet gives instructions to the Seer in Rev 1:10; 4:1. The apocalyptic tradition is behind Matt 24:31 (reflecting Isa 27:13; cf. 1 Cor 15:51–52; and C. A. Evans for the argument that Paul is indebted to Ps 46:6 LXX).

Paul knows the apocalyptic tradition, but he drastically reduces its dramatic elements. In 1 Cor 15:52 (cf. Did 16:6) no angels are involved, and it is simply "at the last trumpet" (*en* here is temporal) that the bodies of Christians will be changed. In 1 Thess 4:16 it is God's trumpet, not in the sense that it is God who blows it, but that it has a quality different from that of other trumpets (*theou* is a genitive of character, as in Rev 15:2; thus von Dobschütz 1909: 196). Paul writes as though he expects his readers to understand the stripped down apocalyptic imagery he uses. What remains in this lean description is a martial element that would have impressed his Greek readers, for whom a trumpet was primarily a means by which to give a signal, and the trumpet of God would to them have been a dramatic signal given at the Parousia that no human could give (G. Friedrich in *TDNT* 7:73, 87–88).

*and the dead in Christ will rise first.* The *kai* ("and") does more than add information; it introduces the result of the Lord's descent. Paul's interest is in Christians, and speculation on the fate of non-Christians is misplaced. Paul is offering encouragement, not a comprehensive eschatological treatise. The phrase "the dead in Christ" (*hoi nekroi en Christō*) describes the dead in their relation to Christ (cf. 1 Cor 15:23), and does not refer to an intermediate state in which they found themselves (Frame, 175), as though the text read *hoi nekroi hoi en Christō* ("the dead who are in Christ") (Best 1972: 197). The phrase is equivalent to "those who have fallen asleep in Christ" (1 Cor 15:18) and "the dead who die in the Lord" (Rev 14:13). Death does not sever their relationship with Christ (cf. Rom 8:31–39). Nor is it in conception the same as the "first resurrection" of the souls of the martyrs of Rev 20:4–5.

What was problematic for the Thessalonians was, not whether they would be raised, but how the living and dead would participate in the events of the end and, as is evident from *ou mē phthasōmen*, how their experience would affect their relationship with each other. Paul addresses the problem by making clear the sequence of events (cf. 1 Cor 15:23–28; 2 Thess 2:3–8). The unusual ending of a clause with *prōton* ("first"), immediately followed by *epeita* ("then"), shows the emphasis he places on sequence.

What is important for Paul here is not the transformation of Christians' bodies, which will take place at this time (1 Cor 15:51–52; Phil 3:20–21), nor that the resurrection will take place instantly (1 Cor 15:52). His temporal interest here is in a sequence in which the dead are not disadvantaged, but rise first in order to participate in the gathering. Paul's use of the intransitive *anastēsontai* ("will rise") rather than *egerthēsontai* ("will be raised") or *zōopoiethēsontai* ("will be made alive"; cf. 1 Cor 15:22) retains the parallelism with v 14.

4:17. *then we who are alive, who are left, will be snatched up together with them in the clouds.* The next event in the sequence is the uniting of all Christians with the Lord and is the culmination of Paul's consolation. He now reverts to the first person, describing what will happen at the Parousia to those who are alive, who are left (cf. v 15). The improper preposition *hama* can have an adverbial force, "simultaneously with," and thus describe when the living are snatched up (Moule, 81–82; BDF §194.3; Rigaux 1956: 545; Best 1972: 198). Although it mostly serves as an adverb, in the two cases that it appears with *syn* (1 Thess 4:17; 5:10) it is a double preposition (Robertson, 638). It strengthens the *syn* ("together with them"), which is at the heart of Paul's consolation (see NOTE on v 14).

The verb *harpazein* carries the sense of sudden, violent action (e.g., Matt 11:12; John 6:15; 10:12; Acts 8:39; 23:10; 2 Cor 12:4; Rev 12:5). The notion of a rapture (from the Latin *raptus*, "snatched") does appear in Jewish apocalyptic literature (e.g., 4 Ezra 6:26; 14:9; see Stone, 172). Of special interest is the consolation tradition, which casts light on Paul's use and shows once more how he turns conventional expressions to a pastoral use. Epitaphs lament Fate's snatching (*harpazein*) away the dead from their loved ones to Hades (e.g., IG II.1062a, 3; 11477, 9; IV.620, 2; V.733, 12). Lucian has the stock figure of a bereaved father use the conventional language as he cries out to his dead son: "Dearest child, you are gone from me, dead, snatched away [*anērpasthēs*] before your time, leaving me behind alone and wretched" (*Funerals* 13). Letters of condolence then use *harpazein* and its cognates in addressing or speaking of the grief stricken (e.g., Plutarch, *A Letter of Condolence to Apollonius* 111D, 117BD; *eripere* in Latin letters, e.g., Seneca, *To Polybius on Consolation* 2.6; 11.1; 18.3; *Consolation to Marcia* 6.1; Ovid, *Pontic Letter* 4.11.5; cf. *abstrahere* in Cicero, *Tusculan Disputations* 1.84).

Cicero, referring to *Iliad* 16.433, has Homer representing Jupiter as complaining that he was unable to snatch his son from death (*On Divination* 2.25; cf. *The Verrine Orations* 2.5.12; Seneca, *To Polybius on Condolence* 14.4). Paul takes death for granted in 1 Thess 4:13–18 and does not make as much of it here as he does in 1 Cor 15:35–37. His purpose is to console, and death receives short shrift. The dead in Christ will rise, and their separation from those who were left is overcome as, ironically, they are snatched up together with them. In a neat twist, Paul uses the conventional language of grief to comfort. He does not say who snatches them up, but v 14 would seem to indicate that it is God who gathers them together by snatching them up.

There is no evidence that Paul had originally spoken to the Thessalonians about the Parousia as a snatching up, which they misunderstood as implying an imminent end (so Giesen, 136, 138) or as abandoning the dead, since only those alive could be gathered around the Lord (Plevnik 1984).

Nor does Paul provide any details about how they will be snatched up except that it will be "in the clouds." Clouds are often associated with theophanies (e.g., Exod 19:16; 24:15–18; 40:34; esp. Dan 7:13) and function importantly in apocalyptic presentations. So, although clouds are not mentioned in the accounts of Enoch's rapture (Gen 5:24; according to Wis 4:11 he was snatched up; cf. 2 Kgs 2:11 of Elijah's transport), in 2 En 3, Enoch describes how the angels elevated him: "And they took me onto their wings, and carried me up to the first heaven, and placed me on the clouds. And, behold, they were moving. And there I perceived the air higher up, and higher still I saw the ether. And they placed me on the first heaven."

The theophanic element is also present in the Son of Man tradition. Mark 13:24–27 is particularly vivid in describing cosmic manifestations at the Parousia, "And then they will see the Son of Man coming in [*en*] clouds with great power and glory. And then he will send out the angels, and gather his elect from the four winds, from the ends of the earth to the ends of heaven" (v 26). The cloud is part of the theophany, but the *en* is instrumental (cf. Matt 26:64, influenced by Dan 7:13: he will come upon [*epi*] the clouds). Paul's description is similar to this tradition, but it is remarkable how much he has reduced the apocalyptic element. Rather than develop the apocalyptic imagery, he retains his focus on the gathering of the Christians to the Lord (Baumgarten, 96–97).

*to meet the Lord in the air.* The word *apantēsis* ("meet") and its cognates in the NT are used in the ordinary sense of meeting (e.g., Matt 8:28; 25:1, 6; 28:9; Mark 14:13; Luke 8:27; 17:12). It is also used frequently in the LXX, and its use in Exod 19:10–18, which shares a number of features (descent of the Lord, meeting, clouds, trumpet) with 1 Thess 4:16–17, has been thought a sufficient background to Paul's description (Dupont, 64–73). Another connotation has also been found, which has been more widely accepted (Peterson).

In this technical sense, the word was used of citizens, or a group of them, going out of the city to meet a visiting dignitary and then escorting him back into the city (see Josephus, *Jewish Antiquities* 11.26–28, for a priest awaiting the *parousia* of Alexander in order to go out and meet [*hypantēsis*] him). The term was so well known in this sense that Cicero did not translate it into Latin (*To Atticus* 8.16.2; 16.11.6), and the rabbis adopted the Greek word as a loan word (E. Peterson in *TDNT* 1.381). It was the dignitary who gave the term its technical meaning; royal connotations did not always attach to the word when it described a group going out to meet a prominent person and escorting him (Acts 28:15).

The technical meaning, which was recognized as early as John Chrysostom (*Homilies on 1 Thessalonians* 8 [PG 62:440]), has been advanced in support of the interpretation that the Lord's people will "go to meet him in the air in order to escort him back to earth and that this is where they shall always be with the Lord" (Marshall 1983: 131). This opinion is strengthened by the connection of *apantēsis* with *parousia* (Gundry, 165–66), but it is improbable nevertheless on a number of counts. The Hellenistic processions were undertaken at the initiative of the welcomers, whereas here they are snatched up, presumably by God. Furthermore, the purpose of the meeting is to bring about their gathering with the Lord and each other, not to escort the Lord, of which nothing is said. Nothing is said about returning to earth, either here or in 1 Cor 15:23–28, 51–57 or Phil 3:20–21. Nor does Paul say that they will go to heaven or, indeed, what will transpire when they meet. He retains his focus on the problem at hand.

*and so we shall always be with the Lord.* The *houtōs* ("so") summarizes what precedes (BAGD, 592; Matt 12:26; Acts 7:8; 1 Cor 14:25) and adds that the association with the Lord will be eternal. In Jewish apocalyptic literature it was expected that the risen or raptured faithful would forever live with the Messiah (4 Ezra 14:9; 6:26; 1 En 39:6–7; 62:13–14; 71:16). The same view is contained in the Gospels, where *meta* ("with") is used (Matt 28:20; Luke 23:43; John 17:24; cf. Rev 3:4, 20–21). Paul always uses *syn* ("with") to describe the relationship with Christ after the resurrection (Rom 6:8; 8:32; 2 Cor 4:14; 13:4; cf. Col 3:3–4, and the problematic Phil 1:23). Here, those who had died in Christ will now be with (*syn*) the Lord forever (see 5:10).

Paul does not in 1 Thessalonians reflect the thought that eschatological existence with the Lord is preceded by dying and suffering with him (Rom 6:3–11; 8:17; Gal 2:19; cf. Col 2:12–3:5). Nor does he say anything about the nature of eschatological life with the Lord, for example, that those snatched up will share in glory (Rom 8:17, 19–21; Phil 3:20–21; cf. 2 Thess 1:9–10, 12) and in judgment (1 Cor 6:2–3; cf. Matt 19:28; Rev 20:11–15), nor that they will share in the messianic banquet (Matt 12:1–10; Luke 14:16–24), nor that they will associate with angels (2:19; 3:13; cf. Matt 25:31). Nor can it be inferred that the cloud and rapture motifs, combined with 1 Thess 5:23, hint at the kind of transformation Paul discusses in 1 Cor 15:51–52 and Phil 3:20–21 (so Gillman). Paul keeps his description lean, focusing on being with the Lord, which is the source of comfort.

Some pagans also thought of association with the gods and virtuous people after death as a pleasure to be anticipated (Plutarch, *That Epicurus Actually Makes a Pleasant Life Impossible* 1101E, 1102A, 1105E). Epitaphs frequently proclaimed that the person buried was "with the heroes" (for the evidence, see Kuck, 126). It is therefore not surprising that rhetorical instruction on how to make consolatory speeches suggested speaking of the departed as dwelling with the gods (Menander Rhetor, *Division of Epideictic Speeches* 3.414, 17–19; 3.421, 17–18 Spengel=Russell and Wilson, 162, 176). The practice became common in consolations (Cicero, *Tusculan Disputations* 1.75; Propertius, *Elegies* 4.11.99–102; Seneca, *Consolation to Marcia* 25.1; 26.3; Plutarch, *A Letter of Condolence to Apollonius* 108D, 120BC, 121F).

Paul's stress on being with the Lord and other Christians would therefore have been recognized by his contemporaries as good consolatory practice. Where he differs from them is in their conviction that it is "souls that have lived in accordance with virtue that have as the crown of their happiness that, being freed from the unreasonable element and purified from all body, they are in union with the gods and share with them the government of the whole universe" (Sallustius, *On the Gods and the Universe* 21; see also the citation from Plutarch, *A Letter of Condolence to Apollonius* 120D, cited on p. 271 in connection with *perileipesthai* in v 15).

4:18. *So, exhort one another with these words.* The *hōste* ("So") is synonymous with *toigaroun* ("Consequently") in 4:8 and *dio* ("therefore") in 5:11. These particles all draw practical consequences from what has just been said, frequently, as here, from eschatological statements (see *hōste* in 1 Cor 15:58; cf. 4:5; 10:12; 11:33; Phil 2:12; 4:1). Paul has provided the basis for their comfort and had earlier provided them with an example of how it was done when he had been with them (2:11–13). Now it is the community that must engage in reciprocal comfort; he will repeat the charge for them to do so in 5:14 (cf. 2 Cor 1:3–4; Phil 2:1). Ancient consolations were thought of as exhortations, hence the translation "exhort" for *parakaleite* (see Chapa 1990: 226–27; 1994: 152–53).

Pagan consolation was by nature traditional, and it was by the words of wise men that people were comforted (Ovid, *Pontic Letter* 4.11.11–12; cf. Plutarch, *A Letter of Condolence to Apollonius* 120B; Ps.-Socratics, *Epistle* 21.1). The tradition of consolation was significantly influenced by Stoicism, whose rationalism required that one exercise moderation and decorum when grieving. Individual writers also, however, made fruitful use of their traditional eschatology (see Plutarch, who ends his *A Letter of Condolence to His Wife* [611C–612A] by drawing attention to ancestral beliefs). Paul also uses traditional material, drawing his one major point from it. Theodoret, who was impressed by Paul's interest in consoling the Thessalonians, nevertheless found it necessary to observe that "we do not use our own words, but teaching that is derived from the Lord" (*Interpretation of 1 Thessalonians* 4 [PG 82:648]).

# COMMENT

In 1 Thess 4:13–5:11 Paul provides the most extensive discussion of the Parousia contained in any of his letters. Viewed superficially, the introductory formula in 4:13 may indicate that Paul is moving from exhortation to instruction. Furthermore, the subject matter, eschatological admonitions, further distinguishes 4:13–5:11 from the paraenesis of the rest of chaps. 4 and 5 (Koester 1979: 39). The didactic nature of this section of the letter appears even more pronounced if one assumes that Paul writes to correct some erroneous teaching, for example, that of Gnostics in Thessalonica (so Harnisch, 46–51). What he corrects, however, is not their theology, but their behavior, namely, that they are grieving. The introductory formula, in addition to introducing a new subject, may do no more than affirm the importance and personal relevance of what Paul goes on to say, and his reason for drawing attention to certain elements of the Parousia is not in the first instance to inform, but to provide a basis for conduct. These verses therefore do not interrupt Paul's paraenesis, but are themselves hortatory (Radl, 154–55).

## Consolation by Letter

In Paul's day, consolation was viewed as belonging to paraenesis or protreptic, which were not yet sharply distinguished (Theon, *Preliminary Exercises* 3.117 Spengel; different: Riedweg, 1.62–70), and instruction was given in how to deliver consolations (Ps.-Menander, *On Epideictic Speeches* 3.413–24 Spengel =Russell and Wilson 160–64, the speech is to contain what is known and is to be hortatory). Similarly, instruction in letter writing included the letter of consolation. The sample of a consolation letter reads as follows in the epistolary handbook of Ps.-Demetrius (*Epistolary Types* 5):

When I heard of the terrible things you suffered at the hands of thankless fate, I felt the deepest grief, considering that what had happened had not happened to you more than to me. When I saw all the things that assail life, all that day long I cried over them. But then I considered that such things are the common lot of all, with nature establishing neither a particular time nor age in which one must suffer anything, but often confronting us secretly, awkwardly, and undeservedly. Since I happened not to be present to comfort you, I decided to do so by letter. Bear, then, what has happened as lightly as you can, and exhort yourself just as you would exhort someone else. For you know that reason will make it easier for you to be relieved of your grief with the passage of time.

In addition to containing some of the standard consolatory themes (cruel fate, death as a common experience to all people, the use of reason to assuage grief), this sample letter demonstrates the hortatory nature of consolation (cf. Seneca, *Epistle* 99.32).

The practice of writing such letters is represented by Papyrus Oxyrhynchus 115, which may or may not have been influenced by the handbooks (Deissmann 1965: 176):

> Irene to Taonnophris and Philo good comfort.
>
> I am sorry and weep over the departed one as I wept for Didymas. And all other things, whatsoever were fitting, I have done, and all mine, Epaphroditus and Thermuthion and Philion and Apollonius and Plantas. But, nevertheless, against such things one can do nothing. Therefore comfort [*paregoreite*] ye one another.
>
> Fare ye well. (Athyr 1)

Of interest in this letter are doing what is fitting, the acceptance of fate, and the final exhortation to comfort each other (cf. 1 Thess 4:18, where *parakaleite* is used).

In the NOTES repeated reference was made to similarities between 4:13–18 and ancient consolations, including letters of consolation. Earlier in 1 Thessalonians, Paul referred to his having consoled the Thessalonians while he was with them (2:12) and revealed that he had borrowed a consolatory method from his contemporaries (see NOTES on 3:3–4). He will also urge his readers to console the dispirited among themselves (5:14). It is therefore not surprising that the church fathers thought of 1 Thessalonians as a letter of consolation (Gregg, 155–56, 194).

In this they have been followed by recent writers who are, however, reluctant to identify Paul's letter as a letter of consolation but instead detect only approximations to the genre in 1 Thessalonians (Donfried 1993: 5, 26; Chapa 1994; A. Smith, 51–59). It would be more accurate to describe 1 Thessalonians as a paraenetic letter that contains a strong interest in consoling as part of its hortatory aim. Given the circumstances and condition of his recent converts, to whose needs he was sensitive, Paul could write in no other way.

## Those Who Are Asleep

The metaphorical use of sleep for death appears in the NT outside Paul (e.g., Matt 27:52; Mark 5:39; Acts 7:60; 13:36; for Christian inscriptions, see Milligan, 56), but considerable discussion has revolved around Paul's possible use of it to say something about the state of an individual after his death. Paul does not here refer to an intermediate state, between death and resurrection, as he is thought by some commentators to do in Phil 1:23, but the very notion of sleep has invited speculation (Wilcke, 37–49, 120–21). One view is that it describes a waiting for the resurrection, in support of which passages such as 4 Macc 7:18–19; 16:25; 1 En 92:3; 100:5; Jub 23:31 are cited (Michel 1936; see also Baumgarten,

112–16; against: Hoffmann, 202–26; Luedemann, 236). Another is that it describes the state of the dead before the coming of the Lord, as an interim, imperfect condition in which the dead have a different time consciousness (Cullmann 1958: 57; contra: R. E. Bailey).

Paul shows no interest in the so-called intermediate state here, and his failure to do so does not indicate that he had not yet developed the doctrine he is thought to have developed by the time he wrote Phil 1:23. He is concerned with two different things in the two passages: here with the relationship between believers at the Parousia and in Phil 1:23 with death as a present option. Here he shows no special interest in the term *koimāsthai* and uses it in a self-evident way (Hoffmann, 206, 235–36). The significance of the language is to be determined from the function it performs in its immediate context rather than from some background that finds no echo elsewhere in this pericope.

Paul writes to assuage the grief of his readers, and it is reasonable to examine his language in the context of the ancient literary tradition of consolation. The appearance of the euphemism in funerary inscriptions is clearly consolatory, and it also appears in letters of consolation (e.g., Plutarch, *A Letter of Condolence to Apollonius* 107DEF; cf. Dio Chrysostom, *Oration* 30.39). Cicero provides the rationale behind some people's use: those who minimize death liken it to sleep (*Tusculan Disputations* 1.92; cf. 97, 117; for the Epicurean attitude, see Lucretius, *On the Nature of Things* 3.919–30).

Paul was familiar with this tradition. At the end of 1 Cor 15, in which he uses sleep as the image for death in his discussion of the resurrection (vv 6, 18, 20, 51), he finishes with a taunt of death (vv 54–55). Although the taunt is a pastiche of Isa 25:8 Theodotion and Hos 13:14, it reflects language from the consolatory tradition that Paul twists into an exclamation of triumph over death. In consolations, there are mentions of the sting or bite of sorrow associated with death (e.g., Seneca, *Epistles* 63.4; 99.14), and taunts of the mighty, who were not able to escape death ("Where [*pou*] are you now?" in Plutarch, *A Letter of Condolence to Apollonius* 110D; cf. Marcus Aurelius, *Meditations* 10.31; 12.27, for the style). Paul, instead, taunts death: "Where [*pou*] is your victory? Where [*pou*] is your sting? You've been swallowed up in victory!"

In 1 Cor 15 the main topics are death and resurrection. Here death does not figure as prominently, but Paul's demonstrated awareness of the consolation tradition strengthens the surmise that his use of the euphemism of death as sleep should be seen as simply consolatory in intention. Theodoret's description of Paul's handling of the problem shows that he thinks Paul is writing a consolation (*Interpretation of 1 Thessalonians* 4 [PG 82:645, 648]).

## Hope and the Hereafter

Paul begins his consolatory exhortation by forbidding his readers to grieve like the rest who have no hope. The reference here is not to the Thessalonian Christians who had died and, since they will not be alive at the Parousia, are in the same situation as pagans who have no hope (Becker, 48), nor are they Thessalonians who have given up hope in the Parousia and were therefore like the pagans (Hyldahl, 122–23, 127). Like those "who do not know God" (4:5) and "the outsiders" (4:12), they are non-Christians. Paul does not thereby mean that pagans have no hope of postmortem existence but that they do not have the hope that Christians have by virtue of God's action through Christ, namely, that after their resurrection and rapture they will be with the Lord always (Giesen, 127; Baumgarten, 97; Hoffmann, 301–15).

It is difficult to determine what the majority of people in the Greco-Roman world thought about the possibility of life after death, for they did not leave behind extensive written reflections on the subject (see Rigaux 1956: 529–32). Not surprisingly, therefore, the view exists that belief in immortality was not widely held (MacMullen 1981: 53–57). Indirect evidence, however, suggests that the belief was widespread. Epitaphs declaring that the deceased were "with the heroes," the rhetorical instruction in making consolatory speeches, and the consolation literature all point in this direction (see NOTE on v 17). The evidence of the rhetorical handbooks is particularly telling, for they did not introduce new ideas but put what was traditional to practical use. In addition, one of the attractions of the mystery cults was that they offered a hope of life in the next world (see Nock 1933: 102–3, despite his statement, "In the first century A.D. the educated commonly doubted survival"). In the first century B.C., Cicero declared himself against the Epicurean view, favoring instead the belief in an afterlife, invoking the support of the ancestral rites for the dead and the positions of philosophers on the subject (On Friendship 12–14).

Of special interest, and closer in time to Paul, is Plutarch's work That Epicurus Makes a Pleasant Life Impossible. After he concludes his criticism of the Epicurean lack of social responsibility (1100CD; see NOTE on v 11), Plutarch turns to criticize the Epicureans for insisting on grieving at the death of their friends (1101A). Epicureans denied postmortem existence and, what they considered an attendant matter, fear of the gods. So Plutarch proceeds to discuss eschatology in order to preserve hope (elpis) of divine favor and the faith (pistis) most people have in the gods (1101C). He classifies people in three groups according to their fear of the gods (1101DE). First, there are a few, the evildoers and the wicked, who fear punishment after death and are the better for having fear to restrain them in their evil (1104AB).

To the second group belong the great majority of people who are ignorant but not very wicked. They revere the gods but harbor an element of fear (1101D). They think that in death the soul is separated from the body and undergoes change but does not perish (1104C). What dismays them most is the Epicurean prospect of insensibility and oblivion (1104E), the dissolution of bodies and souls into emptiness and atoms, which cuts out their hope of incorruption (1105A).

The third group are those of cheerful hope and exultant joy (1101D). In religious observances already they have good hope and a sense of being "in the benign presence of the god and his gracious acceptance of what is done" (1102A), which puts away grief, fear, and worry (1101E). They are "the good, whose lives have been just [dikaiōs] and holy [hosiōs]" (cf. 1 Thess 2:10), who "are inspired by their virtue to a most wonderful confidence when they fix their eyes on their hopes" (1105C). Unlike Epicurus, they hope to be in the company of their friends and family in the hereafter, a view Plutarch shares with Pythagoras, Plato, and Homer (1105E).

As he was similar to Plutarch in v 11, Paul also here is similar to him in a number of respects. First is the sequence of their discussions, moving from social (ir)responsibility to grieving over death. Both discuss the issue in terms of faith in the divine and hope of life after death, and both describe life in the hereafter as an association with the divine and with people dear to themselves. Paul and Plutarch differ radically, however, in how they understood these themes. Plutarch classifies people according to their virtue, which determines how they view life after death, with fear or with confidence and hope of immortality. For Paul, what is determinative is what God has done and will do through the Lord. Furthermore, Paul does not speak of incorruption but of resurrection, first of Jesus and then of the Thessalonians.

"The rest who have no hope" sounds like a reference to Epicureans (De Witt 1954b: 315) and would have been understood as such by persons like Plutarch and his readers, and the Thessalonians. That does not mean that Paul attributes Epicurean views to the Thessalonians; he rather describes their grieving as like that of the Epicureans. He uses the anti-Epicurean description as a foil for the positive exhortation that he gives (see COMMENT on 5:1–10). Nevertheless, there were elements in the Thessalonians' thinking that gave bite to his language.

### The Problem at Thessalonica

There has been no lack of answers to the question as to why the Thessalonians were grieving for their dead (see Best 1972: 181–84). Other than comparing them with people who have no hope, Paul is not explicit about the problem. Reconstructions of the Thessalonians' problem have therefore proceeded from Paul's answer to it, amplified by Jewish and Christian apocalyptic traditions and what is known from other early Christian difficulties with eschatology.

One answer is that the Thessalonians had come under the influence of Gnostic teachers who held that the resurrection had already taken place (2 Tim 2:18; cf. 2 Thess 2:2; Schmithals 1972: 160–64; Harnisch). But there is no evidence in 1 Thessalonians that there were Gnostics in Thessalonica, and Paul does not write as though resurrection were the problem. The latter objection can also be raised to the theory that the Thessalonians had difficulty in accepting the doctrine of the resurrection (Holtz 1986: 191–92).

Another view is that Paul had preached to the Thessalonians about the resurrection of Jesus and his coming, which they were to await. After he left them, some of their number died, and Paul now has to provide new instruction on the resurrection of Christians (Guntermann; Marxsen 1969; Luedemann, 212). Once again, however, it is not clear that Paul's interest is focused on the resurrection; furthermore, it is likely that in the decade and a half that Paul had been preaching to Gentiles before he went to Thessalonica he would have had to teach on the subject and that this teaching had become part of his normal instruction to his converts. Furthermore, the Thessalonians had received extensive eschatological instruction (see NOTES on 1:10; 2:16, 19; 3:13; 4:6), during which the question would naturally have come up. This likelihood is increased by the fact that the problem that Paul addresses was occasioned by apocalyptic speculation (see also NOTE and COMMENT on 5:3).

A more probable explanation is that the Greek Thessalonians found it difficult to bring the apocalyptic expectations of resurrection and Parousia together into a systematic whole (Siber, 20–22; Merklein, 407). The Jewish apocalyptic idea of the eschatological resurrection was present in pre-Pauline Christianity, as was the notion of the Parousia, but they were brought together for the first time in 1 Thess 4:13–18 (Holleman). The immediate cause for combining them in this explanation of the relationship between the two events must be found in the problems at Thessalonica.

It is striking that Paul writes at such length on apocalyptic themes in a letter in which he so consistently uses the conventions of his Greek philosophical contemporaries (cf. also 1 Cor 15). Apocalyptic language was part of his gospel, and his Greek listeners accepted it (Beker, 170–73). The Thessalonians had heard from him about the judgment (4:6) and their deliverance from it (1:10), and Paul uses apocalyptic traditions (e.g., 2:13–16) as though he assumes that his readers were conversant with such teachings. Indeed, from 5:1–3 it would appear that some of the Thessalonians were engaging in apocalyptic speculation that Paul felt it necessary to correct.

From Paul's discussion it would appear that the sequence of eschatological events ("first . . . then") and the relationship between the dead and those alive at the Parousia ("shall by no means have precedence," "together with") were in some way related to the problem. The Thessalonians evidently shared these concerns with those Jews in the first century who discussed at great length the status of the living and the dead at the end of time (see Volz, 232–35; Klijn). It was held in such circles that those alive, "who are left are more blessed than those who had died" (4 Ezra 13:24; cf. 6:25; 7:26–44; Pss Sol 17:44; 18:6). But, despite the fear that the dead would be disadvantaged (4 Ezra 13:16–18; 2 Bar 28), the conviction was that both groups would arrive at the judgment at the same time (4 Ezra 5:41–45) and, after the resurrection at the coming of the Anointed One, would appear together and all would be joyous (2 Bar 30:1–3).

Paul's strong affirmation that those left until the Parousia would by no means have precedence over those who would have died clearly reflects these concerns. The situation in Thessalonica, however, was complicated by the activity of Christian prophets, whose pronouncements, Paul cautions, should be carefully tested (5:20–21). Their activity explains why Paul identifies his own teaching as a message from the Lord, that is, that he speaks as a prophet. He does so to counter the false prophets' calming message of peace and security in this age, which they derived from apocalyptic speculation about times and seasons (see COMMENT on 5:1–3).

The false prophets' teaching would defer the Parousia or at least lessen the sense of crisis associated with an expectation of the imminent end. (Giesen also thinks that the problem had to do with the postponing of the Parousia but thinks that it is Paul who extended the time of the Parousia.) Delaying the Parousia would also pose new questions about the events at the end. If the Thessalonians originally had believed that Christ's return was imminent, their focus would have been on Christ and their association with him at his coming. Their deferral of the Parousia and the intervening death of some of their number would raise new questions about their relationship with them at the Parousia, hence Paul's specification of the chronological sequence of events that would lead to their relationship with Christ and those who had died.

The deferral of the Parousia could also have affected the Thessalonians' self-understanding. It is possible that the death of some of them had shattered the association that they considered central to being the community of the last days and that they therefore no longer considered themselves to be that community (Merklein, 409). Their present existence no longer determined by the Parousia, they grieved, according to Paul, like the Epicureans, who had no hope at all of life in the hereafter. They did not, however, give up their expectation that Christ would come, but their inadequate understanding of what would transpire at the end caused their grief. They deferred the eschatological blessings to the end when, in the last days, they would in a proleptic way enjoy those blessings. This, to their mind, would give them precedence over those who had died, and this conviction caused them to grieve over the dead. Paul uses *phthanein* here, as he does in 2:16 and Phil 3:16, to deny them that precedence at the Parousia. Rather than reflect on the present condition of the dead in a so-called intermediate state, he focuses on the Parousia and the resurrection, which constitute for him the Christian hope and ground for comfort. In 5:1–10 he will give attention to the present quality of their lives in view of the Day of the Lord.

## The Parousia and Consolation

It was observed in the NOTES that Paul radically slims down both the traditional apocalyptic content and imagery in his description of the coming of the Lord. This is striking in the way the theme of judgment appears in the letter.

The Thessalonians' faith from the beginning included an expectation that Jesus would come from heaven to deliver them from divine wrath (1:10). The theme also appears in 2:16; 4:6; 5:9, showing that it was part of Paul's and the Thessalonians' view of Jesus' coming. God will execute judgment when the Lord Jesus comes with all his angels (3:13), and the Lord Jesus himself may share in the judgment (2:19). The coming of Jesus is no cause for fear, however, for God, who calls believers into his kingdom (2:12), will sanctify them blamelessly for that coming (5:23), making them increase in love so that they can stand blameless in holiness before him when Jesus comes with all his angels (3:13). Paul can therefore exultantly exclaim that his readers will prove to be his hope, joy, crown, and glory when Jesus comes (2:19–20).

Paul's view of the Parousia in 1 Thessalonians, then, is a positive one for his readers. The presence of the theme of judgment does, however, have a paraenetic force, just as it did have a protreptic force in his original preaching (see NOTES on 1:6–8). What is striking about Paul's description of the Parousia in 4:13–18 is that there is no mention of the judgment. Paul rather describes the Parousia in terms of a number of dramatic events that culminate in all the faithful being with each other and with the Lord Jesus.

That Paul does not here speak of the judgment in his consolation does not mean that judgment has no place in consolation. When the issues are different, the judgment may figure prominently, as it does in the consolatory section of 2 Thessalonians (1:3–3:5).

## Paul the Consoler

The numerous similarities between 4:13–18 and the Greek tradition of consolation make it understandable why the church fathers thought that these verses belonged to that tradition. Even the basic problem with which Paul deals was well known to the writers of consolations: "of all who are journeying towards Destiny those who come more tardily have no advantage over those who arrive earlier" (Plutarch, *A Letter of Condolence to Apollonius* 113CD; cf. Gregg, 180–81).

But Paul differs from his pagan contemporaries in that he avoids the most common conventions they used, for example, reflecting on suffering and human life, observing that death is common to all, recalling the noble way in which the grieving person had faced loss and was dealing with adverse circumstances, reminding the recipient of the consolation of noble examples of persons who had suffered, warning against excessive sorrow, and urging that reason and decorum prevail.

Paul, by contrast, reaches for traditional apocalyptic language to comfort his readers. Plutarch too values ancestral traditions and eschatology, which come at the end, the high point, of his consolations (*A Letter of Condolence to Apollonius* 120C–122A; *A Letter of Condolence to His Wife* 611D–612B), but there is never any doubt that he writes as a philosopher. Paul thought of prophesy as an activity that edified, encouraged, and comforted (1 Cor 14:3; see Hill, 109–19), and here he acts as a prophet who has received the Lord's message with which to comfort. In this, he is closer to the Baruch of the Pseudepigrapha than to Plutarch: "You, however, Baruch, strengthen your heart with a view to that which has been said to you, and understand that which has been revealed to you because you have many consolations which will last forever" (2 *Bar* 43:1; cf. 54:4).

# 2. ON THE DAY OF THE LORD, 5:1–11

Paul continues to discuss eschatology as he moves from exhortation to behave in a particular manner, not to grieve, to a more general concern for the moral life in view of the impending Day of the Lord. Again he uses diverse apocalyptic traditions and molds them into a form that supports his exhortation.

It is not clear whether Paul here responds to an inquiry the Thessalonians had made or whether he writes because of news Timothy had brought him. If it is the former, it is difficult to determine precisely what they would have asked him. The latter is the more probable, and the *peri de* ("About") therefore introduces a new subject or, better, a new stage in the discussion of eschatological matters relevant to the Thessalonians.

The matter requiring attention was the promises of some Christian prophets in Thessalonica of peace and security (v 3), which Paul thinks could have ruinous consequences. Understood thus, the pericope does not represent Paul's own initiative in taking up a matter of self-evident importance to himself rather than of particular concern to the Thessalonians (Holtz 1986: 210). Nor is it to be understood as merely a general warning against eschatological dangers (cf. Matt 24:27, 37–39, 43–51; 25:1–13, 42–51; Mark 13:33–37; Luke 12:35–48; 17:24–30; 21:34–36), although it fits that pattern. Like the rest of chaps. 4 and 5, this exhortation was occasioned by actual circumstances in the church. The hypothesis that 5:1–11 is a later interpolation (Friedrich 1973) finds no support in the text and has been widely rejected (see Plevnik 1979). Nor does the view that vv 4–8 depend on a common catechetical tradition convince (see COMMENT on 4:1–2).

With *peri de* ("About"), Paul begins a new section that is still eschatological. The section consists of two major parts. In vv 1–3 he speaks to a problem in Thessalonica caused by calculations of the end by reminding his readers of the unpredictability of the Day of the Lord. He then assures them that they belong to the Day (vv 4–5a) and on the basis of this assurance exhorts them to live as belonging to the Day (vv 5b–10). The exhortation is enclosed by references to wakefulness (*grēgorōmen* in vv 6b and 10b) and is structured symmetrically.

The first part of the exhortation (vv 5b–7) begins with an affirmation of Christian identity given in negative form (v 5b). The consequences of what they are (*ara oun*) are drawn in hortatory subjunctives (v 6), followed by a reason (*gar*) stated as a self-evident fact (v 7). The second part (v 8–10), antithetical to the first, also begins with a statement of identity, but is made positively, in the form of a causal participle. It is also followed by a hortatory subjunctive (v 8) and a reason (*hoti*), a theologically self-evident tradition (v 9–10a), and it ends with a final clause that encloses the exhortation in vv 5b–10 (with *grēgorōmen*) as well as the entire eschatological section 4:13–5:10 (the sleeping dead and the living with the Lord Jesus Christ).

The eschatological section proper is followed by v 11, which marks a transition between the eschatological section and the exhortation to communal relations that follows. Verse 11 is similar to 4:18 in inculcating behavior that is to follow from (*dio*, "Therefore") the eschatological instruction just given but probably looks back to all of 4:13–5:10 and forwards to 5:12–22, which specifies how the exhortation and edification should take place.

## TRANSLATION

5 ¹About the times and the seasons, brethren, you have no need to be written to; ²for you yourselves know accurately that the Day of the Lord so comes as a thief in the night. ³When they say, "Peace and security," it is then that sudden ruin comes upon them as birth pangs do upon a pregnant woman, and they shall in no way escape. ⁴But you, brethren, are not in darkness, for the Day to surprise you like a thief in the night, ⁵for you are all sons of light and sons of day. We do not belong to night or darkness. ⁶So then, let us not sleep as the rest do, but let us stay awake and be sober. ⁷For those who sleep do so at night and those who get drunk are drunk at night. ⁸But as for us, since we belong to the day, let us be sober, putting on the breastplate of faith and love and as a helmet the hope of salvation, ⁹because God did not destine us for wrath but to obtain salvation through our Lord Jesus Christ, ¹⁰who died for us in order that, whether we are awake or asleep, we might live with him.

¹¹Therefore, exhort one another and build one another up, one on one, as indeed you are doing.

## NOTES

5:1. *About the times and the seasons, brethren.* The phrase *peri de* ("About") need not introduce a response to an inquiry, whether written or oral, but can mark a change of subject (see NOTE on 4:9), which is marked further here by the use of "brethren" (cf. 2:1, 17; 4:1, 13; 5:12). The change is not radical, for Paul is still speaking of living with a view towards the end, but he now takes up calculations of eschatological chronology and their effect on the Christian life.

The phrase "the times and the seasons" is the first of a number of phrases, words, and images in vv 1–10 that do not appear elsewhere in Paul (Friedrich 1973; Harnisch, 76 n. 83). The two terms, taken together, can have slightly different meanings: *chronos* ("time"), referring to time in its extension, and *kairos* ("season"), to a definite moment in time (see Cicero, *On Invention* 1.27.40; Quintilian 3.6.25–26; Augustine, *Epistle* 197.2). This differentiation has been appealed to in support of a theology that identifies a history of salvation by joining special divine *kairoi* (Cullmann 1950: 39–43; contra: Barr, 20–46). The distinction in meaning, however, does not hold.

Both terms are used eschatologically (e.g., *chronos*: Acts 3:21; 1 Pet 1:20; *kairos*: Luke 19:44; 1 Pet 1:5), and they in fact are a hendiadys, the two expressing the same idea. The two definite articles show that the terms were well known to Paul and his readers (Best 1972: 204). Although they occur together in nonbiblical Greek (Demosthenes, *Oration* 3.16; *Epistle* 2.3; Strabo, *Fragment* 10 [Wehrli, 5.11, 3]; Lucchesi's reference to Philo is unconvincing), their collocation has biblical roots.

The terms appear in Neh 10:34; 13:31; Wis 8:8; cf. 7:18, but especially noteworthy is their occurrence in Dan 2:21; cf. 7:12 Symmachus. The notion of divinely fixed periods of time led to apocalyptic calculations to lay bare God's scheme of things and to determine when the critical events would take place (see the interpretation of Jer 25:11 in Dan 9:24–27; cf. 4 Ezra 4:33–37, 44–47, 51; 2 *Bar* 25–30; Volz, 145–46; Str-B 4.986–1015). A connotation of such apocalyptic curiosity is present in "the times and the seasons" here and in Acts 1:7, the only other place in the NT where the two words appear together (cf. Matt 24:3; Mark 13:4; Luke 21:7).

*you have no need to be written to.* For the epistolary convention and the paraenetic function of the phrase, see NOTE on 2:9. By writing in this way, according to John Chrysostom, Paul was comforting them (*Homilies on 1 Thessalonians* 9 [PG 62:446]). This is not a case of *paralipsis,* as 4:9 is, for Paul does not pretend to refrain from discussing something he in fact goes on to discuss. If calculation of the end is implicit in "the times and the seasons," as it seems to be, then v 2 provides the reason why there is no need to write about the timing of the Day of the Lord. What Paul does go on to write about does not have to do with when the Day would come, but with the life to be lived in light of the certainty and unexpectedness of that Day's coming (vv 4–10).

This differs markedly from Rom 13:11–14, where Paul's emphasis is on the nearness of the end as the motivation for the moral life. In 1 Thess 5:1–3, the coming of the Day of the Lord is unexpected and sudden, which has the effect of ensuring the utter ruin of the false prophets, not the moral life of Paul's readers. The similarities in form and content between the two passages should not obscure the differences (see further, Holtz 1986: 238).

*5:2. for you yourselves know accurately.* The reason Paul need not write is that his readers already know something about the times and seasons. This is the only place in Paul's letters where *akribōs* ("accurately") is used (cf. Eph 5:15). The word and its cognates are used of learning or investigating something with great care (cf. Luke 1:3; Josephus, *Against Apion* 2.175) and of teaching with certainty (Acts 18:25, 26; 22:3; 24:22). Of interest is the use of the verb for ascertaining the time of the Messiah's birth (Matt 1:7, 16, cf. 8). The apocalyptic use of the word appears in Daniel, where the adjective describes a dream vision whose interpretation is also certain (Dan 2:45 Symmachus). Of special relevance is Daniel seeking an accurate interpretation of his vision of the coming of one like a son of man (Dan 7:16 Symmachus; cf. 12, "for a season and a time"). It is this apocalyptic use that informs Paul's description of the Thessalonians' knowledge of the times and seasons. It may be that Paul picked up the word from the Thessalonians, who wanted to know accurately when the Parousia would take place (Best 1972: 204–5).

Paul frequently refers to his readers' knowledge. The diatribal *ouk oidate* ("do you not know?") introduces basic Christian teaching that he assumes his readers know (1 Cor 3:6; 6:3, 9, 15, 16), an OT passage (11:2), and something that is otherwise self-evidently true (Rom 6:16; 1 Cor 9:13, 24) or is proverbial (1 Cor 5:6). He uses *oidate* ("you know") to refer to his readers' own experience, a use that predominates in 1 Thessalonians (see 1:5; 2:1, 2, 5, 11; 3:3, 4; 4:2; cf. 1 Cor 12:2; Gal 4:13). The participle *eidotes* ("knowing") also refers to what they know about eschatological matters (Rom 13:11; 1 Cor 15:58).

It is only in his Thessalonian letters that Paul uses the emphatic *autoi* ("your-selves") with *oidate*. Sometimes he does so for the sake of emphasis (1 Thess 3:3; 2 Thess 3:7), sometimes to draw a contrast (1 Thess 2:1). It is both here, being emphatic and having a paraenetic force in that it instills confidence in the Thessalonians, and it contrasts what Paul's readers know with the message of the false prophets in v 3 (cf. 1 John 2:18–22).

*that the Day of the Lord so comes as a thief in the night.* The content of their knowledge is summarized in a simile about a thief's unexpected coming. The present, "comes" (*erchetai*), is not to be taken as futuristic, but is used to express the certainty of the coming (Lünemann, 545–46; Eadie, 176); its characteristics are in some way already present (vv 4–7). Paul tends to use *hōs . . . houtōs* ("so . . . as") to make a comparison emphatic (Rom 5:15, 18; 1 Cor 7:17), which here heightens the irony: what you accurately know is that you cannot know what you seek to know. The image of the thief is used in the OT (Job 30:5; Jer 2:26; 49:9; Joel 2:9; Obad 5), but it is not used of the Day of the Lord before the NT, although the idea that the Day would come suddenly does (Mal 3:1; cf. Mark 13:33–37; Luke 12:35–40).

In the NT the image is applied to the coming of the Day of the Lord (2 Pet 3:10) and to the Lord's coming (Rev 3:3; 16:5), and it becomes a short parable in Q about the day or hour when the Lord comes (Matt 24:43; par. Luke 12:39; cf. *Did* 16:1; *Gos. Thom.* 21; see Harnisch, 84–116). The relationship between Paul's use of the image and Q is not clear, but it is plausible that Paul reflects a knowledge of the Synoptic tradition (Tuckett, 171). However, while in the Synoptics ignorance of the thief's coming is a motivation for wakefulness, for Paul it is connected with the ruin of those who are not alert to the Day's coming (v 3). It is not obvious that the NT passages where the image is used are part of an early Christian prophetic tradition (see P. Müller, 150–51).

This is the only place where night is mentioned, and it creates an infelicitous metaphor, that the Day is coming in the night. It may be Paul's addition, suggested by the Day of the Lord tradition, in order to provide a broader basis for the exhortation that follows in vv 4–10. Ancient Christians thought that Paul was hinting that the Lord would return at night (e.g., Lactantius, *The Divine Institutes* 7.19), which led to the custom of holding vigils on Easter eve (see Rigaux 1956: 557). Paul's point in using the image is that the Day of the Lord comes as a surprise, that the time of its coming cannot be calculated.

## The Day of the Lord

The background to Paul's use of the term is ultimately the OT, where it describes God's decisive intervention, either to judge or to save (see Langevin, 107–67; Plevnik 1997: 11–39). For the unjust, unholy, and proud, it is a day of darkness, not light (Amos 5:18–20; cf. Isa 2:12; Joel 2:1–2), "a day of distress and anguish, a day of ruin and devastation, a day of darkness and gloom" (Zeph 1:14–15). The day is imminent (Isa 13:6; Joel 1:15; 2:1; 4:14), when the Lord of hosts will come with power and glory and the unjust will flee from him (Isa 2:10, 19–21;

cf. *1 En* 1:1–9; 5:5–10), and he will crush his enemies (Zeph 1:14–18). There is also a positive side to the day. The Lord will come to his temple, preceded by a messenger who will purify the people, and all the unrighteous will be burned up (Mal 3:1–18). "But for you who fear my name the sun of righteousness shall rise, with healing in its wings" (Mal 4:1–2; cf. Joel 3:1–2; 4:18).

What Paul had described in 4:15 as the Parousia of the Lord he describes in 5:2 as the Day of the Lord, a term he uses twice as often as Parousia. The Lord here is Jesus, as is evident from the context (4:15, 16, 17; 5:9). What is said of the Day of Yahweh in the OT is said of the Day of the Lord Jesus by Paul. It is the day of wrath (Rom 2:5; cf. Rev 6:17) and is otherwise associated with judgment (Rom 2:16; 1 Cor 1:8; 3:13; Phil 1:10; cf. 2 Pet 2:9; 3:7, 10; 1 John 4:17). In 1 Thess 5, it is a day of light (vv 5, 8) and darkness (vv 5, 7), of salvation (vv 9–10) and ruin (v 3). The day is so much a part of Paul's language that, in addition to referring to it as the Day of the Lord or of the Lord Jesus (Christ) (1 Cor 1:8; 5:5; Phil 1:6, 10; 2:16; 2 Thess 2:2), he can simply refer to it as the Day (Rom 2:16; 13:12; 1 Cor 3:13; 1 Thess 5:4) or that Day (2 Thess 1:10; cf. Luke 17:31; 2 Tim 1:12, 18; see also "the last day": John 6:39, 40, 44; "the great day": Rev 16:14).

Paul uses the term in 5:2 as though his readers were familiar with it, probably because the subject had been part of his original eschatological instruction to them and was a topic under discussion. The sources of the Synoptic gospels knew the theology of the Day of the Lord, but did not use the formula, rather speaking of the Day of the Son of Man (Luke 17:24–30), the day of judgment (Matt 10:15; 11:22, 24; 12:36), and that day (Matt 7:22). First Thessalonians 5:2 is the earliest occurrence of the term as applied to Jesus. For Paul, like the prophets, the term has a moral dimension (see Rom 2:5, 15–16; 13:11–14).

**5:3.** *When they say, "Peace and security."* Paul continues in v 3 to use words in a way unusual to him (*legōsin, eirēnē*) or uses words that he does not use elsewhere (*asphaleia, aiphnidios, ephistēmi*) but which occur in one context elsewhere (*aiphnidios, aphistēmi,* and *ekpheugein* in Luke 21:34–36), all of which suggest that he is using traditional material.

Paul begins the sentence without a transitional particle, which raises the question of how this verse is related to what precedes. He may be clarifying v 2 (so understood by some manuscripts that supply *gar*), or he may be drawing a contrast with it (so understood by some manuscripts that supply *de*). It is more probable that he intends a contrast, as the content of the two verses shows. To the uncertainty about the Day's coming, of which his readers know, he contrasts the peace and security of which certain people speak. The contrast of his readers to these people is made clear in v 4, when he again addresses his readers. It is unusual for Paul to use an impersonal verb, but he does so in 1 Cor 10:10, also of people of whose actions he disapproves (see 2 Tim 4:3; cf. *inquit* in Seneca, *Epistles* 102.8; 121.14; for the diatribal use, to introduce a statement that is then corrected, see Dalfen, 151–52). Paul does not have to identify these people, for his readers know of whom he is writing. In fact, what he attributes to these people is at the heart of the problem he is addressing. The content of their teaching helps to identify them.

Peace is for Paul a profoundly theological concept that describes a relationship with God that is made possible by Christ (Rom 5:1). God is the God of peace (1 Thess 5:23; cf. Rom 16:20; 2 Cor 13:11) and its source (Rom 1:7; 1 Cor 1:3; 2 Thess 1:2). He calls people in peace (1 Cor 7:15), and his peace passes all understanding and keeps believers' hearts and minds in Christ (Phil 4:7). In 1 Thess 5:3 it is quite different. "Peace and security" (*eirēnē kai asphaleia*) reminds most commentators of the false prophets' cry in the OT (Jer 6:14; 8:11 [not in the LXX]; Ezek 13:10). Such prophets questioned who was in control of history, as though Yahweh were not in charge (Brueggemann, 102). It has been thought that Paul used this critical language to describe the views of people in general (Schlier 1972: 86), of unbelievers (Rigaux 1956: 557), or of the Thessalonians (Holtz 1986: 215–16).

Closer to the mark is the surmise that this is Paul's own ironic formulation to describe the teaching of false teachers (Harnisch, 79–82, who errs, however, in identifying them as Gnostics). The combination of *eirēnē* and *asphaleia* occurs only here in the Bible, but the two words combined to form a political slogan celebrating the *Pax Romana*, and Paul has consequently been regarded as making a political criticism (Wengst, 73–78). Finally, it has been argued that the two words describe Epicurean social values of the sort Paul already alluded to in 4:11 (De Witt 1954b: 41–53). It is most likely that the two words are combined by Paul in a hendiadys to criticize the message of false prophets in Thessalonica (see COMMENT).

*it is then that sudden ruin comes upon them.* Paul uses the construction *hotan . . . tote* ("when . . . it is then") elsewhere to stress a particular point in the eschatological scheme (1 Cor 15:28, 34; cf. Col 3:4). Judgment does not remain a future certainty; it is in some way a present reality that comes upon people when they claim a false security. The verb *ephistatai* ("comes upon") is present and is similar to *erchetai* in v 2. Ironically, it is when peace and security are claimed that sudden ruin comes upon the false prophets. Paul uses *olethros* ("ruin") only in eschatological contexts (1 Cor 5:5; 1 Thess 5:3; 2 Thess 1:9). It is related to *apōleia* ("destruction"; 1 Tim 6:9), but rather than imply annihilation "it carries with it the thought of utter and hopeless ruin, the loss of all that gives worth to existence" (Milligan, 65).

As the Day of the Lord comes unexpectedly (v 2), so the false prophets' ruin is sudden (*aiphnidios*). The notion of suddenness in judgment is common in Scripture (Daube), and the themes in 1 Thess 5:2–3 appear already in Mal 3:1–2. Paul's discussion in vv 2–7 shares much with Mark 13:33–37 (esp. vv 35–36), but the parallels with Luke 21:34–36 are so close (e.g., *ephistēmi* in both; *aiphnidios* appears only in 1 Thess 5:3 and Luke 21:35) that it must be assumed that Paul uses the same tradition as Luke (Hartman, 192–93; Aejmelaeus argues for the reverse: these verses in Luke are a summary of 1 Thess 5:1–11). What is noteworthy is how restrained Paul's description is in comparison with the gospel tradition (see also Matt 24:37–41; Luke 17:26–37). As he had done in 4:13–18, however, Paul uses from the tradition only what is needed for his exhortation. Patristic commentators saw an element of consolation in the certain ruin of those who were enticing Paul's readers with their false message (e.g., Theophylact, *Exposition of 1 Thessalonians* 5 [PG 124:1316]; Oecomenius, *Commentary on 1 Thessalonians* 6 [PG 119:97]).

*as birth pangs do upon a pregnant woman, and they shall in no way escape.* To the simile of the thief coming in the night to convey the unexpectedness of the Day's coming, Paul adds one of a woman in labor to convey the inexorableness of the ruin of those who prophesy falsely. He uses the image elsewhere (Gal 4:19, 27) but does so here in a different way. The image appears in the OT prophetic literature (e.g., Isa 26:17; 66:8; Jer 30:6–7) and became popular in Jewish apocalyptic and rabbinic writings to describe the Messianic Woes (Volz, 147; Harnisch, 62–72), a use also found in Matt 24:8 and Mark 13:8. Paul does not use the image in this way, but rather to stress the inevitability with which ruin comes (cf. 4 Ezra 16:35–39 for the same function; cf. 4:40–42; 1 En 62:1–6), from which they shall in no way escape (for *ou mē* with the subjunctive, see 4:15; for use in other eschatological contexts, see Mark 9:1; 13:30; 14:25). The similar tradition in Luke speaks of the Day as coming suddenly like a snare from which the disciples may pray to escape (Luke 21:34–36), but for Paul, the crisis at hand is inescapable.

*5:4. But you, brethren, are not in darkness.* Having countered the message of the false prophets and threatened them with ruin, Paul now turns to exhort the congregation (vv 4–10). The *de* ("But") has an adversative force, as does the emphatic *hymeis* ("you," contrasted to *autois* in v 3; cf. Rom 8:9; 1 Pet 2:9), and *adelphoi* ("brethren") both marks a transition (see NOTE on v 1) and establishes a warmer tone than that of the preceding verse. Paul begins the exhortation with a reassuring affirmation of their true identity, which will provide the basis for that exhortation.

For the sake of emphasis, Paul begins by describing what they are not. He picks up the image of the thief in the night from v 2 and puts it to paraenetic use by playing on the theme of darkness and light in affirming their identity. The contrasts between night and day, darkness and light to describe the human condition were widespread in philosophy and religion, particularly the religion of Israel (e.g., Job 22:11; 29:2–3; Ps 74:20; 82:5; see Aalen) and Judaism, and became especially sharp in apocalyptic literature (e.g., 1 En 41:8; 4 Ezra 14:20; 1QS 3:13–4:26; T Naph 2:7–10; T Benj 5:3). It is equally well attested in the NT (e.g., 1 Pet 2:9; esp. in the Johannine literature, e.g., John 1:5, 8–9; 12:35, 46a; 1 John 1:5; Rev 8:12). Here, Paul has in mind the darkness associated with the unjust when the Day of the Lord comes (see NOTE on v 2).

*for the Day to surprise you like a thief in the night.* Paul repeats the metaphor from v 2, hence the reference is to the Day of the Lord rather than to daylight (Best 1972: 209). Three Alexandrian manuscripts (A B cop[boh]) read *kleptas* ("thieves," in the accusative) rather than *kleptēs* ("thief," in the nominative), which would mean "surprise you like thieves (are surprised)" (preferred by Field, 200–1; Frame, 184). The variant appears to be the result of conformation to the preceding *hymās* (Metzger: 565). The fact that it is the more difficult reading (Lightfoot 1980: 73–74) does not prevail over the better attestation of the singular and, more importantly, the latter's coherence with v 2. The verb *katalam-banein* can have the sense of hostility ("overtake, seize," so understood here by BAGD, 413), but the meaning "surprise" is consistent with the use of the image in v 2 and in such passages as Euripides, *Iphigenia at Tauris* 1025–26; Plutarch, *Agesilaus* 24.5; Pausanias, *Description of Greece* 10.23.7 (see further, for *kata-lambanein* with *hēmera*, Plutarch, *Crassus* 29.5; with *hespera*, Plutarch, *Marcius Corolianus* 17.2).

5:5. *for you are all sons of light and sons of day.* Unlike Rom 13:11–14, it is not the nearness of the Day and their salvation that are to impel them to the moral life, but who and what they in fact are. With *gar* ("for") Paul provides the ground, now positively stated, for the affirmation he just made. The *pantes* ("all") does not imply that Paul has in mind a particular group (the fainthearted) for special encouragement (so Frame, 184). He uses *pantes hymeis* in a variety of ways that do not require such a reading, for example, when he describes his converts' relationship with God (cf. Gal 3:26, "For you are all sons of God"; 3:28, "For you are all in Christ Jesus"), when he is expansive in the opening and closing of his letters (Rom 1:8; 15:33; 2 Cor 13:12, 13; Phil 1:1; 4:22), and when he encourages them (2 Cor 2:3, 5 [*pantas hymas*]).

The Thessalonians are not in the realm of darkness, where the day can surprise them, for they belong to light and to day. The construction *huios* ("son") in a figurative sense with a genitive describing quality is Hebraic (Moule, 174–75, referring to Mark 2:19; Matt 23:15; see BDF §162.6; cf. *tekna phōtos* in Eph 5:8 and *tekna . . . orgēs* in Eph 2:3). The phrase *hoi huioi tou phōtos* ("sons of light") appears in Luke 16:8; cf. John 12:36, but there is no reason to suppose that Paul is influenced by Jesus (as suggested by Frame, 185). It is a common term in the Dead Sea writings to describe members of the community (e.g., 1QS 1:9; 2:16; 3:13, 24, 25; 1QM 1:90) over against the "sons of darkness," the outsiders who are under the dominion of the spirit of darkness (1QS 3:25–27; cf. 1QM 15:9). This has led to the suspicion that the terminology of Qumran has influenced early Christianity (see Harnisch, 119–20 for discussion). Paul shared this dualism (Rom 13:12; 2 Cor 6:14–7:1). For him, "sons of light" is an eschatological term, as appears from his further specification of his readers as "sons of day," a phrase that appears nowhere else and may be Paul's formulation to describe vividly the eschatological quality of their lives. The phrase has a studied ambiguity, having an eschatological sense of the Day of the Lord and referring to daylight, with its implicit moral dimension, which Paul will play on in the exhortation that follows.

*We do not belong to night or darkness.* Paul begins the first part of his exhortation (vv 5b–7) without syntactically connecting it to the preceding affirmation, a feature characteristic of didactic and paraenetic styles (e.g., 1 Cor 5:9; 6:1, 12; see BDF §462.2; 464). Changing from the second person plural to the first person plural, he lays the foundation for his exhortation by moving from the particularity of the Thessalonian situation to a general statement about all Christians (for the style, see Thyen, 90–94). What he just stated in positive form about them, he now states in negative form, therefore continuing the antithetic style. Night and darkness represent the moral realm for those who are not in the light, who are therefore in danger of being surprised by the Day (v 4). It is not at all certain that in his exhortation Paul uses motifs from a baptismal paraenesis (so P. Müller, 148–55; correctly, Koester 1990: 450).

5:6. *So then, let us not sleep as the rest do.* The introductory phrase *ara oun* ("So then") appears in the Bible only in the Pauline literature, mostly to mark transitions in an argument (Rom 5:18; 7:3, 25; 8:12; 9:16, 18; 14:12; cf. Eph 2:19). It is used with the imperative to introduce paraenesis (2 Thess 2:15; cf. Eph 2:19) and also with the hortatory subjunctive, as it is here (Rom 14:19; Gal 6:10). It therefore functions as other inferential particles do in grounding paraenesis in theological affirmations (see NOTE on 4:18). The hortatory subjunctives are imperatival in force (cf. Heb 4:11, 14, 16; 6:1; *1 Clem* 7:2–3; 33:8; Philo, *Noah's Work as Planter* 131). This preaching style, in which he expresses solidarity with his readers, has a pastoral effect (see P. Müller, 155–56; cf. Thyen, 117–19). A close parallel, as to construction and content, is provided by Rom 13:11–14.

The exhortation is given in the antithetical form Paul uses frequently in 1 Thessalonians, a favorite device to stress the second part of the antithesis (1:5, 8; 2:2, 4, 13; 4:7, 8; cf. 5:9, 15). Paul uses a different word for sleep from the one he used in 4:13, 14, 15 (*koimāsthai*). He uses *katheudein* only here and does so in three different ways: in v 6 it is metaphorical, in v 7 it is literal, and in v 10 it is used like *koimāsthai*, as a euphemism for death. In a fragment of a Christian hymn in Eph 5:14, it describes metaphorically the contrast between being dead and being truly alive (see Lautenschlager for an extensive treatment of the evidence). It is "the rest," those who have no hope (see NOTE on 4:13), who sleep. The nature of the sleep Paul has in mind becomes clear from its opposite, stressed in the second part of the antithesis. In 4:13, "the rest" are non-Christians, those who have no hope. Here, they are described in terms of a quality of life that is in contrast to the sober vigilance of those who do have hope of salvation (vv 8–10).

*but let us stay awake and be sober.* Paul uses *grēgorein* ("stay awake") metaphorically here and in v 10 (the only other occurrence in his letters is in 1 Cor 16:13; cf. Col 4:2). It is well attested in an eschatological sense in the Synoptic tradition that has come under consideration in the interpretation of vv 1–5 (see Matt 24:42–43; 25:13; Mark 13:35–37; Luke 12:37. Luke 21:36 has *agrypnein*. See Lövestam, 45–58). It also appears in eschatological contexts in 2 Tim 4:5; 1 Pet 4:7; cf. Rev 16:15. An important difference between the Synoptic tradition and 1 Thess 5:6–10 is that in the former watchfulness is grounded in ignorance of when the end comes (Matt 25:13–15; 24:42; Mark 13:33–37; cf. Luke 12:40), whereas in the latter it is the true identity of Christians that provides the foundation for the exhortation to be awake and sober (vv 5, 8).

Paul is the first NT writer to combine *grēgorein* with *nēphein* ("to be sober"). The suggestion that Paul found the combination in baptismal paraenesis is unlikely (Harnisch, 122 n. 25; contra: Holtz 1986: 224). The combination appears after Paul in 1 Pet 5:8. The verb and its cognates are always used in a figurative sense in the NT: in 1 Cor 15:34, in 1 Peter (1:13; 4:7; 5:8), and in the Pastoral Epistles (1 Tim 3:2, 11; 2 Tim 2:26; 4:5; Titus 2:2), in the latter instances reflecting a moral philosophical perspective.

The combination of being sober (*nēphein*) and awake (*agrypnein*) is found in the moralists (e.g., Plutarch, *To an Uneducated Ruler* 781D). As Paul in 4:4 had combined a traditional Jewish-Christian idea (*hagiasmos*) with a philosophical one (*timē*) and in 5:3 had formed a hendiadys of a traditional term (*eirēnē*) and a philosophical one (*asphaleia*), so he here forms a hendiadys, with *nēphein* strengthening *grēgorein*, to express sober vigilance (Oecomenius, *Commentary on 1 Thessalonians* 6 [PG 119:97]; Lünemann, 547; von Dobschütz 1909: 209).

5:7. *For those who sleep do so at night and those who get drunk are drunk at night.* With *gar* ("For") Paul introduces a self-evident fact to confirm and clarify v 6 (Ellicott, 73; Holtz 1986: 224 n. 435). He may have in mind the normal experience, that drunkenness is generally associated with night (see Milligan, 68; Bruce 1982: 112; Holtz 1986: 224; cf. Plutarch, *To an Uneducated Ruler* 781D, who contrasts sober [*nēphein*] and awake [*agrypnein*] with being drunk [*methyein*] and asleep [*katheudein*]). Some commentators, however, think that it is figurative (Wanamaker, 185; already John Chrysostom, *Homilies on 1 Thessalonians* 9 [PG 62:450]; Theophylact, *Exposition of 1 Thessalonians* 5 [PG 124:1317]), which may be supported by the fact that what it clarifies is figurative. The motifs of sleep and drunkenness were intimately combined in a wide range of literature (Lövestam, 55–56). The image lent itself to moralistic use, as it does in Philo, *On Dreams* 2.160–62:

> For indeed he who gives way to the intoxication [*mēthen*] which is of folly [*aphrosynēs*] rather than of wine bears a grudge against upright standing and wakefulness [*egrēgorsei*], and lies prostrate and sprawling like sleepers [*koimō-menoi*] with the eyes of his soul closed, unable to see or hear aught that is worth seeing or hearing . . . And that deep and abysmal sleep [*hypnos*] which holds fast all the wicked robs the mind of true apprehensions, and fills it with false phantoms and untrustworthy visions and persuades it to approve of the blameworthy as laudable.

Paul continues the deliberate ambiguity that began with his introduction of the term "sons of day" in v 5 to describe both the eschatological and moral dimensions of Christian existence. What is important here is that it is the quality of life, moral somnolence and drunkenness, that demonstrates whether one belongs to the night. There does not seem to be a significant difference, if any, in meaning between the two words for drunkenness (*methyskesthai* and *methyein*).

5:8. *But as for us, since we belong to the day, let us be sober.* The second exhortation, introduced by the adversative *de* ("But"), contrasts positively behavior that is appropriate to the day to behavior that belongs to the night (cf. Plutarch, *Precepts of Statecraft* 800B). Paul again begins by affirming the identity of Christians, this time with a causal participle (*ontes*, "since we belong") that provides the ground for the exhortation. The exhortation again takes the form of a hortatory subjunctive, as in v 6b, and *nēphōmen* is repeated while *grēgorōmen* is dropped. As Paul added "sons of day" in order to play on it, he also added *nēphōmen* to *grēgorōmen* to give a special meaning to the latter and to prepare to end his exhortation on the note of the sober life. *Nēphein* is also used with military overtones in 1 Pet 1:13; 5:8–9; perhaps 2 Tim 4:5.

*putting on the breastplate of faith and love and as a helmet the hope of salvation.* With the aorist participle *endysamenoi* ("putting on") Paul specifies that they are to be sober by taking up their armor (Findlay, 114; von Dobschütz 1909: 211; P. Marshall, 138). The theme of soberness also appears with martial imagery in 1 Pet 1:13; 5:8. Paul frequently uses military language, always figuratively, in a variety of ways (e.g., Rom 6:13, 23; 13:12–14; 16:7; 1 Cor 9:7; 2 Cor 6:7; 10:3–5; Phil 2:25; Phlm 2; cf. Eph 6:10–20; 1 Tim 1:18; 2 Tim 2:3–4). It is frequently thought that Jewish literature provided him with the imagery.

In the OT, Yahweh is described as a man of war (Isa 42:13; Hab 3:9–15), and in Isa 59:17, a passage important for the NT's use of the imagery, God's armament is described as a breastplate of righteousness and a helmet of salvation. According to Wis 5:17–22, with the creation as an ally, God will battle his enemies, clothed with righteousness (*dikaiosynē*) as his breastplate, impartial judgment as a helmet, holiness as a shield, and wrath as a sword. In the Qumran War Scroll (1QM) the community's eschatological existence is described in martial terms (see A. Oepke and K. G. Kuhn in *TDNT* 5.298–300).

The influence of the Jewish tradition on Eph 6:10–20 is clear, and this passage has influenced the way in which the imagery in 1 Thess 5:8 is viewed. According to Ephesians, the cosmic battle with Satan and his agents, conducted in hand-to-hand combat as well as from a distance, is both defensive and offensive, and requires six pieces of armor. This armor now belongs to God's people rather than to God (for rabbinic literature, see *TDNT* 5.310 n. 11). What 1 Thess 5:8 shares with this passage is not the details about the armor or the battle, but the eschatological nature of the battle (cf. Rom 13:11–14, where the paraenetic interest is more pronounced). With Isa 59:17, 1 Thess 5:8 shares the breastplate and the helmet (the hope) of salvation, but now as qualities of the faithful rather than of God. Unlike Eph 6, the armor here is defensive.

While Paul is indebted to the OT for his description of the Christian's armor, the visibility of the Roman military in daily life made it a natural image with which to describe a person's defense (see W. Weiss, who also ascribes the portrayal of the three-part armor to Paul but whose interest is in the eschatological judgment). There was as well a long tradition in Greek and Latin literature that described the virtuous man, particularly the philosopher, in martial terms, and Paul was intimately familiar with this tradition (cf. 2 Cor 10:3–5, on which see Malherbe 1989: 91–119; contrast Sevenster, 156–64). Paul's readers would have been familiar with the technique of describing the qualities of the desired life in terms of armament.

In their culture, the philosopher, who represented the ideal, stands watch day and night, with anxious thoughts and vigilance (*phrontizonta kai agrypnounta*) (Dio Chrysostom *Oration* 49.10). Virtue in a general sense is his armament (Diogenes Laertius, *The Lives of Eminent Philosophers* 6.12) or his conscience is, as he watches over (*hyperagrypnein*) people (Epictetus, *Discourse* 3.22.94–95). His arms are also more closely specified as bravery (Seneca, *Epistle*

113.27–28; cf. Cicero, *Tusculan Disputations* 2.33) and, more typically, philosophical precepts (Horace, *Satires* 2.3.297; Dio Chrysostom, *Oration* 49.10; Epictetus, *Discourse* 4.6.14), prudence (Cicero, *On the Orator* 1.172; Diogenes Laertius, *The Lives of Eminent Philosophers* 6.13), and reason (Philo, *Allegorical Interpretation* 3.155; *On Dreams* 1.103; Seneca, *On Anger* 1.17.2; *Epistle* 74.19–21; Plutarch, *On Chance* 98DE).

The eschatological armament does not consist for Paul of such rational qualities, but of the three qualities for which he had given thanks at the beginning of the letter (1:3). He uses the military imagery to give specificity to and dramatize the nature of eschatological soberness. He mentions only the two pieces of armor from Isa 59:17 but modifies his source in important ways. Paul ascribes two qualities to one piece of equipment rather than two and is thus much more restrained than Eph 6:10–20. Instead of representing righteousness, the breastplate now represents faith and love, which are epexegetical genitives. Furthermore, what is important to him is not the relationship of the qualities to certain parts of the body, but the qualities themselves.

The triad of qualities in 1:3 and 5:8 forms an *inclusio*, which gives coherence to the intervening discussion (see COMMENT on 1:3). With vv 9–10, these motifs virtually cease to occupy Paul; only love will again appear in the remainder of the letter (5:13). Of the three, Paul displays hope most prominently in four ways. First, it is identified alone with a piece of armor. Second, its syntax is different in that it is an accusative in apposition to *perikephalaian* ("helmet") rather than a genitive. Third, by ending the series it is in the most prominent position. Fourth, it is further specified as being a hope that has salvation as its object, which conforms more closely to Isa 59:17.

5:9. *because God did not destine us for wrath.* With *hoti* ("because"; cf. *gar* in v 7) Paul grounds his statement about the eschatological dimension of their hope of salvation by placing it in the soteriological purpose of God. The reason they must put on their armor and be sober is that God does not want them to experience his wrath, but to obtain salvation. Their end is to be different from those who will not escape judgment because they are not eschatologically alert (v 3). Once more an affirmation is made antithetically, beginning with a negative. The construction *tithesthai tina eis ti* ("to appoint someone to or for something," with the middle serving as an active) is found in the LXX (e.g., Ps 66:9; Micah 1:7; 4:7) and in OT quotations in the NT (e.g., Isa 49:6 in Acts 13:47; cf. 1 Pet 2:8) and has been regarded as Semitic (Rigaux: 1956: 570; 1975: 333).

Furthermore, since the precise formulation occurs only here in Paul, the construction has been thought to support the view that Paul is using traditional material (Rigaux 1975), perhaps a baptismal confession (Harnisch, 123–24). The linguistic evidence, however, is not strong enough to support this hypothesis. Eight of the thirteen times Paul uses *tithesthai* it describes God's action (C. Maurer in *TDNT* 8.157). He also uses *keisthai*, which functions as the passive of *tithesthai*, in a similar construction (3:3; Phil 1:16), and Rom 4:17 quotes Gen 17:5 in a similar if not identical manner.

More significant than the syntactical construction is that Paul picks up the theme of God's initiative that began in 1:4 and has continued throughout the letter (e.g., 1:4; 2:2, 4, 12, 16; 3:3; 4:7, 9, 14; see on 1:2 for the emphasis on God in the letter). He has not mentioned God since 4:14, but now he places all that he has said about living soberly within God's plan of salvation. This statement should be self-evident to the Thessalonians (cf. v 7), for the message they originally accepted promised them deliverance from the coming judgment (1:10). With "us" Paul does not imply a contrast to others who are destined for destruction (see Rom 9:22, *skeuē orgēs katērtismena eis apōleian*, "vessels of wrath prepared for destruction"). The contrast to "the rest" is to their manner of life (v 6), not their place in God's design.

*but to obtain salvation through our Lord Jesus Christ.* The contrast is stated emphatically in a construction that highlights the contrast: *ouk . . . eis orgēn alla eis peripoiēsin sōterias* (lit., "not for wrath but for the obtaining of salvation"). With the power of antithesis Paul defines the object of their hope of salvation as the culmination of God's plan. The noun *peripoiēsis* is rare, and its meaning here has been disputed. It can mean "possession" (Eph 1:14) and, with a genitive following, as here, either "preserving" (Heb 10:39; cf. 2 Chr 14:12) or "obtaining" (2 Thess 2:14). Although the last meaning is rare, it does occur in nonbiblical Greek, and most commentators understand it to have the same significance the cognate verb has (e.g., Acts 20:28; 1 Tim 3:13). Some commentators think it means "preserve" here (Rigaux 1956: 570–71; Holtz 1986: 228–29), but 1:10 would seem to point to a future deliverance from a future wrath.

Paul began the larger eschatological section by referring to what God would do for those who had fallen asleep and then turned to Christ's role in the eschatological drama (4:14). Here too he moves from God's design to Christ as the medium of salvation (*dia*, cf. 4:14). The prepositional phrase goes, not with "destine," but with "to obtain salvation" (cf. Rom 5:9, *sōthēsometha di' autou, apo tēs orgēs*, "we shall be saved through him from wrath"; see further on 1:10). For the full christological title, see 1 Cor 15:57.

5:10. *who died for us.* Instead of referring to what Christ would do at the Parousia, as might be expected, or Christ's resurrection as preparation for the Parousia, Paul refers rather to Christ's death, with which he had begun his eschatological section (4:14). There is no real difference in meaning between *peri* ("for") and *hyper*, which is read by some manuscripts. The Christology reflected in the participial clause (*tou apothanontos peri hymōn* ["who died for us"]) appears in the earliest strata of Christian tradition (H. Riesenfeld in *TDNT* 8.509). It is present in Jesus' words instituting the Lord's Supper (Matt 26:28; Mark 14:24; 1 Cor 11:24) and elsewhere describes Jesus' ministry (Matt 20:28; Mark 10:45). Paul had received and preached the tradition that Jesus died for sins (1 Cor 15:3). The formulation is prominent in Paul's reflection on the saving work of Christ (e.g., Rom 4:25; 2 Cor 5:14, 15, 21; Gal 3:12), but there is no such extended reflection here. Elsewhere in the letter, Christ's death is merely mentioned (2:15; the consequences of his death are not explicitly drawn in 4:14).

*in order that, whether we are awake or asleep, we might live with him.* Rather than reflect on the vicarious nature of Christ's death, Paul continues with a final clause (*hina*, "in order that"; see Dahl 1976: 35, for the formula in preaching). The purpose of Christ's death for us is that whether (*ei*) we are awake or (*ei*) asleep we might live with him. A similar connection of *hina* with *zān* ("to live") is made in Rom 14:9 and 2 Cor 4:15 (see Martin 1986: 129–31, on the theological significance of *hyper* here). For the form of the antithesis (*eite . . . eite*), also of maintaining a relationship with Christ whether living or dead, see 2 Cor 5:6–9 (with *ean*, Rom 14:7–8).

The aorist *zēsōmen* is to be taken as future in sense, but it is not clear whether it simply expresses the fact of future life (Rigaux 1956: 573) or whether it is ingressive ("begin to live"; Best 1972: 218). In antithesis to *apothanontos*, it denotes the life for which Christ died (the similar paradox in 2 Cor 5:14–15 describes life in the present). This life is the salvation that Paul hopes to attain (cf. Rom 13:11; Phil 1:19). It presupposes Christ's resurrection and identification with him in baptism (Rom 6:3–5) as well as life in the Spirit (Rom 8:9–11), but once again Paul retains his focus on the issue at hand.

By concluding his eschatological section in this way, Paul returns to the themes of 4:13–18 and his purpose in providing his readers with ground for comfort. The death of Christ (4:14) now finds a purpose differently and more explicitly stated: life with him. The theme of being with the Lord (4:14, 17) concludes the larger section, but the *esometha* of 4:17 is changed to *zēsōmen* to add the dimension of life as that in which salvation consists. And he returns again to the two groups of believers at the Parousia (*hoi nekroi en Christō* or *hoi koimōthentes* and *hoi zōntes*; 4:13, 14, 16), only now he describes them with two different words (*grēgorein* and *katheudein*). These two verbs do not normally describe life and death (see Lautenschlager, 40–51, who does not, however, do justice to Ps 87:6 and Dan 12:2), but their use here is suggested by their appearance in the exhortation in vv 6–8 and by the use of euphemism in consolation (see NOTE on 4:13). The details having been provided, Paul ends the section with a formulation that expresses triumphant confidence: "whether we are awake or asleep, we (shall) live with him."

5:11. *Therefore, exhort one another and build one another up, one on one, as indeed you are doing.* The eschatological section having come to an end, Paul now makes a transition to the final section of the letter, dealing with the mutual ministry of the congregation. This verse could as well be treated with vv 12–22, as the introduction to that section. In terms of form, however, it belongs with 4:13–5:10. It is in consequence of being the eschatological community that the Thessalonians are to edify each other (see Koester 1990: 446–47, 450–54 on community). The *dio* ("Therefore") connects the sentence to the preceding. It is parallel to *hōste parakaleite allēlous* of 4:18, which draws out the practical consequences of 4:13–17, but *dio parakaleite* here is related to the entire section, 4:13–5:10 (Holtz 1986: 233; Plevnik 1997: 116).

The second bracket of the *inclusio* in 5:8–10 (cf. 4:13–14) has brought the eschatological section to a close, and Paul now turns to draw out the practical consequences of the sober life in communal terms (*parakaleite allēlous*, "exhort one another"). He does not say, "with these words," as he did in 4:18, and it cannot be assumed that he has in mind 4:13–5:10 as the content of the exhortation he urges his readers to engage in (so P. Müller, 157). Exhortation is here much wider in scope than it is in 4:18.

The *parakaleite* picks up the note of comfort implied in 4:18, but it takes on a special meaning by being coupled with *oikodomeite* ("build . . . up"), which interprets it (see NOTE on 2:3). What this edifying exhortation consists of is specified in vv 12–22, where Paul heaps up terms from the lexicon of exhortation that he uses pastorally: beseech (*erōtān*), labor (*kopiān*), care (*proistasthai*), admonish (*nouthetein*), exhort (*parakalein*), admonish (*nouthetein*), comfort (*paramythe-isthai*), help (*antechesthai*), be patient (*makrothymein*), test (*dokimazein*). Theodoret correctly understood that Paul was urging his readers to communal psychagogy, of which paraenesis was part (*Interpretation of 1 Thessalonians* 5 [PG 82:653]; cf. Oecomenius, *Commentary on 1 Thessalonians* 6 [PG 119:100]). Paul's own paraenetic style, with its pastoral function, emerges once more in the complimentary "as indeed you are doing" (see NOTE on 4:1).

Paul claimed in 2:11–12 that he had followed the same practice when he was in Thessalonica, thus providing his readers with a model to follow. The major difference is that in 2:11–12, at the end of his self-presentation, he spoke of what he had done for the congregation; here he is concerned with reciprocity within the congregation. The notion of reciprocity is present in Paul's conception of *oikodomein* (cf. Rom 14:19, *hē oikodomē . . . eis allēlous*), in *allēlous* ("one another"), and in *heis ton hena* ("one on one"). The translation takes *allēlous* as the object of *parakaleite* and *oikodomeite* and understands *heis ton hena* differently from most commentators and translators, who understand it simply as equivalent to *allēlous*. The phrase is difficult, and it may be Semitic (BDF §247.4), but it does appear elsewhere (e.g., *Test. of Job* 27:3). It does not appear to be different in meaning from *heis pros hena* (Plato, *Laws* 1.626C; cf. also *heis hyper tou henos* in 1 Cor 4:6). The closest parallel is that in Theocritus, *Idylls* 22.65 (*heis heni*; cf. Maximus of Tyre, *Oration* 38.4, *anēr andri* ["man to man"]). What is clear, and important, is that it describes individual attention to each other and that it cannot be subsumed under *allēlous*. In 2:11, Paul claimed that he had treated his converts *hena hekaston*, as individuals; now he wants them, as individuals, to build up other individuals.

## COMMENT

Paul continues his eschatological exhortation, but now he provides even less information about the end than he did in 4:13–17. Timothy appears to have brought the news that the Thessalonians were being influenced by false prophets, whose teaching was affecting the way Paul's converts lived. No longer expecting the Parousia to be imminent and, in Paul's eyes, their moral perspective no longer determined by it, their behavior was similar to that of "the rest." In practical terms, it meant that they grieved for their dead like pagans did (4:13) and, more generally, that they lived without eschatological vigilance.

As he had done in 4:13–17, so in 5:1–10, Paul makes extensive use of eschatological traditions from the OT, Jewish, and Christian apocalyptic, and from the Synoptic tradition, particularly a tradition that he shares with Luke 21:34–36. What is striking in his use of these traditions, as it was in 4:13–17, is how restrained he is in using them. His purpose is hortatory rather than didactic, and that determines what he selects and how he reduces it to fit his immediate needs. Equally striking is that with the Jewish and Christian apocalyptic traditions he uses important philosophical terms negatively, to characterize false teaching, and positively, to exhort his readers to the sober life.

## The False Prophets

While Paul's moral exhortation (vv 4–10) is general, his introduction in vv 1–3 provides the most specific information about circumstances in Thessalonica and contains some of the sharpest language in the letter. In 2:16 he declares that wrath comes upon those who prevent him from preaching the gospel; here, sudden, inescapable ruin comes upon those, evidently Christian prophets, who propound a message of peace and security that provided perspective for a life that, in Paul's estimation, is like that of "the rest." To counter their false prophecy, Paul introduces the prophetic expectation of the Day of the Lord, with its themes of imminence, darkness, and judgment and of day and light, which provide the basis for the exhortation that follows.

There were prophets in Thessalonica whose message Paul wanted to be carefully tested (5:20–21), and it is likely that it was they who were seeking more precise knowledge about the eschatological plan and indulged their curiosity about "the times and the seasons." That prophets, Christian as well as those of Israel, sought deeper knowledge of the divine mystery of redemption, which included a knowledge of the divine chronology, is a conviction Paul shared with other NT writers (1 Pet 1:10–12; Eph 3:4–7; 1 Cor 2:6–16; for the same language, see Rom 11:25–35; Hunt, 63–70).

When Paul writes about prophecy in 1 Cor 14, he thinks primarily in terms of edifying, encouraging, and consoling (v 3). But prophets performed these functions as they received revelations (v 30), and it is as a prophet with an apocalyptic message from the Lord that Paul himself comforted the Thessalonians in 4:13–18 by clarifying certain details of the coming of the Lord. According to some scholars, in vv 1–3 Paul also speaks in prophetic form (P. Müller, 148–57), but that is not entirely convincing. What Paul criticizes about some people in Thessalonica is not that they prophesy (cf. 5:19–20), but the content of their teaching, which they derived from calculations about "times and seasons," and the effect it had on their lives. Their teaching had the effect of delaying the Parousia and causing the Thessalonians no longer to live in view of its impending arrival.

## *"Peace and Security"*

An interpretation of this phrase that has gained popularity in recent years holds that Paul uses a slogan that described the *Pax Romana*, the peace imposed by political and military means on the world by Rome and maintained by its authority. The term *Pax Romana* is first used by Seneca, Paul's contemporary, who celebrates the importance of the emperor:

> For he is the bond by which the commonwealth is united, the breath of life which these many thousands draw, who in their own strength would be only a burden to themselves and the prey of others if the great mind of the empire shall be withdrawn . . . . Such a calamity would be the destruction of the Roman peace [*Romanae pacis*], such a calamity will force the fortune of a mighty people to its downfall. (*On Mercy* 1.4.1–2)

Seneca's idealistic view was tempered by others who commented on the bloodshed by which the peace had been attained and was being maintained (see Wengst, 11–19, who stresses military power as the dominant factor). Nevertheless, "peace and security" became a slogan to express both political stability and the beneficence of Roman rule (Tacitus, *Histories* 2.12; 4.74, end; Josephus, *Jewish Antiquities* 14.160; 15.348; OGIS 613; see Hendrix 1991).

In his own life, Paul did not enjoy peace and security. His many hardships included persecution, imprisonment, and flogging by Roman authorities (2 Cor 4:9; Phil 1:14; 2 Cor 11:25; cf. Acts 16:22). This violent character of Roman rule contributed to a negative assessment of the Romans by Paul, which is evident, in one interpretation, in 1 Thess 5:3 (Wengst, 73–78). According to this interpretation, "Peace and security" is a slogan of non-Christians who wish to preserve the present order. Paul does not counter this claim by pointing to his own experience but shows it to be an illusion when viewed from the perspective of the Day of the Lord. In the verses that follow, the apocalyptic Paul claims that the *Pax Romana* stands on the side of night and darkness. The surmise that the slogan here is political is not founded exegetically but is assumed on the basis of the political currency of the slogan, as is the claim that it was proclaimed by non-Christians.

Another reading of "Peace and security" as referring to the Roman peace, indeed, as a frontal attack on it, does give close attention to relevant circumstances in the city of Thessalonica, to the Thessalonian correspondence, and to the relevant passages in Acts (Donfried 1985). The argument is that Thessalonica's fortunes were dependent on Roman interests and that it was to the advantage of the Thessalonians to honor their Roman benefactors alongside their gods. In a climate influenced by this "political theology," it is argued, elements of the Christian proclamation could have been misunderstood and proved confrontational: the term "kingdom of God" (1 Thess 2:12), as well as other terms that could have had political connotations (*parousia, apantēsis*, 4:15–17; even *euangelion*, 1:5; 2:2, 4, 8, 9; 3:2). Such preaching, it is claimed, met with opposition that caused affliction (*thlipsis*) and suffering (1:6; 2:14; 3:3, 4), and probably martyrdom (4:13–18). This would make understandable Paul's attack on the *Pax Romana*, an attack that would have been particularly forceful if Paul had been correctly understood (Elliott, 190) as attacking the Roman order in his preaching!

There are a number of difficulties with this interpretation. Foremost is that the hypothesis of a persecuted church, to a degree that makes martyrdom a likelihood, has no foundation in the text. The texts referred to in support of the hypothesis (e.g., 1:6; 2:14; 3:3–4) can more naturally be understood otherwise. Furthermore, *parousia* and *apantēsis* should not have been provocative, even if they did have political connotations, for they describe actions that result in the departure of Christians to heaven from the arena where they might have been thought subversive. Finally, the apocalyptic context in which the "slogan" is set is not sufficiently taken into consideration with respect to both its meaning and function.

"Peace and security" is Paul's formulation to describe the erroneous message of some people in Thessalonica and is influenced by the cry, "Peace, peace, where there is no peace," of the OT false prophets. Instead of repeating *eirēnē*, however, Paul uses another word, *asphaleia*, that occurs elsewhere in the NT only in Luke 1:4 and Acts 5:23. It has been suggested, without substantial proof, that he derived it from apocalyptic tradition (Rigaux 1975: 324–25), but other explanations have been given more weight. A more likely explanation derives from the fact that *asphaleia* is an Epicurean word that describes an attitude in Thessalonica. As Paul had used Epicurean terms to describe his readers' conduct in 4:11 and 13 (De Witt 1954a: 85; 1954b: 41–53), so he does here.

Epicureans, who sought a peaceful life (Lucretius, *On the Nature of Things* 5.1120), found it in association with friends. According to Epicurus, "The most unalloyed source of security [*asphaleia*] from men, which is attained to some extent by a certain force of expulsion, is in fact the security [*asphaleia*] which results from a quiet life [*hēsychias*] and the retirement from the world" (*Principal Doctrine* 14; cf. 7). This security is provided by friendship (*Principal Doctrine* 28; cf. Philodemus, *On Frankness* Fragment 78; see Epictetus, *Discourse* 2.20.8), and it is confined to this life, for it is a security from people, and there is no security against death (Vatican Fragment 31). Furthermore, "There is no profit in attaining security [*asphaleian*] in relation to people, if things above and things beneath the earth and indeed all in the boundless universe remain matters of suspicion" (*Principal Doctrine* 13). What is in mind is fear of the gods and mythical stories about postmortem existence (*Principal Doctrine* 12). The Epicurean focus is totally on life with friends in the here and now.

By characterizing the existence proclaimed by the false prophets in Epicurean categories, Paul delivers a stinging criticism of them. Given the eschatological dimensions of their fundamental beliefs, the Thessalonians could not have described themselves in these loaded Epicurean terms. It is rather part of Paul's rhetoric, in stating the issues as sharply as possible, that he uses Epicurean characterizations when applying apocalyptic traditions to his readers' circumstances. His readers in his eyes would appear to have been in danger of or even to have succumbed to finding a security in their newfound community and relations with each other that did not sufficiently take into consideration the eschatological dimension of their existence. To counter this misconception, Paul uses the apocalyptic traditions that they knew and in 5:1–10 stresses the eschatological reality of their present existence (Koester 1990: 451–54). Part of that reality is that judgment is present on the false teachers (v 3) as it is on those who oppose Paul's preaching (2:16). Throughout the letter, Paul reminds them of the various eschatological aspects of their faith and existence (1:10; 2:12, 19–20; 3:11–13; 4:6; 5:23).

## The Sober Life

Paul added *nēphōmen* ("let us be sober") to *grēgorōmen* in v 6 and used it by itself in v 8 to describe the vigilant eschatological life. *Nēphein* also takes over the place of *grēgorein* elsewhere in the NT (e.g., 1 Pet 1:13; 4:7; but see 5:8), mostly taking a meaning from moral philosophical discourse (see 1 Pet 4:7, *sōphrōnēsate . . . kai nēpsate*; cf. 2 Tim 4:5; *nēphalios*: 1 Tim 3:2, 11; Titus 2:2) but does not always do so (2 Tim 2:26; 1 Pet 5:8). Paul's use here is to be seen in the context of the philosophical notion of soberness.

In the figurative sense, the subject of *nēphein* is *logismos* ("reason") (Philo, *On Drunkenness* 166; Diogenes Laertius, *The Lives of Eminent Philosophers* 10.132; See O. Bauernfeind in *TDNT* 4.937). It is used in a general moral sense (e.g., Ps.-Crates, *Epistle* 3; Ps.-Cebes, *Table* 9.3; Maximus of Tyre, *Oration* 3.3) but especially describes the quality of mind that philosophy makes possible. In protrepsis, the assumption behind the use of the term is stated by Seneca: "Let us, therefore, arouse ourselves, that we may be able to correct our mistakes. Philosophy, however, is the only power that can stir us, the only power that can shake off our deep slumber. Devote yourself to philosophy!" (*Epistle* 53.8).

The conversion to philosophy is then described in similar terms. So the young Polemo was said to grow sober (*anenēphen*) as he listened to a lecture on virtue and temperance and, sobered up (*anenēpsen*) by philosophy, awakened, as it were, from a deep sleep (Lucian, *The Double Indictment* 16–17; cf. *Hermotimus* 83: "it is as if I sobered up from drunkenness"). Another convert describes his experience as looking up, "as it were, out of the murky atmosphere of my past life to a clear sky and a great light," and his new life as not drunkenness, but sobriety and temperance (Lucian, *Nigrinus* 5; cf. Philo, *Allegorical Interpretation* 2.60). The themes then continue in paraenesis, as in Marcus Aurelius, *Meditation* 6.31: "Be sober [*anenēphe*] and come to your senses, and being roused again from sleep and realizing that they were but dreams that beset you, now awaking [*egrēgorōs*], again look at . . . ."

That the experience of conversion is behind Paul's language, particularly present in the light symbolism (cf. 2 Cor 4:1–6; Acts 13:47; 26:18; Col 1:10–14), has suggested to some scholars that we here have to do with traditional baptismal paraenesis (Baumgarten, 218; Harnisch, 121). However, the way in which Paul has been introducing philosophical elements, particularly Epicurean ones, at decisive points in his eschatological discussion requires us to examine whether the Epicurean viewpoint may not have particular force here.

It was well known in antiquity that for Epicurus pleasure was the beginning and end of the blessed life (Diogenes Laertius, *The Lives of Eminent Philosophers* 10.128). Epicurus himself thought pleasure to be sober (*sobria*) and abstemious (*sicca*) (Seneca, *On the Happy Life* 12.4; further on sobriety, Philodemus, *On the Good King according to Homer* 3.28). It was to be found in company with friends, friendship going "dancing around the world proclaiming to us all to awake to the praises of a happy life" (Vatican Fragment 52). Epicurus's later critics did not hide their snideness in referring to Epicurean soberness (e.g., Plutarch, *Against Colotes* 1123F).

The majority of people simply equated Epicurean pleasure with sensuality, and even Plutarch, who knew better, was content to repeat what was popularly said about the Epicureans (*That Epicurus Actually Makes a Pleasant Life Impossible* 1100CD). Epicurus tried to explain that what he meant by pleasure was not sensuality, but what was produced by sober reasoning (*nēphōn logismos*) (Diogenes Laertius, *The Lives of Eminent Philosophers* 10.132). For most people, however, the slogan "Let us eat, drink and be merry, for tomorrow we die" typified the Epicurean life (Ameling).

Paul joins the anti-Epicurean critics in 1 Corinthians without mentioning them. In 10:7, he uses one form of the slogan, which happens to coincide in form with Exod 32:6, to describe the dissolute life. He uses a different form of the slogan, which coincides with Isa 22:13, in 1 Cor 15:32 in his argument about the resurrection. Paul shows in 15:31–34 that he shares the anti-Epicurean bias of his age, and he uses the slogan in an *ad hominem* manner in assuming that a belief in the eschatological resurrection should govern one's moral life. The quotation from Menander's *Thais* in v 33 warns the Corinthians against evil associations, which, in the context, means those who live an Epicurean-like life. He closes the pericope polemically with the challenge to sober up (*eknēpsate*) and with other terms that have an Epicurean bearing (Malherbe 1989: 84–86). This is the only place outside of 1 Thess 5:6, 8 where Paul uses a form of *nēphein*.

The issue in 1 Thess 5:1–11 is not the resurrection but the danger of living without an expectation of the Parousia that transforms the believers' present existence. By using Epicurean terms, Paul subtly but clearly warns his readers of the danger inherent in their acceptance of the false prophets' message. He therefore uses *nēphein* with an edge, but not yet with the charged anti-Epicurean polemic that would characterize later Christian comment (Schmid, 880–83). The Epicurean elements in the letter are clear enough (see NOTES on 4:11, 13; 5:3), as they are in 1 Cor 15:31–34, but it is not equally clear why Paul introduced them into the discussion. It is unlikely that the Thessalonians thought of themselves as having an affinity with the Epicureans in matters of eschatology and described themselves in Epicurean terms. It is probably Paul who, aware of the general disapproval of the Epicureans, used their language to state matters as sharply as possible.

## Building Each Other Up

Paul provided pastoral care to the Thessalonians when he was with them and in the process provided them with an example to follow. While never diminishing the importance of the relationship between himself and his churches, he gave detailed directions on how they should "pastorally" care for each other (e.g., Rom 15:1–7; 1 Cor 5, 14; Gal 6:1–5; 2 Thess 3:6–15), and such care is assumed as a matter of fact in his letters (e.g., Phil 2:1; see Glad, 185–212). In his own practice, Paul had used the principles and devices of contemporary psychagogy, and he will do so in detail in vv 12–22.

It was Epicurus who had first developed a system of psychagogy, but by the time of Paul it was used by people irrespective of their philosophic allegiance (Malherbe 1987: 81–88; see COMMENT on vv 12–16). The goal of psychagogy was to develop people morally, spiritually, and intellectually, and for the most part this was thought of in individualistic terms. A communal dimension was added when psychagogy took place in settings like the school of Epictetus and especially in Epicurean fellowships. In the latter, practices were developed that aimed at the development of the individual within a circle of friends who exercised individual responsibility for other individuals. In the process, the community itself was strengthened (Glad, 161–81).

It is important to note that this introduction to Paul's psychagogic instructions that follow marks a transition from the preceding eschatological section. The *dio* ("Therefore") in v 11 shows that Paul considers Christian communal psychagogy a consequence of the Thessalonians' eschatological existence and that its goal is not the fulfillment of human capacities, as it was in pagan psychagogy.

According to 2:11–12, Paul had focused his care on individuals, and now he wants the Thessalonians themselves to do the same. He urges other churches to exercise the same concern (e.g., Rom 14:1; 15:1–6; 1 Cor 4:6; 5:5; 2 Cor 2:5–11; Gal 6:1–5; Phil 4:2–3; 2 Thess 1:3). He does not visualize care as flowing in one direction, from a defined group of persons to the larger congregation, but conceives of the activity as reciprocal (see Glad, 171–77, 196–206, on "rotational psychagogy"). The activity is thought of in functional rather than institutional terms and will be given greater precision in vv 12–22. Here he subsumes the entire activity under the rubric of edification (*oikodomein*).

This is the first time in his extant letters that Paul uses the word *oikodomein*, and he does so as though he expected its metaphorical meaning to be understood. The term has an obvious applicability to personal development and was so used by moral philosophers (Epictetus, *Discourse* 2.15.8–9; Plutarch, *On Progress in Virtue* 85F–86A; *On the Fortune of the Romans* 320B). Basic to Paul's use of the term are a concern for another's good (Rom 15:2; 1 Cor 8:1; 10:23–24; 14:17), that it is communal in nature, and that it is a person-to-person activity among all members of the congregation (Rom 14:19; 15:1–2; 1 Thess 5:11; 1 Cor 8:10 [ironic]; 14:17; see Kuck, 172–74; O. Michel in *TDNT* 5.141). In 1 Corinthians, Paul also stresses the relationship between the edification of the individual and the building of the congregation as an entity (3:10–15, the church as a building; 14:4–5, 12, the assembly [ekklēsia]). The special circumstances in Corinth caused him to identify prophecy with edifying in chap. 14, but the other references in the letter show that edification of individuals as well as the assembly should be the goal of all the Corinthians.

Paul does not here show the same interest in the edification of the church that he does in 1 Cor 3 and 14. Thessalonian individuals are to care for individuals without reference to the larger entity of the congregation. The detailed psychagogy that Paul desires of his readers sounds remarkably like that of the moralists from whom he derived the technique. Completely different from them is that Paul's readers are to engage in it as children of the Day who soberly look forward to living with the Lord Jesus Christ. That is to be the goal of their care for each other, not the development of character or the fulfillment of human potential.

# E. ON INTRACOMMUNAL RELATIONS, 5:12–22

◆

Paul devotes the last section of his paraenesis to relations within the church, as he also does at the end of Romans (12:1–15:13) and Galatians (5:1–6:10). Much of the subject matter of this section (particularly vv 14–18) is so similar in content and form to other NT community paraenesis (e.g., Heb 13:1–7; 1 Pet 3:8–12; Jas) that most commentators surmise that Paul is using traditional material of general applicability that is not addressed to specific conditions in the Thessalonian church.

A minority view holds that Paul shapes the traditional material in light of the situation in Thessalonica (Laub 1973: 201; Marshall 1983: 146). Thus the reference to the disorderly in v 14 is thought to refer to 4:10, and vv 12–13 and vv 15–22 also seem to have concrete situations in Thessalonica in view (Holtz 1986: 240–41). Another view is that in referring to the ataktoi ("disorderly"), the oligopsychoi ("discouraged"), and the astheneis ("weak"), Paul is specifying three groups whom he has had in mind since the beginning of his paraenesis in 4:1 (the idlers in 4:11–12; the discouraged in 4:13–18; the weak in 4:3–8) (Frame, 196). This argument has not met with approval, but there is evidence for the view that Paul's advice here is related to the rest of the letter and so to circumstances in Thessalonica.

To begin with, the connection between the ataktoi and 4:12 is strong. The behavior Paul urges there, that the readers behave in seemly fashion (euschēmonōs), is the opposite of being disorderly, and euschēmonōs and its cognates appear with various forms of taxis ("order") to describe social behavior (see NOTE on 4:12). Furthermore, of the Thessalonians' activities that he mentions here, kopian ("labor") and ergon ("work") formed part of his first thanksgiving for his readers

(1:3). In addition to describing the Thessalonians' former conduct, these words described Paul's own ministry, which is presented in the letter as a model for theirs (his work and labor on their behalf [2:9; 3:5] and his comforting of them [2:12]). Finally, Paul's advice on prophecy (5:19–22) is put in perspective by his claim to speak as a prophet (4:15) and his warning against the erroneous message of false prophets (5:3).

The style of this section differs from the rest of the letter. It contains fifteen imperatives in addition to an infinitival construction (*erōtōmen* with *eidenai* and *hēgeisthai* in v 12) that has an imperatival force (see vv 12–14). The imperatives initially stand at the beginning of short sentences of equal length (vv 13b–15); then, apparently for the sake of variety, they stand at the end of such sentences (vv 16–22). After vv 12–13, there is no syntactical connection between these short sentences. These stylistic features, plus the content of the brief statements, which consist of self-evidently good advice, give to the entire section the appearance of a collection of unconnected gnomic sentences haphazardly strung together. The style should not, however, lead to the misperception that the sentences are not related to each other or to the situation in Thessalonica.

The large section of advice falls into two parts. The first part (vv 12–15) specifies how the reciprocal edification (v 11) is to be carried out, giving attention to the nature of the care and the emotional condition or disposition of those who receive the care. The second part (vv 16–22), which ends the paraenesis of the letter, gives directions on one particular function in the church, that of prophecy. It differs from the preceding advice on intracommunal relations in that it is not concerned with individuals and their condition or attitudes, but with a particular spiritual activity and how it is to be evaluated.

# 1. ON "PASTORAL CARE" AMONG MEMBERS OF THE CHURCH, 5:12–15

This section is divided into two parts, the first giving directions on how to treat those individuals who provide "pastoral care" (vv 12–13), the second directing the individuals who provide the care (vv 14–15) (see COMMENT on "Pastoral Care" and "Psychagogy"). The two sections are similarly structured. Each begins with a word describing Paul's wish (*erōtōmen* ["we beseech"] in v 12; *parakaloumen* ["we exhort"] in v 14), followed by *adelphoi* ("brethren") in vv 12 and 14. In the first section, complementary infinitives (*eidenai* ["to give recognition"] in v 12; *hēgeisthai* ["to esteem"] in v 13) have imperatival force; in the second, four imperatives are used (*noutheteite* ["admonish"]; *paramytheisthe* ["comfort"]; *antechesthe* ["help"]; *makrothymeisthe* ["be patient"], v 14).

The symmetry between the two sections is carried to the conclusion of each section, where imperatives (*eirēneuete* ["be at peace"] in v 13; *horāte* ["see to it"] in v 15) introduce cautions about communal relations in light of what has just been said. The conclusion to the second section is longer than that to the first.

It is antithetic in form, and the second member of the antithesis ("but at all times pursue what is good for one another and for all," v 15) may be a summarizing conclusion to the entire section, vv 12–15.

## TRANSLATION

5 ¹²We beseech you, brethren, to give recognition to those who labor among you and care for you in the Lord and admonish you, ¹³and to esteem them very highly in love because of their work. Be at peace among yourselves. ¹⁴And we exhort you, brethren, admonish the disorderly, comfort the discouraged, help the weak, be patient with all. ¹⁵See to it that no one renders evil for evil to anyone, but at all times pursue what is good for one another and for all.

## NOTES

5:12. *We beseech you, brethren, to give recognition to.* The postpositive particle *de* could be resumptive ("now") or adversative ("but"). If it were the latter, it would introduce something in antithesis to v 11, Paul perhaps addressing persons who had a special responsibility to the congregation in contrast to the reciprocal care of the church in general (Masson, 71). The *de* has also been thought to signal a new subject the Thessalonians had raised in a letter to Paul to which Paul now gives his attention (Faw), but the argument that *de* or *peri de* ("now concerning") marks a response to a letter is not persuasive (see COMMENT on 3:6–10). The particle rather signals an expansion of v 11 (Hainz, 42–43; Best 1972: 223), and need therefore not be translated.

Paul uses *adelphoi* ("brethren") in transitions elsewhere in the letter (2:1, 17; 4:1, 13; 5:1; cf. Rom 12:1; 1 Cor 10:1; 15:1; Phil 3:1). For the significance of its use with *erōtōmen* (cf. v 14), see NOTE on 4:1. In encouraging members of the church in their relations with each other, Paul himself sets the tone by being gentle rather than peremptory.

The complementary infinitive *eidenai* does not have the same meaning it does in 4:4 (so Frame, 192), nor does the usual meaning, "to know," make sense in this context. It is best to think of it as meaning "to respect," "to honor," "to recognize," or "to give recognition to" someone. The word has this meaning in Aelius Aristides, *Oration* 35.35, and in Ign *Smyrn* 9:1 it is used interchangeably with *timān* ("to honor"). Paul expresses the same idea with *epiginōskein* in 1 Cor 16:18 and with *entimous echete* in Phil 2:29 (1 Tim 5:17 is not quite the same).

*those who labor among you and care for you in the Lord and admonish you.* The persons to be given recognition are described with one definite article followed by three participles ("labor," "care," "admonish"), each followed by a personal pronoun ("among you," "for you," "you"). Only the second participial clause is further qualified, with the addition of "in the Lord." That only one article is used indicates that Paul has one group of people in mind. They are not described in terms of office but in terms of the functions they perform (Hainz, 37–38; Laub 1973: 31). The repetition of the personal pronouns stresses the personal relationship between those who exhort and those who receive their exhortation (for the personal element, see NOTES and COMMENT on 1:5–6); they do not signal a distinction between the two groups (Rigaux 1956: 576).

The relationship between the functions is not clear. Since the *kai* ("and") is coordinate, all three participles are grammatically on the same level and may simply describe different functions that the individuals in mind perform. If, however, the article is taken to be related particularly to the first participle (*kopiōntas*), which is then understood to describe a comprehensive activity, the other two (*proistamenous* and *nouthetountas*) could be subordinate to the first, giving greater specificity to it (thus Best 1972: 226; Holtz 1986: 242). That only those two functions specify the first could indicate that Paul thought they had particular relevance to his readers (thus Frame, 192).

There is no compelling reason, however, why the last two participles should be subsumed under the first. Paul goes on in v 14 to mention other functions that are performed. The definite article therefore does not refer to a group delimited by the three functions mentioned, but to people who do such things. It is clear that in vv 12–14 Paul is interested in functions that are performed rather than in defining one group of individuals whose prerogative, duty, or special ministry it is to engage in communal care. These functions describe what certain individuals do but are not confined to one group of people from whom care flows to another who receive it. The connection with v 11 must be taken seriously; there Paul is emphatic that the edification, to which he gives precision here, is reciprocal. It is when they give the care that they are to be given recognition. At another time they may be the ones who receive care and admonition. The functions have a profound impact on the community, and Paul is very careful in vv 12–14 to clarify the relationship within which pastoral care is given and how it is to be given.

First in the list of functions, and somewhat different in nature from the others, is labor. Commentators have found it difficult to decide what Paul meant by *kopian* ("to labor"). Paul used the verb and noun of his own hard, painful physical labor (e.g., 1 Cor 4:12; 2 Cor 6:5; 11:23, 27; 1 Thess 2:9; 2 Thess 3:8) and, figuratively, of his own evangelical activity (e.g., 1 Cor 15:10; Gal 4:11; Phil 2:16; cf. Col 1:29) and that of others (e.g., Rom 6:6, 12; 1 Cor 16:16) (see Harnack 1928). The noun is only rhetorically different from *ergon* ("work"), which also describes missionary activity (cf. v 13; 1 Cor 15:58; see NOTE on 1:3). The activity here, however, has been thought to be of a more general nature, perhaps to help the poor or ill (von Dobschütz 1909: 216; cf. Acts 20:35), although even that interpretation has been thought too restrictive (Henneken, 70–71). Earlier in the letter, Paul had used the noun to describe the Thessalonians' (1:3) and his own (3:5) ministry of the word, and this is the most likely activity he has in mind here (cf. 1 Tim 5:17, *hoi kopiōntes en logō kai didaskalia* ["those laboring in word and teaching"]).

The labor here is not directed to the congregation as the other two participial actions are but takes place among them. Had the labor been directed at the church, Paul would have written *eis hymās* ("for you") as he does in Rom 16:6; Gal 4:11. This supports the identification of the labor as missionizing and provides a glimpse of the Thessalonians' congregational life. We do not know that the Thessalonians preached in public or that Christians normally did so; the private settings in which they met were where they evangelized. According to Acts 17:6–9, the church in Thessalonica was identified with the house of Jason, and it is likely that the church was still meeting there or in another patron's house when Paul wrote to them (see pages 60–61, 63–64; Malherbe 1987: 7–17). Paul reminded the Thessalonians in 2:9 of his physical labor and toil (*kopon kai mochthon*) while he preached the gospel to them.

As he had preached among them (*en hymin*, 1:5) when they were still pagans, so now some of their number, those who "labor," still do. Since the household, which accommodated the church, also contained the workshop, Paul's reference to "the outsiders" (4:12) is therefore sociological and not spatial. These pagans, who were in the Christians' sphere of influence, were likely the "all" Paul refers to in 3:12 and 5:14, 15. It should not appear strange that preaching aimed at conversion should be associated with edification of the church, as it is in vv 11–12. According to 1 Cor 14, prophecy, one of whose major functions is edification (vv 3, 5, 12, 17, 26), results in the conversion of an unbeliever who enters the Christian assembly (vv 23–25).

Interpreters, especially in the nineteenth century, have identified those who labor with presbyters (Ellicott, 76; Lightfoot 1908: 79, Milligan, 71; Findlay, 121), and the identification is still made by commentators who find it difficult to conceive of a nonhierarchical church (e.g., Rigaux 1956: 576–78; Staab, 42). It is unlikely, however, that a group of not more than a couple of dozen in number (Suhl, 115) would need such a formal structure. Neither is it likely that in the few months since its founding this group of former pagans would have appointed or had appointed for them by the apostle such leaders. Paul shows no interest in his early letters in a formal church structure (contrast Phil 1:1).

The attempt to make church officers out of "those who labor" is sometimes bolstered by giving a particular meaning to *proistanai* in the clause *(tous)* . . . *proistamenous hymōn* ("[those] . . . who care for you"). Here he turns from activity directed to nonbelievers to activity that has members of the church as its object.

The verb *proistanai* in Titus 3:8, 14 means to devote or apply oneself to something; in these two passages, it is to good works. Two other, more usual meanings are relevant to the NT, where the word occurs only in the Pauline literature. One meaning is to preside, in the sense of leading or governing, and the second is "to be concerned about," "to care," or "to aid" someone (B. Reicke in *TDNT* 6.700–3; BAGD, 707). The verb appears in Paul only in 1 Thess 5:12 and Rom 12:8, and its meaning, especially in the former passage, has been decided on by commentators in light of their views of the nature of Paul's congregations.

Those interpreters who think that the church in Thessalonica already had elders, who would be the persons who "labored," attach great significance to the first meaning. They point to the use of the word to describe various kinds of officials in ancient associations (Milligan, 72; MM, 541; Rigaux 1956: 577–78). Furthermore, they argue that the word clearly carries that meaning in the Pastoral Epistles, where it is used in lists of qualifications of certain officials in the church (1 Tim 3:4, 5, 12) or describes the activity of an official (1 Tim 5:17). In this view, the notion of care is not given up, but care is thought to have conferred leadership in a congregation with a developing structure but whose meetings must have been presided over by a definite group of officials (Hainz, 45–46).

In 1 Thess 5:12, the participles on either side of *proistanai* are not official designations, and neither is *proistanai* (so most commentators). Paul is concerned with activities or functions in vv 12–14, and there is no indication in this context or anywhere else in the letter that he has in view any officials in Thessalonica. The participle describes those who care for others in the congregation. It also does so in Rom 12:8, where extending such care is one of a series of gifts that describes functions that benefit others (exhorting, contributing, performing acts of mercy; see von Campenhausen 1969: 64–66). This is also the meaning of *prostatis*, used of Phoebe in Rom 16:2, the only place in the NT where the noun is used. There it has the more specialized meaning of "patron," someone who aided the church financially and possibly legally, something that Jason seems to have done in Thessalonica (Acts 17:6–9; see Malherbe 1987: 15).

The evidence of the Pastoral Epistles does not speak against such an understanding but in fact supports it. The word is not used a single time in these letters to designate an official but rather describes the way in which officials are to act, and the notion of care is present (Laub 1973: 71–72). The verb is used synonymously with *epimeleisthai* ("to care") in 1 Tim 3:4, 5, of which v 12 is a summary. One of a number of qualifications, it is an activity in which a man must be engaged if he wishes to be a bishop, but those attributes are not confined to aspirant bishops. In 1 Tim 5:17 *proistanai* describes an activity of an elder, which is not more exclusively the prerogative of the elder than laboring in the word and teaching, which are mentioned in the same verse.

The exact nature of the care Paul has in mind is not clear except that, in contrast to the laborers, the caring individuals benefit members of the church directly. It may have been the leadership provided by some of the earliest converts as Stephanas and his household did in Corinth (1 Cor 16:15–16; Laub 1973: 86). Administration was regarded by Paul as a gift (1 Cor 12:28), and their service may have consisted in guiding the church. They may have become leaders through their service to others (cf. Matt 20:25–28; Luke 22:27), but as 4:18; 5:11, 14–15 show, they are not a limited group. The context in 5:12 and in Rom 12:8 suggests, however, that the word more likely is to be understood in a pastoral or psychagogic way.

The notion of caring was firmly embedded in ancient psychagogy. A number of words other than *proistanai* was used to describe it. A common term was *ōphelein* ("to benefit"), which could include the idea of caring (cf. Plutarch, *On How to Tell a Flatterer from a Friend* 70DE; *On How to Profit from One's Enemies* 89B; Isocrates, *Panegyricus* 130). More to the point is that the ideal philosopher was seen as someone who cared for all people (*kēdemōn* and its cognates were frequently used, e.g., Dio Chrysostom, *Orations* 32.11, 26; 77/78.39; Epictetus, *Discourses* 3.22.81; 24.65). The quotation from Dio Chrysostom, *Ora-*

*tion* 77/78.38 in the COMMENT shows that psychagogy was the way in which the philosopher demonstrated his care.

If *proistanai* is understood to mean govern, the qualification that it takes place *en kyriō* ("in the Lord") may specify that the legitimacy or authority of those who engage in it comes from the Lord rather than Paul (Hainz, 45–46). This phrase has also been thought to be in opposition to *en hymin*, stressing that the service is delegated by the Lord rather than performed as a purely voluntary communal activity (Rigaux 1956: 578). There is, however, no hint of authority in the context; furthermore, what is grammatically parallel to *en hymin*, which is the object of the action expressed in the participle *kopiōntas*, is *hymōn*, not *en kyriō*. The phrase characterizes the care as Christian, given by virtue of the caregivers' relationship with Christ (cf. on 4:1; see von Dobschütz 1909: 217; Laub 1973: 72; Best 1972: 225–26). What is further significant is that this is the only theological qualification in vv 12–15 and that it stands at the point where Paul turns to the activity that explicitly has members of the church in view.

Whereas *proistanai* is general in meaning, *nouthetein* ("to admonish") and the Latin word group *admonere* refer to a form of exhortation that was a fixed part of ancient psychagogy (see esp. Seneca, *Epistle* 94.45, cf. 39). Its literal meaning is to instill sense in someone and teach him what should and should not be done (Ps.-Demetrius, *Epistolary Types* 7). The didactic element was thus present, but admonition was addressed more to the will than the mind (J. Behm in *TDNT* 4.1019).

Admonition was thought of as associated with frank and bold speech (*parresia*: Plutarch, *On How to Tell a Flatterer from a Friend* 50B, 72BE) and as such was to be engaged in out of goodwill and a desire to benefit those in error (Dio Chrysostom, *Orations* 51.5, 7; 73.13). Admonition began with self-examination and was particularly successful when the speaker, considering those he wished to benefit even closer than his relatives, spoke openly, "stressing his words as much as possible and increasing the relevance of his admonition [*tēn nouthesian*] and exhortation for himself and them alike" (Dio Chrysostom, *Oration* 77/78.42; Plutarch, *On How to Tell a Flatterer from a Friend* 71E–72A; see further NOTE on 2:2 and COMMENT on 2:3).

Admonition was especially appropriate to those who were making progress in their moral development but still fell short of perfection, who needed someone to lead the way (*praeire*) for them and to say, "Avoid this," or "Do that" (Seneca, *Epistle* 94.50–52). It included rebuke (*epitimān*) and reproof (*elegchein*), and there was thus a harsh element to it, which was to be kept within bounds (Dio Chrysostom, *Orations* 13.1; 72.9–10; 73.10). One cannot improve people without first condemning their present conduct, but "a distinction must be made between accusation, when one denounces with intent to injure, and admonition, when one uses like words with intent to benefit; for the same words are not to be interpreted in the same way unless they are spoken in the same spirit" (Isocrates, *Panegyricus* 130; cf. *On the Peace* 72). The person engaged in admonition should therefore not become angry, for then his admonition would lapse into faultfinding (*Gnomologium Byzantinum* 258, 259; Plutarch, *On How to Tell a*

*Flatterer from a Friend* 66E), nor would he revile and abuse, for then he would offend rather than mend someone (Seneca, *On Anger* 3.36.4). Friends admonish, enemies abuse (Plutarch, *On How to Profit from One's Enemies* 89B). Because admonition can be severe, it is best to admonish people individually (Plutarch, *On Listening to Lectures* 39A; *On How to Tell a Flatterer from a Friend* 71F) and in private (Plato, *Apology of Socrates* 26A; Dio Chrysostom, *Oration* 77/78.38; Plutarch, *On How to Tell a Flatterer from a Friend* 70D–71D).

The didactic element of admonition is present in the deutero-Pauline letters (Eph 6:4; Col 1:28; 3:16), as is the conception of it as harsh (Titus 3:10). For the rest, *nouthetein* is used psychagogically. In Acts 20:31 it describes Paul's emotional admonition of the Ephesians, given individually (*hena hekaston*; cf. 1 Thess 2:11), as he also wishes the Thessalonians to do (1 Thess 5:11, *heis ton hena*). Because of his special relationship with the Corinthians as their father in the gospel, Paul admonished them (1 Cor 4:14–15). He was also convinced that members of the Christian community were able to admonish one another (Rom 15:14), and he reflected on the issues involved in such admonition in Rom 14 and 15. As in 1 Thess 5:11–12, he also there thought that admonition contributes to mutual edification (cf. Rom 14:19; 15:2). The Thessalonians were in precisely that stage of their development to which admonition was particularly relevant: they were making progress but still needed encouragement (cf. 4:1, 10; 5:11).

5:13. *and to esteem them very highly in love because of their work.* Having specified for which functions individuals are to be given recognition, Paul in a parallel statement provides the reason why they are to be honored. The verb *hēgeisthai* normally means "to lead," "to guide," or "to think," "to consider" (BAGD, 343), but the meaning "to esteem," which is required here by the context, has also been documented (MM, 277). For *hyperekperissou* ("very highly"), see NOTE on 3:10, the only other place where it occurs in the NT. The closest parallel elsewhere to this clause is 1 Cor 16:15–16 (cf. Mark 10:42–45; Luke 22:24–27), but here the stress is on function, *ergon* ("work"), which summarizes the three activities of v 12, and the relationship is not one of submission (cf. Heb 13:17), but of love. For evangelistic activity as work issuing from love, see 1:3. Here the workers are to be loved.

*Be at peace among yourselves.* The sentence is not connected grammatically to what precedes, so its meaning is unclear. Ancient copyists (e.g., P30 D* F; cf. Vg: *cum eis*) sought clarity by changing the reflexive pronoun *heautois* ("yourselves") to *autois* ("them"), which would have the sense of urging the readers to be at peace with the persons whose actions have just been mentioned. There is, however, no evidence that members of the congregation opposed the leaders (argued by Frame, 195). Paul does not speak of only two groups, but thinks of the relationship among members of the congregation.

*Heautois* is used here for *allēlois* ("one another") (BAGD, 287, citing, among other passages, Mark 9:50, "Have salt in yourselves [*en heautois*], and be at peace with one another [*eirēneuete en allēlois*]"). In view is the community as a whole, who are to engage in mutual edification (v 11; cf. Rom 12:18, *meta pantōn anthrōpōn*). Paul is aware that such intensely personal exhortation would be in danger of upsetting those on the receiving end, and therefore cautions them (Oe-comenius, *Commentary of 1 Thessalonians* 6 [PG 119:101]; Theophylact, *Exposition of 1 Thessalonians* 5 [PG 124:1320–21]). A church made up of neophytes in the faith would find it challenging to adapt to the scrutiny and correction they received from their fellow members. The statement probably also applies to those who provide the care, especially those who admonish, warning them not to cause enmity by abusing people, a danger we have seen to be present when admonishing. For a similar warning, against retaliation, see NOTE on v 15.

5:14. *And we exhort you, brethren.* As in v 12, with *de* ("and") Paul makes a transition, now to those who provide pastoral care. The form of the exhortation, *parakaloumen de hymās, adelphoi,* is a variation of v 12, (*parakaloumen* instead of *erōtōmen*) (see NOTE on 4:1). The identity of the "brethren" has been disputed. Some patristic as well as modern commentators have argued that Paul now addresses the leaders (the *proistamenoi*) he had mentioned in v 12, giving them directions on the proper way to care for the congregation (e.g., John Chrysostom, *Homilies on 1 Thessalonians* 10 [PG 62:456]; Findlay, 124; Masson, 73).

Best (1972: 229) has effectively countered this interpretation with a number of arguments:

1. The view that the "leaders" of v 12 constituted a defined group is not supported by the evidence.

2. There is no reason why, since in v 16 Paul addresses the church as a whole, he should not do so in v 14.

3. The similarity of the introductory phrases in vv 14 and 16 suggests that the same audience is in view. If Paul in v 14 has a contrast in mind, the word order should have been *hymās de parakaloumen* ("And you we exhort") instead of *parakaloumen de hymās* ("And we exhort you"), as it is here (cf. von Dobschütz 1909: 220).

4. "Brethren" describes the church at large rather than only certain of its members.

*admonish the disorderly.* The sentence continues with the first of four imperatives, each of which is followed only by its object. This sentence differs from the other three in that *nouthetein* is the only verb carried over from the activities mentioned in v 12 and that its objects (*tous ataktous*) are the only persons in v 14 who are described in terms of their action rather than their emotional conditions or psychological dispositions (note the verb [*ataktein*] in 2 Thess 3:7, and the adverb [*ataktōs*] modifying *peripatein* ["to conduct"] in 2 Thess 3:6, 11). This, plus the fact that admonition stands at the head of the list of directions, shows the importance Paul attached to admonition. This is significant in view of the fact that it is the harshest form of exhortation Paul mentions in the letter. Paul presented himself as an example of gentle care for them to follow (see NOTES and COMMENT on

2:6, 11–12), and the strongest term he used to describe his own activity is *(dia)martyresthai* ("to charge"; 2:12; 4:6). The disorderliness that had developed in Thessalonica after his departure was sufficiently serious to require sterner attention.

The verb and adverb of the word group *ataktein* are used in 2 Thess 3:6, 7, 11 of the failure to work, as they are in some papyri, hence commentators and translators render *tous ataktous* here as "the idlers" (cf. Frame, 197; RSV; NIV; Best 1972: 229–30, "loafers"). Paul's concern in 4:11–12 makes certain that a tendency not to work was a real problem in Thessalonica and supports this translation. Had Paul merely been concerned about the idleness of such people, however, he would have used more common words for idleness, such as *argoi* or *apraktoi* to describe them.

The word *ataktōs* literally means "disorderly" and referred to people who refused to submit to accepted forms of behavior (Spicq 1956; 1958: 157–59). Beginning with the church fathers, the disorderly have been thought to be those who act contrary to the will of God, so that the reviler, the drunkard, the covetous—indeed, all who sin—are disorderly (e.g., John Chrysostom, *Homilies on 1 Thessalonians* 10 [PG 62:455]). In Thessalonica, willfulness was expressed in a refusal to work. In 4:10–12 Paul treated the matter of idleness in social terms, and he will do so again in 2 Thess 3:6–15, but here, by using *ataktoi*, he alludes to the character trait that was responsible for their social conduct. He does so in a context in which he matches certain kinds of pastoral care with certain dispositions. Admonition was addressed to the will (see NOTE on v 12), hence Paul uses *ataktoi* rather than *argoi* or *apraktoi*. In this connection, it is also significant that when Paul referred to his paradigmatic behavior (2:1–12), he described his own manual labor as an act of free will (see *eudokein* in 2:8–9).

*comfort the discouraged.* Paul had comforted (*paramytheisthai*) the Thessalonians when he had been with them (2:12) and in 4:13–18 gave them advice on how to comfort (*parakalein*) each other after the death of some of their members. Consolation was a well-known form of ancient psychagogy (see Malherbe 1990b: 387–88) and contained an element of admonition (see Chapa 1994: 152 n. 14), so it is not incongruous that Paul should follow advice on admonition with advice on comfort (cf. Plutarch, *On Superstition* 168C).

In 4:13–17 Paul had provided the basis for comforting the Thessalonians who were grieving; here the objects of comfort are those with a particular psychological condition. The word *oligopsychos* is seldom used in nonbiblical Greek, and this is its only occurrence in the NT. Lexica usually assign the meanings of "fainthearted" and "discouraged" to it (G. Bertram in *TDNT* 9.665–66; BAGD, 564). In PPetrie 2.50a, 12 (Witkowski, 41) the verb *oligopsychein* is the opposite of *andrizesthai* ("to conduct oneself in a manly or courageous manner"; BAGD, 64; cf. Theodoret, *Commentary on 1 Thessalonians* 5 [PG 82:653]). The word is similar in meaning to Aristotle's *mikropsychos*, the small-souled person who claims less than he deserves, who is the opposite of the *megalopsychos*, the great-souled person who claims and deserves much, who is self-sufficient and confident (*Nicomachean Ethics* 4.3.3, 1123b; cf. John Chrysostom, *Homilies on 1 Thessalonians* 10 [PG 62:457]). On this reading, the people Paul has in mind feel inadequate and diffident (Bruce 1982: 123; cf. von Dobschütz 1909: 221). Paul probably derived the form of the word from the LXX, where *oligopsychos* means "fainthearted" or "anxious" (e.g., Isa 25:5; 35:4; 54:6; 57:15; Sir 4:9; cf. *1 Clem* 58:4, where *oligopsychos* appears with *asthenein*, "to be weak").

The meaning of *oligopsychos* is thus clear, but the reason for the Thessalonians' discouragement is not clear. Reasons have been found in the text of the letter: persecutions (2:14), most frequently, concern over the dead (4:13–18), temptation to sin (4:3–8), and uncertainty about salvation (5:1–11). It is futile to focus on one of these items, for Paul's interest is in a psychological condition, one that allows a wide range of experiences that create a need for comfort. Paul had already comforted his converts when he was with them (2:12), and it was necessary for him to do so then in view of the distress experienced by recent converts (see COMMENT on 1:6; 3:3–4). *Oligopsychoi* perfectly describes the state of such persons, which would have been aggravated by what they experienced after Paul's departure.

*help the weak.* Numerous attempts have been made to identify the "weak" persons (*asthenōn*) Paul has in mind, some interpreters likening them to the Romans and Corinthians who had scruples about matters of diet and the religious calendar (Rom 14; 1 Cor 8, 10; see Best 1972: 231), others identifying them with those in need of instruction in sexual behavior (4:3–8; Frame, 198; Marshall 1983: 151), and others with persons who worried about the delay of the Parousia (thought to be reflected in 5:1–11; D. A. Black, 45–53). This is the first time in his writings that Paul uses the verb or adjective (see especially Rom 14:1, 2, 21; 1 Cor 8:7, 9, 10, 11, 12; 9:22), and nothing in the context points to a particular group in Thessalonica as weak. In the immediate context, Paul is concerned to match certain types of exhortation to psychological conditions or dispositions, and it is the psychagogic tradition that illuminates this sentence. For Paul, this weakness is moral and intellectual as well as religious, and it is not true, as is claimed (G. Stählin in *TDNT* 1.492), that "weakness does not appear in this sense before Paul's time" (for what follows, see Stowers 1990; Malherbe 1990b; 1995b; Glad, index, s.v., "weak").

Philosophers of many schools referred to people who found it hard to live virtuously as weak. The notion of weakness became part of the Stoic theory of cognition as early as Chrysippus (third century B.C.), who spoke of souls as weak or strong, diseased or healthy, just as bodies are (*SVF* 3.471). Stoics held that because of our weakness, we give assent to false judgments (*SVF* 1.67; 3.177; Plutarch, *Against Colotes* 1122C; Cicero, *Tusculan Disputations* 4.15), and wrong conduct, they said, is due to slackness and weakness of the soul (*SVF* 3.471, 473). Weakness is the inability of the rational faculty to bear virtue's hardships (Cicero, *Tusculan Disputations* 3.34; 5.3) and is the condition or disposition of the self-indulgent (Diogenes Laertius, *The Lives of Eminent Philosophers* 7.115; Cicero, *Tusculan Disputations* 4.29, 42). The weak, knowing that their own judgment could be perverted by the crowd (Seneca, *Epistles* 7.1; 44.1), should avoid the crowd and not expose themselves to things by which they might be seduced (Seneca, *Epistle* 116.5). It was not only Stoics who described people as weak, but it was they who analyzed the human condition in infinite detail and drew out its moral implications. For example, weakness was described as a moral illness, exemplified by a fond imagining of something seemingly desirable, such as fame, love of pleasure, and the like (Cicero, *Tusculan Disputations* 4.29, 42; Diogenes Laertius, *The Lives of Eminent Philosophers* 7.115).

Moral philosophers considered their major goal to be to help people in their moral development, after analyzing them (see Malherbe 1987: 81–88). The weak (*astheneis* or, in Latin, *inbecilliores*) were in special need of the philosophers' care (Seneca, *Epistle* 94.50–51, cf. 30–31) and would be helped by philosophical principles (Seneca, *Epistle* 95.37). It was difficult to help the weak, for the weak feared what was unfamiliar (Seneca, *Epistle* 50.9; cf. Cicero, *De finibus* 5.43) and were prone to want to reform everything and everyone else rather than themselves (Seneca, *Epistle* 107.12). The moralists recognized that people were not weak in the same way. Seneca thought that anger was a sign of weakness but that people are angered by different things, so that the moral counselor should treat them accordingly (*On Anger* 1.20.3; 3.10.4). They generally thought that fear of death was a weakness, and mourning a sign of it (Seneca, *Epistle* 82.23; Plutarch, *A Letter of Condolence to Apollonius* 116E; Cicero, *Tusculan Disputations* 4.60; Pliny, *Epistle* 1.12.12).

The Epicureans, who engaged in mutual care, gave close attention to how the weak in their communities should be counseled. The evidence provided by Philodemus (first century B.C.) in his work *On Frankness*, reveals the concern for the weak (*hapaloi, astheneis*). They should be treated with kindness and gentleness, always taking into consideration their capacity to endure admonition (2, 10, 38), for only then could the counselors be helpful (18, 43, 67, 86). For example, young people, who could be counted among the weak, are easily irritated and must be made amenable to correction, for they are not cured by frankness (7, 59, Tab IIIG; cf. IX, XXII, XXIV).

Paul uses *astheneis* in the philosophical sense in 1 Cor 8 (Malherbe 1995b), but not in 1 Thess 5:14. Both the context and the command to help the weak show that it is the pastoral usage that is represented here. The verb *antechesthai*, which he uses here, can mean "to cling to," "to hold fast to" something or someone and "to take an interest in," "to pay attention to," or "to help" (BAGD, 73). It is one of a number of terms Paul uses of helping someone (cf. *antilēmpsis*, 1 Cor 12:28). Most of these words have the connotation of welcoming, accepting, or receiving someone, and thus helping that person. This is evident in letters of recommendation (e.g., Rom 16:2 [*prosdechesthai*]; Phlm 17 [*proslambanesthai*]; see Malherbe 1983b: 102–10).

Of particular interest is the use of such words in contexts where Paul describes pastoral care, for example, *syllambanesthai* ("to help") in Phil 4:3, *tōn asthenounta . . . proslambanesthai* in Rom 14:1, and *proslambanesthai allēlous* in Rom 15:7, which is a summary of the pastoral care described in vv 1–6, with Christ as the example (cf. also Acts 20:35, *antilambanesthai tōn asthenountōn* ["to help the weak"]). In these occurrences of *proslambanesthai*, the verb is usually translated "to receive," but in its pastoral use it has the connotation of helping someone (see LSJ, s.v. 3.3). The same is true of *bastazein* ("to bear"), as in Rom 15:1 (*ta asthenēmata . . . bastazein* ["to bear the weaknesses"]) and in Gal 6:2 (*ta barē bastazete* ["to bear the burdens"]).

Paul's language clearly belongs to the psychagogic tradition, and once more he describes a condition or disposition rather than particular experiences. He is more interested in matching appropriate pastoral care to persons with such dispositions than in elaborating on particular actions that result from them.

*be patient with all.* In nonbiblical Greek, *makrothymein* and its cognates appear fairly late, are rare, and frequently, but not always, have the sense of resignation (see J. Horst in *TDNT* 4.374–87). Paul's use of *makrothymeisthe* ("be patient") is influenced by Jewish usage. An insignificant word in nonbiblical Greek, it takes on a profound significance in the LXX, where it describes God's relationship with his people. The basic passage is Exod 34:6 ("The Lord God, compassionate and merciful, patient [*makrothymos*] and full of pity"), which becomes a refrain in later Jewish literature (e.g., Ps 102:8; Joel 2:13). In the Wisdom literature, it is also a quality of the wise man (Prov 16:32; 17:27; Sir 5:11).

Paul thinks of God as patient and, without allowing God's patience to eliminate the reality of divine anger (Rom 9:22), thinks that it aims at human repentance and salvation (Rom 2:4; cf. 1 Tim 1:16; 1 Pet 3:20; 2 Pet 3:9, 15). It is a Christian quality, is a gift of the Spirit (Gal 5:22), and is exercised through love (1 Cor 13:4). It is not a passive quality; like the other verbs in 1 Thess 5:14, it describes action intended to benefit certain types of persons. The deutero-Pauline letters pick up this communal dimension of patience (cf. Eph 4:2, "with patience, forbearing one another in love" [*meta makrothymias anechomenoi en agapē*]; 2 Tim 4:2).

*Makrothymein*, which does not appear in pagan psychagogy, is thus heavy with theological content. However, the idea that people in need of care should be treated with patience underlies the entire endeavor to benefit people. Just as a physician who diagnoses his patients repeats and modifies his treatment as he progresses, the counselor should be patient and repeat his therapy (Philodemus, *On Frankness* 63, 64, 67, 69; Plutarch, *On How to Tell a Flatterer from a Friend* 74DE).

The objects of the other kinds of care commanded in v 14 are matched with the nature of the care that is specified. Patience, however, is always appropriate, regardless of the persons who are addressed. To be "patient with all" is one of the series of injunctions directed to members of the church as a means by which to edify each other (v 11). The "all" refers either to all the members of the Thessalonian church (Findlay, 125; Best 1972: 232), not only the disorderly, discouraged, and weak (Bornemann, 238), or, more likely, the entire community, including non-Christians (see NOTE on *en hymin* in v 12). This attitude is quite different from Titus 3:10, where one is to shun a divisive Christian after a second admonition (cf 2 Tim 4:2; see Malherbe 1989: 137–45).

5:15. *See to it that no one renders evil for evil to anyone.* This verse corresponds to the command to be at peace in v 13. Like that command, it concludes a section dealing with communal relations, but is twice as long. It consists of an antithesis, the first part of which, in the negative, is a warning against retaliation. This is the only place where Paul uses *horāte mē (tis)* ("See to it that [no one]"; cf. Matt 18:10), but the related expression, *blepete mē*, with the same meaning and also dealing with intracommunal relations, occurs in 1 Cor 8:9 and Gal 5:15 (cf. Eph 5:15; Col 2:8).

The prohibition expresses a general principle of conduct, and the change from the plural *horāte* to the singular *tis* ("one") does not mean that Paul addresses the leaders to take care that certain individuals in the church not retaliate (so Bornemann, 238). The warning is addressed to all the readers, and the principle has reference to the pastoral functions mentioned in v 14. There is no reason to limit it to the command to be patient, as many commentators do, on the ground that that command is also general in scope (correctly, Wanamaker, 198). The use of *tis* and *tini* ("one" and "anyone") in fact makes the prohibition as general as possible (von Dobschütz 1909: 223).

The natural urge to retaliate finds expression in OT mandates (e.g., Lev 24:19–21; Deut 19:21; Prov 21:22–25) as well as conventional Greek morality (e.g., Theognis 867–72; Ps.-Isocrates, *To Demonicus* 26; Xenophon, *Anabasis* 1.9.11). The same sources also rejected retaliation. Thus in the Jewish moral tradition, as exemplified by Proverbs (20:22; 24:29; 25:21) and *Joseph and Aseneth* (23:9; 28:5; 29:3), retaliation is warned against. Among the Greeks, retaliation was regarded negatively (e.g., Plato, *Gorgias* 509C; *Crito* 49A–D), and in Paul's time, the moralists regularly rejected the notion that the philosopher might retaliate rather than suffer wrongs (e.g., Musonius Rufus, Fragments 3, 6, 10; Epictetus, *Discourse* 1.18, 28; Seneca, *On Anger* 2.34.1, 5; 3.24.1; 25.1; see Fitzgerald 1988: 103–7).

The NT consistently teaches against retaliation, beginning with the teaching of Jesus on the proper attitude towards enemies (Matt 5:44–48; Luke 6:27–36), which is also the context in which Paul warns against it in Rom 12:17 (see vv 14–21). In 1 Pet 3:9, the principle is applied to relations between members of the church, and it is also present in this sense in 1 Cor 6:7, although it is not explicitly cited. Because of *pantas* ("all") in v 14 and in the second part of the antithesis in v 15, some commentators think that Paul is warning against retaliation against all people without restriction. The *pantas* in v 14, however, refers to those mentioned as receiving the care specified in v 14. Similarly, the warning against retaliation is to be seen in the context of the pastoral care described in v 14.

The moral philosophers, too, were sensitive to the tendency to retaliate when people were admonished (Plutarch, *On How to Tell a Flatterer from a Friend* 72EF; Dio Chrysostom, *Orations* 51.4, 7; 72.9–10). This was particularly true of the weak, who were easily offended (Seneca, *On Anger* 1.5; 2.34.1; Dio Chrysostom, *Oration* 77/78.40). Paul's own experience taught him that bold speaking could irritate people (Gal 4:16; cf. Plutarch, *On How to Tell a Flatterer from a Friend* 56A). A danger attending frank speech was that, when the speaker was attacked by those he offended, he might lash out in retaliation. Then, it was pointed out, his speech sprang from his having been wronged and having a grievance rather than from goodwill, as it should have been. When it proceeds from self-regard, it is not admonition but faultfinding (Plutarch, *On How to Tell a Flatterer from a Friend* 66E; cf. 67BC). The one who wishes to help others should not reply to admonition with admonition (72E–73C).

In v 15, the warning against retaliation is addressed to those who exhort rather than those who receive the exhortation. But, since comforting, helping, and being patient would hardly result in retaliation, Paul must primarily have in mind admonition, the only type of exhortation mentioned twice in vv 12–14 as that which might make people want to get even. It is this type of exhortation that, moralists were aware, resulted in retaliation. Understood thus, the evil not to be repaid with evil is harsh speech that is self-assertive and self-justifying rather than speech that is intended to benefit the listener.

*but at all times pursue what is good for one another and for all.* Paul does not think that passivity is a proper response to being wronged. The second part of the sentence is positive and intensive ("at all times," "pursue"; cf. Rom 14:19; 1 Cor 14:1) and concludes the entire section on pastoral care (vv 12–15). This is the sixth time in the letter that Paul uses *pantote* ("at all times") to describe continuity or persistence (see NOTE on 1:2). The words *agathos* ("good"), used here, and *kalos* (v 19) are used interchangeably (e.g., Rom 7:13, 18, 21; Gal 6:9–10), without any apparent difference in meaning (he uses *kalos* in prohibiting retaliation in Rom 12:17). Some commentators think that the good is expressed by acting in love (Best 1972: 235; Holtz 1986: 256), but "good" does not appear in the texts cited to support this contention (Rom 13:8–10; Gal 5:14). Perhaps more to the point is that the good is discovered through testing (Rom 12:2; 1 Thess 5:21). If the first part of the verse deals with the pastoral care just described, it is likely that the second part does so as well and that the good in mind is that which is achieved through pastoral care, carried out with discrimination. Thus, the good is "what is beneficial, as opposed to *kakon* in the sense of injury or harm" (Lightfoot 1980: 81).

In his prohibition of retaliation in Rom 12:17, Paul's application is universal: "Repay no one evil for evil, but take thought for what is noble in the sight of all people [*kala enōpion pantōn anthrōpōn*]," and commentators have thought that *pantas* in 1 Thess 5:15 is similarly universal, Paul requiring nonretaliation within the church and towards all people. If *pantas* in 3:12 refers to non-Christians who were present in the Christian assembly (see NOTE on *en hymin* in 5:12), it could also do so here, which would mean that, while the primary focus is on the edification of the Christians in Thessalonica ("for one another"; cf. v 11), in a secondary way, pagans also are in view (for the principle, see Gal 6:10, also at the end of paraenesis on pastoral care in the Christian community).

# COMMENT

Paul continues completing what was lacking in the Thessalonians' faith (3:10). After encouraging them in a general way in 5:1–10 to live sober lives as children of the Day, he now gives very specific directions on how they should conduct themselves in their relationships with each other. Paul's interest in communal relations, in evidence at the very beginning of the letter (1:5–6), surfaced again in the transition to chaps. 4 and 5 (3:12, see COMMENT) and has been a concern throughout these last two chapters (4:6, 9, 18; 5:10). Paul has just described the eschatological existence that should characterize the church. This could have a destabilizing effect (cf. 2 Thess 2:1–2), and he therefore gives practical directions on how the church is to be edified and kept stable.

These detailed instructions open a window on how he expected members of a newly founded church to nurture each other. They were to follow his example in doing so. It is not quite precise to refer to that care as "pastoral," for Paul never referred to himself as a pastor nor to his converts' care as pastoral; furthermore, the modern term "pastoral care" has connotations that are quite different from what Paul encouraged his churches to do (Best 1988: 1–2, 10, 22).

## Psychagogy

Ancient philosophers described what Paul is concerned with here as psychagogy, and it is best to retain that word as far as possible (see NOTES on 2:11–12; 5:11). Psychagogy (*psychagogia*), according to Plato, is an art that leads the soul by means of words (*Phaedrus* 261A). It has in common with the art of medicine that both begin by diagnosing the person to be helped and being timely in teaching him (270E, 271A, 272A). Philosophers assumed that people differed in what vices they were prone to (Cicero, *Tusculan Disputations* 4.81; cf. 4.27). Stoics, in characteristic fashion, engaged in detailed analysis of people's dispositions and emotional states, but Epicurus (fourth–third centuries B.C.), who first developed a psychagogic system, had already done so (Seneca, *Epistles* 52.3–4; cf. 71.30–37). By the time of Paul, psychagogy had become widespread, and its basic principles and techniques were accepted by people regardless of their philosophical allegiance (Malherbe 1987: 81–88).

The medical metaphor became very common in the early Empire to describe psychagogy (Malherbe 1989: 140–42). For example, it was thought that frank speech should be therapeutic, that, like a physician, the philosopher should act at the right moment and that, as a physician continues his treatment after surgery, so the philosopher should not abandon people after stinging them with harsh words (Plutarch, *On How to Tell a Flatterer from a Friend* 73D–74E). The medical imagery was useful when stressing that the philosopher should vary his speech as he adapted it to different circumstances. This principle is illustrated by three contemporaries of Paul who in the following citations do not all use medical imagery.

Seneca, a Stoic, assumes that "human life is founded on kindness and concord, and is bound into an alliance for common help, not by terror, but by mutual love" (*On Anger* 1.5.3). He instructs the teacher,

to heal human nature by the use of words, and these of the milder sort, as long as he can to the end that he may persuade [*suadet*] someone to do what he ought to do, and win over his heart to a desire for the honorable and the just, and implant in his mind hatred of vice and esteem of virtue. Let him pass next to harsher language, in which he will still aim at admonition [*moneat*] and reproof [*exprobet*]. Lastly, let him resort to punishment [*poenas*], yet still making it light and not irrevocable. (*On Anger* 1.6.3)

Dio Chrysostom, also a Stoic but with a strong Cynic inclination, describes the ideal philosopher's life as being spent in caring (*kedomenos*) for people and trying to lead them to virtue,

partly by persuading [*peithōn*] and exhorting [*parakalōn*], partly by abusing [*loidoroumenos*] and reproaching [*oneidizōn*] in the hope that he might thereby rescue someone from low desires and intemperance and soft living, taking them aside privately one by one [*idia hekaston*] and also admonishing [*noutheton*] them in groups every time he finds the opportunity, with gentle words at times, at others harsh. (*Oration* 77.78.38)

Plutarch, a Platonist, is aware that speaking to people individually (see NOTE on 2:11; 5:11) may be counterproductive:

yet if anybody draws them to one side and tries to teach [*didaskē*] something useful, or to advise [*parainē*] them of some duty, or to admonish [*nouthetē*] them when in the wrong, or to calm [*katapraunē*] them when incensed, they have no patience with him; but, eager to get the better of him if they can, they fight against what he says, or else they beat a hasty retreat . . . . (*On Listening to Lectures* 39A)

The impression should not be left that psychagogy proceeded in one direction, from one class of persons, the philosophers, to the rest. The philosophers who would presume to correct others were first to examine themselves, purging their minds with the aid of reason, and throughout their lives would strive to preserve their individuality (Dio Chrysostom, *Oration* 77/78.40, cf. 38; Epictetus, *Discourse* 3.22.13). They would therefore be open to correction themselves, and that knowledge would affect the way in which they corrected others (Plutarch, *On How to Tell a Flatterer from a Friend* 72F). In the Epicurean communities, reciprocal care was institutionalized (see Glad, 124–32).

The need to fine-tune psychagogy to match the condition of the hearer resulted in the classification of numerous styles of exhortation. They are discussed extensively in the moral literature (e.g., Seneca, *Epistles* 94; 95; Clement of Alexandria, *Christ the Educator* 1.1, 8). In 1 Thess 5:11–15 Paul reflects knowledge of psychagogic principles and applies them to the church in Thessalonica.

## The Thessalonian Church and Its Psychagogy

The church Paul writes to was small and probably met in a home that also provided space for the Christians and their manual laborers to practice their trade.

Paul's readers had been Christians for about six months, and as yet they had no appointed officials to lead them. It is remarkable that Paul mentions none of his readers by name, as he does in most of his other letters in which he writes of mutual edification (cf. Rom 16:1–5; 1 Cor 16:15–18; Phil 4:2). He is evidently more interested in how the church as a whole should function than in particular individuals.

Neither the brevity of his directions nor the fact that they are somewhat similar to Rom 12:9–21 proves that this is merely traditional paraenesis (so Dibelius 1937: 31). Several factors suggest that his directions had circumstances in Thessalonica in view. Paul nowhere else mentions the disorderly, discouraged, and weak together, as he does here, and only the weak are mentioned elsewhere (1 Cor 8, 10; Rom 14) but with different meanings than the word has here. The way in which he writes suggests that his readers were familiar with the substance of what he says and that he writes in order to lay stress on certain aspects of their psychagogy. That he repeats *nouthetein* indicates that he knows of circumstances, most probably the refusal to work, that called for more severe admonition than he himself had given.

The care about which Paul writes was not something new to the Thessalonians. Paul carefully sketches in the letter a process of nurture that began with the church's founding, when he cared for them (2:11–12). Then he sent Timothy to do the same (3:2–3). Now Paul does so again as he writes this pastoral letter, and he urges them to continue their care of one another (see Malherbe 1987: 61–94). Although Paul does not use the paraenetic "as you are doing" (cf. 4:1, 10), there is every indication that they were already engaged in mutual care.

The normal experiences of converts required such consistent attention (see COMMENT on 1:6–8). New converts experienced distress and anxiety as their new commitment alienated them from family, friends, and frequently, business associates, although this may not have been the case with the Thessalonians. In addition, they experienced intellectual and religious dislocation as they reconstructed a new conceptual world. They were challenged to conform to new standards of living, which could lead to discouragement and even dejection and despair (Malherbe 1987: 36–46). Paul's departure from Thessalonica soon after their conversion, the social ostracism they experienced (see COMMENT on 2:14), and the death of some of their number would have added to their distress and made pastoral care all the more necessary.

From the very beginning of the church in Thessalonica, Paul had stressed the communal dimension of their new life and especially the importance of relationships among individuals within the church (see NOTE and COMMENT on 1:4–5). The detailed directions in 5:12–15 show how, as individuals speak to other individuals, they are to edify each other (cf. v 11). To people who were already engaged in communal spiritual care, Paul describes how it should be done properly, thus providing us with a view of a mission church in the process of self-formation. That he begins his directions with cautions to give recognition to those who provide spiritual care and to esteem them very highly, to be at peace among themselves, and ends with a warning against retaliation, shows that he is conscious of the tension inherent in the psychagogical enterprise. This was particularly true when, as in Thessalonica, the kinds of care he describes were delivered in a rotational manner in which those exhorting would on another occasion themselves be exhorted (Glad, 208–12).

The repetition of *nouthetein* in his instruction shows that Paul is particularly concerned with this kind of speech. Admonition was harsh, and those on the receiving end would be tempted to dismiss it as denunciation and reviling rather than an attempt to do good. Isocrates warns against such a response and describes the proper one:

> while abhorring those who revile you to your harm as inimical . . . you ought to commend those who admonish you for your good and to esteem them as the best of your fellow-citizens, and him most of all, even among them, who is able to point out most vividly the evils of your practices and the disasters which result from them. For such a man can soonest bring you to abhor what you should abhor and to set your hearts on better things. (*On the Peace* 72–73)

In 1 Thess 5:12–14 Paul similarly gives advice on the proper response to people who admonish and also advises the admonishers how to do so properly.

An example of a Pauline admonition is found in Rom 14:1–15:13, which is Paul's paraenetic reminder to the Romans of how they are to carry out their admonition of each other (cf. 15:14). It illustrates the communal dimension that admonition had for Paul. On the positive side, admonition urges acceptance of each other (14:1, 3; 15:7), and thus the Thessalonians should aim at edification (14:19; 15:2), which requires that they live in peace (14:19), think the same thing (15:5), and bear the weaknesses of those who are themselves unable to do so (15:1).

Paul draws attention to relationships among them by using the word *adelphoi* ("brethren"). That relationship derives from their relationship with Christ, who died and was raised for them (Rom 14:8–9). Brothers are therefore not to judge each other (14:4, 10, 13), despise each other (14:10), be stumbling blocks to each other (14:13, 21), cause each other to grieve (14:15, 21), or destroy each other (14:15, 20). Paul is thus fully aware of the dangers in admonition and attempts to ameliorate them by situating admonition in a community that belongs to the Lord (14:8), with the result that relationships within it are determined by that fact.

Paul's extended directions on the treatment of the idlers in 2 Thess 3:6–12 and his command that the church admonish them in 3:13–15 provide an insight into how he applied such commands practically.

The similarities between Paul's directions and contemporary psychagogy are numerous and were obvious to early commentators. John Chrysostom, for example, used the image of the physician, adapting his treatment to the condition of his patient in commenting on the passage (*Homilies on 1 Thessalonians* 10 [PG 62:455–57]). Paul never, however, uses that imagery in his instructions on communal care, and his directions are always qualified theologically (e.g., Rom 15:1–7; Gal 6:2; Phil 2:1). So here, the perspective for the communal care is provided by the Day of the Lord and the sober life lived in consequence of that expectation, care is given in the Lord, and it is to be responded to in love because of the work of those who encourage.

The difference between Paul and the philosophers is nowhere as clear as in the way they thought about the reception of psychagogic speech. The ideal response to a philosopher's speech was turning or coming to oneself (see NOTE on 1:9). Plutarch in his tractate *On Listening to Lectures* describes how a person would evaluate a speech. The listener:

> should begin with himself and his own state of mind, endeavoring to estimate whether any one of his emotions has become less intense, whether any of his troubles lays less heavily upon him, whether his confidence and his high purpose have become firmly rooted, whether he has acquired enthusiasm for virtue and goodness. (42B)

> he should be grateful if by pungent discourse someone has cleansed his mind teeming with fogginess and dullness, as a beehive is cleared by smoke. (42C)

Gratitude for benefits received from speakers motivated by goodwill was also a characteristic of the Epicurean communities (see Malherbe 1987: 87).

Rather than the benefit of individuals, the goal of Paul's care, which provided a model for the Thessalonians, was a life worthy of God. It was God, who, through Paul's preaching, called them into his kingdom and glory (2:11–12; cf. 4:1). When gratitude is expressed, it is by Paul, who gives thanks to God for the way the Thessalonians had received God's word, which still had force in their lives (2:13; but see 5:18). The focus is not on themselves, but on God, through whose word their relationship with Paul came about (see NOTE and COMMENT on 1:5–6). Nor is there any hint they should be grateful when they are nurtured; they are to respond with recognition and esteem to persons whose activity is described theologically.

# 2. ON THE EVALUATION OF PROPHECY, 5:16–22

In three of his letters, Paul exhorts his readers to pray constantly (Rom 12:12, 14; Phil 4:4–6; 1 Thess 5:16–18), and in one (1 Cor 7:5) constant prayer is viewed as the norm in the Christian life (Wiles, 284–85). The final section of this letter (5:16–28) is shot through with liturgical elements. Paul visualizes his letter being read while the church is gathered for worship, and these elements will contribute to the use of the letter in the assembly. In vv 16–22 Paul is still concerned with the communal behavior of his readers, but he now moves from their pastoral relations to their more properly spiritual and religious conduct. He specifies this concern by continuing to use imperatives, which he had begun to do in v 11. This section consists of eight imperatives, each of which is preceded by some modification, mostly adverbial, or by an object. The switch in order from v 14, where the imperatives stand first, is probably made for the sake of variety.

With the exception of v 21 (*de*, "but"), there is no syntactical connection between the imperatival sentences, and comparisons are frequently made between vv 16–22 and other collections of organized exhortation united only by their communal interest, such as Rom 12:9–16 (Best 1972: 234, 241–42). Viewed as traditional in character, the section is then thought not to reflect actual concerns in the Thessalonian church. That would also be the result if one stressed the liturgical character of the section, either regarding it as a hymn (Boismard, 13) or, impressed by the rhythmic quality given to the section by the recurrence of the letter *p* (see NOTE on 1:2), regarding it as the headings of a worship service (Martin 1964: 135–36). The whole section has also been described as a short church order (F. Lang in *TDNT* 7.168).

The section is, however, not as loosely or arbitrarily structured as might appear from a strophic arrangement or from the imperatives, which are diatribal in style and therefore naturally asyndetic (Henneken, 105). The first three imperatives (vv 16–18) exhort the readers to rejoice, pray, and give thanks, thus forming a unit as to its content. The rhetorical pattern of three elements is found elsewhere in the letter (cf. 1:3, 5; 2:4; 5:21–22). Its form further sets it apart from vv 19–22. Each imperative is preceded by an adverb or *en panti*, which could be adverbial, but probably means "in everything," "in every circumstance" (see NOTES). This subsection closes with the addition of "for this is God's will in Christ Jesus for you," which marks the only break in the strophic structure.

The five imperatival sentences in vv 19–22 form another subsection, which also constitutes a unit between the affirmation of God's will in v 18 and a prayer in v 23. The imperatives instruct the readers in the proper attitude towards prophecy. These verses are arranged in parallel, vv 19 and 20 being negative and complementary in sense and structure, with *mē* ("not") in the middle of the sentence, and vv 21 and 22 being positive and antithetic to vv 19 and 20, but complementing each other.

The addressees are the same as those addressed throughout the letter, that is, the entire church, rather than a special group within the church. The section further specifies how the edification Paul spoke of in v 11 is to take place, and Paul still focuses on behavior within the community. In vv 16–18, therefore, he does not deal with something that is personal before dealing with a communal matter (so Rigaux 1956: 587; Best 1972: 234–36). Paul's threefold statement on prayer has the Thessalonian community, gathered for worship, in mind (see NOTE on 1:1). His words introduce his final commands in the letter, on what is to be the proper attitude towards prophecy.

## TRANSLATION

5 16Rejoice at all times,
17pray without ceasing,
18in everything give thanks, for this is God's will in Christ Jesus for you.

¹⁹Do not quench the Spirit,
²⁰do not despise prophecies,
²¹but test every thing,
    hold fast to what is good,
²²keep away from every form of evil.

# NOTES

**5:16. *Rejoice at all times.*** The Thessalonians had received the gospel with joy (1:6), and Paul had used the noun to express his exceptionally close relationship with them (2:19–20; 3:9). Paul thought of joy as issuing from faith (Phil 1:26) and associated with hope (Rom 12:12; 15:13), as a major fruit of the Spirit (Gal 5:22), and as one of the elements constituting the kingdom (Rom 14:17). Paul also spoke of the ability to rejoice in adversity (2 Cor 6:10; 7:4; Phil 2:17), and some commentators have seen the connection with v 15 thus: The ability to accept wrong (v 15) makes it possible to rejoice at all times and in all circumstances (see Lünemann, 554), which would be particularly appropriate to the Thessalonians, who had suffered affliction (1:6; 3:3–4).

However, the connection of joy and tribulation or affliction is made only in 1:6 in this letter, and there is no indication that Paul's exhortation has anything to do with tribulation or any other hardship. Paul in general paraenesis frequently urges his readers to rejoice (e.g., Rom 12:12; 2 Cor 13:11; Phil 2:18; 3:1; 4:4), so care should be taken when attempting to relate joy to particular circumstances. That does not mean, however, that Paul is here describing a general Christian attitude (so von Dobschütz 1909: 223–24; Eadie, 206; Rigaux 1956: 582).

This is the first of three commands to pray, and this triad of injunctions should not be separated. They introduce Paul's directions on prophecy and become more emphatic in v 18. The command to rejoice (*chairete*) focuses the more general one to pray (*proseuchesthe*) in v 17. It qualifies, with v 18, the nature of prayer as joyous acceptance. That the Thessalonians are to rejoice *pantote* ("at all times," "always") is a characteristic of Pauline statements on prayer (see NOTE on 1:2).

**5:17. *pray without ceasing.*** Paul stresses the practice of constant prayer in 1 Thessalonians (1:2–3; 2:13; 3:10; 5:17, cf. 25), employing different words for prayer (*eucharistein, mnēmoneuein, deisthai*) and qualifying them with different adverbs (*pantote, adialeiptōs, nyktos kai hēmeras*). There was need for Gentile converts to be instructed to pray (cf. Luke 11:1) and to do so constantly (cf. Luke 18:1; see also Eph 6:18; Col 4:2).

**5:18. *in everything give thanks.*** Attention is drawn to this imperative by its being the last in the series of imperatives dealing with prayer, by being qualified by *en panti* ("in everything") rather than an adverb, and by the fact that the strophic arrangement is broken by the addition of "for this is God's will in Christ Jesus for you." Paul frequently speaks of giving thanks in prayer and normally uses an adverb with the verb (*pantote*: 1 Cor 1:4; Phil 1:3; 1 Thess 1:2; 2 Thess

1:3; 2:13; Phlm 4; cf. Eph 5:20; Col 1:3; *adialeiptōs*: 1 Thess 2:13; *aei*: 2 Cor 6:10). This is the only place where he uses *eucharistein* with *en panti*, which normally in Paul means "in any circumstance," "in everything" (1 Cor 1:5; 2 Cor 4:8; 6:4; 11:6, 9; Phil 4:12). The closest parallel, also in connection with prayer, is Phil 4:6 (cf. 2 Cor 9:8, *en panti pantote*; contrast Phil 1:28, *en mēdeni* ["in nothing"]). Had Paul wished to express a temporal notion with *pās*, he could have used the Septuagintally influenced *dia pantos* ("forever"), as he does in Rom 11:10 (cf. 2 Thess 3:16), or complemented *pās* (e.g., Eph 6:18, *proseuchomenoi en panti kairō* ["pray at all times"]).

*for this is God's will in Christ Jesus for you.* Other than here the construction *touto gar (estin) thelēma (tou) theou* appears in Paul only in 4:3, and in John 6:39–40, in both of which *touto* ("this") points forward. In 1 Thess 4:3, it points to the first paraenesis, on the life sanctified by the Spirit (4:3–8). The *touto* could also point forward here, to the last paraenesis in the letter, on the proper attitude towards the Spirit in prophecy. On such a reading, the two references to God's will would form the two brackets of an *inclusio* that encompasses all the paraenesis contained in chaps. 4 and 5.

When the phrase does point forward, it is made clear that it does so by the use of a noun (*hagiasmos*) in apposition to *thelēma* (4:3) or by a *hina* construction (John 6:39–40). Here, it would have been clearer if Paul had used infinitives in vv 19–22 (cf. 4:4). But that would have broken the diatribal style, which depends on imperatives for effect and which does not, in any case, require that the clauses be syntactically connected. The *gar* introduces an explanation of why they should give thanks in every circumstance: it is God's will that they do so, and the circumstance in which they are to do so is identified as prophecy in what follows.

Most commentators, however, think that the phrase "for this is God's will in Christ Jesus for you" points backwards, but there is disagreement as to whether the reference is to all of vv 16 and 17 (thus Lünemann, 554; Best 1972: 236; Holtz 1986: 258) or only the last imperative, to give thanks (so Ellicott, 81, with reference to patristic commentators; Eadie, 208). The latter is more likely if *en panti* is taken, as it should be, to mean "in every circumstance." Then *eucharisteite* stands out more emphatically than the other two imperatives in vv 16 and 17.

That God's will is said to be *eis hymās* ("for you") means that Paul is not giving a general admonition to lead a prayerful life as part of God's design for his elect. Taken with *en panti*, it points to a particular circumstance in Thessalonica. The emphasis on the need to give thanks suggests that Paul thinks that there were things in Thessalonica for which some Thessalonians might not wish to give thanks. The warnings that follow show that he has in mind prophecy (so also Richard, 273; cf. Matt 7:21, for doing the Father's will in the context of a discussion of prophecy).

**5:19.** *Do not quench the Spirit.* As the context shows, Paul has in mind the Holy Spirit rather than the human spirit (contrast v 23). He has mentioned the Holy Spirit only twice elsewhere in 1 Thessalonians, in connection with his readers' conversion (1:5–6) and their sanctification (4:8). In view of the latter, it is possible that he may also here be referring to the activity of the Spirit in the moral life (cf. Gal 5:18, 22–24; see 1 Cor 6:19), particularly if vv 21 and 22 are understood ethically. The connection with prophecy (v 20), however, suggests to the vast majority of commentators that Paul has in mind the charismata, the gifts of the Spirit.

Opinions diverge on whether he here refers to the gifts in general (1 Cor 12:4–11; cf. Rom 12:6–8, where the Spirit, however, is not mentioned), without restriction to a particular gift (thus Ellicott, 81; Frame, 205; F. Lang in *TDNT* 7.168; Best 1972: 238; Wanamaker, 202), and only moves from the generic (note the article with *pneuma*) to the specific in the next verse (cf. 1 Cor 14:1), or whether he is already speaking of prophecy, which is an utterance prompted by the Spirit (1 Cor 12:10–11; thus Bruce 1982: 125; Holtz 1986: 259). Again, the context as well as the verb used (*sbennynai*, "to quench") indicate that Paul is already referring to prophecy.

The notion of the Spirit as hot or fiery and thus capable of being quenched appears elsewhere in the NT (e.g., Matt 3:11; Luke 3:16; Acts 2:3; 2 Tim 1:6; see also Rom 12:11 and Acts 18:25, which may refer to the human spirit). However, the imagery and the language had a firm place in contemporary discussions of inspiration, and Paul's command is illuminated by those discussions (see COMMENT). Other NT references describing actions against the Spirit, such as resisting (Acts 7:51; cf. Isa 63:10 [provoking]) or grieving (Eph 4:30) the Spirit, do not help to determine Paul's meaning here. Those who interpret the word ethically think that it is an impure life that quenches the Spirit (e.g., John Chrysostom, *Homilies on 1 Thessalonians* 11 [PG 62:461, 462]).

Other commentators, who think that Paul is referring to prophecy, nevertheless also think that Paul is prohibiting his readers from quenching the Spirit within themselves because of their dread of "enthusiasm" (Ellicott, 82; Roosen 1971: 123; Bruce 1982: 125, refers to Jer 20:9; Gillespie, 36–44). It is also possible, indeed likely, that Paul thinks of suppressing the Spirit in others, in whatever way the Spirit moves them to exercise a gift (Frame, 205; Bruce 1982: 123, refers to Mic 2:6; Aune, 219; Wanamaker, 202–3).

The context shows that Paul is prohibiting his readers from keeping others from prophesying (see COMMENT). The vast majority of commentators understand the present prohibition (*mē sbennyte*, "do not quench") to command the cessation of action already in progress (e.g., Best 1972: 237). That is the general grammatical rule, but the rule is extremely fluid (Moule, 135). In many cases, *mē* with the present imperative "does not refer to the interruption of an action already begun, but to an action still in the more or less distant future against which the speaker urges resistance. Sometimes the reference to the future is directly or indirectly indicated by the context" (Smythe, 1841.a). The general rule should not be pressed here; like the other imperatives it describes what should be habitual (Bruce 1982: 125).

The larger context in which the prohibition appears (5:3) shows that Paul does not visualize a situation in which his readers were already rejecting prophetic claims; the danger lay precisely in their being susceptible to such claims, and he had inveighed against them. Now he cautions that his readers not on principle reject the utterances that some people claimed they made in the Spirit. He will go on to specify more clearly what the appropriate response should be.

5:20. *do not despise prophecies.* Paul again uses a present prohibition, thus creating a complementary parallelism to v 19: the despising of prophecies specifies further how the Spirit may be quenched. By *prophēteia* Paul may mean the gift of prophecy (as in 1 Cor 12:10; 13:2), but as the plural suggests, he has in mind prophetic utterances (as in 1 Cor 14:6, 22; thus NEB and most commentators). This supports the opinion that he has in mind an attitude towards someone else's activity rather than one's own.

It is remarkable that Paul has to warn against despising prophecies, for he thought of prophets as appointed by God (1 Cor 12:28–29) and as receivers of revelation through the Spirit (1 Cor 14:29–31; cf. 12:10), and one expects that his congregations shared his view. Yet in 1 Cor 14 (cf. 2:6–16) he is at great pains to stress the superiority of prophecy over speaking in tongues (cf. 1 Cor 14:1). He was in Corinth when he wrote 1 Thessalonians, and it is possible that it was the Corinthian situation that caused him to write the way he does about prophecies, especially since in 1 Corinthians (chap. 14 in particular), he gives preeminence to prophecy (Holtz 1986: 259).

It is more likely, however, that it was circumstances in Thessalonica that were responsible for his warning. The word *exouthenein* is a strong one, ranging in meaning from "to view with disdain" (Rom 14:3, 10; 1 Cor 1:28; 6:4; 16:11) to "to despise" or "to reject with contempt" (Acts 4:11; 2 Cor 10:10; Gal 4:14). Commentators who think that Paul's readers were already despising prophecies (on the basis of the present prohibition; see NOTE on v 19) have identified various reasons for their rejection: apocalyptic speculations that resulted in a failure to work (4:11; 2 Thess 3:6–11; thus Best 1972: 239; cf. Schlier 1972: 102); the demand for money by the idlers claiming to speak in the Spirit (Frame, 203–4) more generally, charismatics who led people astray and brought discredit upon this gift (Ellicott, 82); and a scorn of ecstasy (see Best 1972: 239).

Given the standing prophets enjoyed, it is not surprising that prophetic pretenders arose and were warned against (e.g., Matt 7:15; 24:11, 24; 2 Pet 2:1; 1 John 4:1). Paul warned against false prophets in 5:3, and v 20 should be seen in that context. If "Peace and security" is Paul's formulation of the message of false prophets in Thessalonica (see COMMENT on 5:3), we have a hint as to the kind of utterances he has in mind: they were eschatological messages (contrast Horn, 130). Paul does not want his sharp language about the false prophets (5:2–3) to be taken as justification for rejecting all prophecies about the end. He does not say anything about how the despising might be expressed, whether only in attitude, or by not heeding what was said, or by not allowing the utterances to be made (see von Dobschütz 1909: 226). The Thessalonians continued to be upset by the messages of people claiming to speak in the Spirit (2 Thess 2:2).

5:21. *but test every thing.* To the two prohibitions, Paul now contrasts actions that should be taken. The *de* ("but") is omitted by some manuscripts (א* A 33 syrp, pal), perhaps because of assimilation to *do* in the following *dokimazete*, or because the scribe did not see the connection of the verse to the preceding one

(Best 1972: 240), or because he wanted to make the verse a terse and disconnected maxim (Eadie, 211). The better attestation ($\aleph^c$ B D G it syr$^h$) and the sequence of Paul's thought in vv 19–22 argue for *de* as the better reading. The *de*
is adversative: Despite the misuse of the Spirit, the Spirit is not to be quenched
nor prophecies to be despised, but all things are first to be tested.

The *panta* ("everything") is problematic and has been thought by some to
have reference to everything, even beyond spiritual gifts in general (Morris 1991:
178), by others to all spiritual gifts (Ellicott, 82), by still others as all things expressed in inspired speech (Lünemann, 556), by yet others to all spiritual gifts including prophecy (Rigaux 1956: 592; Dautzenberg 1975: 131; Best 1972: 240;
Wanamaker, 203), and, correctly, to prophecy (Eadie, 211; Holtz 1986: 261).
Rather than rejecting prophetic utterances out of hand, they should be tested in
every respect.

The word for testing (*dokimazein*) is used by Paul for judging moral behavior
(Rom 12:2; 1 Cor 11:28; 2 Cor 13:5; Gal 6:4). Early Christian writers thought
that Paul was here dependent on a saying of Jesus not recorded in the NT, which
read: "Act as experienced exchangers [*dokimoi*]," but *dokimazein* and its cognates were too current to justify the connection (correctly, Rigaux 1956: 592; Jeremias 1964: 100–104).

Paul knew of persons who had a gift, made available by the Spirit, to test
prophets (1 Cor 12:10), and he may also have thought that prophets could test
what other prophets said (1 Cor 14:29–30). Paul uses *diakrisis* and *diakrinein*, respectively, in these passages in 1 Corinthians. A large number of commentators
hold the opinion that it is such charismatics that he has in mind as the ones to do
the testing (e.g., Ellicott, 82–83; Lünemann, 556; Eadie, 211; von Dobschütz
1909: 226). There is no reason, however, why the imperative *dokimazete* should
not be addressed to the same people the other imperatives are addressed to, namely all of Paul's readers (Dautzenberg 1975: 132). According to other passages in
the NT that deal with judging or testing false prophets, the testing is not limited
to certain people within the church (see Matt 7:15; 1 John 4:1–3; cf. *Did* 11).

Paul, however, is here concerned with testing the utterances of prophets rather
than the prophets themselves (probably also in 1 Cor 14:29–30, although he is
not explicit). Elsewhere, when prophets are to be tested, the criterion to be applied is their behavior (Matt 7:15–23; cf. *Did* 11:3–11) or an element of the
creed (1 John 4:2–3). Here, Paul does not explicitly state what criterion should
be applied. If v 22 is understood ethically, the criterion would also be their behavior. If, however, vv 21–22 still deal with prophetic utterances, then the criterion is to be sought elsewhere. Since Paul has corrected false prophecies in
5:1–10, his teaching there provides a standard by which to test. So also does the
eschatological teaching that his readers had received from him earlier (1:10;
2:12, 14–16; 3:11–13; 4:6, 13–17; 5:23). When he confronts eschatological error
in 2 Thessalonians, he explicitly refers to what they had been taught by him (2:5,
6, 15).

*hold fast to what is good.* A consequence of the testing is that it identifies what
is to be held on to. This is therefore not a general, disconnected saying, although

Paul does use *kalon* with an ethical sense elsewhere (e.g., Rom 12:17; 2 Cor 8:21; 13:7), but is the culmination of his directions on how prophecies are to be treated. The verb *katechein* frequently has the sense of holding fast to something that is authoritative (1 Cor 11:2; 15:2; cf. Luke 8:15; Heb 3:6, 14; 10:23), and it probably has that connotation here. The context demands that "the good" be that which meets the criterion used in testing. Secondarily, it will be found to be that which edifies the church (v 11; cf. 1 Cor 14:3–5, 12, 26; Dibelius 1937: 31).

5:22. *keep away from every form of evil.* As v 18 does, this verse echoes 4:3: It is God's will to keep away from evil. This verse is antithetically parallel to the preceding command, and is sometimes thought to be more general than it actually is (e.g., Eadie, 212; Lünemann, 556). The meaning of the command, which is influenced by the OT (Job 1:1, 8; 2:3; cf. 1QS 1:4), depends on how *eidos* and *ponēros* are understood.

*Eidos* could mean "appearance" (2 Cor 5:7), which would render the meaning that everything that even appears to be evil should be avoided. This would support an ethical interpretation of the verse. It is more likely, however, that *eidos* means "form" or "kind" (BAGD, 221). The word does not appear in the OT passages that influence this verse but is combined by Paul with *pās* ("every"), as is frequently done in Hellenistic Greek (Milligan, 76–77). Paul thus enjoins his readers to abstain from everything that is actually evil. The *pās* picks up on *pās* in v 21 and emphasizes the deliberateness with which evil should be avoided after a thorough testing shows it to be evil. *Ponēros* could be read as either an adjective or a noun. Read as a noun, "every form of evil," the antithesis to *to kalon* is kept more clearly. The reference is still to prophecy, and the subsection ends on a warning note.

## COMMENT

The history of the exegesis of vv 16–22 shows a tendency to isolate vv 16–18 from vv 19–22, to stress the traditional character of Paul's directions, and consequently to question whether these verses are related to a particular situation in Thessalonica. Evidence has been presented in the NOTES to support the interpretation that vv 16–22 constitute a unit, that their content coheres, and that it is directed to a specific situation in Thessalonica having to do with prophecy.

In vv 12–15 Paul specified ways in which the Thessalonians should edify each other (v 11). In vv 16–22 he concludes the paraenesis in his letter by giving directions on how his readers should respond to prophecies. He does so here for two reasons.

First, it is natural that he take up prophecy after the psychagogical instructions in vv 12–15, for prophecy, although it is a gift of the Spirit, had the same goal and methods (edification, exhortation, comfort) as psychagogy (1 Cor 14:3; see NOTE on 4:15; COMMENT on 4:13–18: Paul the Consoler). Prophecy thus belongs to a discussion of the community's edification (Laub 1973: 91–95).

The second reason Paul discusses prophecy is revealed in the form of his commands on prophecy. He does not view prophecy, as he did the various psychagogical activities in vv 12–15, from two sides, that of those who engage in an activity and that of those who receive it. In fact, he does not mention an activity (prophecy) but rather what is produced by it (prophecies). His focus is more narrow than it was in vv 12–15. It was particular prophecies, of which his readers knew, that caused him to conclude his paraenesis in this way. Furthermore, that he begins by prohibiting his readers from summarily rejecting what prophets say shows that he feared that they had a tendency to do so.

False prophetic utterances, which had fatal consequences, had engaged Paul's attention in the verses immediately preceding his paraenesis on the community's edification (5:1–10). He had been extremely sharp in his references to an existence that took its character from these utterances, which deferred the Parousia. Paul had warned, not too subtly, that, with the imminence of the Parousia removed, their existence was Epicurean in character (see COMMENT on 5:3, 6; 4:13; cf. 4:11–12). Having thus charged that prophecies could be dangerous, Paul now wants to keep his readers from rejecting all prophecies out of hand.

There were therefore circumstances in Thessalonica that called forth Paul's injunctions (see COMMENT on 4:13–18: The Problem at Thessalonica). But that does not support the hypothesis that the false prophets' success had met with a backlash in the congregation, which Paul now seeks to ameliorate lest all prophecy be rejected (Henneken, 105). Paul's readers were not already rejecting false prophecy; the problem was precisely that they were in thrall to the false prophets and that Paul had to be very emphatic to separate his readers and their life from the false prophets and the type of existence that was consistent with their teaching (5:1–10). Although the present prohibitions (vv 19–20) would normally command that a present action cease, they could also describe what should take place in the future, what should be habitual, which is what they do here.

Paul's prohibition not to quench the Spirit (*to pneuma mē sbennyte*) is made in language that also appears in discussions of the inspiration of the oracle at Delphi (see esp. van Unnik 1968; for some reason Forbes does not treat 1 Thess 5:19–22). A widespread theory was that the oracle's inspiration was effected by a subterranean spirit or vapor that entered the prophet as she sat on a tripod over a crack in the earth (Cicero, *On Divination* 1.38, 115; Strabo, *Geography* 9.3.5). Although this explanation is rationalistic, Plutarch thought that the spirit came from the gods and demigods (*On the Obsolescence of the Oracles* 438D).

The spirit entered the prophet's soul, enkindling and setting it aflame (Cicero, *On Divination* 1.114; Plutarch, *On the Obsolescence of the Oracles* 438C). Plutarch advances as one reason why, in his own time, the prophet no longer performed as she had done before, that the spirit had been quenched (*tou pneumatos . . . apesbesmenou*; *The Oracles at Delphi* 402BC). The language is similar to Paul's, but it is already evident that Paul's view of the Spirit differs from that of Plutarch, which is materialistic. Plutarch's view of prophetic inspiration has nevertheless been thought helpful in understanding 1 Thess 5:19–20.

Briefly stated, the psychology of inspiration Plutarch represents is as follows: Souls have an innate capacity to prophesy, but they prophesy when they are withdrawn from the body. A temperament or disposition must be attained "through which the reasoning and thinking faculty of the souls is relaxed and released" before they can prophesy (Plutarch, *On the Obsolescence of the Oracles* 432C). The prophet withdraws from the present "by a temperament and disposition of the body as it is subjected to a change [called] inspiration." What foretells the future is irrational and indeterminate in itself; it receives impressions when the prophetic spirit enters the body. Then "the soul becomes hot and fiery, and throws aside the caution that human intelligence lays upon it, and thus often diverts and quenches the inspiration" (432DEF). The prophet can be imposed upon to prophesy, but when she does not first attain the appropriate disposition, the results are likely to be disastrous and even fatal (Plutarch, *On the Obsolescence of the Oracles* 438A-D; Lucan, *Civil War* 5.120–97).

This language of inspiration has led to the view that Paul is prohibiting the Thessalonians from despising the gift of prophecy and suppressing the prophetic spirit in themselves (van Unnik 1968, followed by numerous commentators). It is not to be doubted that Paul uses the language of inspiration, but the numerous differences between his and Plutarch's views of prophecy caution against this interpretation. In addition to having a different view of the Spirit who inspires prophecy, Paul does not think that prophecy is irrational but considers it to be rational (1 Cor 14:15, 19) and susceptible to control by the prophet (1 Cor 14:32). For Paul it is therefore not reason that quenches the Spirit, for prophecy itself is rational.

Paul is not reflecting on the phenomenon of prophecy but focuses on certain prophetic utterances. The Spirit in v 19 is the prophetic Spirit, but the complementary parallel in v 20 shows that Paul's real interest is in prophetic utterances, as the plural *propheteias* also makes clear. Furthermore, the parallels show how quenching is to be understood, as despising prophetic utterances. This naturally means utterances spoken by someone else, which is in keeping with the communal interest Paul has shown throughout his paraenesis (4:6, 9, 18; 5:11, 12–15). That is absent from the pagan discussions of prophetic inspiration. Also in keeping with his communal perspective is that the congregation is to assess the value of prophetic statements that are made and so determine which ones are to be accepted as valid.

# IV. CONCLUSION, 5:23–28

◆

Paul concludes his letter with a prayer (vv 23–24), a request (v 25), a greeting (v 26), a command on the reading of the letter (v 27), and a benediction (v 28). Most of these elements are epistolary conventions that are also found in the conclusions of other letters of Paul, but his prayer in vv 23–24 differs sufficiently from the other elements in the conclusion that it may be considered apart from them. Opinion is divided over whether, from the perspective of epistolary form, the prayer is the end of the body of the letter and is therefore to be read as part of the preceding paraenesis (e.g., Rigaux 1956: 602–6; Bruce 1982: 164–66; Holtz 1986: 275; M. Müller, 112–17) or whether it is the beginning of the letter closing and is therefore one of a number of items with which Paul winds down his letter (e.g., Best 1972: 242–47; Wanamaker, 205–9; Weima 1994: 175–86).

The major reason usually advanced in support of the former position is that the prayer parallels 3:11–13, which concludes the first half of the letter. To this might be added that the designation of God as the God of peace (v 23) immediately after directions concerning prophecy is paralleled in 1 Cor 14:33. The major reasons for understanding the prayer as part of the letter closing are form critical. The peace and health wishes of Greco-Roman and Semitic letters are part of the letter closings. Furthermore, "peace" and "grace" in the conclusion (vv 23, 28) form an *inclusio* with 1:1. The evidence is slightly in favor of the latter position.

# TRANSLATION

5  23Now may the God of peace himself sanctify you completely, and may your whole spirit and soul and body be preserved blamelessly at the coming of our Lord Jesus Christ. 24He who calls you is faithful and he will do it.
25Brethren, pray also for us.
26Greet all the brethren with a holy kiss.
27I adjure you by the Lord that this letter be read to all the brethren.
28The grace of our Lord Jesus Christ be with you.

# NOTES

*5:23. Now may the God of peace himself.* For the formulation *autos de ho theos* ("Now may God himself"), see NOTE on 3:11. As it does there, *de* ("Now") marks a transition and is not adversative, for it introduces a distinction between what God does and what Paul had called on the Thessalonians to do (Frame, 210; for the Pauline peace wish, see Gamble 1977: 67–73). Insistence that the background of these words is epistolographic practice rather than liturgical (M. Müller, 112–17) sharpens a distinction that is not useful for understanding how Paul expected the letter to be received. Paul transforms an epistolographic convention to serve his pastoral purpose (see COMMENT).

Paul uses the same phrase elsewhere at the end of his letters (Rom 15:33; 16:20; Phil 4:9; see Heb 13:20; cf. 2 Cor 13:11, *ho theos tēs agapēs kai eirēnēs* ["God of love and peace"]; 2 Thess 3:16, *ho kyrios tēs eirēnēs* ["the Lord of peace"]). In Judaism, the phrase appears only in *T. Dan* 5.2, where it is analogous to "angel of peace" (*T. Dan* 6.2, 5; cf. *1 En* 40:8; 60:24; see Delling 1975: 78). For peace in Paul's thought, see NOTES on 1:1 and 5:3.

*sanctify you completely.* This prayer differs from the other places where Paul uses the formula, "May the God of peace be with you" in the way it is expanded. He picks up the theme of sanctification from the prayer in 3:13. He had de-

scribed sanctification (*hagiasmos*) as God's will, from the perspective of the
Thessalonians' actions (4:3). In the earlier prayer and now he describes sanctification from the perspective of God's actions (cf. 4:7), expressed in the optative
(see NOTE on 3:11), and he emphasizes the degree to which God sanctifies.

The very rare *holotelēs* ("completely") was used by Aetius (first or second century A.D.) of the fully formed human embryo (*Compendium of Tenets*, preserved
by Ps.-Plutarch, *On the Opinions of Philosophers* 5.21 [H. Diels, *Doxographi
Graeci*, 433, a21]). Paul thus uses current physiological terminology to stress the
thorough sanctification for which he prays. Although translated adverbially
("completely"), *holoteleis* is an adjective, and some commentators have understood it ethically, of the result of sanctification. It is better, in view of what follows, to understand it as describing the totality of sanctification, extending
throughout the person.

*and may your whole spirit and soul and body be preserved.* The second part of
the prayer amplifies the petition for sanctification. In the Greek, the two synonymous adjectives denoting entirety (*holoteleis kai holoklēron* ["completely and
wholly"]) are put together before the more common anthropological terminology. This places an emphasis on them, as does the chiasmus that results (*hagiasai
. . . holoteleis, kai holoklēron . . . tērētheiē*). The *kai* ("and") is epexegetical ("indeed"), introducing a fuller statement of the prayer-wish expressed in v 23.

*Holoklēros* too appears in Aetius with a meaning similar to that of *holoteleis*
(according to Ps.-Plutarch, *On the Opinions of Philosophers* 5.18; 5.19.5 [428,
25; 430, 23 Diels]; see also Plutarch, *On Stoic Self-Contradictions* 1047E, *holo-
klēria tou somatos* ["wholeness of the body"]). It and its cognates are also used in
letters of the health of his readers for whom a letter writer prays (see COM-
MENT). Grammatically, the singular *holoklēron*, here in the predicate position,
modifies only *pneuma*, which stands for the entire person in Pauline benedictions at the end of letters (Gal 6:18; Phil 1:23; Phlm 25). However, its physiological meaning supports the view that *holoklēron* modifies all three of the nouns
that follow, which in Paul's view constitute a unity. The passive optative *tērētheiē*
("may . . . be preserved") resumes *hagiasai*; its logical subject is God (for *tērein*
of God's preserving, see John 17:11, 12, 15; Rev 3:10; cf. 2 *Bar* 13:3, " . . . you
will surely be preserved until the end of times.").

This is the only place in Paul's letters where the tripartite division of human
nature into spirit, soul, and body appears, and this particular division appears
nowhere before him. Plato speaks of mind or intelligence (*nous*) in the soul, and
of the soul in the body (*Timaeus* 30B), and the Stoic Marcus Aurelius a century
after Paul has the division body, soul, and mind (*Meditation* 3.16), but Paul's trichotomy in 1 Thessalonians is the earliest occurrence of that precise formulation. Scholars have been divided since antiquity over whether this trichotomy
represented Paul's view of human nature or whether he held to the more traditional dichotomist view of body and soul (see von Dobschütz 1909: 230–32;
Rigaux 1956: 596–600).

Paul's use of anthropological terms is neither original, systematic, nor consistent. Most of the time, he speaks of the body and the spirit (e.g., Rom 8:10, 13;

1 Cor 5:3; 7:34; cf. Jas 2:26), but he also speaks of the flesh and the spirit (1 Cor 5:5), and the flesh and the mind (Rom 7:25). He distinguishes spirit and soul in 1 Cor 14:45, but the distinction is due to the way he develops an argument based on Gen 2:7. When Paul uses another tradition, the conventional description of friends as being one in soul (Aristotle, *Nicomachean Ethics* 9.8 1168b6ff.; Diogenes Laertius, *The Lives of Eminent Philosophers* 5.20), he uses spirit and soul in parallel, "one soul" further specifying "one spirit" (Phil 1:27). In Acts 4:32, where the same convention is used, it is expanded differently: *kardia kai psychē mia* ("one heart and soul").

That Paul was not interested in precise anthropological classification appears from the different ways in which he uses anthropological terms to describe the entire person. In 2 Cor 7:1, "flesh and spirit" do so, but in Rom 13:1 and 16:4 "soul" does, as does "spirit" in 1 Cor 16:18; 2 Cor 2:13; 7:13 (synonymous with "flesh" in v 5). In some of his salutations, "spirit" is equivalent to "you" (Gal 6:18; Phil 4:23; Phlm 25; cf. 1 Thess 5:28). Paul used "soul" in 1 Thess 2:8 to describe his total self (and perhaps "heart" in the same way in 2:4, 17; 3:13), but here he elaborates in order to emphasize the totality of God's sanctifying (cf. the elaboration of Deut 6:5 in Mark 12:30). Despite frequent claims to the contrary, Paul is writing rhetorically, and it is unnecessary to posit some liturgical tradition (Holtz 1986: 264) or popular psychology (E. Schweizer in *TDNT* 6.435) behind his words, or to separate "spirit" grammatically from "soul and body." Similarly, there is no need to have the latter explicate "spirit" (thus Masson, 77–78) or to see reflected in the tripartite formulation a Gnostic separation of the spirit from corrupt body and soul (Jewett 1971b: 175–83).

*blamelessly at the coming of our Lord Jesus Christ.* The temporal clause states when the readers' sanctification for which they are to be kept will come to fruition. The *en* ("at") shows that Paul does not here think of the process of sanctification (as though he used *eis*) that begins with baptism (1 Cor 6:11) and continues throughout life, but that his focus is on the final result of God's action. The adverb *amemptōs*, used only here in the NT, may thus be interpreted as an adjective (Frame, 214), with which Paul further describes their condition of being *holoteleis* and *holoklēron*. The perspective is the same as that of 3:13. For the comforting way in which Paul refers to the Parousia in this letter, see COMMENT on 4:13–18.

5:24. *He who calls you is faithful and he will do it.* The rhetorical force of the prayer is paralleled by the emphatic nature of this affirmation, which is similar in function to an "Amen." The adjective *pistos* begins the sentence ("Faithful is he"), thus emphasizing the reason why Paul's readers may be assured that his prayer for them will be fulfilled. Furthermore, the second part of this short sentence accentuates the affirmative in two ways. First, the word order (*hos kai*, "who also" or "who indeed") does so. Second, the verb *poiēsei* ("will do") has no object, which makes the affirmation more striking (cf. Num 23:19; Ps 36[37]:5). Rather than being a general statement, that God will act in accordance with his call, the context, which has to do with God's sanctifying, supplies the meaning (cf. also Rom 4:21).

Paul does not explicitly say that God is faithful, but there is no doubt that he is referring to God. The formula *pistos ho theos* ("God is faithful") appears elsewhere in Paul's letters (1 Cor 1:9, with God's call; 10:13, with God who will do; cf. 2 Cor 1:18; 2 Thess 3:3, with "the Lord"; see also Heb 10:23; 11:11) and is a succinct statement of the faithfulness of God (see Rom 3:4; 2 Tim 2:13). The theme is expressed in the OT in a similar formulation (Deut 7:9 LXX; cf. Isa 49:7 LXX, "Holy One of Israel"; see *Pss Sol* 14:1, with "Lord"). The formal character of the epithet has led to the supposition that it has a liturgical background, perhaps originally associated with baptism (von Osten-Sacken), but that is beyond proof. The liturgical ring to the verse here is due to Paul's anticipation that the letter would be read when the church met to worship, not to a liturgical practice from which it was derived.

Instead of saying that God is faithful, as he does elsewhere, Paul identifies *ho kalōn* ("he who calls") as the faithful one. It is always God who calls (cf. 2:12, also in the present; see NOTE there, and NOTES on 1:4, 5), and his call is to a life of holiness (4:7). But once more, and most emphatically, it is God who is faithful, who will render them completely holy and blameless at the Parousia.

5:25. *Brethren, pray also for us.* After the prayer (vv 23–24), Paul returns to using imperatives. No connecting particle ties this sentence to what precedes, but if the variant reading *kai* ("also") is read, there is a connection. The textual evidence for including (P³⁰ B D* 33 81) and omitting (ℵ A D<sup>c</sup> G) *kai* is evenly balanced, but most editors include it, albeit without great confidence (Metzger, 565). The *kai* could have reference to v 17, its significance being that the Thessalonians' ceaseless praying should not be so general that it does not include Paul. The connection could also, and more likely, be to v 23, in which event Paul wants his readers to pray on his behalf as he has just prayed on theirs.

Paul frequently requests the prayers of his correspondents (Rom 15:30–32; 2 Cor 1:11; Phil 1:19; 2 Thess 3:1; Phlm 22; cf. Eph 6:18–20; Heb 13:18; Ign *Magn* 14:1; Ign *Trall* 12:3). He does not here say what they are to pray for. If the connection with v 24 is accepted, he could be requesting prayers for his own sanctification and preservation. Given the content of his other requests for prayers, however, it is more likely that he has in mind his ministry (Wiles, 262–63). In that event, the request would recall the circumstances of his ministry of which he reminded his readers in chaps. 1–3 and, particularly, those circumstances of which Timothy would have informed them (2:15–3:1).

5:26. *Greet all the brethren with a holy kiss.* Letter writers conveyed two kinds of greetings. Greetings to addressees were expressed in the beginning of the letter, mostly in the prescript, while greetings involving third parties were expressed in the conclusion. The verb most commonly used was the one Paul uses here (*aspazesthai*); see the examples cited in COMMENT on vv 23–24, where the greeting is combined with the health wish (cf. Gamble 1977: 59–60). Of all Paul's letters, Galatians alone lacks greetings. Paul uses the noun on the two occasions that he sends his personal greetings (Rom 16:21; 2 Thess 3:17; cf. Col 4:18; contrast Rom 16:22). He uses the verb in the third person when he conveys the greetings of third parties (Rom 16:16, 21, 23; 1 Cor 6:19, 20; 2 Cor 13:12;

Phil 4:21, 22; Phlm 23; cf. Col 4:10, 12, 14; 2 Tim 4:21; Titus 3:15) and in the second person when he sends greetings to a third party (frequently in Rom 16; 1 Cor 16:20; 2 Cor 13:12; Phil 4:21; 1 Thess 5:26; cf. Col 4:15; 2 Tim 4:19; Titus 3:15; Heb 13:24; 1 Pet 5:14). It is noteworthy that he does not convey the greetings of anyone in the church in Corinth, from where he writes, or of any coworkers, as is his normal practice, excepting, also, 2 Thessalonians and Galatians.

In three instances when a third party is in view as the recipients of the greeting, the greeting is strengthened, as it is here, by the injunction that it be executed with a holy kiss (1 Cor 16:20; 2 Cor 13:12; 1 Thess 5:26; see also 1 Pet 5:14, a kiss of love). Paul's reference to the practice assumes that it was not new, but there is no certainty as to what its origin may have been. That it was liturgical in origin and reflects a practice at certain points in the worship of Pauline churches (G. Stählin in *TDNT* 9.136, 139; Bruce 1982: 133–34) may have the support of the practice in Rome after the middle of the second century (Justin, *Apology* 65.2), but there is nothing in Paul's letters to support the hypothesis (see Thraede 1968–69).

It is likely that Paul introduced the practice to his churches. The kiss in Greco-Roman as well as Jewish custom was, among other things, a form of family greeting (*TDNT* 9.119–20, 126), and given the importance of fictive family relationships in the Pauline churches (see NOTE and COMMENT on 1:4; Malherbe 1987: 48–51), it became the natural form of greeting in the churches. The kinship language is present here, *adelphoi* ("brethren") appearing in vv 25, 26, and 27.

The kiss is not an ordinary one but is to be holy, Paul again picking up on a major theme of the letter (see NOTE on v 23). Such a greeting may have been given at different points in the church's worship (Klauck, 352–56), but here its function is not liturgical but epistolary (Klinghardt, 336–38). As part of the greeting, the kiss expresses Paul's desire for a close tie among those in view in the letter. Chrysostom's understanding of Paul's injunction is on the mark: "Because absent he could not greet them with the kiss, he greets them through others, as when we say, 'Kiss him for me.' " (*Homilies on 1 Thessalonians* 11 [PG 62:465]).

It is not clear what situation Paul visualizes. Some commentators have the impression that Paul writes to the leaders of the church who are asked to extend Paul's greetings to the other members of the congregation (thus Frame, 216; Masson, 79; cf. Phil 4:21). The majority think that *tous adelphous pantas* ("all the brethren") is the equivalent of *allēlous* ("each other"; cf. v 11) and that Paul has the entire congregation in mind (e.g., Milligan, 80; von Dobschütz 1909: 232; Best 1972: 245). There is no reason why Paul's injunction to greet should not be seen as directed to the entire church, as the rest of the letter is. But it is unlikely, however, that the phrase "all the brethren" is equivalent to "each other," for it is immediately repeated in v 27, where it could not mean "each other."

The natural way to understand Paul's command is that "all the brethren" has in view Christians beyond the primary recipients of the letter. The letter is addressed to the church in Thessalonica, whom he asks to extend his greetings to other Christians. These Christians most probably were those persons in the environs of Thessalonica who had been converted by Paul's converts after he had left the city but whom Paul included in his care (see COMMENT on 1:1, 7–8; 5:27; the situation would be analogous to that represented in Colossians, e.g. 1:7–8; 2:1, 5; 4:13, 15–16). Greeting this secondary group with a holy kiss at Paul's behest would strengthen the solidarity between Paul and both groups. The kiss would thus have a social function rather than a primarily liturgical function.

5:27. *I adjure you by the Lord*. Instead of simply using another imperative, Paul makes his final exhortation with exceptional earnestness. Again he lapses into the singular for the sake of emphasis (but without *egō*; see on 2:18; 3:5; cf. 2 Thess 2:5; 3:17; pages 86–89). If this is where Paul takes the pen to conclude the letter in his own hand (see COMMENT), it shows that he considers the letter to be his own composition, not a joint one with his cosenders, Silvanus and Timothy. Greater weight is laid on his command by *enorkizō* ("I adjure"), the only place in the NT where the compound form of the verb is used. The language means, "I put you on your oath as Christians" (Morris 1991: 187). The reasons for the notable power of this charge are not immediately clear (see COMMENT).

*that this letter be read to all the brethren*. On the reading of the letter to its primary and secondary recipients, see pages 352–57. Again Paul specifies that "all the brethren" are to be taken into consideration (see COMMENT). According to many textual witnesses, the brethren are described as *hagiois* (א^c A K P Ψ 33 sy), but the adjective is almost certainly to be omitted (Metzger, 565–66). This is the only explicit statement Paul makes about the reception of the letter. It is not clear, however, what form of the letter was to be read to "all the brethren," whether it would be the original or a copy, who would take the letter to them, or who was to do the actual reading (see COMMENT). The reading was aloud and in public, as the community met for worship (see 2 Cor 1:13; cf. Col 4:16; Justin, *Apology* 1.67), but it is not known whether the courier of the letter or someone else would do the reading (cf. 1 Tim 4:13; Rev 1:3); the office of reader developed towards the end of the second century (see Gamble 1995: 211–31). The reading of Paul's letters in the churches cannot be compared to the reading of sacred texts in the synagogue or to the reading of Scripture in the church a century and a quarter later.

5:28. *The grace of our Lord Jesus Christ be with you*. As he had begun his letter (1:1), so Paul ends it with a grace benediction. All of his letters end with such a benediction, but no two benedictions are the same (see Gamble 1977: 65–67). Paul replaced the conventional *errōsthe* ("Farewell"; cf. Acts 15:29; 2 Macc 11:38) with the benediction, for which there are no precise parallels. "Peace" and "grace" from 1:1 are repeated in 5:23, 28, which enclose the final greeting.

## COMMENT

In the conclusion of the letter, Paul further strengthens his relationship with his readers. Whereas in chaps. 1–3 he did so by recounting the history of his relationship with them, in 5:23–28 he does so by adapting epistolographic conventions to his purpose and to the context in which he expected the letter to be read. That context was the church gathered for worship, a gathering that would hear his prayer on their behalf and his request for their prayer on behalf of himself, that would hear his greetings and his letter being read, and that would listen to his closing benediction.

The epistolographic conventions Paul adapts were originally designed to express a writer's goodwill towards his correspondents and to overcome the limitations imposed on both parties by their physical separation. Paul's conclusion does the same thing, but his modifications of the conventions intensify their social function of binding the founder of the church more closely to his converts and, in turn, binding them to their converts. In this way, the conventions aid Paul's pastoral purpose.

From an epistolary perspective, vv 23–24, whether they mark the closing of the body of the letter or the beginning of the conclusion, are important, for they summarize the main themes of the letter. The themes of call or election (1:4; 2:12; 4:7; 5:24; cf. 3:3; 5:9) and sanctification (4:3, 7; 5:23–25) are of major importance in the letter and are connected in 4:7. The prayer therefore functions epistolographically by forming an *inclusio* with 1:4 and reminding the readers of Paul's two major themes.

The epistolographic features in the conclusion are more extensive than has been recognized. Writers of letters used various literary devices to express their interest in the setting in which their letters would be read (see Koskenniemi, 186–89). Paul uses these conventions in vv 26–27, but the prayer in vv 23–24 already adapts a convention according to which a writer expresses his interest in his correspondent's health. In earlier Greek letters, the interest was expressed by asking for information about the reader's health, but by the early Roman period interest was expressed in the health wish at the beginning of the letter (see NOTE on 1:2), and by the first century A.D. the prayer for health had become part of the farewell, as it is in vv 23–24 (White 1986: 200–2). The following two examples illustrate the practice:

Greet [*aspasai*] Heliodorus and Exakon. Greet [*aspasai*] Apollonios the cobbler, and Plouton. I pray for your health with that of your children. (PAmherst 2.135, 20–24)

All my household greet [*aspazontai*] you. Greet [*aspasai*] all your friends, each by name. I pray that you are well. (PMich 8.479, 19–22; cf. 482, 34–37; 499, 16–19)

The words for health most frequently used are the noun *sotēria* and the verb *errōsthai*, but *holoklēros* and its cognates also appear frequently (see Koskenniemi, 71–72, 134–47, 151–54). Paul thus uses a contemporary epistolographic convention, but what is striking is the elaborateness of his prayer, that it deals with spiritual rather than physical soundness, and that the prayer is separated from the greeting in v 26.

As Paul had prayed for his readers, he requests that they pray for him. The principle of reciprocity, which was to govern relationships within the church to which he writes (3:12; 4:9, 18; 5:11, 12–15), should also govern his relationship with them. Paul had assumed that his converts were sufficiently concerned about his difficulties for him to send Timothy to them lest they be emotionally shattered by his afflictions (3:2–3, cf. 6), and he now asks for their continuing concern. That Paul acts pastorally towards his converts does not mean that pastoral care flowed in only one direction. As members of the Thessalonian church at different times gave and received such care, so Paul expected to be encouraged by other Christians with whom he would be in contact (Rom 1:12), and he was not reticent to say how much he was comforted by reports that his churches continued to be concerned about him (3:8; cf. 2 Cor 7:5–7).

Paul's petition for the Thessalonians' prayer would further strengthen his bond with them. He extends that bond to "all the brethren," evidently Christians beyond the immediate circle to whom the letter is addressed. In addition to the prayer he requests, which would most probably be congregational, the clearest indication of the letter's reception Paul envisages is provided by this command that the letter be read to "all the brethren."

Numerous reasons have been offered for the intensity with which Paul gives this command, the most prominent ones being the following:

1. Paul wanted all the members of the recently founded church to know of his goodwill towards them.

2. The church was profoundly divided, and Paul wanted to ensure that all Christians in Thessalonica would hear his words.

3. Not all members of the church could read, hence the command to have the letter read publicly for all to hear.

4. Paul was already suspicious that letters claiming to have been written by him were circulating in Thessalonica (see 2 Thess 2:2; 3:17), and his adjuration was intended to authenticate this letter.

5. Paul's primary readers were the leaders of the church, and he wanted to make certain that the entire church would hear what he had to say.

6. The "brethren" in vv 26 and 27 were coworkers of Paul's who were preaching in the neighboring areas, who should be aware of what he wrote to the church he had founded.

7. There were separate Gentile and Jewish churches, and Paul wanted this letter, although primarily addressed to Gentiles, also to be heard by Jews.

The social realities of first century Christianity suggest a different explanation. Given the rapid spread of the new faith from the original converts in Thessalonica (see COMMENT on 1:1, 7–8), it is likely that a number of house churches, each consisting of not more than a couple of dozen members, had come into existence in and around Thessalonica by the time Paul wrote 1 Thessalonians. The evidence is far from conclusive, but a picture of house churches emerges from scattered evidence that provides a possible explanation of these verses.

From Rom 16 it would appear that there were at least three house churches in Rome (vv 5, 14, 15) and perhaps as many as five (vv 10, 11); churches are associated with the households of a number of individuals in Corinth (e.g., Acts 18:1–3, 7, 8; Rom 16:23) in addition to other churches in the immediate area (Rom 16:1; 1 Cor 1:2; 2 Cor 1:1); and there may have been more than one church in Colossae (Col 4:15, 17; Phlm 2). We cannot be certain about the relationships among these churches in one area, but important for our present purpose is that in each instance one letter was written to a number of churches in one area (Malherbe 1983b: 100–101). Such a situation in Thessalonica would well explain Paul's references to "all the brethren" in vv 26 and 27: he wanted his letter to be read to all the Christians in the environs of Thessalonica.

Adolf von Harnack (1910) argued that the church in Thessalonica was divided between a Gentile majority and a Jewish minority, which met separately, and that 1 Thessalonians was written to the former and 2 Thessalonians to the latter. Nevertheless, he argued, 5:27 shows that Paul wanted to make certain that this letter would be read to all the Christians in Thessalonica. It is not improbable that Christians of different ethnic backgrounds and theological perspectives would meet in their own groups, but it is highly unlikely that Paul wrote separate letters to two groups (see COMMENT on 2 Thess 3:4, 6–10).

Paul would have preferred to be with the Thessalonians in person (2:17–18) but instead had sent Timothy to them, perhaps with a letter. Timothy had now returned to Paul, probably with a letter from Paul's Thessalonian converts, in which they asked for advice on some practical matters. In addition, Paul would have heard from Timothy about circumstances in Thessalonica about which they did not write. In response, Paul writes 1 Thessalonians, which was to be carried by an unknown emissary, who supplemented what Paul had written in this letter (see 1 Cor 4:17; cf. Eph 6:21; Col 4:7 for the practice).

This letter is therefore part of an ongoing process of communication, and Paul wants to ensure it as wide a distribution as possible. This is not the same as Gal 1:2, which addresses the churches in an entire region and is thus a circular letter. Nor is it quite the same as Col 4:15–16, which has to do with exchanging letters with a church in the next town. Paul's letters appear to have been circulated soon among churches other than those to whom they were written, and this practice contributed to their being copied and collected (Gamble 1995: 96–100). The passage 2 Pet 3:15–16 represents a stage further down the road.

The letter Paul wrote to his converts would naturally be the one read to them, but it is not certain what form of the letter, the original or a copy, would be read to the second group or groups, or who would have transmitted the letter to them. The following considerations make it likely that it was a copy. Paul dictated his letters (Richards) and signed them in different ways. On some occasions, he drew attention to the greeting that he himself wrote (1 Cor 16:21; 2 Thess 3:17;

cf. Col 4:18); on others he mentioned that he was writing in his own hand (Gal 6:11; Phlm 19).

There is no reason to doubt his claim in 2 Thess 3:17 that he always ended his letters in his own hand, even when he did not draw attention to it (Gamble 1977: 76–80). That would then be the case with 1 Thessalonians. Judging from Gal 6:11, the autographic conclusion could be quite long, and it is impossible to be sure where it begins in 1 Thessalonians, although the suggestion that he signals in 5:27 that he is taking up the pen has some merit (Best 1972: 246; Bruce 1982: 135; Marshall 1983: 164). But an equally good case could be made that the entire conclusion, beginning with v 23, could have been written by Paul.

A copy of the autograph would bear no such identifying feature. The possibility that such a copy of 1 Thessalonians became available to its secondary readers helps to explain the situation in 2 Thessalonians, where Paul is at great pains to certify the genuineness of the letter (3:17). He does so because he suspects that a letter purporting to have been written by him was advocating views contrary to his own (2:2). Copies of letters would have been more easily susceptible to glosses attributed to the original author (see pages 353–54 and COMMENT on 2:2; 3:17).

# PAUL'S SECOND LETTER TO THE THESSALONIANS

◆

# 2 THESSALONIANS:
# INTRODUCTION

◆

The circumstances that led to the writing of 2 Thessalonians must be determined in the first place from the letter itself. Unlike the case with 1 Thessalonians, the value of Acts for determining this letter's occasion is minimal. The manuscript tradition and patristic comment claim that Paul was the author and that it was the second letter Paul wrote to the Thessalonians. Both claims have been disputed, however, increasingly during the last three decades, and it has been argued that problems of authorship and occasion are much more complex for this letter than they are for 1 Thessalonians. The way the letter is understood depends on whether it is assumed that Paul wrote it or that someone else did so in his name. The discussion that follows assumes the integrity of the text (see pages 79–80; Sumney).

## I. PAULINE AUTHORSHIP

### A. OCCASION AND AUTHORSHIP

The issue of authorship is closely related to what is understood to have occasioned the letter. Although there is no information in 2 Thessalonians of the sort there is in 1 Thess 2:17–3:13, the letter does refer to certain circumstances in Thessalonica the writer had in mind when the letter was written.

On the assumption that the letter is genuine, we can learn a considerable amount of information concerning how Paul stayed in contact with the Thessalonians after 1 Thessalonians, to which 2 Thessalonians may refer (2:15; 3:17). Conditions in Thessalonica had deteriorated and called for a different response from what Paul had given in 1 Thessalonians. Unlike in his earlier letter, Paul here gives no indication of how he had learned of the conditions in Thessalonica that led to his writing 2 Thessalonians. There is no evidence, as there seems to be in 1 Thessalonians, that his converts had written to him (see pages 75–77), although this has been suggested (see Frame, 8–19 and his commentary on 2 Thess 1:2, 11; 3:1–5). We are left to reconstruct the situation from incidental remarks in 2 Thessalonians itself.

Paul includes Silas and Timothy as cosenders of the letter, as he had done in the first letter (1:1; 1 Thess 1:1), and from at least as early as Marcion the same authorship was attributed to both letters (see the evidence cited in Bornemann,

3 19–20; for the use of 2 Thessalonians in the early church, 547–57; Rigaux 1956: 112–20, for the use of both letters in early Christian literature). Paul's two coworkers who, according to Acts, accompanied him only during the second missionary journey, joined him in preaching the gospel in Corinth (2 Cor 1:19) after they brought him financial aid from Macedonia (2 Cor 11:7–11; Acts 18:5). Timothy delivered his report on the church in Thessalonica (1 Thess 3:1–10). In response to that report Paul wrote 1 Thessalonians, and it was probably while the three were together in Corinth that Paul wrote the second letter as well, perhaps in A.D. 51 (see pages 71–74). How soon after the first letter he wrote the second cannot be determined. Five to seven weeks (thus Frame, 19) may be too short a time, and it is highly unlikely that Paul wrote only a few days after he had dispatched the first letter (thus Graafen, 45–51). Paul most probably wrote the second letter a few months after 1 Thessalonians had been received and been circulated in accordance with his wish (1 Thess 5:26–27) and after the conditions addressed in 2 Thessalonians had developed.

With two exceptions (2:5; 3:17) the plural is used throughout the letter, as it is in 1 Thessalonians. The plural here also is to be understood as an authorial plural (see pages 86–89). While this letter is not as autobiographical as the first one, it is more explicit in referring to Paul's personal example as the basis for the directions he had given on how the Thessalonians were to behave and, now, on how the congregation should exercise discipline (3:6–16). Such features do not lay claim to apostolic authority for the letter, as is sometimes alleged (see pages 369–70), but they do mark an increase over 1 Thessalonians in the self-consciousness with which Paul makes demands.

Paul was experiencing persecution or at least opposition for preaching the gospel at the time he wrote (3:1–2). The circumstances he mentioned in 1 Thess 2:15–16 thus still obtained (cf. Acts 18:5–17). His request for his readers' prayers that the word might spread through his efforts as it did through theirs recalls the report of their evangelizing in 1 Thess 1:7–8.

## B. THE RECIPIENTS AND THEIR CIRCUMSTANCES

Paul says that he had heard about some Thessalonians' disorderliness (3:11) but does not say from whom. Presumably he had also heard about their behavior under persecution (1:4) and of the eschatological error of some of them from someone (2:1–2), but whether all his information came from the same person or persons is not clear. Nor is it clear that all the issues that were brought to his attention were related, for example, that the refusal of some to work (3:6–12) was due to the view that the Parousia had already taken place (2:1–2). Paul, as did early churches in general, depended to a considerable extent on oral reports for their knowledge of conditions in other churches (cf. Acts 14:27; 3 John 3). Such reports could be straightforward (e.g., Phil 2:26), but sometimes the significance Paul saw in what was reported makes it difficult to recover what he had actually been told (e.g., 1 Cor 1:11). He also lapsed into hyperbole about something that was reported (1 Cor 5:1) and wryly accepted it (1 Cor 11:18). We should, then, on principle, be cautious in the conclusions we draw about what Paul may have learned about the Thessalonians.

The basic facts about the Thessalonians, however, emerge clearly from what Paul writes and are ones we have already encountered in the first letter. They were being persecuted as they had been when he wrote the first letter (see 1 Thess 2:14), but the attention Paul now devotes to the problem (1:3–10) suggests that the persecution had increased or that his readers' consternation in the face of it required more attention. This is the major reason for writing the letter. In addition, some of them had adopted or were in danger of adopting eschatological views in need of correction (2:1–2), as they had been when Paul wrote 1 Thessalonians (see 1 Thess 5:3; cf. 4:15), but the erroneous views were now different. In all of this, Paul's first letter may have contributed to the difficulties he now addresses (see COMMENT on 2 Thess 1:3–4). Finally, the problem of idleness (1 Thess 4:11–12) had become aggravated, and Paul now finds it necessary to demand that the congregation discipline the loafers (3:6–15).

It is not only the subject matter that shows that this letter represents a further stage in Paul's communication with the Thessalonians; Paul is at great pains to underline the continuity with what had gone before. He refers to what he had written and had taught them when he was with them (2:5, 15). He also advances his own practice of working to support himself, which they knew from having seen him at work when he was with them, to justify the directions he now gives them (3:7–8).

Although there is thus continuity with what had gone before, this letter is not as warm in tone as the earlier one, for the circumstances that called forth 2 Thessalonians were not the same in all respects as those which had occasioned 1 Thessalonians. Before, a major concern of Paul in chaps. 1–3 had been to cultivate a warm relationship with his readers, on the basis of which he would give the practical advice of chaps. 4 and 5. In 2 Thessalonians, the issues were sharper, and in one instance—his directions on working—his earlier command had not been heeded. But it would be wrong to emphasize this difference to the point of overlooking the warmth that there is in Paul's language in this letter (e.g., 1:3, 4; 2:13; 3:13, 15) or to stress his reference to his authority (3:9) and the normative tradition (2:15; 3:6; see Dautzenberg 1969: 98–100; Laub 1990: 403–17) without taking note of the places where he identifies with his readers (1:7), refers to God's calling them through his preaching (2:14; cf. 1:10), which according to 1 Thess 1:4–6 had brought about his special relationship with them, and asks them to pray for him (3:1–2) as he prays for them (1:11). Furthermore, it cannot be stressed too strongly that the readers of 2 Thessalonians had also read 1 Thessalonians not too long before and that, indeed, Paul suspects that they misunderstood certain parts of that letter. He could assume that they had responded positively to his effort to cultivate a cordial relationship with them (see 1 Thess 3:6–9), and there was no need to repeat his earlier effort to that end.

The major doctrinal element at issue in Thessalonica when he wrote this letter was the erroneous teaching that the Parousia had already come (2:1–2). Much attention has been devoted to 2:2, primarily because it identifies the eschatological error, which has been thought to be Paul's main concern in the letter. This is an unjustified assumption that minimizes the importance Paul attached to behavior in chaps. 1 and 3. Paul does not say how he had learned of this problem, nor is he certain how the false teaching had come to the Thessalonians, nor, indeed, is he clear whether the false doctrine had already made inroads into Thessalonica or whether he is only alerting his readers to it. For our present interest, to learn as much as possible about the recipients of 2 Thessalonians, it is 2:2b, despite its obscurity, that is important. The obscurity of this verse may, however, be lessened when it is read in light of 1 Thess 5:26–27 and the ancient practice of "publishing" and circulating one's letters.

For various reasons (see pages 364–74), some scholars have thought that 1 and 2 Thessalonians were written to different sets of readers, suggestions ranging from the churches in Beroea (Goguel, 4.327–37) and Philippi (Schweizer; contra: Michaelis 1945) to different readerships within the church in Thessalonica. Thus one suggestion has been that 1 Thessalonians was written to the leaders of the congregation, and 2 Thessalonians, written soon after the first letter, was intended for the entire church, to be used primarily during its communal worship (Dibelius 1937: 58). There is no evidence to support the hypotheses of Beroea and Philippi as the destination of the second letter, and the passages usually adduced in arguing that Paul had two groups in view in one Thessalonian church, namely the congregation and its leaders (1 Thess 5:12–13, 26–27), admit of a different interpretation (see COMMENT on these passages).

Adolf von Harnack (1910) made a proposal that comes closest to the view of this commentary, that there was more than one group in Thessalonica. The letters are thought to be so similar that it has often been suggested that 2 Thessalonians was dependent on 1 Thessalonians (see pages 356–58) and Harnack thought that the major problem in the relationship between the two letters was more than merely literary. He sought to explain why the letters are so similar in many respects but are so different in mood and tone by arguing that the two letters were written at the same time, 1 Thessalonians to the entire church and 2 Thessalonians to a Jewish faction in it.

The differences between the two letters primarily reflect the ethnic background of their readers, in Harnack's view, but with few exceptions (2 Thess 3:6, 13–15) Paul does not add anything new in 2 Thessalonians, and at the significant points in the letter (2:5; 3:6ff., 10) he claims that his readers had been instructed by him in these details when he was with them. Paul had thus converted this group of Jews and wanted to make sure that 1 Thessalonians would be read to them also (see 1 Thess 5:26–27). He then decided to write a letter to them, because of their peculiar position as Jewish Christians in the city and the attendant dangers that that circumstance brought. Although Paul had converted them, he did not have as cordial a relationship with them as he did with the Gentiles. The Jewish group accepted the validity of the Gentile mission but had not yet become completely assimilated in the larger church.

Harnack's hypothesis has been almost universally rejected (an exception: Lake, 83–86). The reasons most frequently advanced in judging this theory improbable are that both letters are addressed to the entire church, that there is no evidence of the division in the church that Harnack suggests, and, most important, that had there been such factions, it is inconceivable that Paul would have encouraged the division by writing a second letter to one (e.g., Manson; Jewett 1986: 22).

In addition, it has also correctly been claimed that the Jewish elements in 2 Thessalonians on which Harnack based his hypothesis are not as pervasive as he asserted them to be (Best 1972: 39; see page 365). The Jewish elements, to which there are no parallels in the first letter, appear mostly in the apocalyptic section (1:5–2:12). But 1 Thessalonians, having primarily Gentiles in mind, shows that Paul had instructed them in apocalyptic themes right from the start (1:10; 4:6, 14), that they continued to reflect on them (4:15; 5:3), and that Paul could continue to use such traditions (2:15–16).

It is true that both letters were addressed to the entire church, but that does not necessarily lead to the conclusion that the church consisted of only one group. The social reality of first-century Christianity and Paul's compliment to the Thessalonians for their part in the spread of the gospel (1 Thess 1:7–8) make it highly probable that there was more than one group of Christians in Thessalonica already when he wrote 1 Thessalonians. Indeed, if Paul's ministry in Thessalonica lasted as long as two or three months, as is likely (see pages 59–61), it is probable that more than one Christian house church came into existence during his stay. Paul's claim that he had converted the readers of 2 Thessalonians need therefore not refer only to the primary audience of 1 Thessalonians.

It was evidently Paul's custom to write one letter to all the groups when there were a number of groups (see COMMENT on 1 Thess 1:1, 7, 8; 5:27; Gamble 1995: 97). It is therefore not incongruous at all that Paul wrote both letters to the entire church but focused on each of at least two groups as the initial recipient of a letter. Although 2 Thessalonians does not contain a command to have it read to "all the brethren," its concluding benediction does end with "you all" (3:16, 18), which could refer to the secondary readers of the letter.

Harnack partly anticipated the objections that there was no disunity of the sort he posited and that Paul would not have tolerated it, much less implicitly sanctioned it by writing 2 Thessalonians to one group. He argued (1910: 566 n. 1) that Paul could not have expected Jewish converts to give up immediately all their customs and adopt those of their Gentile fellow converts. There must have been a transition period. Although Paul's letters do not deal with this situation, Harnack saw it reflected in Gal 2:11ff., which is indeed a not improbable interpretation of that text.

More light is thrown on the circumstances of the recipients of 2 Thessalonians by reading 2:2b ("either by a spirit or by a spoken word or by a letter purporting to be from us, to the effect that the Day of the Lord has come") in the context of the ancient practices of the "publication" and circulation of letters. In the absence of a postal service for private correspondence, people in the Roman Empire made do with messengers who carried letters between writer and addressee (see White 1986: 214–16; OCD, 1233–34; Epp 1991). Even when messengers were selected with great care, the experience of so wealthy and important a person as Cicero in the late Republic shows that writers were constantly concerned that their letters might arrive late or not at all and that confidentiality, whenever it was important, might be breached when carried by sometimes not-disinterested persons (Nicholson). In the case of people of Cicero's standing, the letter carriers, who were familiar with the contents of the letters, might add to or clarify the letters when delivering them (White 1986: 216; Nicholson, 42 n. 16; see Cicero, *To Atticus* 15.4a; *To His Friends* 3.1.1–2).

Paul seems not to have been concerned about the safety of his letters or whether they would arrive on time. And although it is possible to surmise who delivered certain of Paul's letters (e.g., Phoebe [Rom 16:1]; Stephanas, Fortunatus, and Achaicus [1 Cor 16:17]; Epaphroditus [Phil 2:25–30]), it is striking that he never explicitly says that the persons he names were performing this service. Presumably, these individuals were well known to or were prominent in the churches to which the letters were written, and there was no need to identify or introduce them, although he did so in the case of Phoebe. For the same reason, Paul was not concerned about the letters' safety, and since the letters were public documents in the sense that they would be read to churches, confidentiality was not an issue.

Another reason why Paul did not identify the persons who carried his letters is that his messengers were likely to have supplemented or explained his letters orally (see Eph 6:21; Col 4:7 for the practice in post-Pauline churches), and there was therefore no need to identify them as the letter carriers. The Christian letter bearers were an integral part in the process of communication by letter. There are indications that Paul's letters sometimes needed to be explained. He protests too much in 2 Cor 1:13–14, when he asserts that he only wrote what was readily understandable (contrast 2 Pet 3:16).

The Corinthians, for example, on one occasion clearly needed clarification of a requirement that Paul had made of them. Paul supplied this clarification in 1 Corinthians (see 5:9–13). And in 1 Corinthians Paul informs them that Timothy would supplement what he was writing (4:17), evidently when Timothy would arrive in Corinth (16:10–11) some time after 1 Corinthians had been delivered by Stephanas, Fortunatus, and Achaicus (1 Cor 16:17). Paul would rather have seen his correspondents in person; it was when that was impossible that he turned to writing letters, as he did when he wrote 1 Thessalonians (see 2:17–18; 3:10). Paul shared this reticence about writing letters with other writers (e.g., Demosthenes, *Epistle* 1.3; Isocrates, *Epistle* 1.2; *To Philip* 25–26). So although Paul's letters are all that remains of his communication with his churches, we should be sensitive to the fact that they constituted only part of that communication.

We do not know who the bearer of 1 Thessalonians was or who would have read the letter to its primary audience, but it is safe to assume that the bearer would have done more than merely deliver the letter. According to the ancient understanding of publication, 1 Thessalonians was published when it was first read in Thessalonica. The custom in literary circles was that an author's letter would be read aloud to a circle of his acquaintances and might then be discussed or commented upon. This appears to have been the custom in Paul's churches (see NOTE and COMMENT on 1 Thess 5:27). "In any event, the text, once placed in the hands of the recipients, was no longer under Paul's control and might be used as the community or its members saw fit" (Gamble 1995: 96). This would have been even more likely if the letter were intended to be circulated (see Rom 1:7; Gal 1:2), as Paul's letters were assumed to have been by his successors (see Col 4:16). The natural thing would have been to circulate copies of the original letter rather than the letter itself.

This epistolary practice is the ground for the following hypothesis that explains the references to letter writing in 2 Thessalonians. Paul's adjuration in 1 Thess 5:27, that the letter be read to all the brethren in the congregations in Thessalonica and its environs, was followed. Paul assumes this in 2 Thess 2:2b, but the tentativeness of his language there shows that he may be uncertain about the form in which the primary recipients of 2 Thessalonians had received 1 Thessalonians. There is no way of knowing who carried the copy of 1 Thessalonians to its secondary audience, but since the command in 1 Thess 5:27 is addressed to the primary audience, it suggests that it was they rather than the original bearer(s) who disseminated it. Paul further reckons with the possibility that 1 Thessalonians was interpreted by individuals who did so claiming that they were representing Paul's prophetic proclamation that he made as he was moved by the Spirit or who simply claimed that they could do so because they knew Paul's teaching (see NOTE and COMMENT on 2:2).

The fact that what Paul meant in his letters was not always clear to his readers suggests that the comment or explanation that accompanied the reading of 1 Thessalonians need not have been an attempt to introduce teaching contrary to Paul's (see COMMENT on 2:2). If Paul thought that someone had done so, one would expect him to have responded with the sharpness he exhibited in Galatians and 2 Cor 10–13, when he was confronted with doctrines contrary to his own. It is more likely that there was a misinterpretation of his teaching. It is also worth noting that it is not clear from 2 Thess 2:1–2 whether the Thessalonians had already succumbed to the error or whether Paul's clarification was intended to be prophylactic (so also Wanamaker, 40).

Paul's emphasis in drawing attention to the subscription written with his own hand (2 Thess 3:17) suggests that he suspected that his readers had received a copy of 1 Thessalonians rather than the original. The subscription therefore performs an authenticating function: he wants to make it abundantly clear what his teaching and its application are. It may also hint that he suspects that the copy his audience had read to them had been glossed. That is beyond proof, although not impossible. Before Marcion, already, Christians felt free to emend texts in order, ironically, to preserve their true meaning (see the perceptive discussion by Gamble 1995: 125–27). In principle, therefore, the letter Paul refers to could have been a glossed or emended copy of 1 Thessalonians.

There is also another possibility to be considered. The reference to a "Pauline" letter should be seen in the context of the epistolary activity of Paul and his followers. The Pauline wing of the early church engaged in intense literary activity, and a few decades after Paul's death letters were written in his name. It is possible that such letters were already circulating by the early 50s, which should not be surprising, since Paul had probably already written letters to churches he had founded during the fifteen years or so since his call to preach to the Gentiles. When he left Thessalonica, it could already have been known that he used letters as a medium of instruction and spiritual care when he was separated from his newly established churches.

Such letters and those of his later followers would have been distributed to churches other than the ones to which they were addressed. Such a situation would have facilitated the writing and circulation of letters in his name. However, evidence in favor of understanding 2:2 to refer to such a pseudonymous letter eludes us. The situation as reconstructed here makes it likely that Paul is referring to 1 Thessalonians and an interpretation of it. To eliminate any possible doubt about 2 Thessalonians, he draws attention to his signature and further appeals to the traditions he had taught them either when he was with them (2:5, 15) or in 1 Thessalonians (2 Thess 2:15; cf. 3:6). His strategy is therefore to circumvent the possible sources of the error.

## C. THE STRUCTURE, STYLE, AND PURPOSE OF 2 THESSALONIANS

This reconstruction of the epistolary situation goes a long way towards explaining the literary relationship between 1 and 2 Thessalonians. That relationship has been a bone of contention, especially after William Wrede (1903) made a synoptic comparison of 1 and 2 Thessalonians, which proved to him that the second letter was literarily dependent on the first. The judgment has been made that as much as one-third of 2 Thessalonians is derived from 1 Thessalonians (e.g., von Dobschütz 1909: 45). We are concerned here with the question of literary relationship, primarily for what it may say about the structure and purpose of 2 Thessalonians.

The comparison that follows demonstrates that, when placed in parallel columns according to the order of 2 Thessalonians, similarities between the two letters seem to emerge. References in boldface are of epistolary conventions that are sometimes thought to reveal the structure of the letter. The references not in bold type represent similarities in language or content, but they are of less importance for our purpose.

| | *2 Thessalonians* | | *1 Thessalonians* |
|---|---|---|---|
| **1:1–2** | Paul, Silvanus, and Timothy to the Thessalonians . . . grace to you and peace. | **1:1** | Paul, Silvanus, and Timothy to the Thessalonians . . . grace to you and peace. |
| **1:3** | We ought to give thanks to God always for you. | **1:2–3** | We give thanks to God always for you. |
| 1:4 | | 1:3 | |

| | | | |
|---|---|---|---|
| 1:5 | | 2:12 | |
| 1:7 | | 3:13 | |
| 1:8 | | 4:5–6 | |
| 1:10 | | 3:13 | |
| 1:11 | | 1:2–3: 2:12 | |
| 2:1 | | 4:15–17; 3:13; 5:12 | |
| 2:2 | | 4:15 | |
| 2:5 | | 2:9; 3:4 | |
| **2:13** | We ought to give thanks to God always for you. | **2:13** | We give thanks to God without ceasing. |
| 2:14 | | 1:4–5; 2:12; 5:9 | |
| 2:15 | | 3:8 | |
| 2:16 | | 3:11 | |
| **3:1** | Brethren, pray for us. | **4:1** | Well, then, brethren, we beseech and exhort you in the Lord Jesus. |
| 3:3 | | 5:24 | |
| **3:5** | May the Lord direct your hearts to the love of God and to the steadfastness of Christ. | **3:11** | May our God and Father himself and our Lord Jesus direct our way to you. |
| 3:6–14 | | 4:11; 5:14 | |
| 3:8 | | 2:9 | |
| 3:9 | | 1:6–7 | |
| 3:10 | | 4:11 | |
| 3:12 | | 4:1, 11 | |
| 3:15 | | 5:13–14 | |
| **3:16** | May the Lord of peace himself give you peace continually in every way. | **5:23** | May the God of peace himself sanctify you completely. |
| **3:18** | The grace of our Lord Jesus Christ be with you all. | **5:28** | The grace of our Lord Jesus Christ be with you. |

There are similarities between the two letters, but they are not as great as is frequently thought, and they differ in importance. The phrase *to loipon* ("For the rest"; 2 Thess 3:1) or *loipon oun* ("Well then"; 1 Thess 4:1), is not peculiarly epistolary and occurs at different places in the letters, so may be omitted from consideration in a structural comparison.

It is frequently claimed that the most striking feature in comparing 1 and 2 Thessalonians is the similarity in their structure, as represented by the boldfaced items above, which appear in the same sequence (e.g., Frame, 46). To these might be added the prayers in 2 Thess 2:16–17 and 1 Thess 3:11–13 (Menken 1994: 39; but the instruction in eschatology [2 Thess 2:1–12, 15; 1 Thess 4:13–5:11] and the faithful saying [2 Thess 3:3; 1 Thess 5:24], also adduced by Menken, are out of sequence). Beyond these formal features, there are echoes of 1 Thessalonians in 2 Thessalonians. What is characteristic of 2 Thessalonians, however, is that the reminiscences of the first letter are incorporated "in original ways into new settings" (Frame, 47), and they do not appear in the same order as in 1 Thessalonians (von Dobschütz 1909: 45).

In terms of substance, the similarities are confined to the importance of eschatology in both letters (e.g., 1 Thess 4:13–5:11; 2 Thess 1:5–2:12) and the issues of manual labor and disorderliness (1 Thess 2:9; 4:11–12; 5:14; 2 Thess 3:6–12). Rather than merely repeat the concerns of the first letter, however, 2 Thessalonians reveals that there were further developments in Thessalonica in these matters and that, although the subjects were the same, the details about them were no longer the same, and so Paul's responses to them were accordingly also different (see NOTES and COMMENT on 1:3–4).

Attempts to explain the relationship between the two letters have frequently been marked by methodological error. Since Wrede, the comparison between them has been dominated by the narrow problem of the inauthenticity of 2 Thessalonians. The procedure has been to follow the structure of 2 Thessalonians and compare scattered references from 1 Thessalonians to it (e.g., Menken 1994: 36–38; Richard, 20–25). This method has also been used by defenders of the authenticity of the letter (e.g., von Dobschütz 1909: 45). In the absence of large blocks of similarities, critics focus on words and phrases, which appear so numerous that they are led to the conclusion of a recent commentator on 2 Thessalonians (Menken 1994: 39; cf. Marxsen 1982: 34):

> There is only one explanation for these similarities: between 1 and 2 Thessalonians there is a literary dependence: the author of one letter wrote making use of the other letter. He had the other letter, so to speak, on his desk.

This view was already rejected by von Dobschütz (1909: 46–47), who suggested, more persuasively, that the similarities were more likely due to Paul's mind being flooded by memories of what he had written in 1 Thessalonians not too long before. The major methodological problem with using 1 Thessalonians in the comparison merely as a source to be mined in service of the hypothesis of the inauthenticity of 2 Thessalonians is that the first letter loses coherence and its inherent structure does not emerge; one may then not speak of a true comparison of letters. When the two letters are compared, respecting the coherence of each, what stands out are not their similarities but their differences (see Frame, 46–51). The following outline assumes the integrity of 2 Thessalonians and views it on its own terms (see pages 79–80 for compilation theories):

I.   Address, 1:1–2
II.  Thanksgiving and Exhortation, 1:3–2:12
     A.   Thanksgiving Proper, 1:3–12
          1.   Thanksgiving, 1:3–4
          2.   Encouragement of the Discouraged, 1:5–10
          3.   Petition for Worthy Conduct, 1:11–12
     B.   Exhortation: The Day of the Lord, 2:1–12

III. Thanksgiving and Exhortation, 2:13–3:5
    A. Thanksgiving Period Proper, 2:13–14
    B. Exhortation, 2:15–3:5
        1. Admonition, 2:15
        2. Prayer for Encouragement, 2:16–17
        3. Request for Prayer, 3:1–2
        4. The Faithfulness of God, 3:3–4
        5. Prayer for Faithfulness, 3:5
IV. Commands, 3:6–15
    A. Discipline of the Disorderly, 3:6–12
    B. Congregational Admonition, 3:13–15
V. Conclusion, 3:16–18
    A. Prayer for Peace, 3:16
    B. Greeting, 3:17
    C. Benediction, 3:18

It is not clear that attempts to understand 2 Thessalonians in light of ancient rhetorical systems (Jewett 1986: 81–87; Hughes 1989: 68–93; Wanamaker) gain much over the form-critical approach, although the two methods are not mutually exclusive. When 2 Thessalonians, outlined as above, is compared with 1 Thessalonians as outlined on pages 78–79, a number of things emerge as to their structure. First is that, aside from the address and conclusion, the differences between the letters are far more striking than their similarities (see also Best 1972: 53; Murphy-O'Connor 1996: 111). The major section of 1 Thessalonians, the autobiography (chaps. 1–3), does not appear in 2 Thessalonians at all. Furthermore, the other epistolary elements thought to be similar in fact appear in 1 Thessalonians in this autobiographical account (1 Thess 1:2–3; 2:13; 3:11). The way the possible literary dependence of 2 Thessalonians on 1 Thessalonians has occupied the discussion is particularly unfortunate in that the structure of the second letter has not emerged clearly, and this has obscured the purpose of the letter.

In 1 Thessalonians Paul used three thanksgivings (1:2–3; 2:13; 3:9); in 2 Thessalonians he uses two, but in totally different ways. In 1 Thessalonians, the thanksgivings frame and develop the autobiography, which forms the basis for the exhortation in chaps. 4 and 5. In 2 Thessalonians, by contrast, the two thanksgivings begin the letter by introducing two sections of exhortation that together constitute two-thirds of the letter.

The first exhortation is dominated by eschatology, and it encourages the discouraged and exhorts those who are in danger of being unsettled by false teaching (see Weiss 1959: 289–90). The first main part of the letter, then, is hortatory or, more precisely, comforting. According to the ancient classification of letters, it would so far appear to be a letter of consolation (see COMMENT on 1 Thess 4:13–18). Paul's tone here is encouraging and caring, as is appropriate in such a letter. The second thanksgiving introduces exhortation on a number of matters, but primarily having to do with mutual concern and with the reception of the word and faithfulness to Paul's traditions.

After these exhortations, Paul turns finally to command the church with respect to the disorderly, those of its members who refuse to work (3:6–15). His tone is now different. He begins his directions to the church with a peremptory command, "We command [*parangellomen*] you, brethren, in the name of the Lord Jesus Christ" (3:6; cf. 3:12), and throughout this subsection (3:6–12) his tone has the force of the ancient "commanding letter" (*parangelmatikē epistolē*) of the epistolary handbooks, such as Ps.-Libanius, *Epistolary Styles* 62:

> You have frequently wronged your farm laborer as if you did not know that the insult [was sure to] get back to us. Stop it right away, lest we bring suit against you also for your earlier injustice.

The sample shows that the tone is appropriate when considering judicial procedure. In the second subsection (3:13–15), Paul then directs the disciplining congregation not to abandon those they discipline, but to act pastorally towards them, which nevertheless means that they are to be made ashamed and admonished (*nouthetein*), that is, to have sense instilled in them and be taught what should and should not be done (Ps.-Demetrius, *Epistolary Types* 7). In the final part of the body of the letter, Paul thus takes a harder stance towards the church than he does in the rest of the letter, and he demands that the church also do so towards the idlers in its midst.

The language that Paul uses in this concluding part belongs to and recalls the psychagogic tradition he used so freely in the first letter, although he uses it here with a harder edge. Nevertheless, his language does reveal his pastoral intention in writing this part of the letter. His pastoral concern already becomes evident in chap. 1, where he uses apocalyptic traditions rather than the psychagogical language in a consoling manner. Psychagogical language does, however, appear in 2:1–3:4: *erōtōmen* ("we beseech" in 2:1); *mē . . . saleuthēnai* ("not . . . to be shaken") and *mēde throeisthai* ("not to be troubled" in 2:2); *stēkete* ("stand") and *krateite tas paradoseis* ("hold to the traditions" in 2:15); *parakalein* ("to comfort" in 2:16, of God); *stērizein* ("to establish" in 2:17; 3:3, of God); *phylassein* ("to guard" in 3:3, of God). This language is not used in precisely the same way it was in 1 Thessalonians, for the circumstances that called forth 2 Thessalonians required a different psychagogic adaptation than it did in Paul's first letter (for adaptation, see COMMENT on 1 Thess 2:11–12; 5:12–15). The differences between the ways the traditions are used should not be accentuated to the point that Paul's aims in the two letters are considered radically different.

It is frequently thought that the main purpose of 2 Thessalonians was to correct the error of 2:2. One mistake in this view is that it arbitrarily diminishes the importance Paul attaches to the issues he addresses in chaps. 1 and 3. Another is that it effectively, if not explicitly, isolates 2:1–12 from what precedes and makes it didactic in nature, whereas it is more closely related to the consolatory section of 1:3–12 and is paraenetic (see Trilling 1972: 75–76). And as has been observed, the ancients thought of consolation as belonging to paraenesis (see COMMENT on 1 Thess 4:13–16).

It is preferable not to assign 2 Thessalonians exclusively to one particular epistolary type. It has been suggested that 2 Thessalonians belonged to the category of the letter of advice (Wanamaker, 48; see Ps.-Demetrius, *Epistolary Types* 11), but advice and paraenesis were not as sharply differentiated at this time as they would be later (see Ps.-Libanius, *Epistolary Styles* 5). But elements of the letters of command and admonition are also present, and it would therefore be more precise to describe the letter as belonging to the mixed type that draws from many styles (Ps.-Libanius, *Epistolary Styles*, 45). It is with this understanding that the broad term "exhortation" has been used in this commentary to describe the letter.

Second Thessalonians is hortatory and pastoral, as 1 Thessalonians also was. There are differences in structure between the letters, as Paul carefully adapted to new circumstances. But in doing so, he followed the directions he had given his readers in his first letter. (This explains why, with the exception of 2:1–12, the impression may be left that there is not much new in 2 Thessalonians [Wrede, 17].) In 1 Thess 5:14 he had told them to "comfort the discouraged"; this he does in 2 Thess 1:3–3:5, but in a way different from 1 Thess 4:13–5:11. He had also told them to "admonish the disorderly"; this he does in 2 Thess 3:6–12, and his readers are told to do the same in v 15. These are the two purposes of 2 Thessalonians (see also Frame, 52).

# D. AN ALTERNATIVE SEQUENCE OF THE LETTERS

As early as Hugo Grotius, it has been suggested that if 2 Thessalonians were written before 1 Thessalonians, a number of problems would be solved. Grotius thought that such an order best explains Paul's reference in 2 Thess 3:17 to his custom of signing his letters (1641: 1.1032; 1646: 2.651; see Hughes 1989: 75–76, on Grotius). Johannes Weiss (1959: 1.289) suggested that 2 Thessalonians was a letter Timothy took along when Paul sent him to Thessalonica from Athens (1 Thess 3:1–5). Its present position in the canon is due to the principle that longer letters stood first in order; the titles of the letters were added by later editors. Thomas W. Manson judged that, if 2 Thessalonians is read by itself, it is little more than a note, but if it is read in relation to 1 Thessalonians, it reveals a young community, fervid in its expectation of the Parousia (270). Manson has provided the most extended argument for the primacy of 2 Thessalonians and has been followed by a number of scholars who sometimes added arguments of their own. The following are Manson's major arguments.

1. The persecutions mentioned in 1 Thess 2:14 are clearly in the past, but are at their peak in 2 Thessalonians. Second Thessalonians 1:4–5 is "merely a hopeful and friendly mode of expression, for the whole letter shows that they were in the most urgent need of encouragement" (271; see also Weiss 1959: 289–90). There is nothing in 1 Thessalonians to indicate that the persecution was still going on. In response, it has been countered that the argument would have force, except if the persecutions were intermittent (Jewett 1986: 24) and that persecutions were in fact a reality when 1 Thessalonians was written (Best 1972: 43,

who refers to 1 Thess 3:3, which may, however, not have in mind the Thessalonians' persecutions; but see 2:15).

2. The internal difficulties of the church are a new development in 2 Thessalonians but familiar to all concerned in 1 Thessalonians. Thus, the situation depicted in 2 Thess 3:11–15 sounds new. But in 1 Thess 5:14 the full force is not appreciated unless Paul had in mind what he said in 2 Thess 3:11–15. The specific command (*parangellein*) referred to in 1 Thess 4:10–12 is the one he gave in 2 Thess 3:12. This is inconclusive, for it is natural that Paul in a second letter deals at greater length with an issue that had become inflamed since the first letter was written (also Jewett 1986: 25).

3. Similar to Grotius's suggestion, it is proposed that the emphasis on Paul's signature (2 Thess 3:17) makes sense only if it appears in the first letter. Paul signed other "first letters" in the same way (e.g., Gal 6:11; Phlm 19). However, if 3:17 was written because of Paul's suspicion about a letter purporting to have been written by him, it would imply that the Thessalonians had already received such a letter before his first genuine letter was written, which is unlikely.

4. Paul's reference to times and seasons in 1 Thess 5:1 would be very much to the point if they had already received 2 Thess 2. The argument is inconclusive, for 1 Thess 5:1 could, and probably does, refer to oral teaching rather than instruction by letter (Best 1972: 44); besides, it is inconclusive for the same reasons advanced to Manson's second argument.

5. In 1 Thess 4:9–5:11 Paul responds to inquiries made in a letter from the Thessalonians or via Timothy, which arose from their having read 2 Thessalonians. Thus 1 Thess 4:9–12 refers to 2 Thess 3:6–15; 1 Thess 4:13–18 responds to a question that arose because of 2 Thess 2:1–12; 1 Thess 5:1–11 responds to questions about the signs that will precede the end. This is forced reasoning; the normal experience of new converts would give rise to the issues Paul addresses.

6. Another argument is based on a perception of the theology of the letters. Manson thinks that 1 Thessalonians, a letter of joy, is a more mature form of thought than 2 Thessalonians, a letter of anxiety, with its references to judgment and punishment. This misunderstands 2 Thessalonians and is, besides, a modern understanding of what constitutes a mature theology. (Buck and Taylor, 140–45, also are concerned with the development in Paul's theology, which they consider unlikely to have taken place in so short a period.)

Manson had been preceded (West) and was followed by other advocates (e.g., Gregson) for 2 Thessalonians being written first, but his is the most thoroughgoing argument in favor of it. Defenders of the traditional sequence, who have been more numerous, have found it convenient to engage him as the prime representative of the view he proposes (e.g., Best 1972: 42–45; Jewett 1986: 24–26). Charles Wanamaker has recently written the only commentary based on the hypothesis of the primacy of 2 Thessalonians, and he has insisted that, rather than simply refute Manson's arguments, a positive case should be made for the priority of 1 Thessalonians (39). If such a case can be made, then the counterclaims against Manson would be implicitly proven.

Jewett (1986: 26–30) had earlier set out to do precisely that, putting forth three arguments:

1. There are three references in 2 Thessalonians (2:2, 15; 3:17) to previous correspondence, but there is no reference in 1 Thessalonians to an earlier letter, which is *prima facie* evidence that 2 Thessalonians was written later.

2. "Paul provides in 1 Thessalonians an elaborate explanation of the apocalyptic significance of persecution," whereas "nowhere in 2 Thessalonians is concern expressed about how the congregation is responding to persecution" (28).

3. Paul's references to his direct relationship with his readers "in 1 Thessalonians are exclusively in connection with the founding of mission" (29). In contrast, the only reference in 2 Thessalonians to the founding mission is in 2:15.

All Jewett's arguments are not equally persuasive, and Wanamaker subjects them to close scrutiny. He concludes that the "strongest piece of evidence, in fact virtually the only evidence of any real merit for the precedence of 1 Thessalonians, turns out to be the possible reference to a previous letter in 2 Thess 2:15" (45), but which he thinks is a reference to 2 Thessalonians itself. The arguments in the debate are essentially exegetical and will be considered in the exegesis of 2 Thessalonians below. Suffice it here to note that Wanamaker has attempted to refute Jewett's arguments but has not himself made a coherent case for the primacy of 2 Thessalonians.

Such a case must take into consideration evidence in 2 Thessalonians of Paul's contact with the Thessalonians as the background to the letter, and in his discussion of the sequence of the letters Wanamaker is much too modest in exploiting that evidence. In focusing on the relationship between the two letters, he has lost sight of the following references which, taken together, could suggest a sequence of events that led to the writing of 2 Thessalonians, Paul's first letter to the church after he had established it: Paul had converted the Thessalonians (2:14) and taught them eschatological doctrine (2:5) as well as social responsibility (3:10) and perhaps other matters (2:15). He remained with them long enough to expect that his personal example would carry weight (3:7–9). After leaving them, he received alarming news that there was a threat of doctrinal error (2:2), that some of his converts were disobeying his command that they should work (3:11), and that the Thessalonian believers were being persecuted (1:4). He then writes 2 Thessalonians, long enough after he had left Thessalonica for him to suspect that a letter had been written in his name (2:2). On such a reading, 1 Thessalonians does not appear anywhere in this letter.

This reading pulls together scattered references to reconstruct the history of Paul's relationship with the Thessalonians. Most frequently, that is the only kind of evidence available for a historical reconstruction of Paul's mission, but the evidence for the primacy of 1 Thessalonians is of a different sort and is much stronger. In the introduction to 1 Thessalonians (page 80) and in the commentary, especially on 1 Thess 2:17–3:10, it was seen that Paul's major concern in the first three chapters of the letter was to remind his readers of his relationship with them and to develop it further. That relationship had come into existence when Paul had preached the gospel to them (1:5–6), and beginning at that point, Paul reminds them of what had transpired up to that point when he wrote 1 Thessalonians. This historical reminiscence serves as the basis for the entire letter, but particularly of the paraenesis he gives in chaps. 4 and 5.

## E. CONCLUSION

Paul wrote 2 Thessalonians soon after 1 Thessalonians, around A.D. 51, from Corinth, when Silas and Timothy were with him. He had heard of certain conditions in Thessalonica, learning that his converts were discouraged by persecution, that there was danger of their being unsettled by erroneous teaching about the Parousia, and that some refused to work. In response, he wrote a pastoral, hortatory letter that was encouraging as well as admonishing.

Paul addressed 2 Thessalonians to all the believers in Thessalonica, as he had 1 Thessalonians, with the primary audience being a group he had converted. It was different from the primary audience of 1 Thessalonians, but there is insufficient evidence to support Harnack's theory that this group was Jewish. They had heard a copy of 1 Thessalonians read to them, accompanied by amplification or comment on what Paul had meant by the Day of the Lord. In writing 2 Thessalonians, therefore, Paul could assume that his readers knew 1 Thessalonians and that he only needed to refer to those elements from it that were germane to his immediate purpose.

# II. NON-PAULINE AUTHORSHIP

## A. ARGUMENTS FOR PSEUDONYMITY

Paul had always been considered the author of 2 Thessalonians until the beginning of the nineteenth century (see Bornemann, 498–537; Rigaux 1956: 124–52; Trilling 1972: 11–45, for the history of research). The hypothesis of a pseudonymous authorship was first proposed by J. E. C. Schmidt in 1801, on the basis of the eschatology of the letter, particularly with 2:1–12 in view, and received fuller critical support throughout the nineteenth century. William Wrede gave important support to the claims for pseudonymity in 1903, attaching greatest importance to the literary relationship between 1 and 2 Thessalonians, which has figured prominently in the discussion ever since.

The majority of scholars still hold to the genuineness of 2 Thessalonians, but after the publication of Trilling's canvassing of the issues in 1972, an increasing number of critical scholars have come to regard the letter as pseudonymous. The currency of this view is reflected by the number of commentators who hold it, only one of whom wrote before Trilling's book (Masson in 1957), the rest after (Krodel, 1978; Marxsen, 1982; Laub, 1985; Menken, 1994; Richard, 1995; Légasse, 1999) and by other, extensive studies (e.g., P. Müller, 1988). The major arguments advanced in support of pseudonymity are the following (summaries by J. A. Bailey, 131–40; Trilling 1981).

## 1. Literary Relationship

Proponents of pseudonymity consider the literary relationship to be the major issue in solving the "riddle" of 2 Thessalonians (e.g., Marxsen 1982: 18–28; Menken 1994: 36–40). It is claimed that answers to all other questions depend on a satisfactory explanation of this relationship (Trilling 1980: 23). Conversely, if the relationship between the letters is shown to be not as close as it has been made out to be, the other arguments supporting the claim of pseudonymity lose considerable force. It was demonstrated above (see pages 356–59), that the relationship is not as close as has been claimed and that the structure of 2 Thessalonians can be explained as due to Paul's addressing two problems in Thessalonica, namely his readers' discouragement in the face of persecution and the refusal of some to heed Paul's command that they work to earn their own living. It remains to consider the other arguments.

## 2. Language and Style

The argument on the basis of the linguistic evidence has taken into consideration matters of vocabulary, style, and tone.

The number of words that are unique to each letter does not support the view of two different authors (see Milligan, lii–liii). Seventeen words occur only in 1 Thessalonians, of which nine come from the LXX, six represent ordinary Greek usage, and two seem to be Paul's own formulations. Ten words are unique to 2 Thessalonians, of which five are from the LXX and five are not unusual.

The OT does not directly influence either letter, for neither quotes from it. The closest possible allusions to the OT appear in 2 Thess 1:9 (Isa 2:10; cf. 19, 21) and 2:8 (Isa 11:4 in apocalyptic contexts). For the rest, the stronger OT allusions are formulaic (2:3; cf. Deut 7:9; Isa 49:7) or liturgical (3:5 [cf. 1 Chr 27:18]; and 3:16 [cf. Num. 6:27; Ruth 2:4]), thus in traditional material. It is true that there is a more Septuagintal cast to 2 Thessalonians, which is probably due to the apocalyptic elements throughout chaps. 1 and 2, but there are more OT phrases in 1 Thessalonians than is generally recognized (Holtz 1983: 56–57; Penna, 2.89–91). Language therefore does not help much in determining the relationship between the letters, and it is generally thought that the language throughout both letters is that of Paul (von Dobschütz 1909: 39–44; Frame, 28–37; Rigaux 1956: 80–94; Trilling [1972: 46–66] remains unpersuaded).

Certain terms seem to some scholars to be used in different ways in the two letters, for example, *thlipsis* ("tribulation") is the basis for retribution in 2 Thess 1:4–6 but is the confirmation of the Thessalonians' election in 1 Thess 1:6–10; *basileia tou theou* ("the kingdom of God") is present in 1 Thess 2:12 (cf. Rom 14:17; 1 Cor 4:20), but future in 2 Thess 1:5; *klēsis* ("calling") has a future orientation in 2 Thess 1:11 but is used of the Christian life in the world in 1 Thess 4:7. Such judgments erroneously assume that there is only one dimension to words for Paul, and such judgments are based on unfirm exegetical grounds.

On the other side of the ledger are the facts that some unusual terms occur only in 1 and 2 Thessalonians (*Thessalonikeus* in 1 Thess 1:1 and 2 Thess 1:1; *euthynein* in 1 Thess 3:11; 2 Thess 3:5) and that unusual turns of phrase, probably derived from the LXX and from apocalyptic literature, are used about the same number of times in both letters (see the list in Frame, 32–33). Because of such evidence, there has been a hesitancy to draw far-reaching conclusions on the basis of vocabulary (e.g., Milligan, liv–lv; Rigaux 1956: 87). Proponents of pseudonymity, however, consider certain kinds of linguistic use cumulative evidence for their position (e.g., Trilling 1972: 46–51; P. Müller, 11–12). At least one such proponent, however, does not think that the vocabulary of 2 Thessalonians is any less Pauline than that of the recognized letters (Menken 1994: 32).

A number of stylistic features have also been brought into the discussion. Paul frequently uses pictorial or figurative language in 1 Thessalonians, whereas in 2 Thessalonians such language appears only twice (1:7, rest or relief; 3:1, the word running). Beda Rigaux (1956: 90), who drew attention to this phenomenon, ascribed no great significance to it, but Trilling (1972: 56) thought it pointed to pseudonymity. The significance of the images that Paul uses in 1 Thessalonians is considerably diminished when it is observed that almost all of them are derived from the traditions Paul uses and are therefore hardly characteristic of his style: psychagogy (nurse [2:7]; father [2:11]), consolation (those who are asleep [4:14–15]), apocalyptic (the trumpet [4:16], birth pangs [5:3], the thief in the night [5:4], darkness and light, day and night [5:4–5]; to sleep and be awake [5:6, 10]).

It is also alleged that the long sentences in 2 Thessalonians (e.g., 1:3–12; 2:5–12; 3:7–9) differ from the short sentences in 1 Thessalonians and are not Pauline. Paul does, however, use long sentences in, among other places, 1 Cor 1:4–8; Phil 1:3–11, which appear at the beginning of his letters, as does, indeed, 1 Thess 1:2–5 (perhaps 1:2–7, if the sentence is punctuated differently). It is true that the sentences in 2 Thessalonians are generally longer, but the stress should rather be on the shortness of the sentences in 1 Thessalonians, which is due to the paraenetic style of that letter.

The short, asyndetic sentences, characteristic of paraenesis, appear frequently there (e.g., in 1 Thess 4:4–10; 5:1–11, 14–22) but seldom in 2 Thessalonians (3:2b, 17, which are not paraenetic). The second letter is also hortatory, but its style is closer to the apocalyptic traditions Paul uses when he encourages or consoles. When he consoles in 1 Thess 4:13–5:11, his sentences are also long, and he uses no antitheses in 4:13–18, although antitheses of different kinds are used in the apocalyptic paraenesis (5:1–11). The argument based on the length of sentences, therefore, does not take into consideration the different literary characteristics when comparisons are made, and are consequently without validity.

Paul's language in the second letter is fuller than in the first. He repeats words more often (Trilling 1972: 62–63), although that is partly due to the subject matter (but see the formulations with *pās* ["all," "every"] and *pantote* ["always"]: 1:3, 4, 10, 11; 2:9, 13, 17; 3:2, 6, 16, 17). On the other hand, in 1 Thessalonians he uses triadic formulations (e.g., faith, hope, love [1:3]; power, Spirit, full conviction [1:5]) three times as often as he does in the second letter (see Rigaux 1956: 89).

Finally, attention is drawn to the more formal or impersonal tone of 2 Thessalonians, which is thought to be expressed in the formulation "We ought to give thanks" (1:3; 2:13); in the use of "brethren," which is only used in the structural formulas supposedly taken from 1 Thessalonians (2 Thess 1:3; 2:1, 13, 15; 3:1, 6, 13; but see 3:15) in contrast to the way it is used eighteen times in 1 Thessalonians, and by the use of "we command" to introduce paraenesis in 2 Thess 3:6 (cf. 3:4, 10, 12) instead of "we beseech and exhort" in 1 Thess 4:1 (cf. 4:10; 5:11, 14).

In addition, it is remarked that 2 Thessalonians does not have the warmth of the first letter and that it does not dwell on Paul's cordial relationship with the Thessalonians (Krentz, 520). Here scholars are led astray by the warm relationship that Paul cultivates in 1 Thess 1–3, which is not in 2 Thessalonians and is, indeed, unique among all of Paul's letters. The tone of 2 Thessalonians is not as impersonal as is often claimed (see page 351), but there is a greater formality. This is due to the impression Paul wishes to make on his readers because of the new situation in the church. Even so, not all the elements marshaled to demonstrate Paul's formality in fact do so, and will be taken up in the commentary.

Although the argument of a difference in tone is very weak, it has nevertheless been pressed into service to argue for pseudonymity (Trilling 1972: 63–64). The assessment of the argument by a commentator who thinks Paul did not write the letter is telling: "The difference in tone *per se* is not a sufficient reason to deny Pauline authorship to 2 Thessalonians, but in combination with other factors, it has some weight" (Menken 1994: 31). That is, the evidence is cumulative in nature and ultimately depends on the argument of literary structure.

In conclusion, it needs to be stated that it is fundamentally wrong to compare the language of the two letters in this way. The investigation is shaped by the question of pseudonymity, which means that differences are concentrated on and their significance is exaggerated. There is either no, or at the most insufficient, attention given to how the changes in the situation in Thessalonica may have caused Paul to consciously adopt a different style at points to achieve his present goal, not the one he had when he wrote 1 Thessalonians. All Paul's letters, after all, have their peculiarities (von Dobschütz 1909: 43).

The most serious shortcoming of these linguistic investigations is their purely statistical character. They do not take into consideration the literary style of 1 Thessalonians or the traditions that Paul uses in it. They are therefore insuffi-

ciently sensitive to Paul's derivation of the language that comes into consideration and to how it functions in the various sections of the letter. The language of
1 Thessalonians becomes a conglomeration of words, phrases, and sentences to
be manipulated to prove a hypothesis. At best, the results of this approach can
only be inconclusive.

## 3. Theology

The major theological difference between the two letters, to the mind of those
who reject the genuineness of 2 Thessalonians, is to be found in their escha-
tologies, which also has consequences for other theological elements in the author's thought (see Braun; Trilling 1972: 124–28; full discussion in P. Müller,
41–67; summarized by Krentz, 521). The argument is basically that apocalyptic
traditions dominate 2 Thessalonians and that their effect is to present an eschatology that differs from what Paul taught in 1 Thessalonians as well as in his
other letters. So, salvation in 2 Thessalonians is completely future, where judgment also plays a major role (1:7–10; 2:8), but before the Parousia certain
events must occur (2:3–12). This eschatology reinforces the encouragement
that is given to the faithful, namely, that they will be vindicated (1:5) when
those who persecute them will be condemned (1:8–9; 2:11–12). The apocalyptic schema of 2:1–12 thus urges them to remain faithful and so serves a moral-
izing function.

It is claimed that this eschatology differs from Paul's in a number of ways. Paul,
it is said, held to an imminent coming of the Lord in the first letter (1 Thess 4:15,
17; 5:1–5; cf. Rom 13:11–12; 1 Cor 7:29, 31; Phil 4:5), whereas in 2 Thessalonians the author holds an opposite view, in connection with which he commands his readers to stand firm and be faithful (2:15). Paul, it is said, does not
stress judgment as much as this letter does and never uses the idea of retribution
to comfort believers who are being persecuted.

What is most striking about these arguments is, once again, that they do not
consider the changed situation between 1 Thessalonians and that portrayed in
2 Thessalonians. In dealing with Paul's theology, the particularities responsible
for the contours of his theology are slighted. In consequence, dubious statements
are made about what his views are, particularly as expressed in 1 Thessalonians,
or the evidence is read one-sidedly.

A few examples will suffice. First Thessalonians also speaks of judgment (1:10;
2:16) and of future deliverance from it (1:10). Paul does not speak of an imminent Parousia in 1 Thess 4:15, 17, although he expected Christ to come during
his lifetime; nor does he do so in 5:1–5, where, more precisely, he speaks of the
suddenness of the coming of the Day of the Lord (vv 2–3) with connotations of
judgment, which has moral implications (5:4–7). He there counters a view that
defers the Parousia with one that stresses the proleptic nature of the Day (see
COMMENT on 5:2–7; cf. 2:16). The persons he has in mind in 2 Thess 2:2
most likely misunderstood this (see pages 371, 373 and COMMENT on 2 Thess
2:2). That he uses a "timetable" to correct this error is not unique; he does so too

in 1 Cor 15:23–28, where he also counters a radically realized eschatology (see v 19; cf. 4:8). And Paul's combining the notion of judgment with the comfort of believers who are being persecuted is due to the situation in regard to which he is writing, one where persecutions and eschatological anxiety confounded his readers.

It is also thought that the eschatology of 2 Thessalonians influences its Christology. In this letter, Christ acts only in the future. The judgment will take place at his revelation from heaven (1:8), when he will destroy the Lawless One (2:8), and believers will be gathered to him at his Parousia (2:1). There is also a tendency to use language about Christ that is used elsewhere by Paul of God (cf. 2 Thess 2:13 with 1 Thess 1:4; 2 Thess 2:14 with Rom 1:23; 3:7; 1 Cor 10:31, etc. of God's glory; 2 Thess 3:12 with 1 Thess 5:23; see Menken 1994b). But this phenomenon is already present in 1 Thessalonians, especially in eschatological sections, where Christ appears to engage in eschatological judging (see COMMENT on 1 Thess 2:19; 3:11–12; cf. 2 Cor 5:10), and the Day of the Lord (God) becomes the Day of the Lord (Christ), where it retains its OT association with judgment (see COMMENT on 1 Thess 5:2–3).

It is completely unrealistic to expect Paul to write in exactly the same way in all circumstances. It is clear from 1 Thess 4:13–18 that he used material from the traditions available to him, both apocalyptic and consolatory, selecting only what was useful to him as he tried to comfort his readers in their particular circumstances. He does the same thing in 2 Thessalonians. In this regard, the assessment of a defender of the pseudonymity of 2 Thessalonians is to the point as regards the difference in eschatological outlook:

> I believe that this difference alone is not a sufficient argument, but that it may be an argument in combination with other pieces of evidence . . . . In general, Paul is able to express his ideas in various ways, dependent upon the situations of his audiences and of himself . . . . This means that, as far as eschatology is concerned, it is *possible* that Paul wrote 2 Thessalonians. Whether it is *probable* is another matter. (Menken 1994a: 29–30)

We have, thus, once more what is regarded as cumulative evidence. We have seen, however, that the foundation for the argument of inauthenticity, the hypothesis of literary dependence, is unstable and that each bit of evidence has proved to be inconclusive or unpersuasive when viewed on its own.

## 4. Apostleship, Tradition, and Ethics

Observations on these three topics cannot be said to be arguments for pseudonymity; they are rather interpretations based on the assumption of pseudonymity. A good example is the claim that 2 Thessalonians stresses Paul's apostolic authority. The fact that the word "apostle" appears only once in 1 Thessalonians (2:7) and is completely absent from 2 Thessalonians has not been a deterrent to the assertion. Assuming that the letter was written generations after Paul, when the figure of Paul was invoked as a means by which legitimacy could be claimed for Paulinists who sought to apply Paul's teachings to new situations (e.g., Col 1:24–28; Eph 3:1–9), elements in 2 Thessalonians are identified to demonstrate that the letter belongs to a later period characterized by such tendencies.

The argument goes as follows: The call of the Thessalonians is connected with Paul's preaching (2:14), which brings about faith in the truth (2:13) in contrast to those who do not love the truth but believe in falsehood (2:10–12). If Paul's hearers hold to this truth they will be saved and attain to the glory of the Lord (2:14). Since the apostolic message provides this guarantee, it is incumbent on them to hold to the apostolic tradition, whether taught orally or by letter (2:15), and 2 Thessalonians contains the tradition (3:17). The apostolic tradition is to govern the conduct of the readers (3:6), and the normative apostolic example (3:7–9) reinforces the commands on how to behave in particular ways (3:10, 12). What is striking is that all the ethical demands are related to the person and teaching of Paul (2:15–3:15).

If one drops "apostolic" from the previous paragraph, which does not appear in the text, and refuses to be scared by "tradition," what is said to be so different in 2 Thessalonians turns out to be quite similar to 1 Thessalonians. In that letter as in no other Paul through his gospel forms a relationship with the Thessalonians that could provide them with security in the faith (see COMMENT on 1 Thess 1:5–6; 3:6). When he introduced the paraenetic section proper (4:1–2), Paul reminded them of the tradition of paraenetic precepts that he had transmitted to them when he was with them. And he reminded them of his own manual labor (2:9), which reinforced his command for them to earn their own living in similar fashion (4:10–12).

The judgment of Menken is once more on target:

> These differences are not immediately visible, but they are the result of a certain amount of interpretation; the very limited size of the letter (only forty-seven verses) makes it difficult to verify such interpretation. The differences are easily exaggerated by those who are already convinced that Paul did not write 2 Thessalonians, or minimized by those who are convinced that he did. (Menken 1994a: 30)

Exegesis of the text will determine which conviction is correct.

## B. OCCASION, PURPOSE, AND DATE

Those scholars who advocate pseudonymity frequently focus on the apocalyptic matter in the letter, particularly 2:1–12, on the ground that it reveals the major purpose for writing. They consequently discover the occasion for the letter in a context in which especially that passage is intelligible. One view identifies the context as a renewed interest in apocalypticism after A.D. 70, and especially before the turn of the first century, citing as evidence 4 Ezra, Mark 13, Matt 24–26, and Revelation.

Some persons, it is argued, appealing to the authority of Paul, proclaimed an apocalyptic kerygma, "The Day of the Lord is at hand" (2 Thess 2:2), which 2 Thessalonians corrects (Koester 1971: 244–45). Another view rejects the claim that 2:2 could be apocalyptical, for then a series of cosmic events would have had to have taken place; instead, the problem is identified as Gnostic, an interpretation that is further supported by referring to the idle life (3:6–16), which, it is asserted, was Gnostic (Marxsen 1968: 39; so also J. A. Bailey, who cites 2 Tim 2:17–18). These views have in common an approach that attempts to fit 2 Thessalonians into a broad history-of-religions context.

Different answers have been given for why the pseudonymous letter is addressed to Thessalonica. Wrede suggested that the eschatological "enthusiasts" whom the letter opposes appealed to 1 Thessalonians for their views, hence the letter was associated with Thessalonica, but it was written at some distance from Thessalonica (37–38). Willi Marxsen (1982: 34–35, 80), however, held that the letter was addressed to the Thessalonians because 1 Thessalonians was read in the church there and the enthusiasm 2 Thessalonians corrects may have been based on an interpretation of 1 Thess 4:13, 17. Wolfgang Trilling (1980: 25–27) also found the reason in 1 Thessalonians, which deals with the Parousia more than any other Pauline letter (4:13–5:11), but for Trilling that did not mean that the letter was written to Thessalonica. It was written, rather, to a church or churches where the conditions reflected in the letter existed and was thus written out of the author's situation rather than that of the Thessalonians.

First Thessalonians itself has also been named as the occasion for 2 Thessalonians. Rather than simply correcting erroneous apocalyptic ideas for which the first letter was responsible or which it could be understood to be justifying, the author of 2 Thessalonians wrote to replace 1 Thessalonians, in effect treating it as inauthentic. Lindemann picked up an older argument but gave it more precision, arguing that 2 Thessalonians was written to eliminate the expectation of an imminent Parousia, which could be supported by 1 Thessalonians. Although the author uses 1 Thessalonians, he does not quote from it, but refers to it in 2:2, thus associating it with the error he opposes. He wants 2 Thessalonians to be accepted as Paul's only letter to the Thessalonians (2:15; 3:17).

One cannot help but be impressed by this imaginative and skillful proposal, yet in the final analysis it does not convince. Not only is the exegesis of the relevant passages forced, but the notion, that someone should write under the name of Paul to secure apostolic authority in order to undermine a genuine Pauline letter, is stunning in its boldness. And it exhibits an understanding of what the use of apostolic "authority" meant in pseudonymous letters that does not do justice to the phenomenon. It was not so much a grab for apostolic power as it was a device with which writers could apply what they considered apostolic teaching to a new context.

Marxsen (1982: 30–35, 80) has offered a somewhat related but still different proposal. Marxsen argues that the author faced a concrete problem (2:2) that he answered by referring to Paul's teaching in person rather than engaging what Paul had written (2:5; 3:10). The author knows 1 Thessalonians, but he writes as

if it did not exist. He does not mention 1 Thessalonians because it must have
been preserved in Thessalonica and the enthusiasts in Thessalonica may have
appealed to it for support. He alludes to it in 2:2 without explicitly referring to it
and passes it off as a forgery. The letter his readers must heed is 2 Thessalonians,
but anticipating that this letter might be questioned, he adds 3:17. Marxsen's proposal has the advantage, as does that of Lindemann, that it engages the major
texts exegetically, but his reading too does not deliver the most natural meaning.
In addition, his proposal that 2 Thessalonians was written to Thessalonica raises
the question how a pseudonymous letter could displace a genuine Pauline letter
that had been written to the same church less than three decades earlier and was
still preserved in Thessalonica.

Trilling has denied that 2 Thessalonians was meant to replace 1 Thessalonians; rather, it was meant to supplement it. He maintains that 2 Thessalonians
was written to dampen the expectation that the Day of the Lord was imminent,
to encourage the faithful in time of persecution, and to give directions concerning the disorderly. Strictly speaking, however, Trilling asserted, the letter deals
with only one theme, the Parousia; the reference to persecution is vague and
confined to the first thanksgiving (1:2ff.), and it is not clear that disorderliness
was an actual problem.

It is not Paul but the interpretation of Paul's teachings that 2 Thessalonians
wishes to correct, according to Trilling. The people the author has in mind probably found support for their view in 1 Thess 4:15, 17, where the Day of the Lord
is not mentioned, but the idea of an imminent coming *is* present. Trilling is on
the right track when he suggests that the problem lay with the interpretation of
Paul's teachings. It is not clear, however, why the problems could not have existed in Thessalonica soon after Paul's first letter was received (see page 351).
The clearest connection with the first letter is the question of disorderliness in
3:6–15 (cf. COMMENT on 1 Thess 4:10–12), and Trilling's judgment that it
was not an actual problem is arbitrary.

Most scholars date the pseudonymous letter in the last two decades of the first
century A.D., although Marxsen (1968: 44) thinks that it was written soon after 70.
Various reasons for the late date are adduced: Paul's writings were known widely
enough for the writer to be able to write under the cover of Paul's name (Wrede,
91; J. A. Bailey, 143; Trilling 1980: 27–28, 152), the delay of the Parousia had
become a problem (Laub 1985: 40), the renewal of interest in apocalypticism
(Koester 1982: 244–46). Other considerations sometimes brought into the discussion of the letter's date have not carried much weight. Persecutions of Christians, for example, by Domitian, do not help to determine the date, for there were
persecutions earlier, indeed, Paul mentions some of them earlier in 1 Thess
2:14–16 (Wrede, 91). It has sometimes been thought that, if 2:4 refers to the temple in Jerusalem, the letter would have to have been written before 70 (see discussion by Wrede, 36–37, 96–113), but that is not a strong argument against a late
date, "for the apocalyptists often write as if things are still in existence when they
are not (cf. Rev. 11:1ff. re the temple)" (Best 1972: 58). If 2 Thessalonians was not
written by Paul, a dating late in the first century is a reasonable conjecture.

# C. CONCLUSION

The arguments against the authenticity of 2 Thessalonians are not persuasive. When they do rest on the interpretation of particular passages, they slight or reject the more natural meanings of the texts. The judgment that the major (sometimes that the only) theme in the letter is eschatology is totally arbitrary. By neglecting the attention the letter gives to the disorderly and to the persecution of the readers and their conduct under it, the pastoral dimension of the letter is missed. Furthermore, when the letter is seen primarily as a theological discussion that could have taken place wherever Paul was accepted as an authoritative figure who wrote letters, the connection with 1 Thessalonians that 3:6–12 makes is slighted at too high a price: it sacrifices the major point at which continuity with Paul's ministry in Thessalonica and with 1 Thessalonians can be demonstrated.

It is much more likely that Paul was writing to correct some of his readers' misunderstanding of 1 Thessalonians. He makes certain in 2 Thess 3:17 that his readers would know that this was his letter, which could be checked against 1 Thessalonians and against what he had taught them in person. There "is no need to resort to elaborate theories about this letter displacing others or claiming primacy" (Jewett 1986: 185).

It is unreasonable to expect that the following hypothesis be accepted: A letter (1) that registers concern about what had been communicated in an earlier letter, possibly attributed to the author of this letter (2:2), (2) that refers to what the author had taught both orally and in a letter (2:15), and (3) that draws attention to its own genuineness (3:17) is pseudonymous. Someone writing such a letter would have been audacious to a degree beyond belief.

Finally, insufficient attention has been given to the difficulty of bringing such a letter into circulation (see Zahn, 1.159). Marxsen is aware of the problem but offers no satisfactory solution to it. Having suggested that 2 Thessalonians was written to Thessalonica (1982: 34–35, 80), he becomes ambivalent when he briefly discusses the question of how the letter could have circulated in Thessalonica two decades after the first letter (35 n. 9). Surely recipients of the new letter would have been skeptical when the new letter suddenly appeared.

After raising the question, Marxsen unsuccessfully flails about in search of an answer:

1. *The problem would have been the same for all the other pseudonymous letters in the NT.* But none of the other letters draws attention to the problem of letter writing the way 2 Thessalonians does. Furthermore, none of those letters is purportedly written to the same church to which a genuine one had already been written.

2. *Apocalypses were frequently written under the names of ancient worthies (e.g., Isaiah, Ezra, Enoch) and brought into circulation much later by their authors.* However, 2 Thessalonians is not an apocalypse but a letter that has concrete circumstances in view (e.g., 3:6–12).

3. *First Thessalonians was not canonical and in regular public use, so the introduction of another letter would not have been problematic.* How does one know that it was not in regular public use? Marxsen and Lindemann argue that 2 Thessalonians was written precisely in view of problems 1 Thessalonians had caused or might exacerbate, which would presumably mean that the letter was, at the very least, accessible. More important, the argument for pseudonymity is predicated on the acceptance of Paul's apostolic authority, of which, we have seen, much is made. Such authority in Thessalonica would have been based on 1 Thessalonians.

It is easier, at first glance, to imagine how a pseudonymous letter might have originated much later, far away from Thessalonica, as Wrede did. The main thing would have been that the letter be considered doctrinally correct. When the letter arrived in Thessalonica around A.D. 90–100, the persons in the church who had been alive when Paul was there would have been very young at that time. They would now, with the appearance of 2 Thessalonians, mistrust their memory of Paul and his teaching rather than the genuineness of the new letter, which was similar to the first one, unobjectionable as to its content, and otherwise unsuspicious (Wrede, 90–91).

This is certainly imaginative, but raises serious questions. Would the Thessalonians not have been suspicious of a letter written to them but whose delivery was delayed for more than forty years, especially when the letter itself raises issues about letter writing? Would they not, on the basis of 3:17, have compared the signatures of the two letters, or why must we assume that the original copy of 1 Thessalonians was no longer available? How would the pseudonymous letter actually have been delivered to the Thessalonians? This is a problem for all theories of epistolary pseudonymity, but particularly for this letter, for the reasons mentioned. And how could a letter addressed to the Thessalonians have been in circulation elsewhere before being delivered to its addressees? By the last decade of the first century, Paul's letters were widely circulated; it would have been difficult for 2 Thessalonians to escape the notice of the church to which it was addressed.

Finally, the argument is based on the assumption that the author had a better knowledge of 1 Thessalonians, which he essentially rewrote, than did the people to whom it was written and who probably had it read regularly in their assemblies. It also assumes that while the pseudonymous author (and the modern scholar) could discern the differences between the two letters, the original readers could not. Which raises a question about the nature and extent of the differences and whether they naturally lead to the hypothesis of pseudonymity. It is more reasonable to interpret 2 Thessalonians on the basis of the hypothesis that Paul wrote it to Thessalonica not too long after he had written 1 Thessalonians, to the same city but with a different primary audience in view.

# III. SUMMARY: PAUL'S SECOND LETTER TO THE THESSALONIANS

Paul's second letter to the Thessalonians was written from Corinth, probably early in A.D. 51, a very few months after his first letter. Silas and Timothy are still with Paul, but other than being mentioned in the address, they play no role in the letter. Paul had received news that conditions in the Thessalonian church had deteriorated since he wrote the first letter: persecution of the new converts was continuing, erroneous eschatological doctrine was being taught, and some of the Thessalonians refused to earn their own living. Paul writes this pastoral letter to encourage the discouraged, correct the doctrinal error, and direct the church in how to discipline the idlers.

# 2 THESSALONIANS: TRANSLATION, NOTES, AND COMMENTS

◆

# I. ADDRESS, 1:1–2

◆

## TRANSLATION

1 ¹Paul, Silvanus, and Timothy to the church of the Thessalonians in God our Father and the Lord Jesus Christ: ²grace to you and peace from God [our] Father and the Lord Jesus Christ.

## NOTES

The address is identical to 1 Thess 1:1, with the exception that God is described as "our" Father and that the phrase "God [our] Father and the Lord Jesus Christ" is added to specify the source of grace and peace.

It is impossible to decide with certainty whether in the latter phrase "God the Father" or "God our Father" (v 2) should be read, for the textual evidence is evenly split (Metzger, 567). The pronoun *hēmōn* ("our") could have been the original and later omitted for stylistic reasons, since it appears in v 1, or the shorter reading could have been original, with *hēmōn* being added to conform to v 1 and the other Pauline addresses (see NOTE on 1 Thess 1:1). The appearance of "our" in the formulas in 1:11 and 2:16 may support its inclusion here, but could also argue against inclusion because the formulaic character may have influenced a scribe to include it here.

The differences from 1 Thessalonians make 2 Thessalonians more like the addresses in Paul's other letters. If a later writer were using 1 Thessalonians to produce a letter of his own (see pages 356–59), the addition of the entire phrase could be taken as evidence of an attempt to bring the letter into greater conformity with Pauline usage. In that event, the "our" would have been original and was later omitted.

## COMMENT

Paul mentions Silas and Timothy as cosenders, as he does in 1 Thess 1:1, and again addresses the letter to "the church of the Thessalonians" rather than to "the church in Thessalonica," which would have been more in line with his later practice (see NOTE on 1 Thess 1:1). That Silas and Timothy were still with him suggests that he wrote the letter shortly after he wrote 1 Thessalonians. That they are not mentioned again in the letter is of no significance; neither was Sosthenes mentioned in 1 Corinthians after the address (1:1). The assumption that they are mentioned to lend authority to the letter, as they were supposed to have done in 1 Thess 1:1 (Trilling 1980: 36) is without foundation and misunderstands why they are mentioned in the first letter (see page 89). Paul does not call himself an apostle, and there is not the slightest hint of an appeal to authority (see COM-MENT on 1 Thess 1:1).

The address shows that the letter is written to all the Thessalonian Christians, as the first letter had been, but we should probably visualize a number of groups in Thessalonica and its environs, which to Paul's mind together constituted the church (see COMMENT on 1 Thess 1:1; 5:26–27). The primary group to whom the first letter was addressed was Gentile, and they were to ensure that the letter be read to all the other groups in the area. That appears to have been done, and Paul now again writes to the entire church, but with a different primary group in mind as recipients of the letter (see page 353).

Harnack (1910) thought that this group was Jewish, but that theory is not assured. Slight support for the theory, however, might just be found in v 1 in the addition of the pronoun *hēmōn* to *en patri* to read "God our Father" instead of "God the Father" (1 Thess 1:1), which would have normally connoted God the Creator, a particular-ly apt way of reminding the Gentile Thessalonians of the terms, partly borrowed from Jewish propaganda to Gentiles, in which Paul had preached to them (see COMMENT on 1 Thess 1:1, 9). Here, however, the addition of the pronoun brings out the relational rather than the creative dimension of God: the Thessalonians have God as their Father (see also v 2 and 2:16; cf. "our God," 1:11; see 1 Thess 1:3; 3:11, 13; 2:2 and 3:9; Rom 8:15–16; Gal 4:6–7; Matt 6:8–15). In any event, "God our Father" here and possibly in v 2 is part of the language Paul uses to describe fic-tive kinship, which is important for him in 1 Thessalonians (see NOTES and COMMENT on 1 Thess 1:4; 4:9; Malherbe 1987: 48–51) and also in 2 Thessalo-nians, especially when he has relationships within the church in mind (3:6, 13, 15).

The phrase "grace and peace" appears only here and the words appear sepa-rately in the benediction in this letter. Elsewhere in the letter, "grace" and "peace" appear separately only in formulas (for "grace" alone, see 1:12; 2:16; 3:18, all formulaic, as also in 1 Thess 1:1; 5:28; for "peace" alone, see 1 Thess 5:3, 23; but note *eirēneuete*, "be at peace," in 5:13). Paul thus uses the words sep-arately or in combination only formulaically in these two letters. He may have created the formula in view of the setting in which the letter would be read, namely when the congregation met for worship (see Kramer, 151–53). Since the first letter had been read to his readers, this part of the address would not be new to them (see NOTES on 1 Thess 1:1; 5:3, 23).

What would have been new was the addition of the phrase specifying God and Christ as the sources of grace and peace. The phrase was not added to make the address conventionally Pauline (so Trilling 1980: 36); it merely represents Paul's normal practice. It is rather the omission of the phrase from 1 Thess 1:1 that is unique and requires explanation, not its presence in 2 Thess 1:2. It is striking that God and Christ are equally sources of grace and peace, as is the case elsewhere in Paul. God is a source of grace for Paul (see Rom 3:24; 5:15; 1 Cor 1:4; 3:10), and so is Christ (see 1 Cor 16:20; 2 Cor 8:9; 13:13; Gal 1:6); God is a source of peace (Rom 15:33; 16:20; 1 Cor 14:33; Phil 4:9; 1 Thess 5:23), and so is Christ (2 Thess 3:16; cf. Col 3:15). This is part of Paul's tendency to ascribe qualities to Christ that are also used of God (see page 369).

# II. THANKSGIVING AND EXHORTATION, 1:3–2:12

◆

This section begins with the first of two thanksgivings in the letter (the other is in 2:13–14), both of which introduce exhortation (see page 359). These two thanksgivings are not similar to the thanksgivings in 1 Thessalonians, as is frequently claimed (see pages 356–57). The only similarity is that both letters contain more than the normal one thanksgiving, but they function in different ways in the structures of the letters. In 1 Thessalonians, two thanksgivings (1:2–3; 3:9) enclose Paul's autobiographical account, within which a third one (2:13) introduces a short discussion on the reception of the word and suffering persecution for it. The entire first three chapters are an autobiographical thanksgiving that prepares for exhortation on specific matters. One of these is comfort, necessitated by the death of some Christians at Thessalonica (4:13–18), which is followed by correction of an erroneous eschatological expectation (5:1–11), clarifying the eschatological framework within which comfort may be found, and is to that extent itself consolatory.

A similar consolatory concern occupies Paul in this letter, and it surfaces already in the first thanksgiving, in the beginning of the letter, which leads to encouragement of the discouraged readers. Here Paul uses apocalyptic material, as he had also done in 1 Thess 4:13–18. Here also he follows the apocalyptic matter with a correction of erroneous eschatological claims in 2:1–12. Thus, while there are similarities between the two letters, they are not found in the overall structures of the two letters and clearly not in the way the thanksgivings contribute to their structures, but rather in the way that encouragement and correction of eschatological doctrine go hand in hand. That Paul immediately turns to encourage believers in distress by adducing apocalyptic traditions shows how important he thought the matter was in Thessalonica.

The limits of this thanksgiving are clear. It begins with v 4 and concludes with v 12, on an eschatological note, which is normally characteristic of Pauline thanksgivings (Schubert, 4–9; see O'Brien 1977: 261, on Rom 1:8ff. and Phlm 4ff., which do not have such endings). The first words of 1:3, "We ought to give thanks," mark the beginning of the thanksgiving, and the first words of 2:1, "Now we beseech you, brethren," show that a new phase of the letter is being entered. Within the thanksgiving, a new section, eschatological in thrust, begins with v 5 and extends through v 10. It is followed by a prayer report in vv 11–12, which is also eschatological in perspective and rounds off the thanksgiving period (see O'Brien 1977: 169–70). In the Greek, vv 3–10 constitute one long sentence; it is broken down in the translation for the sake of clarity.

# A. THANKSGIVING PROPER, 1:3–12

◆

## 1. THANKSGIVING, 1:3–4

The beginning of the thanksgiving is similar to 1 Thess 2:13 in form, but as to its context it is much more like 1 Thess 1:2–3, yet with significant differences dictated by the different situation Paul is now addressing. He does not mention hope, which was very important in the first letter, and he is more emphatic in his praise of his readers, thus establishing a special relationship with them. In addition to the pastoral and paraenetic functions the thanksgiving performs, it also performs the epistolary functions of setting the tone of the letter and introducing some of the main themes of the letter.

## TRANSLATION

1 ³We ought to give thanks to God always for you, brethren, as is proper, because your faith grows abundantly and the love of each individual one of all of you for one another is increasing, ⁴so that we ourselves do boast about you in the churches of God about your endurance and faith in all your persecutions and the tribulations that you are bearing.

## NOTES

1:3. *We ought to give thanks to God.* It is only here and in 2:13 that *opheilomen* ("we ought") is added to *eucharistein* ("to give thanks") in Paul's letters (cf. *charin opheilomen*, Xenophon, *Cyropaedia* 3.2.30). Commentators who consider 2 Thessalonians pseudonymous regard this as colder in tone than the simple thanksgivings of Paul's other letters and think that what was spontaneous on the part of Paul has now become part of the church's obligations (thus Trilling 1980: 43–44; Laub 1985: 43–44). That the obligation is assumed by someone writing in Paul's name would mean that the apostolic paradigm is invoked to substantiate church practice.

The phrase is neither colder nor more impersonal than the simple *eucharistoumen*. Personal obligation is expressed by *opheilein* (cf. Rom 13:8, of the obligation to love); had Paul wished to express an impersonal obligation, something that was required by the very nature of things, he would have used a form of *dein* ("to be necessary"). What he goes on to say further shows that he is anything but impersonal or cold. Furthermore, the expression, together with *kathōs axion estin* ("as is proper") that follows, has a liturgical background in Judaism that was continued by the Apostolic Fathers (see *1 Clem* 38:4; *Barn* 5:3; 7:1). In the liturgical formula a number of terms describing obligation were used, of which *opheilein* was the most personal (Aus 1973: 436, 438). The phrase in this context expresses emphasis, which is continued, especially by *kathōs axion estin* and *autous hēmās* ("we ourselves").

*always for you, brethren.* This is standard in Paul's thanksgivings (see NOTE on 1 Thess 1:2) except for the addition of "brethren" at this point. In other thanksgiving periods, "brethren" appears later (e.g., 1 Thess 1:4; 1 Cor 1:4; 2 Cor 1:8). In this verse and throughout the letter, it is used primarily in the vocative, at the beginning of new sections (cf. 2:1, 13, 15; 3:1, 6, 13). This is not more stereotypical than 1 Thessalonians (so Trilling 1972: 76–77, 98), where the vocative is similarly used (2:1, 14, 17; 4:1, 13; 5:1, 12, 14, 25). Nor is the charge justified that the absence of such accompanying self-designations as "saints," "the called," "the elect," etc. makes the letter more stiff and formal. Such judgments are predetermined by the perspective from which the letter is read.

When read as a continuation of Paul's communication with his recent Thessalonian converts, the use of "brethren" here is a natural continuation of the kinship language that figured so importantly in 1 Thessalonians (see NOTE and COMMENT on 1 Thess 1:4). Paul uses it here for the same reason that he emphasizes "we" in v 4, to stress their affectionate relationship in the context of suffering (cf. 1 Pet 5:9). It is also important to note that "brethren" is qualified in 2:13 ("beloved by the Lord") in much the same way that it is qualified in 1 Thess 1:4 ("whom God loved"). And as it describes communal relations in 1 Thessalonians (4:6, 10; 5:26), so it does in 2 Thessalonians, where "brother" describes a relationship that demands special attention and care (3:6, 15 ["as a brother"]).

*as is proper.* This phrase (*kathōs axion estin*) occurs only here in Pauline thanksgivings (cf. Phil 1:7, *kathōs dikaion estin* ["as is right"]), and it too is liturgical (Aus 1973). It does not refer to the degree or manner in which thanks is to be given, nor is it a mere parenthesis inserted between "brethren" and the *hoti* ("because") that follows, but it continues the idea of personal obligation expressed in *opheilomen*.

Some commentators have seen the relationship between the two phrases as follows: *opheilomen* expresses the subjective obligation, *kathōs axion estin* introduces the objective basis, the experience and progress of the Thessalonians (Eadie, 229; Lünemann, 577). Connecting the latter phrase with the *hoti* that follows makes sense of the fact that *kathōs* is frequently causal in Paul (BDF §453.2), but its connection with *opheilomen* adds to the emphasis with which Paul is writing. The reason for the emphasis is found in the situation to which Paul writes (see COMMENT). Much to the point is that such expressions occur in connection with suffering (e.g., Herm *Sim* 9.28.5).

*because your faith grows abundantly.* The *hoti*, having its causal sense, introduces the ground for the obligation and propriety of giving thanks to God (contra: von Dobschütz 1909: 236). As in 1 Thess 1:3, faith is mentioned in the thanksgiving, but with some differences. In 1 Thess 1:3, faith issues in the work of preaching the gospel, while here the focus is on faith itself; but see the different sense in 1:11, which is the second bracket of the *inclusio* that envelops this thanksgiving period. In both thanksgivings faith is introduced as a theme that re-occurs in the letters.

The faith of Paul's readers had been a major concern for him since his abrupt departure from them, and was one of the reasons why he had sent Timothy to them, to strengthen them in their faith (1 Thess 3:2, 5). It is noteworthy that faith and tribulation (*thlipsis*) appear together there. Although Paul was overjoyed by Timothy's report about their faith (1 Thess 3:6–7), he still wished to supply what was lacking in it, that is, to discuss some practical applications of it (3:10), which is evidently what he did in 1 Thessalonians.

Now he is overjoyed by the abundant or luxuriant growth of their faith in their present persecutions and tribulations. His fulsome praise of their growth in faith does not mean (as it had not meant in 1 Thess 1:3) that he was not concerned about their faith. In 2 Thess 1:11 he prays for it, he reminds them of their con-version to it in 2:13, and he calls them believers in 1:10. Faith in this letter is the same as it was in 1 Thessalonians, faith in God, to whom they were converted by Paul's preaching (1 Thess 1:9–10). Paraenetic reminders in the letter strengthen them in their daily life and distinguish them from those who do not believe the truth (2:11–12), some of whom oppose Paul in his preaching of the gospel (3:2).

The compound verb *hyperauxanein* ("to grow abundantly"), which John Chrysostom drew attention to (*Homilies on 2 Thessalonians* 2 [PG 62:473]) and which appears only here in the NT, emphasizes the growth. Compounds with *hyper* ("over," "more than") are characteristic of Paul's style to express emphasis (e.g., *hyperperisseuein* ["to overflow, be in greater abundance"], Rom 5:20; 2 Cor 7:4; *hyperhypsoun* ["to raise to the loftiest height"], Phil 2:9; *hyperekteinein* ["to stretch out beyond"], 2 Cor 10:4; *hypernikān* ["to win a most glorious victory"], Rom 8:37). The simple *auxanein* is also used of growing faith (2 Cor 10:15) and of God causing growth to occur (1 Cor 3:6, 7; 2 Cor 9:10). The word describes organic growth, such as of a seed (Matt 6:28; 13:32; Mark 4:8) or of a person (Luke 1:80; Col 2:19; 1 Pet 2:2). Here it is in the durative present tense, indicat-ing that the inner growth of the Thessalonians' faith was continuing (von Dob-schütz 1909: 237).

*and the love of each individual one of all of you for one another is increasing.* Paul again mentions one of the members of the triad of Christian qualities from the thanksgiving in 1 Thess 1:3. He elsewhere also speaks only of faith and love as he does here (1 Thess 3:6; Phlm 5; 1 Cor 16:13–14; 2 Cor 8:7). While the growth of the Thessalonians' faith is here described as internal, their increasing love for one another is an external ground for Paul's thanksgiving (Rigaux 1956: 613), but he does not make the connection that faith works through love (Gal 5:6).

In 1 Thessalonians, Paul had thanked God for his readers' love expressed in their evangelism (1:3) and for himself (3:6) and other members of the church (4:9), yet he exhorted them to continue doing so in their relationship with one another (5:13) and to put it on as part of their eschatological armor (5:8). Signif-icantly, he prayed that the Lord might cause their love "for one another and for all" to increase and abound (*pleonāsai kai perisseusai*; 3:12). It is not certain that the "all" in that passage stands for all people in general or whether, more probably, it refers to those non-Christians who associated with Christians in their assemblies (see COMMENT on 1 Thess 3:12; 5:12, 15). What is clear is the emphasis with which he prays for communal love in a text that serves as a hinge connecting the two parts of the letter.

Paul expresses himself even more emphatically about their love in the thanksgiving in 2 Thessalonians. The durative present tense of the verb *pleonazei* contributes to this emphasis, as does its synonymous parallelism with *hyperauxanei*. Because of the parallelism, he does not have to use the compound *hyperpleonazei* (cf. 1 Tim 1:14, in a thanksgiving, referred to by O'Brien 1977: 173 n. 42). Elsewhere in Paul, *pleonazein* always occurs in connection with a form of *perisseuein* ("to abound": Rom 5:20; 6:1; 2 Cor 4:15; 8:14–15; Phil 4:17–18; 1 Thess 3:12).

The greatest emphasis lies in the overloaded phrase *hē agapē henos hekastou pantōn hymōn eis allēlous*. Paul stresses both the individual and communal dimensions of love. The love of every individual member of the entire congregation for each other was increasing. This appears unrealistic, and it has been argued that this could not have been a reference to a particular church but is directed to all churches everywhere (Trilling 1980: 45). It should be noted, however, that thanksgivings have a paraenetic function that allows a writer to give thanks for something that the readers are in fact still to develop (see COMMENT on 1 Thess 1:2–3).

It is frequently argued that the change from *tē agapē eis allēlous kai eis pantas* ("love for one another and for all") in 1 Thess 3:12 to the formulation here, in particular, the omission of *eis pantas*, marks a limiting of love to Christians and exclusion of all others (e.g., Trilling 1980: 45), but as we have seen, it is unlikely that "all" in 1 Thess 3:12 or in 5:12, 15 refers to non-Christians in general. Furthermore, the parallel text to 2 Thess 1:3 is not 1 Thess 3:12, but 4:9–10 (see COMMENT). By mentioning love in the thanksgiving in 1 Thessalonians, Paul introduced a theme that would reoccur in important ways in the letter, but that is not the case here.

Love does not occur again in the second bracket of the *inclusio* as faith does (v 11), and the noun as well as the verb appear only in formulas in the letter, and in those places, they do not refer to the love of the Thessalonians (2:13, 16, of God's love; 2:10, the heretics' refusal to love the truth). It is particularly striking that love does not appear in the discussion of the idlers (3:6–15), since it figured so prominently in Paul's treatment of work in 1 Thessalonians (see COMMENT on 1 Thess 2:9; 4:9). The reason for the extraordinary stress on love here must be found in the situation Paul was addressing (see COMMENT).

1:4. *so that we ourselves do boast about you.* The result (*hōste* with the infinitive; see 1 Thess 1:7) of their conduct was that Paul was continuing to boast about them. The emphasis is continued in the compound form of the verb *egkauchāsthai* ("to boast"), which occurs only here in the NT and a mere four times in the LXX (Ps 51:3; 73:4; 96:7; 105:47; cf. *1 Clem* 21:5). The simple verb appears frequently in Paul, for example, in Rom 5:2–4, where it is related to *thlipsis* ("tribulation") and *hypomonē* ("endurance"), as it is here.

Emphasis is most strongly expressed in the construction *autous hēmās* ("we ourselves") and by its position at the head of the clause. The *autous* with the pronoun (see *autos egō* ["I myself"] in Rom 7:25; 2 Cor 10:11) creates so strong an emphasis that commentators have seen here a contrast with someone else who is not explicitly identified. Numerous suggestions have been offered as to whom or what Paul contrasts himself: (1) Other people were praising the Thessalonians (e.g., 1 Thess 1:9), so Paul stresses his relationship with his converts (Lünemann, 578; Findlay, 141; Bruce 1982: 145). (2) He stresses his apostolic authority (thus Wrede, 85) or his role as founder of the church (Lightfoot 1980: 98). (3) Somewhat differently, he contrasts his present boasting to his former silence about their efforts (1 Thess 1:9; Morris 1991: 194). The most likely possibility is that he contrasts his boasting to the Thessalonians' reluctance to speak about themselves, because they felt they were not worthy of being boasted about (John Chrysostom, *Homilies on 2 Thessalonians* 2 [PG 62:474]; von Dobschütz 1909: 238; Frame, 223–24; see COMMENT).

*in the churches of God.* This is reminiscent of 1 Thess 1:7, 9, where Paul claims that the Thessalonians' preaching and their relationship with him were spoken of so widely that there was no need for him to say anything. Here, however, the situation is different: Paul boasts, not about their preaching, but about their conduct under persecution and affliction. He had already referred to the Thessalonians as his "crown of boasting," that is, the crown in which he would boast or, better, exult (see NOTE on 1 Thess 2:19). There he had in mind exultation before the Lord at the Parousia, when he would have finished his race and received his prize. Here, the boasting continues (present tense) in the present and is about his readers' conduct (cf. 2 Cor 7:4, 13; 9:2, for boasting about a church or individual; see 8:1–5, for boasting without using the word itself).

It is not clear to which churches he is referring in his talk about boasting. He does not explicitly say that they are the churches in Achaia, and the phrase "churches of God" is unusual for Paul. With the exception of 1 Cor 11:16, the plural "churches" is always qualified by the addition of a geographical location: Judea (1 Thess 2:14; Gal 1:22), Galatia (Gal 1:2; 1 Cor 16:1), Macedonia (2 Cor 8:1). When used in the singular, "the church of God," there is usually no such qualification (1 Cor 10:32; 11:22; 15:9; Gal 1:13), but sometimes there is (1 Cor 1:1; 2 Cor 1:1). Paul does refer to the Jerusalem church as the church of God (Gal 1:13; 1 Cor 15:9), but the evidence does not support the contention that it is primarily that church that is meant by "the church of God," which Paul persecuted, and that "the churches of the Gentiles" (Rom 16:4) were later given the appellation (Bruce 1982: 145). Paul also speaks of "the churches of Christ" (Rom 16:16) and "the churches of the saints" (1 Cor 14:33).

It has been argued that Paul could not be thinking of the churches in Achaia in 2 Thess 1:4 on the grounds that evidence of churches in the area other than Corinth is found for the first time in Rom 16:1, with reference to Cenchreae. Before that, three years after 2 Thessalonians, 2 Cor 1:1 still speaks of one church, together with the saints in all of Achaia (von Dobschütz 1909: 239). This is to overlook 1 Cor 1:2, which already seems to visualize more than one church. Furthermore, Paul's churches spread quickly, and it is highly likely that there were other Christian conventicles in and around Corinth by the time Paul wrote 2 Thessalonians, all of which would be included in the designation "church of God" or "churches of God" (see COMMENT on 1 Thess 1:1; 5:26–27; pages 352–53). Paul's readers would have understood the reference to be to all the churches with which Paul was in contact, primarily those in Achaia, especially since there is no generalizing hyperbole here as there is in 1 Thess 1:8.

*about your endurance and faith.* In this second part of the result clause Paul explicates *en hymin* by identifying endurance and faith as the qualities about which he was boasting. Ancient commentators understood the construction, which has one definite article with both nouns, as a hendiadys, which is then to be understood as "your faith that endures" or "your endurance in faith" (e.g., Theodore of Mopsuestia 2.43 Swete), but modern commentators have for the most part correctly insisted that *hypomonē* ("endurance") and *pistis* ("faith") must each retain its own identity.

Endurance stands first after the article and is followed by *hymōn* ("your"), which means that it is the major of the two qualities. If one holds to the view of pseudonymity, this could be seen as evidence since *hypomonē*, a Greek virtue present in 2 Pet 1:6, only attains its decisive significance in the later NT writings (e.g., 1 Tim 6:10–11; 2 Tim 2:10, 12; 3:10; Titus 2:2; Heb 10:32, 36; 12:1–3; Jas 1:3–4, 12; 5:11; 1 Pet 2:20; Rev 2:2–3, 19; 13:10; 14:12) to which 2 Thessalonians is supposed to belong. These writings have a strong paraenetic tenor (Trilling 1980: 48). Paul used the word extensively elsewhere, however, as he did in 1 Thess 1:3. Sometimes he used it of his own endurance in hardship (2 Cor 6:4; 12:12) and associated it with eschatological trials (2 Cor 1:6), which he viewed from the perspective of hope (Rom 5:4; 8:23–24; 15:4; 1 Cor 13:7).

What is striking here is that *hypomonē* seems to take the place of the third member of the triad of qualities for which Paul had given thanks in 1 Thess 1:3. There endurance was qualified by hope, but there is no reference to hope in this thanksgiving, and hope, which is so important in 1 Thessalonians, appears only once in 2 Thessalonians, in a formulaic text (2:16). The difference between the letters in this respect is so stark that its omission must have been deliberate and caused by the situation Paul was addressing (see COMMENT). What is impressive to Paul here is actual conduct, the fortitude of the Thessalonians that would be proof of their afflictors' judgment (v 6).

Paul's emphasis on endurance has tempted commentators to give *pistis* here the meaning of "faithfulness" or "fidelity," thus somewhat similar in meaning to *hypomonē* (e.g., Lünemann, 579). But there is sufficient reason to give it the usual meaning it has for Paul, particularly in view of the way he has just described it so emphatically in v 3. Endurance may be uppermost in Paul's mind in v 4, but by connecting it closely to faith he shows that it is something more than mere dogged persistence (see Rev 13:10, where the two words are also joined).

*in all your persecutions and the tribulations that you are bearing.* Paul states the circumstances in which they demonstrated their endurance and faith. The construction is similar to the preceding clause: one definite article stands before *diōgmois* ("persecutions"), which is immediately followed by the pronoun *hymōn* ("your") and then by *tois thlipsesin* ("tribulations"). The presence of *pāsin* ("all") before the article, regardless of whether it also belongs with *thlipsesin*, weights the sentence further in favor of *diōgmois* and may place a special emphasis on the persecutions. This may be putting too fine a point on the matter, however, for the *hymōn* belongs to both *diōgmois* and *thlipsesin*, and in what follows Paul mentions affliction rather than persecution (v 6).

These are the circumstances that called for the encouragement that will follow in vv 5–10. *Diōgmos* is the more specific term, "persecution" (Rom 8:35; 2 Cor 12:19), and *thlipsis* a more general one that could refer to a wide range of oppression or distress. *Thlipsis* can, but need not, have an eschatological connotation, and in 1 Thessalonians it does not refer to persecution as is usually assumed (see COMMENT on 1 Thess 1:6). Paul does not reveal the nature of the mistreatment the Thessalonians were receiving, but the present tense of *anechesthe* ("you are bearing") shows that it was ongoing (see also *paschete* ["you are suffering"] in v 5). The present tense of *thlibō* ("to suffer affliction") in v 6 points in the same direction.

If *thlipsis* in 1 Thessalonians does not refer to persecution but to internal distress (cf. Phil 1:17, caused by Christians), the only reference to the Thessalonians' persecution would be 1 Thess 2:14, where the aorist *epathete* ("you suffered") does not convey ongoing oppression. The situation in Thessalonica should therefore be seen as one in which Christians were victims of intermittent periods of oppression, one of which was going on at the time Paul wrote 2 Thessalonians. The *anesis* ("rest," "relief") that they could expect (v 7) suggests that the oppression was more along the lines of social ostracism and criticism than of physical persecution (see COMMENT on 1:7).

## COMMENT

The beginning of the thanksgiving proper is extraordinary for the emphatic ways in which Paul modifies the conventional epistolary form to suit his immediate purpose. Patristic commentators thought that Paul's words in the thanksgiving were pastoral and prepared for the more demanding instructions he will give later in the letter (so Theodoret, *Interpretation of 2 Thessalonians* introduction [PG 82:657]; see also Calvin, 311). More particularly, they understood Paul in these two verses to be consoling and encouraging his readers by writing of the obligation and propriety of giving thanks for them because of their faith and love for one another (John Chrysostom, *Homilies on 2 Thessalonians* 2 [PG 62:475]; Theophylact, *Exposition of 2 Thessalonians* 1 [PG 74:1329]). For Theodoret, the thanksgiving amounted to praise of the Thessalonians (PG 82:658–60). Some modern commentators have shared the view that the thanksgiving was intended to encourage and console the Thessalonians (e.g., Lünemann, 557; von Dobschütz 1909: 235).

This thanksgiving, as did the one in 1 Thess 1:2–3, performs the usual functions of setting the tone of the letter, introducing basic themes to be treated, and is paraenetic, strengthening the relationship between Paul and his readers. Two features of this thanksgiving suggest that it was carefully constructed to speak pastorally to the condition of Paul's readers. The first feature is the constant emphasis in his language, achieved through word order, intensive compound verbs, parallelism, repetition, intensifying pronouns, and the strong pathos that pervades the thanksgiving. The second feature, partly related to the first, is that a contrast between Paul and his readers shimmers just below the surface: it *is* right and proper that Paul gives thanks, and he *does* have cause to boast of them.

Paul writes as if someone were denying the appropriateness of his thanksgiving and boasting, or at least had to be convinced of it. Indications are that the Thessalonians themselves were in need of such persuasion. Paul's emphatic assertion of the appropriateness of his thanksgiving is justified by their extraordinary faith and love, and his boasting in the churches is about their endurance and faith while they are persecuted and afflicted, even if they have not themselves boasted about how they stood up in difficult circumstances. That explains the contrast implicit in the emphatic *autous hēmās . . . egkauchāsthai* ("we ourselves . . . do boast") in v 4. Paul's pastoral intent thus stretches far beyond his assurance that he gives thanks for them (v 3) to everything else he says in the thanksgiving.

One is reminded by the almost extreme, excessive language of the pathos with which Paul wrote in 1 Thess 2:17–3:13 in describing his relationship with the Thessalonians. This thanksgiving has the same effect of confirming Paul's relationship with the Thessalonians. He also did so in the thanksgiving in 1 Thess 1:2–6, but with one notable exception. There he used the first and second personal pronouns in describing the relationship with them; here, five second personal pronouns are used, while Paul is confined to *opheilomen* ("we ought") and *autous hēmās*, the emphatic statement that implicitly draws attention to the Thessalonians. The focus then remains on them.

That the Thessalonians needed encouragement appears clearly from 1:4–10, and Paul will encourage them in other parts of the letter (Frame, 220, thought that encouragement is the purpose of the entire section, 1:3–2:17). But that does not sufficiently explain the fullness of his characterization of their faith, love, and endurance, which is not only complimentary but also hortatory. The answer must be found in the condition of the Thessalonians.

The Thessalonians to whom Paul wrote were still new to the faith and would still be experiencing the difficulties of new converts. Paul's first letter and Timothy's visit may have helped in some matters, but as 3:6–15 show, not in all. Paul's converts required time to gain certainty in the new faith, both as to its central beliefs and to the moral conduct it required (see COMMENT on 1 Thess 1:6, 9–10). Paul's letters testify to how difficult it was for new converts to do this (e.g., 1 Cor 8:7, of Christians; cf. 2 Thess 3:2, of pagans). One of the problems of all converts to a new system of belief and practice that requires a transformation of the total person was uncertainty by the convert that he knew enough about the new way of life and its requirements, and that he was making sufficient progress (see Malherbe 1987: 39–40). Paul was aware that his converts shared these problems, and in 1 Thessalonians he adopted the paraenetic style to serve his pastoral purpose, stressing what they knew and complimenting them for how they were conducting themselves (see pages 85–86). That is also what he does in 2 Thess 1:3–4, but without the paraenetic clichés.

The Thessalonians' uncertainty, and perhaps dissatisfaction, with themselves, may have had another, more surprising source, namely Paul's first letter to them. Some of them may have misunderstood its teaching about the Parousia (see COMMENT on 2:1–2; page 355), and they may also have misunderstood the consequences of Paul's eschatological teaching for their lives. Paul had countered the false prophets' teaching that deferred the Parousia by stressing the suddenness with which the Day of the Lord would come, which required that believers now live as children of the Day (1 Thess 5:1–11). Paul had also written of being blameless at the Parousia of the Lord Jesus (1 Thess 3:13; 5:23; cf. 2:12), when there would be judgment for the lives they now lived (4:6; cf. 1:10). The message that Paul initially preached, which had brought them to conversion, was already distressing in its effects (see COMMENT on 1 Thess 1:6; Malherbe 1998), and his attempt at reassurance (1 Thess 4:9; cf. Rom 5:9) must not have been successful.

Paul had sent Timothy to Thessalonica to stabilize the Thessalonians' faith lest they be unsettled (sainesthai) by tribulations (1 Thess 3:2), and now they were experiencing tribulations, as he had predicted that they would (1 Thess 3:4). But their distress was now more intense, because some persons thought that Paul had taught that the Day of the Lord had already come (2 Thess 2:2), that they were now living in the time when they would be expected to be blameless. Even if Paul was only warning against their accepting such a doctrine, they would nevertheless have felt more uncertain and inadequate because of their awareness of the claim.

In addressing the problem, Paul does a number of things. He tries to calm them down: they are not to be so quickly shaken (saleuthenai) or nervously wrought up (throeisthai) by the erroneous doctrine. He makes a sharp distinction between them and their opponents at the judgment (1:8–10), affirms that Satan will be destroyed (2:9–10), and stresses that God called them, is faithful, and will preserve them (2:13; 3:3, 5; on all of this, see the perceptive comments by von Dobschütz 1909: 28–29). He also does so in good paraenetic fashion at the beginning of the thanksgiving, in effect complimenting them for those qualities about which they themselves were still feeling inadequate. Hence his emphatic language.

Paul's stress on the luxuriant growth of their faith expresses his confidence that they have not veered from their commitment to God and to the message they had accepted at their conversion (1 Thess 1:8–10). Similarly, the almost ecstatic description of their love at the very least shows that Paul's prayer in 1 Thess 3:12, that the Lord increase and abound their love was fulfilled, and they could be assured of the Lord's working in their lives. His emphatic language could be designed to strengthen that conviction. It is noteworthy, however, that the emphasis does not reside in the verb that describes the growth (pleonazein ["to increase"]; cf. the compound, hyperauxanei, of faith), which is actually a lessening of emphasis from the prayer in 1 Thess 3:12 (pleonāsai kai perisseusai ["to increase and abound"]), but in the specification of the communal character of their love: every single individual in the entire congregation was loving the other members.

The parallel is therefore not 1 Thess 3:13, but the hyperbolic 1 Thess 4:9–10, where he praises them for their *philadelphia* ("love for the brethren"), about which they had been taught by God and which they were practicing in the whole of Macedonia. Paul only needed to encourage them to do so more and more, and to specify how they were to express their love, by earning their own living and thus living quietly, which would ensure approval from the larger society (1 Thess 4:11–12). Paul himself had provided an example of how economic self-sufficiency was an expression of love (1 Thess 2:8–9).

Paul's directions in 1 Thess 4:9–12 were most probably a response to an inquiry from the Thessalonians about the extent of the practical expression of their love, whether it should include financial support of the idlers. Instead of answering their question in the way they had probably expected, he addressed his directions to the entire church, commanding them to work. He therefore placed no limits on love but described its expression in practical, social terms (see COMMENT on 4:9–12). It is only later in the letter that he singles out the idlers, calling them the disorderly, that is, persons who do not conform to the accepted norms of behavior, and advises that they be admonished (*nouthetein*; 5:14), the sharpest pastoral action mentioned in the letter.

As the Thessalonians had continued to love each other while some of their members sponged off them when Paul first wrote to them, so they still do now. Paul's thanksgiving in 2 Thess 1:3 calls to mind the extraordinary statements, not without hyperbole, he had earlier made about their love (1 Thess 4:9–10). They still demonstrate the love that lies at the base of communal psychagogy (cf. Phil 2:1–2), in which each member has a responsibility (cf. Gal 6:4–5; Rom 15:2; see COMMENT on 1 Thess 5:11). His praise of them has a hortatory function, to continue loving each other, but its immediate purpose is to encourage them in their present difficult circumstances by referring to their demonstrated behavior. As he had separated harsh treatment of the idlers (5:14) from the celebration of their love (4:9) in 1 Thessalonians, so does he in 2 Thessalonians (3:6–15).

While Paul elaborates on two of the three Christian qualities found in the thanksgiving in 1 Thess 1:2–3, here he omits the third one, hope, which appears only once in 2 Thessalonians, in a prayer (2:16). This is extraordinary in view of the importance of the subject in 1 Thessalonians, especially 4:13–5:11, and of Paul's intensifying what he says about the other two qualities (v 3). It is significant that *hypomonē* comes last in the order of the qualities, the position that is usually most emphatic in the triad (see NOTE on 1 Thess 1:3), and that when it is here coupled with faith, it has the definite article and is followed by *hymōn*, which gives further emphasis to it (see NOTE on v 4). Paul stresses endurance because it is the prime quality that is demonstrated in persecution and is what he is implicitly encouraging them to continue.

Endurance is closely related to hope for Paul. In 1 Thess 1:3, it was the Thessalonians' endurance informed by hope, or that issued from hope, for which he gave thanks. In Romans, endurance appears in sequences of experience which culminate in hope (Rom 5:3–4; 15:4). Its eschatological dimension is evident in Rom 2:5–8, "to those who by endurance in good work seek glory, honor, and immortality he will give eternal life, but for those who are factious and do not obey the truth, but obey wickedness, there will be wrath and fury": God will render righteous judgment on the day of wrath according to each person's works. This statement could stand as an introduction to 2 Thess 1:5–10.

The omission of hope nevertheless remains odd but can be explained by the situation of the people to whom Paul is writing. Paul knows of the teaching that the Day of the Lord has come (2:2). According to Paul, hope has no place in such a view, for we only hope for what we do not yet see, and we hope for it with endurance (Rom 8:24–25; cf. 1 Cor 13:7). He could therefore not boast about his readers' hope, for he was writing to the entire church, some of whom may have held to a view that, by his definition, excluded hope (2:2). But he could boast about their endurance, and combining it with faith, he reminds them of the premise of their eschatological hope, their faith in God (see 1 Thess 1:8–10; 4:14).

# 2. ENCOURAGEMENT OF THE DISCOURAGED, 1:5–10

The thanksgiving ends with a prayer report in vv 11–12, but before then it is expanded considerably by the insertion of vv 5–10, which places the tribulation of the Thessalonians in the context of God's just eschatological judgment, with both its positive and negative aspects. The thought progresses as follows: v 5 states the goal, the kingdom of God, for those who are presently suffering, vv 6–7a remark on the two sides of divine judgment, vv 7b–9 describe the Parousia with judgment for the believers' enemies, and v 10 returns to the salvation of believers at the end (von Dobschütz 1909: 241).

In addition to being set off grammatically from its context, this section has literary and grammatical characteristics that give it a certain unity (Roosen 1971: 131–32):

1. The Greek has a strong Septuagintal cast, and one of the two clearest allusions to the OT appears in v 9 (Isa 2:10; cf. also v 8 [Isa 66:15]), but it would be going too far to speak of "implicit citations" in v 10a (Ps 88:8 LXX) and v 10b (Ps 67:36 LXX) as Roosen, 131, does.

2. There is frequent parallelism between verses (vv 6, 7) and within verses (vv 8, 9, 10).

3. Verses are connected by catchwords: "righteous judgment of God" (tēs dikaias kriseōs tou theou) in v 5 is picked up by "just in God's sight" (dikaion para theō) in v 6; "to repay" (antapodounai) in v 6 with "repaying with

vengeance" (*didontos ekdikēsin*) in v 8, cf. "they will pay the penalty" (*dikēn tisousin*) in v 9; "glory" (*tēs doxēs*) in v 9 with "to be glorified" (*endoxas-thēnai*) in v 10; "in all who have believed" (*tois pisteusasin*) with "for our testimony to you was believed" (*episteuthē to martyrion hēmōn eph' hymās*) both in v 10.

The pervading parallelism suggests the following structure of the text (see Bruce 1982: 147; Giblin, 4–5):

## TRANSLATION

1 ⁵ This is a clear proof of the righteous judgment of God, that you be made worthy of the kingdom of God, for which you are indeed suffering,
⁶since indeed it is just in God's sight to repay
those who afflict you with affliction,
⁷and you who are being afflicted with relief with us
at the revelation of the Lord Jesus from heaven with the angels of his power,
⁸with flaming fire, repaying with vengeance
those who do not know God
and those who do not obey the gospel of our Lord Jesus.
⁹They will pay the penalty of eternal ruin
from the face of the Lord
and from the glory of his might,
¹⁰when he comes
to be glorified in his saints
and to be marveled at in all who have believed
(for our testimony to you was believed)
on that day.

The linguistic and formal features of vv 5–10 have been considered evidence that Paul was making use of material formed before him. Bornemann (329, 336–39) thought that vv 6–10 were a slightly revised Christian psalm or hymn. Dibelius (1937: 41–43) held the opinion that Paul used Christianized Jewish apocalyptic material dealing with a judgment theophany. This text is not didactic, as he thought 1 Thess 4:13–18 is, but is a confession with the content of a traditional Jewish apocalyptic scene. Dibelius could imagine the chapter being read to the congregation gathered for worship, which would explain to him the cool tone he detected in it. Roosen (1971: 132) partially accepted Dibelius's views, but suggested that the material could have originated in Christian apocalyptic missionary preaching (cf. 1 Thess 1:9–10; Rom 1:18–32). Roger Aus (1971: 113–14) argued that vv 5–10 were a mosaic of OT passages, a view that could be reconciled with Bruce's contention (1982: 148–49) that Paul was drawing from a "testimony book," a collection of OT passages dealing with an eschatological subject. Such a collection would have originated in pre-Pauline Christianity and continued to develop in the centuries that followed. Most commentators have correctly rejected such theories and held that Paul or whoever else wrote the letter composed the section himself (e.g., Rigaux 1956: 623–25; Trilling 1980: 55 n. 167; Marxsen 1982: 65).

# NOTES

1:5. *This is a clear proof.* The grammatical connection with what precedes is unclear. "This is" is an attempt at clarification for the English reader that assumes an elision (*ho estin*) on analogy to *hētis estin* ("which is") in Phil 1:28, which is the closest parallel in thought in the NT (cf. BDF §480.6). On such a reading, *endeigma* ("a clear proof") would be a nominative. It is more likely an accusative in direct apposition to the preceding (cf. Rom 8:3; 12:1; see Milligan, 88; Frame, 226). This is the only place where *endeigma* appears in the NT. This passive form of the noun may be taken to denote a result that has been reached or something that has been proved, but it cannot really be distinguished from the active form, *endeixis*, which is used elsewhere (Phil 1:28; Rom 3:25–26; 2 Cor 8:24; see Milligan, 87, followed by most commentators).

   *Endeigma* could be in apposition to the Thessalonians' persecutions and tribulations, which stand closest to it in the sentence (Bassler; Wanamaker, 221) and which have an eschatological referent in apocalyptic traditions (Matt 24:21; Mark 13:19, 24; Rev 7:14), but Paul is not yet concerned with the proximity of the end, which will be characterized by such events (Rigaux 1956: 620; Best 1972: 254). *Endeigma* could also be in apposition to endurance and faith, but Paul does not speak of such qualities in general. *Endeigma* is most likely in apposition to "your endurance and faith in all your persecutions and the tribulations that you are bearing," that is, those aspects of the Thessalonians' conduct about which Paul is boasting. As his reference to his boasting had a consolatory function, so does his placing of their conduct in God's eschatological scheme, which he now begins to detail insofar as it relates to his readers (see John Chrysostom, *Homilies on 2 Thessalonians* 2 [PG 62:475]). Paul does not say to whom their experience is a proof (in Phil 1:28 it is to the persecutors), but the consolatory function of his language here suggests that it is a proof to his readers.

   *of the righteous judgment of God.* The phrase "the righteous judgment" (*hē dikaia krisis*) occurs elsewhere in the NT of Jesus' judgment (John 5:30; cf. 7:24), and "to judge . . . in righteousness" (*krinein . . . en dikaiosynē*) appears in Acts 17:31 of eschatological judgment. The notion of just judgment is also associated with persecution, as it is here, in 1 Pet 2:23; Rev 16:5, 7; 19:2, 11. The closest parallel to *dikaia krisis*, however, is *dikaiokrisia* ("righteous judgment") in Rom 2:5, where it clearly refers to eschatological judgment. A major exegetical problem is whether the judgment in view in 2 Thess 1:5 is present or future.

   The majority of commentators think that the reference is to the eschatological judgment, pointing in vv 7–9 to the definite article *hē*, which designates a definite judgment that does not have to be defined any further, and adducing Rom 2:5 (cf. 3:8, *krima endikon*, "just condemnation") and Luke 16:25 as parallels (see Lünemann, 580; von Dobschütz 1909: 242; Rigaux 1956: 620;

P. Müller, 56). However, that vv 7–9 and Rom 2:5 refer to the future does not require that v 5 also do so, and that the definite article is used proves nothing (Eadie, 235; Lenski, 382); it is in fact not used in Rom 2:5 in its reference to the future.

Some commentators think that the judgment is present and find similar thinking in 1 Pet 4:17–19 (e.g., Ohlshausen, 463; Lenski, 382; Marshall 1983: 173). The two possibilities are not mutually exclusive, however, and those commentators are correct who see a connection between the present and the future judgments. Without diminishing the importance of the future judgment in this passage, Paul's view is that judgment, which is just because God dispenses both reward and punishment, is already working out proleptically in the present (Trilling 1980: 50). As is the case with the kingdom of God, the Day of the Lord, and other eschatological concepts, the judgment is in some way already present, preparing for the final judgment (Wohlenberg, 132; Marshall 1983: 173; Alford, 285: "this being an earnest and token of it"). For the proleptic element in Paul's eschatological thinking, see 1 Thess 2:16; 5:1–8; 2 Thess 2:7. An overinterpretation of it led to the problem that Paul addresses in 2 Thess 2:1–12, but rather than shying away from it, he here uses it in a pastoral manner (see COMMENT).

*that you be made worthy of the kingdom of God.* The construction *eis to* plus the infinitive could describe either purpose, as it does in the translation "that you be made worthy" (e.g., Wohlenberg, 132; von Dobschütz 1909: 243; Frame, 226), or result, "with the result that you are made worthy" (e.g., Ellingworth and Nida, 138; Eadie, 580; see BDF §402.2). It could also describe the content of God's judgment (Theophylact, *Exposition of 2 Thessalonians* 1 [PG 124:1333], who places a heavy emphasis on the consolatory intention of Paul's word). A close parallel is 1 Thess 2:12, *eis to peripatein hymās axiōs tou theou tou kalountos hymās eis tēn heautou basileian kai doxan* ("to conduct yourselves in a manner worthy of God, who calls you into his kingdom and glory"). This passage, which deals with ethical conduct, does not differ from 2 Thess 1:5, which deals with suffering (so von Dobschütz 1909: 243). As the *paramythoumenoi* ("comforted") in 1 Thess 2:12 shows, Paul is also concerned with their conduct in distress. The compound *kataxiōthēnai* ("to be made worthy"), in the passive to denote God as the one who makes them worthy, intensifies the simple *axioun* ("to make worthy"; see v 11).

It is notoriously difficult to distinguish between purpose and result in NT Greek, and in this case the judgment of Eadie is to the point: "Surely it is a refinement to debate in such a case whether *eis to* refers to result or purpose, as the result is simply the embodied purpose, and the purpose by appointed and fitting means works out the result" (236). The practical point is that Paul places the Thessalonians' experience within the divine purpose and attributes to it a positive significance, not that they would inherit the kingdom (1 Cor 6:9) or through tribulations enter it (Acts 14:22), but that their endurance and faith are proof of God's righteous judgment that they are already being made worthy of the kingdom.

The compound *kataxiousthai* occurs only here and in Luke 10:35 and Acts 5:41 in the NT (cf. 3 Macc 3:21; 4 Macc 18:3; *Ep Arist* 175), in all of which it is understood to mean "to deem worthy," rather than "to make worthy," as in the translation adopted here. Acts 5:41, "that they were counted worthy to suffer dishonor for the name" (*hoti katexiōthesan hyper tou onomatos atimasthēnai*) is frequently cited in support of such an understanding. But the parallel is more apparent than real. The syntactical constructions are quite different. The idea of deeming something or someone worthy has its analogy in *dikaia krisis* in 2 Thess 1:5 and not in *kataxiōthēnai*, and the simple form of the verb in v 11 clearly means to make worthy (see also Rev 3:4, of those who will be with the Lord because they are worthy).

*for which you are indeed suffering.* With *paschete* ("you are suffering") Paul picks up the idea of endurance (v 4), and the present tense (cf. *anechesthe*, v 4) shows that he is still concerned with their present experience. The clause makes clear that the suffering about which he is speaking was not suffering in general, but suffering related to the kingdom. Precisely how it is related to the kingdom depends on how *hyper hēs* is understood, whether it is "because of which" (Rigaux 1956: 621, referring to Phil 1:27b–30 as a commentary on this passage), similar to "on behalf of which" (Eadie, 230, citing Acts 5:41; 9:16; Rom 1:5; 15:8; 2 Cor 12:10; 13:8), or whether it is "for the establishment, promotion and maintenance of which" (Lightfoot 1980: 102), or whether it is to be understood as indicating a motive or goal, "obtaining or achieving which" (Lünemann, 581; von Dobschütz 1909: 243; Trilling 1980: 51; Rom 8:17 is frequently cited).

Given Paul's intention to help his readers make sense of their present experiences, the last possibility is most likely correct. But Rom 8:17–18 is not a precise parallel (cf. Luke 24:26; 1 Pet 1:11; 5:1; Acts 14:22), for Paul does not contrast present suffering with future glory (see vv 9, 12). He compliments them, not for mere stick-to-itiveness that will ensure a future reward, but for already beginning in some sense to achieve their goal. Understood in this way, the *kai* is emphatic ("indeed") and does not anticipate v 7 ("with us"), there associating ("and") their suffering with Paul's suffering. The *kai* also has a consecutive force, hinting at the connection between suffering and being made worthy of the kingdom (Ellicott, 98). Paul retains the focus on the Thessalonians and the meaning of their suffering.

1:6. *since indeed it is just in God's sight to repay.* Paul only now widens his focus to include the Thessalonians' oppressors in God's just decree, but they are included with the Thessalonians within the rubric of God's eschatological repayment of their present conduct. The conditional particle *eiper* ("since indeed") introduces a condition about which there can be no doubt (cf. Rom 3:30; 8:9, 17). According to John Chrysostom, Paul used this expression rather than one that conveyed his own opinion because the statement is self-evidently true (*Homilies on 2 Thessalonians* 2 [PG 62:475]). Paul uses it for the sake of emphasis (Theodoret, *Interpretation of 2 Thessalonians* 1 [PG 82:660]). By introducing his thought this way he carries forward his effort to comfort them and encourage them to greater endurance (Lünemann, 581).

This positive intention is evident in that *dikaion para theō* ("is just in God's sight") connects with *tēs kriseōs tou theou*, which had as its purpose that the Thessalonians be made worthy of the kingdom. It is this practical, pastoral purpose that drives Paul's language, not an interest in divine retribution as part of theodicy. Paul writes against a background in which retribution was thought to be a constituent part of God's just judgment and considered to be reserved for God (see also Rom 2:6–8; 12:19; 2 Cor 5:10; cf. Col 3:25; Luke 16:25). Such thinking forbade human retribution or vindictiveness (Rom 12:19; 1 Thess 5:15; cf. Matt 5:38–48); it was sufficient to rely on God's justice for vindication, which was the source of comfort.

The image of the divine tribunal is present in the phrase *para theō* ("in God's sight," "before God"; cf. Rom 2:11, 13; Gal 3:11). The verb *paradidosthai* ("to render," "to repay") can be used in a nonjudicial sense (see 1 Thess 3:9; cf. Luke 14:14) and when used judicially can have a negative (Rom 12:19; Heb 10:30, both of which depend on Deut 32:35) or a positive (1 Macc 10:27) sense. Here it has both *thlipsin* ("affliction") and *anesin* ("relief") as objects. Echoes of Isaiah are heard in this section, and Isa 63:4 or 66:6 may be behind Paul's language here, but other OT texts (e.g., Ps 136:8 LXX; Obad 15) express the same idea (Aus 1971: 62–63; Bruce 1982: 149–50; Aus 1976 detects influence of Isa 66 throughout 2 Thess 1).

*those who afflict you with affliction.* Paul specifies God's repayment in two parallel statements. Unlike 1 Thess 4:13–18, where he also comforts, he here speaks of the judgment of the oppressors, which he describes as afflictions caused by them. Unlike v 4, here *thlipsis* is eschatological (cf. Matt 24:9, 21, 29), and Paul uses apocalyptic traditions to comfort his readers. The notion of judgment is central to Jewish apocalyptic thought, which, in the midst of despair, expresses the conviction that on the day of judgment "all wrongs will be set right; justice will not only be done, it will also be seen to be done" (D. S. Russell, 380). The justice of God's decree is the foundation of comfort (see Stone, 318–20, on 4 Ezra 10; cf. 12:8; 14:13), and the apocalyptist, by revealing the eschatological benefits, renders comfort (2 *Bar* 54:4).

From here on, Paul will use apocalyptic matter more intensively, yet it is noteworthy how relatively restrained he is in doing so, as he had also been in 1 Thess 4:13–18. When he conducts an extended argument about judgment, he can be very vivid in his description (Rom 2:1–11, esp. v 9), but when he comforts his readers, he retains only those elements that serve his immediate end. He provides no information about the nature of the tribulation the oppressors will endure, but it is natural to think that it will be of the same kind with which they themselves were afflicting the Thessalonians (see v 4). Paul will elaborate on the oppressors in vv 8–9; at present, judgment is simply brought up in the first line of a claim made in parallel, with the stress coming in the second line.

1:7. *and you who are being afflicted with relief with us.* Up to this point, Paul had spoken of the present qualities and experiences of the suffering Thessalonians. Now he turns to the payment they will receive for the way they are presently conducting themselves. It is tempting to hold that *antapodounai* ("to repay") must here have a different meaning than it has with *thlipsin*, such as "to grant," "to guarantee," "to provide" (so Trilling 1980: 52). But there is no reason why the verb should have different meanings in the two parallel lines, unless it is feared that "repay" may support the notion of earning or meriting relief. That a Christian's behavior had direct eschatological consequences, however, is not an idea foreign to Paul (cf. 1 Cor 3:14; 2 Cor 5:10; see COMMENT on 1 Thess 2:19; cf. 3:5). "Repay" also fits Paul's immediate, pastoral intention better. As he had assured his discouraged readers that they were in some way already being made worthy of the kingdom for which they were suffering, he now assures them that they will be repaid for their suffering.

The repayment of oppressors will be *thlipsis* ("tribulation"); that of those now afflicted, *anesis* ("relief"; for the reversal of conditions, cf. Luke 16:19–25). The anticipation of eschatological peace and rest is common in apocalyptic literature (e.g., 4 Ezra 7:36, 38, 75, 85, 95; 2 Bar 73:1; cf. Heb 3:18–19; 4:1). Paul uses *anesis* with *thlipsis* and its verb in 2 Cor 2:13; 7:5; 8:13. *Thlipsis* describes emotional pressures or distress, *anesis* their relaxation. *Anesis* is thus appropriate in letters of consolation to describe mitigation of grief as their intention (*anesis tēs lypēs*; Plutarch, *A Letter of Condolence to Apollonius* 102B). Also part of the consolatory tradition is the phrase *meth' hēmōn* ("with us"; see NOTE on 1 Thess 4:17, where *syn* is used instead of *meta*). Patristic commentators already recognized the consolatory nature of Paul's words (cf. John Chrysostom, *Homilies on 2 Thessalonians* 2 [PG 62:469–70]; Theophylact, *Exposition of 2 Thessalonians* 1 [PG 1243:1333]). It therefore really misses the point in assuming that the plural is real and not authorial, to wonder, as some commentators do, whether Paul has in mind eternal association with all Christians or primarily with the writers of the letter.

*at the revelation of the Lord Jesus from heaven.* The function of the judgment scene, which begins here and extends through v 9, is similarly to console the Thessalonians (see Theodoret, *Interpretation of 2 Thessalonians* 2 [PG 82:660]). The preposition *en* ("at") could be instrumental, "in and through" (for the idea, without *en*, see 2:8), thus repayment would not only be associated with the revelation but would actually form a part of it (so Milligan, 89). More probably, it is temporal, describing when the repayment takes place (see v 10, "when he comes"; Rom 2:5, *en hēmera orgēs kai apokalypseōs dikaiokrisias tou theou* ["in the day of wrath and the revelation of God's just judgment"]; cf. *en* with *parousia* in a temporal sense in 1 Thess 2:19; 1 Cor 15:23; and *en apokalypsei* in a temporal sense in 1 Pet 1:7).

Instead of speaking of Christ's *parousia*, as he had in 1 Thessalonians (2:19; 3:13; 4:15; 5:23) and would again in 2 Thessalonians (2:1, 8, 9 [the latter of the Lawless One]), Paul speaks of Christ's revelation (see also the verb, in the passive, in 2:3, 6, 8, all of the Lawless One). He thus stresses the visual rather than the auditory aspect, as he had done in 1 Thess 4:16 (cf. also *epiphaneia* [2:8], *endoxazesthai* [1:10, 12], *doxa* [1:9; 2:13]; see Milligan, 141–51, on *parousia*, *epiphaneia*, *apokalypsis*). This is the first occurrence of *apokalypsis* as equivalent to the technical sense of *parousia*. The revelation of the Messiah was spoken of in Jewish apocalyptic literature (e.g., 4 Ezra 7:28; 13:32), the idea being that the Messiah was hidden before God, to be revealed at the proper time (*1 En* 48:6; 62:7; *2 Bar* 39:7). The fundamental notion may have been the revelation of what already exists (so Milligan, 150–51; Eadie, 239), in which Theophylact found consolation (*Exposition of 2 Thessalonians* 1 [PG 124:1333]).

Elsewhere, *en apokalypsei* refers to revelation granted as a special gift already possessed in the present (1 Cor 14:6; cf. also v 26; 2 Cor 12:1, 7; Gal 1:12; 2:2; 1 Cor 2:10), but it is also used eschatologically in 1 Cor 1:7, *apekdechomenous tēn apokalypsin tou kyriou hēmōn Iēsou Christou* ("awaiting the revelation of our Lord Jesus Christ") and Rom 2:5, "the day of the wrath and the revelation of God's just judgment." The phrase also appears in 1 Pet 1:7, 13 and, of special interest, in 4:13, suffering with Christ, "in order that you may also rejoice and be glad at the revelation of his glory" (see Herzer, 107–19).

The judgment is described with three prepositional phrases. The first is "from heaven" (see NOTES on 1 Thess 1:10; 4:16). As God comes in judgment from heaven in the OT (Ps 18:9; Isa 64:1), so the Lord Jesus shares the divine prerogative of judging (see NOTES on 1 Thess 2:19; 3:13).

*with the angels of his power.* The second prepositional phrase describes an attending circumstance of the judgment: the Lord will be accompanied by angels. The genitive *dynameōs* could be qualitative, and the phrase *angellōn dynameōs autou* could be a Hebraism, which would be rendered "mighty angels" (RSV; NIV: "powerful angels"). Another suggestion is that the phrase means "angelic host," with an appeal to 2 Kgs 21:5 LXX and Ps 32:6 LXX for this meaning of *dynamis*. The NT does not make use of this meaning, however, and this suggestion also makes *autou* ("his") go with *didontos* ("repaying") in v 8 and refer to God (for the grammatical improbability of this proposal, see Lünemann, 582).

The most probable meaning of the phrase is that the angels who will accompany the Lord are the agents through whom he executes his power (so most commentators). God's repayment is carried out by the Lord Jesus and his angels (cf. *1 En* 61:10 for God's angels). For the angels who will be in attendance at the judgment (cf. Mark 8:38–9:1), see NOTE on 1 Thess 3:13; for Paul's limiting of what the angels do at the *parousia*, see NOTE on 1 Thess 4:16 (contrast Matt 24:30–31; 25:31; Mark 8:38; 13:27; Luke 12:8–9); and for the frequency with which angels appear at the End in apocalyptic literature, see Zech 14:5; 1QM. Elsewhere, Paul speaks of power in connection with the resurrection and transformation of human bodies that will occur at the *parousia* (1 Cor 6:14; 15:43; cf. Phil 3:10), but here Christ's power and might (*ischys*, v 9) have to do with the way he executes judgment.

1:8. *with flaming fire, repaying with vengeance.* The third prepositional phrase describes the form of the Lord's revelation and again does so in terms of OT theophanic language, that he comes with fire (Exod 19:18; Deut 5:4; Dan 7:9–10; see F. Lang in *TDNT* 6.935–36). A variant reads *en phlogi pyros* ("in a flame of fire": B D F G) instead of the more difficult *en pyri phlogos* ("in a fire of flame"), which is preferred by the majority of commentators and the Nestle text, and is accepted here. The latter reading appears in the B text of Exod 3:2

(cf. Sir 8:10). Best (1972: 258) is right that the easier reading is under the influence of Isa 66:15; 29:6; Dan 7:9, etc., but Aus (1976: 266) argues that it is correct precisely because it agrees with Isa 66:15, which he implausibly thinks is
part of a mosaic of Isaian texts that lie behind 2 Thess 1, although it may indeed
be alluded to in the very next phrase in v 8.

More important is the punctuation after the phrase. The comma in Nestle
makes clear that the flaming fire qualifies *apokalypsis*, specifying another element of it (Eadie, 241; Findlay, 147). Christ is revealed in or is surrounded by
fire (cf. Rev 1:13–16). In the apocalyptic tradition, fire is associated with the eschatological judgment (see Volz, 318–19; F. Lang in *TDNT* 6.936–38; cf. Matt
25:41; Mark 9:43, 48; thus Trilling 1980: 55). If there is no comma here, it may
be taken with what follows and be understood similarly. There is, however, no
indication that this fire either destroys or purifies (cf. 1 Pet 1:7; 4:12; Aus 1971:
81), and the phrase may be understood in a revelatory sense (as in Acts 7:30).
Nevertheless, most commentators hold that the flame is both a manifestation of
the divine presence and an instrument of vengeance (cf. Mal 3:2; 4:1–2; Lightfoot 1980: 102; von Dobschütz 1909: 247; Best 1972: 259), which is supported
by 1 Cor 3:13–15 (see F. Lang in *TDNT* 6.944–45). What is striking, though, is
the restraint with which Paul uses the apocalyptic element of fire, reducing it to
a mere mention.

In v 6, Paul had described judgment as God's repayment or retribution in negative and positive terms; he now continues the thought of repayment, but attributes the action to Christ and expresses it in language that has overtones of Isa
66:15. He now draws attention only to the negative aspect of the eschatological
judgment. He elaborates on repayment in three ways. The first is in the phrase
*didontos ekdikēsin* ("repaying with vengeance"), which is loosely attached to *tou
kyriou Iēsou*. The exact phrase occurs only here in the NT, but is not an unusual LXX expression (e.g., Num 31:3; 2 Sam 4:8 LXX; 22:48; Ezek 25:14, 17).

The word group describes various dimensions of retribution for deeds done.
*Ekdikēsis* is punishment for a wrong committed (Rom 13:4; 1 Pet 2:14) and
could be eschatological (Luke 21:22), when punishment will be meted out at the
final judgment in accordance with God's justice (Rev 19:2; cf. 6:10). Justice is
ultimately received from God (Luke 18:3, 5, 7–8), and humans are not to seek
vengeance, for it belongs to God (Rom 12:19; cf. Heb 10:30, both quoting Deut
32:35). John Chrysostom points out that those who are being repaid are not described as oppressors of the Thessalonians but as those who do not believe and
who disobey the gospel (cf. 2 Cor 10:6); it is therefore on the Lord's account that
they are punished, not on account of the Thessalonians (*Homilies on 2 Thessalonians* 2 [PG 62:470]). Already in his instructions to the Thessalonians when he
was with them, Paul had warned them that the Lord would punish (avenge) immoral sexual conduct (1 Thess 4:6).

*those who do not know God and those who do not obey the gospel of our Lord
Jesus.* These are the second and third ways in which Paul elaborates on the judgment. The major exegetical difficulty is whether he has two groups in mind,
each introduced by the definite article *tois* ("those"), and if so, who they were.

Many commentators advance two major arguments to support the contention that Paul has two groups, Gentiles and Jews, in mind (e.g., Ellicott, 100; Lightfoot 1980: 103; Lünemann, 583; von Dobschütz 1909: 248):

The first argument places great weight on the repetition of the article, which normally might, but need not, indicate two classes of people.

The second argument makes much of the different descriptions of the persons with whom the articles go. Those who do not know God are usually Gentiles in the OT (e.g., Jer 10:25; Ps 78:6 LXX) and in Paul (1 Thess 4:5; cf. Rom 1:28), while Jews are described as disobedient (e.g., Rom 10:16, 21).

There is a degree of plausibility to this view, but the arguments are not as persuasive as they might initially appear. To begin with, the two descriptions are not exclusively applied to two different groups. Jews are also described as not knowing God in the OT (e.g., Jer 9:6 LXX; John 8:55) although not in Paul. Furthermore, while Paul in 1 Thess 4:5 specifies that it is Gentiles who do not know God, he does not do so here. In addition, Gentiles and Jews are indiscriminately referred to as disobedient (Rom 10:16; 11:30).

The grammatical argument would be stronger were it not for the Hebraic character of Paul's language here, which suggests synonymous parallelism (see also v 10), as, for example, in Jer 10:25a: "Pour out thy wrath upon the nations that know thee not, and upon the peoples that call not on thy name" (cf. Ps 36:10). If read thus, the second part of the parallel enhances or more precisely defines those who do not know God as those who disobey the gospel (thus Findlay, 148; Bruce 1982: 151; for the formulation, see Rom 10:16; for the thought, see Rom 15:18–20; cf. 2 Cor 10:5–6). This is supported by Paul's understanding that the knowledge of God is communicated through the gospel of the Lord Jesus Christ, whom he preaches (2 Cor 4:4–6).

It is not clear whom Paul has in mind on either reading. Commentators who think that he refers to two groups sometimes limit the Gentiles he has in view to those who had not heard the gospel and, in addition, rejected the natural revelation available to them (Rom 1:19–28; Lightfoot 1980: 103; Findlay, 149; Bruce 1982: 151). But there is nothing in the text to support this limitation. There is also a tendency to identify all persons in v 8 with the oppressors of v 6, but that does insufficient justice to the fact that, as Chrysostom maintained, they are punished on God's account, not the Thessalonians'. In reassuring his readers that justice will prevail Paul moves to a higher level of consideration: the relation of those to be punished to God. Fundamental to their culpability is their rejection of God, which will have dire consequences for them.

*1:9. They will pay the penalty of eternal ruin.* "They" renders the indefinite pronoun *hoitines*, which some grammarians think was no longer clearly distinguished from the definite relative *hoi* (so BDF §293), while others hold that it sometimes still was (see the discussion in Moule, 123–25). But the indefinite relative does on occasion retain a qualitative sense "to indicate that persons . . . belong to a certain class" (BAGD, 587; see Ellicott, 100–101; Eadie, 243; Milligan, 90–91; cf. Rom 1:25; Gal 4:24, 26; Phil 4:3). It does that here, explaining the character of its antecedents by telling what they will experience in the judgment.

The phrase *dikēn tisousin* ("will pay the penalty") is common in classical Greek but is not used anywhere else in the Bible, although similar phrases do occur (e.g., *ekdikein dikēn* in Lev 26:25; *ekdikein ekdikēsin* in Ezek 25:12). It is noteworthy that Paul uses such a classical idiom in a context so suffused with apocalyptic language. The explanation may reside in Paul's interest to stress the justice of God's judgment (cf. *dikaia krisis* in v 5; *dikaion* in v 6), for "*dikē* connotes justice in the penalty, punishment determined by a lawful process" (Findlay, 149, distinguishing *dikē* from *kolasis* ["chastisement"], Matt 25:46; Acts 4:21; 2 Pet 2:9; *timōria* ["satisfaction"], Heb 10:29). This by no means implies that divine justice was not considered to be the foundation of eschatological judgment in Jewish apocalyptic thought also (see Volz, 288–90; cf. 4 Macc 12:12, "justice will hold you in store for a fiercer and an everlasting fire and for torments which will never let you go for all time").

The translation "eternal ruin" renders *olethron aiōnion*, which is in apposition to *dikēn*. The phrase occurs in Jewish literature in 4 Macc 10:15 (A) and elsewhere in the NT, as it does here, always in eschatological contexts (1 Thess 5:3; 1 Cor 5:5; 1 Tim 6:9). It sometimes seems equivalent to *apōleia* ("destruction"; Rom 9:22; Phil 1:28; 3:19; cf. *apōleia aiōnios, Pss Sol* 2:31, 34; see also 3:11–12; 15:12–13, and Volz, 325) and belongs to the realm of such expressions as "eternal fire" (Matt 18:8; 25:41; Jude 7), "eternal chastisement" (Matt 25:46), and "eternal judgment" (Heb 6:2; cf. *1 En* 91:15; see Volz, 272–309, 325–27). It does not mean annihilation, but everlasting ruin. What is striking, once more, is that Paul does not dwell on the eschatological pains so vividly described in Jewish apocalyptic literature reflected elsewhere in the NT, but describes ruin as separation (see Volz, 320–25; cf. Matt 5:29–30; Luke 16:23–26; Rev 14:10–11; 19:3; 21:8; contrast John Chrysostom's justification for emphasizing the judgment in moral exhortation, *Homilies on 2 Thessalonians* 2 [PG 62:470–80]).

*from the face of the Lord.* The preposition *apo* ("from") admits of a number of possible meanings (see Eadie, 244–45; Rigaux 1956: 632), in the following order of escalating probability:

1. Patristic commentators understood *apo* temporally, the ruin occurring "at," "from," or "immediately after" the Lord's manifestation, which would make the phrase parallel to *en tē apokalypsei* ("at the revelation") in v 6. The references to Rom 1:20 and Phil 1:5, marshaled in support of this interpretation are not, however, apt, for in them *apo* is used with an event or epoch that makes clear the temporal significance.

2. *Apo* was interchangeable with *ek* ("from"; cf. 1 Thess 2:6; Matt 3:16; John 1:44–46; see GNTG 3.259), and it has been suggested that the face of the Lord would be the ultimate source of eternal ruin (for the same construction, *apo tou prosōpou tou kyriou* ["from the face of the Lord"], but emphasizing eschatological blessings, see Acts 3:20).

3. A more probable interpretation takes *apo* to be causal, the Lord bringing about ruin "by his presence and glory" (Findlay, 150). The OT speaks of the destructive effect of the Lord's presence (e.g., Ps 34:16; Jer 4:26), and in late Greek *apo* was used interchangeably with *hypo* ("by") of the agent (GNTG 3.258),

though most frequently in this sense with passive verbs (e.g., Acts 2:22; 15:33; 20:9; 2 Cor 7:13; the manuscripts frequently replace *apo* with *hypo*). For a similarity in thought but not wording, see 2 Thess 2:8c.

4. A number of considerations suggest that *apo* should be understood spatially, as reflected in the translation. This is the normal meaning of the phrase (e.g., Acts 5:41; 7:45; Rev 12:14; 20:11). Furthermore, this is one of the strongest allusions to the LXX, the refrain in Isa 2:10, 19, 21, where it is predicted that the unrighteous would try to hide themselves in rocks and caves *apo prosōpou tou phobou kyriou kai apo tēs doxēs tēs ischyos autou* ("from the presence of the fear of the Lord and from the glory of his might") when he rises to terrify the earth. In Isaiah God is Lord; here Jesus is Lord.

In addition, and most important, is that the spatial understanding of *apo* points to the contrast of those who do not know God and do not obey the gospel to those who believe, who will be with the Lord Jesus forever (see NOTES on 1 Thess 4:14, 17; 5:10; cf. 2 Thess 1:7). The Thessalonians will appear before God and the Lord Jesus at his coming (1 Thess 2:19; 3:13; for the blessed who will see the face of God, see Ps 11:7; 18:10; Heb 12:14; 1 John 3:2; Rev 22:4). Paul's omission of *tou phobou* ("of the fear") from Isaiah makes the parallelism with the following phrase stronger and again shows Paul's relative reticence to stress judgment in comparison with contemporary apocalyptic. This is also in contrast to Rev 6:15–17, which alludes to these passages from Isaiah, combined with Hos 10:8, and to the Son of Man tradition, e.g., Matt 15:41, "Depart from me [*ap' emou*] . . . into eternal fire"; cf. "into eternal chastisement" (*eis kolasin aiōnion*, v 46; cf. Matt 7:23; Luke 18:27). Paul continues to strip the apocalyptic traditions of elements that do not directly serve his consolatory purpose.

*and from the glory of his might.* In the second part of the parallelism, "face" becomes "glory" and "Lord" becomes "might" as Paul continues to use the language of Isaiah to emphasize the powerful, dramatic nature of the Lord at his coming. This phrase is a periphrasis for the person of Jesus and describes his glory and the power associated with it (Bornemann, 392). Glory, with the connotation of brightness (see Luke 9:29–32; 1 Cor 15:41), is a manifestation of the divine presence (Luke 2:8), and for Paul, as for the Son of Man tradition (e.g., Matt 24:30; Mark 13:26), it is also an eschatological notion that he utilizes in comforting his readers.

Paul contrasts present sufferings to the glory that is to be revealed in its fullness (Rom 8:18), but in a certain sense, those whom God has called and justified he has already glorified (Rom 8:30). They will be given all things with Christ, and nothing will be able to separate them from the love of Christ (Rom 8:31–39; cf. 2 Cor 4:17, "For this slight momentary affliction is preparing for us an eternal weight of glory beyond all comparison").

God calls people into his kingdom and glory through the preaching of the gospel, which evokes faith (2 Thess 2:13–14; cf. 1 Thess 2:12). According to 2 Cor 4:4–5, the light of the glory of Christ, who is the image of God and himself has glory (3:18), is transmitted through the gospel that has him as its content. Behind this preaching stands the mighty Creator himself (4:6): "For it is the God who said, 'Let light shine out of darkness,' who has shone in our hearts to give the light of the knowledge of the glory of God in the face of Christ [*tēs doxēs tou theou en prosōpō Christou*]." But unbelievers are kept from seeing that light of the glory of Christ; their minds are blinded by the god of this world (v 4). It is these persons, who do not know God and disobey the gospel, who will be separated from the glory of the Lord's might. This will ultimately take place when the Lord comes.

1:10. *when he comes to be glorified in his saints.* Having in vv 7b–9 described the judgment of those who reject God and oppress the Thessalonians, Paul now returns to what his readers may look forward to. In v 5 he had introduced his encouragement by claiming that the purpose of their experiences was to make them worthy of God's kingdom, for which they were suffering. In 1 Thess 2:12, Paul had connected kingdom and glory, and he has just described the oppressors' exclusion from that glory. He now concludes by describing the purpose of the Lord's coming as the Lord's own glorification. The focus has moved from the Thessalonians to their oppressors to the Lord.

The phrase "when he comes" designates the time of the judgment just described. It is also the time when the Lord will be glorified. In this section Paul wants to specify the events that lie in the future (cf. "at the revelation," v 7; "on that day," v 10). The phrase introduces another synonymous parallelism, each member beginning with an infinitive, to express the purpose of the Lord's coming.

The compound infinitive *endoxasthēnai* ("to be glorified") is used only here and in v 12 in the NT, but it occurs in the LXX (Exod 14:4; Isa 14:25; 49:3). The phrase recalls Ps 88:8 LXX but does not quote it. Here, it makes an emphatic contrast to v 9: *apo tēs doxēs* versus *endoxasthēnai*. The saints could be the angels of v 7 (see NOTE on 1 Thess 3:13), but since they are parallel to the believers in the next member of the parallelism, they must be Christians. *Hagioi* ("saints") was a common designation for Christians (1 Cor 16:1–2; 2 Cor 9:1; cf. Rom 15:25, 31), who were *klētoi hagioi* ("saints by calling"; Rom 1:7; 1 Cor 1:2) because God called them in sanctification (see NOTES and COMMENT on 1 Thess 4:7; cf. 2 Thess 2:13–14).

Precisely what it means that the Lord will "be glorified in his saints" is not clear. The *en* may be instrumental (cf. Isa 49:3) as many patristic commentators held, meaning that the Lord would be glorified through his saints. The preposition could also be taken spatially (cf. Ps 88:8; 1 Macc 3:14) so that the Lord would be glorified among Christians, which would, incidentally, make a further contrast to v 9. *En* could also be causal, as it is in v 12, where Christ's glorification is grounded in that of the saints. There is something analogous in 1 Thess 2:20, where Paul says that the Thessalonians are his eschatological glory, in this way expressing his pastoral concern for them by complimenting them. In addition to what was said above about glory, it is important to note that Paul stresses that Christians will share glory with Christ (Rom 8:17–18; Phil 3:21; cf. Col 3:4). Paul's statement here, that the Thessalonians will be the ground of Christ's glory, may be his way of going a step further than the notion of participation in order to strengthen them by complimenting them, as he had done in 1 Thess 2:20.

*and to be marveled at in all who have believed.* The second member of the parallelism continues the thought of the first. The language is again inspired by the OT without quoting it (Ps 67:36), and *en* is again causal (cf. Isa 61:6; see Cramer, 6.384). The verb *thaumazein* ("to marvel") here does not mean astonishment, but admiration (see Sir 38:3, 6, for *thaumazesthai* and *endoxasthēnai* in the same context). Paul does not specify "all" the believers because of divisions of some sort among the Thessalonians, for example, between those who would be alive and those who would have died by the time of the Parousia (1 Thess 4:13–17) or between Jews and Gentiles. He does so for the sake of emphasis, emboldening those of his readers who may still have been uncertain about their salvation (see NOTE and COMMENT on vv 4–5), so the phrase *pāsin tois pisteusasin* has the sense "all who have believed, you included" (Lightfoot 1980: 105; Wohlenberg, 137; von Dobschütz 1909: 251). He uses the articular aorist participle because he views things from the perspective of the end, when the Lord comes: because the Thessalonians had believed, they will be cause for the Lord to be marveled at.

*(for our testimony to you was believed).* He stresses that his readers belong to those who believed by making a parenthetical affirmation introduced by the causal *hoti* ("for"; for this as a parenthesis, see already Theodore of Mopsuestia, 2.47 Swete; for a similar interruption of a thanksgiving, see 1 Cor 1:6). The testimony (*to martyrion hēmōn*) of which he speaks was the gospel (v 8) he had preached to them (cf. *to euangelion hēmōn* ["our gospel"], 2:14; 1 Thess 1:5; 2 Cor 4:3; *to kērygma hēmōn* ["our preaching"], 1 Cor 15:14).

The phrase *eph' hymās* is awkward. It can go either with *episteuthē* ("was believed") or with *to martyrion hēmōn* ("our testimony"). It is more natural to take it with the latter, for *epi* with the accusative normally describes motion towards an object. Paul introduces the parenthesis, which is occasioned by *pisteusasin*, to further strengthen the Thessalonians' confidence that they will be among the believers at the Parousia (Lünemann, 585). The parenthesis is an echo of 1 Thess 2:13 (Findlay, 152), and it continues to draw attention to Paul's special relationship with them expressed earlier in the letter (vv 4–5, 7).

*on that day.* For the phrase (also in 2 Tim 1:18; 4:8), see NOTE on 1 Thess 5:2. Its use here was probably inspired by Isa 2:11, 20, which also informed the language of v 9. By virtue of its position at the end of the sentence that began in v 3 and because of the parenthesis, which further accentuates it, the phrase stands in a position of strong emphasis.

Paul begins and ends v 10 with temporal specifications of when Christ's glory will be fully and finally manifested. He knows that some of his readers may think that the Day of the Lord has already come (2:2). They would likely also have assumed that they were already in full possession of eschatological glory (cf. 1 Cor 4:10, for Paul's ironic comment about some of his readers who also hold to an overrealized eschatology [see v 8]). Such teaching would have discouraged some Thessalonians who did not share that confidence in the midst of persecution and tribulation. Paul therefore specifies exactly when the eschatological glory will be realized.

# COMMENT

In vv 5–10 Paul addresses the practical problems of the Thessalonians' discouragement, particularly as it was exacerbated by the suffering they were enduring. Social ostracism and persecutions of other sorts would discourage recent converts under any circumstances. For some of the Thessalonians, these experiences must have caused greater consternation because they were already unsettled or were in danger of being unsettled by the erroneous teaching that the Day of the Lord had already come (2:2). Presumably, that would have meant that they should be experiencing the blessings of the kingdom and glory into which God had been calling them (1 Thess 2:12) rather than the tribulation and oppression that was their present lot. To encourage them in these circumstances is the first major purpose of the letter, and in vv 5–10 Paul does so by placing them and their experiences in the larger plan of God's scheme of things.

In his encouragement, Paul uses apocalyptic traditions, as he had also done when he consoled his readers in 1 Thess 4:13–5:11, although the reasons why they required consolation then differed from the present circumstances. Then the problem had been an intracommunal one, whether those Thessalonians who would be alive at the Parousia would have an advantage over those who would have died when the Lord comes (4:13–18). There was an erroneous eschatological teaching that affected those who grieved, to which he would give attention after his consolation proper (5:1–11). Now the practical problem at hand is the suffering of the Thessalonians at the hands of unbelievers (2 Thess 1:5–10). Again there is erroneous eschatological teaching that contributes to the problem Paul is attempting to alleviate, to which he will give closer attention in 2:1–12.

It is thus the practical needs of his readers that Paul seeks to meet by applying to their situation apocalyptic traditions he considers appropriate. In the first letter, his consolation stressed that at the Parousia all believers will be gathered to be with each other and the Lord; in the second letter, the emphasis is on God's justice in judging the oppressors and on their separation from the Lord, although the theme of the association of believers is continued (v 7). In fact, the differences between the two letters should not be accentuated. If Paul wrote 2 Thessalonians soon after 1 Thessalonians, which appears to have been the case, his readers would recently have heard the earlier consolation read to them and would have understood the present one as a supplement called for by their present crisis. Indeed, Paul had used various means of comforting his converts as early as when he was still with them (see NOTES and COMMENT on 1 Thess 3:3–4). What stands out in this consolation is his stress on the comforting security of God's design (Dibelius 1937: 41).

Some scholars, while recognizing that Paul is here engaged in comfort, have nevertheless detected sharp differences between Paul's apocalyptic views and those thought to be represented in 2 Thessalonians, which they regard as pseudonymous (see pages 368–69). Marxsen (1982: 44–52), for example, who may be taken as representative, argues that the apocalyptic thought in this letter is more like that of traditional Jewish apocalypticism than Paul's. A major part of his argument is that 2 Thessalonians lapses into a dualism that is more characteristic of that thought than Paul's.

Like the apocalyptists, Paul believed in a final judgment (1 Thess 1:10), but he thought of it as already present in some way (1 Thess 2:16). He speaks of the apocalyptic events of the coming of the Lord and resurrection, but combines them and is not as vivid in his description of those events as the apocalyptists were. He speaks of the Day of the Lord (1 Thess 5:1–11), but unlike the apocalyptists he rejects speculation about when it would come, for doing so deflects believers from the possibility of already living as children of the light and the Day.

In this stress on the present, Marxsen asserts, Paul differed from Jewish apocalyptists, who required that the faithful live in a manner now that will enable them to stand in the Judgment and thereafter share the glory, which the coming Day will bring. Furthermore, in such contexts Christology is soteriological (1 Thess 1:10; 4:14; 5:9–10). Future salvation is secured by what Christ has already done and is always a present possibility. Marxsen (1982: 67) maintains that 2 Thessalonians is different and that, as in Jewish apocalyptic thought, the two ages are sharply distinguished and there is no anticipation in the first of the second, with the lone possible exception found in 1:5a. The present holds consequences for the future, but the future does not break into the present. Nor is the letter's Christology soteriological, for the judgment that God brings (1:5–7a) is carried out by Christ (1:7b–10). Nowhere in Paul is judgment used in comforting the faithful.

In the NOTES it has been shown that the sharp dualism that Marxsen discerns in 2 Thessalonians is in fact not present. It is the presupposition that the letter was written by someone other than Paul, at a considerably later time than 1 Thessalonians, that drives his interpretation. In 2 Thessalonians 1:5–10 God's judgment is already present (v 5a); the Thessalonians are already being made worthy for the kingdom (v 5b). In saying this the author does not encourage his readers to risk suffering for which they will be rewarded, thus introducing a doctrine of merit (so Marxsen); they are already suffering, and Paul is comforting them by telling them what God is already doing to them, making them worthy (the passive of *kataxiōthēnai*).

What appears to be especially offensive to some commentators is the emphasis on judgment and Christ's role in dispensing it. Paul wrote in a context in which divine retribution was accepted as part of the notion of divine justice by Jews as well as Gentiles (cf. Plutarch, *On the Delay of the Divine Judgment*). To stress that divine justice required judgment and punishment provided no justification for human retribution or vindictiveness. And the notion of an eschatological reversal of fortune is not restricted to Jewish apocalyptic thinking and 2 Thessalonians. It is true that in 2 Thessalonians what is usually associated with God is associated with Christ, for example, the Day of the Lord, his coming with angels, judgment, separation of the unjust. But as is clear from the NOTES, the same elements appear explicitly or implicitly elsewhere in Paul (Kreitzer, 93–129).

This commentary rejects the interpretation that the author of 2 Thessalonians has lapsed into apocalypticism to such an extent that Paul could not have written it, but that does not mean that Paul did not appropriate theological insights from contemporary apocalypticism to comfort his readers. He appears to have done so in his assertion that God had decreed that they be made worthy of the kingdom (v 5b). Paul does not think that God deemed them worthy of the future kingdom because of their endurance and faith in their present hardship. As the eschatological judgment is in some way already present, so is the kingdom (see NOTE on 1 Thess 2:12), and their endurance already has a transforming effect on them (cf. Rom 5:1–4). Paul's thinking is related to a contemporary theology of suffering and shares much with 1 Pet 4:17–19 and Phil 1:28.

This theology of suffering took into consideration God's justice, which requires judgment and punishment while affirming God's acceptance of his elect. It differs from the law of retribution (Exod 21:23–25), which requires that evil actions now performed be recompensed in the eschaton (cf. 1 Cor 3:17). This is how some scholars understand the teaching in vv 5–10. This theology of suffering, in contrast, finds value in the sufferings of the faithful in the present, rather than deferring that value to the eschaton.

In this theology of suffering, God's punishment in the present is a sign of his mercy (*Pss Sol* 13:9–10), for he does not wait to punish them as he does the nations (2 Macc 6:12–16). He punishes them now, for he is just: "he afflicted them as his enemies because they sinned, therefore, they were once punished that they might be forgiven" (2 *Bar* 13:8–10). The thought is also expressed clearly in the words of Baruch to the tribes that were carried across the Euphrates:

> Therefore, I have been the more diligent to leave you the words of this letter before I die so that you may be comforted regarding the evils which have befallen you, and you may also be grieved regarding the evils that have befallen your brothers, and then further, so that you may consider the judgment of him who decreed it against you to be righteous, namely, that you should be carried away into captivity, for what you have suffered is smaller than what you have done, in order that you may be found worthy of your fathers in the last times. (2 *Bar* 78:5)

The similarity of this theology to 2 Thess 1 has been recognized for some time (e.g., Wichmann, 27–29; Aus 1971: 71–75; Bassler), but it is also clear that in his appropriation of this tradition Paul was very selective. He focuses on one element, God's just judgment, that through their suffering the Thessalonians be made worthy. He does not speak of their suffering as punishment for their sins and is not interested in developing a theology of suffering. He is rather concerned to comfort his readers who were suffering for the kingdom, and that determines the way he uses this tradition, as it does the other traditions reflected in this consolation.

# 3. PETITION FOR WORTHY CONDUCT, 1:11–12

The prayer report in vv 11–12 ends this section of the letter as the prayers in 1 Thess 3:11–12; 5:23–24 end sections of that letter. This marks the end of the thanksgiving proper, which began with v 3, as is customary in most Pauline thanksgivings, and it closes on an eschatological note. In addition, the conclusion continues to comfort the readers by interceding for them and laying stress on God's activity in their lives. Paul makes his petitions with two subjunctives, *axiōse* ("may make . . . worthy") and *plērōse* ("may fulfill"), which introduce the members of a synonymous parallelism. He concludes with a statement of purpose that once more focuses on the theme of glorification.

## TRANSLATION

1 ¹¹To this end we also pray for you always, that our God
    may make you worthy of his call
    and may fulfill every resolve to do good and work of faith in power,
    ¹²so that the name of our Lord Jesus may be glorified in you, and you
in him, according to the grace of our God and the Lord Jesus Christ.

## NOTES

1:11. *To this end.* This phrase (*eis ho*) has been thought to refer to *kataxiōthēnai* in v 5 (Lightfoot 1980: 105), which is, however, too distant, or to mean "in view of" (Wohlenberg, 139; von Dobschütz 1909: 254), which unnecessarily avoids the phrase's usual, obvious meaning, which expresses purpose, "in order that." Paul prays that the *endoxasthēnai* ("to be glorified") and *thaumasthēnai* ("to be marveled at"), about which he has just spoken, be realized in the Thessalonians, for they do not take place automatically (Lünemann, 586; Findlay, 153; O'Brien 1977: 177).

*we also pray for you always.* The *kai* ("also") has caused much mischief among commentators. Some have thought that it signifies a contrast to someone else, in addition to Paul, who might have been praying. One theory is that Paul has in mind a letter from the Thessalonians, who had written to him that, despite their discouragement, they were praying that God would prepare them for the coming Day (Frame, 249, 252). That they were praying, especially in view of their lack of confidence and uncertainty (see COMMENT on vv 4–5), is quite likely, and that they had mentioned this in a letter to Paul is not improbable (see pages 175–77; Malherbe 1990a), but it is highly unlikely that the *kai* would refer to a comment in a letter so distant as to antedate 1 Thessalonians.

A different view is that *kai* after a relative pronoun is so weak that it can be fairly left untranslated (e.g., Rom 5:2; 1 Cor 1:8; Phil 2:5; thus Best 1972: 268). The most probable solution is that *kai* qualifies *proseuchometha* ("we . . . pray"): Paul also prays, interceding for them in addition to giving thanks for them (von Dobschütz 1909: 254; O'Brien 1977: 178). More specifically, the prayer is added to the glorification that the Lord will experience in his saints. That Paul always (*pantote*) intercedes for them is the counterpart to his assurance that he always gives thanks for them (see NOTE on v 3) and performs the pastoral function of expressing his constant care.

*that our God may make you worthy of his call.* Paul states the content of the prayer in the form of a purpose clause (*hina* plus the subjunctive *axiōse*). In the Greek, *hymās* ("you") stands immediately after "that," a position of emphasis, thus focusing on the readers and connecting the prayer closely to v 10b: Paul is praying for those to whom his testimony was directed and who believed it. His close relationship with his converts, expressed in the parenthesis in v 10, is continued in the description of God as "our God" (see NOTES on 1 Thess 1:3; 2:2; 3:9, 11).

The first petition is that God "make them worthy" (*hymās axiōse*). The same issues that are involved in the meaning of *kataxiōthēnai* in v 5 are present here. The issues involved in the interpretation of that verse also apply to *axioun*: the word means "to make worthy" rather than "to deem worthy." God is the subject implicit in the passive *kataxiōthēnai*; here he is explicitly the one who is to make the Thessalonians worthy. Thus, the glorification of the Lord on that Day, which will be grounded in his saints, is ultimately God's action.

The calling (*klēsis*) of which God is petitioned to make them worthy may be either past or future. Most commentators think that it is the eschatological call, finding support in one Pauline passage, Phil 3:14, and in Matt 22:3, 8. The reason for this interpretation is that *axiōse*, which points to the future, is taken by them to mean "might deem worthy." However, with the exception of Phil 3:14 (cf. Eph 1:18), Paul thinks of God's call as having taken place in the past (e.g., 1 Cor 1:9; 7:20; Gal 1:6; 5:13; 1 Thess 4:7; 5:24; 2 Thess 2:14) or as continuing in the present (1 Thess 2:13; see NOTE there; cf. Matt 22:3, where the verb is used of past and eschatological action). Paul's reference to the Thessalonians' call effectively requires that they conduct themselves in accordance with their call (see 1 Cor 1:16; cf. Eph 4:1). The member of the parallelism that follows clarifies this member.

*and may fulfill every resolve to do good.* Paul petitions God to make the Thessalonians worthy of his call by bringing to fulfillment their resolve to do good. Older commentaries referred the phrase *pāsan eudokian agathōsynēs* to God, as though Paul were praying that God fulfill his own good pleasure, but that interpretation is generally rejected (e.g., Lünemann, 587; Eadie, 251–52; Rigaux 1956: 639–40). The notion of God effecting human conduct is common in Paul (e.g., Phil 4:19 [*plēroun*]; 1 Thess 3:10 [*pleonazein, perisseuein*]; see the passive *peplērōmenoi* in Phil 1:11, where God is the implied subject; cf. Col 1:9). In Phil 2:13, *eudokia* ("goodwill," here "resolve") refers to God (cf. Eph 1:5, 9), but it also refers to human goodwill (e.g., Phil 1:15; Luke 2:14). Paul had used the verb *eudokein* in 1 Thess 2:8; 3:1 of his free decision in conducting his ministry, so God's action does not eliminate human freedom of choice or resolve. Furthermore, the grammatically parallel phrase that follows (*ergon pisteōs* ["work of faith"]) refers to the Thessalonians, which suggests that *pāsan eudokian agathōsynēs* ("every resolve to do good") also does so (in Gal 5:22, *agathōsynē* is a fruit of the Spirit). The thought here is similar to Phil 2:13 (except for the referent of *eudokia*), where God is said to be effective in the Philippians' wishing and doing.

*and work of faith in power.* The phrase "work of faith" (*ergon pisteōs*) is similar to *ergon tēs pisteōs* in 1 Thess 1:3, where the genitive is subjective, as it also is here. There the Thessalonians' work for which Paul gave thanks was their evangelistic activity; here the reference is more general, its association with *agathōsynē* perhaps indicating a moral dimension to the work that is to issue from faith. Paul has moved from resolve to action (O'Brien 1977: 181). Lest his readers focus too narrowly on the effort that is required of them, Paul appends *en dynamei* ("in power") in the emphatic position at the end, though it goes adverbially with *plērōse*. The second petition is thus bracketed by references to God's activity, which rules out any possible claim to merit, yet it requires human action (note the substitution of *en ergō* for *en dynamei* in 1 Thess 1:5).

1:12. *so that the name of our Lord Jesus may be glorified in you, and you in him.* Paul ends by stating the purpose of the prayer, substituting *hopōs* ("so that") for the more usual *hina* (v 11) for the sake of variety. The purpose is formulated in language reminiscent of Isa 66:5 LXX, "in order that the name of the Lord be glorified [*doxasthē*]." The composite *endoxasthē* in v 12 is influenced by *endoxasthēnai* in v 10, which may connect the two verses and support the contention of some commentators that Paul has in mind the eschatological glorification of the name (e.g., Frame, 241; Masson, 91; Best 1972: 270–71; O'Brien 1977: 182). That does not, however, take into sufficient consideration the present conduct of the Thessalonians that is in view in v 11 (so von Dobschütz 1909: 257; Trilling 1980: 64; Wanamaker, 235).

It is through their conduct now, as they are empowered by God, that the name of the Lord Jesus will be glorified. The *en hymin* ("in you") describes the ground of the glorifying, that is, "by virtue of you," as it did in v 10 (cf. *en tois hagiois*, "in his saints"; cf. Gal 1:24, *kai endoxason en emoi ton theon* ["and they were glorifying God because of me"]). There is a reciprocity between Christians and Christ; they too will be glorified in him (*en autō* refers to the Lord and not his name) when his name is glorified. Exactly how this occurs in the present is not clear (see NOTES on vv 9–10), but the addition of this phrase adds comfort to the implied exhortation of the prayer report (Theodoret, *Interpretation of 2 Thessalonians* 1 [PG 82:661]).

There is no need to see in the reference to the name the significance some commentators do, as for example, "The glorification of the *name* of the Lord Jesus thus implies the showing forth of the Lord Jesus as He really is, in all the fulness of His person and attributes (cf. Phil. ii.9., Heb. i.4)" (Milligan, 94). "Name" stands for the person and is used with a variety of verbs, e.g., *hagiazein* ("to sanctify"), Matt 6:9, frequently in quotations from or allusions to the OT: *blasphēmein* ("to blaspheme"), Rom 2:24 (cf. Isa 52:5); *apangellein* ("to proclaim"), Heb 2:12 (cf. Ps 21:23); *diangellein* ("to proclaim"), Rom 9:17 (cf. Exod 9:16); and *doxazein* ("glorify"), Rev 15:4 (Ps 86:8); Herm *Vis* 2.1.2; 3.4.3 (cf. Ps 85:9, 12 LXX; Isa 24:15; 66:5). In 2 Thess 1:12, *endoxazein* may also be influenced by Isa 66:5, but the reference here need not be to glorification at the Parousia, as was the case in v 10.

To glorify God through one's conduct is a common idea in the NT. Paul speaks of glorifying God in one's body (1 Cor 6:20) and of doing all things to the glory of God (1 Cor 10:31), and reports of people who had glorified God because of him (lit., "in him," Gal 1:24). Glorifying God is associated with doing good works (Matt 5:16; 1 Pet 2:12; 4:16) as it is in 1 Thess 2:12. This passage is thus another instance of applying to Christ what has been said of God (cf. Ign *Eph* 2:2; Ign *Smyrn* 1:1; Ign *Pol* 8:2).

*according to the grace of our God and the Lord Jesus Christ.* Again Paul specifies the divine source of the glorifying: it is in consequence of or because of grace that the name is glorified (*kata tēn charin*; see BAGD, s.v. *kata* II.5.a.δ; cf. Milligan, 94), which once more excludes human merit (Rom 4:16; 11:5–6; cf. Eph 2:5, 8). In Greek there is one article before "our God" (*tou theou hēmōn*) and none before "Lord Jesus Christ" (*kyriou Iēsou Christou*), which may mean that God and Christ are viewed as the same person, as they are in some late NT writings (Titus 2:13; 2 Pet 1:1, 11). This could be taken as evidence that this letter belongs among those letters, but it does not need to do so. Another solution has been to regard *kai kyriou Iēsou Christou* as a gloss by a later reader (von Dobschütz 1909: 258).

While Paul does elsewhere refer to Jesus as God only once (Rom 9:5), he ascribes to Jesus attributes usually regarded as God's prerogatives, and he does so in both letters, e.g., Jesus judges (1 Thess 3:13; 4:6; 2 Thess 1:7–8), and the gospel is described as his (1 Thess 3:2; 2 Thess 1:8) and is the same as his word (1 Thess 1:8; 2 Thess 3:1). The NOTES have indicated how frequently in vv 5–10 Paul makes such attributions to Christ. It is therefore possible that he might identify God and Christ in v 12. Other considerations, however, suggest otherwise.

Not much weight can be attached to the use or nonuse of the article in connection with God and Christ. In our letters, *ho theos hēmōn* ("our God") with the article is frequently used (e.g., 1 Thess 1:1; 2:2; 3:9, 13; 2 Thess 1:1, 11; 2:16), as is *kyrios* ("Lord") without the article (e.g., 1 Thess 3:8; 4:1, 6, 17; 5:2; 2 Thess 1:1, 2; 2:13; 3:4, 12). "Lord" has practically become a proper name requiring no article. It is appropriate that at the end of his thanksgiving proper Paul return to God, with whom he had begun it (v 3). The prayer report with which the thanksgiving ends used *ho theos hēmōn* as the subject of the petitions (v 11), and the same epithet is used in the conclusion of the purpose clause (v 12). It is for the sake of fullness of expression that Paul adds "and the Lord Jesus Christ," which had already become formulaic (see Trilling 1980: 64–65).

## COMMENT

The concluding prayer report continues the pastoral, comforting thrust of the thanksgiving period. Paul had stressed his readers' moral behavior at the beginning of the thanksgiving, and he does so again here at the end. He also picks up the themes of worthiness and glorification from vv 5–10. The consolation that he offers them does not permit them to wait, as victims, for God's deliverance.

Verses 5–10 do develop dramatically a picture of reversal, when God in his justice will set things right, but that does not allow them to wait passively for their vindication. They are to decide freely to do good, their faith is to issue in work, and they are to bring glory to the name of the Lord.

As we have seen, Paul has a view of glory as a present factor in the Christian's life. Through preaching, the glory of Christ is transmitted (2 Cor 4:4–5), and those who behold the glory of the Lord are themselves progressively transformed from one degree of glory to another (2 Cor 3:18). Their total identification takes place when they suffer hardships, in which the life of Jesus is made manifest (2 Cor 4:10–11). Despite hardships, there is a daily renewal: affliction produces an eternal weight of glory as the believer looks beyond what is transitory (2 Cor 4:17–18). There is thus a present dimension to glory in a life that makes Christ manifest in this world. The thought in 2 Thess 1:12 seems to be along the lines of 1 Cor 6:20, "So glorify God in your body"; cf. Phil 1:20, "Christ will be manifested in my body."

In 2 Thess 1:12 Paul has this practical, everyday dimension in mind, of the Christian moral life bringing glory to Christ. The spirit of what he says is very similar to 1 Pet 4:14–16, "If you are reproached for the name of Christ, you are blessed, because the spirit of glory and of God rests upon you. But let none of you suffer as a murderer, or a thief, or a wrongdoer, or a mischief maker; yet if one suffers as a Christian, let him not be ashamed, but under that name let him glorify God." That is not to say that the eschatological dimension is completely absent. In the preceding verse the author made that clear: "But rejoice insofar as you share Christ's sufferings, that you may also rejoice and be glad when his glory is revealed" (1 Pet 4:13). And in the succeeding verse he describes the present as already an age of judgment for Christians: "For the time has come for judgment to begin with the household of God; and if it begins with us, what will be the end of those who do not obey the gospel of God?" The view of 2 Thess 1:5–12 is not dissimilar.

Paul, then, is pastoral and comforting, but the ethical imperative is not diminished. In fact, by combining Christian responsibility with eschatological glory and reciprocity with the Lord, moral demands assume a weight that would appear impossible to bear. However, his pastoral intercession that God make them worthy of his call and powerfully bring to fulfillment their decision to do what is good reminds his readers of the divine assistance to which they have access.

# B. Exhortation: The Day of the Lord, 2:1–12

◆

Paul continues to treat the subject of the Lord's coming as he extends his pastoral concern, already begun in chap. 1. In 1:3–12 he had comforted his readers in the form of a thanksgiving; in 2:1–12 he does so in the form of a warning. The first chapter, particularly 1:6–10, is the presupposition for the second, much as 1 Thess 4:13–18 was for 5:1–11, and in both letters the second section deals severely with purveyors of false doctrine. After 2:1–2, which connects the two chapters, in vv 3–12 Paul lays out an apocalyptic schema, the didactic elements of which are not offered for their own sake, but rather to support his practical purpose of exhorting them to live calmly and faithfully (Bornemann, 349–51).

The limits of this pericope are marked by the paraenetic beginning in v 1, *erōtōmen de hymās, adelphoi* ("Now we beseech you, brethren"), and the concluding warning of judgment in v 12. A new section is introduced in 2:13 with the second thanksgiving in the letter (cf. 1:3). Sometimes the pericope is thought to encompass vv 13–14 or vv 13–17 as well (e.g., von Dobschütz 1909: 260; Giblin, 41–49; Trilling 1980: 69–70; Menken 1990: 375–77), but the overall structure of the letter supports the limitation to vv 1–12 (see pages 356–57).

Within this section, Paul first introduces the doctrinal error and its possible sources, which he feared might pose a threat to the emotional stability of the Thessalonians (vv 1–2). To demonstrate that the Day of the Lord could not already have come, as some erroneously claimed, he then lays out, in nonchronological fashion, a scheme in which future and present events alternate: vv 3–5, what must take place before the end; vv 6–7, what is taking place now; vv 8–10, what will take place at the end; vv 11–12, what is taking place now.

## TRANSLATION

2 ¹Now we beseech you, brethren, with reference to the coming of the Lord Jesus Christ and our gathering to him, ²not to be quickly shaken in mind nor to be emotionally wrought up, either by a spirit or by a spoken word or by a letter purporting to be from us, to the effect that the Day of the Lord has come.

³Let no one deceive you in any way. For [the Day of the Lord will not come] unless the apostasy comes first and the Man of Lawlessness is revealed, the Son of Perdition, ⁴who opposes and exalts himself over every so-called god or object of worship so that he takes his seat in the temple of God, proclaiming himself to be God. ⁵Do you not remember that while I was still with you I used to tell you these things?

⁶And you know now what it is that is exercising a restraining force, so that he may be revealed at his [proper] time. ⁷For the mystery of lawlessness is already at work; only until he who is now restraining will be out of the way.

⁸And then the Lawless One will be revealed, whom the Lord Jesus will slay with the breath of his mouth and destroy by the appearance of his coming. ⁹His coming will take place by the working of Satan, attended by all power and signs and wonders of falsehood, ¹⁰and by all deceit of wickedness for those on the way to perdition, because they did not receive the love of the truth so as to be saved.

¹¹And for this reason God sends them a power working to delude them, so that they should believe the lie, ¹²that all should be judged who had not believed the truth but delighted in wickedness.

# NOTES

2:1. *Now we beseech you, brethren.* The *de* ("Now") marks a transition from the thanksgiving of 1:3–12 to the exhortation of 2:1–12, which is addressed to the same people (Frame, 244). Paul uses *erōtōmen* ("we beseech") three other times in his letters, sometimes in a literary form of petition that he modifies to make it less formal (see NOTE on 1 Thess 4:1). In 1 Thess 4:1 *erōtōmen* is used in combination with *parakaloumen* ("we exhort"), and the form is modified by the addition of "in the Lord Jesus" to give it theological weight and of *adelphoi* ("brethren") to make the appeal more cordial. In Phil 4:2 it follows two occurrences of *parakalein* (v 1) and instead of *adelphoi* is followed by *gnēsie syzyge* ("true" or "genuine yokefellow"), thus conveying warmth (cf. Grabner-Haider, 10). In 2 Thess 2:1 *erōtān* is used without *parakalein*, with which it is used interchangeably in the papyri (see Bjerkelund, 34–39). It is also used here with *adelphoi*, which in this letter, with one exception (3:15), is always in the vocative and at the beginning of major sections of the letter (1:3; 2:1, 13, 15; 3:1, 6, 13). Paul's use of *erōtān* here is similar to that in 1 Thess 5:12.

*with reference to the coming of the Lord Jesus Christ and our gathering to him.* Instead of *peri*, which might have been expected (see 1 Thess 1:2, 9; 3:9; 4:9; 2 Thess 1:3; 2:13; 3:1), Paul uses *hyper* ("with reference to"; cf. 1 Thess 3:2; the variant reading in 5:10; 2 Thess 1:4). The two prepositions were equivalent in meaning at the time when Paul wrote (cf. 1 Thess 3:2, *parakalesai hyper*, but *hyper* is used seldom with *erōtān* in the papyri [Bjerkelund, 40]). In 1 Thess 4:14–17 Paul had comforted his readers by holding out the hope that they would be gathered at the coming of the Lord to meet him and be with him forever (see NOTES and COMMENT there).

He succinctly refers here to that discussion: the one article *tēs* ("the") combines *parousias* (cf. *apokalypsis* in 1:7) and *episynagogēs*, showing that they are closely related in his thinking, and the *ep' auton* summarizes *eis apantēsin tou kyriou* ("to meet the Lord") and perhaps recalls the sequel "to be with the Lord" as well (1 Thess 4:17). The noun *episynagogē* (2 Macc 2:7; *Pss Sol* 17:50) and its verb (2 Macc 2:18; Matt 24:3; Mark 13:27) were technical terms for the eschatological gathering (Isa 27:13). According to John Chrysostom, this is paraenesis combined with encomium and encouragement (*protropē*; *Homilies on 2 Thessalonians* 3 [PG 62:481]). Paul's concern in 2 Thess 2:1–12, then, is practical, to comfort his readers by reminding them of the eschatological teaching they had received in the first letter.

2:2. *not to be quickly shaken in mind nor to be emotionally wrought up.* Paul's reason for returning to his earlier consolation in 1 Thessalonians becomes clear in his expressed purpose (*eis* plus the infinitive) for beseeching them on the matter. His warning is given in a tightly constructed clause in which one article governs two infinitives, *saleuthēnai* ("to be shaken") and *throeisthai* ("to be emotionally wrought up"). An edge is given to his warning by the adverb *tacheōs* ("quickly"), which is to be taken temporally, referring to the short period of time that had elapsed since they had previously heard from him on the subject, rather than of manner, "with little reason" (Alford, 288; Trilling 1980: 75, who adduces Gal 1:6; 1 Tim 5:22 in support).

Besides its obvious literal sense, *saleuein* was used extensively of intellectual instability (a collection of material in Kemmler, 179–89, as it is here, *saleuthēnai hymās apo tou noos*), "shaken out of your wits" (the rendering of Bruce 1982: 163). Under normal circumstances, converts would feel unsettled (see Malherbe 1987: 46–48), and when he was separated from the Thessalonians, Paul was aware that they needed to be established and encouraged lest they be agitated (1 Thess 3:2–3). It is likely that they were still in this state when he wrote 2 Thessalonians (see NOTE 1:3–4), and he repeatedly urges them to stand firm and hold to the tradition they had received (2:15, 17; 3:3, 6).

The reason Paul here fears for their stability, however, is his suspicion of the erroneous eschatological doctrine that he goes on to correct. Acceptance of the false doctrine would shake them (*saleuthēnai*, aorist). The verb *throeisthai* ("to be emotionally wrought up") occurs in the NT only here outside the Synoptic apocalypse (Matt 24:6; Mark 13:7; cf. the variant reading in Luke 24:37), where it is also warned against. This condition would continue (*throeisthai*, present) as a result of their having been shaken (Wohlenberg, 142 n. 6).

*either by a spirit or by a spoken word or by a letter purporting to be from us.* Paul proceeds to mention three possible sources which might upset the Thessalonians. The negatives *mē* ("not") and *mēde* ("nor") in the preceding clause are followed by the reptetition of *mēte* with three nouns in this clause ("either . . . or . . . or"), thus strengthening the warning. The exegetical challenge is twofold, to properly understand the meaning of the three nouns, all used without an article, and to determine the relationship of the phrase *hōs di' hēmōn* ("purporting to be from us") to them.

It is generally agreed that "spirit" (*pneuma*) refers to the prophetic Spirit, as it does in 1 Cor 2:10, 13; 12:10; 1 Thess 5:19–20, and to false prophets, as in 1 John 4:1–3. The reference here could be to false prophets who might have propounded the false doctrine (cf. on 1 Thess 5:3) or, more likely, a prophetic teaching of Paul's that had been misunderstood (for Paul as prophet, see NOTE and COMMENT on 1 Thess 4:15). The "word" (*logos*) would appear to be oral speech as distinct from communication by letter (cf. 2:15), and uninspired speech as distinct from inspired prophecy (but see 1 Thess 1:5 for the Spirit in connection with the *logos* of mission preaching). Because of the connection between *logos* and *epistolē* in 2 Thess 2:15, some commentators see a contrast between these two means of communication and the spirit Paul mentions (e.g., Zahn, 1.234). That cannot be justified grammatically, however, nor does the larger context support the suggestion. The letter Paul mentions could have been one falsely attributed to him or, more likely, 1 Thessalonians, an interpretation of which, he suspected, could have been responsible for the erroneous doctrine (see COMMENT).

The relationship of the phrase *hōs di' hēmōn* (lit., "as though through or by us") to what precedes is not immediately clear. It could refer only to *epistolē* and be interpreted to mean *hōs di' hēmōn gegrammenēs* ("as though it were written by us") or *hōs hēmōn gegraphotōn autēn* ("as though we had written it"; see BDF 425.4; Zahn, 1.235). It could also, in light of 2:15, refer to *logos* as well as *epistolē*, but there is no grammatical ground on which it should not be taken with *pneuma* as well, and the majority of commentators correctly take it with all three (see Frame, 247).

*to the effect that the Day of the Lord has come.* Paul now identifies the erroneous teaching, introducing it with *hōs hoti* ("to the effect that"). The *hos* does not imply the falsehood of the statement (understood so, e.g., by Lünemann, 595; Eadie, 259), nor does it denote a quality wrongly attributed to someone (Wanamaker, 238); it is the context that does so. The combination of *hōs* and *hoti* is simply the equivalent of *hoti* (cf. 2 Cor 5:19; 11:21; see GNTG 3.137).

The Thessalonians would have been upset by the assertion that "the Day of the Lord has come." Paul first used the term "Day of the Lord" in his correspondence with the Thessalonians in 1 Thess 5:1–11, where he corrected the speculative teaching of some false prophets that deferred the end, thus lessening the impact of eschatological hope on the Thessalonians' daily life. In response, Paul stressed the suddenness with which the Day will come (5:2, 4) and argued that the Thessalonians were already children of the Day and the light (5:5, 8) and that they should live accordingly (see COMMENT).

In contrast, in 2 Thess 1:10, "that day" is stressed to lie in the future, when a series of events will visibly occur. In 2:2, the present error appears to be a radical interpretation of 1 Thess 5:5, 8. The perfect *enestēken* means "has come" or "is present." In Rom 8:39; 1 Cor 3:22; 7:26; Gal 1:4 the verb in its participial form is contrasted to the future, and most commentators correctly hold to the perfect meaning here (see the discussion in Eadie, 258–64). It does not mean "is coming" (*erchetai*, 1 Thess 5:2), "is at hand" (*ēngiken*, Rom 13:12), or "is near" (*engys estin*, Phil 4:5), as is assumed by a few scholars (e.g., Lightfoot 1980: 110; Stephenson; Koester 1990: 455; correctly, Sellin, 235–37), which would hardly have called for correction (cf. 1 Pet 4:7; Rev 1:3; 22:10). Such a view is based less on lexicographical or grammatical grounds than on assumptions of what the Thessalonians could not have thought (Rigaux 1956: 653).

*2:3. Let no one deceive you in any way.* In laying out a chronological scheme to counter the false teaching (see COMMENT), Paul turns to the future (vv 3–5) and begins with a warning. He uses the unusual subjunctive in the third person with the negative (*mē tis hymas exapatēsē* ["Let no one deceive you"]; cf. 1 Cor 16:11) to extend his warning. A more common term is *planān* ("to lead astray"; cf. 1 Cor 6:9; 15:33; Gal 6:7), which is used particularly in apocalyptic warnings (e.g., Mark 13:5–6; Matt 24:4–5, 11, 24; Rev 2:20; 12:9; 20:3, 8, 10). There is no indication that Paul is here thinking of intentional deception (so Lünemann, 595; Eadie, 264; von Dobschütz 1909: 269; Best 1972: 280) any more than he did in v 2. But he does more than recapitulate what he has just said. The abrupt beginning of the sentence, without an introductory *blepete* or *horāte* ("See to it that"; cf. Mark 13:5; 1 Thess 5:15), adds emphasis, as does the perfective *ek* in *exapatēsē*. He also expands the possible sources of error from himself to *tis*, "anyone" (*mē tis*, "no one"), and generalizes the means by which error might be disseminated ("in any way"), which makes the readers more responsible for what they accept (von Dobschütz 1909: 268).

*For [the Day of the Lord will not come] unless the apostasy comes first.* "For" (*hoti*) introduces the reason why Paul's readers should not be deceived, but only the protasis ("if the apostasy does not come first") is expressed. It has been clear since the earliest commentators that the apodosis has to be supplied along the lines suggested in the brackets (see Eadie, 264). Paul begins to correct the erroneous doctrine by enumerating two things that must happen before the Day of the Lord comes. The *prōton* ("first") is to be taken with both the apostasy and the revelation of the Man of Lawlessness. The two events are closely related to each other (Lünemann, 596; von Dobschütz 1909: 269; most commentators), but that does not mean that they will succeed each other (as suggested by Findlay, 167; Milligan, 98). After an interruption in vv 5–7, Paul will return to this topic in vv 8–10.

The article with "apostasy" shows that the readers already knew the apocalyptic view, probably taught them by Paul (v 5), that the pressure under which the faithful will find themselves will cause many of their number to defect. The noun *apostasia* and its cognates are used of political as well as religious rebellion (see Rigaux 1956: 654). In the LXX, it is used of apostasy from or rebellion against God (Josh 22:22; 2 Chr 28:19; 33:19; Jer 2:19) and came to describe apostasy from Judaism (1 Macc 2:15). Although the occasional commentator thinks that the apostasy mentioned in 2 Thess 2:3 is an assault on governing authorities, and thus on God who ordained them (Rom 13:1–2; cf. Bruce 1982: 167), the vast majority of commentators correctly regard the apostasy as religious and ethical in nature (e.g., Lünemann, 596; von Dobschütz 1909: 270–71; Frame, 251).

This is part of a view that anticipated an age in which evil would assume cosmic proportions (4 Ezra 5:1–13). There can be no hope that the good in this age would be realized before the evil also present in it reached its fruition:

[The age] will not be able to bring the things that have been promised to the righteous in their appointed times, because this age is full of sadness and infirmities. For the evil about which you ask me has been sown, but the harvest of it has not yet come. If therefore that which has been sown is not reaped and if the place where the evil has been sown does not pass away, the field where the good has been sown will not come. (4 Ezra 4:27–29)

For evils worse than those you have now seen happen shall be done hereafter. For the weaker the world becomes through old age, the more shall evils be multiplied among its inhabitants. For truth shall go farther away, and falsehood shall come near. (4 Ezra 14:16–18)

The end will come to its own planned fulfillment (2 *Bar* 27), when civil oppression will be accompanied by moral degradation (1 *En* 91:5–7) and apostasy from God's teaching (1QpHab 2:1–10).

*and the Man of Lawlessness is revealed, the Son of Perdition.* Paul continues the visual imagery he had begun in 1:7, but now uses it of the evil figure. He substitutes *apokalyphthē* ("be revealed") for *elthē* ("comes") and places it at the head of the clause. In addition to *apokalyptein*, which reoccurs in vv 6 and 8, he speaks of the "appearance of his coming" in v 8. In view of the teaching that the Day of the Lord had already come, unobserved by all, Paul now insists that it will be preceded by a series of visible events. The revelation of the Man of Lawlessness is an analogy to the revelation of the Lord Jesus from heaven (1:7; cf. also *parousia* in 2:9), but no indication is given of where he is now hidden, whether on earth or in Sheol (cf. Mark 8:28; Matt 16:14; Luke 9:19, for the possibility of persons returning from the dead).

Paul does not name the person, but begins a series of characterizations that lend a particular quality to the age that person will dominate. The formulation *ho anthrōpos tēs anomias* ("the Man of Lawlessness") is Semitic (*GNTG* 3.307–8), the genitive being one of relationship or quality. The "man" would signify to the Greek reader the representation in which *anomia* comes to fullest expression. The phrase may have been suggested by Ps 88:23 LXX (for the idea, see Ps 5:6; 6:9) and is abbreviated in v 8 to *ho anomos* ("the Lawless One"). Some manuscripts, ancient translations and citations read *hamartias* ("of sin") rather than *anomias* ("of lawlessness"; A D F G Ψ lat sy Ir^lat Eus), but *anomias* is preferred for two reasons: (1) *anomia* is rarely used by Paul and *hamartia* often, so the latter could be an attempt to conform to more usual Pauline usage, and (2) *anomia* in v 7 and *anomos* in v 8 presuppose *anomia* in v 3 (Metzger, 567).

The lawlessness in mind here is not antinomianism, the rejection of the Mosaic law, but is more general, conduct against the will of God, the practical equivalent of sin (cf. 1 John 3:4). In Judaism, lawlessness came to describe the influence of paganism on Jews (*Pss Sol* 1:8; 2:3; 3:13), especially as it was embodied in a person like Pompey (*Pss Sol* 17:13, cf. 20), and in Matt 24:12 and *Did* 16:4 it signifies the decay of the end time.

The phrase *ho huios tēs apōleias* ("the Son of Perdition") may have been derived from Isa 57:4. The Semitic *huios* ("Son") does not differ from *anthrōpos*, to which it is in apposition. The genitive again describes relationship and not origin, signifying what the person belongs to or what characterizes him (BDF §162.6). It describes the ultimate fate of the "sons of doom" (see 1QS 9:16, 22; Damascus Document [CD] 6:15; 13:14; Best 1972: 284). For "son" in this sense, see NOTE on 1 Thess 5:5 (cf. Mark 3:17; for the genitive, Heb 10:39). The phrase is used of Judas in John 17:12. "Perdition" (*apōleia*), which in Paul's letters is contrasted with salvation (1 Cor 1:18; 2 Cor 2:15; Phil 1:28), is used of eschatological doom in 2 Pet 3:7. The characterization of the Man of Lawlessness as the Son of Perdition anticipates v 8, which spells out his doom.

2:4. *who opposes and exalts himself over every so-called god or object of worship.* Two further characterizations follow, with one article combining two participles (*ho antikeimenos kai epairomenos* ["who opposes and exalts himself"]). Satan is sometimes described as *ho antikeimenos* (1 Tim 5:14; 1 Clem 15:1; Mart Pol 17:1; cf. Zech 3:1), but in v 9 this figure is distinguished from Satan. The participles describe actions rather than identify persons (see NOTE on 1 Thess 5:12). Behind these characterizations of the Man of Lawlessness is the figure of Antiochus IV Epiphanes, whose self-aggrandizement assumed apocalyptic significance (Dan 11:36–37 Theod). It is not said whom the Man of Lawlessness opposes, and it has been thought, on the basis of v 8, that he is the opponent of Christ (Lünemann, 597; Eadie, 268), but the rest of v 4 suggests that he opposes God.

The arrogance of this figure knows no bounds. He exalts himself *epi panta legomenon theon*, which can mean "over every being called god" or "over every so-called god." The latter would be a reference to beings who are thought to be gods but in fact are not (cf. 1 Cor 8:5; Gal 4:8); the former would be more comprehensive, including God himself. Restricting the reference to the latter is attractive in view of *sebasma* ("object of worship"), which refers to altars, images, and the like (e.g., Acts 17:23; cf. Wis 14:20; 15:17). But it is difficult to see how opposition to and exaltation only over such beings and their cult objects would call for criticism. It is therefore preferable to understand the characterization as of someone who is so self-aggrandizing that he vaunts himself against all gods whatsoever, perceived and real.

*so that he takes his seat in the temple of God, proclaiming himself to be God.* The extent of his arrogance becomes evident in its result (*hoste* plus the infinitive; cf. 1:4; 1 Thess 1:7). He (*auton* is emphatic) takes his seat (*kathisai* is intransitive) in God's temple. What Paul means by "temple," or more precisely "shrine," (*naos*) is not clear. The word is used of the physical body (1 Cor 6:19), but that does not fit this context. The church also is called God's temple (1 Cor 3:16; 2 Cor 6:16; Eph 2:21), and this interpretation has had its patristic as well as modern proponents (see Giblin, 76–80). It has also been thought by some patristic and modern commentators that Paul is referring to the heavenly temple, where God sits (Ps 10:4, "The Lord is in his holy temple; the Lord, his throne is in heaven"; cf. Isa 66:1; Mic 1:2; Hab 2:20; 1 En 14:17–22; 2 Bar 4:2–6; cf. Frame, 256).

The most obvious identification is the Jerusalem temple and it is held by most commentators, but problems attach to it. Although certain individuals in the OT (Isa 14:3–4; Ezek 28:2) and Nero (Sib Or 5.29–34) made divine claims for themselves, and Gaius Caligula considered himself a god and wished to have his statue erected in the temple (Josephus, *Jewish War* 2.184–85), nobody actually entered the temple proclaiming himself to be God. It would appear that it is still the figure of Antiochus IV Epiphanes as described in Daniel that is behind Paul's language here. The figure so described will halt worship to God and install the abomination that makes desolate (Dan 9:27; 11:31; 12:11) and speaks against God (11:36–37). Paul uses this language apocalyptically, as Matthew also does (24:15).

The destruction of the temple in A.D. 70 has also posed problems for interpreters who think that Paul had the Jerusalem temple in mind. Patristic commentators overcame the problem by claiming that the temple would be rebuilt. Some commentators, who hold that the letter is pseudonymous, have seen in this a difficulty for their theory, if the letter were written after the temple was destroyed (see discussion in Wrede, 94–114; Trilling 1972: 126). This problem is more apparent than real; other writings dating after A.D. 70, including Hebrews, convey an impression that the temple was still standing (cf. Attridge, 8). Irenaeus, who thought that Paul was referring to the Jerusalem temple and also echoed the passages in Daniel, saw no problem in his position (*Against Heresies* 5.25.4; see von Dobschütz 1909: 276–77). The usurpation of the temple of God as the locus for claiming himself to be God symbolizes the gravest act of defiance imaginable, and to express that is Paul's intention as he writes in starkly apocalyptic language.

2:5. *Do you not remember that while I was still with you I used to tell you these things?* Paul abandons his comments on the Man of Lawlessness as he breaks in with the important reminder that he had instructed his readers in these matters during his stay with them. Greek editions of the NT (and the NIV) begin a new subsection with v 5, but the verse goes better with what precedes (so also Rigaux 1956: 662), the antecedent of *tauta* ("these things") being found in vv 3–4. The style changes: Paul lapses into direct speech, asks a question, and uses the singular for the first time in the letter, as he does in 1 Thess 2:18; 3:5 (with *egō*) and in 2 Thess 3:17 (see pages 86–89). But this does not make the question a parenthesis (so Trilling 1980: 88–89).

The appeal to memory (*ou mnēmoneuete*) here is not the equivalent of the paraenetic *mnēmoneuete* ("you remember") in 1 Thess 2:9, nor is it the equivalent of the repeated paraenetic *oidate* in 1 Thessalonians (e.g., 3:3–4; 4:2, 5; see page 82). It is rather similar to the more chiding *ouk oidate* ("do you not know") that Paul uses when he refers to something that is a proverbial, traditional teaching or is self-evident (e.g., 1 Cor 3:16; 5:6; 6:2–3, 9, 15–16, 19; 9:13, 24). This is sharper language than the *erōtōmen* of v 1 and even the warning in v 3.

In 1 Thess 3:4 Paul had also reminded his readers of instruction that he had given them when he was with them (cf. 4:2), but there he was more encouraging. In 2 Thessalonians, on the other hand, he is more pointed in his reminiscence (cf. 3:10) as he writes to a situation that has deteriorated. This is further demonstrated by the imperfect tense of *elegon* ("I kept on telling you"), which is a strong affirmation that they had received ample apocalyptic instruction from him. Furthermore, they had received it while he was still (*eti on*) with them, which means that they should regard his oral teaching as their source of knowledge of the matters about which he is writing. That excludes any other source, even Timothy or another intermediary (cf. 3:6).

Paul does not here take into consideration 1 Thessalonians, which does not treat the subject matter with which he is presently dealing. When he writes more generally, however, his teaching in his first letter is placed on the same level as his oral teaching (2 Thess 2:15). These references to oral teaching are not made by a pseudonymous author to invoke the authority of the Pauline tradition to support elements in 2 Thessalonians that are found nowhere else in Paul's writings (so Trilling 1980: 88) but are dictated by the circumstance that Paul was countering an error about whose source he was uncertain. By going back to his oral instruction, he circumvents all possible sources of error.

2:6. *And you know now what it is that is exercising a restraining force.* Paul now turns from what will take place just before the end to the present (vv 6–7). He had instructed the Thessalonians while he was with them about the revelation of the Man of Lawlessness before the end, but they also now know of an eschatological force already at work. The *kai nyn* ("and . . . now") could be logical ("now then," or "and now, these things being so"; cf. Acts 3:17; 10:5; 22:16; 1 Cor 14:6; BDF §442.15; Eadie, 275) or temporal. If temporal, it can go with *eti ōn*, perhaps in contrast to it, or with what follows (Frame, 262–63; Bornemann, 365–67; Best 1972: 290–91). Given the temporal markers in the passage, it is more natural to take it temporally. There is no need, however, to consider it as being in contrast to *eti ōn* (e.g., by Trilling 1980: 88–89), which would have required *nyn de* ("But now"), but as being complementary to it.

The sense is, "You know what I told you then, about the Man of Lawlessness, and you know now about restraint and the restrainer." The *kai nyn* stands in the position of emphasis, at the beginning of the sentence, underlining the present knowledge of the Thessalonians. Paul gives no indication of how they came to have this present knowledge; it is part of the mystery of vv 6–7. There is much to commend the suggestion made by Giblin (159–66), that Paul does not have in mind conceptual or speculative knowledge but experiential knowledge "in which some form of immediate personal awareness, realization, recognition and the like is stressed" (160). But such an existential knowledge does not rule out the likelihood that Paul had instructed them about the forces that were presently at play in God's scheme of things (Roosen 1971: 148; Best 1972: 291).

Paul here uses the enigmatic neuter articular participle *to katechon* ("what is exercising restraint") and in v 7 the masculine articular participle *hō katechōn* ("he who exercises restraint") as though the language was familiar to his readers. The meaning of the verb *katechein* has been difficult to determine (see discussion in Best 1972: 295–302; Barnouin). It can mean "to suppress" (e.g., Rom 1:18), but in view of the temporal qualifications in this context, which describe a sequence of events, the majority of commentators understand it to mean "to restrain."

Grammatically, matters are complicated by the fact that *to katechon* ("what restrains") has no object, although there can be little doubt that the *auton* ("he") in the second part of the sentence is already in mind. The major problem that has faced interpreters through the centuries is that a neuter articular participle is used here but a masculine one in v 7. The difficulties are illustrated by one twentieth-century translation that merely transliterates *katechon* and renders the rest of the text in unintelligible English: "And now you know the *katechon* so as him to be revealed in his own time" (Best 1972: 273). What does emerge clearly is that the meaning of *to katechon* is to be discovered in the context about an eschatological timetable (see COMMENT).

*so that he may be revealed at his [proper] time.* The purpose of the restraint (*eis* plus the infinitive) is so that the revelation of the Man of Lawlessness takes place at the proper time. It is implied that it is God's purpose that is being worked out, and the context shows that the subject is the revelation of the Man of Lawlessness (cf. vv 3, 8). It is characteristic of apocalyptic schemes that persons and events have their proper times or seasons in God's plan (cf. 4 Ezra 4:34–37; 7:74; 2 Bar 21:8; 48:2–5; 56:2), an idea also behind 1 Thess 2:16, where Paul had also assumed that his readers were familiar with this teaching (cf. 1 Tim 6:15; Mark 13:32). The function of the statement is to tap into the apocalyptic knowledge of Paul's readers in order to put the coming of the Day of the Lord in proper eschatological perspective. To prevent them from relegating the Day so far to the future, however, that it would have no practical effect on the present (see NOTES and COMMENT on 1 Thess 5:1–3), he turns to the present.

2:7. *For the mystery of lawlessness is already at work.* Paul explains ("For") his statement about restraint: Lawlessness is at work (cf. 1 John 4:3 of the Antichrist) but is being held in check. In contrast to the future revelation, what is already occurring is a mystery. The phrase "mystery of lawlessness" is used nowhere else (contrast 1 Tim 3:16). In the Qumran scrolls, the "mysteries of sin" appears (1QH 5:36; 1Q27 1, 2, 7; 1QM 14:9; cf. Josephus, *Jewish War* 1.470), but "mystery of lawlessness" appears to be an *ad hoc* formulation by Paul, who wishes to underline the mysteriousness of the present lawlessness. The genitive *anomias* is epexegetic (Bornemann, 367): the secret that has lawlessness as its content (Frame, 263). The character of what is at work is known only to those who have knowledge of God's scheme, who know about the present restraint (v 6; von Dobschütz 1909: 281); its true significance is hidden from others (cf. 1 Cor 2:7).

The verb *energeitai* could be passive ("is made to be active"; Wanamaker, 253) and thus have God as its subject or, as most interpreters hold, could be middle ("be at work"), which simply describes lawless activity (cf. v 11). In either case, the context shows that the activity takes place within and is circumscribed by God's eschatological plan.

*only until he who is now restraining will be out of the way.* There is an ellipsis here. The Greek literally reads, "only he who now restrains until he is out of the way." Something must be supplied, and the context suggests that it is *energeitai* ("is at work"), with "the mystery of lawlessness" as its subject (for the grammatical structure, see Gal 2:10). The meaning, then, is that there is a limit to the present working of the mystery of lawlessness: it will only continue as long as the restrainer is present. The eschatological drama is being played out according to the divine script.

Now Paul uses a masculine articular participle instead of the neuter (v 6). The personification has its counterpart in *anomia* (v 7), which is personified as *ho anthrōpos tēs anomias* (v 3) and *anomos* (v 8). The mysterious lawlessness is always under constraint; only when the restrainer departs from the scene will there no longer be any mystery and will matters finally come to a head (vv 8–10). Paul does not say how the restrainer will depart from the scene (for the meaning of *ek mesou genetai*, see Fulford; Bruce 1982: 170) and does not imply that his removal will be violent (see von Dobschütz 1909: 282), which would be unlikely, since the restrainer is viewed positively. Paul's exposition of the eschatological scheme acknowledges the presence of evil in it, but establishes its limitations. Paul's purpose is pastoral: his readers should view their experiences from an eschatological perspective, which promises a decisive end to the evils from which they are suffering (cf. 1:7–10).

2:8. *And then the Lawless One will be revealed.* Paul returns to the events that will occur at the end (vv 8–10), which had been the subject of vv 3–5. Here he expands on the condition he had laid out in v 3 for the revelation of the Man of Lawlessness. The *kai tote* ("And then") balances *kai nyn* ("And . . . now") of v 6. It will be the proper time ("then") for the Lawless One to be revealed (see NOTE on v 6b), when the purpose of the restraint (vv 6–7) is fulfilled. The Lawless One is the same person described in the Semitic formulation Man of Lawlessness (v 3), and for the third time it is said that he will be revealed (vv 3, 6, 8), the verb again in the passive, indicating that the event takes place at God's behest. This revelation stands in contrast to the mystery of lawlessness that is presently at work.

*whom the Lord Jesus will slay with the breath of his mouth and destroy by the appearance of his coming.* The textual tradition differs on a number of readings, primarily on whether "Jesus" should be read or omitted (see Metzger 1994: 568). The sentence is one of the two closest allusions to the LXX in 2 Thessalonians (see NOTE on 1:9), but even so there is little scholarly agreement about the precise text that Paul used or how different manuscript readings of this verse later came about. It would appear that behind Paul's language is Isa 11:4, where it is said that the root from the stump of Jesse "shall smite the earth with the rod of his mouth, and with the breath of his lips he shall slay the wicked." Paul has here compressed the two clauses into one, possibly under the influence of Ps 32:6, "By the word of the Lord the heavens were established; all the hosts of them by the breath of his mouth" (Frame, 265–66). "Jesus" may have been dropped by later copyists to conform Paul's words to the OT, but the tradition on this text is too complex and inconclusive for us to be certain about this or the other disputed readings in the sentence. The image that nevertheless emerges is of the destruction wrought upon the Lawless One by the Lord Jesus.

The second part of the sentence, in synonymous parallelism to the first, emphasizes this destruction (cf. 1 Cor 15:24, 26 for *katargein* ["to destroy"]; also 2 Tim 1:10) but now merely by the "appearance [*epiphaneia*] of his coming [*parousias*]." This is the only place where *epiphaneia* is used in the NT outside the Pastoral Epistles, where it is used both of Jesus's incarnation (2 Tim 1:10) and his eschatological coming (1 Tim 6:14; 2 Tim 4:1, 8; Titus 2:13). It is also the only place where *epiphaneia* and *parousia* are combined. Whereas *epiphaneia* in the Pastorals has the connotation of an appearance to help humanity, here it destroys the Lawless One (Best 1972: 304, refers to the hostile sense in which the word is used in Jewish Greek, e.g., in 2 Macc 2:21; 3:24; 12:22; 14:15, but these passages describe how the divine manifestation aided God's people by routing the enemy). What Paul says about Jesus' *parousia* here describes the negative side to what he had said about it in v 1.

2:9. *His coming will take place by the working of Satan.* The syntax of the Greek is difficult, but the sense is clear. The relative pronoun *hou* ("His") resumes *hon* ('whom") and refers to the Lawless One. Paul now moves from the description of the Lord's actions at his coming to those of the Lawless One at *his* coming. As the Lawless One and the Lord Jesus both are revealed (1:7; 2:3), they both will have a coming (2:1, 8, 9). Paul uses *estin*, literally "is," but translated here "will take place," because it describes the certainty of the future event (cf. 1 Thess 5:2 [*erchetai*, "comes"], v 3 [*ephistatai*, "comes upon"]; 1 Cor 3:13 [*apokalyptetai*, "is revealed"]; Lünemann, 603).

A number of loosely connected statements characterize this coming. First, it will take place by Satan's working. In 1:7, Paul had referred to the power that Christ would exercise at his revelation through the angels who would accompany him. Similarly, although the mystery of lawlessness is already at work (*energeitai*, 2:7), there will be a mighty working associated with the coming of the Lawless One, but it will be Satan's working (cf. Rev 13:2; for God's power, see NOTE on 1:7 and cf. Eph 1:19–21). The Lawless One will thus be an agent of Satan.

*attended by all power and signs and wonders of falsehood.* The second feature of the Lawless One's coming is that it will be accompanied by a number of phenomena. Here and in v 10a *en* goes with datives of accompaniment ("attended by") that further specify how his coming will take place. It is not certain whether *pasē* ("all") goes only with *dynamis* ("power") or with the other two nouns as well. The parallel of the construction *en pasē . . . pseudous* (v 9) to *en pasei . . . adikias* (v 10a), both ending with a genitive, suggests that it goes with all the three intervening nouns and contributes to the fullness of expression.

There is no justification for the view that "all power" stands apart from signs and wonders, and is what works them (as in Rom 15:19), for they all belong to a series of terms traditionally used to describe miraculous phenomena. It is true that "power" is normally used in the plural in such cases (e.g., in Matt 13:58; Mark 6:2, but cf. 5; Acts 8:13), but its occurrence here with the two other words that normally denote supernatural phenomena (see John 4:48; Acts 2:43; 4:30; 2 Cor 12:12) suggests that it has the same meaning here. Furthermore, all three words appear together elsewhere (in the same order as here in Acts 2:22, in a different one in Heb 2:4).

What stands out is that the singular *dynamis* is used with the plural of the other two nouns. But elsewhere "signs" and "wonders" are also used in both the singular (Deut 13:1–2) and plural (Deut 28:46; 29:3; Ps 134:8 LXX), although the plural does predominate, so the use of the singular *dynamis* here is not unique. The singular may be due, on the one hand, to an affinity in meaning with *energeia*, and on the other to its parallelism with *apatē* in v 10a.

The clause ends with the genitive *pseudous* ("of falsehood"), which may qualify only the last noun ("wonders") or, more probably, all three, as *pasē* does. The genitive may describe (1) the origin of the miraculous works, that is, they belong to the realm of him who is false (so Findlay, 182; cf. John 8:44), (2) the quality of the miracles, that is, that they are not truly miracles, or (3) the intention of the miracles, that is, to convince people of falsehood. There is no indication that Paul thinks of the miracles as anything but real, and while it is possible that (1) may be included in his thought, the context, particularly v 10b, argues for (3).

2:10. *and by all deceit of wickedness for those on the way to perdition.* With "and" Paul loosely attaches a clause parallel to v 9a that directs attention to the effect of the Lawless One's wonders. The *en* ("by") is still dependent on *kat' energeian*: it is by Satan's working that people are deceived and thereby destroyed, but they are not coerced to act against their will (see NOTE on v 11). While *apatē* ("deceit") need not have an apocalyptic sense (see NOTE on 1 Thess 2:3; Col 2:8), it does so here (cf. *planē* in v 11). In Hellenistic Greek, it is frequently used as a synonym for pleasure and luxuriousness (Spicq 1991: 157–59), often associated with sensuality (cf. Eph 4:22) and money (cf. Matt 13:22; Mark 4:19), but here it appears to be more comprehensive, denoting the quality of wickedness (for the genitive, see NOTES on vv 3, 9b), which Paul also generalizes and accentuates by adding *pasē* ("all"), as he does in Rom 1:29.

The present articular participle *tois apollymenois* ("those on the way to perdition," Bruce 1982: 173; Roosen 1971: 119) is a dative of disadvantage. It can go only with *apatē adikias*, which would mean that the rest of the sentence would have a wider reference that included other people as well. More probably, it goes with *estin* and identifies those who are affected by the Lawless One's coming as described in vv 9–10. The Lawless One, the Son of Perdition (v 3), by his coming and through his actions will ensure the perdition of those who heed him. Once again, the present is used for the future, which is already decided (cf. 1 Cor 1:18; 2 Cor 2:15; 4:3; see NOTE on *estin*, v 9).

*because they did not receive the love of the truth so as to be saved.* Although there has been an element of predeterminism in the drama sketched so far, Paul does not absolve those who are lost of responsibility. The rest of the pericope, beginning with *anth' hōn* ("because") has the purpose of emphasizing precisely this. Only here does *anth' hōn* occur in the NT outside Luke's writings (Luke 1:20; 12:3; 19:44; Acts 12:23). The receiving (*dechesthai*) Paul has in mind has the connotation of welcoming (see NOTES on 1 Thess 1:6; 2:13, which describe the Thessalonians' reception of the gospel). The aorist *ouk edexanto* ("they did not receive") looks at their failure to accept the gospel from the perspective of the end (Best 1972: 307).

This is the only place in the Bible where the phrase "the love of the truth" is used. It contrasts the full devotion to the truth with the falsehood and deceit to which they instead succumb (cf. Rom 1:25, the love of God contrasted with a lie). For Paul, the truth is found in the gospel (see Gal 2:5, 14; cf. Col 1:5). The infinitival construction *eis to sōthēnai* can express either purpose (as in vv 6, 11) or result. For the notion of receiving the preacher of the gospel in order to be saved, see 1 Thess 2:15–16. The immediate context, however, suggests that Paul is concerned with the result of their unwillingness to love the truth. Rather than being saved, they find themselves on the way to perdition.

2:11. *And for this reason God sends them a power working to delude them.* The *kai* ("And") has a consecutive force, "and so," further strengthened by *dia touto* ("for this reason"; on the phrase *kai dia touto*, see NOTE on 1 Thess 2:13). It is because of their refusal to love the truth that God acts in the way he does. God's action is thus in consequence of theirs (cf. Rom 1:24, 26, 28; Richard, 353, in addition refers to Rom 11:7, 25; Mark 4:11–12; Rev 9:20–21; 16:9, 11). Some ancient manuscripts and versions read *pempsei* ("will send") instead of *pempei* ("sends"), which has stronger support. Even the present may have a future sense, as it does in *estin* (v 9) and *tois apollymenois* (v 10), but it is more likely that it is a true present, describing what is happening now, and carries a note of warning. The phrase "a power to delude" renders *energeian planēs*, literally, "a working of error." As the work of the Lawless One is both future and present (vv 9, 7), so is that of God. The conditions that will eventuate have their roots in the present, and everything takes place according to God's scheme of things. Because they did not love the truth, God designs them to be deluded on eschatological matters (*planē, exapatān* [v 3], and *apatē* [v 10] are synonymous; see NOTES).

*so that they should believe the lie.* Paul makes quite clear what God's purpose (*eis to* plus the infinitive) is: Because they did not deign to love the truth (*tēs alētheias*), God sends a power to delude them into believing the lie (*to pseudei*), which is not falsehood in general, but specifically the claim by the Lawless One to be God (v 4), who will come, empowered by Satan to perform supernatural works of falsehood (*pseudos*, v 10; the article with *pseudos* also appears in Rom 1:25, where Paul also speaks of rejecting the truth about God).

2:12. *that all should be judged who had not believed the truth but delighted in wickedness.* Love of the truth would have resulted in salvation (v 10). When that did not happen, God worked out the balance of his purpose, that all people be judged according to whether they believed or not. This is the final purpose (*hina pantes krithōsin* ["that all should be judged"]). Judgment here is condemnation, without any of the nuance with which it is treated in chap. 1. That "all" will be judged lends weight to the warning.

Those who had not welcomed the love for the truth, who had believed the lie, are now described as those who had not believed the truth. The force of the statement lies in the second member of the antithesis, which once again stresses their volition (*eudokēsantes* ["delighted"]). Paul used forms of *eudokein* in 1 Thess 2:8; 3:1 of decisions he made freely about his ministry, and in 2 Thess 1:11 he used *eudokia* for the Thessalonians' free resolve to do good. We see here the antithesis to 1:11–12: the free decision to indulge in the wickedness that will characterize the coming of the Lawless One will earn divine condemnation and ensure perdition (v 10).

# COMMENT

There is nothing like 2 Thess 2:1–12 anywhere else in Paul's writings or in the NT (Milligan, 95, draws attention to Rev 18:5–8, 12–17; 16:9–11). It has been regarded as doctrinal information intended to correct a misunderstanding (Lünemann, 592; Holland, 43) and as the main reason why 2 Thessalonians was written (e.g., Ohlshausen, 470; von Dobschütz 1909: 261; Staab, 50; Roosen 1971: 138; Bruce 1982: 162). More recently, however, it has correctly been seen that this section is not dogmatic in character but is intended to calm the congregation and provide it security in the way that comfort had been the intention of chap. 1 (Trilling 1972: 67, 72).

The following statement by Charles H. Giblin well describes the purpose of the section:

> What seems to have been neglected in studying this passage is attention to the repeated subordination of apocalyptic flights to a point of pastoral concern or pastoral reaction. Paul seems to be more concerned with the pastoral problem of correcting the Thessalonians' outlook than he is with describing the coming of the Antichrist or even the coming of the Lord. He seems to be trying to make them realize that the present attack on their faith, on their fidelity to the Gospel as he preached it to them, is the verification at least in part of the total eschatological perspective he first presented to them and to some extent now re-presents in apocalyptic terms. (41)

The same pastoral intention is evident in Paul's relatively sparse use of apocalyptic traditions in 1 Thess 4:13–5:11 and in 2 Thess 1:5–10.

Paul's words of comfort in 1 Thess 4:13–18 had at their heart a clarification of the Parousia and the Thessalonians' gathering with the Lord at it, which constituted their hope. In that section of the first letter Paul elaborated what he had taught them in person and applied it to the problem reflected in 4:15, the question of the relation between those who would have died and those who would still be alive at the Parousia. Now Paul is fearful that his earlier efforts to comfort them might be undone and that his readers might be wrought up as their grasp on his teaching was loosened.

Paul is clear that the reason for his concern is a teaching that the Day of the Lord had already come. It is important to observe that the problem revolves around the Day of the Lord, discussed in 1 Thess 5:1–11, and not the resurrection. Paul assumes in 1 Thessalonians (4:15, 17; cf. 1:10) that his readers believe in the resurrection of Christ and of Christians, and there is no evidence in 2 Thessalonians that the belief in the resurrection had in some way become problematic. To interpret v 2 in light of passages like 2 Tim 2:18 (cf. Col 2:12; perhaps 1 Cor 4:8), which refers to the resurrection as past, or to understand the doctrine he refers to as influenced by Gnosticism, a mystery theology, or Alexandrian Wisdom speculation is to miss the mark (correctly, Sellin).

The Day of the Lord is the third major item from 1 Thess 4:13–5:11 that Paul mentions in the same sequence in 2 Thess 2:1–2: (1) The Parousia of the Lord Jesus (1 Thess 4:15; 2 Thess 2:1), (2) assembling to meet Christ (1 Thess 4:17; 2 Thess 2:1), and (3) the Day of the Lord (1 Thess 5:1; 2 Thess 2:2). It is therefore to 1 Thessalonians that one must go for clarification.

In opposition to those persons who deferred the Parousia, Paul had stressed that the light of the Day was already proleptically present and required a special quality of life (1 Thess 5:5, 8). Furthermore, he had emphasized that the Day would come suddenly and unexpectedly (5:2, 4). He had also earlier in the letter spoken of a proleptic realization of eschatological judgment (2:16; see COM-

MENT). Indeed, the present dimension of the eschatological future is so much a part of Paul's thinking that he does not mute it, even in 2 Thessalonians, where his teaching had been taken to an extreme (see COMMENT on 1:5). The Thessalonians had received extensive eschatological and apocalyptic instruction from Paul (see 1 Thess 1:10; 2:15–16; 2 Thess 2:5), raised questions about it (1 Thess 4:15), and speculated on it (1 Thess 5:1–3). Paul suspects that some of them may have overinterpreted what he had said about the Day, which would easily have caused some of his readers great distress, even though they persevered in tribulation and persecution (see COMMENT on 2 Thess 1:3–4).

The theological reason for distress is intelligible when one considers what the erroneous doctrine would have implied to those who held it. A frequently cited example of a bishop of Pontus, who predicted that the judgment would come within a year (Wrede, 49–50; Trilling 1980: 79–80), is not to the point. We must look for evidence closer to hand, in 1 Thessalonians, rather than even the Synoptic apocalyptic texts (appealed to by Menken 1994: 100–101). On the basis of 1 Thess 5:1–11, they would have claimed that they had escaped the judgment of the Day of the Lord and that they were living in the light of the Day. Fully clad with faith, love, and hope, they were already in possession of salvation and in full association with the Lord Jesus, which they had attained at his Parousia, which they presumably understood as a spiritual event. It is not difficult to see how such a view could raise problems for believers confronted by continuing persecution and tribulation.

Paul's suspicion of the attitudes based on the erroneous doctrine explains much in chap. 1, which is pastoral in intent. The readers whom he encouraged had extraordinary faith, love, and endurance, and their conduct was truly worthy of boasting about. It is true that they were being persecuted, but that was proof, not that they were beyond judgment, but, paradoxically, of God's righteous judgment that they were being made worthy of the kingdom for which they were suffering. The eschatological judgment is still to come, on that Day when the Lord will be revealed for all to see, to be glorified in them, while unbelievers will receive their punishment. Paul thus stresses the future in the most vivid, comforting way while encouraging his readers by finding meaning in their present experiences. In this way he prepares for 2:1–12.

Paul clearly writes with a view towards the doctrinal error that could have a deleterious effect on his readers, but beyond that, absolute confidence about the situation and its background eludes us. Paul does not explicitly say that someone had in fact taught this error, and he may simply be writing to prevent them from succumbing to the false teaching should someone teach it (cf. Wanamaker, 40). Furthermore, he does not say how he had learned of this matter or how much he knew about it, nor is he sure how such a doctrine could be justified, except that in some way it could be or was being justified by laying it at his door, when he was supposed to have made a prophetic utterance, taught without inspiration, or instructed in a letter. The proposal offered in the INTRODUCTION, pages 352–56 combines the limited evidence to form a scenario that is as credible as any we are likely to draw.

On that understanding of the evidence, a copy of 1 Thessalonians would have been taken by its first readers to other Christians in Thessalonica. As at its first reading to its primary recipients, a copy of 1 Thessalonians would again have been amplified by comments from whoever now carried or read the letter. The new messenger would claim to represent Paul's thought or be able to clarify its meaning to the secondary recipients. In addition to 1 Thessalonians itself, the commentator could also adduce Paul's prophetic utterances and his uninspired teaching.

It is most likely that in this process an erroneous interpretation of Paul's view of the proleptic nature of the eschaton arose. Paul is not sure how it may have arisen but he knows how it could have arisen and denies that he was the actual source of the teaching in any of the three ways he mentions. At the same time, he expresses no anger, which suggests that he did not think that he had been deliberately misrepresented. It is also noteworthy that the objects of divine judgment in 1:8–9 are not teachers of theological error, as they were in 1 Thess 5:1–3, but unbelievers. There was a misunderstanding or misinterpretation rather than willful deception or "opponents" (Koester's description [1990: 455]).

Some interpreters have discovered here the firmest ground for denying that Paul wrote 2 Thessalonians (see pages 368–69), as well as for their assessment that 2:1–12 represents the reason why the letter was written. Koester's argument is nuanced and forceful, and proceeds with a cogent view of eschatology in 1 Thessalonians (1990: 435–37; cf. P. Müller, 65–67) but errs in the interpretation of 2:1–12.

Koester maintains that in 1 Thessalonians the eschatological future is realized in the life of the believers, whereas in 2 Thessalonians "opponents" work with a radicalized apocalyptic timetable according to which the Day of the Lord is near, the tribulations are eschatological, and the believers' change will only come after the Day arrives. The author, Koester avers, accepted the timetable, but he connected the tribulations with the coming judgment. Viewed thus, 2 Thess 1:3–12 lays the foundation for 2:3–12, consoling those under tribulation and expecting them to wait patiently for the coming of the Lord (1:7), which will bring judgment. Traditional elements from widespread apocalyptic schemata that periodize the eschatological future are then used "to fix stages of events that will lead from the present to the future" (1990: 456), yet the believer is at a point just before the decisive end. Eschatological existence in Paul has thus been changed to apocalyptic expectation (Müller 1962: 66).

This interpretation errs in a number of respects. Very important is that *enestēken* (2:2) does not mean "is near," but "has come," so the perception of the error that is supposed to have included an apocalyptic timetable that was accepted by the author of 2 Thessalonians is wrong. The view Paul rejects is the result of a radical interpretation of his realized eschatology (1 Thess 5:1–11), and rather than accept the new timetable this view implies, Paul uses apocalyptic elements to divide up the time that remains before the Parousia.

That Paul should do so is natural because of the error he corrects. He would also periodize in 1 Cor 15:20–28, where he again opposed a radicalized eschatology (cf. v 19). He takes the same approach to a similar problem in 1 Cor 4:5–13 (cf. v 8), where temporal qualifiers are important to his argument, as are his present sufferings (cf. 5, 8, 11, 13). That he periodizes in 2 Thess 2:3–12 does not mean that he thereby does away with the present as a time of eschatological existence (see COMMENT on 1:5; 2:7) any more than it does that his realized eschatology in 1 Thessalonians (5:1–11; cf. 2:16) obviated his futuristic eschatology elsewhere in the same letter (1:10; 2:19; 3:13; 4:6, 13–18; 5:23).

The text does not identify those who will apostatize (v 3). Numerous possibilities have been suggested (see Best 1972: 281–82). There is no evidence that Jews are particularly in mind, and it is not clear what Paul could have thought that Gentiles would apostatize from (Rom 1:18–32 does not apply). Cyril of Jerusalem (*Catecheses* 15.9) thought that the Christian heretics of his own day fulfilled Paul's words. Although Cyril's identification of heresy has been rejected (e.g., by Frame, 251), it may not be far off the mark if it is seen within a broader context.

If Paul had taught the Thessalonians the apocalyptic view of apostasy, they would not have thought that only a part of humanity would be deceived but that the whole world would be in jeopardy (cf. Rev 13:3). Yet in Christian circles the focus was on the apostasy of Christians, particularly in their following false prophets and their teachings (Matt 24:11–12) or heeding the claims of false Christs (Matt 24:24; 1 John 2:18, 22; 4:3; 2 John 7). The appearance of such deceivers was a sign of the last days (1 Tim 4:1–2; cf. 2 Pet 2:1–2; 3:3; 1 John 2:18; Jude 18), when general lawlessness would be rampant (Matt 24:12; *Did* 16:4). That Paul returns to deceit (*apatē*) and perdition (*tois apollymenois*) in v 10, coupled with a failure to love the truth, suggests that such Christian apostasy is Paul's principal focus as he counters a false teaching. This error should not unsettle his readers for the paradoxical reason that things will get much worse before the end, when the source of evil will be destroyed.

The Man of Lawlessness is neither a demon nor Satan, but is the tool through whom Satan achieves his ends, someone of satanic power (v 9). Because of the analogy between 1:7 and 2:3, he is sometimes thought of as being in some sense a rival Messiah, the Antichrist of 1 John (2:18, 22; 4:3; 2 John 7; thus Bruce 1982: 167), but in this context he is, more precisely, anti-god and Anti-God. This person shares features with the later Antichrist figure, perhaps because the later development, especially in patristic writers, made use of 2 Thess 2 (Jenks, 216). At the same time, 2 Thess 2 shares parallels to the Synoptic apocalypses (see Hartman, 195–205), a fact that reflects the wide interest in the conditions at the end, when seductive forces will be active. Paul had instructed his converts about this, evidently teaching them about the Man of Lawlessness.

The Man of Lawlessness has been identified with various historical figures, such as one or another Roman emperor, particularly Nero, while he was still alive or appearing again after his death in a supernatural form. From the Reformation on, the popes have also been so identified. All such historical identifications fail because Paul has in mind an eschatological personification of lawlessness, the ultimate representative of those in whom lawlessness comes to expression. There is a Jewish background to the view that a human being, not a demon or Satan, epitomizes such evil (see Isa 14:4–27; Ezek 28:1–19; Dan 11:24–45), and it is irrelevant whether this eschatological figure will be Jewish or Greek.

What is enigmatic to the modern reader was known to Paul's readers, and his reminders of what they were told or knew show that he was not informing them of details about the eschatological drama, but rather speaking to them as persons with inside knowledge of the mystery (cf. Mark 13:14). The apocalyptic images confirm them in what they already know, which thus performs a pastoral function (see COMMENT on 1:3–4) when the readers are confronted by false teachers. They are surrounded by evil, and although the Anti-God is not yet present, the evil of the future is already at work proleptically. Paul will be explicit in his exhortations and prayers for their stability (2:15, 17; 3:3, 5), but he already acts pastorally in laying out the apocalyptic scheme (see Trilling 1980: 93). It is important to remember this function of what is said, even when the meaning of the details eludes us.

Paul appeals to the present knowledge of his readers about what restrains the Man of Lawlessness in order that he be revealed in his proper time. When he is revealed, he will be destroyed (v 8), and Paul's statement here carries a note of warning not to expect or wish for premature action against the Anti-God. Revelation at the proper time is the main theme of the section. Within this scheme a restraining force is being exercised, but Paul does not say on whom restraint is being exercised or what that person is being restrained from. The context would seem to suggest that it is the Man of Lawlessness being restrained in his lawlessness. That would imply that evil had not yet attained the absolute proportions it would assume in the final apostasy (see NOTE on v 3). The restraining function is therefore positive, a reason why the Thessalonians need not despair.

The restraint in view, whether as an activity (the neuter articular participle) or as embodied in a person (the masculine articular participle), has been variously identified, the following being the more popular ones (see Frame, 259–62; Best 1972: 295–301; Marshall 1983: 196–99):

1. The most popular view through the centuries has been that the neuter refers to "the restraining power of law and order, especially as these were embodied in the Roman Empire and its rulers" (Milligan, 101).

2. Another popular interpretation sees in the neuter a reference to the limit of time fixed by divine decree, and in the masculine a reference to God (Roosen 1971: 148–49).

3. An interpretation advanced as early as Theodoret and revived in recent decades holds that the neuter refers to preaching, and the masculine to Paul, the preeminent preacher of the eschatological message (revived by Cullmann 1966; see Munck 1959: 36–42).

4. Another type of interpretation sees in the references a supernatural spirit or person, like the devil, who controls the forces of evil (see Frame, 259), or the Holy Spirit, or an angel (see Roosen 1971: 149–50).

Surveys of such interpretations "only emphasize the fact that we do not know what Paul had in mind" (Frame, 262). It may indeed be that this is an *ad hoc* formulation by Paul, since there is nothing in the rich Jewish apocalyptic literature exactly like the *katechon* (2:7) (von Dobschütz 1909: 283).

Although *katechon* does not appear in Jewish literature, there was a conception in the OT (e.g., Isa 13:22; Ezek 12:21–25) and in the later apocalyptic literature that accommodated it well. In these texts, it is stressed that God is in control of human events and that what might appear to be a delay in bringing things to an end is in fact God's working out his mysterious purpose. A significant example of this kind of thinking is the commentary of the Qumran sect on Hab 2:3 (Strobel, 7–14, 98–116; Menken 1994: 110–11):

> *For there is yet another vision relating to the appointed time; it speaks of the end and does not deceive.*
> The explanation of this is that the final time will last long and will exceed everything spoken of by the Prophets; for the Mysteries of God are marvellous.
> *If it tarries, wait for it; for it will surely come and will not delay.*
> The explanation of this concerns the men of truth who observe the Law, whose hands do not slacken in the service of Truth when the final time delays for them; for all the seasons of God come to pass at their appointed time according to this decree concerning them in the Mysteries of His Prudence. (1QpHab 7:5–14; trans. Dupont-Sommer, 262–63)

A similar understanding of Hab 2:3 is also found in Heb 10:35–39, and the idea is present in 2 Pet 3:8–9. That the concern was not confined to Jews and Christians is clear from Plutarch, *On the Delay of the Divine Judgment*.

There is also an apocalyptic view that the range of evil is limited until the proper time (Job 7:12; Rev 13:1; 2 *Bar* 29:4; 4 Ezra 6:52). In Revelation, this restraint takes the form of the binding of Satan by an angel (20:1–3, 7–10; cf. 9:13–15), which has supported the unnecessary surmise that the restrainer in 2 Thess 2:7 is an angel (e.g., by Roosen 1971: 149–50). What is significant is that evil, often personalized in Satan, serves a function within God's redemptive scheme, but under strict limitations (e.g., Job 2:1–7; 1 Cor 5:5; 2 Cor 2:10–11). The Man of Lawlessness is active now, and that should alert Paul's readers to the superhuman forces with which they were dealing. But evil's being under restraint was also a reason for comfort (cf. 1 Cor 10:9–13).

When Paul returns to the events that will transpire at the end (vv 8–10), he elaborates on vv 3–5. When there is no longer any restraining force and all is revealed, Paul asserts, the Lawless One will be destroyed and those seduced by him will undergo the perdition towards which they are already headed. In vv 3–5 Paul had dwelt on the action of the Lawless One, here he will say more about what the Lawless One will do, but he begins his description by stressing the divine action. As the passive "will be revealed" indicates, it is God who is responsible for the revelation; furthermore, the Lawless One is revealed only to be destroyed by the Lord Jesus. The initiative resides with God and the Lord Jesus, and all actions will be visible (see NOTE on 1:7). This point is missed by commentators who think the expression "appearance of his coming" is pleonastic or clumsy; it rather describes the coming in terms central to Paul's purpose.

The coming of the Lord will be visible to all, which is stressed to counter the false view he refers to in 2:1–12. If that erroneous view had been based on a wrong understanding of 1 Thess 5:1–10, Paul might have feared that those holding it would think that they were already safe, enjoying the ultimate eschatological bliss. That would be why he stresses eschatological judgment, as he had also done in 1 Thess 5:1–2, where he used images associated with the tradition of the Day of the Lord. The Parousia here is different from the way it is viewed in the first letter, where it has predominantly positive connotations (see NOTE on 1 Thess 2:19; see COMMENT on 4:15).

In addition to the Day-of-the-Lord imagery, Paul uses other apocalyptic traditions in his description of the events of the end. Thus, that Satan will lead people astray belongs to such traditions (e.g., *Sib Or* 3.64.70), and that signs and wonders would be used to lead people astray had a firm place in apocalyptic thinking, both in the NT (e.g., Mark 13:22; Matt 24:24; Rev 13:11–18) and elsewhere (see Meeks 1967: 47–53). And Isa 11:4, which Paul uses to describe the Lord's annihilation of the Lawless One, is also used in apocalyptic writings (e.g., 4 Ezra 13:10; *1 En* 62:2; cf. 14:2; 84:1; *Pss Sol* 17:24, 27). But here, as elsewhere in 1 and 2 Thessalonians, Paul radically reduces the apocalyptic elements. This is vividly illustrated by a comparison with Rev 19:11–21, where Isa 11:4 is also used in a dramatic heavenly battle scene, which Paul lacks. He retains only those elements that serve his immediate purposes of correcting the erroneous teaching and comforting his readers by promising them that their great opponent will be destroyed (see NOTES on 1:6–7).

In addition to comforting his readers, Paul shows his pastoral concern in the way he concludes this section of the letter. He warns them of the deceit of wickedness and that it is possible already to be in danger of perdition. He demands adherence to the truth but speaks of love for it rather than holding to tradition (contrast v 15). And he concludes the section in good hortatory fashion with the emphatic statement that the ultimate choice is between believing and deliberately deciding in favor of wickedness.

# III. THANKSGIVING AND EXHORTATION, 2:13–3:5

## A. THANKSGIVING PERIOD PROPER, 2:13–14

◆

This is the second thanksgiving period in the letter. Like the first (1:3–4), it introduces exhortation, here on a number of different matters (see page 359 and discussion of 1:3–4), and to that extent performs one of the epistolary functions of thanksgiving periods (see discussion of 1 Thess 1:3–5; contrast O'Brien 1977: 184). The similarity to 1:3 has supported the contention that this was the introductory thanksgiving to a separate letter (Schmithals 1972: 193–94), a fragment of which was incorporated in the composite of epistolary fragments that now constitute 1 and 2 Thessalonians, but the hypothesis has not met with favor.

### TRANSLATION

2 ¹³But we ought to give thanks to God always for you, brethren beloved by the Lord, because God chose you as firstfruits for salvation through sanctification by the Spirit and belief in the truth. ¹⁴To this he called you through our gospel, that you might obtain the glory of our Lord Jesus Christ.

### NOTES

2:13. *But we ought to give thanks to God always for you, brethren.* This introductory clause is exactly the same as the beginning of 1:3 (see there), except that *hēmeis de opheilomen eucharistein* replaces *eucharistein opheilomen*. The emphasis Paul achieves by using *opheilomen* (see NOTE on 1:3) is enhanced by moving it into a position of prominence and placing *hēmeis* ("we") at the head of the sentence, which gives it the sense "as for us" (so Bruce 1982: 189). The pronoun in so emphatic a position is reminiscent of the emphasis gained by the use of *autous* in 1:4 (see COMMENT there for Paul's pastoral intention). The *de* ("But") could be merely transitional, as it is in 2:1 ("Now"; so Best 1972: 311), or it could be resumptive, picking up the thought of 1:3 (so von Dobschütz 1909: 297; Frame, 278). Most commentators, however, correctly see it as contrastive, in particular to vv 11–12 (see COMMENT).

*beloved by the Lord.* This is also an addition to 1:3. The phrase may be a reminiscence of Deut 33:12, but "the Lord" would refer to Jesus, as it frequently does in Paul, especially in his letters to Macedonia (see Frame, 279; e.g., Phil 1:14; 2:24, 29; 3:1; 1 Thess 1:6; 3:8; 4:15; 2 Thess 2:2; 3:3, 4, 16). That Jesus is in mind may be further confirmed by the fact that God has just been explicitly named and will again be named in the clause that follows (Best 1972: 311). However, two factors suggest that the reference here is to God. Verses 13–14 are in contrast to vv 11–12, and both sections have God's action as their subject. Furthermore, the topic in both sections is faith and God's action in relation to it.

In vv 13–14 Paul uses terms that are used elsewhere in statements about people who are brought to faith by God through preaching. The same complex of terms and ideas occurs in 1 Thess 1:4–5, the only other place Paul uses the perfect passive participle *ēgapēmenos* ("beloved") instead of *agapētos*, as he also does here. There he is explicit that the brethren have been loved by God, a notion central to his thinking that God had called Gentiles and that God called them through the gospel (see NOTES on 1 Thess 1:4–5). It may be that, because for him this notion is grounded in the OT, he modifies *adelphoi* ("brethren") with a term from the LXX (cf. Deut 33:12).

*because God chose you as firstfruits for salvation.* With the causal *hoti* ("because") Paul introduces the grounds for his thanksgiving. Paul frequently refers to God's choice of believers, using different words for it (Rom 8:29–30: *proginoskein* ["to foreknow"], *proōrizein* ["to predestine," cf. 1 Cor 2:7]; 1 Cor 1:27–28: *eklegesthai* ["to choose," cf. Eph 1:4]; 1 Thess 5:9: *tithenai* ["to destine"]). Here he uses *heilato*, the aorist indicative of *haireisthai*, which is used of divine election only in this place (cf. Deut 7:6–7; 10:15 for a compound form). The compound *eklogē* ("election") is used in 1 Thess 1:5, where it also has to do with preaching.

The translation "as firstfruits" renders *aparchēn*, which is the reading adopted by all major editions of the Greek NT. The textual evidence for this reading is not significantly stronger than that for *ap' archēs* ("from the beginning"), which is preferred by most commentators. Arguments in favor of *aparchēn* have therefore been made on grounds other than the textual witnesses (see Metzger, 568): (1) *aparchē* occurs six other times elsewhere in Paul's writings (Rom 8:23; 11:16; 16:5; 1 Cor 15:20, 23; 16:15), although in only one (Rom 11:16) is it used without a qualifying genitive, as it is here; (2) with one exception (Phil 4:15), *archē* means "power" in Paul; (3) there is evidence elsewhere that copyists changed *aparchēn* to *ap' archēs* (see the variant readings of Rom 16:5; Rev 14:4). Such arguments are inconclusive, however, and it is more profitable to ask what each reading might mean.

Proponents for *ap' archēs* ("from the beginning") for the most part think that it means that from the beginning of time God intended to save those whom he chose (e.g., Wanamaker, 266; O'Brien 1977: 188). This is the meaning of *archē* in such passages as Isa 63:16; Sir 24:9; Matt 19:4; 1 John 2:13. It could also be taken to be the beginning of the preaching of the gospel in Thessalonica, and Paul in this way would encourage his readers by referring to their own history.

There are also different ways in which to understand *aparchēn* ("firstfruit"). It could not be taken absolutely, for the Thessalonians were not the first people ever to accept the gospel, nor the first even in Macedonia to do so. Harnack, however, thought that this was a reference to the Jewish converts, who were the first in Thessalonica to believe and to whom 2 Thessalonians was written, a hypothesis that has been widely rejected (see pages 352–53). Nevertheless, despite the difficulties in making the choice, editors of the Greek NT are correct in deciding in favor of *aparchēn*.

Interpreters usually stress that *aparchēn* denotes priority in a sequence of events and that it can therefore not be applied to the Thessalonians. They neglect the meaning of the OT's offering of the firstfruits as the means by which the products of the harvest were sanctified to God, and that the firstfruits thereby had a qualitative aspect and also looked forward. A wider perspective than that of a sequential marker is also found in the NT. The future aspect is present in Rom 8:23, where the Spirit is said to be the *aparchē* Christians possess as they await eschatological redemption (*apolytrōsis*). The connection with redemption (*agorazein*) is also made in Rev 14:4, where it is the faithful who are the *aparchē* by virtue of their having been redeemed. And in Jas 1:18, God's generative power is exercised through the preaching of the gospel: "Of his own will he brought us forth by the word of truth that we should be a kind of firstfruits of his creation." The same themes of sanctification, eschatological redemption (here called "salvation"), and the preaching of the gospel appear in 2 Thess 2:13–14.

What defines *aparchē* is that God chose it *eis sōtērian* ("for salvation"), which is further described in v 14b (*eis peripoiēsin doxēs*; cf. v 10b, *eis to sōthēnai* ["so as to be saved"]) and 1 Thess 2:16; 5:9.

*through sanctification by the Spirit and belief in the truth.* Paul specifies the means by which God chose them for salvation (*en* is equivalent to *dia*; see already John Chrysostom, *Homilies on 2 Thessalonians* 4 [PG 62:488]). One *en* goes with both *hagiasmō* and *pistei*, which indicates that sanctification and belief belong together and are not to be separated. Grammatically, the clause could go with either *heilato* or *sōtēria*, but most commentators correctly hold that it goes with the entire statement, "God chose you as firstfruits for salvation."

Sanctification is brought about by the Spirit (*pneumatos* is a subjective genitive). Paul had already in 1 Thessalonians made the connection between his readers' election, the activity of the Spirit, and their reception of the gospel (1:4–5), and reminded them of the moral consequences of God's having called them *en hagiasmō* ("in sanctification") when he bestowed the Spirit on them (4:7–8; see NOTES there). See 1 Cor 2:4; 2 Cor 3:3; Gal 3:1–5 for the activity of the Spirit in his preaching. The phrase "in the truth" translates *pistei alētheias*, in which the genitive describes the object of the faith. Paul understood faith to be brought about by the Spirit (1 Cor 2:4–5; cf. 12:13, for the resulting confession). Here he draws a contrast to v 12.

*2:14. To this he called you through our gospel.* For the phrase *eis ho* ("To this"), see NOTE on 1:11. The antecedent of "this" (*ho*, neuter) cannot be "salvation" (*sōtērian*, feminine), but refers to the entire preceding clause, beginning with "salvation." Paul now makes explicit what was implicit in that clause: the election takes place through the gospel he preached (so already Theophylact, *Exposition of 2 Thessalonians* 2 [PG 124:1348]), which is the mode by which the Spirit sanctifies and faith is engendered (cf. Rom 10:14–17).

*that you might obtain the glory of our Lord Jesus Christ.* The phrase *eis peripoiēsin doxēs* ("that you might obtain the glory") is in apposition to *eis ho* ("To this") and therefore states the goal of the process by which God calls. For the construction as well as the thought, see 1 Thess 5:9 (see NOTE; cf. Eph 1:14), where "salvation" is used instead of "glory." For the importance of "glory" for Paul in this letter, see NOTES on 1:8–10, 12.

## COMMENT

The first striking thing that the thanksgiving does is to contrast Paul and his readers to the unbelievers about whom he had just spoken. This appears already in the contrastive *de* ("But") and then in the contrasting way in which Paul uses the same terminology: those on the way to perdition will not be saved (v 10) but will be judged (v 12), while the readers are the firstfruits for salvation (v 13); the former live in wickedness (vv 10, 12), while the latter are sanctified (v 13; cf. 1 Thess 4:3, 7 for a similar contrast); the former did not believe the truth (vv 10, 12), the latter did (v 13). In contrast to the willfulness of those whose actions result in God's sending delusion on them so that they believe in falsehood (v 11), here the initiative is totally God's: he loved them, chose them, sanctified them, and called them to share in the Lord Jesus' glory.

Once again, such language is pastoral and has a comforting effect. Believers, who are aware of the mystery of lawlessness already at work and who know of the wickedness and deception still to come, may be comforted as they are reminded that they have been chosen by God and are at the center of his saving purpose. The thanksgiving is remarkable for the way in which it brings together the main themes of the two letters, thus capturing the hortatory and comforting elements of Paul's communication to his recent converts. As the NOTES indicate, this is true not only of the similarity to the other thanksgivings in the two letters, especially 1 Thess 1:3–5 and 2 Thess 1:3, but also in such terms and themes as "brother," God's choice and call, salvation, sanctification, faith, the gospel that Paul preached, and the obtaining of eschatological glory (see O'Brien 1977: 191–93).

It is frequently pointed out that the thanksgiving offers a broad theological sweep, especially if *ap' archēs* is read, and reference is often made to James Denney's comment that these two verses

are a system of theology in miniature. The apostle's thanksgiving covers the whole work of creation from the eternal choice of God to the obtaining of the glory of our Lord Jesus in the world to come. (342; cf. Bruce 1982: 192; O'Brien 1977: 184; see also Rigaux 1956: 680)

This is true, but attention should also be given to the functions of the theological summary in its epistolary context. In relation to what precedes, it provides a basis for comfort and confidence, and to what follows, it is the basis for exhortation.

# B. EXHORTATION, 2:15–3:5

◆

Having countered the false doctrine that he suspected might be infecting the church, and in the process comforting his readers, Paul now turns to exhort them. The thanksgiving looked backwards as it comforted, but a comforting strain will continue through 3:5. Nevertheless, the hortatory tone prevails in this section. This is evident from the imperatives with which the section begins (2:15; cf. 3:1), which lead up to imperatives commanding the readers to specified behavior (3:6–12, 13–15). What is most striking about this section, however, is how prayer and the request for intercessory prayer dominate the section. Paul wishes his commands on Christian responsibility to be read in the context of his and the church's dependence on God. After his detailed directions, he will return to prayer (3:16).

## 1. ADMONITION, 2:15

### TRANSLATION

2 ¹⁵So then, brethren, stand fast and hold onto the traditions which you were taught, whether by our oral teaching or our letter.

### NOTES

2:15. *So then, brethren, stand fast and hold onto the traditions which you were taught.* For the characteristic Pauline *ara oun* ("So then"), see NOTE on 1 Thess 5:6. Here it establishes the commands it introduces in what precedes: it is because of God's actions for which Paul has just given thanks that he commands his brethren who have been loved by God. He uses the military term *stēkein* ("to stand fast"; see NOTE on 1 Thess 3:8) to contrast the proper Christian emotional condition to the instability that he suspects may have been caused by the false teaching (see v 2 and NOTE). This is the only place in Paul's letters where the verb is used absolutely (see, e.g., Phil 1:27, "in spirit"; 4:1, "in the Lord"; 1 Thess 3:8; 1 Cor 16:13, "in the faith"; "freedom" is to be understood in Gal 5:1). The context, however, shows that Paul's concern here is not general moral constancy, but emotional stability in the face of the erroneous eschatological teaching.

The *kai* ("and") is explicative: the way to stand firm is to hold to the traditions. *Kratein* ("to hold onto") can, with *paradoseis* ("traditions"), have the sense of holding onto the moral teaching of Paul; it is evidently equivalent to *katechein* ("to hold onto"), which is used with *paradosis* of ethical teaching in 1 Cor 11:2. Indeed, in 3:6 he deals with an ethical aspect of the tradition. But here, holding onto the traditions explains how they are to stand fast, by continuing to heed the teachings they had received from him that, against the background of vv 1–2, have to do with the coming of the Lord.

There is nothing negative about the notion of tradition (cf. Gal 1:14; Mark 7:8–9; Col 2:8). Paul elsewhere uses the language to describe the transmission of tradition in a positive manner (cf. 1 Cor 11:23; 15:1). Here the tradition is further identified as that which they were taught. There is no reason, on the basis of a very broad understanding of what tradition is thought to have signified in the later rabbinic literature, to understand Paul's reference here to include what was generally passed on by missionaries (so Best 1972: 317).

*whether by our oral teaching or our letter*. The tradition Paul has in mind is what he had taught them orally, therefore when he was with them, or by letter, when he was separated from them. By appealing to his oral teaching he circumvents any possible misattribution to him that might have given rise to or supported the erroneous teaching (see NOTE and COMMENT on v 2). Similarly, the letter he refers to is 1 Thessalonians itself, and neither a glossed copy (see discussion of 3:17) nor an interpretation of it (see pages 350–51).

## COMMENT

In this verse Paul intensifies his directions on how to counter the false teaching by returning to two of the putative sources for it, his own teaching and 1 Thessalonians (cf. v 2). He does not mention the Spirit, probably because it was unnecessary for his present purpose to do so. Paul had already, in 1 Thess 5:21, spoken of testing prophetic utterances, one of the criteria of which evidently was his teaching (see NOTE).

Here the stress is on the traditions that he has taught, which must include his gospel, to which he has just drawn attention (v 14). He could simply have mentioned his earlier teaching or what his readers had learned from him (see 1 Cor 4:17; Phil 4:9; cf. Rom 16:17), so there must be a reason why he refers to his teachings as traditions. Reference to his teaching (cf. 1 Cor 4:17) and the tradition he taught (cf. 1 Cor 11:2, 7) sometimes serves to stress the wide currency of his teaching, and that may be implicit here: there is nothing secret about his teaching, everyone knows it.

The word *paradosis* further has the connotation of continuity, presupposing the transmission of what has been known or of what becomes known in the process of transmission. The thought is present in 1 Thess 4:1–2, where Paul uses the technical terminology for the transmission of tradition rather than the word "tradition" itself. His readers should, in doctrinal matters, hold to what they know to have been his teaching rather than be led astray by people who make novel claims. Elsewhere in 2 Thessalonians he refers to what his readers already know (2:6) or what he had commanded them (3:6, 10).

The means by which he seeks to maintain this continuity is to refer to what he had taught orally (lit., "by word") and "by letter." There is nothing strange about Paul's referring to what he had taught them. In addition to the passages in 2 Thessalonians just referred to, 1 Thessalonians does so (4:6, 11) and is replete with assurances that his readers already know what he is urging them to do. This is characteristic of paraenetic style, which Paul puts to pastoral use (see pages 81–86). Nor is there anything peculiar about Paul's reference to his letters or his letter writing, particularly when the letters were misunderstood (cf. 1 Cor 5:8–10) or when there was something else problematic about them (cf. 1 Cor 4:14; 9:15; esp. 2 Cor 1:13–14; 10:10), as there was when he wrote 2 Thessalonians (see NOTE and COMMENT on 2 Thess 3:17).

Despite acknowledging, however, that this sentence makes perfectly good sense on the assumption of the authenticity of 2 Thessalonians, proponents of the pseudonymity of the letter have maintained that it makes better sense if it is placed later, at a time when references were made to the transmission of the faith (Jude 3) and of holy commandments (2 Pet 2:21). It is further maintained that the combination of "word" and "letter," singular in the NT, is somehow more intelligible in a period when there was a developing respect for apostolic tradition and letters thought to be written by apostles (Trilling 1980: 128–29). But the assertion is based on generalizations about apostolicity and not exegesis of 2 Thessalonians (see pages 365–66).

# 2. PRAYER FOR ENCOURAGEMENT, 2:16–17

## TRANSLATION

2 16Now may our Lord Jesus Christ himself and God our Father who has loved us and given us eternal encouragement and good hope by grace 17encourage and establish your hearts in every good work and word.

## NOTES

2:16. *Now may our Lord Jesus Christ himself and God our Father.* It is unlikely that the *de* ("Now") is slightly adversative, Paul distinguishing what his readers are to do (v 15) from what he prays that Christ and God do (so Frame, 285). The *de* is part of the prayer form, in which it appears with the emphatic *autos* ("himself"; cf. 1 Thess 3:11; 5:23; 2 Thess 3:16), and is merely transitional. As to its form, the prayer is similar to 1 Thess 3:11–13, which concludes the long thanksgiving that begins in 1:3. Some commentators think that it does the same thing here (e.g., Best 1972: 319). Most striking is that Christ is mentioned before God, as he is in Gal 1:1 and the benediction in 2 Cor 13:13. This may be due to the fact that in 2:13–3:5 as a whole Christ is more prominent than God (so Rigaux 1956: 690). It is also possible that God is mentioned last in order to accommodate the long participial clause (so Trilling 1980: 131). The formula *ho theos ho patēr hēmōn* ("God our Father"), with the article before *patēr*, is unique.

   *who has loved us and given us eternal encouragement and good hope by grace.* The two articular participles are in the singular (*ho agapēsas hēmās kai dous* ["who has loved and given us"]) and would appear to describe God, but the fact that they take singular verbs (*parakalesai* ["encourage"] and *stērixai* ["establish"]) does not rule out the possibility that they refer to both Jesus and God (cf. 1 Thess 3:11, for a similar instance). Paul speaks frequently of the love of God (e.g., Rom 5:5; 2 Cor 13:13) and the love of Christ (Rom 8:35; 2 Cor 5:14). Their love is so intertwined that it cannot be separated (Rom 8:35, 37, 39). The two aorist participles, governed by one article, refer to a specific past event. That event may have been Christ's saving death (cf. Gal 2:20, "who loved me and gave himself for me"), but the closer reference to God's love in v 13 suggests otherwise. There God's love is demonstrated in his election and call through the preaching of the gospel, and the perfect tense of the participle shows that the result of that act of God's love continues.

   Paul's pastoral interest is further exhibited in what he specifies as God's gifts and how they are modified. In view of the persecutions the Thessalonians were enduring (1:4), it is appropriate that he mentions encouragement (*paraklēsis*; for the verb, *parakalein*, with the sense of "comfort," see 1 Thess 3:7; cf. Rom 15:5 [2 Cor 1:13], for the God of [all] comfort). That it is eternal means that it has been active since its bestowal and will be so throughout all eternity. The expression has the ring of prayer to it.

   The expression "good hope," which does not appear elsewhere in the Bible (cf. 2 Cor 1:7, "firm hope"; Titus 2:13, "blessed hope"; 1 Pet 1:3, "living hope"), is frequently attested in secular Greek (e.g., Julian, *Epistle* 20.452C [LCL], "you will give me still greater good hope for the future life") and, as epitaphs show, was adopted by Jews (Légasse, 414–15). The adverbial phrase "by grace" goes naturally with "has given," but it more likely modifies both participles. The relation of the phrase to "who has loved us" becomes clear when the latter is taken as reference to God's call (cf. Gal 1:6, "who called you by the grace of Christ" through the preaching of the gospel).

   2:17. *encourage and establish your hearts in every good work and word.* Although in the singular, the verbs have Christ and God as their subjects (for the same use of the singular and the optative in prayers, see NOTE on 1 Thess 3:11). For the meaning of *parakalein* ("to encourage") and *stērizein* ("to establish") in contexts like this, see NOTES on 1 Thess 3:2–3, where they are used of Paul's sending Timothy to strengthen the Thessalonians lest they be shaken emotionally and abandon their faith. See NOTE on 1 Thess 3:13 for the Lord establishing their hearts at the Parousia. Here the reference is to the present and is comprehensive: "heart" denotes the entire person, and "work" and "word" encompass all human activity. For the significance of the combination of the two, see NOTE on 1 Thess 1:5. The repetition of "good" and its place at the end of the sentence lend emphasis to it. For similar concerns of Paul in a prayer on behalf of the Thessalonians, see 2 Thess 1:11 and NOTE.

## COMMENT

Paul's pastoral approach to the Thessalonians continues in this prayer. The language of emotion, which begins with v 13 and is reminiscent of the pathos of 1 Thess 2:17–3:13, continues. There Paul had used such language to strengthen the bond between himself and his readers before advising them on particular matters. Here he stresses God's and Christ's actions on their behalf. They are admonished to stand firm and to hold to the traditions they had been taught, but these imperatives are bracketed, first, by a thanksgiving that God had totally transformed them when he called them through the gospel and, second, by the prayer that God and Christ enable them to live the life to which they had been called.

The entire section, vv 12–17, and particularly vv 16–17, is well suited to Paul's readers. They evidently lacked confidence that they were living up to God's expectations as they faced persecution. That was not an unusual concern of converts, and Paul began the letter by focusing on it and complimenting them on their conduct (1:3–5; see COMMENT). Here, his focus is on the divine aid available to them, able to make them sufficient to the task.

# 3. REQUEST FOR PRAYER, 3:1–2

## TRANSLATION

3 ¹For the rest, brethren, pray for us, that the word of the Lord may speed on and be glorified, as it does with you, ²and that we may be delivered from the perverse and wicked men, for not everyone has faith.

## NOTES

3:1. *For the rest, brethren, pray for us.* For *to loipon* ("For the rest"), see NOTE on 1 Thess 4:1. Rather than being temporal ("Finally"), it is transitional, introducing important injunctions (cf. Phil 3:1; 4:8). For Paul's request for prayer on his own behalf, see NOTE on 1 Thess 5:25, and for the literary form of the prayer request, see Wiles, 292.

*that the word of the Lord may speed on and be glorified, as it does with you.* Paul's readers are to pray for him with a twofold object expressed by *hina . . . hina* ("that . . . that"). Paul had earlier described the active, dynamic character of the gospel as the Thessalonians had received it (1 Thess 2:13) and then proclaimed it (1 Thess 1:8). The first object of their prayer should be that, as had been the case with them (*kathōs kai pros hymās*), it might be with him. The image of the word of the Lord running has overtones of Ps 147:4 LXX, which speaks of the word running swiftly, but it was also an athletic metaphor popular in Paul's day that he frequently used (Rom 9:16; 1 Cor 9:24–27; Gal 2:2; 5:7; Phil 2:16; cf. 2 Tim 4:7; see further, NOTE on 1 Thess 2:19). Some commentators make the inference, partially based on Psalms and on Matt 24:14 and Mark 13:10, that Paul has in mind the swiftness with which the gospel is to be spread (Findlay, 198; Marshall 1983: 213; Best 1972: 324–25). This is supported by the rapidity with which the gospel was spread by the Thessalonians (see NOTE on 1 Thess 1:8) and by Paul's reference to them here. This interpretaton would be further strengthened if *treche* ("speed") and *doxazetai* ("be glorified") were taken as a hendiadys (thus von Dobschütz 1909: 305).

Nevertheless, an alternative understanding presents itself if another aspect of the metaphor is considered and *doxazetai* is taken as the reward received upon winning the race. The race is viewed in terms of its having been run unhindered (so John Chrysostom, *Homilies on 2 Thessalonians* 4 [PG 62:489]; Theodoret, *Interpretation of 2 Thessalonians* 2 [PG 82:669]), an interpretation supported by the second object of the prayer Paul requests (for the idea, see 2 Tim 2:9).

3:2. *and that we may be delivered from the perverse and wicked men.* The second object of the prayer provides some information about Paul's circumstances at the time of writing. It was not unusual for Paul to be opposed in his preaching, and in 1 Thess 2:14–16 he alluded to Jews as his opponents in Corinth at the time he wrote that letter. Acts 18:5–17 suggests that Jewish opposition in Corinth continued for a while (cf. Rom 15:30–32, a prayer for deliverance from unbelieving Jews in Jerusalem). The description of his opponents has a biblical ring (cf. Isa 25:4, "you will deliver them from wicked [*poneron*] men"), but in the OT *poneros* is associated with words other than *atopos* ("perverse"; e.g., Ps 139:1, *adikos* ["unjust"]; Isa 9:17, *anomos* ["lawless"]; Jer 15:21, *loimos* ["pestilential"]). The definite article indicates that he has a definite group of people in mind whom he expected his readers to know.

*for not everyone has faith.* What distinguishes Paul's opponents for him is not their ethnic identity, but their lack of faith. In 2:11–12, Paul had spoken of those who did not believe in terms of God's eschatological plan (cf. also 1 Thess 2:14–16); here he simply advances their lack of faith as the reason (*gar* ["for"]) for their actions against him.

## COMMENT

The pathos with which Paul has been writing continues, as he asks his readers, after his prayer on behalf of them, to pray for him. He can have empathy with them, for as they are suffering (1:5), he too is in circumstances from which he wishes to be rescued. Yet even as he asks for their prayers, he commends them and comforts them by reminding them of the active word of the Lord and of God's deliverance (see John Chrysostom, *Homilies on 2 Thessalonians* 4 [PG 62:489]). In 1 Thess 1:6–8, they had been imitators of him and became an example when they preached the gospel; here they exemplify the action he wishes.

But he solicits their prayer for him only insofar as he is the bearer of the word of the Lord, and even that he does not state explicitly. The only reference to himself is in terms of his need to be delivered from evil opponents, yet even that petition does not mention his own hardships, but rather the lack of faith that is evidently responsible for his opponents' hindering of his preaching the gospel.

# 4. THE FAITHFULNESS OF GOD, 3:3–4

## TRANSLATION

3 ³But the Lord is faithful, who will establish you and guard you from the Evil One. ⁴We have confidence in the Lord about you, that what we command, you indeed are doing and will continue to do.

## NOTES

3:3. *But the Lord is faithful.* The *de* ("But") is more than transitional, as it is in vv 4–5, where it is left untranslated. Here it marks a change in the objects of God's action, from Paul to the Thessalonians, and contrasts the lack of faith of Paul's opponents with the faithfulness of the Lord. Paul plays on the kinship of *pistis* ("faith," v 2) and *pistos* ("faithful"), which describes a divine quality that will be exhibited to their benefit. The phrase "the Lord is faithful" (*pistos . . . estin ho kyrios*) is similar to but not the same as "God is faithful" (*pistos ho theos*), which is the form elsewhere in Paul (1 Cor 1:9; 10:13; 2 Cor 1:18; see also 1 Thess 5:24 and NOTE there).

One difference is the presence of *estin* ("is"), which emphasizes the faithfulness of the Lord. The other is that the Lord, not God, is called faithful. Most commentators take the reference to be to Christ, mostly on the basis that *kyrios* is used so frequently in this letter of Christ. But this identification elsewhere in the letter can be disputed (see NOTE on 2:13); furthermore, "Lord" is most frequently more fully identified as "the Lord Jesus" (1:7; 2:8), "our Lord Jesus" (1:8, 12), "our Lord Jesus Christ" (2:14, 16), and "the Lord Jesus Christ" (1:12; 2:1; 3:6, 12 [but see 1:9; 2:2]). In addition, since the simple *kyrios* in 2:13 and 3:1 refers to God, it is natural to suppose that it also does so here. Paul thus continues to dwell on God's saving, one might say pastoral, action, which he had introduced in 2:16.

*who will establish you and guard you from the Evil One.* What was part of a prayer wish in 2:17 is now a confident assertion: God will establish (*stērixei*) you (see NOTES on 2:17 and 1 Thess 3:2–3). Paul uses *phylassein* ("to guard") only in Rom 2:26 and Gal 6:13, where it applies to the law (cf. 1 Tim 5:21; 6:20; 2 Tim 1:12, 14, of guarding the tradition; 2 Tim 4:14, in the sense of being on one's guard). The word is used in the OT of the Lord guarding the just from all evil and from the snare of iniquity (Ps 120:7; 140:9 LXX, resp.). Paul's use is similar, but it is likely that he uses *tou ponērou* ("the Evil One") as masculine rather than the neuter ("evil"). The issue is debated (e.g., Dibelius 1937: 53, argues that it is neuter; Best 1972: 327–28, that it is masculine). This characteristic of Satan became a proper name elsewhere in the NT (Matt 6:13 [cf. *Did* 8:2]; 13:19, 34; Eph 6:16; 1 John 2:13–14; 1 John 5:19), just as an activity has in 1 Thess 3:5 ("the Tempter"). Paul was very conscious of Satan while he was in Corinth (see 1 Thess 2:18 and NOTE there) and had commented on his eschatological activity in 2:9.

3:4. *We have confidence in the Lord about you.* Having expressed confidence in what the Lord will do, Paul now expresses confidence in the Thessalonians (cf. the transition from 2:13–14 to v 15). But his confidence is "in the Lord" (for the formal *en kyriō*, see Rom 14:14; Gal 5:10; Phil 2:24). The thought is expressed in 2 Cor 3:4–5: "Such is the confidence that we have through Christ towards God. Not that we are sufficient of ourselves to claim anything as coming from us; our sufficiency is from God." Nevertheless, Paul on occasion expresses confidence about his readers as a hortatory or paraenetic device, urging upon them precisely what he says he is confident about (see 2 Cor 1:15; 2:3; 8:22; Phlm 24). That is what he does here, as the following clause shows.

*that what we command, you indeed are doing and will continue to do.* In 1 Thessalonians the noun (*parangelia* [4:1]) and the verb (*parangellein* [4:11]) had the sense of giving moral precepts or instructions. The verb is used in vv 4, 6, 10, 12 in this chapter, and in each case can be translated "command," which could be justified by the sharper tone that begins with v 6. We would do well, however, to be sensitive to nuance, particularly when paraenetic features are present, as they are here. The statement that the Thessalonians were indeed (the *kai* is used for emphasis) doing what Paul had told them to do is paraenetic (cf. 1 Thess 4:1, 10; 5:11), as is the confident assertion that they will continue to do so (cf. 1 Thess 4:1–2, 10b, and NOTES). Paul adopted the paraenetic style for pastoral purposes in 1 Thessalonians (see pages 85–86), and that is what he does here (see John Chrysostom, *Homilies on 2 Thessalonians* 5 [PG 62:493], for the hortatory function of the sentence).

# COMMENT

Paul again turns to focus on his readers, to assure them of God's faithfulness in caring for them. He solicits their prayers for his deliverance from evil people but is confident that God will guard them from the Evil One. The comforting nature of such statements is evident in light of the circumstances described in 1:4–5 (see NOTES and COMMENT) and is accentuated by the emphatic assertion that God *is* faithful.

Verses 3–4 look backward as well as forward, as they begin to close the exhortation that began in 2:13 and prepare for the commands that will begin in 3:6. In the paraenetic manner, although vv 1–4 are in a sense themselves hortatory, they describe the relationship between Paul and his readers that will form the basis of his directions that will follow. The sharp tone and the commands in vv 6–15 may cause one to expect an assertion of his apostolic authority already here. Instead, he is in need of their prayers for God's deliverance, of which he is confident because of God's faithfulness. And he is confident in their compliance with his mandates. His pastoral manner could not be clearer.

# 5. PRAYER FOR FAITHFULNESS, 3:5

## TRANSLATION

3 ⁵May the Lord direct your hearts to the love of God and to the steadfastness of Christ.

## NOTES

3:5. *May the Lord direct your hearts to the love of God and to the steadfastness of Christ.* The prayer marks the end of the second section of exhortation in the letter. For the aorist optative and *kateuthynai* ("may . . . direct") in prayers, see NOTE on 1 Thess 3:11. The phrase "direct your hearts" is from the LXX, where it is used of people turning their hearts to the Lord (2 Chr 12:14; 19:3; 20:33; Sir 49:5; 51:20 ["soul" instead of "heart"]) or the Lord turning people's hearts to himself (1 Chr 29:18; Prov 21:2). It has this spiritual rather than literal sense (cf. 1 Thess 3:11), "heart" referring to the total inner person (see 1 Thess 2:4 and NOTE). Most commentators take "Lord" to refer to Christ, and some, especially patristic commentators, to the Holy Spirit (see Theodoret, *Interpretation of 2 Thessalonians* 3 [PG 82:669]). If *kyrios* elsewhere in vv 1–5 refers to God, however, as has been argued above, it would be natural to understand it as doing the same here, reflecting the OT use. Yet in 1 Thess 3:11 the singular *kateuthynai* has God the Father and the Lord Jesus Christ as subjects.

The principal exegetical difficulty is how to understand the two genitives, "of God" and "of Christ." The first could be objective and mean that Paul prays that his readers love God. The phrase "love of God," however, elsewhere in his letters refers to God's love for people (Rom 5:5; 8:39; 2 Cor 13:13). Furthermore, he had begun this thanksgiving, which began in 2:13 and ends with this verse, by addressing his readers as "brethren beloved by the Lord," that is, God (see NOTE there). And in 2:16 he again referred to God's love (see NOTE). The meaning here is that the Thessalonians are to direct themselves totally to God's love and to depend on it.

It is natural, then, to take "of Christ" as similarly subjective, referring to the steadfastness that Christ demonstrates, which in a sense parallels God's faithfulness (cf. the extensive discussion by Eadie, 307–9, of the different possibilities of meaning). It is possible that *hypomonē* ("steadfastness") could mean "endurance," as it does in 1 Thess 1:3; 2 Thess 1:4 (see NOTES), and that Christ's example should inspire the Thessalonians to endure in their sufferings. The immediate context, however, which deals with God's faithfulness as the basis for confidence, recommends the meaning adopted here.

## COMMENT

Paul concludes the second section of thanksgiving and exhortation (2:13–3:5) by showing his concern for his converts in a prayer. Before he admonishes them (3:6–15), he urges them by means of an intercessory prayer to incline their hearts to God's love and Christ's steadfastness, a constant source of encouragement (cf. Rom 15:4–5).

# IV. COMMANDS, 3:6–15

◆

After comforting and exhorting his readers up to this point in the letter, Paul now turns to direct them in how they are to treat erring members of the congregation. His tone changes from consolation and exhortation to command, as he now comes to the second purpose for writing 2 Thessalonians (see pages 360–61).

# A. DISCIPLINE OF THE DISORDERLY, 3:6–12

◆

Paul had been at great pains to instruct his converts in socially responsible behavior when he was with them and then in 1 Thessalonians (see 4:9–12). That he reserved admonition, the harshest type of moral exhortation he mentions in that letter, for members of the church who conducted themselves in a disorderly manner by not earning their own living (1 Thess 5:14) indicates how important he considered the matter to be. Despite those efforts, however, Paul learned from an oral report, some Thessalonians refused to work (2 Thess 3:11). So, once more he writes on the subject. But now he writes, in greater detail and more sharply than he had done in 1 Thess 4:9–12; 5:14, on the action the congregation should take towards the idlers.

The tone of this section is exhibited in the *inclusio* formed by the phrases "we command [*parangellomen*] you, brethren, in the name of the Lord Jesus Christ" in v 6 and "we command [*parangellomen*] and exhort [them] in the Lord Jesus Christ" in v 12. And within this section he reminds his readers that he used to give them instruction (*parēngellomen*, "instructed" or "commanded") when he was with them (v 10). The section begins with a command to the entire church about what they should do with respect to the idlers (v 6). Most of the section then states the reasons for his command: it is in keeping with the tradition they had received from him (v 6c), with the example he had set for them to follow (vv 7–9), and with his command at that time that they earn their own living (v 10). Only in v 11 does he reveal the reason why he writes on the subject, the report he had received about the situation in Thessalonica. He concludes by commanding the idlers, in a somewhat indirect manner, to live in quietness and work to earn their own living (v 12).

## TRANSLATION

3 ⁶Now, we command you, brethren, in the name of the Lord Jesus Christ, withdraw from every brother who conducts himself in a disorderly manner and not in accordance with the tradition that you received from us. ⁷For you yourselves know how you ought to imitate us, for we were not disorderly among you, ⁸nor did we accept bread from anyone without paying, but in labor and toil, night and day, we kept at our work in order not to burden any of you. ⁹It was not that we had no right [to be supported by you], but to present ourselves as an example for you to imitate. ¹⁰Indeed, when we were with you, we used to give you this instruction, "If someone does not wish to work, let him not eat." ¹¹For we hear that there are some who are conducting themselves among you in a disorderly manner, doing no work at all, but being busybodies. ¹²Such persons we command and exhort in the Lord Jesus Christ that, by working quietly, they are to eat their own bread.

## NOTES

3:6. *Now, we command you, brethren, in the name of the Lord Jesus Christ.* With a transitional *de* ("Now") Paul begins a new section, for which he had prepared in v 4. There he had, in paraenetic fashion, expressed confidence in his readers' compliance with his instructions; here he particularizes that general statement and does so by appealing to Christ's authority. The formula *en tō onomati tou kyriou Iēsou Christou* ("in the name of the Lord Jesus Christ") specifies the authority by which Paul speaks, and makes clear that *parangellomen* here expresses a command (cf. 1 Cor 7:10; 11:17).

He uses the same formula in 1 Cor 5:4, where he also introduces instructions on congregational discipline (see also, for a milder use of almost the same formula, 1 Cor 1:10 [*parakalō . . . dia tou onomatos tou kyriou hēmōn Iēsou Christou*, "I exhort you through the name of our Lord Jesus Christ"]; 1 Thess 4:2 [*tinas parangelias edōkamen hymin dia tou kyriou Iēsou*, "what precepts we gave you through the Lord Jesus"]; cf. Eph 5:20; Col 3:17). The authority inherent in the formula is most evident when it is used in exorcisms (e.g., Acts 16:18; cf. 19:13). For *adelphoi* ("brethren"), see NOTE on 2:1. It does not make the tone cordial here, but does lessen the harshness of the sentence. There is no evidence that the "brethren" were a special group within the congregation (so Ellis, 19–21; Bruce 1982: 204). The command that follows makes sense only if the entire congregation is in view.

*withdraw from every brother who conducts himself in a disorderly manner.* The verb *stellesthai* ("withdraw") in the middle appears in the NT only here and in 2 Cor 8:20, where its meaning is not clear. It appears in Mal 2:5 LXX, where it is used in parallel to "fear." It seems to differ little from *hypostellein* in Gal 2:12, *hypestellen kai aphōrizen heauton* ("he withdrew and separated himself"), where the two verbs form a hendiadys. Theodoret comments that Paul used *stellesthai* instead of *chōrizesthai* ("to separate oneself," *Interpretation of 2 Thessalonians* 3 [PG 82:669]; see also Theodore of Mopsuestia, *Commentary on the Epistles of Paul* 2.61 Swete). That this is the meaning here is clear from v 14, where *mē synanamignysthai* ("not to associate with") is used instead. The disorderly are those who willfully reject the accepted norms by which the church is expected to live (see NOTE on 1 Thess 5:14).

*and not in accordance with the tradition that you received from us.* Disorderly behavior is that which does not have Paul's tradition as its norm (*mē kata tēn paradosin*). In 2:15, he referred to tradition as something that he taught verbally, either orally or in writing, the reference there being primarily to his eschatological teaching. What he now refers to is a matter of conduct, as he will go on to specify (vv 7–12), but it too had been the subject of oral and written instruction (1 Thess 4:9–12; 5:14).

3:7. *For you yourselves know how you ought to imitate us.* By introducing his own behavior, Paul shows that he understands tradition to encompass more than verbal teaching. In vv 7–11 Paul uses *gar* ("For") three times (vv 7, 10, 11) to introduce various aspects of the reason for his command that the congregation withdraw from the disorderly. These aspects are in fact specifications of the tradition by which he measures his converts' conduct.

The first reason is introduced by the emphatic *autoi gar oidate* ("For you yourselves know") and enclosed by references to the need to follow his example (vv 7, 9). Paul used the phrase in 1 Thess 2:1 (cf. vv 2, 5, 11) to call to mind features of his ministry of which they knew, in order to lay a foundation for his later instructions (see COMMENT on 1 Thess 2:1–12). The phrase is part of the paraenetic style of 1 Thessalonians (other references to their knowledge in that letter are 1:5; 3:3–4; 4:2; 5:2), reminding them as he exhorts them (cf. 1 Thess 2:9 for reminder; see NOTE and COMMENT on 2:1–12; pages 84–85). Imitation is similarly part of paraenetic style. What was implicit in 1 Thess 2:9 is now made explicit: Paul expected to be imitated and had specified how that should be done (see v 10, below; cf. 1 Cor 4:16–17, more generally). But his use of the remembrance-imitation motif here is not hortatory; it is advanced as a reason for church discipline.

*for we were not disorderly among you.* Paul clarifies why they were to imitate him. The *hoti* ("for") introduces the reason, which is stated fully in an antithesis: "we were not disorderly . . . nor did we accept bread . . . but in labor and toil . . . ."

The first statement is simple and straightforward, and does not reveal how he conceived of his manual labor as part of his apostolic self-understanding (see COMMENT on 1 Thess 2:9). It is negative in form to apply to the situation at hand, the discipline of those who live disorderly lives (v 11). Since it is Paul's teaching that is the norm for orderly living, this assertion implies a claim that his behavior agreed with his teaching.

3:8. *nor did we accept bread from anyone without paying.* The second negative statement is equally straightforward, requiring no proof: He did not receive his subsistence gratis while preaching. Instead, Paul preached the gospel gratis (2 Cor 11:7).

*but in labor and toil, night and day, we kept at our work in order not to burden any of you.* The second part of the antithesis, introduced by the strong adversative *alla* ("but"), is where the emphasis lies and contains what Paul is most interested in affirming, namely that his behavior was not only impeccable (working laboriously, long hours, continuously) but that it was from the beginning intended to be paradigmatic. But unlike 1 Thess 2:9, where the pathos with which his example is described makes vivid his love for his converts, here it serves to give greater weight to his paradigmatic conduct itself. This paradigmatic significance he then elaborates in the rest of vv 8b–10. Verse 8b and 1 Thess 2:9 (see NOTE) are more similar than any other texts in the two letters. Verse 8b, however, mentions neither love nor the proclamation of the gospel nor his free decision to work (1 Thess 2:8), which are central to the earlier text, so that what predominates is Paul's purpose not to burden those to whom he preached.

3:9. *It was not that we had no right [to be supported by you].* The elaboration of his paradigmatic practice continues in another antithesis that brings to an end the first ground for his command to withdraw from the idle members. The Greek of the sentence is compressed and must be expanded in terms of the subject discussed (see 2:3 for another ellipsis; cf. Phil 3:12; 4:11, 17 for *ouch hoti* ["It was not that"]; for the phenomenon, see BDF §480.5). The negative member of the antithesis is again brief and self-evident. Paul discusses his right or authority to financial support at great length in 1 Cor 9, where he also begins the heart of his argument with self-evident reasons for this right (1 Cor 9:7–12a; Malherbe 1995b). Paul mentions his right here, not because he had been challenged on the subject, but precisely because he can take for granted that his readers would accept it and he could use his waiving of it as part of another argument.    ·

*but to present ourselves as an example for you to imitate.* The first antithesis ended in a purpose clause, "in order not to burden you" (v 8), and so does the second, "for you to imitate," which is parallel to the first. In contrast to 1 Thess 2:9, where three motifs (love, preaching, self-sufficiency) are present, Paul here limits himself to self-sufficiency. His practice is now explicitly stated to have been paraenetic: what was implicit in 1 Thess 2:9 (see NOTE and COMMENT: Introduction on 1 Thess 2:1–12), now is made explicit as a ground for his command on church discipline. The self-confidence of the assertion is heightened by the emphatic position in which *heautous* ("ourselves") is placed (*hina heautous typon dōmen* [lit., "in order ourselves as an example to present"]).

3:10. *Indeed, when we were with you, we used to give you this instruction.* The reason for the command to withdraw from the idlers began in v 7 with *autoi gar oidate* ("for you yourselves know") and ends with a clause introducted by *kai gar* ("Indeed"; lit., "For also") and with a verb in the imperfect to describe continuing instruction (*parēngellomen* ["we used to instruct"]). The same pattern is used in 1 Thess 3:3–4. The *kai* could be a simple connective, Paul thereby adding that when he was with them he taught that they should work (Best 1972: 338). It is more likely, however, that it is ascensive, as it is in 1 Thess 3:4 (cf. Phil 2:7), Paul emphasizing that as he kept on working he kept on instructing them (imperfect *parēngellomen*; contrast the aorist in 1 Thess 4:11). The example he set to be imitated was reinforced by instruction that he now clearly specifies (*touto parēngellomen* [lit., "this we used to instruct"]), with the *touto* in the emphatic position, pointing to the saying that follows in v 10b.

*"If someone does not wish to work, let him not eat."* The content of the instruction is given in what has been called the Golden Rule of work (von Dobschütz 1909: 314) and "a bit of good old workshop morality" (Deissmann 1965: 314), a sentiment that was widespread in Jewish and Greek sources (see Str-B, 3.641–42; Wettstein, 2.314). The various forms of the saying inculcate the virtue of work and sometimes connect work with earning one's living, as in Ps.-Phocylides, *Sentences* 153, "Work hard so that you can live from your own means" (see van der Horst, 216–17). These sayings are not precisely the same as Paul's, which lays stress on the will not to work (Rigaux 1956: 709). Paul may reflect a popular sentiment, but it is not at all clear that he is quoting something. His waiving of his right not to work was an act of his free will, and this aspect of his decision was integral to his understanding of his apostleship (see NOTES and COMMENT on 1 Thess 2:8–9; for the issue behind 1 Cor 9:18–19, see Malherbe 1995b). Here the exercise of will is seen from a different perspective, that of an ethical imperative.

3:11. *For we hear that there are some who are conducting themselves among you in a disorderly manner.* With the third *gar* ("For"), Paul introduces his explanation for his directions on church discipline. The present *akouomen* ("we hear") is perfective, "we have heard" (BDF §322.1; cf. 1 Cor 11:18), and the accusative and participle used with it describe what was going on at the time. This is the clearest indication in the letter of circumstances in the Thessalonian church. The same unidentified persons who told him about this matter may also have told him about the erroneous eschatological teaching he corrects in 2:1–12. But there he does not say how he had learned of the error nor that he knows that someone was actually teaching it, and his response is calm and comforting.

The report on disorderliness, in contrast, moves him to speak passionately and in detail about what the congregation should do. He does not say how he had learned about the situation, by letter or oral report, but he is sufficiently confident of his information to demand harsh action (cf. 1 Cor 1:11; 11:18, for hearsay information). In 1 Cor 5:1 a general report occasions a similar response. In that passage as well as here, Paul knows the identity of the offenders, even though he uses the indefinite pronoun in referring to them (for this practice, see

2 Cor 2:5; 10:2, 12; Gal 1:7; 2:12). It is impossible to determine how large a group the "some" were, but there is no indication that there were very many (so Best 1972: 339, and most other commentators).

Paul does not say that "some of you" (*tinas hymōn*; cf. *tina hymōn* ["any of you"], in v 8) or "some from among you" (*tinas ek hymōn*; cf. Rom 11:14) were conducting themselves in this manner. Rather, *en hymin* ("among you") goes with the disorderly behavior and is thus in contrast to Paul's practice, which was not disorderly among them (v 7, *ouk etaktēsamen en hymin* ["we were not disorderly among you"]). Paul's concern is that this behavior is taking place in their midst, where he had set a different example (see 1 Thess 1:5 and NOTE; 2:7 [*en mesō hymōn*]).

*doing no work at all, but being busybodies.* Paul clarifies what the disorderliness consists in with a play on words that is difficult to render in English. The most successful attempt is Moffatt's "busybodies [*periergazomenous*] instead of busy [*ergazomenous*]." With the charge that the idlers were busybodies, Paul is again using language from the discussions of social attitudes that informed his advice in 1 Thess 4:11–12.

The description of the idlers shows that they did not follow that advice. The Thessalonians had been told to make it their ambition to "live a quiet life and to mind [their] own affairs [*hēsychazein kai prassein ta idia*] and to work [*ergazesthai*] with [their] hands . . . so that [they] may conduct [themselves] becomingly [*peripateite euschēmonōs*] in the eyes of the outsiders." Here *euschēmonōs* is the equivalent of *en taxei* or *kata taxin* ("in orderly fashion" [see NOTES]). In 2 Thess 3:11, the idlers are conducting themselves in a disorderly manner (*peripatountas . . . ataktōs*), but their conduct is viewed solely from the perspective of Christian intramural relations. And instead of working, they do not work at all (*mēden ergazomenous*), but are busybodies (*periergazomenous*).

Paul says *mēden ergazomenous alla periergazomenous* rather than the more natural *mēden ergazomenous mēde prassontes ta idia* ("nor minding their own affairs"), which would have reflected 1 Thess 4:11 more clearly. That he does so shows the significance of the second member of the antithesis. The emphatic position and sharpness of *periergazesthai* show the importance that this offensive behavior has for Paul.

Meddlesomeness was a common notion, as were the other terms he uses in 1 Thess 4:11–12, in the society at large in Paul's day. Philosophers were frequently accused of being busybodies (*periergoi* and its synonym *polypragmones*; cf. Plutarch, *On Being a Busybody* 516A; Lucian, *Icaromenippus* 20). They could claim that they had given up their professions in order to better serve humanity in their teaching (Dio Chrysostom, *Oration* 80.1), but the slur that they were busybodies meddling in other peoples' affairs was constantly hurled at them. The persistence of this criticism is evident from the defensiveness with which it was insisted that the genuine philosopher is not a busybody (e.g., Epictetus, *Discourses* 3.22.97; cf. 1.21; Dio Chrysostom, *Oration* 21.2–3). Thus Paul uses a well-known term of opprobrium that was applied by his contemporaries to people who thought of themselves as representing higher values.

3:12. *Such persons we command and exhort in the Lord Jesus Christ.* With an untranslated *de* Paul turns to address the idlers themselves, albeit in an indirect way. The pronoun *toioutois* ("Such persons") retains its qualitative aspects (cf. Rom 16:18; 1 Cor 16:16, 18) without expressing contempt. Its emphatic position in the sentence, followed immediately by *parangellomen* ("we command"), makes for sharpness, and it shifts the focus that has so far been on the larger congregation and the action it is to take. This is the second bracket to the *inclusio* that begins with v 6. There he used *adelphoi* to soften the tone; here he adds *parakaloumen* ("we exhort"). This may be understood as softening his command, but usually it is the verb accompanying *parakalein* that gives specificity (see NOTE on 1 Thess 2:3).

*that, by working quietly, they are to eat their own bread.* Paul couches his command in language that recalls 1 Thess 4:11 (*hēsychazein*) and implicitly demands that they follow his example and teaching (vv 6, 10). That Paul returns to quietness (*hēsychia*) is to be expected in view of the fact that it was often associated with descriptions of the busybody, for example, that he cannot endure *hēsychia* (Plutarch, *On Being a Busybody* 518E) or that the worthless man, untrained in *hēsychia*, is alert in meddlesome curiosity (Philo, *On the Life of Abraham* 20–21; cf. Chion, *Epistle* 16.5, *hēsychia* vs. *polypragmosynē*). It is, indeed, to be expected that he would bring up *hēsychia* here, for in 1 Thess 4:11, minding one's own affairs by engaging in manual labor explains what he means by living quietly (see NOTE on the explicative use of *kai*).

# COMMENT

In the COMMENT on 1 Thess 4:9–12 it was argued that the passage attains clarity when it is set in the context of conventional ancient social and political discussions, and one interpretation was set forward. In recent years, other sociological interpretations, especially as applied to 2 Thess 3:16–12, have been offered. Ronald Russell thought that the situation behind this passage was one in which poor Christians entered into a patron-client relationship with wealthy members of the church and, rejecting the idea of working, took advantage of brotherly love in the congregation to propagate their viewpoints among the members of the church.

Bruce Winter (1994) saw the issue not so much as one of poverty but of some members of the church reverting to patron-client relationships. He supposes that there were Christians wealthy enough to be potential patrons and even public benefactors. Paul's reason for working, in his view, was to break the patron-client relationship, requiring everyone to work. Idleness was clearly more of a problem when 2 Thess 3:6–12 was written than before, and a possible reason for this, it is suggested, was a famine that caused some Christians to seek patronage from their wealthy contributors. At the same time, Winter acknowledges that they did not want to work, but how that unwillingness is related to the need caused by the hypothetical famine he does not make clear.

A third sociological interpretation to illuminate the text, by Robert Jewett (1993), focuses on the space in which Christians met and the activities within that space. Jewett visualizes tenement churches, where Christians of modest means would pool their resources in potluck meals. The literary form of the command in 2 Thess 3:10 is that of casuistic law, which required community discipline for its application. It reflects settings in which communities exercise social coercion through deprivation of food. Jewett envisages a kind of Christian commune or cooperative, which is told by Paul to exercise discipline on those who do not want to work and so be able to contribute to the common meal.

Such sociological interpretations have been rejected, sometimes for methodological reasons but mostly because they do not do justice to traditional eschatological interpretations (Romaniuk; see COMMENT on 1 Thess 4:9–12). The latter argument is not strengthened by a failure to give due consideration to the observations (1) that Paul had already laid stress on work when he was with the Thessalonians, thus before any erroneous eschatological view could have developed that caused or justified idleness, and (2) that there is no connection made anywhere in the Thessalonian letters between eschatology and work or idleness.

The latter objection to the eschatological interpretation especially carries weight with respect to 2 Thess 3:6–12. The traditional interpretation is that because of the Thessalonians' expectation of the imminent coming of Christ, they gave up working and sponged off others. The difficulty with this is that there is no evidence in 1 Thessalonians that they held to such an expectation (see COMMENT on 4:13–18; 5:1–11). Furthermore, if there were a connection between eschatology and the unwillingness to work, 2 Thess 2:1–2 poses a problem, for the eschatological error mentioned there is not an imminent futuristic expectation, but an already realized eschatology.

M. J. J. Menken (1993) has made the most creative suggestion in addressing this objection. He suggests that the disorderliness of some Thessalonians consisted in their not living according to the command of God in Gen 3:17–19, which in Jewish tradition was God's imposition of the requirement to work in order to eat. They were unwilling to work because, thinking that the Day of the Lord had come, paradise was restored. The order in 2 Thess 3:10c, Menken thinks, may very well be a reflection of Gen 3:17–19, and may claim that God's command has not been annulled. Attractive as the hypothesis is, it does not overcome the objection that there is no eschatological reference in 3:6–12. Rather than a reference to 2:1–2, the reference is to Paul's work and its paraenetic function. We are thus pointed to 1 Thess 2:9 and 4:9–12 as the background to this passage.

There are literary connections between 2 Thess 3:6–12 and 1 Thess 2:9 (*kopos kai mochthos, nyktos kai hēmeras, pros to mē epibarēsai*); 4:11 (*hēsychia*); 5:14 (*ataktōs*), showing that the passage on congregatoinal discipline is the culmination of instruction on working that Paul had given, which began with his establishing of the church. Scholars who consider 2 Thessalonians pseudonymous judge this to be evidence that a later writer used 1 Thessalonians to make Paul a paradigm for social behavior in his own day (e.g., Trilling 1980: 144–47). It is more likely that, as Paul in other ways has emphasized continuity between his letters and his earlier instruction (e.g., 2:5, 15), he does the same thing when repeating the language he used before. In addition, continuing discussion of the subject guaranteed a certain degree of repetition.

The texts dealing with the subject were written at two different times and reflect three different occasions. The texts reveal a clear progression that culminates in 2 Thess 3:6–12.

1. First Thessalonians 2:9, although written to serve Paul's paraenetic purpose at the time he wrote, nevertheless identifies things that were central to his conception of work as part of his apostolic self-understanding: he decided out of his own free will to work, it was a demonstration of his love for his converts, allowing him not to burden them financially, it accompanied his preaching, and it provided his converts with an example to follow. The perspective is totally that of Paul and the church, with outsiders receiving no mention (see NOTES on 2:8–9).

2. In 1 Thess 4:9–12, those themes are reduced to two: love and self-sufficiency. Paul here probably responds to an inquiry from the Thessalonians about the practical limits of fraternal love in the congregation, whether love was to extend to material support of fellow members. In response, he addresses the entire congregation, not two groups, those who work and those who do not. His tone is calm and didactic. To a compliment on their love he adds the notion of quietness, which is then explained in social and political terms (minding their own affairs, manual labor as he had instructed them, self-sufficiency), and the opinion of outsiders. While there is no evidence that the failure to work constituted a major problem in the church, 1 Thess 5:14 shows that Paul considered it a real one, and his directive to admonish them shows how serious he considered it to be. That he describes it as disorderliness rather than idleness shows that for him willfulness lay at the heart of the problem.

3. The situation addressed in 2 Thess 3:6–12 shows a connection with what is reflected in 1 Thessalonians, but there are marked differences which reveal that matters had deteriorated. Paul now knows that some Thessalonians are not working, and he attributes it to their wish not to do so. It is impossible to know with certainty how they justified their decision. It is quite possible, perhaps even likely, that they presumed on the extraordinary love of the Christian community for their support (cf. 1:3; see COMMENT on 1 Thess 4:9–12). That would mean that the supporters in the congregation were contributing out of love to a situation that Paul addresses with striking sharpness. Whatever the motivation of the idle members may have been, Paul reduces it to willfulness and describes their behavior as disorderliness that should not be tolerated.

It is important to note that Paul's sharp comments are addressed almost entirely to the church as a whole. Only v 12 is directed to the shirkers, and even then he speaks to them indirectly. There is no way of knowing how many idlers there were or what proportion of the entire church they constituted. Paul's attention, in any case, is devoted to the congregation and the action they are to take. They were allowing an intolerable situation to exist, and Paul writes to move them to take an unpleasant action (cf. 1 Cor 5 for a similar situation). This is his sole purpose in writing to those who are to withdraw.

Some of the themes that were present in his earlier discussions of work are used, but in a different, nonparaenetic way. He does not mention love or proclamation of the gospel, and the focus is entirely on what is taking place within the congregation. His own example of self-sufficiency and his teaching on the subject are used, not paraenetically, but to justify withdrawing from the idlers. Free will comes up, but as a perverse decision *not* to work. The closest that he comes to his earlier paraenetic speech is, ironically, in his command to the disorderly to work in quietness to earn their own bread (v 12).

The reason for Paul's sharpness is to be found in the nature of the Thessalonian church. He ended 1 Thessalonians with an extended series of directions on how the church was to be edified, through caring for each other (5:11–22). Based on respect and love for those who would do the work of the gospel in their midst (*en hymin*, vv 12–13), members of the congregation were to engage in reciprocal individual instruction and exhortation (v 11; see NOTE). This very personal psychagogy that Paul details in 5:11–22 could easily cause tensions that would tear the fabric of the community, and he warned against hostility (v 13) and retaliation (v 15). In 2 Thess 3:11, Paul ends this section of instruction to the church with another kind of conduct *en hymin* ("among you") that would be destructive of relations within the church, namely meddlesomeness.

Paul's interest in this section is not primarily in the economic policy of the church. It is, rather, in mutual responsibility within the church, which some Thessalonians were threatening by being disorderly and meddlesome. His own behavior was exemplary for its orderliness and self-giving concern for others, and constituted the tradition by which they were to conduct themselves.

# B. CONGREGATIONAL ADMONITION, 3:13–15

◆

The limits of this conclusion to the body of the letter are clearly marked by the vocative *adelphoi* ("brethren") in v 13, with which each section of the letter begins (1:3; 2:1, 13, 15; 3:1, 6, 13), and *autos de ho kyrios tēs eirēnēs* ("the Lord of peace himself") in v 16, which is the beginning of the letter closing (Weima, 187–91). The section contains four imperatives that are not general paraenesis without any concrete reference (Trilling 1972: 98–99; 1980: 153–54), but are

Paul's concluding commands on how the congregation should conduct itself with respect to the situation created by the disorderly.

## TRANSLATION

3 ¹³But as for you, brethren, do not become weary of doing good. ¹⁴But if anyone disobeys what we have communicated through this letter, that person you must mark so as not to associate with him, in order that he might be put to shame; ¹⁵nevertheless, do not regard him as an enemy, but admonish him as a brother.

## NOTES

3:13. *But as for you, brethren, do not become weary of doing good.* With the emphatic *hymeis de* ("But as for you") Paul returns to addressing the entire community. With the first of four imperatives he warns that his instruction in vv 6–12 does not mean that they are to refrain from doing good. Paul had concluded his instructions on pastoral care in 1 Thess 5:11–15 with a command to continue to do good, which in that context probably referred to the good achieved through such care (see NOTE). The context here suggests that the reference is to the material support the church had given to their fellow members in need rather than to doing good in general (P. Müller, 166) or to doing what is right (*poiein* with *kalon* or *kalos*; Rom 7:21; 1 Cor 7:37–38; 2 Cor 13:7).

Paul is rather warning against overinterpretation of his directions. The phrase *mē egkakēsēte kalopoiountes* is similar to Gal 6:9 (cf. 10), where it appears at the end of advice on the support of teachers. A prohibition expressed with the aorist subjunctive (*mē egkakēsēte*) normally forbids an action not yet begun, in this case, "do not begin to be weary of doing good." Paul had been chagrined that the church did not follow his instructions that all should earn their own living, but he does not want them now to stop doing good altogether.

3:14. *But if anyone disobeys what we have communicated through this letter.* Paul qualifies what he has just said, perhaps because he anticipates that, just as some individuals in the church had not obeyed his earlier instruction, so they might not heed what he has said in this letter (*tō logō hēmōn dia tēs epistolēs*). There is no reason to think that the reference is to the entire letter, including the doctrinal teaching in 2:12 (thus Trilling 1980: 154–55; P. Müller, 166; Légasse, 436–37). Disobedience is one possible response to Paul's command in this chapter, particularly v 12; it is of a piece with being disorderly and unwilling to work.

*that person you must mark, so as not to associate with him.* Paul continues to think in terms of individuals rather than a group and now gives more precision to what is meant by withdrawal (v 6). Presumably the marking is to be done when the congregation is gathered (cf. Matt 18:17–18; 1 Cor 5:4, 12; 2 Cor 2:5–11), but it is not clear how the marking is to take place. Some older commentators took *tēs epistolēs* with *sēmeiousthe* ("mark") and thought that Paul wanted the Thessalonians to write him a letter about the individual(s) from whom they withdrew, thus marking those disciplined by the congregation (see Eadie, 317–18;

Lünemann, 629–30, for cogent arguments against taking "letter" with "mark"). The definite article poses the greatest difficulty for such an understanding, for it could hardly refer to a letter yet to be written; furthermore, it normally refers to the letter at hand, as it does in 1 Thess 5:27 (cf. Rom 16:22; Col 4:16).

The Textus Receptus sought to alleviate the syntactical abruptness of *sēmei-ousthe mē synanamignysthai* ("mark so as not to associate closely with," read by ℵ A B D¹ Ψ 33) by adding *kai* and changing the infinitive to an imperative (*synanamignysthe*), thus balancing the two imperatives ("mark and do not associate with"). There is little difference in meaning, except that the close connection between the two verbs in the preferred reading is loosened. The infinitive is not imperatival (so Frame, 308–9, citing Rom 12:15; Phil 3:16), but final, stating the purpose for the marking. The verb *synanamignysthai* is rare and occurs in the LXX only in Hos 7:8 and Ezek 20:18. The only other occurrences in the NT are in 1 Cor 5:9, 11, where an association close enough to eat together is prohibited.

*in order that he might be put to shame.* The purpose of withdrawal is to shame the idle person. The verb (*entrapē* ["might be ashamed"]) is in the aorist passive, with the congregation being the unexpressed subject. Shame is intended by the congregation and is not a by-product of its withdrawal (cf. Titus 2:8; for the active with the same sense, see 1 Cor 4:14; for *entropē*, the noun, see 1 Cor 6:5; 15:34). Withdrawal is designed to have both social and emotional effects which, according to other Pauline texts, will ultimately have a positive outcome (cf. 1 Cor 5:4–8). Such a congregational action is a punishment that produces grief (cf. 2 Cor 2:6–7), which, if it is godly, in turn produces repentance that leads to salvation (2 Cor 7:10). Here, however, Paul is silent on such an outcome.

*3:15. nevertheless, do not regard him as an enemy, but admonish him as a brother.* Paul does not want the congregation to give up on the disobedient member. The *kai* ("nevertheless") adds something that is surprising or unexpected ("and yet," "in spite of that"; BAGD, s.v. *kai* I.1.g). It is as a brother that the individual errs and as a brother that he continues to be admonished. Withdrawal does not mean avoidance; a relationship is maintained in which the congregation, in addition to having shamed the idler, continues (the present tense of *noutheteite* ["admonish"]) to admonish him (contrast Titus 3:10, where two admonitions are allowed before avoiding a divisive person). Admonition was to be finely calibrated, according to the ancient psychagogists, if it was to benefit the person admonished. It is an appropriate accompaniment to congregational withdrawal, for admonition, too, engenders repentance, shame, and grief (Plutarch, *On Moral Virtue* 452CD). As a type of exhortation directed to the will, it was a particularly appropriate response to the disorderly, willful persons in the congregation (see NOTES and COMMENT on 1 Thess 5:12, 14).

## COMMENT

Paul becomes more specific about how the church is to address the problem at hand. His command to withdraw is harsh (v 14), but it is flanked by cautions that his commands not be overinterpreted: his readers are not to understand him to be prohibiting help to persons in need (v 13), and they are not to be hostile to the persons disciplined (v 15).

Much remains unclear about the procedures that Paul wanted followed. It is unlikely that when he was with them an occasion calling for such action arose, so that the Thessalonians would be familiar with the procedure, nor is there any indication that he had instructed them in the subject of church discipline. It is most likely that he expected the person who carried this letter to its recipients to supply the details or that he left matters of procedure to the church, so long as his commands were carried out. It is noteworthy, nevertheless, that the Corinthians, who misunderstood Paul on other matters (see, e.g., 2 Cor 1:13), also misunderstood what he meant by not associating with erring members (1 Cor 5:9–11).

We are left to speculate about how someone was "marked" for discipline; indeed, it is quite possible that Paul had no particular procedure in mind. The weight of evidence suggests that, however it was done, it was a congregational action (1 Cor 5:4; Matt 18:19–20; cf. Deut 19:15–21; 1QS 5:24–6:1).

Withdrawing from an individual at the very least meant that he would not be admitted to the church's fellowship meals. This is a reasonable inference one may draw from v 10 (see 1 Cor 5:11; 1QS 8:16–18). If the church met in the house of someone like Jason (see pages 60, 63–64; Malherbe 1987: 12–17), entrance could easily be controlled (cf. 2 John 10; for a power play exercised in this regard, cf. 3 John 9–10, on which see Malherbe 1983b: 92–112). Nonbelievers could be present when the church met for worship (1 Cor 14:24), but Paul held Christians to a higher standard in order for them to enjoy the fellowship of the church (1 Cor 5:11). Paul's argument in 1 Thess 4:11–12 assumes that outsiders would have a fair amount of knowledge about the Christian community, perhaps because some of them were present in the church's assemblies (see 1 Thess 3:12; 5:12, 15 and NOTES), and 1 Corinthians (7:12–16; 10:27–28) reflects a situation in which Christians continued social relations with the larger society. The social boundaries being so permeable, it is not surprising that the Corinthians had difficulty in understanding how to withdraw from Christians and at the same time not withdraw from unbelievers.

This distinction would have made Paul's injunction to withdraw from or deny close association to a member of the fictive Christian family especially invidious and harsh. His command assumes that great value was attached to membership in this family (see NOTE on 1 Thess 1:4), so harsher treatment of erring Christians than of unbelievers would have been particularly painful. Paul knows this, and makes it explicit: withdrawal by the congregation is designed to cause shame. In addition to the emotional and social difficulties experienced by the recent converts (see COMMENT on 2 Thess 1:4), those withdrawn from are now to experience the admonition of their fellow converts.

This admonition was continuous and probably, as suggested by John Chrysostom, who was familiar with psychagogical practices, given in private (Homilies on 1 Thessalonians 5 [PG 62:495]). That is what friends did when they corrected their friends one on one (Plato, Apology of Socrates 26A; Dio Chrysostom, Oration 77/78.38; Plutarch, How to Tell a Flatterer from a Friend 70E–71A [see

NOTES on 1 Thess 2:11; 5:11]). Paul has fellow Christians rather than friends in mind, but he uses the same psychagogical methods friends used. That he calls the offending Christian a "brother" rather than "disorderly" here, the only place in the letter where "brother" is not used in the vocative, shows that he is emphasizing the continuing relationship within which admonition is to take place.

Despite Paul's two cautions in vv 13 and 15, his command is harsh. Here he does not mention salvation as a goal of the church's discipline, as he does in 1 Cor 5:5, nor is restoration of the erring, either to their former condition (Gal 6:1) or to the fellowship of the congregation (2 Cor 2:6–11), in prospect. Paul is writing to a congregation that has been too permissive, neglecting his example and teaching on work, with the result that there were individuals who were meddlesome in their midst. He wants to move the congregation to taking disciplinary action and admonishing their brethren, as he in fact is admonishing them.

# V. CONCLUSION, 3:16–18

◆

Paul concludes the letter with a prayer (v 16), a greeting (v 17), and a benediction (v 18). Commentators differ on whether the background of the conclusion is liturgical (Jewett 1969; M. Müller) or epistolographic (Weima 1996: 187) practice. They also differ on whether, form critically, the prayer in v 16 is the conclusion of the body of the letter (Bruce 1982: 211–13; Légasse, 438–39) or the beginning of the letter closing (Best 1972: 345–46; Weima 1996: 187). As to background, the two possibilities are not mutually exclusive, and as to epistolary form, the latter view has slightly more evidence in its favor (see the introductory comments to 1 Thess 5:23–28).

## A. PRAYER FOR PEACE, 3:16

◆

### TRANSLATION

3 ¹⁶ May the Lord of peace himself give you peace continually in every way. The Lord be with you all.

### NOTE AND COMMENT

See NOTE on 1 Thess 5:23, where, however, "God of peace," the more usual designation, is used. Most commentators think that "Lord" refers to Jesus, which is possible but not necessary (see NOTE on 3:3). The prayer wish for peace opens the conclusion of the letter as it had been a part of the opening of the letter (1:2). The form here is reminiscent of the priestly blessing in Num 6:26 LXX, "May the Lord . . . give you peace." The background of Paul's phrase is liturgical, but he adapts it to his own epistolary purpose. Paul visualizes the context, the congregation assembled for worship, in which the letter will be read and crafts the conclusion rhetorically to fit that context. His predilection for the alliterative use of labials (e.g., 2 Cor 1:3–7; 9:8) is especially evident in his prayers (see 1 Thess 1:2 and NOTE), as it is here with its alliterative play on various forms of *pās* (*dia pantos* ["continually"]; *panti tropō* ["in every way"], *pantōn* ["all"]). "The Lord be with you all" is likewise liturgical (see Rom 15:33; Phil 4:9, where "the God of peace" is the subject; cf. Judg 6:12; Ruth 2:4).

Because of the liturgical quality of this verse and because it appears in the letter closing, most commentators do not think that it has any relation to what precedes (cf. Rom 15:33; 16:20; 2 Cor 13:11; Phil 4:7, 9; 1 Thess 5:23–24, where God's peace is the subject and where the prayer is generally thought to be unrelated to the body of the letter). A number of factors, however, suggest that here there is a connection between the prayer and what precedes. First, Paul strengthens his usual closing prayer by asking that the Lord of peace himself give them peace continually in every way. This emphasis makes sense in light of Paul's caution in v 15 that the congregation not act with hostility towards the disorderly. Then, too, it has been observed that admonition, even when given with good intentions, could provoke a hostile reaction (see NOTE on 1 Thess 5:13, where "be at peace among yourselves" also comes after the command to admonish (cf. NOTE on 5:15).

This does not mean that there was already conflict among the Thessalonians (so Weima 1996: 189); on the contrary, Paul has just spurred them to take action that they had not taken. Rather than conflict, extraordinary love characterized relationships within the church. Paul is anticipating strained relations and prays that peace may prevail. That the addition to the peace wish has a general reference is due to its liturgical character, which in no way lessens its relevance to what precedes.

# B. GREETING, 3:17

◆

## TRANSLATION

3 17The greeting with my own hand—of Paul, which is a sign in every letter, this is the way I write.

## NOTE AND COMMENT

The same salutation ("The greeting with my own hand—of Paul") occurs in 1 Cor 16:21 and Col 4:18. This is one of the ways Paul signed his letters (see Gal 6:11; Phlm 19 for alternative ways). A stenographer would have written the letter at his dictation up to this point (cf. Rom 16:22); now Paul takes the pen to write the last few lines as a kind of signature. We may assume that he did so even when he did not draw attention to the fact. What is unusual is that here, in addition to drawing attention to his signature, he insists that it is an identifying sign in every letter that he wrote.

Paul's reason for doing this is to be found in 2:2, his suspicion that a letter containing doctrinal error was circulating under his name (see COMMENT there). His concern would have had further grounds if, as is probable, his original letter to the Thessalonians had remained with the first recipients while a copy not bearing his signature was circulated among other Christians in the area (see COMMENT on 1 Thess 5:27; page 351).

# C. BENEDICTION, 3:18

◆

## TRANSLATION

3 ¹⁸The grace of our Lord Jesus Christ be with you all.

## NOTE AND COMMENT

The benediction is identical to 1 Thess 5:28 (see NOTE), with the exception that "all" is added. Since no two benedictions in Paul's letters are exactly the same, not much weight should be attached to this difference (see Rom 16:29; 1 Cor 16:23; 2 Cor 13:13; Gal 6:18; Phil 4:23; cf. Eph 6:24; Col 4:18). The addition may have been suggested by *meta pantōn hymōn* ("with you all") in v 16. It may also have in view other than the primary recipients of the letter (see page 353).

# INDEX OF COMMENTATORS AND MODERN AUTHORS

◆

# INDEX OF BIBLICAL AND OTHER ANCIENT REFERENCES

◆

| | |
|---|---|
| 1:8 | 185 |
| 1:10-12 | 302 |
| 1:11 | 396 |
| 1:12, 15 | 173 |
| 1:13-22 | 223 |
| 1:13 | 295, 297, 305 |
| 1:14-16 | 120, 231 |
| 1:15 | 238 |
| 1:18 | 260 |
| 1:20 | 288 |
| 1:21-22 | 109 |
| 1:22 | 243, 256 |
| 1:26 | 167 |
| 2:2 | 146, 384 |
| 2:8 | 298 |
| 2:9 | 293 |
| 2:11 | 225 |
| 2:12, 15 | 260 |
| 2:12 | 259, 412 |
| 2:14 | 400 |
| 2:20 | 387 |
| 2:21 | 114 |
| 2:23 | 394 |
| 3:1-6 | 259 |
| 3:1, 16 | 260 |
| 3:7 | 227, 229 |
| 3:8-12 | 308 |
| 3:8 | 243 |
| 3:9, 15-16 | 173 |
| 3:9 | 321 |
| 3:20 | 320 |
| 4:1-2 | 225 |
| 4:7 | 295, 305, 417 |
| 4:8-9 | 256 |
| 4:12 | 198, 400 |
| 4:13 | 272, 413 |
| 4:14-16 | 413 |
| 4:16 | 412 |
| 4:17-19 | 395, 408 |
| 5:1 | 396 |
| 5:3 | 145 |
| 5:4 | 185 |
| 5:7 | 202 |
| 5:8-9 | 297 |
| 5:8 | 295, 297, 305 |
| 5:9-11 | 192 |
| 5:9 | 383 |
| 5:10-11 | 191 |
| 5:10 | 205 |
| 5:12 | 87, 98, 194 |
| 5:14 | 341 |
| 5:16 | 173 |

**2 Peter**

| | |
|---|---|
| 1:1, 11 | 412 |
| 1:6 | 387 |
| 1:7 | 243 |
| 1:11 | 118 |
| 1:16 | 272 |

| | |
|---|---|
| 2:1-2 | 431 |
| 2:1 | 332 |
| 2:3, 14 | 142 |
| 2:9 | 291, 402 |
| 2:18 | 139, 140 |
| 2:21 | 441 |
| 3:3 | 431 |
| 3:4 | 272 |
| 3:7, 10 | 291 |
| 3:7 | 419 |
| 3:8-9 | 433 |
| 3:9, 15 | 320 |
| 3:10 | 290 |
| 3:12 | 272 |
| 3:15-16 | 345 |
| 3:16 | 354 |
| 3:17 | 139, 140 |

**1 John**

| | |
|---|---|
| 1:5 | 293 |
| 2:13-14 | 446 |
| 2:13 | 436 |
| 2:18-22 | 290 |
| 2:18, 22 | 431 |
| 2:18 | 431 |
| 2:28 | 272 |
| 3:2 | 403 |
| 3:4 | 419 |
| 3:18 | 111 |
| 4:1-3 | 333, 416 |
| 4:1 | 332 |
| 4:2-3 | 333 |
| 4:3 | 423, 431 |
| 4:17 | 291 |
| 5:19 | 446 |
| 5:20-21 | 121 |

**2 John**

| | |
|---|---|
| 7 | 431 |
| 10 | 460 |

**3 John**

| | |
|---|---|
| 1 | 67 |
| 2 | 106 |
| 3 | 350 |
| 8 | 199 |
| 9-10 | 460 |

**Jude**

| | |
|---|---|
| 1 | 110 |
| 3 | 441 |
| 7 | 402 |
| 9 | 274 |
| 18 | 431 |

**Revelation**

| | |
|---|---|
| 1:3 | 342, 417 |
| 1:9 | 115 |
| 1:10 | 274 |

| | |
|---|---|
| 1:13-16 | 400 |
| 2:2-3, 19 | 387 |
| 2:2 | 109 |
| 2:20 | 417 |
| 3:3 | 290 |
| 3:4, 20-21 | 277 |
| 3:4 | 121, 396 |
| 3:10 | 338 |
| 4:1 | 274 |
| 5:1 | 274 |
| 6:10 | 400 |
| 6:15-17 | 403 |
| 6:17 | 291 |
| 7:2 | 274 |
| 7:14 | 394 |
| 8-9 | 274 |
| 8:12 | 293 |
| 9:13-15 | 433 |
| 9:20-21 | 427 |
| 9:20 | 265 |
| 10:22 | 120 |
| 11:1ff | 372 |
| 12:5 | 275 |
| 12:9 | 417 |
| 12:14 | 403 |
| 13:1 | 433 |
| 13:2 | 425 |
| 13:3 | 431 |
| 13:10 | 387 |
| 13:11-18 | 434 |
| 14:4 | 436, 437 |
| 14:10-11 | 402 |
| 14:12 | 387 |
| 14:13 | 266, 275 |
| 15:2 | 275 |
| 15:4 | 411 |
| 16:5, 7 | 394 |
| 16:5 | 290 |
| 16:9-11 | 427 |
| 16:9, 11 | 427 |
| 16:14 | 291 |
| 16:15 | 295 |
| 18:5-8, 12-17 | 427 |
| 18:11 | 264 |
| 19 | 274 |
| 19:2, 11 | 394 |
| 19:2 | 400 |
| 19:3 | 402 |
| 19:11-21 | 434 |
| 20:1-3, 7-10 | 433 |
| 20:3, 8, 10 | 417 |
| 20:4-5 | 275 |
| 20:11-15 | 278 |
| 20:11 | 403 |
| 21:3 | 212 |
| 21:8 | 402 |
| 22:4 | 403 |
| 22:10 | 417 |

# INDEX OF MAJOR SUBJECTS

◆

emphasis achieved
  by using "all" 334
  through antitheses 91, 136, 140, 145, 147, 155, 159, 167, 451
  with articles 231, 245
  through chiasmus 338
  by coinage of a word 245
  through comparisons 91
  by collocation of verbs 212
  through compounds 204, 384, 385, 404
  with confident assertions 339, 400, 446
  with unusual construction 267
  with denials 293
  through elaboration 91
  by emphatic constructions 213
  through emphatic formulations 91
  with epistolary clichés 262
  by explicit statement 143
  with litotes 58
  by mentioning his own name 91, 184, 195
  with overweighted clauses 385
  with phrases expressing obligation 383
  by quoting own words 194
  by using an oxymoron 247
  with paraenetic phrases 157, 194, 218,
  with parrallelism 385
  with particles 91, 141, 183, 185, 194, 245, 272, 396, 446
  with pathos 183
  with powerful assertions 152
  by using pronouns 91, 115, 167, 182, 202, 212, 244, 273, 290, 386, 420, 435, 441, 450, 451
  through repetition 91, 117
  with rhetorical questions 91
  by lapsing into singular 342
  through syntactical position 58, 107, 108, 109, 114, 116, 121, 135, 149, 165, 169, 171, 186, 190, 193, 194, 212, 224, 275, 386, 391, 405, 410, 411, 417, 422, 435, 450, 451, 453, 454
  *see also* page 204
emphasis by Paul on
  appropriateness of thanksgiving 389
  Christian conduct 56
  continuity between his instruction and letters 455-56
  on endurance 387, 391
  epistolary inscription in his own hand 355, 362
  ethical dimension of God's call 233-34, (cf. 241)
  God 123, 132, 180, 197, 299
  God's action 273
  God's judgment 407
  God's justice 406
  God's sanctifying 338, 339
  God's vengeance 233
  God's word 244
  hardships as inevitable 198, 199

Thessalonians' imitation of himself 130
love as basis for church's life 257
modifying conventional epistolary form 388
nearness of the end 289
on need for thanksgiving 330
his own manual labor 452
the powerful coming of the Lord 403
his readers' knowledge 235
reciprocal edification 311
the unexpected coming of the Day 428
unique relationship 89
endurance
  informed by hope 108-9
Epicureans 215, 243-45, 247, 249, 253, 257-59, 281, 282, 283, 292, 304, 305-6, 307, 319, 323, 324, 327, 335
  *see also* anti-Epicurean
epideictic 96
epistolary clichés and conventions 75-76
  absence in body, presence in spirit 90
  "but concerning" 75
  desire to see reader's needs fulfilled 90
  joy upon receiving a letter 75, 90
  no need to write 90
  prayer to see one's reader 90
  prescript 91, 148
  supplying needs of reader 76
  thanksgiving period 75, 91, 134-35, 164-65, 172
  yearning to see readers 76, 90, 96, 146, 182
  *see also* thanksgiving as epistolary convention
epistolary or literary plural
  *see* authorial plural
epistolography
  epistolary theory 95, 96, 145
  Paul's freedom towards contemporary 90-91, 95, 97
  *see also* conventions, epistolary clichés and letters
error
  as ignoble motive to preach 140-41
eschatological exhortation 260-308, 359, 368, 381-434
eschatological thinking
  blamelessness in 150, 213
  the church in 261, 307-8
  deliverance in 122, 132
  supposed differences between 2 Thess and Paul's 368-69
  error in 350, 413-34, 439, 452, 455
  false prophets' 288-92
  gathering of believers in 261-86
  God as witness in 163
  holiness in 213, 215, 238
  nature of hope in 107, 281-83
  idleness combined with 253-54, 455
  instruction of Paul's converts in 333, 363, 450
  about Jesus 121
  judgment in 393-408
  metaphors in Paul's 185, 288-307

the moral life in 293-307
Paul's mission informed by 170, 177
distinguishes Paul from philosophers 80
problems in Thessalonians 283-85
proleptic realization in Paul's 177
reward in Paul's 188, 195-96
Satan in 390, 419, 424-27, 431-34, 446
trials, tribulations, or woes in 108, 115, 127-
28, 193, 382-92
divine wrath in 126, 132, 171, 176
*see also* apocalyptic theology, apocalyptic
traditions, Day of the Lord, glory,
Parousia, proleptic, tribulations
example (personal)
of Christ 319, 447
of churches 167
described antithetically 155
of leaders 66
normative apostolic 370
in paraenesis 82-84, 126, 146, 155, 161, 207,
208, 248, 286
of Paul 56, 65, 80-81, 126, 129, 131, 134,
157, 161, 175, 208, 215, 249, 278, 307,
316, 323, 363, 391, 449-54, 456-57, 461
of the Thessalonians 68, 78, 115-17, 130
exhortation (*paraklēsis*)
of Paul characterized 142-64
variegated character of 139-40
*see also* lexicon of exhortation

faith, hope, and love 108-9
father
in apocalyptic consolation 408
God as 99, 101-2, 107, 212-14, 330, 379-80,
441-42
in paraenesis 83, 140, 155, 221
Paul as 86, 92, 98, 101, 151-52, 160, 163,
164, 187, 199, 221, 315, 366
in psychagogy 163, 366
*see also* kinship language
fictive kinship
admonition and discipline in 459-60
as basis for giving advice 83
"brotherly love" used only of 243
developed by Paul 110, 191
the holy kiss in 341
*see also* brothers, kinship language
First Thessalonians
adapted to Thessalonian needs 85
authenticity of 13
form and function of 78-81
integrity of 79
occasion and date of 72-75
as a pastoral letter 78, 85-86
purpose of 77-78, 132
as response to Timothy's report and a letter
75-77
style and language of 82-92
written out of Paul's emotional need 77,
179-210

*see also* language and style
flattery 143
frankness (*parrēsia*) 137, 138, 145, 147, 155
friends, friendship 63, 65, 76, 80, 84, 88, 90,
95-96, 101, 105, 107, 137, 142, 148, 155,
158, 181, 183, 186, 190, 196-97, 201, 202,
203, 215, 220, 222, 242-43, 245, 248-49,
251-52, 256-59, 283, 304, 306-7, 325, 339,
343, 361, 460-61
*see also* letter types (friendly)

Gallio inscription 72-73
Gentiles
calling of 436
conversion of in Thessalonica 56-61, 66, 119
evangelization of hindered by Jews 171,
176-78
Gentiles and Jews in church in Thessalonica
344, 352, 401
as not having hope 265
judgment of Gentiles and Jews alike 128,
171, 230-31, 407
as not knowing God 230, 401
preaching to 120-22, 170, 285
gentleness
in speech and demeanor 145-50
glory
attaining the Lord's 370, 438
Christ's 153, 278, 404-7
the Thessalonians as Paul's crown of 186-88,
285, 404
eschatological 392, 399
judgment as exclusion from God's 403-4
God's 141, 143, 150, 152, 327, 369, 395,
404, 412-13
the Lord coming in 290, 402-3
a present factor in Christian life 412-13
seeking (reputation) 141, 143-45, 159-60,
246
Son of Man coming in 276
God
as calling 107, 109-10, 124, 125, 134, 143,
150, 152, 153, 156, 165-67, 175, 177, 215,
224, 233-34, 238, 327, 339-40, 343, 390,
395, 403, 404, 406, 410, 413, 436-38, 442-
43
as creator 99-100, 107
as electing (choosing) 111-12, 153
as father of the church 99-100, 213-14
as father of proselytes 128
frequently referred to 106, 108, 123, 124,
133-34
Jesus as 412
Jesus as exercizing prerogatives of 185-86,
212, 214, 233, 399, 407, 412
living and true 122-23
loving 110, 442
Paul's reliance on 138
pleasing or displeasing 142, 170, 175-76,
220

by the Lord Jesus 185-86, 214, 233, 399, 407
paraenetic force of the theme of 286, 402
in Paul's mission instructions 233, 284, 285, 299, 390
of persecutors 177, 387, 397-98, 406
rendered through Christ 266
the suddenness of eschatological 292
of unbelievers 427, 430
in 1 and 2 Thessalonians 368-69
*see also* proleptic, wrath of God

kingdom
called into God's 153-54
kinship language
used to foster close relations 159-60
used to make feel secure 85
used by non-Christians 110
strong concentration of in 1 Thess 102, 125, 160, 182, 191, 198, 215, 243, 341, 380
*see also* brothers, fictive kinship

language and style 89-92
alliteration 91, 106-7, 462
apocalyptic starkness 178, 179
asyndeton 91, 149, 231, 328, 366
diatribe 239, 289, 291, 328, 330
hyperbole 116, 118, 130, 179, 202, 206, 245, 350, 387, 391
hendiadys 153, 288, 292, 296, 387, 444, 450
*inclusio* 87, 88, 89, 92, 104, 139, 142, 151, 167, 180, 189, 192, 196, 200, 217, 219, 224-25, 228, 234, 237, 261, 298, 300, 330, 337, 343, 383, 385, 448, 454
irony 173, 258, 259, 276, 290, 297-307, 355-405, 457
litotes 58
Paul's liveliness of style 91
parallelism 171, 275, 332, 385, 389, 392, 393, 401, 403-5, 409-10, 424-25
variety 113, 139, 150, 294, 309, 328, 411
vituperation 179
*see also* antithesis, emotive language, emphasis, images (literary), paraenesis, pathos, pronouns
Lawless One 272, 369, 398, 414, 419, 424-27, 433-34
*see also* Man of Lawlessness, Son of Perdition
letter types:
admonition 361
advice 361
command 361
consolation 279, 359
friendly 96, 123, 180-83, 184, 201
mixed 361
paraenetic 83, 84-86
letters
authority in 101
circulation of 103, 344-45, 352-53, 355-56, 373-74, 463

copying of 103, 342, 345-46, 355, 364, 374, 430, 440, 463
Jewish influence on Paul's 100
as means of communication 95-96, 416
oral element in 96
paraenesis in 83-84
prescripts of 90, 97, 106, 117, 340
salutations in 97, 99-101, 123, 339, 463
setting in which Thessalonian letters read 89, 90, 91, 96, 100-1, 103, 342-43, 354-55, 380
as surrogates 95
and worship 90, 96, 100, 106, 123, 211-12, 213, 327-28, 337, 339-42, 352, 365, 380, 382, 393, 460-62
*see also* epistolary clichés and conventions, epistolography, letter types, thanksgiving as epistolary convention
lexicon of exhortation 139, 151-52, 218-19
*see also* exhortation
love
of God 110, 436, 447
for Paul 200-1, 206-7
of Paul for Thessalonians 147-48
within the Christian community 108-9, 212-13, 215, 297, 315, 384-85, 391
*see also* brotherly love

Maccedonia
Christians associated with 66-68
churches in 103, 130
contributions of churches in 173
Silas and Timothy's arrival in Corinth from 60, 71-72, 89, 102, 245, 350
spread of the gospel in 68, 116-18, 130
Paul in 68-71, 73
Paul's references to 68
poverty of 65, 173
Thessalonians' evangelizing in 62
Thessalonians' love for all 244-45, 391
Thessalonica as metropolis of 14
prominent women in 63
Man of Lawlessness 418-22, 424, 431-43
*see also* Lawless One, Son of Perdition
manual labor
discipline of those who cease 450-59
and disorderliness 358
and love connected 145-50, 161, 162, 242, 252, 255
low esteem of 64, 148, 160-61, 256
of Paul 60, 63, 65, 92, 144
of Paul as an act of free will 256-57, 317
of Paul and his apostolic self-understanding 60-61, 134, 141, 162
of Paul not to burden converts 161
of Paul as extended 163
of Paul as paradigmatic 149, 161, 242, 249, 256, 451
of Paul as proof of his love 148, 162, 242, 258

relationships within the church 81, 91, 215, 228-29, 232, 237, 241-61, 307-36, 443-61
*see also* kinship language
remembrance, reminders, memory
in epistolary formula 107, 221-22
in paraenesis 82-83, 84, 123, 155, 199, 201, 207, 244, 286
Thessalonians' of Paul 75, 77-78, 104, 114, 148, 161, 197, 198, 201, 207-8, 219, 374, 421
reminders by Paul 55, 56, 84, 85, 89, 90, 92, 101, 103, 104, 113, 118, 124, 126, 127, 130, 131, 132, 133, 137, 148, 149, 152, 156, 157, 160, 161, 163, 170, 179, 208, 215, 221, 222, 234, 237, 241, 244, 251, 255, 256, 287, 305, 312, 326, 340, 343, 364, 370, 380, 384, 392, 415, 421, 432, 437, 438, 444, 448, 450
*see also* remembrance, memory
restraining force 414, 422-24, 432
restraining one 414, 422-24, 432-33
resurrection
of Christians 153, 262-63, 266, 275, 277, 280-85, 306, 399, 407, 428
of Jesus 58, 117, 121-22, 129, 132, 261, 265-66, 270, 299-300, 428
rhetoric
ancient systems of 359
church 96
devices and techniques of 111, 136, 145, 149, 172, 184, 231, 328, 339, 462
epideictic 96
epistolary theory in handbooks on 96, 147
handbooks on 135
instruction in 278, 282
in oral reading of letters 107
rhetorical overstatement 65, 68
passion of 234, 304, 339
Paul not dependent on 113
elements of in Paul's letters 96
to philosophers 96
rhetorical questions 91, 184, 185, 203, 204, 236
of vituperation and hyperbole 79
*see* paralipsis

saints
as angels 214, 404
as Christians 215, 234, 383, 386, 404, 410-11
*see also* sanctification
sanctification (holiness)
as setting Christians apart 237, 239
constantly comes to realization 216
viewed corporately 239
viewed eschatologically 213, 215, 238, 285, 337-39
God the main actor in 238
as God's will 224-25
in the moral life 92, 217, 224-41

a punctiliar event 216
saints by virtue of 404
a life of required to serve God 120, 340
of the Spirit 153, 213, 215, 228, 330, 437
*see also* saints
Satan 179, 180, 181, 184, 188, 189, 195
(Tempter), 196, 197, 297, 390, 419, 424-27, 431-32, 433-34, 446
Secundus 67
self-description
antithesis in 84
eschatological perspective in 143
paraenetic function of Paul's 153-63
of Paul 84, 104-5
of Paul's ministry in Thessalonica 149
philophronetic purpose of 104-5
to establish trustworthiness 80
self-sufficiency 161, 243, 252, 253, 257-58, 391, 451, 457
Seneca
on adaptation of paraenesis 81, 82
as using authorial plural 88-89
as writer of paraenetic letters 83-84
Silas
background of 57-58
as co-author 87-88, 98, 148
movements of after Thessalonica 70-71
also named Silvanus 97-98
with Paul in Thessalonica 57
sleep
as metaphor for death 280-81
in moral discourse 295-97, 305
*see also* images (literary)
sober life 305-6
social aspects 56, 63-66, 102, 125, 128, 132, 152, 161, 170, 172-73, 193, 215, 218, 240-60, 282-83, 292, 308, 317, 325, 342, 344-45, 353, 363, 388, 391, 448-61
Son of Perdition 419, 426
*see also* Lawless One, Man of Lawlessness
Stoics 99, 107, 111, 126, 138, 139, 152, 158, 203, 220, 229, 230, 239, 246, 248, 249, 278, 318, 323, 324, 338
synagogue 58-60, 63, 69, 175-76, 342
Synoptic and pre-Synoptic traditions
of the Day of the Lord 291
of eschatological watchfulness 295
of emotional instability 416
of a statement made by Jesus 267-68
of killing the prophets 174-75
of filling up the measure of sins 176
similar to 2 Thess 2:1-12 431
about the Son of Man descending 274
of the thief in the night 290
"wrath" in 171

textual variants 58, 67, 111, 112, 145, 152, 165, 191, 219, 226, 235, 243, 245, 263, 291, 293, 315, 332, 340, 342, 379, 419, 424, 427, 436